Broad Is My Native Land

Broad Is My Native Land

Repertoires and Regimes of Migration in Russia's Twentieth Century

Lewis H. Siegelbaum

and

Leslie Page Moch

CORNELL UNIVERSITY PRESS

Ithaca and London

Publication of this book was assisted by a grant from the Jack and Margaret Sweet Professorship in History, Michigan State University

First published 2014 by Cornell University Press

Library of Congress Cataloging-in-Publication Data

Siegelbaum, Lewis H., author.
    Broad is my native land : repertoires and regimes of migration in Russia's twentieth century / Lewis H. Siegelbaum and Leslie Page Moch.
        pages cm
    Includes bibliographical references and index.
    ISBN 978-0-8014-5333-5 (cloth)
    ISBN 978-0-8014-7999-1 (pbk.)
    1. Migration, Internal—Russia (Federation)—History—20th century. I. Moch, Leslie Page, author. II. Title.
    HB2068.2.A3S535   2014
    304.80947'0904—dc23   2014022384

Cornell University Press strives to use environmentally responsible suppliers and materials to the fullest extent possible in the publishing of its books. Such materials include vegetable-based, low-VOC inks and acid-free papers that are recycled, totally chlorine-free, or partly composed of nonwood fibers. For further information, visit our website at www.cornellpress.cornell.edu.

Cloth printing   10 9 8 7 6 5 4 3 2 1
Paperback printing   10 9 8 7 6 5 4 3 2 1

This book is dedicated to
Sami, Sarah, and Sasu,
our peripatetic children.
As we wrote this book,
they resided in

Angol
Antofagasta
Bozeman
Buenos Aires
Chicago
Columbia
Los Angeles
Paris
St. Paul
Vienna
and Williamsburg.

Contents

Maps and Tables

Maps

Tables

Acknowledgments

E rnest Hemingway once said, "Writing, at its best, is a lonely life." Both of us have experienced much loneliness in writing, but we decided to try something different. This book represents the realization of what at first seemed an improbable idea— that coming from different intellectual backgrounds and having different areas of expertise, we could find common ground and write together about migrants in Russia. We are grateful to those institutions and individuals whose skepticism did not outweigh their supportiveness. To say we could not have completed this experiment in collaboration without such support may not be true, but having received it unquestionably made collaborating less stressful and even at times fun.

We acknowledge with gratitude the support of the Jack and Margaret Sweet Professorship at Michigan State University and the George Kennan Institute of the Woodrow Wilson Center for International Scholars for funding our research in libraries and archives. For their permission to reproduce images, we thank the U.S. Holocaust Museum and the Krasnoiarsk Regional Studies Museum. We also wish to thank the librarians and archivists who frequently extended themselves to assist us. They include Vadim Altskan, Michael Gelb, and other experts at the U.S. Holocaust Memorial Museum library and the staff of the Library of Congress's European Reading Room in Washington, DC; the Russian State [Lenin] Library, the Russian State Archive of the Economy, and the Russian State Archive for Social and Political History in Moscow; and the Russian National Library and the Russian State Historical Archive in St. Petersburg. David Anderson of the University of Aberdeen and the 1926/27 Polar Census Project helped to light our way in the Far North. Joe Welsh of RS & GIS at Michigan State, who prepared our maps; Peter Berg, the director of MSU's Special Collections; and virtually everyone who works at our home library also deserve our thanks, as do the staff of the National Library of Finland and especially Irina Lukka, who made its Slavic collection feel like a home away from home.

Many individuals both near and far gave us encouragement and tips, shared the fruits of their research with us, read all or parts of our manuscript, and otherwise went out of their way to be helpful. Among them were Natalie Belsky, Kate Brown, Victoria Donovan, Dirk Hoerder, Lynn Lees, Leo Lucasscn, Roger Markwick, Alex Öberlander, Anna Eva Peck, the late Anatolii Remnev, Madeleine Reeves, Jeff Sahadeo, Andrey Shlyakhter, Ben Sawyer, and Anika Walke. Our project benefitted from presentations to the Midwest Russian Historians' Workshop at Northwestern University, the students in REEES 395 at the University of Michigan, the graduate students in HST 824 and HST 854 at Michigan State University, the Social Science History Association meetings in Vancouver and Chicago, the European Social Science History Association conference in Vienna, IAS 384 and students and faculty in International and Area Studies at Washington University, and the colloquium in honor of Lynn Lees at the University of Pennsylvania.

Once the manuscript reached the press Karen Laun guided it through production with aplomb, and our copy editor Mary Petrusewicz saved us from ourselves. Finally, words fail us (which is a good thing because he probably would have wanted to edit them out) in expressing our gratitude to John Ackerman for his willingness to take on our book just as he was preparing to transition to a life of relative leisure after serving as director of Cornell University Press for several decades.

Russian Terms and Abbreviations

artel	semi-formal work associations originating among Russian peasants
besprizornik/besprizornyi	homeless orphan
bomzh	acronym for "person without definite place of residence," a homeless person
brodiaga	vagrant, tramp
edinolichnik	independent farmer outside collective and state farms
Gulag	Main Administration of Labor Camps; the labor camps themselves
kolkhoz	collective farm
krai	outlying administrative unit or territory within Russian political space
kulak	prosperous peasant, ostensibly the enemy of Soviet power
limitchik	worker given temporary residence permit by a Moscow enterprise (1970s–1980s)
lishentsy	"enemies of the working people" disenfranchised by law (1918–36)
meshchane	lower estate of townspeople; petite bourgeoisie
Narkomzem	Soviet People's Commissariat of Agriculture, until 1947
NKVD	Soviet People's Commissariat of Internal Affairs, until 1947
obkom	regional committee of the Communist Party
oblast'	administrative unit corresponding to province
OGPU	Joint State Political Administration (1922–34), absorbed by NKVD in 1934

okrug	administrative division within oblast' or krai, often defined in ethnic terms
orgnabor	organized labor recruitment
otkhodnik	peasant working for wages outside the village or kolkhoz
propiska	residence permit
raion	administrative district subordinate to oblast' or krai
RGAE	Rossiiskii Gosudarstvennyi Arkhiv Ekonomiki (Russian State Economic Archive)
RGASPI	Rossiiskii Gosudarstvennyi Arkhiv Sotsial'no-Politicheskoi Istorii (Russian State Archive for Social and Political History)
RGIA	Rossiiskii Gosudarstvennyi Istoricheskii Arkhiv (Russian State Historical Archive)
RSFSR	Russian Soviet Federated Socialist Republic
samotek	a term critical of party functionaries for allowing social processes to proceed on their own; literally "drift"
samovol'nyi	irregular migrants who made their own arrangements and traveled without state permission or assistance
shabashnik	temporary worker earning money off the books in the late Soviet period
soslovie	legal estate in tsarist Russia with corresponding civic rights and responsibilities
sovkhoz	Soviet state farm employing wage labor
Sovnarkom	Council of People's Commissars
teplushka	boxcar containing stove and bunks for human transport
uchastok	parcel or section of land designated for settlement
uezd	secondary administrative unit within tsarist Russia corresponding to county
volost'	unit of peasant self-government in tsarist Russia; township
VTsIK	All-Russian Central Executive Committee of the Congress of Soviets
VUZ	higher education institution
zemliak/zemliachka	fellow countryman/countrywoman; compatriot
zemstvo	local and provincial self-governing institution in tsarist Russia (1864–1917)

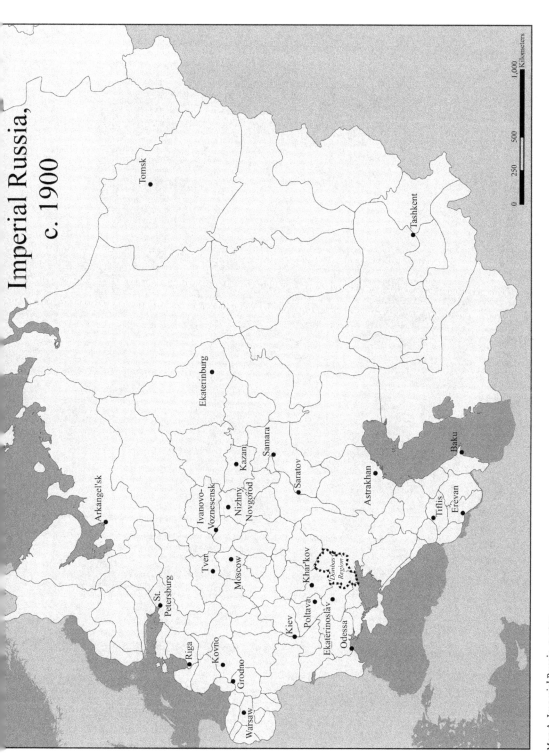

Imperial Russia, c. 1900

Arkangel'sk

St. Petersburg

Riga

Kovno

Grodno

Warsaw

Tver'

Moscow

Ivanovo-Voznesensk

Nizhny Novgorod

Kazan

Samara

Saratov

Ekaterinburg

Kiev

Poltava

Ekaterinoslav

Odessa

Khar'kov

Donbas Region

Astrakhan

Tiflis

Erevan

Baku

Tomsk

Tashkent

0	250	500	1,000

Kilometers

Map A Imperial Russia, c. 1900

Soviet Union 1974

R. S. F. S. R.

Iakut ASSR

Chukotka NO

Koriak NO

Kamchatka Oblast

Magadan

Sea of Okhotsk

Sakhalin Oblast

Khabarovsk Krai

Amur Oblast

Maritime Region

Jewish AO

Agin Buriat NO

Chita

Buriat ASSR

Irkutsk

Ust-Ordyn Buriat NO

Tuva ASSR

Tamyr NO

Evenki Krai

Krasnoiarsk Krai

Khakass AO

Kemerovo

Novosibirsk

Tomsk

Gorno-Altai AO

Altai Krai

Eastern Kazakh Oblast

Semipalatinsk

Yamalo-Nenets NO

Khanty-Mansi NO

Nenets NO

Komi ASSR

Komi-Permi NO

Perm'

Sverdlovsk

Cheliabinsk

Kurgan

Omsk

Pavlodar

Severo-Kazakhstan Oblast

Kustanai

Karaganda

Kokchetav

Akmolinsk

Tselinograd

Semipalatinsk

Aktiubinsk

Turgai Oblast

Dzhezkazgan

KAZAKH S. S. R.

Taldi-Kurgan

Alma-Ata

Dzhambul

KIRGIZ S. S. R.

Frunze

TADZHIK S. S. R.

Gorno-Badakhshan Oblast

Kzyl-Orda

Chimkent Oblast

Tashkent

UZBEK S. S. R.

Samarkand

Bukhara Oblast

Surkhandar'ia Oblast

Kashkadar'ia Oblast

TURKMEN S. S. R.

Ashkhabad

Mary

Chardzhou

Karakalpak ASSR

Khorezm Oblast

Mangyshlak Oblast

Gur'ev

Ural'sk

Western Kazakhstan Oblast

Astrakhan'

Elista

Kalmyk ASSR

Groznyi

Dagestan ASSR

Makhachkala

Chechen-Ingush ASSR

North Ossetia ASSR

Kabardin-Balkar ASSR

GEORGIAN S. S. R.

Tbilisi

ARMENIAN S. S. R.

Erevan

AZERBAIJAN S. S. R.

Baku

Nakhichevan ASSR

Nagorno-Karabakh AO

Caspian Sea

Black Sea

Bashkir ASSR

Ufa

Udmurt ASSR

Tatar ASSR

Kazan'

Kuibyshev

Orenburg

Mari ASSR

Chuvash ASSR

Mordovian ASSR

Saratov

Volgograd

Rostov

Krasnodar Krai

Stavropol' Krai

Voronezh

Tambov

Penza

Ul'ianovsk

Gor'kii

Vladimir

Moscow

Tula

Riazan'

Lipetsk

Kursk

Belgorod

Orel

Briansk

Kaluga

Smolensk

UKRAINIAN S. S. R.

Kiev

Khar'kov

Donetsk

Dnepropetrovsk

Crimea

Odessa

MOLDAVIAN S. S. R.

Kishinev

BELORUSSIAN S. S. R.

Minsk

LITHUANIAN S. S. R.

Vilnius

LATVIAN S. S. R.

ESTONIAN S. S. R.

Leningrad

Pskov

Novgorod

Vologda

Arkhangel'sk

Murmansk

Karelian ASSR

Kalinin

Iaroslavl'

Kostroma

Kirov

Baltic Sea

0   375   500   750   Kilometers

—— Oblast, Krai or Autonomous Republic (ASSR) Boundary

········ Union Republic (S.S.R.)

- - - - Autonomous Oblast (AO) or National Okrug (NO)

Post Soviet States (Commonwealth of Independent Republics)

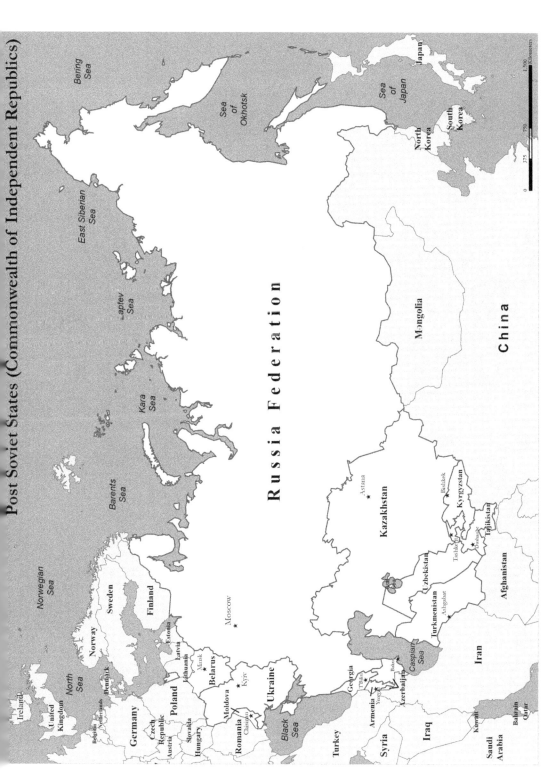

Map C Post-Soviet states

Broad Is My Native Land

Introduction

"Peasants from the warm areas of the Ukraine are being sent to the farthermost northern regions of the USSR," wrote Stephan G. Prociuk, a son of Ukraine who wound up in New York. A senior analyst at the American Association of Aeronautics and Astronautics, Prociuk had contributed earlier articles to the British-based journal *Soviet Studies*. In 1967, while writing about "the manpower problem in Siberia," he lamented not only his fellow Ukrainians "being sent" to northern Russia but also the presence of "nomadic peoples" (presumably from Central Asia) in the metallurgical plants of the Dnieper area and the coal mines of the Donbas (that is, in Soviet Ukraine). He went on to note Lithuanians and Estonians "found" in the Urals and the Far East; Russians from the "cold northeast" descending on the Crimea, North Caucasus, and Trans-Carpathia; Carpathian mountaineers "recruited" for forestry work in the taiga flats of the Komi Autonomous Republic," and flatland Ukrainians "transplanted" to the Altai mountains. Worst of all, perhaps, people from "forsaken villages in the Kostroma and Vologda oblasts with a nineteenth-century or even eighteenth-century way of life" had been "brought" to "cities which, up to 1944, were the outposts of Western European culture in those parts of Eastern Europe imbued with the heritage of Austrian and German influences and traditions." For Prociuk, the predictable result of all this unnatural movement of people was "chaos and general dissatisfaction."[1]

To his credit, the aeronautical engineer from L'viv recognized the extent, variety, and importance of territorial displacements within the Soviet Union. But like most who have written on the subject, he cast the role of the migrants in their migration almost entirely in

---

1. S. G. Prociuk, "The Manpower Problem in Siberia," *Soviet Studies* 19, no. 2 (1967): 207. The papers of Prociuk (1916–84) are in the Ukrainian Academy of Arts and Sciences in the United States, in New York.

passive terms. Among the peoples who from his perspective were out of place, some had been "recruited," and others had been "sent," "brought," "transplanted," and "found"; only the Russians from the "cold northeast" had agency—they were "coming."

In this book we analyze the varieties of migration practiced in Russian political space during the twentieth century.[2] Collectively, and for the most part anonymously, migrants changed Russia's landscape. They animated rural areas, and left them flat; they built cities and provided the labor power to keep them going; they swelled universities and training schools as teachers and students. They suffered displacement in wartime; they continued to suffer from prison camps, internal exile, and hard labor long after many nations had stopped using distance to punish. Along the continuum from seasonal movement to city-ward migration and beyond to colonizing and coerced migration, people in Russia had every kind of migratory experience.[3] Dirk Hoerder has pointed out that migration, "once defined as a crossing of borders between states, is now understood as a social process and appears as a basic condition of human societies."[4] As basic as human mobility may be, people in Russia had a particular history of movement in the twentieth century.

We have chosen a twentieth century that has flexible boundaries for several reasons. First, patterns of movement in tsarism's last decades did not start in the year 1900, nor did the scale and direction of post-Soviet migration change discernibly in the year 2000. Second, the censuses of 1897 and 2002 offer some of the few data points to which we can refer. More important, we are concerned with the transitions from one political configuration to another and aspire to a study that will help discern what is peculiar to Russia and the three political systems encompassed here. Why the twentieth century at all? This was the century that inherited a strong impulse to improve on the past. Empires, technologies, and political ideologies spawned in the nineteenth century all pointed in that direction. The results of their application in the twentieth century often proved unimaginably catastrophic. Russia in this respect played a crucial role, one that is reflected in the way its people moved and were moved.

We use Russia to refer to the more accurate, but unwieldy, label of Russian political space, meaning Imperial Russia, the Soviet Union, and the Russian Federation. We recognize that the boundaries of this political space expanded and contracted throughout the century, and that each of these political entities contained a multiplicity of peoples whose attitudes toward Russian-based political power were varied and complicated. Germans, Poles, Kazakhs, and Chinese, to take but a few examples, had distinct histories of dwelling

---

2. Henceforth, we will use Russia to refer to the more accurate, but unwieldy, label of Russian political space.

3. Charles Tilly, "Migration in Modern European History," in *Human Migration: Patterns and Policies*, ed. W. McNeill and R. Adams (Bloomington, 1978); Leslie Page Moch, *Moving Europeans: Migration in Western Europe since 1650* (Bloomington, 2003).

4. Dirk Hoerder, *Cultures in Contact: World Migrations in the Second Millennium* (Durham, 2002), xix.

and moving within (and crossing borders of) Russian political space. Nevertheless, political authorities assumed the right and wherewithal to move them regardless of their historical ties to particular places.

Each iteration of state power—the tsarist, Soviet, and post-Soviet—engendered a variety of *migration regimes*, that is, policies, practices, and infrastructure designed to both foster and limit human movement.[5] Each carried a distinct and evolving approach to how and where people should move. Tsarist officials sought to slow definitive departures of peasants from the village by reinforcing communal authority at the same time as they made seasonal migration possible and paternalistically guided resettlement. The Pale of Settlement served to keep Jews away from the Russian interior—until World War I sent hundreds of thousands of them streaming eastward. Similar restrictions kept Chinese settlers confined to border regions in the Far East. Distinguished administrators and lowly soldiers alike found themselves assigned far from home; and thousands of revolutionaries and ordinary criminals went into exile in the Far North, to Siberia and beyond.

Some practices of Imperial Russian migration regimes reappeared in Soviet times: the state continued to organize resettlement and assign soldiers, prisoners, and administrators far from home; newcomers to the cities required permission both to leave the countryside and to take up urban residence; passports once again governed internal migration. Yet, in the Soviet era, and particularly under Stalin, state attempts to control the movement of people assumed unprecedented proportions.[6] For example, the way the Soviet government handled the threat that enemy occupation posed to civilians during the Great Patriotic War was fundamentally more ambitious than what its tsarist predecessor had done during the First World War.[7] The goal of the Stalinist state became the rational distribution of population in accordance with the location of natural resources and in contrast to its vision of bourgeois societies in which people moved about willy-nilly. An elaborate hierarchy of "regime" and nonregime cities with corresponding registration procedures substituted for the price structures of a capitalist housing market to bar some categories of people and permit others. Only at the end of the Stalin era did compulsory resettlement and deportation give way to moral suasion and material incentives, which predominated in subsequent decades.

Some of the Soviet administrative mechanisms that determined legality of residence survived into the post-Soviet era, although not only bribes but also the dictates of capital

---

5. For the use of the term "regime" in this way, see A. V. Viatkin, N. P. Kosmarskaia, S. A. Panarin, eds., *V dvizhenii dobrovol'nom i vynuzhdennym: Postsovetskie migratsii v Evrazii* (Moscow, 1999), 14.

6. Kate Brown, *A Biography of No Place: From Ethnic Borderland to Soviet Heartland* (Cambridge, MA, 2003), 82–83, 91, 115–16.

7. Cf. Peter Gatrell, *A Whole Empire Walking: Refugees in Russia during World War I* (Bloomington, 1999); Rebecca Manley, *To the Tashkent Station: Evacuation and Survival in the Soviet Union at War* (Ithaca, 2009), esp. 7–47.

adulterated migration regimes. The breakup of the Soviet Union paradoxically both complicated and facilitated movement across what had become international boundaries. Job-seekers, students hoping to improve educational qualifications, and people visiting relatives in what had been just another Soviet republic found it necessary to pull strings and bribe their way to their desired destinations. At the same time, the formation of "ethnocracies" in many of the newly independent states accelerated the out-migration of Russians and other Slavs, many of whom Russian Federation authorities designated as "forced migrants."[8]

In addition to political forms, Russia's spaciousness shaped mobility. A Stalin-era song celebrated the boundlessness of Soviet space, encompassing vast and varied terrains— "from Moscow to the hinterlands / from the southern mountains to the northern seas"— the largest landmass under a single political administration in the world. Anywhere else, covering such distances would have meant crossing international boundaries (if not oceans). We have appropriated the first line of this song, "Broad is my native land," as our title in recognition of its dual meaning, for it also could express a lament for being far from home.[9] Moreover, not everyone separated from home considered their new place to be their native land. The multiplicity of national subjectivities militated against identification with "Russia" and even more so the supranational space defined successively as Empire, Union, and Federation.

At the same time, the vastness of Russia limited political control from the center. Thanks to the immensity of the country, many people managed to evade surveillance. Conscripts, exiles, and forced settlers, among others, disappeared, only sometimes reappearing at home. On the other hand, migration within Russian political space often did resemble crossing international boundaries: one had to submit papers (i.e., internal passport, and sometimes authorization to travel) as if entering a new country, and the sheer ethnic and linguistic diversity made it seem as if one had indeed moved abroad.

We aspire to make this complex story sufficiently lucid to engage the student of migration who is not an expert in Russia and thereby to connect the history of Russian migration to that of migration worldwide. This requires attention to both what is characteristic of Russia and what patterns, practices, and principles are widely shared. Our desire to "bring Russia in" to the global migration picture is inspired by a double impulse: On the one hand, the view of Russian migration is generally limited to the great emigrations from its western

---

8. Rogers Brubaker, *Ethnicity without Groups* (Cambridge, MA, 2004), 153–54.

9. "Song of the Motherland," from the 1936 musical comedy *Circus* (Tsirk), contained the refrain "Broad is my native land/Many her forests, fields, and rivers!/No other such land do I know/Where a man can breathe so free" that prisoners sang ironically as they were being transported through Siberia in 1950, according to N. N. Boldyrev, "The Crooked Path of Fate," in *Voices from the Gulag*, ed. Aleksandr Solzhenitsyn (Evanston, 2010), 131–32.

territories to Western Europe and North America at the turn of the twentieth century and to the forced migrations of the Soviet era, and we desire to extend that very partial picture. On the other hand, we aspire to "bring migration in" to studies of Russian history—expanding the utility of migration history by applying it to Russia. We cannot possibly match the richness of microhistories—of particular places over the *longue durée*—or broader-gauged studies of particular moments. What we can do is convey how political decisions, socioeconomic processes, and even international war were reflected in migration, and even how these macroforces were embodied in individuals through migration. Migration thus serves as a fairly sensitive barometer of the political, economic, and social "weather," its vectors registering the winds of change blowing over one area or another and at times the entire country.

A state-centered history presents a great temptation to this study because the state defines migration and enumerates those who move, making migration, as Charles Tilly observed decades ago, one of those "apparently crisp concepts that owes its crispness to bureaucracy."[10] Archival documents and published studies lead scholars to focus on the ambitions and disappointments of state officials and on bureaucrats' observations about people who take to the road that often emphasize disorder and judge migrants as lacking desirable qualities or resources. Our consideration of *regimes* of migration gives due importance to state plans and perspectives. In seeking to organize and structure migration, the state categorized migrants according to its own lights. State officials inscribed people as resettlers, special settlers, refugees, evacuees, bearers of temporary residence permits, recipients of special pay increments, young specialists assigned for a given number of years to a particular job and place, and so forth.

But we also argue that migration resulted from migrants' *repertoires* and itineraries. These could coincide with but also be in opposition to migration regimes even when they partook of the technologies (postal system, railroads, telegraph, telephone, and more recently, air travel and the Internet) on which the regimes depended. By repertoires we have in mind migrants' own practices, their relationships and networks of contact that permitted adaptation to particular migration regimes. Marked by geographic origin, confession, gender, kinship, friendship, and professional identity, these are visible, for example, in the peasant practice of sending men to the city and the congruent pattern of families in which husbands and wives lived separately. They also can be seen in rhythms of seasonal mining and harvest migration and the social institution that transcended changes in political regimes of scouts sent out ahead by resettling families.[11] As Mark Edele writes, "These

---

10. Tilly, "Migration in Modern European History," 48.

11. On the scouts, see Lewis H. Siegelbaum, "Those Elusive Scouts: Pioneering Peasants and the Russian State, 1870s–1953," Kritika: Explorations in Russian and Eurasian History 14, no. 1 (2013): 31–60.

patterns were not accidental, but they followed the lead of precedent. They had, in other words, their own histories . . ."[12] To contextualize such repertoires, we consider whom the culture allowed to depart and who remained behind, the resources (cultural as well as material) at the disposal of migrants, and the means for maintaining connections with the community back home as well as establishing new ones at destination—in short, the elements that are crucial underpinnings to human mobility worldwide.

Migrants overcame distance by every means: villagers seeking work walked and were carted along tracks to high roads leading to provincial and capital cities; others boarded barges and steamers that plied the rivers; convicts trod well-worn paths into exile; sleds carried the Arctic reindeer herders in their annual rounds whereas camels and horses bore Kazakh *auls* from summer to winter pasture. The culminating feat of transport binding European Russia to Siberia and the Far East was the Trans-Siberian Railroad. Built between 1891 and 1916, it represented perhaps the premier example of migratory regimes coinciding with migrant repertoires. Even before World War I, millions had traveled east along its tracks.[13] In the Soviet period a web of railroad routes came to cover European Russia, while the Trans-Siberian sent out spurs. Roads lagged behind.[14]

To emphasize the agency of migrants is not so very innovative within the field of migration history, but it breaks new ground for Russianists. Part of our agenda is to recover and listen to the voices of migrants, however constrained they were in expressing themselves. But we also examine their collective agency. Having set target figures for how many people to move in the interests of a managed redistribution of the population, the state often found itself overwhelmed by the irregularity (*samovol'nost'*) that migrants brought to the process. Without the unregistered peasant settlers of the late nineteenth century and the self-dekulakizing peasants in the 1930s, the escapees from the Gulag (Main Administration of Corrective Labor Camps) and the self-evacuees during the Great Patriotic War, the itinerants who populated railroad stations, the independent seasonal workers and temporary hires of the 1960s–1970s and their post-Soviet Caucasian and Central Asian descendants, the history of migration in modern Russian political space would be far simpler but impoverished.

We not only acknowledge, but also insist on the limitations of what we—or anyone else—can know about migration in Russia. The numbers of those who rode the rails, sat

---

12. Mark Edele, *Stalinist Society, 1928–1953* (Oxford, 2011), 72.

13. Steven V. Marks, *Road to Power: The Trans-Siberian Railroad and the Colonization of Asian Russia, 1850–1917* (Ithaca, 1991); Donald W. Treadgold, *The Great Siberian Migration: Government and Peasant in Resettlement from Emancipation to the First World War* (Princeton, 1957).

14. Ian Frazier, *Travels in Siberia* (New York, 2010); Lewis H. Siegelbaum, "Roadlessness and the 'Path to Communism': Building Roads and Highways in Stalinist Russia," *Journal of Transport History* 29, no. 2 (2008): 277–94; Siegelbaum, *Cars for Comrades: The Life of the Soviet Automobile* (Ithaca, 2008), chap. 4.

on horseback or were pulled in carts, hitched rides or simply walked to get away from danger or toward a desired destination are incalculable because so many fell through the cracks, inadvertently or otherwise. Migrants, as Hoerder has observed, "have minds of their own and plans for their futures," and it is precisely migrants' wills and plans that are of interest to us.[15] But to paraphrase a great nineteenth-century thinker, they did not make their plans under circumstances chosen by themselves. We are most curious about the experience of those who moved, but recognize the necessity of understanding this as a function of the interplay between regimes and repertoires of migration. This dynamic varied over time, and differed from one political system to another, as well as within any one of them. It also varied among the different forms of migration that structure our study: resettlement, seasonal migration, rural-to-urban migration, career migration, military migration, evacuation, exile and deportation, and itinerancy. We trace the arc of each form across the twentieth century. The order in which we present them represents a compromise between chronological emphasis and the shifting balance between voluntary and coerced forms of migration.

Yet we understand that writing about different kinds of migration as if they were mutually exclusive does not do justice to the unruliness of a phenomenon that resists tidy categories. And so some qualifications are in order. First, one person can experience multiple moves and more than one kind of movement in a lifetime. The best-documented villager in the Imperial city, Semën Kanatchikov, relocated to a second city and was then a political exile in a remote settlement in the Far North, a worker in Saratov, then a prisoner in Siberia—all before the age of forty.[16] Millions of peasants, dislocated by collectivization during the 1930s, engaged in violent migrations as soldiers during the Great Patriotic War, after which—if they survived—they settled in some place other than where they had lived before the war. Likewise, evacuees from the western borderlands could travel farther to the east to become resettlers during the war when benefits proffered by recruiters represented a life-saving choice for them and their children. Finally, some of the Russians fleeing penury and persecution in the post-Soviet near abroad settled in state-sponsored rural areas rather than the cities they had left behind to make careers during the last decades of the USSR.

Second, different categories belie similarities of logistics. Already early in the century, convoys of converted boxcars called *teplushki* became the state's preferred method of transporting people by the hundreds. Initially used for soldiers, the wagons subsequently served resettlers to Siberia and the Far East, returnees traveling westward after the Revolution and

---

15. Hoerder, *Cultures in Contact*, xx.
16. Semën Kanatchikov, *A Radical Worker in Tsarist Russia: The Autobiography of Semën Ivanovich Kanatchikov*, trans. and ed. Reginald Zelnik (Stanford, 1986); 360–88.

Civil War, peasant "kulaks" bound for special settlements, deportees and evacuees during the Second World War, and others. Along with the formation of convoys went the compilation of lists containing the names and vital information of passengers, baggage, and animals; the provision of food, water, and (sometimes) medical care; and arrangements for disembarkation and assignment to new "homes." These procedures typically were accompanied by the consumption of a great deal of paper on which officials from one office recorded and sent details to another.

Third, what the serial presentation of migratory forms can obscure is their simultaneity, spatial convergence, and even mutual constitution. Just as millions of peasants from the Black Earth provinces of European Russia and Ukraine resettled on land beyond the Urals in the late nineteenth and early twentieth centuries, so others, mainly from farther to the north, were migrating to cities, either on a seasonal or longer-term basis. Ambitious young people in Siberian towns prepared for entrance exams to far-flung universities tutored by the best-educated members of their society, political exiles.[17] Prisoners built railroads alongside locals and itinerant laborers. In the 1930s, tourists, prisoners, and the so-called special settlers traveled on the same rail lines, but only tourists had decent food and clear windows. There even was at least one instance when demobilized Red Army soldiers recruited for settlement in Siberia traveled on the same train as a contingent of deportees.[18] During the war, evacuees en route to Kazakhstan sometimes found themselves on the same train as ethnic German and Polish deportees. Such disparate groups appeared (literally) alongside each other in memoranda on "arrivals and placements" as well as allocations of fuel for transport from railroad stations to final destinations.[19] As for functional relationships, one of the reasons demobilized soldiers and collective farmers from "overpopulated" regions migrated to the Kuban, Dnepropetrovsk, and other parts of southern Russia and Ukraine in 1933 was to repopulate land from which Cossacks and kulaks had been deported.[20] And in a more benign sense, one reason collective farm villages throughout Central Russia needed the services of seasonal laborers in the late Soviet period is that too many of their able-bodied residents had joined the rural exodus to cities that offered better educational opportunities and marital prospects.[21]

---

17. Anna Bek, *The Life of a Russian Woman Doctor: A Siberian Memoir, 1869–1954* (Bloomington, 2004), 39.

18. Diane Koenker, *Club Red: Vacation Travel and the Soviet Dream* (Ithaca, 2013); V. Danilov, R. Manning, and L. Viola, eds. *Tragediia sovetskoi derevni, kollektivizatsiia i raskulachivanie: Dokumenty i materialy v 5 tomakh, 1927–1939* (Moscow, 2002), 3: 274–75.

19. United States Holocaust Memorial Museum, Record Group 74.002, Tsentral'nyi Gosudarstvennyi Arkhiv g. Almaty (TsGA Almaty), f. 1137, Reel 1, op. 6, d. 1279, l. 180; [Reel 4], op. 9, d. 141, ll. 93, 97.

20. For a report that remaining peasants were warning the resettlers about Cossack vengeance, see Rossiiskii Gosudarstvennyi Arkhiv Ekonomiki (RGAE), f. 5675, op. 1, d. 48, ll. 42, 47; d. 52, l. 25; d. 79, l. 55.

21. Timur Ia. Valetov, "Mekhanizmy samoorganitsii sezonnykh trudovykh migrantov v SSSR i na postsovetskom prostranstve," in *"Sovetskoe nasledstvo": Otrazhenie proshlogo v sotsial'nykh i ekonomicheskikh praktikakh sovremennoi Rossii*, ed. L. Borodkin (Moscow, 2010), 253–59.

Finally, we recognize that all forms of migration are coerced to a degree; moreover, they are often mutually constituted in the sense that the greater, or more widely spread, the use of coercion, the more likely people on the receiving end will resort to evasive action including escape, itself a form of migration.[22] Increased restrictions breed increased numbers of outliers and outlaws. We thus have no illusions that writing about one kind of migratory practice means that it existed in splendid isolation. On the contrary, it was precisely because of these temporal, spatial, and functional links among migratory practices that we decided to separate them for heuristic purposes.

Although this is a large-scale study, individuals matter, not only because it is only through personal statements that we are able to hear the voice of the migrant, but also because individual demographic traits make a difference to the migration experience. Gender most fundamentally shapes the migration process. Perceptions of appropriate work, levels of independence, and capacity to travel—themselves changeable and variable over time and space—vary by the meaning of gender. Who migrates is affected by the labor market and by state policies, and these are in turn shaped by perceptions of appropriate work and activity for men and women. We can infer some of these constructions from the ratio of men to women in migrating groups, but we cannot always know precisely what proportion of a group on the move is male or female, because bureaucrats only sometimes concerned themselves with sex ratios.[23] In Imperial Russia, for example, men predominated among newcomers to the city and worked in production and trade, whereas migrant women labored primarily in domestic service and the needle trades, as they did in cities elsewhere.[24] In the great cities of post-Soviet Russia, Central Asians would work at many of the jobs Russian peasants had taken at the beginning of the century, and once again most were men. Between these two, Soviet state policy would promote a wide range of places in the urban workforce for women. It will be obvious that some kinds of mobility—that of refugees (mostly women and children) and seasonal laborers (mostly men), for example—proved to be more gendered than others.

---

22. For an analogous interpretation, see Tom Brass and Marcel van der Linden, eds., *Free and Unfree Labour: The Debate Continues* (Bern, 1997).

23. Among the most recent and relevant considerations of migration and gender are Donna R. Gabaccia and Katherine M. Donato, *Gender and Migration over the Long Durée* (New York, forthcoming); Katharine Donato, Joseph Alexander, Donna Gabaccia, and Johanna Leinonen, "Variations in the Gender Composition of Immigrant Populations: How They Matter," *International Migration Review* 45 (2011): 495–526; Katharine Donato, et al., "A Glass Half Full? Gender in Migration Studies," *International Migration Review* 40 (2006): 3–26; Nancy Green, "Changing Paradigms in Migration Studies: From Men to Women to Gender," *Gender and History* 24, no. 3 (2012): 782–98; Dirk Hoerder, "Transcultural Approaches to Gendered Labour Migration: From the Nineteenth-Century Proletarian to Twenty-First Century Caregiver Mass Migrations," in *Proletarian and Gendered Mass Migrations: A Global Perspective on Continuities and Discontinuities from the 19th to the 21st Centuries*, ed. Dirk Hoerder and Amarjit Kaur (Leiden, 2013), 27–33; Moch, *Moving Europeans*, chap. 4.

24. Gijs Kessler, "Migration and Family Systems in Russia and the Soviet Union, Nineteenth to Twentieth Centuries," in Hoerder and Kaur, *Proletarian and Gendered Mass Migrations*, 133–50.

The following individuals exemplify some of the people on the move in twentieth-century Russia. Semën Kanatchikov came to Moscow at age sixteen in the mid-1890s, driven by his father who had followed the same trajectory in his youth. Fulfilling his burning desire to leave the countryside, Kanatchikov roomed at first with fellow villagers. In about 1930, a young woman student named Masha left Moscow for Magnitogorsk—the new steel town rising east of the Urals—not recruited like so many thousands of others, but lured by her sister's attractive descriptions of the new city and determined to pay her own way in order to avoid obligation to the employment bureau. Eighteen-year-old Genya Batasheva, a Soviet Jew, embarked on a wartime odyssey after escaping from Nazi-occupied Kiev. She and her friend Manya traveled to Tashkent, to a former Cossack settlement on the steppe, to Omsk where they found work in an evacuated shipbuilding factory, and finally to a town in southern Siberia's Altai region where she rejoined her father, evacuated there as a worker from the Khar'kov Tractor Factory. During the Great Patriotic War and in the years that followed, the Soviet government deported millions of Soviet citizens, among them Aili Valdrand, who in 1949 accompanied her "kulak" mother from their farm on Saaremaa island off the Estonian coast to a special settlement in Novosibirsk oblast'. She made the return journey as a young woman of twenty-two in 1958. At the end of the twentieth century, Moscow's burgeoning economy drew Central Asians and people from the Caucasus such as Akhmed, who left the Azeri enclave in Karabakh to sell fruit and nuts in the Danilevskii market, earning enough to return periodically to his family back home.[25]

A vast range of scholarship has helped to shape our project. We drew our inspiration from Hoerder and other historians of migration who demonstrated the possibility of thinking in broad and comparative terms without losing sight of the cultural specificities and individuality of migrants.[26] We stand on the shoulders of several generations of scholars who have written about people on the move in Russia—from the demographer Eugene Kulischer, who interpreted war as "violent movement of masses of people which stems from differential population pressures," to Donald Treadgold's splendid account of trans-Siberian migration; the social scientists who viewed Soviet urbanization and industrialization within the modernization paradigm regnant in the 1970s; the cluster of social

---

25. Kanatchikov, *Radical Worker in Tsarist Russia*; Pearl S. Buck, *Talk about Russia with Masha Scott* (New York, 1945), 91; USHMM, RG-50.226.0008 Oral History Interview with Genya Batasheva; "Aili Valdrand (1936)," in *Estonian Life Stories*, ed. and trans. Tiina Kirss and Rutt Hinrikus (Budapest, 2009), 439–55; Irina Sandul, "Time Runs Out for Russia's Foreign Workers," *The Russia Journal*, May 13, 2002, http://russiajournal.com/node/6205 (accessed November 23, 2012).

26. In the introduction to their edited volume, John Randolph and Eugene M. Avrutin refer to this approach as "agent-centered studies" (*Russia in Motion: Cultures of Human Mobility since 1850* (Urbana, 2012), 11). See also Moch, *Moving Europeans*; Jan Lucassen and Leo Lucassen, "The Mobility Transition Revisited, 1500–1900: What the Case of Europe Can Offer to Global History," *Journal of Global History* 4, no. 3 (2009): 347–77; Lucassen and Lucassen, "From Mobility Transition to Comparative Global Migration History," *Journal of Global History* 6, no. 2 (2011): 299–307.

historians who studied labor migration of the late nineteenth century through the prisms of class formation, gender, and family history; and the historians of Stalinist and post-Stalinist Russia who emphasized the "peopling" of its cities and the rural exodus.[27] We are indebted as well to the scholarship on Russia of more recent years that has concerned itself with empire, colonization, and nationality; the socially catastrophic effects of war, internal as well as international; and emerging patterns of migration in the wake of the Soviet Union's termination.[28]

Regimes of migration are reflected in the paperwork of the institutions responsible for their implementation and surveillance. We found much evidence of such paperwork in the state's archives as well as in published documents.[29] In reading bureaucrats' mail, we also found traces of migrants' repertoires in the form of requests, complaints, and other solicitations of the state's interest or mercy. But we also relied on migrants' diaries, personal correspondence, and memoirs.[30] Interviews with migrants in print, on video, and on the

---

27. Eugene M. Kulischer, *Europe on the Move: War and Population Changes, 1917–47* (New York, 1948), 18; Treadgold, *Great Siberian Migration*; Robert A. Lewis and Richard H. Rowland, *Population Redistribution in the USSR: Its Impact on Society, 1897–1977* (New York, 1979); Robert E. Johnson, *Peasant and Proletarian: The Working Class of Moscow in the Late Nineteenth Century* (New Brunswick, 1979); Joseph Bradley, *Muzhik and Muscovite: Urbanization in Late Imperial Russia* (Berkeley, 1985); Barbara Alpern Engel, *Between the Fields and the City: Women, Work, and the Family in Russia, 1861–1914* (Cambridge, 1994); Jeffrey Burds, "The Social Control of Peasant Labor in Russia: the Response of Village Communities to Labor Migration in the Central Industrial Region, 1861–1905," in *Peasant Economy, Culture, and Politics of European Russia, 1800–1921*, ed. Esther Kingston-Mann and Timothy Mixter (Princeton, 1991), 52–100; Stephen Kotkin, "Peopling Magnitostroi: The Politics of Demography," in *Social Dimensions of Soviet Industrialization*, ed. William G. Rosenberg and Lewis H. Siegelbaum (Bloomington, 1993), 63–104; David Hoffmann, *Peasant Metropolis: Social Identities in Moscow, 1929–1941* (Ithaca, 1994); L. N. Denisova, *Ischezaiushchaia derevnia Rossii: Nechernozem'e v 1960–1980-e gody* (Moscow, 1996).

28. See among recent publications, Willard Sunderland, *Taming the Wild Field: Colonization and Empire on the Russian Steppe* (Ithaca, 2004); Nicholas Breyfogle, Abby Schrader, and Willard Sunderland, eds., *Peopling the Russian Periphery: Borderland Colonization in Eurasian History* (London, 2007); V. I. Diatlov, ed., *Migratsii i diaspory v sotsiokul'turnom, politicheskom i ekonomicheskom prostranstve Sibiri: Rubezhi XIX–XX i XX–XXI vekov* (Irkutsk, 2010); Joshua A. Sanborn, "Unsettling the Empire: Violent Migrations and Social Disaster in Russia during World War I," *The Journal of Modern History* 77 (June 2005): 290–324; Lynne Viola, *The Unknown Gulag: The Lost World of Stalin's Special Settlements* (Oxford, 2007); Vladimir Mukomel', *Migratsionnaia politika Rossii: Postsovetskie konteksty* (Moscow, 2005); Iu. V. Roshchin, *Migratsiia naseleniia v sud'be Rossii* (Moscow, 2008).

29. For a request for more paper, see USHMM, RG 74.002, TsGA Almaty, f. R-1137, op. 6, d. 1279, l. 53. For a list of archival holdings used in this study, see the bibliography. Among published document collections, the most valuable to us were M. V. Shilovskii, ed., *Sibirskie pereseleniia: Dokumenty i materialy*, 2 vols. (Novosibirsk, 2003–6); Danilov, Manning, and Viola, *Tragediia sovetskoi derevni*, 5 vols. (Moscow, 1999–2003); *Evakuatsiia v Kazakhstan: Iz istorii evakuatsii naseleniia zapadnykh raionov SSSR v Kazakhstan, 1941–1942*, ed. I. Grinberg, G. Karataev, N. Kropivnitskii (Almaty, 2008); *Stalinskie deportatsii 1928–1953 gg.*, ed. N. L. Pobol' and P. M. Polian (Moscow, 2005).

30. For example, Mukhamet Shayakhmetov, *The Silent Steppe: The Memoir of a Kazakh Nomad under Stalin*, trans. Jan Butler (New York, 2007); M. V. Sumkin, *V Sibir' za zemlei (iz kaluzhskoi gubernii v semipalatinskuiu oblast')*, zapiski khodoka (Moscow, 1908); A. A. Tatishchev, *Zemli i liudi: V gushche pereselencheskogo dvizheniia, 1906–1921* (Moscow, 2001); USHMM, RG-31.053 Memoirs of Abram Tseitlin; USHMM, RG-31.113 Diary of Anna Dashevskaya; USHMM, RG-31.089 Sigal Family Papers, 1920–1947.

Internet have grown exponentially in the past few years. They have powerfully affected us, both intellectually and emotionally.[31]

Our decision to focus exclusively on internal migration *within* Russian political space means that some people who left their homes for whatever reason drop out of our study because they crossed international boundaries never to return, or because the boundaries changed, placing them outside Russian governance. Among these people are the millions of Jews, Ukrainians, and other emigrants from tsarist Russia who ended up in Europe and North and South America; the "White" émigrés who left in the years immediately after the October Revolution; refugees from the western borderlands who returned to their newly independent homelands after 1917; Kazakhs escaping over the southern border with China to avoid forced settlement ("sedentarization") from the late Imperial period through the years of collectivization; Poles "repatriated" after World War II; the some four hundred thousand Karelians evacuated to Finland in 1944; those who accompanied the German army as it retreated from occupied Soviet territory, as well as Ostarbeiter, who did not return to the USSR; Soviet soldiers stationed in postwar Eastern Europe; ethnic Germans, Jews, Greeks, and others belonging to diasporic nationalities who emigrated to the United States, Israel, and Western Europe; "shuttle" traders buying goods on one side of an international border to sell them on the other; and the millions who migrated within or between former Soviet republics other than the Russian Federation after 1991. Nonetheless, because our scope is long and the space expansive, and because as Gijs Kessler points out, migration was almost exclusively internal during much of the twentieth century, the omission of international migration leaves us with plenty to do.[32]

We also do not address occasional travel such as tourism or commuting that did not involve changing one's domicile, although these practices unquestionably entailed moving in Russia and sometimes have been treated by scholars alongside or as part of migration.[33]

---

31. V. Gal'chenko with Nina Maksimova, "Zhitie odnogo shabashnika," *EKO*, no. 3 (1987): 101–36; oral interviews in USHMM, RG-50; and at "Ia Pomniu/I Remember: Vospominaniia veteranov VOV," www.ire member.ru. See also the Oxford Russian Life History Archive, www.ehrc.ox.ac.uk/html/ehrc/lifehistory/ar chive.htm; and Jeff Sahadeo, "The Accidental Traders: Marginalization and Opportunity from the Southern Republics to Late Soviet Moscow," *Central Asian Survey* 30, nos. 3–4 (2011): 521–40.

32. Kessler, "Migration and Family Systems," 139. Cf. Eric Lohr, *Russian Citizenship: From Empire to Soviet Union* (Cambridge, MA, 2012), 9: "In the context of a war scare, autarkic industrial mobilization, and an intensive campaign against the flight of hard currency and people, Stalin closed down the citizenship border, making it extraordinarily difficult to immigrate, emigrate, or denaturalize."

33. See for example Anne E. Gorsuch and Diane P. Koenker, eds., *Turizm: The Russian and East European Tourist under Capitalism and Socialism* (Ithaca, 2006); Anne E. Gorsuch, *All This Is Your World: Soviet Tourism at Home and Abroad after Stalin* (Oxford, 2011); Koenker, *Club Red*; Lewis H. Siegelbaum, "Soviet Car Rallies of the 1920s and '30s and the Road to Socialism," *Slavic Review* 64, no. 2 (2005): 247–73; B. S. Khorev and V. N. Likhded, *Zhitel' sela—Rabotnik goroda* (Moscow, 1982). Commuting is known as "pendular migration" (*maiatnikovaia migratsiia*) in Russia. For a discussion of the issues involved in "migration" as opposed to "mobility" studies, see the editors' introduction to Randolph and Avrutin, *Russia in Motion*, 1–16.

Finally, writing in the wake of the enormous outpouring of scholarly literature on the Gulag occasioned by the opening of Soviet archives, we decided not to include the forced journeys of prisoners to the camps. These in their essentials—the Black Marias that took arrestees to prison; the lorries transporting them to the railroad stations; and the long trips aboard convoys of boxcars bound for a labor camp, and transfers between camps—are so well known that they require no emendation from us.[34]

We have chosen to organize this study by a typology of migrations, modifying the categories discussed by Charles Tilly years ago.[35] A focus on the migrants themselves, rather than the state, allows us to investigate the experiential dimension of mobility without forcing an unnecessarily tidy narrative. We begin with settlers—the colonizers of the great spaces of Siberia, the Kazakh steppe, and the Far East in Imperial and Soviet times. Millions took long paths and broke from their home area definitively by engaging in "resettlement" (pereselenie), although at least before 1914 one in five "re-resettled" back home. Resettlement, we argue, had two dimensions: for the state—both tsarist and Soviet—it was a colonial project, but for resettlers themselves it had the fundamentally conservative objective of reproducing conditions that had become increasingly difficult to maintain at home.

We next move to the least disruptive of migratory movements—seasonal work in the field, the mine, the forest, or the city to find what the home district could not provide in monetary or material terms. State efforts—especially in the Soviet period but also in post-Soviet Russia—to organize or regulate seasonal migration were doomed by the informality of arrangements between migrant and direct employer. Structurally similar to those found in many other parts of the world, these arrangements took on culturally specific qualities because seasonal migrants enjoyed relative autonomy and freedom of movement.

With chapter 3, our attention turns to migration to the city. We argue that urban areas were the great victors of the twentieth century. They attracted people who wanted to get ahead or start a new life, because both the tsarist and Soviet states privileged the city and its denizens. The break with rural life became more definitive as the century progressed, although precisely because cities swallowed rural migrants so quickly, village ways persisted even in the most metropolitan districts.

Career migrants—organized by the employing institution—are the subjects of our fourth and fifth chapters. In administering and policing the movement of people to and

34. For an outstanding review of this literature, see Kate Brown, "Out of Solitary Confinement: The History of the Gulag," *Kritika: Explorations in Russian and Eurasian History* 8, no. 1 (2007): 67–103. For return journeys from the Gulag, see Nanci Adler, *The Gulag Survivor: Beyond the Soviet System* (New Brunswick, 2002); Adler, *Keeping Faith with the Party: Communist Believers Return from the Gulag* (Bloomington, 2012); Miriam Dobson, *Khrushchev's Cold Summer: Gulag Returnees, Crime, and the Fate of Reform after Stalin* (Ithaca, 2009).

35. Tilly, "Migration in Modern European History"; Charles Tilly, "Transplanted Networks," in *Immigration Reconsidered*, ed. V. Yans-McLaughlin (New York, 1990), 79–95.

within their domain, state officials themselves traveled away from home, often for years, sometimes forever. They too, according to our lights, deserve to be considered migrants. Men and women assigned after graduation to a specific locale according to the system of distribution (*raspredelenie*) introduced in the 1930s belong with career migrants, as do officials assigned to administer settlers and collective farmers, and employees of the penal system. With military migrants, we enter the territory of conflicts that plagued the century—from the Russo-Japanese War in 1904–5 to the Chechen wars that poisoned the 1990s. For officers, their service may have been a career, but for soldiers, less so. The military both mobilized and isolated; it exposed soldiers to peoples and places remote from their past experience and inculcated a culture of violence that set them apart. With career and military migrations, we cross the watershed separating less from more coerced forms of migration. We therefore are particularly interested in the agency of people in response to their assignments.

The refugees and evacuees of the century, for whom coercion played an enormous role, provide the focus of chapter 6. We trace their movements from the first and second world wars up through the Chernobyl nuclear accident and the flight of ethnic Russians from the former Soviet republics (the "near abroad") to the Russian Federation in the wake of the Soviet Union's disintegration. We pursue both the regimes of evacuation—the principles and procedures by which the state removed people and determined where they should go—and the repertoires enacted by refugees and evacuees to mitigate hardship. We trace the arc from refugees fleeing more or less unaided during World War I and the Russian Civil War, to evacuees removed from harm's way in the Great Patriotic War and late Soviet disasters, to refugees escaping from post-Soviet ethnic fallout. The trajectory corresponds closely to the capacities and ambitions of respective state administrations, although in practice the distinction between evacuee and refugee often was blurred. Both the state and evacuees, we argue, relied heavily on the family to lessen the burdens.

Chapter 7 focuses on an extreme case of coerced migrations: the movements of deportees to and among remote settlements. This, unlike other migration practices we cover, started modestly in the late Imperial period; it expanded during World War I when tsarist officials became concerned about the loyalties of western borderland peoples, but grew by leaps and bounds under Stalin. We emphasize that, from the economic standpoint, deportation replaced planned voluntary resettlement programs as the primary method of colonizing and harvesting resources in remote regions. Yet the deportation of one group created the need to resettle others to fill the void. Mostly rural in origin, people subjected to deportation adapted with varying degrees of success to the rigors of exile, but many, longing to return home, escaped. We conclude the chapter by assessing the long-term effects of deportation on those who were subjected to it and later returned.

Our final chapter considers those itinerant men, women, and children who did their best to elude the notice of authorities—prison and labor camp escapees, homeless orphans, Roma, and the mobile pastoralists of Kazakhstan and the Far North. Here, repertoires of migration confronted regimes of "sedentarization," in effect, the opposite dynamic from that operating in the cases of evacuation and deportation. In seeking to rein in itinerancy, state officials had several advantages, including inducements of manufactured goods, technologies of identification and capture, and the collaboration of nonitinerant society. But their capacity to encroach on and curtail the lifeways of itinerants was not unlimited, and as the upsurge in itinerancy during the last decade of the century suggests, it could in fact recede.

Thus, the Ukrainians whom Stephan Prociuk lamented leaving "warm areas" of their country for northern Russia and the Central Asians who wound up in Ukraine were far from anomalous. Their synchronous geographic mobility represented but a moment in a history of migratory practices that transcended political systems. Some of these practices had analogues elsewhere in the world; others appear to be unique functions of Russian spatial or political configurations. Our project, then, is to interrogate what difference size and politics made to the nature and extent of migration, what difference migrants made to governmentality, and, no less important, what migrants made of their own experiences.

~CHAPTER ONE~

Resettlers

They come, and come, and come, these people from Samara, Tula, Ekaterinoslav, Chernigov, Kiev, and Podolia—from early spring to late fall, to the east and back. The wealthy and the poor, the strong and ill, the smart and stupid, older folks and those just married. Russians and Tatars, Mordvins and Chuvash, Ukrainians and Germans. Where are they going? To Kustanai, Turkestan, and Merv, to Tomsk Cabinet Land, Akmolinsk, Semipalatinsk, Semirechia, some to look for the Chinese salient and others to seek land in India. Why? What drives them? This question is so important that I must consider it.

—V. L. Dedlov, *Pereselentsy i novyia mesta*

They left for the most basic of reasons—because of "land hunger," because the terms of the Emancipation Statute of 1861 had burdened them with redemption payments and cut them off from some of the best lands close to home, because of corrupt local officials, limited employment opportunities, and usurious interest rates on loans. They came to Siberia and the Kazakh steppe because land was plentiful, and making a new start seemed preferable to continuing to eke out an existence back home. This process was known as resettlement (*pereselenie* in Russian) because it consisted of already settled people moving to a different, usually distant, site. Peasants had been resettling themselves for centuries, but never in such numbers. More than a million crossed the Ural Mountains dividing the European from the Asian portions of the Empire before the end of the century. After a lull during the war against Japan and the 1905 revolution, the numbers reached unprecedented proportions. Over half a million resettled in 1907, and even more migrated in each of the next two years.[1]

---

1. Adam McKeown names migration to Siberia, Manchuria, Central Asia, and Japan from northeast Asia and Russia as one of the three great long-distance migration flows of the period 1840–1940 in *Melancholy*

They came also because the Imperial Russian state now encouraged newcomers. It was eager to colonize its sparsely populated and "wild" Asian territories with Orthodox Slavic peasants, among other reasons, to "forestall territorial encroachment" by the Chinese to the south.[2] It established favorable conditions for departure. The Ministry of Internal Affairs and later the Ministry of Agriculture's Resettlement Administration identified, surveyed, and marked off parcels or plots (*uchastki*) of land for settlement. They also set up way stations to assist and count the number of travelers and provided reduced fares on steamships and the railroad and start-up loans to those who registered in advance. The progressive extension of the Trans-Siberian Railroad, from the 1890s until the second decade of the twentieth century, reduced the time and expense in transit and helped to shape the direction of resettlement. These and associated measures designed to control resettlement comprised a *regime* of migration.

Tsarist officials frequently modified and occasionally suspended parts of their resettlement regime. After the hiatus created by the 1917 Revolution, Soviet officials sought to revive what their predecessors had established, but also gave latitude to regional authorities who pursued alternative regimes. Beginning in the early 1930s and extending over the remainder of the Stalin era, the state became more proactive. It recruited Red Army soldiers, recently collectivized peasants living in more densely populated regions, and, during the Second World War, evacuees for resettlement not so much in Siberia but elsewhere on lands designated for development or from which local inhabitants had been deported. Fundamental to these practices and extending over the remainder of the Soviet period was the assumption of responsibility by the state to align population with natural resources, which it pursued not only via resettlement, but also other migration regimes. Nevertheless, with the exception of the Virgin Lands program of the 1950s, post-Stalin era resettlement regimes were more modest in ambition and scope.

The practices settlers pursued to bend regimes of resettlement to their purposes we refer to as their *repertoires*. They included determining when in the family's life-cycle resettlement made the most sense, choosing who if anyone would remain behind, and evaluating information about where to settle from occasional travelers, relatives and neighbors who already had resettled, scouts (*khodoki*) sent to inspect territory, and state officials. Decisions about what time of the year to depart and the disposition of property also entered into settlers' repertoires, as did whether to seek the state's assistance or travel and settle by one's own devices.

Order: Asian Migration and the Globalization of Borders (New York, 2008), 47–50. On peasant resettlement in earlier centuries, see David Moon, "Peasant Migration and the Settlement of Russia's Frontiers, 1550–1897," *The Historical Journal* 4, no. 4 (1997): 859–93. For the numbers from 1885 to 1913, see A. A. Kaufman, "Pereseleniia i pereselencheskii vopros v Rossii," in *Entsiklopedicheskii slovar' tovarishchestva "Br. A. i I. Granat i Ko,"* 7th ed. (St. Petersburg, 1914), 31: 548.

2. Adam McKeown, "Global Migration, 1846–1940," *Journal of World History* 15, no. 2 (2004): 158, 174.

Among those who wrote about peasant resettlement to Siberia in the late nineteenth and early twentieth century, some were astounded at peasants' willingness to undertake long and arduous journeys into the unknown. A report that appeared in a St. Petersburg journal of populist (narodnik) persuasion cited a group that abandoned their homes in Kursk province to resettle in Siberia's Tomsk province despite the lack of government approval. The peasants allegedly comforted themselves with the thought "if we sit on the pot, they won't throw us off."[3] A. A. Kaufman, one of the most respected of contemporary experts whom we shall meet many times in these pages, used the pathological metaphor of a "fever" (goriachka) to convey the "spontaneous character" of peasant resettlement. People departed, he claimed, "without any clear image of where they intend to settle."[4] Others, such as the journalist V. L. Dedlov, cited far-fetched "rumors" impelling peasants—"the smart and the stupid"—to set out for "the Chinese salient" or "land in India."[5]

Aside from a yawning cultural gap between peasants and educated society, these comments suggest that settlers' repertoires did not sit well with the resettlement regime. But it would not do to exaggerate the difference. Each adapted syncretically to the other. The tsarist state accommodated the peasant institution of scouting, and many settlers did abide by and benefit from the regime's strictures. In Soviet times and especially under Stalin the rules became more stringent, but settlers asserted their priorities too, returning home when conditions proved intolerable, and extracting other concessions. Above all, both regimes and repertoires relied heavily on the family as the essential unit of resettlement.

Russian resettlement was far from unique in these respects. As José Moya points out, the transatlantic migrations of the nineteenth and early twentieth centuries that also inspired the use of the fever metaphor were "accomplished basically by the primary, microsocial networks of humble folks, by kin and friends, and by friends of friends." But "the power of this popular, microsocial revolution . . . came from its interaction with the macrostructural revolutions [of] macadamized roads, trains, steamers, and . . . the expanding apparatus of the liberal state."[6] Minus the roads and the state's liberality, the same held for resettlement in Russian political space.

The movement of peasants across the vast Eurasian steppe might also be compared to settlers making their way across the North American plains. Both entailed families of

3. The quotation comes from *Severnyi vestnik*, no. 11 (1888): 195, as cited in M. K. Churkin, " 'Situatsiia riska' kak faktor formirovaniia i realizatsii migratsionnogo potentsiala zemledel'cheskogo naseleniia evropeiskoi chasti Rossii vo vtoroi polovine XIX—nachale XX v.," in Diatlov, *Migratsii i diaspory*, 72.

4. A. A. Kaufman, *Sibirskoe pereselenie na iskhode XIX veka, istoriko-statisticheskii ocherk*, 2nd ed. (St. Petersburg, 1901), 19.

5. V. L. Dedlov, *Pereselentsy i novyia mesta* (St. Petersburg, 1894), 102. For the widespread use of the "fever" metaphor, see José Moya, *Cousins and Strangers: Spanish Immigrants in Buenos Aires, 1850–1930* (Berkeley, 1998), 95–96.

6. Ibid., 116–17.

European origin traveling overland to take up the plow anew. Both in their colonizing thrust brought much distress and irrevocable change to indigenous non-Europeans' way of life.[7] Yet not all frontiers are alike. The settlement of Siberia, the steppes of Kazakhstan, and the Russian Far East depended to a far greater degree on deportees and exiles than did the American interior, and whereas the state dictated the terms in the Russian case, in America bankers and real estate speculators loomed large. Nevertheless, as the historian Kate Brown pointed out, the "gridded lives" led by newcomers to both Kazakhstan and Montana resembled each other to such an extent that they found themselves in "nearly the same place."[8]

Resettlement to Siberia in the Late Nineteenth and Early Twentieth Centuries

One "fine spring day" in May 1907, a peasant by the name of Sumkin—we know only his surname and that his given name began with the letter "M"—left his native village in Kaluga province in search of "open land" in Siberia. He hoped to build "a good peasant life without eternal need, without frequent harvest failures, and without cruel bondage to rural kulaks." He traveled aboard a "resettlement train" that headed east through the central Russian towns of Tula and Riazan', dipped south to Tambov, and then east again through Penza, before crossing the Volga and proceeding east-northeast through Ufa and across the Urals into Siberia.[9] He continued traveling by train as far as Omsk, where he boarded a steamer for a six-day journey to Semipalatinsk province. Proceeding another 400 miles to the east, he visited a number of potential sites for settlement, including the Zaisan district (uezd) up against the Chinese border.

Sumkin was one of some five million peasants whom officials recorded as resettling in Siberia between 1885 and 1913. Slightly over a million, including Sumkin, were registered as "scouts," people dispatched by families to identify and lay claim to land appropriate for settlement. Most peasants seeking to resettle did so because, like Sumkin, they

---

7. Nicholas Breyfogle, *Heretics and Colonizers: Forging Russia's Empire in the South Caucasus* (Ithaca, 2005), 6–7; Willard Sunderland, "The 'Colonization Question': Visions of Colonization in Late Imperial Russia," *Jahrbücher für Geschichte Osteuropas* 48, no. 2 (2000): 219–20; Andrei Znamenskii, "'The Ethic of Empire' on the Siberian Borderland: The Peculiar Case of the 'Rock People,' 1791–1878," in Breyfogle, Schreider, and Sunderland, *Peopling the Russian Periphery*, 108.

8. Kate Brown, "Gridded Lives: Why Kazakhstan and Montana Are Nearly the Same Place," *The American Historical Review* 106, no. 1 (2001): 17–48.

9. M. V. Sumkin, *V Sibir' za zemleiu (iz kaluzhskoi gubernii v semipalatinskuiu oblast')*, zapiski khodoka (Moscow, 1908), 3, 8–9.

had grown weary of neediness and bad harvests and hoped they could do better in Siberia on land made available for farming. When asked in the mid-1890s why they had left their homes to settle in Siberia's Tomsk province, peasants most frequently cited the shortage of arable land (malozemel'e), lack of hay, the inaccessibility of forests, and crop failures.[10]

In at least two respects, however, Sumkin was unusual. First, his native province of Kaluga, located southwest of Moscow in the heart of the Central Industrial region, provided relatively few settlers to Siberia. Peasants populating Siberia in the late nineteenth and early twentieth centuries tended to come from the Black Earth provinces of Kursk, Tambov, Chernigov, Voronezh, and Poltava farther to the south, or from provinces closer to Siberia such as Perm, Samara, and Viatka. Kaluga peasants were far more likely to engage in seasonal labor migration over shorter distances or cottage industry to supplement their farming activities. Second, Sumkin was one of few peasants seeking land in Siberia who left a written account of his experience. Scouts more frequently sent letters shortly after arriving at their destinations. Like others from relatives who had settled earlier, the letters were intended to convince the folks back home to make the long journey to Siberia and thus, as Willard Sunderland has noted, "their accent is mostly (though not exclusively) on the positive."[11] Some exulted ("You will die where you are, but here you will be resurrected"; "Enjoyment—what hay!"); others more modestly contended that "here it is quite possible to live."[12] Settlers in Tomsk cited such letters—as well as orally transmitted descriptions by wanderers and fellow villagers who had returned from periods of exile, military service, or working for wages—in their explanations of what had persuaded them to leave.[13]

Sumkin's account conforms to Sunderland's observation that, unlike letters, first-person narratives "were produced expressly for publication by peasant authors who wished to discourage other peasants from resettling." Sumkin claimed to have been misled by a Resettlement Administration booklet that seemed to indicate an abundance of grain in the Semipalatinsk region. He envied earlier settlers who had taken the best plots of land and were living "in such outstanding well-being," while he was compelled to search in an area

10. A. A. Kaufman, Khoziaistvennoe polozhenie pereselentsev vodvorennykh na kazennykh zemliakh tomskoi gubernii po dannym proizvedennago v 1894 g. po porucheniiu g. tomskago gubernatora, podvornago izsledovaniia (St. Petersburg, 1895), vol. 1, pt. 1, 5, 16, 37, 42, 49, 72.

11. In his analysis of Russian peasant settlers' written accounts, Willard Sunderland draws on roughly fifty letters and "a small handful of first-person . . . accounts printed in journals or in pamphlet form." See Willard Sunderland, "Peasant Pioneering: Russian Peasant Settlers Describe Colonization and the Eastern Frontier, 1880s–1910s," Journal of Social History 34, no. 4 (2001): 902.

12. V. N. Grigor'ev, Pereseleniia krest'ian riazanskoi gubernii (Moscow, 1885), 106–8.

13. Kaufman, Khoziaistvennoe polozhenie, vol. 1, pt. 1, 23, 33, 67, 84, 150, 155, 297, 341; vol. 1, pt. 2, 2, 11, 44.

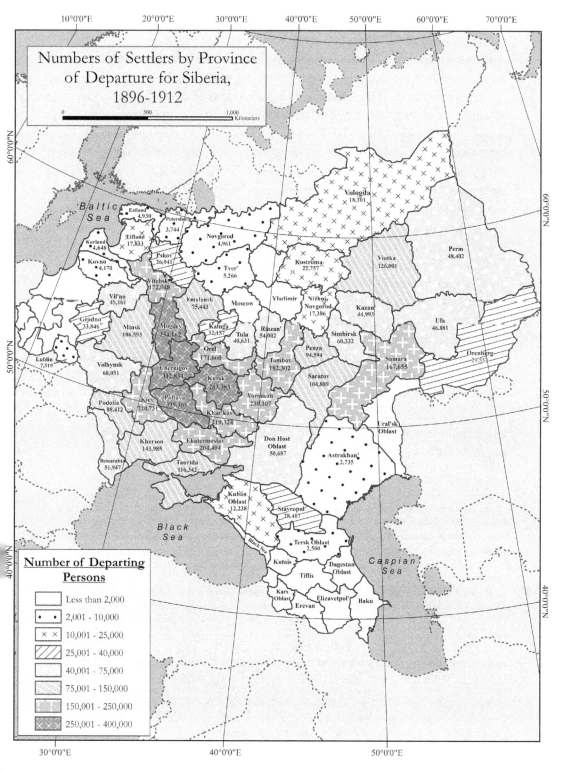

Numbers of Settlers by Province of Departure for Siberia, 1896-1912

0   500   1,000
Kilometers

Number of Departing Persons

- Less than 2,000
- 2,001 - 10,000
- 10,001 - 25,000
- 25,001 - 40,000
- 40,001 - 75,000
- 75,001 - 150,000
- 150,001 - 250,000
- 250,001 - 400,000

Baltic Sea

Estland 4,930
Liiland 17,833
Kurland 4,648
Kovno 4,170
St. Petersburg 3,744
Pskov 26,941
Vil'no 45,161
Grodno 33,846
Vitebsk 172,048
Novgorod 4,961
Tver' 5,266
Smolensk 75,443
Moscow
Vladimir
Kostroma 22,757
Nizhni-Novgorod 17,386
Vologda 18,101
Viatka 126,001
Perm 48,402
Kazan' 44,993
Ufa 46,881
Simbirsk 60,332
Orenburg 29,55?
Minsk 106,593
Mogilev 254,162
Kaluga 32,157
Tula 40,631
Riazan' 54,002
Penza 94,594
Samara 167,655
Lublin 7,519
Volhynsk 68,051
Chernigov 312,834
Orel 171,660
Kursk 263,383
Tambov 182,302
Saratov 104,889
Ural'sk Oblast
Podolia 88,412
Kiev 220,731
Poltava 399,461
Khar'kov 219,324
Voronezh 236,107
Kherson 143,985
Ekaterinoslav 204,404
Don Host Oblast 50,687
Astrakhan' 2,735
Bessarabia 51,947
Taurida 116,342
Kuban' Oblast 12,238
Stavropol' 28,407
Black Sea
Tersk Oblast 2,500
Caspian Sea
Kutais
Tiflis
Dagestan Oblast
Kars Oblast
Erevan
Elizavetpol'
Baku

Map 1.1 Areas of departure of settlers for Siberia from European Russia, 1896–1912

populated largely by "Kirgiz" who often resorted to stealing settlers' livestock. "Having seen and learned all this," he returned home empty handed.[14]

In this respect as well, Sumkin was not at all unusual; most scouts did not succeed. Of the 150,000 whom the authorities recorded crossing into Siberia during 1907, only 27 percent registered land. This was slightly less than the average of 30 percent for the years 1896 through 1913, perhaps reflecting the fact that more scouts went in search of land in 1907 than in any other year.[15] Scouts' ability to find land also depended on its availability, which in turn required the state's surveyors to designate parcels for settlement. Before the opening of the Trans-Siberian Railroad, which greatly facilitated overland travel, good land could be had in the western Siberian provinces of Tomsk and Tobol'sk.[16] But as Sumkin found out to his chagrin, surveyors had difficulty keeping up with the pace of settlement, which pushed relentlessly farther south into the Kazakh steppe and Central Asia as well as Enisei province in eastern Siberia and the Amur and Maritime oblasts.

Some settlers journeyed to the Far Eastern edge of the Empire entirely by sea. Embarking at Odessa, they traveled through the Suez Canal and across the Indian Ocean, around the Malaysian peninsula and up the coast of Indochina and China, putting in at Constantinople, Port Said, Colombo, Singapore, Shanghai, and Nagasaki, before reaching Vladivostok some forty-five days later. Of the more than two thousand who sailed in 1897 aboard the ships of the Volunteer Fleet, half originated in Kiev province while nearly a third hailed from Chernigov.[17] Georgii Terent'evich Khokhlov, who made the trip the following year on behalf of his community of Uralsk Cossack Old Believers, went in search of the mythic "Land of White Waters" (Belovod'e), reputed to be somewhere in Indochina. Like Sumkin, he left an account of his journey, and like Sumkin he failed to find what he was looking for.[18]

---

14. Sunderland, "Peasant Pioneering," 902; Sumkin, V Sibir' za zemleiu, 46–47, 60–61. Like virtually all Russians, Sumkin uses the term "Kirgiz" to refer to people who from the 1920s onward would be known as Kazakhs. We use the term "Kazakh" throughout unless referring to people whom Russians in Imperial times called Kara Kirghiz, and thereafter Kyrgyz.

15. A. A. Kaufman, "Pereselencheskaia statistika," in Entsiklopedicheskii slovar' tovarishchestva "Br. A. i I. Granat i Ko," 31: 7–8.

16. On the railroad's impact on migration, see Treadgold, Great Siberian Migration, 131–52; Steven G. Marks, "Conquering the Great East: Kulomzin, Peasant Resettlement, and the Creation of Modern Siberia," in Rediscovering Russia in Asia: Siberia and the Russian Far East, ed. Stephen Kotkin and David Wolff (Armonk, NY, 1995), 23–39.

17. Rossiiskii Gosudarstvennyi Istoricheskii Arkhiv (RGIA), f. 391, op. 2, d. 211, ll. 7, 76, 79. The eight deaths reported among them (seven of whom were children under two years old) represented a rate similar to what overland travelers experienced. On death rates from 1895 to 1899 among migrants traveling through Cheliabinsk, the main checkpoint of the Resettlement Administration, see Komitet Sibirskoi Zheleznoi Dorogi, ed., Kolonizatsiia Sibiri v sviazi s obshcheim pereselencheskim voprosom (St. Petersburg, 1900), 188.

18. G. T. Khokhlov, "Puteshestvie Ural'skikh kazakov v 'Belovodskoe tsarstvo,'" Zapiski imperatorskago russkago geograficheskogo obshchestva po otdeleniiu etnografii 28, no. 1 (1903): 3–101.

Figure 1 Settlers one week after arrival in Maritime province, *Aziatskaia Rossiia*, vol. 1 (St. Petersburg: A. F. Marks, 1914), 525.

But millions of peasants did. Which peasants? A survey that Kaufman conducted of the economic condition at point of origin, cost of travel, and experiences after arrival of households in 131 settlements in Tomsk province found that former state peasants were slightly more likely to leave than former serfs. Middling families predominated among resettlers. The explanation for the latter finding conforms to patterns of long-distance migration elsewhere. A household elder put it succinctly in explaining why only 18 of 231 families receiving permission to leave a district in Kursk province actually departed for Siberia: "there was no point for the rich to go; and the poor had nothing."[19]

Households with "nothing" could not resettle because, although the state provided assistance in the form of reduced railroad fares, loans, and deferments on taxation and military service, resettlement could cost each household quite a bit.[20] The Kursk settlers who embarked on their journey in late April and arrived in early July 1890 spent an average of 130

19. Kaufman, *Khoziaistvennoe polozhenie*, vol. 1, pt. 1, 11.

20. The "state" consisted of the Ministry of Internal Affairs' Land Section before 1896 and its Resettlement Administration thereafter. In 1906 the Resettlement Administration was transferred to the Ministry of Agriculture.

rubles per family. Despite the unusual length of time on the road (caused by having to wait an entire month for a steamer at Tiumen), their travel expenses came to less than those of the families from another district in Kursk province, which amounted to an average of 160 rubles.[21] The railroad significantly reduced both the time and cost of travel. Donald Treadgold cites an average of 57 rubles per family for a trip from central Russia to Tomsk in 1890, but only 15 rubles in 1898 after the introduction of rail service.[22] Still, new settlers had substantial start-up costs for which many went into debt or hired themselves out to old settlers.[23]

As often occurs in long-distance migration, many who sought to resettle beyond the Urals did so illegally; moving from one place to another was common, and for all those whose managed to adjust to conditions on the frontier, a substantial proportion returned home. The legality of migration of course depended on the conditions imposed by the state. These initially were quite stringent. Peasants had to obtain permission from both their own commune and the one they wished to join. Certain regions remained off limits. Officials eventually began to look more favorably on resettlement as a means of alleviating population pressure in the central Russian heartland and strengthening the Russian presence in the Asian part of the Empire to counterbalance what they perceived as growing threats from Japanese expansionists and Chinese migrants. The problem then became how to ensure "correct colonization," that is, matching resources to population and rationally distributing services.[24]

"Irregular" (samovol'nye; literally, "self-willed") migrants shadowed the state's regime at every stage of its long, tortured evolution. Even after 1896 when the Resettlement Administration made reduced fares and other assistance contingent on following proper procedures for registering land, a significant proportion of migrants did not do so. If slightly over one in every four passing through Cheliabinsk in 1895 lacked authorization to settle, then in the following year irregulars made up 44 percent of all settlers and by 1899 over half (53 percent) of the total.[25] The proportion would decline thereafter but rarely dip below 20

---

21. Kaufman, Khoziaistvennoe polozhenie, vol. 1, pt. 1, 7, 11.

22. Treadgold, Great Siberian Migration, 131.

23. Andrei Stankevich, Materialy dlia izucheniia byta pereselentsev tobol'skoi gubernii za 15 let, s kontsa 70-kh godov po 1893 g., 2 vols. (Moscow, 1895), 1: 18, 26, 28, 53, 67, 82; A. A. Khramkov and A. N. Klychnikov, "Pereselentsy i starozhily v sele Anisimovo (Borovlianskoe) Barnaul'skogo uezda (opyt analiza Vserossiiskoi sel'skokhoziaistvennoi perepisi 1917 g.)," in Demograficheskoe i khoziaistvennoe razvitie altaiskoi derevni vo vtoroi polovine XIX–nachale XX v. (na materialakh massovykh istochnikov): Sbornik statei, ed. V. N. Razgon and I. G. Silina (Barnaul: Azbuka, 2002), 101–21. The term "old settler" generally referred to someone who had arrived before the emancipation of the serfs in 1861.

24. Treadgold, Great Siberian Migration, 67–81; Francois-Xavier Coquin, La Sibérie: Peuplement et immigration paysanne au xixe siècle (Paris, 1969), 349–85; Sunderland, Taming the Wild Field, 177–220; Peter Holquist, "'In Accord with State Interests and the People's Wishes': The Technocratic Ideology of Imperial Russia's Resettlement Administration," Slavic Review 69, no. 1 (2010): 151–80.

25. Kaufman, Sibirskoe pereselenie, 51.

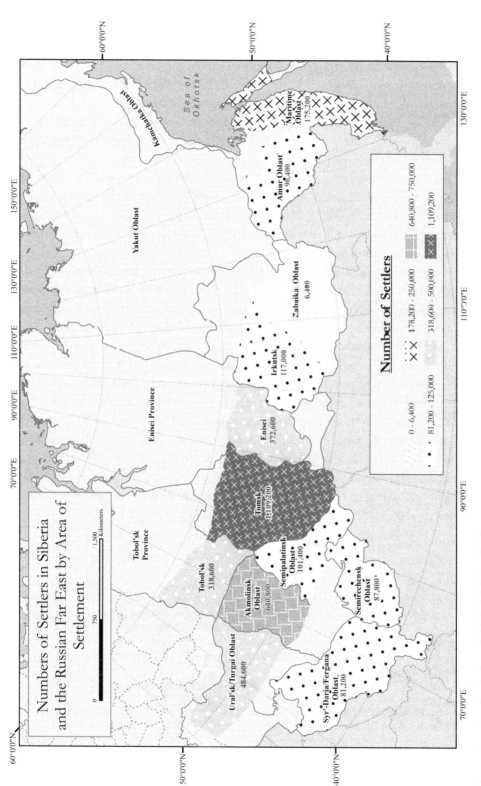

Map 1.2 Location of settler households in Asiatic Russia, 1893–1912

percent. It would be overly romantic to ascribe such behavior to a longing for freedom or the persistence of resistance against the weight of the tutelary state. For every group of settlers who squatted on land in remote regions undetected—at least for a while—by agents of the state, or who had decided from the beginning to have nothing to do with officialdom, most migrated irregularly for quite mundane reasons.[26] Some migrants abused the system by registering for a certain parcel, but only to take advantage of the reduced fare in order to have a look around, perhaps settling somewhere else or working for wages.[27] More often, they set out for a parcel on which they were registered, only to run out of funds or otherwise change their minds en route, causing them to end their journey somewhere else. Other settlers sought to follow the rules, only to be confronted by local officials' refusal to grant them permission to leave their commune, or delays in the processing of requests that could drag on for years (by which time applicants might already have sold their property), or assignments to places the applicants had not requested.[28]

Whatever the reason, irregular settlers violated the Resettlement Administration's commitment to rational settlement as well as officials' own amour propre. No less troublesome for officials were settlers who had registered with a particular commune or received permission to form their own but who, after awhile, picked up stakes again and moved on. In some cases, according to ethnographers' investigations, this was because new settlers wore out their welcome with old settlers or grew weary of being exploited by them. In others, relations among new settlers became intolerably fractious, causing some families to abandon the settlement where they were registered and seek a new one.[29] But Kaufman thought he detected a more worrisome development. "Within the Altai okrug so beloved by settlers," he wrote shortly after the turn of the century, "some 22,000 moved from one place to another between 1889 and 1892 and in the district of Tomsk almost 15 percent of all settlers changed location." Interpreting such movement as a measure of declining economic well-being and noting that as older areas of colonization filled up and conditions for settling in (*vodvorenie*) had worsened, he predicted that such turnover of households would increase.[30]

---

26. For instances of settlements discovered post hoc by authorities, see *Kolonizatsiia Sibiri*, 202–3; N. Iadrintsev, "Nashi vyseleniia i kolonizatsiia," *Vestniik Evropy*, no. 6 (1880): 473–74; A. A. Kaufman, *Pereselentsy-Arendatory turgaiskoi oblasti (2-ia chast' otcheta starshago proizvoditelia rabot Kaufmana po komandirovke v turgaiskuiu oblast')* (St. Petersburg, 1897), 27–28, 33 (of attachment). For the earlier "peculiar case of the 'rock people" of the Altai, see Znamenski, " 'Ethic of Empire' on the Siberian Borderland," 106–26.

27. *Sbornik uzakonenii i rasporiazhenii o pereselenii*, 16 (circulars of Ministry of Internal Affairs, no. 34, 1894, and no. 1, 1897).

28. Kaufman, *Khoziaistvennoe polozhenie*, vol. 1, pt. 1, 11, 16, 33, 37, 82, 84, 118, 129, 181, 257, 269; vol. 1, pt. 2, 44; vol. 1, pt. 3, 2; Stankevich, *Materialy dlia izucheniia byta pereselentsev*, 1: 117.

29. Settlers who rented land from Kazakhs in the steppe region were notorious for being peripatetic, moving every year. See Kaufman, *Pereselentsy-Arendatory turgaiskoi oblasti*, 33.

30. Kaufman, "Pereseleniia i pereselencheskii vopros," 515.

We are fortunate to have traces of peasants' own explanations in the form of petitions requesting the right to move from one parcel to another. For example, in October 1907—just about the time Sumkin had returned to his native village—three peasants representing a recently settled community in Tomsk province addressed Her Highness Mariia Fedorovna. They had left their "dear homeland" with "hopes of improving our condition," but the parcel assigned by the Resettlement Administration had proven "less beneficial and even unsuitable." They asked for one "near the Gulinsk River at the site of the Nikolaev yurt." More desperate still were peasants from Vitebsk province who had settled in a district of Tomsk province on a parcel that turned out "to be without water." "Cattle and people are dying," wrote their spokesman, who reported that the petitioners intended to abandon the parcel for state land in "the Martynov ravine." Another plenipotentiary, Pavel Efimov Tsvikh, saw fit to address his petition to the tsar. His clients, ten families with over a hundred members, had settled in 1908 in another district of Tomsk but the parcel's swampiness and complete unsuitability for grain cultivation "forced" them to seek another section. Tsvikh claimed that both the local resettlement official and surveyor had assisted them in locating and moving to "the only available parcel in the district," but it turned out not to be available after all. Ejected from the parcel, the families were "dispersed, living in utter dependence, wherever and however."[31] Like letters to authority in general, these petitions conformed in both the choice of words and their content to certain conventions, one of which undoubtedly was to exaggerate the neediness of the petitioners. Nevertheless, it would be unwise to minimize the disappointment these people must have felt after resettling and the challenges they confronted in re-resettling.

According to the law of 13 July 1889, the state reserved the right to expel and return to their homes peasants who migrated to Siberia without permission. The law, however, was "without practical application" because rounding up such individuals and their families and supervising their expulsion went far beyond the state's capacities.[32] Ironically, much of the state's campaign against irregular settlers stemmed from its assertion that they were more likely to return home than those who followed prescribed procedures.[33] That may have been, but as so often occurs with migrants, actual experience defied official categories. Take for example the five families with twenty-eight members from Berdichev district in Kiev province who, having received permission to migrate to the Southern Ussuri territory, left Odessa by ship in early February 1901. Arriving in Vladivostok on 20 April, they set

---

31. RGIA, f. 391, op. 2, d. 417, ll. 3, 12, 58–59. All three petitions were rejected by the Resettlement Administration.

32. Kaufman, *Sibirskoe pereselenie*, 23.

33. For example, whereas 4.9 percent of registered settlers (amounting to 14,877 individuals) returned home in 1909, 11.9 percent (33,139) of irregulars returned. See N. Turchaninov, "Pereselencheskoe dvizhenie v 1909 godu," *Voprosy kolonizatsii* 6 (1910): 20–21.

out to inspect the parcels assigned to them, only to discover to their horror that the land was under water because of seasonal flooding. Succumbing as well to rumors of the high cost of bread, meat, and horses, they requested from a local resettlement official permission to inspect land in the Amur or elsewhere, but were refused and instead given travel papers to return home. Their average expenses came to 1,000 rubles per family, which they were able to afford only because they had sold off everything before departing.[34]

Those who could not bear the conditions to which they were exposed and had the means to return comprised a sufficient number of people to constitute the official category of "returnees." The most detailed statistical material on returnees appeared in volumes compiled by the statistician G. A. Priimak and published periodically by the Resettlement Administration. Covering settlers who passed through the Cheliabinsk and Syzran' checkpoints, Priimak's data show that of a total of nearly three million individuals who migrated to Siberia between 1896 and 1909, close to four hundred thousand (13 percent) returned. The proportion fluctuated from a high of 37 percent in 1901 to a low of 6 percent in 1907, the very year of Sumkin's unsuccessful search for land.[35]

Much about returnees defied explanation. Writing in 1906, Kaufman noted the gradual and seemingly inexorable rise in the percentage of returnees from 3 to 4 percent in the 1880s and early 1890s, to nearly 14 percent in 1894–98, and nearly 19 percent between 1899 and 1903. Migrants, he surmised, were finding it increasingly difficult to set themselves up successfully because of a diminution of good land in western Siberia and the Kazakh steppe. He also argued that the quality of migrants had declined.

> If in the late 1880s and early 1890s investigators described a type of "settler-pioneer" . . . who prayed to God and relied on himself, not fearing the severity of the Siberian climate, and despite government antipathy or maybe because of it was able to overcome all obstacles, now weaker and less capable people consider migrating. . . . The migrant-pioneer of old has become the gray, commonplace, migrant mass.[36]

But if this were so, why did the rate of return plummet in subsequent years? Data from different provinces show not only gyrations of greater magnitude but also trajectories in opposite directions. For example, returnees from Chernigov province who passed through the Syzran' checkpoint varied from a low of just 3.5 percent of migrants in 1906 to a high of nearly 52 percent in 1911. Returnees to Kursk represented nearly 12 percent of migrants

34. V. V. Kir'iakov, *Ocherki po istorii pereselencheskago dvizheniia v Sibir' (V sviazi s istoriei zaseleniia Sibiri)* (Moscow, 1902), 179–80, citing *Russkie vedomosti*, no. 172, 1901.

35. N. Turchaninov, *Itogi pereselencheskago dvizeniia za vremia s 1896 po 1909 gg. (vkliuchitel'no)* (St. Petersburg, 1910), 44–45.

36. A. A. Kaufman, *Pereselenie: Mechty i deistvitel'nost'* (Moscow, 1906), 7, 18.

from that province in 1900, but 20.5 percent (of a much smaller number) in 1905, and only 3 percent in 1908.[37] Overall, as indicated by a zemstvo-sponsored study from 1913, the proportion of returnees dropped from almost 18 percent between 1896 and 1905 to about 12 percent between 1906 and 1912. Perhaps part of the explanation lay in the increased assistance that the zemstvos provided to migrants, for those from the eight southern Russian provinces represented by zemstvo agents in Siberia had lower return rates than from other European Russian provinces.[38] Then again, this was just what the zemstvos desired to demonstrate.

These studies listed up to fifteen different reasons for migrants returning. They included such entries as "did not have permission to stay," "plot of land was occupied," "insufficiency of means to set up farm," "farm was too far from market," "lack of timber for housing," and "severity of climate."[39] Based on returnees' responses to standard surveys conducted by officials at Cheliabinsk and Syzran', the list represented a panoply of calamities experienced by settlers. One wonders, though, what the unfortunates returning to Berdichev uezd would have told officials, for "land under water" did not figure in the list. Inquiries conducted by Kaufman and others among settlers elicited a slightly different set of explanations for the departure of neighbors. Typical of their responses were those given in the Vladimir settlement in Tomsk province. Founded in 1888 by sixty-six families—all state peasants from Kursk province—the settlement had accommodated a total of seventy-two families by the time Kaufman arrived in 1894. Of these, eleven had departed, seven of which had left immediately because they considered Vladimir a "wild place, [with] no church, and the midges frightened them."[40] Reports from other settlements mention abandonment by families "frightened" by midges, mosquitoes, and the wildness of the location, but also simply defeated by the poor quality of the land, lack of hay and forest, and poor grain harvests—reasons that echoed those given by settlers *seeking* land in Siberia.[41]

Dedlov described a family of returnees he encountered in the steppe region of Akmolinsk in the mid-1890s as a "heap of rags"; another group of families queried a few years

---

37. For Chernigov, see E. Dobrovol'skii, ed., *Pereselenie iz chernigovskoi gubernii v 1909–1911 gg.: Po materialam cheliabinskoi i syzranskago pereselencheskikh punktov* (Chernigov, 1913), 33. The average over seventeen years was 13.5 percent. For Kursk, see Turchaninov, *Itogi pereselencheskago dvizheniia*, 2–3.

38. Trudy statisticheskago otdela biuro iuzhno-russkoi oblastnoi zemskoi pereselencheskoi organizatsii, *Pereselenie v Sibir' iz vos'mi gubernii, vkhodiashchikh v sostav Iuzhno-Russkoi Oblastnoi Zemskoi Pereselencheskoi Organizatsii za 1906–1912 gg. Uchet semeinago pereseleniia. Tekst i svodnye tablitsy. Vypusk 1* (Poltava, 1913), 3–6. The eight provinces—Volhynia, Saratov, Kherson, Khar'kov, Voronezh, Kiev, Chernigov, and Poltava—sent just over one million migrants to Siberia between 1906 and 1913.

39. G. A. Priimak, *Tsifrovyi material dlia izucheniia pereselenii v Sibir' sobrannyi putem registratsii pereselentsev, prokhodivshikh v Sibir i vozvrashchikhsia iz Sibiri cherez Cheliabinsk v 1898 godu* (Moscow, 1904), 242.

40. Kaufman, *Khoziaistvennoe polozhenie*, vol. 1, pt. 1, 7.

41. Ibid., 15, 22, 50, 89. Settlers sometimes were intent on demonstrating their moral superiority, as in the case of those from Alekseevskii who described the twenty families that had returned "for stupid reasons."

later were described as "completely ruined but still not having quite succeeded in adjusting to their ruin." When queried about what they would do when they returned home, only the few fortunate families that had not sold all their property before departing for Siberia could bring themselves to answer the question.[42] It might be assumed that the families that stuck it out despite such hardships were tougher or more resourceful than those who returned. But even this assumption did not hold in all cases, for as Dedlov himself pointed out, only the most energetic among those that had failed had the strength to make the return journey.

These glimpses of returnees and the reasons why they abandoned settlements they once had risked so much to inhabit are tantalizingly suggestive. We would want to know additionally whether the families that returned had been among the more solid or marginal ones before departing for Siberia; whether deaths, births, and household divisions had figured among the burdens that made remaining in a settlement intolerable; and what other events or factors had intruded. In the absence of such information, about the only thing one can say with any confidence is, to paraphrase Tolstoy's dictum in *Anna Karenina*, every returnee family's situation was unhappy, but each was unhappy for a different reason.

Two final points about resettlement to Siberia are in order. The first is that in the minds of state officials and sections of educated society, Russian peasant settlers represented valuable assets in the mission to civilize the Empire's Asiatic peoples, "a wonderful and powerful colonizing element," in the words of Prime Minister Petr Stolypin.[43] Thus, when a contributor to the Resettlement Administration's journal *Voprosy kolonizatsii* wrote in 1907 that resettlement could assist in "the conversion of the Kirgiz to agriculture and the development of trades," he was only expressing a widely held view. In this case it was all the more fervently advanced because of disappointment with Siberian Cossacks who "not only have not influenced the steppe Kirgiz, but themselves have been subjected to their influence in their way of life and economic relations."[44] As for complaints that the pressure of settlers for more land was antagonizing the Kazakhs, the director of the Resettlement Administration G. V. Glinka told the Duma that "if there were two or three brawls last year, then

---

42. Dedlov, *Peredelentsy i novyia mesta*, 99. S. F., "K khronike pereselencheskago dvizeniia v Sibir' za poslednie gody," *Russkoe bogatstvo*, no. 6 (1901): 136.

43. P. A. Stolypin, "Iz perepiski P. A. Stolypina s Nikolaem Romanovym," *Krasnyi arkhiv* 5, no. 30 (1928): 82, cited in Charles Steinwedel, "Resettling People, Unsettling the Empire: Migration and the Challenge of Governance, 1861–1917," in Breyfogle, Schrader, and Sunderland, *Peopling the Russian Periphery*, 128. For analyses of changing and contested meanings of "colonization" in late Imperial Russia, see A.V. Remnev, "Vdvinut' Rossiiu v Sibir': Imperiia i russkaia kolonizatsiia vtoroi poloviny XIX-nachala XX vv.," *Ab Imperio*, no. 3 (2003): 135–58; Alberto Masoero, "Territorial Colonization in Late Imperial Russia: Stages in the Development of a Concept," *Kritika: Explorations in Russian and Eurasian History* 14, no. 1 (2013): 59–91.

44. O. R. Shkapskii, "Pereselentsy i agrarnyi vopros v semirechenskoi oblasti," *Voprosy kolonizatsii* 1 (1907): 81.

this still doesn't mean that all Kirgiz regard Russians with hostility." After all, he added, "the majority of the Kirgiz masses do not use the land especially often."[45] It was necessary to reinforce the settlement of the Kazakh steppe for another reason, asserted a Duma deputy: to counter the plans of the Chinese, who, as Dmitrii Mendeleev had warned years earlier, were bent on colonizing the region.[46]

But the point is that as culture bearers, peasant resettlers did not always fulfill the mission assigned to them (and in most cases were unaware of it). Kaufman observed that at least in Irkutsk and Enisei provinces, they "not only do not implant the economic practices of their homelands, but on the contrary completely assimilate to the economic relations of the native inhabitants, and cannot but assimilate, because such assimilation is a necessary condition of their very survival in the harsh Siberian environment."[47] The early twentieth-century historian of Siberian resettlement V. V. Kir'iakov extended this point to the cultural-spiritual realm, noting that given frequent and close contact with those of other faiths, "the Russian becomes indifferent to his own faith."[48] Fears of "nativization," or at least the atrophying of positive qualities associated with Russian ethnicity, appeared frequently enough to warrant the label "panic."[49]

The second point is that in resettling, peasants were seeking to reproduce elsewhere a familiar way of life associated with extensive grain cultivation on household plots held either in communal or familial tenure. The ability of peasants to perpetuate this kind of agriculture at home had become seriously degraded in the years following the abolition of serfdom. "Resettlement," argued Kaufman, stemmed from "the given density of population require[ing] conversion to a more intensive culture," an impossible task given "the inertness of the masses."[50] Thus, if the migration of five million peasants to the east constituted a "resettlement revolution," it was in intent a profoundly conservative revolution.[51] Whether by transplanting themselves these peasants managed in fact to break their "cruel bondage to rural kulaks" is beyond the scope of our story.

---

45. *Voprosy kolonizatsii* 3 (1908): 321.

46. A. K. Tregubov, "Pereselencheskoe delo v semipalatinskoi i semirechenskoi oblastiakh," *Voprosy kolonizatsii* 6 (1910): 172.

47. A. A. Kaufman, "Organizatsiia i glavneishie vyvody khoziaistvenno-statisticheskago izsledovaniia irkutskoi i eniseiskoi gubernii," in *Sbornik pravovedeniia i obshchestvennykh znanii* 4 (1895): 144, cited in *Kolonizatsiia Sibiri*, 368–69.

48. Kir'iakov, *Ocherki po istorii pereselencheskago dvizheniia*, 327.

49. A. V. Remnev, N. G. Suvorova, "Upravliaemaia kolonizatsiia i stikhiinye migratsionnye protsessy na aziatskikh okrainakh rossiiskoi imperii: Otsenki i prognozy imperskikh ekspertov," in Diatlov, *Migratsii i diaspory*, 62–63. See also Willard Sunderland, "Russians into Iakuts? 'Going Native' and Problems of Russian National Identity in the Siberian North, 1870s–1914," *Slavic Review* 55, no. 4 (1996): 806–25.

50. Kaufman, "Pereseleniia i pereselenskii vopros," 508.

51. P. P. Vibe, "Vliianie germanofobskikh nastroenii na pereselencheskuiu politiku v Sibiri na rubezhe XIX–XX vv.," in Diatlov, *Migratsii i diaspory*, 79.

Resettlement in the Interwar Years

Like so many other things, the resettlement of land-hungry peasants suffered with the outbreak of World War I. The number of peasants recorded by the Resettlement Administration as settling on its designated plots beyond the Urals shrank from about 336,000 in 1914 to 28,000 in 1915 and less than 6,000 during 1917.[52] The decline undoubtedly had more to do with the rapid shift in the bureaucratic institution's priorities—from making land available for settlement to absorbing prisoners of war and refugees—than from any diminution of peasants' desire to resettle.[53] As for recently resettled peasants, archival sources testify to the efforts of the Resettlement Administration to adjust to the uncertain circumstances that followed the overthrow of the tsar in February 1917.

On more than one occasion it announced its intention to replace the institution of the peasant land captain (krest'ianskii nachal'nik, Siberia's equivalent to the zemskii nachal'nik of most European Russian provinces) with local self-government. In June, it urged all land committees and commissars of the Provisional Government as well as local administration personnel to "use all your authority and influence to persuade resettlers" not to abandon their new property and return home in anticipation of an immediate division of landlords' property.[54] But as suggested by at least some requests to return home that have survived in the archives, the longed-for "black repartition" (chernyi peredel) of peasant legend did not motivate all those seeking to return. Some complained in terms identical to those lodged by settlers in earlier decades—of land that turned out to be too hilly, too stone laden, too dry, too salty, too sandy, too lacking in forest resources—as if war and revolution meant little. Only the response they received—that "your petition can be resolved only after the resolution of the agrarian question by the Constituent Assembly"—differed.[55]

More fraught were relations between settlers and Kazakhs in the wake of the massive Turkestan revolt of 1916. The tsarist government's conscription of Central Asian men into labor brigades sparked the revolt. But the systematic conversion of grazing land into parcels for settlement and settlers' illegal encroachments on remaining pastureland, the rejection of numerous appeals from Kazakh representatives to cease further Russian

---

52. N. I. Platunov, *Pereselencheskaia politika sovetskogo gosudarstva i ee osushchestvlenie v SSSR (1917–iiun' 1941 gg.)* (Tomsk, 1976), 35.

53. RGAE, f. 478 (Narodnyi komissariat zemledelii RSFSR), op. 6, d. 1332, ll. 12–18. This is a communication from the "Commissariat [*sic*] of Agriculture, Resettlement Administration," dated March 29, 1917 to local officials lamenting the "significant supply of settlers' plots not being put under settlement (*zaselenie*)" owing to a lack of surveying, road building, well drilling, and other measures.

54. RGAE, f. 478, op. 6, d. 1331, ll. 8, 17, 53.

55. RGAE, f. 478, op. 6, d. 1347, ll. 4, 13, 40, 84.

settlement, the wartime conscription of livestock, and the further deterioration of the Kazakh economy already had provided plenty of tinder. In the course of the revolt, Kazakhs
attacked settlements large and small, killing several thousands of inhabitants and seizing
their livestock.[56] Soon after the overthrow of the tsar, the Provisional Government stopped
the conscription of Central Asians, amnestied those arrested during the rebellion, and
returned some land confiscated by tsarist authorities. But it drew the line at any further
concessions to the Kazakhs, again invoking the Constituent Assembly as ultimate
arbiter.[57]

The new Soviet government had no wish to do away with the Resettlement Administration or jettison its staff. As one Commissariat of Agriculture (Narkomzem) official pointed
out in February 1918, "To destroy the technical apparatus of the local resettlement bodies
that contain experienced and needed personnel would be extremely undesirable."[58] The
official, a Socialist Revolutionary by the name of A. E. Feofilaktov, may have been responding to news from Turkestan that congresses of Kazakh soviet deputies had disbanded the
resettler bureaucracy and transferred its funds to their own regional soviet. Soviets elsewhere seemed to have followed Turkestan's lead. By late March Feofilaktov described the
work of the Resettlement Administration over which he presided as "in complete ruin,"
and called for a Siberian Resettlement Congress to meet in Omsk in a month's time to resolve the issue.[59]

The revival of the resettlement apparatus had become urgent because the tide of migration between the Russian heartland and Siberia began to flow in the other direction. If in
1917 officials had feared the return of settlers to stake their claims on confiscated property
in European Russia, then already in the first months of 1918, workers seeking to escape
from food shortages in the cities began casting their eyes eastward. By early April an official
in Petrograd could "affirm that the flow of settlers . . . if not greater than in 1907–9, will
soon be so." This projection probably did not come to pass, but other reports referring to
the unavailability of transport, the hostility of the indigenous population to further

56. See P. G. Galuzo, *Turkestan-Koloniia (Ocherk istorii Turkestana ot zavoevaniia russkimi do revoliutsii 1917 goda)* (Oxford, 1986); B. S. Suleimenov and Ia. Basin, *Vosstanie 1916 goda v Kazakhstane* (Alma-Ata, 1977); Martha Brill Olcott, *The Kazakhs* (Stanford, 1987), 101–26; Daniel Brower, "Kyrgyz Nomads and Russian Pioneers: Colonization and Ethnic Conflict in the Turkestan Revolt of 1916," *Jahrbücher für Geschichte Osteuropas* 44, no. 1 (1996): 41–53.
57. RGAE, f. 478, op. 6, d. 1332, l. 34.
58. RGAE, f. 478, op. 6, d. 1331, ll. 26, 24–25. The Council of People's Commissars tried to give teeth to this commitment by approving annual pay scales for all employees of local resettlement organizations from directors (*zaveduiushchie*) down to couriers and kitchen help (ll. 24–25). See also Platunov, *Pereselencheskaia politika*, 36, which cites a report from this time claiming that "the Resettlement Administration was the sole department of the former Ministry of Agriculture that did not interrupt its work for a single day during the October Revolution."
59. RGAE, f. 478, op. 6, d. 1332, ll. 130, 164.

settlement, and general disorder reflected the actual difficulties of accommodating in Siberia a lot of hungry and frightened people.[60]

Should we regard these desperate migrants and the many who followed them as resettlers or refugees? Soviet authorities seeking to dilute the Cossack-dominated Southern Don region in 1919 with more politically reliable "peasant elements from Central Russia" assumed those elements would respond to the call as resettlers. But the majority of volunteers, at least in Viatka province, turned out to have been uprooted from elsewhere.[61] The contribution of refugees to resettlement only grew with the famine of 1921–22. After the All-Russian Central Executive Committee (VTsIK) issued a resolution permitting free settlement to Siberia from the most afflicted areas (mid- and northern Volga), more than 540,000 people registered and the actual number probably exceeded a million.[62] But even as some peasants fled eastward, others were pleading for assistance to move *from* Siberia back home. Special commissions organized convoys to transport peasants from west to east and east to west.[63] From one standpoint, E. H. Carr's, these were "chaotic" movements that "flowed and ebbed"; from another, they represented a "compensatory survival technique" that Russian peasants had been deploying since before the time of serfdom.[64]

By contrast, the expulsion of several thousand Russian settlers from the Kazakh ("Kirgiz") Autonomous Republic represented something new.[65] In Terry Martin's view, it epitomized the "Kazakh variant" of affirmative action in the Soviet East during the 1920s. This variant, Martin writes, "ha[d] strong popular support given the region's poverty, ethnic conflict over land possession, and deeply felt invidious estate divisions."[66] Yet another variant, articulated by a Special Commission for Tajikistan Affairs in the mid-1920s, proposed resettling highlanders to correct a "historical injustice," the earlier conquest of the Tajik lowlands by semi-nomadic Uzbeks. If in the Kazakh case the injustice was colonization by Slavic peasants, then in Tajikistan, the long-forgotten retreat of Tajiks into the mountains

60. RGAE, f. 478, op. 6, d. 1332, ll. 157–59, 174.

61. See Peter Holquist, *Making War, Forging Revolution: Russia's Continuum of Crisis, 1914–1921* (Cambridge, MA, 2002), 184–86; Aaron Retish, *Russian Peasants in Revolution and Civil War: Citizenship, Identity, and the Creation of the Soviet State, 1914–1922* (Cambridge, 2008), 251–52.

62. Platunov, *Pereselencheskaia politika*, 44.

63. RGAE, f. 478, op. 7, d. 699, ll. 2, 4–12, 19–20, 52; d. 700, ll. 4–5, 12, 15, 52, 96, 102, 118; d. 704, 6, 19, 37; d. 2949, l. 55; d. 2958, l. 13.

64. E. H. Carr, *Socialism in One Country, 1924–1926* (Harmondsworth: Macmillan, 1958), 1: 554; Retish, *Russian Peasants*, 245.

65. RGAE, f. 478, op. 7, d. 699, ll. 32, 51; d. 700, l. 90. See also *Sovetskoe stroitel'stvo v aulakh i selakh Semirech'ia, 1921–1925 gg.: Sbornik dokumentov i materialov*, ed. A. G. Bagriantsev and Sh. Ia. Shafiro (Alma-Ata, 1957), 221–22.

66. Terry Martin, *The Affirmative Action Empire: Nations and Nationalism in the Soviet Union, 1923–1939* (Ithaca, 2001), 57. See also Pavel Polian, *Ne po svoei vole . . . istoriia i geografiia prinuditel'nykh migratsii v SSSR* (Moscow, 2001), 54–55.

served as the wrong to be righted. As Botakoz Kassymbekova recently has argued, sending these highland Tajiks to farm cotton in the Vakhsh Valley near the border with Afghanistan also potentially yielded for the Soviet state political, military, and economic benefits.[67]

Ironically, in 1922, the same year in which some of the Slavic colonists in Kazakhstan were sent packing, VTsIK established an Institute of Scientific Research on Colonization (Goskolonit) to investigate future colonizing possibilities.[68] Its formation was followed two years later by a decree from the Council of Labor and Defense ushering into existence a Central Colonization Committee answerable to VTsIK. Its task was to determine which areas of the country could be brought into cultivation and industrial development via the rational redistribution of the population.[69]

Goskolonit experts and Narkomzem personnel were at pains to differentiate socialist *kolonizatsiia* from the colonialism practiced by tsarist Russia and overseas empires even if some of them had worked for the Imperial-era Resettlement Administration.[70] "Our colonization," affirmed a publication from 1925, "involves railroad construction, the building of industry, culture, etc."[71] Soviet policy, it was insisted, sought to raise the culture and economic condition of indigenous peoples by means of what Francine Hirsch has called "state-sponsored evolutionism."[72] How differently Kazakhs and other Central Asians experienced the policy is an open question. Soviet authorities must have wearied of the comparison, for in 1925 they began to retire colonization from the names of the relevant institutions—Goskolonit became the Institute of Land Organization and Resettlement; and in 1927 Narkomzem RSFSR's Department of Colonization and Resettlement turned into the Resettlement Committee.[73] By 1929, when P. G. Galuzo published his account of

---

67. Botakoz Kassymbekova, "Humans as Territory: Forced Resettlement and the Making of Soviet Tajikistan, 1920–38," *Central Asian Survey* 30, nos. 3–4 (2011), 354–57.

68. Francine Hirsch, *Empire of Nations: Ethnographic Knowledge and the Making of the Soviet Union* (Ithaca, 2005), 87. Goskolonit's short-lived journal, *Trudy gosudarstvennogo kolonizatsionnogo nauchno-issledovatel'skogo instituta* (1924–26), served as a laboratory for ideas about colonization.

69. Platunov, *Pereselencheskaia politika*, 66–71.

70. On personnel who transcended the revolutionary divide, see Holquist, "'In Accord with State Interests,'" 151–79. For the nexus between resettlement and colonization in tsarist Russia, see Sunderland, *Taming the Wild Field*; and Sunderland, "The Ministry of Asiatic Russia: The Colonial Office That Never Was but Might Have Been," *Slavic Review* 69, no. 1 (2010): 120–50.

71. RSFSR Severo-Zapadnoe Oblastnoe Ekonomicheskoe Soveshchanie, Kolonizatsionnaia Komissiia Pravlenie Murmanskoi zhel. dor., *Kolonizatsiia karel'sko-murmanskogo kraia—Spravochnaia kniga dlia zheliaiushchikh vodvorit'sia na pereselencheskikh uchastkakh v karel'sko-murmanskom krae* (Leningrad, 1925), 10.

72. Hirsch, *Empire of Nations*, 87–94. For the "spectrum of meanings implicit in the words *colonie* and *colon* in the French empire," see Anne Laura Stoler and Carole McGranahan, "Refiguring Imperial Terrains," in *Imperial Formations*, ed. Ann Laura Stoler, Carole McGranahan, and Peter C. Perdue (Santa Fe, 2007), 3.

73. Platunov, *Pereselencheskaia politika*, 66, 71; Nick Baron, *Soviet Karelia: Politics, Planning, and Terror in Stalin's Russia, 1920–1939* (London, 2007), 265. The name of this institution would change again more than once, but for the sake of clarity we continue to refer to the Resettlement Committee throughout the Soviet period.

the history of Turkestan from its conquest by the Russians until the 1917 Revolution, it was sufficient to call the book "Turkestan—Colony" to connote that colonies could not exist in Soviet territory.[74]

Nevertheless, American Jewish supporters who helped send "toiling Jews" from the *shtetls* of the former Pale of Settlement to cultivate crops and raise animals in Crimea and southern Ukraine continued to refer to them as colonists throughout the remainder of the decade and even into the 1930s.[75] Each family cultivated 12 hectares of wheat, rye, and barley fields in the case of a settlement in the Kalinindorf Jewish Autonomous District in southern Ukraine, according to Roman Lazebnik, whose family resettled there in 1923 when he was three years old.[76] Colonists, settlers, migrants—what is the difference? As Joshua Sanborn notes in another context, most people known as migrants "leave their homes and enter a social realm in which barriers of language, class, and/or culture inhibit the acquisition of power by new arrivals. . . . Privileged migrants generally do not refer to themselves as migrants or immigrants, preferring instead terms like 'expatriate' or 'colonist.' "[77] But what about the colonized, that is, those who already were living in places to which colonists migrated? According to a recent history of the enterprise, Jewish "colonization sparked quick, grassroots reactions," particularly among Germans, themselves the descendants of colonists who had arrived in the late eighteenth century. Also put out were Tatar Communists, for whom Jewish settlers "seemed to impinge on the national integrity and political legitimacy of the Crimean Tatar Oblast."[78]

---

74. Galuzo, *Turkestan-Koloniia*.

75. Jonathan L. Dekel-Chen, *Farming the Red Land: Jewish Agricultural Colonization and Local Soviet Power, 1924–1941* (New Haven, 2005), 117. Dekel-Chen uses the term "colony," "settlement," and "cooperative" interchangeably. See also Dina A. Amanzholova, "Iz istorii zemleustroistva Evreev v SSSR," *Cahiers du monde russe* 45, nos. 1–2 (2004): 209–40. A Narkomzem document from 1934 lists arrivals and departures of "Jewish settlers" in Crimea for each year from 1923 to 1933 and plans for the period 1934–37. See RGAE, f. 5675, op. 1, d. 48a, l. 50.

76. "I Remember/Ia pomniu: Vospominaniia veteranov VOV," http://iremember.ru/partizani/lazebnik-roman-evseevich.html, 1 (accessed March 17, 2012).

77. Sanborn, "Unsettling the Empire," 296–97.

78. Dekel-Chen, *Farming the Red Land*, 99, 126. On colonization in southern Ukraine (New Russia) in the eighteenth and nineteenth centuries, see Roger P. Bartlett, *Human Capital: The Settlement of Foreigners in Russia, 1762–1804* (Cambridge, 1979); Leonard G. Friesen, *Rural Revolutions in Southern Ukraine: Peasants, Nobles, and Colonists, 1774–1905* (Cambridge, 2008), 49–59. According to a Jewish American correspondent who visited the village of Royteh Shtern near Khar'kov in 1933—the famine year—"Christian villages looked upon the Jews with a bitter envy" because the Jews received help from relatives in America. See Roman Serbyn, "Harry Land of the Jewish Daily Forward (*Forverts*) on Ukraine in the Autumn of 1933," *Holodomor Studies* 2, no. 2 (2010): 237.

Whether they thought of it as colonization or resettlement, Soviet officials committed themselves to managing migration through planning.[79] This involved identifying areas of surplus rural population, unoccupied or thinly populated areas to be developed, and what it would take to move people from the former to the latter. The principle was simple. As Lenin told the Eighth Congress of Soviets in December 1920, "No socialist country is possible . . . if it cannot move tens and hundreds of thousands of workers wherever they are needed."[80] E. H. Carr cites a five-year plan developed by Narkomzem in 1923 as the "first attempt at official organization of migration." It envisioned moving 630,500 people to the Volga, the Urals, and Siberia at a cost to the state of twenty-five million rubles.[81] Additional estimates that Carr characterizes as "ambitious" and "more utopian" followed suit. Probably the most ambitious was the Resettlement Committee's ten-year projection of over five million people migrating from areas of excess population in the Russian, Belorussian, and Ukrainian republics to regions of "Union significance," namely, the Far East, Siberia, the mid-Volga, and Karelo-Murmansk.[82]

Bold though the projections were, the procedures for peasants to resettle bore striking resemblance to what tsarist authorities had stipulated in the laws of 1896 and 1904. Once again, the state relied on peasants' scouts to represent the interests of their clients ("not less than five and not more than ten peasant households," according to a Narkomzem directive from 1925) by making application for scouting certificates that gave them the right to reduced fares on the railroad and to choose parcels of land. If a scout did not find suitable land in a particular district, he was given access to information about available land elsewhere and a reduced fare to travel there.[83] As under the tsars, so in the 1920s, higher authorities "categorically" enjoined those on the ground to "struggle against irregular resettlers" whose actions disrupted the rational distribution of land among those from overcrowded areas.[84] But as before, a substantial number of peasants traveled at their own initiative and bore the expenses associated with irregular resettlement.[85]

79. L. I. Borodkin and S. V. Maksimov, "Krest'ianskie migratsii v Rossii/SSSR v pervoi chetverti XX veka (makroanaliz struktury migratsionnykh potokov)," *Otechestvennaia istoriia*, no. 5 (1993): 127. Borodkin and Maksimov argue that "planned settlement" referred to state regulation rather than the more ambitious kind of planning that predominated from the late 1920s onward.

80. V. I. Lenin, *Polnoe sobranie sochinenii*, 55 vols., 5th ed. (Moscow, 1970), 42: 150.

81. Carr, *Socialism in One Country*, 555.

82. Baron, *Soviet Karelia*, 81; Polian, *Ne po svoei vole*, 58–59. Kassymbekova, "Humans as Territory," 351, cites the Resettlement Committee's "five-year prospective plan" from RGAE, f. 5675, op. 1, d. 7, ll. 4–6. This called for moving five million people by 1933.

83. Platunov, *Pereselencheskaia politika*, 73–76.

84. See for example the memo distributed in Samara province in 1925 in RGAE, f. 478, op. 7, d. 2958, ll. 1–4.

85. According to Carr, who cites "almost certainly exaggerated" data from *Ekonomicheskoe obozrenie*, 80 percent of the 111,000 settlers in 1924–25 were irregulars. A year later, the number of settlers "was said to have reached 120,000 of whom more than half were planned and aided" (*Socialism in One Country*, 556, 558).

Between the spring of 1924 and the autumn of 1929, Soviet authorities tallied some nine hundred thousand resettlers. Cheliabinsk, with its extensive facilities to register, feed, bathe, disinfect, educate, and in other ways minister to settlers, remained the main entry point for travel to Siberia and the Far East. Among areas of resettlement, Siberia garnered the lion's share of migrants, between 36 percent (in 1926–27) and 63 percent (in 1928–29) of the annual totals. The Far East, which accounted for only 5 percent in 1924–25, received nearly 30 percent of resettlers in 1927–28. As for sending regions, the Central Black Earth provinces initially led all others, as they had before the revolution, but beginning in 1926–27 the Mid-Volga and the West (Belarus, Briansk oblast') overtook them, and in 1928–29 Leningrad oblast' did as well. New sources of nonagricultural employment closer to home undoubtedly affected these changing rates of outmigration, but closer inspection might reveal additional factors.[86]

Iu. V. Pikalov, a Khabarovsk-based historian, has pointed out that many of those registered on parcels of land did not in fact turn up. In the Far East, only 30 percent did so in 1927. Pikalov surmises that the state's failure to invest in infrastructure dissuaded potential settlers. He also argues that in the rough and ready conditions of the Far East settlers preferred to send ahead working teams to prepare the land independently of resettlement personnel rather than parties of scouts, which he describes as "an outdated method."[87] Outdated it might have been, but the difference between a scout and a working team could have been nominal—a working team might have been a group of scouts by another name.

As before the revolution, some settlers could not stick it out and decided to return home. Often, they appealed to the state for assistance to offset costs that otherwise would have been beyond their means. Judging by what survives in the archives, the state turned down most such requests, arguing, as it did repeatedly, "that in general, migration from Siberia to the European part of the RSFSR is undesirable."[88] Even so, at first glance, the letter sent by a man named Dobrinskii to VTsIK and Narkomzem in February 1925 would seem likely to have elicited support. Dobrinskii wrote his letter on behalf of 14 families whose 118 members, listed by name, lived in the village of Dobroe ("Good") on the banks of the Amur River. Fifteen years earlier in 1909, these families had arrived in the Russian Far East from the Kuban. An article from *Amurskaia Pravda* that Dobrinskii helpfully pasted to the letter explained why they desired to return. Entitled "How Long Will This Continue?" the article

86. Platunov, *Pereselencheskaia politika*, 80–85. For a discussion of differential rates of outmigration from sending regions, see Carr, *Socialism in One Country*, 561–62. Siberia may have become more desirable for people from western regions because emigration westward was severely constrained.

87. Iu. V. Pikalov, *Pereselencheskaia politika i izmenenie sotsial'no-klassovogo sostava naseleniia dal'nego vostoka RSFSR (noiabr' 1922–iiun' 1941 g.)* (Khabarovsk, 2003), 102.

88. RGAE, f. 478, op. 7, d. 2949, ll. 31, 3, 7, 11–12, 55, 56.

reported that on the night of January 18, some 150 Chinese "fell upon" the small unarmed village, seizing horses, icons, knives, and "everything else they could lay their hands on." They also reportedly raped women, "especially the young ones." Two months later, an official from Narkomzem's Division of Colonization and Resettlement informed the citizens of Dobroe that their motive for abandoning the settlement "is hardly sufficient, as you are not deprived of the possibility of turning to your local executive committee with a request to take necessary measures to protect yourselves and your property from similar attacks in the future."[89] The archives unfortunately are silent about what Dobrinskii and his neighbors thought of this suggestion.

Decisions about whether and when to return could not have been taken lightly, but they by and large are beyond retrospective scrutiny. Carr indicates that 120,000 settlers arrived at their destinations and 22,000 (18 percent) returned in 1925–26. In the Far East—a notoriously tough place to survive—about 10 percent of the number of settlers who arrived during 1926 returned. By 1928 the rate had risen to nearly one in four, and in 1929, more than one in three (60,000 of a settler population of 156,000). Not all necessarily had intended to stay in the first place. Thanks to a decree of September 1926, settlers could remain registered in their former communities for up to three years, enabling family members to try out the new location without severing ties with the old. The more unscrupulous also could travel to the new location at a reduced fare and pocket the 400 rubles they received as a loan rather than using it to offset the costs of settling in.[90]

Thus far, we have presented resettlement as a form of migration in which peasants sought to sustain their rural-based way of life by relocating themselves and their families, typically at a considerable distance from their original home, and with the state setting the rules and providing direction and assistance. Not unlike homesteading in the American West, peasants who resettled chose to do so often with neighboring families but rarely as an entire village. It is important to recognize, though, that not only need drove peasants to relocate; state coercion, often couched as encouragement, played a role as well.

Usually, the researcher looks in vain for hard evidence of coercion, for state officials typically cast settlers as responsive volunteers. However, both in the 1920s and again in the 1950s, documentation of coercion in the resettlement of Tajik peasants from their mountain homes to collective farms in the southern valleys is clear. In 1930 the Central Committee of the Tajik Communist Party rebuked an overzealous administrator for having relocated 40 percent of the 10,000 households resettled against their will. Twenty-five years later, 450 Tajik families, officially listed as volunteers, moved to the lowlands. But according to a

89. Ibid., ll. 27–31. These were the feared Red Beards (*Khunkhuzy* in Russian, often rendered as *Honghuzi* in English).

90. Pikalov, *Pereselencheskaia politika*, 104; Platunov, *Pereselencheskaia politika*, 75–76.

former storekeeper, "Nobody volunteered! The district authorities forced us to leave. Their method was simple. Once in May 1955, they ordered the closure of all grocery stores. . . . With no store where we could buy food, there was no way to survive." But 40 percent coerced means that as many as 60 percent may have volunteered, and volunteers from the highlands in the mid-1950s had preceded those forcefully "transferred."[91] Nevertheless, the voluntary resettlement of some often was made possible by the involuntary resettlement of others. This symbiotic relationship of some people being moved out and others being moved in, of deportation and resettlement, of depopulation and repopulation, would become endemic to resettlement policy in the 1930s and 1940s.

Occasionally, the interface between the two groups of migrants became uncomfortably close. The history of the Life and Labor Commune as recounted by some of its surviving members nicely illustrates this point. Formed in 1921 in Teplyi Stan on the edge of Moscow, the Life and Labor Commune was one of several consisting primarily of peasants who committed themselves to living according to the tenets of Leo Tolstoy. Initially, Soviet authorities tolerated the commune's existence, but with the onset of full-scale collectivization, its version of collectivist agriculture became anathema. Voluntary resettlement in the East was still, though, a possibility, and in February 1930, the presidium of the Central Executive Committee granted permission for several such communes to relocate there. In accordance with procedures originating in the 1880s, the Commissariat of Agriculture issued land-scouting tickets for the communes' representatives to travel to sites of free land, providing them with addresses and maps of available parcels. Thus, in May 1930, three peasant scouts—two from the Life and Labor Commune and another from the World Brotherhood colony in Stalingrad province—departed on their mission.[92]

According to Boris Mazurin, one of the two from the Life and Labor Commune, they started inspecting land near Tashkent before visiting Auliye-Ata (now Taraz), Bishkek, Alma-Ata (now Almaty), Semipalatinsk, and Ust-Kamenogorsk. They then turned north up the Irtysh River to Novosibirsk and northeast to Shcheglovsk (now Kemerovo) and Novokuznetsk, a journey by train, on horseback, and by foot of at least 9,300 miles. It was in Alma-Ata where they first encountered evidence of another migration regime, specifically in the form of an offer from "the head of the agricultural agency for the [Kazakh] republic" to occupy "a whole village on the very outskirts of the city, with houses ready for use . . . in a word, come on in, settle down, and start eating apples." Tempting as the offer was, the

---

91. Kassymbekova, "Humans as Territory," 359. Quotation from Olivier Ferrando, "Soviet Population Transfers and Interethnic Relations in Tajikistan: Assessing the Concept of Ethnicity," *Central Asian Survey* 30, no. 1 (2011): 42–43. Ferrando tendentiously translates *pereselenie* as "population transfer" rather than resettlement.

92. Borís Mazurin, "The Life and Labor Commune: A History and Some Reflections," in *Memoirs of Peasant Tolstoyans in Soviet Russia*, ed. William Edgerton (Bloomington, 1993), 28–46.

scouts refused. The village owed its emptiness to the deportation of peasants who had refused to join a collective farm, and as Tolstoyans, Mazurin and his comrades would not take advantage of the violence inflicted on the village's previous residents. Yet in 1931, by which time the commune had reconstituted itself on the banks of the Tom River near Novokuznetsk, it sent four men "with money and axes" upriver to buy, dismantle, and float downstream houses and barns abandoned by peasants who had fled collectivization, "scattering in all directions." Some of these people had gone to work in factories, others were engaged in building the gigantic Kuznetsk industrial complex, while still others prospected for gold.[93]

It did not take long before the Tolstoyans found themselves at loggerheads with local officials. Some, Mazurin reports, considered going "still further off, break[ing] away from the world with its bustle" to find "a new settlement where no one would bother them." Three from the former Stalingrad commune sought a new location in the taiga but soon returned, for "the only people who wandered through the taiga were hunters and gold prospectors." Instead, "all able-bodied males" engaged in seasonal work at the Kuznetsk project and returned on holidays when "everything was full, merry, and crowded."[94] Thus, in focusing on a single commune of several hundred members over the course of some two years, we encounter their own repertoires of semi-voluntary resettlement, rejection of one location in Central Asia in favor of another farther north in western Siberia, an abortive attempt at settlement farther to the east, and seasonal migration to a burgeoning construction site. But that is not all. We also hear about peasants forcibly removed from their village, others who have engaged in rural-to-urban migration, and still others who have vagabonded in the taiga.

The all-out drive for collectivization that began in the winter of 1929–30 gave Soviet authorities an unprecedented opportunity to move people around. Nearly two million peasants labeled as "kulaks" were expropriated and deported as "special settlers" (*spetsposelentsy*) to regions with harsh climates and resources to be developed. "Cast in layers of secrecy, deceit, and human cruelty," this massive undertaking stood at the opposite end of the spectrum from voluntary resettlement.[95] We therefore situate it in chapter 7. Here we concentrate on the complementary process of ordinary peasant households and the families of soon-to-be demobilized Red Army soldiers recruited for resettlement on collective farms. What made the recruitment complementary is that the recruits would take up residence in areas from which kulaks had been deported, sometimes occupying houses they had vacated.

---

93. Ibid., 47–48.
94. Ibid., 57.
95. Viola, *Unknown Gulag*, 2. See also V. P. Danilov and S. A. Krasilnikov, eds., *Spetspereselentsy v zapadnoi Sibiri*, 4 vols. (Novosibirsk, 1992–96); Polian, *Ne po svoei vole*, 76–84; V. N. Zemskov, *Spetsposelentsy v SSSR, 1930–1960* (Moscow, 2003), 1–121.

Red Army soldiers about to complete their terms of service became one of the chief groups recruited for collective farms located in strategically sensitive border regions such as the Far Eastern krai, Karelian Autonomous SSR, and Leningrad oblast'.[96] Already accustomed to taking orders and not yet having returned to their homes, they represented to Soviet authorities an attractive alternative to the Cossacks who had performed similar functions in earlier centuries. As with so many other tasks assumed by the Soviet bureaucracy, including population removal, this exercise in population insertion proceeded on the basis of quotas. In 1930, Narkomzem was supposed to have sent 10,600 Red Army veterans accompanied by their families to twelve collective farms located in seven different Far Eastern districts, or an average of over 800 families per collective farm. During 1931, its quota amounted to another 10,000 families distributed among twenty-seven farms in fourteen districts, and in 1932, slightly fewer families on ten machine-tractor stations (MTS).[97]

Such substantial numbers of people required a significant commitment of resources and their coordination among nearly a dozen different state agencies. Problems inevitably arose. Recruiters were unsure whether to dispatch soldiers directly from their units without giving them a chance to collect their belongings and family members or to allow them to return home and thereby risk losing them. Indeed, many recruits failed to show up at the designated time and place for departure, either because they had been poorly informed or had had second thoughts. In 1930, although recruiters signed up 90 percent of the 10,600 soldiers, only 70 percent had reached Irkutsk by the beginning of 1931, and a mere 44 percent actually arrived in the Far East. Some found themselves sharing the same trains with special settlers, an embarrassing occurrence that authorities clearly did not want repeated. Things improved slightly in 1931 when an additional 2,000 families above the target of 10,000 had been recruited. However, only 6,900 had departed for the Far East, and of these less than 5,800 actually had arrived as of December 25. Moreover, owing to administrative confusion, poaching by other organizations, and "kulak agitation," nearly 1,000 had gone missing since arrival. Preparations for receiving the newcomers lagged and older settlers often treated them with coldness if not hostility.[98]

---

96. Arrangements for Red Army collective farms were systematized by a resolution passed on May 17, 1931 by the RSFSR's Council of People's Commissars. See Danilov, Manning, and Viola, *Tragediia sovetskoi derevni*, 3: 123–24.

97. Ibid., 3: 123, 169–70. In October 1931 the Politburo raised the figure for 1932 to 18,000 families plus 2,000 in the Eastern Siberian krai, 195.

98. Ibid., 3: 196, 207, 247–48, 274–75. The sharing of trains by settlers and deportees is eerily similar to the Nazis' resettlement program in which the same vans used by VOMI (Main Office for Ethnic Germans, a subdivision of the Reich Commission for the Strengthening of Germanism) to bring *Volksdeutsche* settlers to their new homes in Poland sometimes transported the previous owners of those homes eastward. See Valdis O. Lumans, *Himmler's Auxiliaries: The Volksdeutsche Mittelstelle and the German National Minorities of Europe, 1933–1945* (Chapel Hill, 2010), 204.

Some recruits not surprisingly felt deceived and expressed their disappointment within earshot of authorities. For example, in a conversation among wives someone was overheard saying, "It would be better if we went back now, but they took our papers. . . . We don't have anything to eat except bread. We'll survive somehow until summer and then leave." "We fought for Soviet power for two years," said a "middle peasant" named Pomarskii, "but now we'll fight against it. We were deceived, brought here and left to rot. We'll talk with those deceivers, and urge them to deceive the defenders of the Soviet regime."[99]

The program nevertheless expanded. By 1933 nearly 2,000 veterans, the overwhelming majority of whom were party and Komsomol members, were living on four collective farms in the Kuban. Their spirits in January were reported to be "buoyant, firm," although by the middle of May, one in eight had deserted. Commissar of Defense Voroshilov reported in October that over 15,000 new recruits had been signed up—110 percent of the quota—and convoys had started to leave for their destinations.[100] Sufficiently encouraged, the Politburo issued guidelines to the Resettlement Committee for recruiting civilian collective farmers in the RSFSR and Belorussian Republic and, with the assistance of military officers who had organized the resettlement of Red Army veterans, settling them in Ukraine.[101]

Between October 1933 and April 1934, the Resettlement Committee moved some 59,000 Red Army and collective farm families to "southern districts," including Odessa oblast', eastern Ukraine, the north Caucasus, and Stalingrad. These families represented over 80 percent of the 77,000 recruited and resettled between 1933 and 1937, not only to southern districts but also eastern Siberia and the Russian Far East.[102] One can follow in the archives the daily progress of these operations—ten convoys carrying 611 families on January 11, twelve convoys moving 785 families on January 12, twenty-three convoys transporting 1,598 families on January 14, and so forth. Actually, the reports also include information on the railroad stations through which the convoys passed, the number of women, children, horses, cows, and poultry on board, the weight of the baggage, and less frequently, problems, measures taken to overcome them, and the disposition of the resettlers: "the attitude of the collective farmers is lively" (January 14); "All left on time. Convoy no. 50052 left from Semenovka without food, but measures were taken to supply it on the way. Attitude is good" (January 15).[103]

The resettlement effort entailed meticulous recording of data, organization of transport, provision of food and other supplies for the journey, and arrangements at destination. No

99. Danilov, Manning, and Viola, *Tragediia sovetskoi derevni*, 3: 276.

100. Ibid., 3: 761, 808.

101. Ibid., 3: 809–10.

102. RGAE, f. 5675, op. 1, d. 48a, l. 16, from a report by Volkov, director of the Southern District Sectors, dated October 14, 1934; Polian, *Ne po svoei vole*, 80–81.

103. RGAE, f. 5675, op. 1, d. 33, ll. 4–14.

wonder that upon the conclusion of operations that went off without any disasters responsible officials received bonuses.[104] Despite the Resettlement Committee's own resettlement—from Narkomzem and VTsIK to the NKVD in 1936—its shared responsibilities with the security police, the army, and the Commissariat of Transport remained constant. So similar were these operations that a mishap such as the one that befell a group of settlers in November 1933 could prompt awkward comparisons. "The kulaks who were deported in 1930 were better supplied than these collective farmers," wrote the head of the Southern Railroad's Political Section on the failure of local organizations to provide food to the settlers.[105]

The obvious difference between special settlers and resettlers was that resettlement depended on recruitment of volunteers. "The resettlement of collective and individual farmers who express a desire to join collective farms will proceed exclusively on a voluntary basis," stated the Resettlement Committee's plan for 1936.[106] The committee by this point had amassed considerable experience in encouraging volunteers. In October 1933, the Council of People's Commissars approved measures designed to attract settlers to Ukraine—recently depleted by famine—from among collective farmers in the Russian heartland. Repeated in February 1935 when 4,000 families from central Ukraine were sought for settlement in the border region to the west, the measures offered a waiver on all tax arrears, cancellation of obligatory milk and meat deliveries for a year, use of horses from the common stables, provision of free transportation to destination, a loan of up to a 100 kg of grain to each family, and provision of credits to purchase domestic animals.[107] Not just anybody qualified. According to a report from the Ivanovo Industrial oblast', which sent 3,500 households to the Donetsk oblast' in Ukraine, "During the recruitment, troikas from village soviets and the districts undertook a review of each household and rejected anyone who had been a class enemy or had a criminal record."[108]

Generally, though, recruiters overfulfilled their plans (as indeed did those who expropriated and banished kulaks). Instead of sending 14,000 Red Army families to the Kuban, they sent 14,801; assigned the task of recruiting 3,000 households to resettle in eastern Siberia, they came up with 3,065. The results did not depend so much on recruiters' persuasiveness, for many more families sought to resettle than were recruited, and some who joined the convoys did so outside official strictures (samovol'no). A report to the Communist

---

104. See for example the effusive congratulations and bonuses bestowed on several officials in the December 19, 1933 and January 1, 1934 protocols of All-Union Resettlement Committee sessions in RGAE, f. 5675, op. 1, d. 33, ll. 60–63. We thank Kate Brown for making copies available to us.

105. RGAE, 5675, op. 1, d. 48, ll. 58–58obv. The transfer of the Resettlement Committee to the NKVD was made via temporary residence in the Council of People's Commissars in 1933.

106. Danilov, Manning, and Viola, Tragediia sovetskoi derevni, 4: 605.

107. Ibid., 4: 387–88.

108. RGAE, f. 5675, op. 1, d. 48, l. 4.

Party's Central Committee referred to "a lot of 'unplanned settlers' . . . as many as planned [ones]" among families resettling from the Western oblast' to Dnepropetrovsk. Another report claimed, "if the number of people refusing to go is very small, the number of those going outside planned settlement is enormous."[109]

The question is why. Why did peasants from the Western oblast' want to leave their homes for Dnepropetrovsk? Authors of the above-cited reports worried that independent householders (edinolichniki), kulaks, and other anti-Soviet elements were trying to sneak away without fulfilling their tax and other obligations to the Soviet state. They were not entirely wrong. Everyone, not only anti-Soviet elements and not only in the Western oblast' but also peasants throughout the newly collectivized countryside of central Russia, desperately sought relief from the obligations imposed on them. Many of them must have seen resettlement to Ukraine, the Kuban, and other parts of the country that were sparsely populated thanks to the recent famine and deportations as their only chance for survival.

Some barely made it. The demobilized soldiers and their families sent to the Kuban experienced such shortages over the winter of 1933–34 that the Politburo was moved to instruct Anastas Mikoian, Commissar of Supply, to provide massive quantities of grits, sugar, fish, and cooking oil within ten days. It also instructed the Council of People's Commissars (no less!) to come up with 10,000 square meters of glass to "repair" settlers' homes, presumably because they had lacked windows (during the winter!), and to take other measures of a similar nature. The problem, it seems, was that suppliers had been squandering, most likely selling off, materials intended for the settlers.[110]

No wonder that despite the proffered privileges, some peasants remained cautious. The authorities considered as class enemies not only those trying to evade restrictions to become settlers but also the purveyors of rumors about the dangers settlers faced. They reported that the demobilized soldiers bound for the Kuban had encountered such rumors as that "the Cossacks will take revenge [because] they won't forgive you for coming to replace them," and "you will die from malaria and hunger just like the others did." Settlers about to embark for eastern Siberia heard that "at night the Japanese attack homes."[111] Authorities' attribution of both eagerness and rumormongering to enemies of Soviet power belied their morbid fear of losing "total control over the distribution and composition of populations." Here Nick Baron identifies controlling migration regimes as a key objective of the Stalinist state.[112]

109. Ibid., d. 48, ll. 28–29, 54, 73; Danilov, Manning, and Viola, Tragediia sovetskoi derevni, 4: 448.

110. Danilov, Manning, and Viola, Tragediia sovetskoi derevni 4: 73. Judging by measures adopted in September 1935 to grant them privileged access to materials and to lower their supply quotas, Red Army kolkhozes remained serious underperformers in general. See ibid., 4: 579.

111. RGAE, f. 5675, op. 1, d. 48, ll. 42, 47; d. 52, l. 25; d. 79, l. 55. The rumors about malaria and unwelcoming Cossacks seem to have been accurate in at least two cases.

112. Baron, Soviet Karelia, 237.

Rumors rather reflected peasants' own worries about the operations. An "opportunity for anonymous, protected communication," they were part of the repertoire of potential resettlement, one of the "arts of political disguise" characteristic of subaltern peoples.[113] To check things out, to reassure themselves, peasants also relied on the familiar ("outdated") practice of sending ahead scouts. Sometimes, as when 25 of 133 families recruited from one Western oblast' district refused to go to Ukraine, it was because scouts reported problems. In other instances, scouts "disorganized" the recruitment plan by reporting favorably on collective farms in one district even though the households they represented had been assigned to another. They continued to hit the road, arriving "every day in large numbers" at the oblast' offices of the Resettlement Committee with requests for information and permission to settle.[114] In its plan for 1936, the Resettlement Committee made provision for scouts—five to each district in Cheliabinsk and Omsk oblasts, where collective farms were accepting settlers.[115]

In addition to sending scouts, peasants tried to keep in touch with countrymen who had resettled earlier. They also sought information about opportunities for resettlement via another time-tested method—pestering authorities for information and assistance via letter. They wrote to the People's Commissar of Agriculture, the Resettlement Committee, far-off land departments, the editor of Krest'ianskaia gazeta, and anyone else they could think of to inquire about resettling in the Saratov region, the Azov-Black Sea region, Karelia, Siberia, the Far East, the Jewish Autonomous oblast', "or," as one particularly desperate letter writer put it, "anywhere else without bad conditions because on our kolkhoz we have little land and very few labor days and an inadequate supply of bread."[116]

The list of desired destinations included several "land-rich" regions to which the authorities had sent convoys in 1933 and 1935, but otherwise the letter writers tried to shape the resettlement regime to their needs. For example, the spokesman for a group of twenty-five householders wrote to the Resettlement Committee in July 1935, "After receiving permission to resettle, we will inspect the place and, finding one that we like, will inform you of its location." Other peasants related hard-luck stories of personal hardship and family separation. Nobody persisted more than Efim Goncharov, who originally described himself as a "planned settler" desirous of migrating from the North Caucasus to the Russian Far East. After receiving the standard reply that "no resettlement is planned at present," he wrote again, this time, after completing his army service. Rejected again, he wrote a third

---

113. James C. Scott, Domination and the Arts of Resistance: Hidden Transcripts (New Haven, 1990), 145.

114. RGAE, f. 5675, op. 1, d. 48, ll. 52, 56; Siegelbaum, "Those Elusive Scouts," 56–57.

115. Danilov, Manning, and Viola, Tragediia sovetskoi derevni, 4: 606–7.

116. RGAE, f. 5675, op. 1. d. 105, ll. 28, 29–30, 38–39, 40, 50, 63, 74, 77, 110, 115, 125, 129; d. 106, ll. 1, 3, 8, 33, 59.

letter identifying the region, the oblast', the district, and even the village where he wanted to settle. "I request to resettle, although not by planned settlement, on the railroad at a reduced rate because I am a poor collective farmer with a family of seven," he wrote.[117]

The persistence of these practices despite the state's radically revised resettlement regime illustrates one of the fundamental truths about this form of migration, namely, its dependence on cultural repertoires that could translate the state's grandiose schemes into terms both comprehensible by potential migrants and to their perceived advantage. From the peasants' perspective, the state's ways were mysterious. Its selection of places to permit settlement was unpredictable, and its willingness to grant material support, arbitrary. Best to try whatever methods had worked before and hope that the state eventually would make the necessary adjustments.

On at least two occasions—in 1934 and again in 1936—the Resettlement Committee indulged settlers by asking them to "help us by letting us know" what "shortcomings" they experienced during their journey and upon arrival at their destination. In this remarkable Stalinist version of a customer satisfaction questionnaire, settlers were provided with a form listing nine questions and urged to respond because, as was written near the bottom of the form, "we want . . . to eliminate the problems and punish the guilty." Most respondents limited themselves to laconic expressions of contentment or gratitude. Only the occasional note of alarm disrupted the litany, such as the following from Ivan Ianchuk, who traveled all the way from Arkhangel'sk to Ukraine's Vinnitsa oblast': "it's good to say that everything was well done, but when we arrived at the kolkhoz we discovered that collective farmers receive nothing, no bread for labor days, and I would like to know how is it possible to live without bread?"[118]

These interactions occurred amid—and, as already indicated, thanks to—more coercive forms of migration. This relationship recapitulated an older pattern that dated back to the nineteenth century when Imperial Russian authorities viewed resettlement as the mechanism to colonize lands previously in the possession of the Empire's nomadic Asian subjects but deemed to be in excess of what they needed to graze their herds. In logistical terms, the Stalinist version of resettlement shared several practices with more coerced forms of migration. Each had quotas assigned to local authorities, transported migrants to their destinations in convoys consisting of boxcars, and made demands on authorities at receiving points for housing, schools, and other infrastructure that proved impossible to meet.

Sometimes they also shared geographic proximity. The Far Eastern krai, site of numerous corrective labor camps and a destination for special settlers, also served as a

---

117. Ibid., d. 106, ll. 109–15.
118. Ibid., d. 90, ll. 9–10; d. 164, ll. 1–152.

mythological frontier—an underpopulated region (partly because of the earlier deportation of Koreans) that needed protection from potential invaders and the rapid development of its resources. Thence between 1937 and 1939 went 25,000 Khetagurovites, three-quarters of whom were women. All volunteers, they left their jobs as factory workers, teachers, secretaries, and nurses to travel thousands of kilometers to the East. What prompted them to do so was the call of the eponymous Valentina Khetagurova, a Komsomol activist and wife of a Soviet military officer stationed in the Far East. She urged her Soviet sisters to join her "to pacify nature, so that all of the region's riches can be exploited for socialism," and to defend the Soviet Motherland. Judging from the letters and memoirs in Elena Shulman's account, Khetagurovites were motivated by a spirit of adventure and the strong desire to demonstrate that women were no less capable than men, even—or especially—in previously all-male fields. According to a list from March 1938 that Shulman cites, agriculture garnered the largest share of Khetagurovites—1,546 of slightly over 8,000. The railroad, industrial enterprises, the army, the NKVD, the fishing industry, and others followed in that order.[119]

Elsewhere, the projects attracting settlers—or making settlers of displaced peasants—were less heroic. The resettlement of 700 households in the fertile Krasnodar krai related to stepping up champagne production rather than border security. Overall, between 1939 and June 1941, about half a million peasants were resettled in the Far Eastern and Maritime territories, Siberia, and Kazakhstan, not for any specific purpose, but to make more rational the distribution of population.[120] Barely receiving notice outside their own oblast' or republic, thousands of peasant families took part in "micro-migrations," that is, resettled "internally" for a variety of reasons—to avoid inundation due to dam construction (Vologda, Kuibyshev, Kalinin, and Yaroslavl' oblasts), cultivate recently irrigated land (Azerbaijan), and consolidate fishing operations (Arkhangel'sk oblast').[121]

119. Elena Shulman, *Stalinism on the Frontier of Empire: Women and State Formation in the Soviet Far East* (Cambridge, 2008), 1, 87–93, 119–39, 232. See also Shulman, " 'Those Who Hurry to the Far East,' Readers, Dreamers, and Volunteers," in Breyfogle, Schrader, and Sunderland, *Peopling the Russian Periphery*, 213–37.

120. O. M. Verbitskaia, *Naselenie rossiiskoi derevni v 1939–1959 gg.: Problemy demograficheskogo razvitiia* (Moscow, 2002), 195. For an account of the dispatch of 151 families from the Chuvash ASSR to Kustanai oblast' in northern Kazakhstan in June 1940, see the report by the director of the convoy to Evgenii Mikhailovich Chekmenev, the director of the Resettlement Administration of the Council of People's Commissars, in USHMM, RG-22.020 Gosudarstvennyi Istoricheskii Arkhiv Chuvashskoi Respubliki (GIAChR) f. 1263, op. 1, d. 51, l. 274.

121. Danilov, Manning, and Viola, *Tragediia sovetskoi derevni*, 5: bk. 2, 536–37. For the concept of micromigrations, see John S. Schoeberlein, "Shifting Ground: How the Soviet Regime Used Resettlement to Transform Central Asian Society and the Consequences of This Policy Today," in *JCAS Symposium Series No. 9: Population Movement in the Modern World III*, ed. Komatsu Hisao, Obiya Chika, and John S. Schoeberlein (Osaka, 2000), 51.

Resettlement, 1941–91

With the outbreak of war in Europe, the symbiosis between population dislocation and relocation grew stronger. Soviet territorial annexations at the expense of Poland in 1939 and Romania in 1940 brought on large-scale deportations into the Soviet interior. In the case of rural areas of the former Polish eastern provinces (western Ukraine and western Belarus), Soviet authorities targeted ethnically Polish *osadniki*, veterans of the Soviet-Polish War of 1920 to whom the Polish government had granted land. Entire villages were emptied out.[122] Some resettlers from the Soviet interior replaced the banished peasants, and authorities permitted Ukrainian families to occupy the former estates on which they previously had worked as laborers. They also dispatched border guards and military colonists to convert the farms to kolkhozes and sovkhozes.[123]

Matters differed in the Karelian territories, which came into Soviet hands in March 1940. Soviet occupiers found few people to deport because the overwhelming majority of Karelians—over four hundred thousand people—already had deported themselves to Finland with the assistance of the departing Finnish military forces. The first settler-collective farmers from the Russian interior arrived in Vyborg in July. Greeting them were the assistant director of the Resettlement Administration, recently appointed city officials, and a newsreel team that recorded the event. By fall, collective and state farms were popping up all over the Karelian countryside, populated by resettlers from Tula, Riazan', and Kiev oblasts, and the Chuvash ASSR.

Thanks to a report from the head of the convoy of settlers from the Chuvash Republic, we know something about their journey. They departed just before midnight on July 30. A doctor and two nurses accompanied them along with the convoy's leader, Stepanov, who did not mention the presence of military or security personnel. They stopped at Yaroslavl' and four other stations, where they were served hot food. They arrived a week after departing at Elisenvaara, located midway between Lake Ladoga and the new border with Finland, some 125 miles north of Leningrad. They had covered a distance of about 1,000 miles. At Elisenvaara, they were assigned to various settlements, some especially built for them. Those finding themselves near the border expressed alarm at the possibility of attacks from Finns. Rather than offering assurances about their safety, soldiers from the Red Army (possibly border guards) appealed to their patriotism and asked them to assist in strengthening the defense of the Motherland.[124]

---

122. See Zemskov, *Spetsposelentsy v SSSR*, 84–91.

123. Jan T. Gross, *Revolution from Abroad: The Soviet Conquest of Poland's Western Ukraine and Western Belorussia* (Princeton, 2002), 215; David R. Marples, "The Ukrainians in Eastern Poland under Soviet Occupation, 1939–1941: A Study in Soviet Rural Policy," in *The Soviet Takeover of the Polish Eastern Provinces, 1939–41*, ed. Keith Sword (New York, 1991), 236–52.

124. USHMM, RG-22.020 GIAChR, f. 1263, op. 1, ll. 282–83.

What were they like, these resettlers who populated the newly formed Karelo-Finnish Soviet Socialist Republic? Fortunately, the observations of two contemporary witnesses have survived. I. P. Kurteev, a junior artillery officer, described those from the central Russian oblasts who had just arrived at Elisenvaara station as "pitiable—poor, badly dressed, with many children." "I couldn't believe," he continued, "that in 1940 when suburban collective farms, for example in Kirov oblast', were raising themselves up little by little, there were people traveling in goods wagons, dirty and wearing patches, with their goods and cattle on the platform, the cattle looking gaunt." "Poor, without cows . . . and for the most part lacking domestic animals," the Mordvin settlers whom another witness encountered seemed to doubt the finality of their move.[125]

They, of course, were right. We do not know all the places where these and other settlers went after Finnish troops reconquered Karelia in July–August 1941.[126] Some of them wound up in the Chuvash Republic, although we cannot be sure they were the same folks who had departed for Karelia in July 1940. In any case, not long after Soviet troops retook the territory in 1944, the USSR Council of People's Commissars ordered the transport ministry to "reevacuate" and the commissariat of trade to feed up to 43,000 people.[127] Each territorial unit that had accommodated evacuees from Karelia in 1941 received its quota of people to send back. In the case of the Chuvash Republic, that was 1,390. Chuvash authorities produced a plan that overfulfilled the quota, rounding up applicants from twenty-six different districts and the capital city of Cheboksary.[128]

Better documented is the resettlement between 1945 and the early 1950s of more than six thousand collective farm families in the Karelian Isthmus, which had become incorporated within the Leningrad oblast'. Indeed, thanks to the researches of the local historians Viktor Stepakov and Evgenii Balashov, we can reconstruct the process, almost step-by-step, beginning with the State Defense Committee's decision of January 15, 1945 to resettle "a thousand of the best collective farm families from Vologda, Yaroslavl', and Kirov oblasts." This relatively close look starkly reveals the complexities of selecting people, moving them, satisfying their needs, and enabling them to become productive, which, it turns out, was the whole point . . . or nearly so.

---

125. V. N. Stepakov and E. A. Balashov, V "novykh raionakh:" Iz istorii osvoeniia karel'skogo peresheika, 1940–1941, 1944–1950 gg. (St. Petersburg, 2001), 35–38, 42.

126. One of the places they went at least temporarily was to Podporozhskii district bordering on Lake Onega in the extreme east of Leningrad oblast'. For a letter by kolkhozniki inquiring about their compulsory evacuation so that the employees of a sovkhoz from the Karelian Isthmus could be accommodated, see USHMM, RG-22.030 Tsentral'nyi Gosudarstvennyi Arkhiv Sankt-Peterburga (TsGA SPb.), f. 7179, op. 11, d. 814, ll. 164–65.

127. A copy of the decree is in USHMM, RG- 22.027M Gosudarstvennyi Arkhiv Rossiiskoi Federatsii (GARF), f. A-327, op. 1, d. 2, l. 139.

128. USHMM, 22.020 GIAChR, f. 1263, op. 1, d. 81, l. 69. The Chuvash Council of People's Commissars drew up similar plans for reevacuating people to the Latvian and Estonian SSRs. See ll. 72, 75.

The Leningrad party obkom responded almost immediately to the announcement by ordering state and party officials in six districts to "put in order all residential and business structures reserved for the resettled collective farmers by February 5." This was a tall order because, as the Leningrad Oblast' Executive Committee chairman Solov'ev noted, "the majority of homes and businesses have been subjected to varying degrees of damage." But there was no time to lose because at least eight recruiters, ranging in age from twenty-one to forty-seven and all but one party members, were fanning out across Yaroslavl', Vladimir (not Vologda), and Kirov oblasts in search of worthy settlers.[129]

Some of the resettlers who followed in the wake of party organizers, agronomists, and other *nomenklatura* personnel found conditions to their liking. Judging by the group letter that settlers from four collective farms in the Iaskii (Jääski) district wrote in March 1945 to their former neighbors in Kirov oblast', they definitely were among the fortunate. "We were greeted with music and warm words," the letter stated in the best propagandistic tradition. "We all have received good homes with outbuildings. . . . The stoves, windows, and doors are in complete working order. . . . We will energetically be ready for spring sowing and develop animal husbandry." This too was fortunate, because, as Solov'ev told a meeting of the Leningrad oblast' soviet in August, "we recovered the isthmus not only to colonize it, but in order to provide Leningrad with foodstuffs." Not so fortunately, Solov'ev made his comment as part of a dressing down of district soviet executives, the majority of whom had to admit that their collective farms had not "given" Leningrad anything. "Only the best people were selected for the Karelian Isthmus, but under you, it seems, they have gone rotten," an obviously displeased Solov'ev concluded.[130]

By December some 1,800 of these "rotten" settlers had begun working in industrial enterprises and elsewhere in the urban economy as seasonal laborers. Recruiters meanwhile turned to a familiar source of recruits. Hundreds of demobilized soldiers were signed up, including several who "expressed a desire to inspect districts in the isthmus"—that is, to scout out the territory. Propitiated with loans of 5,000 rubles per family and other incentives, recruits came from as far away as Kazakhstan and Siberia's Altai and Omsk territories.[131] Even now, new twists occurred in the symbiotic relationship between depopulation and repopulation. In May 1947 the Council of Ministers issued instructions to remove from Leningrad oblast' anyone of Finnish or Ingrian nationality who had returned to their

129. Stepakov and Balashov, V "novykh raionakh," 68, 98. Seven of the eight recruiters were male.
130. Ibid., 66–68, 70–71, 107–8.
131. For the State Defense Committee resolution of June 1945, see USHMM, RG-22.027M GARF, f. A-327, Reel 309, op. 2, d. 429, l. 1; for the processing in 1946 of refusals by demobilized Red Army soldiers "subject to" (podlezhashchikh) resettlement, see ibid., dd. 431–34; and for the selection and transport of 1,500 kolkhoz families in 1947, see d. 440, ll. 47, 49–52, 119–25.

homeland after the Great Patriotic War. Consistent with the "national bolshevism" of Stalin's last years, in July 1948, the Leningrad oblast' soviet executive committee was told by its vice chairman, "We have instructions from the party's central committee, if you like, personally from Comrade Stalin, that the districts of the Leningrad oblast' should be settled first of all by Russian people."[132] What had been implicit thus rose to the level of articulated policy: when available, ethnic (or "Great") Russians should be relied on as settlers, particularly in areas once inhabited by nationalities of doubtful loyalties.[133]

One might imagine that the war effort superseded resettlement plans, but it is more appropriate to view the war as having reshaped them. Although saddled with the enormous task of arranging the accommodation, provisioning, and employment of millions of evacuees (the subject of chapter 6), the Resettlement Committee also bore responsibility for organizing two major resettlement campaigns. Each involved moving thousands of peasant families considerable distances at state expense. Both had large implications for food production so vital to sustaining the Red Army at the front and the civilian population in the rear. One was devoted to expanding the fishing industry; the other to replacing agriculturalists deported because of their nationality.

The recruitment of peasants from European Russia to work in fishing kolkhozes and processing plants of the Far North, the Volga delta, the Baikal region, the Amur basin, and Kamchatka occurred in three phases: April–July 1942, March–August 1943, and early 1944.[134] The logistics of these efforts were virtually identical to the prewar campaigns discussed above. But no matter how experienced it was at this sort of thing, the regime reproduced its pathologies. What might have seemed routine and straightforward from the Olympian heights of the Kremlin inevitably became enmeshed in bureaucratic push and pull as one descended from oblast', krai, and autonomous republic to district and thence to individual kolkhoz. File after file in central and regional archives document the tug of war in painful detail. What made the war years different was the availability of a large group of people even more vulnerable to the blandishments of resettlement officials—evacuees. Soviet authorities, who never seemed to tire of moving people, drew on this source.

Territories in central and northern European Russia were designated to supply settlers for the fishing industry. They included five autonomous republics (Chuvash, Marii, Mordvin, Tatar, and Udmurt) and nine oblasts (Gor'kii, Yaroslavl', Kalinin, Kirov, Penza,

---

132. Ibid., d. 440, ll. 97, 110, 128, 132–33. Mark Edele cites a RSFSR Council of Ministers report from GARF (f. A-259) that only 320 Red Army families had settled in Karelia by March 1946. See Edele, "Veterans and the Village: The Impact of Red Army Demobilization on Soviet Urbanization, 1945–1955," *Russian History* 36 (2009): 170. On national bolshevism, which lauded ethnic Russians as the elder brothers of other Soviet peoples, see David Brandenberger, *National Bolshevism: Stalinist Mass Culture and the Formation of Modern Russian National Identity, 1931–1956* (Cambridge, 2002).

133. This issue will be revisited in more detail in the chapter on deportation and return.

134. USHMM, RG-22.027M, GARF, f. A-327, Reel 303, op. 2, d. 388, ll. 1–2, 42, 46–54.

Riazan', Tambov, Tula, and Vologda). Because each of these territories absorbed several hundred thousand evacuees, it would be reasonable to assume that authorities would move out indigenous peasants so that people evacuated from farther to the west could be accommodated more easily. This indeed may have been part of the calculus of the authorities in Moscow, but it was not the reality on the ground.

The typical campaign to send settlers to fishing kolkhozes and factory communities began with a request to the USSR Council of Ministers by the Commissariat of Fisheries for the allocation of a certain number of additional workers and the distribution of quotas among authorities in territories targeted for recruitment. Regional authorities could—and did—challenge these quotas, claiming they could not afford to lose the labor force or spare activists to recruit workers.[135] Once established, quotas were subdivided among districts and, within them, individual village soviets. Territorial governments bore responsibility for publicizing the opportunity for resettlement and associated benefits. Articles describing the expansion of the fishing industry as "an important state task" vital to the war effort appeared in regional newspapers and were reproduced at the district level.[136] Village soviets sponsored meetings intended to elicit applications that they then forwarded to district and oblast' commissions for verification. In the meantime, the Resettlement Committee negotiated with relevant commissariats (transport, food supply, health) to develop schedules for convoys to take the settlers to their new homes and made arrangements for them to be distributed among local kolkhozes, much as had occurred before the war.

The memoranda, inquiries, and reports filed by inspectors and plenipotentiaries from territorial administrations—the sinews of this particular regime of migration—allow us to retrace virtually every stage in the formation, dispatch, and arrival of nearly every convoy of settlers. Few went off without incident. Especially in the first months, recruitment lagged behind quotas; some who signed up had last-minute second thoughts or did not show up at train stations for other reasons; trains arrived late at embarkation points, so that food ran out even before departure; some cars lacked heating and accommodation for baggage and livestock.[137] Upon arrival at destination, settlers discovered they would have to share

---

135. For example, officials from Penza, Voronezh, Riazan', and Yaroslavl' oblasts and the Tatar ASSR declared their opposition to (or in their terms, the impossibility of) fulfilling the quotas assigned to them in connection with a resolution of the RSFSR Council of Ministers from December 1943 to send some 8,500 families to fishing grounds in Arkhangel'sk and Murmansk oblasts. USHMM, RG-22.027M, GARF, f. A-327, Reel 303, op. 2, d. 388, ll. 56, 57, 59, 67, 68a. For earlier opposition by the Tatar ASSR's Council of People's Commissars prompting a letter of warning from the party's Central Committee, see ibid., d. 386, l. 137.

136. For examples, see USHMM, RG-22.027M, GARF, f. A-327, Reel 303, op. 2, d. 386, ll. 56, 70, 219.

137. See memoranda to N. V. Zhukov, chairman of the department of employment of evacuees under the Chuvash ASSR Council of People's Commissars on late arrival of trains, lack of food, etc. among convoys bound for Irkutsk oblast' and the Buriat-Mongol ASSR in 1942, in USHMM, 22.020, GIAChR, f. 1263, op. 1, d. 51, ll. 64, 108–108ob. For households backing out of resettling in Murmansk oblast' in 1944, USHMM RG-22.027M, GARF, f. A-327, Reel 1, op. 1, d. 78, ll. 20, 48, 52.

accommodation with other families because not enough new houses were built, that garden plots were unavailable, or that payment of start-up loans had been delayed. They also received no training in the fishing trade and sometimes were subjected to discrimination, taunting, and open hostility from locals.[138] No wonder a substantial proportion of families refused to stick it out.[139]

These hitches were not peculiar to the war years. They had occurred in the 1930s and would recur during the late 1940s and early 1950s. What was unique had to do with the nature of the settlers. It becomes apparent from the thousands of application forms that have survived in the archives that they consisted of a preponderance of evacuees over applicants indigenous to the region of recruitment, of women over men, and of families with a relatively high proportion of dependents compared with able-bodied members. In a sample taken from some two hundred applications in the Chuvash ASSR to resettle to the Buriat-Mongol ASSR far to the east during the summer of 1942, thirty-four of fifty-five emanated from evacuees—eleven from either Moscow or the Moscow oblast', six from the Belorussian SSR, and three each from Voronezh oblast' and Latvia. Similarly, among a sample of fifty applying to populate the fisheries of Irkutsk oblast', thirty-five came from evacuees— eight from Moscow or Moscow oblast', seven from Leningrad oblast', six from Kalinin oblast', and five from the Belorussian SSR.[140] The fact that fishing rarely entered into the vocations of these or other applicants did not seem to matter to the authorities.

Information from elsewhere suggests their absolute typicality. Commenting on the demographic data he had provided on families resettled in the Irkutsk oblast' during 1942, an executive committee official wrote, "As you can see, the majority of families have many young children and only one able bodied [literally, "work able"; this term excluded women with young children] member. . . . There are even 123 families in which nobody is able bodied."[141] A report from the Bratsk district of Irkutsk oblast' noted that the vast majority

138. See the report from L. T. Dmitriev, chairman of the department of employment of evacuees under the RSFSR Council of People's Commissars on settlers' housing and living conditions and treatment by locals in the Buriat-Mongol ASSR in 1943, in USHMM, RG-22.027M, GARF, f. A-327, Reel 303, op. 2, d. 388, ll. 35–37. On lack of training, this in the Bratsk district of Irkutsk oblast', see USHMM, RG-22.027M, GARF, f. A-327, Reel 44, op. 2, d. 42, l. 55.

139. USHMM, RG-22.027M, GARF, f. A-327, Reel 303, op. 2, d. 387, ll. 35–37. In this particular case, one-third of the families, 521 of 1574, sent to the Buriat-Mongol ASSR in 1943 applied to leave.

140. USHMM, RG-22.020, GIAChR, f. 1263, op. 1, d. 103, ll. 1–239. The basis of sampling was to choose every other applicant. The application consisted of a two-sided sheet, on the reverse side of which the applicant listed information about accompanying dependents. According to a report from August 1942, only 14 of the 272 families resettled in the Bratsk district of Irkutsk oblast' as part of the effort to expand fishing were indigenous to the Chuvash Republic and Kirov oblast'. The overwhelming majority consisted of evacuees from Moscow and Leningrad oblasts. USHMM, RG-22.027M, GARF, f. A-327, Reel 44, op. 2, d. 42, l. 54.

141. USHMM, RG-22.027M, GARF, f. A-327, Reel 44, op. 2, d. 42, l. 2.

of the settler families that had arrived from the Chuvash ASSR and Kirov oblast' in 1942 consisted of evacuees, mostly from Leningrad and Moscow.[142]

Why were evacuees far more likely to wind up as settlers than indigenous collective farmers? Part of the explanation may lie in the desire among local officials to hold onto their own people. One inspector claimed that chairmen of kolkhozes in the Chuvash ASSR did not publicize the opportunity to resettle among collective farmers because the labor supply was already short and they feared losing more of it.[143] But we also should recognize the agency of collective farmers themselves in not making themselves available. The repertoire of how they dealt with authorities included the claim that with planting or harvesting to be done and with so many of their husbands and sons at the front, they could not commit themselves to leaving.

Evacuees also had agency, but were in a tighter spot than collective farmers. Some, hopeful of soon returning home, did not apply to be resettled elsewhere. But for others, waiting was not an option. For Nikifor Rebrii, a primary schoolteacher of Russian, remaining in a rural district east of Kazan was as impossible to imagine as was returning to his native Odessa, far off and still under occupation. "I am without work," he wrote from a village without a school, "and cannot go on living here. Conditions are awful." Someone among the seven families evacuated to a district in the Mordvin Republic reported that they had sold off most of their possessions (shirts, cups, lace), having failed to receive sufficient quantities of bread and other goods from authorities. "I request the representative [of the resettlement office] either provide us with bread or send us more quickly to a place in Erkutsk [sic] oblast'." Others simply wrote that they "lived badly," and, promising to fulfill all assigned work, requested inclusion in the next detachment of settlers.[144] Among those filing applications in the sample cited above, 70 percent were mothers of children below working age, if not toddlers. The small amount of baggage most registered hints at penury as a key motive.[145]

The difficulty of recruiting non-evacuees is illustrated by a case of arm-twisting recorded in unusual detail by one of the inspectors of the Chuvash Republic's office of employment. When ("without any explanation of benefits") peasants from the Bronevik (Armored Car) kolkhoz in the Kalinin district were asked who wanted to go to the Buriat-Mongol ASSR, all were silent. Comrade Fedorov from the village executive committee then allegedly told

---

142. USHMM, RG-22.027M, GARF, f. A-327, Reel 303, op. 2, d. 386, l. 63. That is, 258 of 272, or 94 percent.

143. Ibid., l. 219.

144. Ibid., ll. 102, 167–69.

145. USHMM, RG-22.020, GIAChR, f. 1263, op. 1, d. 103, l. 219. By comparison, when in December 1944 the State Committee on Defense issued its plans for resettling collective farmers in the Karelian Isthmus, it stipulated that each family was entitled to take "up to 2 tons" of personal property. See USHMM, RG-22.027M, GARF, f. A-327, Reel 1, op. 1 d. 3, l. 10.

them if nobody went voluntarily, some would be exiled. To the question of the conditions of travel, Comrade Kulikov, a teacher and stockkeeper in charge of the meeting, replied, "I don't know, but they can't be bad." At this point, Comrade Fedorov proposed to Comrade Kulikov to write down names. He read out five, after which a vote (of not only adults but children too) was held. Citizens Lesovskaia and Kaluzhnaia, whose families had been chosen, protested. Lesovskaia cited her husband at the front, her invalid brother, and two young children. Immediately after the meeting she and Kaluzhnaia left for Kalinino ("despite the fact that it was nighttime") to seek justice from the NKVD.[146]

In a later report "on the question of the violation of the principle of voluntariness in the selection of resettlers to the Buriat-Mongol ASSR," the same inspector noted that "an explanation of the conditions for resettlement and associated benefits" had satisfied all five household heads including Lesovskaia and Kaluzhnaia, who agreed to join a convoy. Moreover, the statement allegedly uttered by Fedorov to the effect that the lack of volunteers would precipitate impressment could not be confirmed.[147] On the one hand, the record that has survived in the archive certainly does not tell the whole story. We will never know why those particular families were chosen and why, after protesting, Lesovskaia and Kaluzhnaia capitulated. In all likelihood, the first report bore a closer relationship to actual events in the village; the latter smacks of a cover-up. On the other hand, this is the sole instance of even alleged coercion in the recruitment of settlers, and the very fact that it precipitated an investigation and a report that reached much higher in the bureaucratic hierarchy suggests its abnormality.

By 1944, the Astrakhan, Murmansk, and Arkhangel'sk oblasts—whose fishing industries needed more workers—had replaced Irkutsk oblast' and the Buriat-Mongol ASSR as the primary destinations of resettlers.[148] Then after the RSFSR Council of People's Commissars had issued the appropriate order in March 1944, the Saratov oblast' replaced Murmansk and Arkhangel'sk.[149] Why Saratov? Because it needed repopulating after the removal of the ethnic German population and the disappointing results of ad hoc resettlement efforts up to that point.[150] Saratov oblast' thus resembled Groznyi oblast' in the North

---

146. USHMM, RG-22.020, GIAChR, f. 1263, op. 1, d. 51, ll. 143–44.

147. Ibid., l. 150. The first report is undated. The second, which went to the chairman of the Council of People's Commissars of the republic, is dated July 28, 1942.

148. For a plan to send one hundred families to the Astrakhan oblast' at the mouth of the Volga to assist in that region's fishing industry, see USHMM, RG-22.020, GIAChR, f. 1263, op. 1, d. 78, l. 63.

149. For reference to the RSFSR Council resolution of March 11, 1944, see USHMM, RG-22.020, GIAChR, f. 1263, op. 1, d. 81. l. 66.

150. According to a summary report, over 500,000 hectares of previously cultivated land remained uncultivated as of January 1943. This was nearly twice as much as anticipated, largely because the number of able-bodied settlers was far below the expected amount. See USHMM, RG-22.027M, GARF, f. A-327, Reel 303, op. 2, d. 386, ll. 12–14.

Caucasus and Crimea as destinations that, following upon the deportation of indigenous people or those resident for generations, warranted the special attention of resettlement authorities.

Simultaneously, forced repatriations of Germans from Kaliningrad oblast' (formerly Königsberg) and Japanese from southern Sakhalin created the opportunity/necessity for planned resettlement of collective farm families from the Russian heartland. Sixteen oblasts and three autonomous republics were tapped to provide settlers mainly to expand the fishing industries. Attracted by the offer of various benefits, the first settlers—about twelve thousand families—arrived in Kaliningrad in August 1946. More than two hundred thousand people from various parts of the RSFSR were living in rural areas of the oblast' by the early 1950s, including over eighty-one thousand in collective farms.[151] Along with the Karelian Isthmus, Kaliningrad attracted more settlers than anywhere else in the RSFSR in the postwar years—some 40 percent. The Far East, including southern Sakhalin and Kamchatka, absorbed another 30 percent, while smaller numbers moved to Crimea and elsewhere.[152]

It should be clear by now that desperation drove many of these families to faraway places. Likewise, desperation and despair must have driven many to return. For return they did. Compared with settlers in Sakhalin, who appear to have been provided with decent accommodation, those in Kaliningrad suffered—and returned to their native villages in substantial numbers.[153] According to the resettlement office's man in Kamchatka, 44 percent of the nearly 2,500 families that had arrived between 1939 and 1944 did not stay. Kamchatka is about as harsh and remote as it gets in the Soviet Union, hence its figurative use by teachers when referring to students sitting in the back of the class. But Crimea, where some 18,000 families settled between 1944 and 1948, lost an even higher proportion—52 percent—by July 1948, mostly because of unprecedented drought in the previous two years. Incomplete data from the former German lands in Saratov oblast' indicates an even less successful resettlement effort. Of the over 4,000 families settling since 1944, less than a

151. Progress in the recruitment of collective farmers and their settlement in Kaliningrad and Sakhalin can be followed in USHMM, RG-22.027M, GARF, f. A-327, Reels 311–12, op. 2, d. 440, ll. 191–92, 197, 216, 231, 250; d. 441, ll. 19, 42, 54, 130, 179–88; d. 442, ll. 28–34, 124.

152. O. M. Verbitskaia, "Planovoe sel'skokhoziaistvennoe pereselenie v RSFSR v 1946–1958 godakh," *Voprosy istorii*, no. 12 (1986): 17–19; USHMM, RG-22.027M, GARF, f. A-327, Reel 340, op. 2, d. 626: Dokladnye zapiski i spravki komissii i oblispolkomov ob itogakh obsledovaniia sostoianiia pereselencheskikh kolkhozov krymskoi oblasti za 1947 g. [November–December 1947]. Crimea was part of the RSFSR until 1954.

153. Inna Penkhvaevna Kim, "Razvitie territorii, prisoedinennykh k SSSR posle vtoroi mirovoi voiny (Vostochnaia Prussiia, Iuzhnyi Sakhalin, Kuril'skie ostrova), 1945–pervaia polovina 1949 gg.," synopsis of Iuzhno-Sakhalinsk University dissertation (2010), 21, 16; Verbitskaia, *Naselenie rossiiskoi derevni*, 198. Part of the problem in Kaliningrad had to do with a shortage of glass for windows. See USHMM, RG-22.027M, GARF, f. A-327, Reel 337, op. 2, d. 610, l. 13. The housing situation remained strained—even by Soviet standards—well into the 1950s. See USHMM, RG-22.027M, GARF, f. A-327, Reel 2, op. 1, d. 142, ll. 36–38.

quarter remained by October 1949.[154] In returning, these families deprived the state not only of their labor but also repayment of the loans extended to them at the time of their settlement. The archives contain some fascinating instances of the state tracking down "irregular" returnees and trying to collect on them as well as a draft edict tightening the terms of loans to future settlers. But as with other instances of irregularity cited above, this was a battle the state probably did not win.[155]

Not all resettlement involved such huge efforts and costs and not all settlers were Russian. In the case of the border with Turkey, a country fast becoming a client state of the United States, Soviet authorities found another solution. They enacted the transfer—officially described as based "on voluntary principles" but evidently experienced as deportation—of Azerbaijani peasants living near the Turkish border to the lowlands of central Azerbaijan. Very little reliable information is available about this resettlement. Current sources from Azerbaijan claim either that Stalin was put up to deporting Azerbaijani peasants by Armenians determined to ethnically cleanse their own republic, or that Stalin himself, increasingly concerned about the possibility of conflict with Turkey, came to regard the Turkic-speaking Islamic Azerbaijanis as a potential fifth column. Whatever the precipitant for their removal, in the years after Stalin's death, some 40–45 percent managed to return to their homes in Armenia.[156]

Even before Stalin's death in 1953, resettlement was losing its association with deportation and assuming its place as a key ingredient in agrarian development schemes. Archival records of meetings among resettlement personnel afford brief glimpses of such internal (within the boundaries of a single republic, oblast', or krai) projects as resettling collective farmers displaced by the construction of the Kuibyshev reservoir in the Middle Volga and bringing thousands of peasant families from mountainous to lowland territories in Azerbaijan, Georgia, and Tajikistan. Both did not involve much voluntariness. Even when the distances were small—an average of less than five miles in the case of the nearly seven thousand collective farm households whose land would be submerged—a special commission consisting of district party committee secretaries and soviet executive committee chairs, the chief architect of the reservoir project, a representative of the hydroelectric

---

154. USHMM, RG-22.027M, GARF, f. A-327, Reels 340, 317, op. 2, d. 630, ll. 31, 144; d. 473, l. 11.

155. USHMM, RG-22.027M, GARF, f. A-327, Reel 317, op. 2, d. 475, ll. 4–10 (Aleksandr Salov), 16–21 (Nikolai Belousov), both of whom left Kaliningrad oblast' in 1947–48. The draft resolution sent by the RSFSR Council of Ministers' chairman M. I. Rodionov to Lavrentii Beria is in USHMM, RG-22.027M, GARF, f. A-327, Reel 337, op. 2, d. 610, ll. 33–34.

156. For the resolution of December 23, 1947, see "O pereselenii Azerbaidzhantsev," http://www.hrono.info/dokum/194_dok?19480310azer.html (accessed May 17, 2012); for a recent interpretation by a historian from Azerbaijan, see Sabir Asadov, "Deportatsiia azerbaidzhantsev iz Armianskoi SSR (1948–1953 gody)," http://azerbaycanli.org/ru/page136.html (accessed May 20, 2012).

power station, and several agronomists decided for the collective farmers where they would live.[157] One imagines that adjusting to the different ecology of the lowlands would have been more difficult, but in the absence of available documentation, imagine is all we can do.

Archival material concerning longer-distance resettlement suggests that personnel did try to ameliorate difficulties experienced by their clientele. They discussed the comparative advantages and costs of housing materials, whether Koreans who "independently" (that is, irregularly) came to Stavropol' krai to cultivate rice should receive exemptions from taxes and other benefits accorded to regular settlers, and how to improve the performance of the Amur Rural Construction trust, whose record of constructing houses at cost and on time was described as "miserable."[158] Yet at least to settlers from Belarus, the Amur seemed no worse as a destination than the Karelo-Finnish SSR, according to a report received by the Belorussian Council of Ministers and Communist Party Central Committee. Recruitment to the Karelo-Finnish Republic started in October 1952 when district executive committees in "areas of excessive labor" began to advertise in local newspapers, clubs, and libraries. They also distributed letters from earlier settlers, a well-rehearsed method of recruitment, to relatives and former neighbors. But, as the report indicated, "a lot of people had returned," which spurred recruiters to advertise the availability of state farms in the Amur. By the end of 1953, an equal number of settler families—568—had departed for Karelia and the Amur.[159]

Resettlement officials throughout the Belorussian Republic cited several reasons for their rather unimpressive record of recruitment during 1953—barely half of a planned ten thousand families. Previously, recruits came mainly from those who had wound up in Belarus as a result of war-related dislocations—thus again blurring the distinction between resettlers and refugees—but that pool had been exhausted. A shortage of staff—only thirty employed in the entire republic—did not help. Another factor, "very bad preparations at destinations," apparently led to settlers "returning in massive numbers." Bureaucratic heartlessness, a perennial favorite of those seeking to burnish their populist credentials, played a role too. Finally, as V. Shkliarik, the director of the republic's Resettlement Bureau, had to acknowledge, "such an important and justified method as sending scouts" was "quite poorly used."[160]

157. RGAE, f. 5675, op. 1, d. 566, ll. 2–3; d. 670, ll. 1–3, 132; d. 633, ll. 5–20. For comparable resettlement distances in the case of the Stalingrad oblast' dam project, see USHMM, RG-22.027M, GARF, f. A-327, Reel 1, op. 1, d. 76, l. 34; d. 91, ll. 106, 162–66.
158. Ibid., d. 586, ll. 88–89; d. 627, ll. 3–5, 39, 108.
159. Ibid., d. 633, ll. 61–70.
160. Ibid., d. 633, ll. 61, 67–69, 71, 75, 83, 85.

Since the official line on scouts had been ambivalent at best, Shkliarik's subordinates could be excused for quite poorly using them. The Council of Ministers' resolution from December 1951 "On Benefits for Resettlement for 1952" mentioned neither scouts, nor representatives, nor plenipotentiaries, nor any other term connoting someone chosen by prospective settlers to inspect conditions. However, the 1953 version approved in February (and repeated word for word in the 1973 resolution) did refer to the right of "representatives of settler collective farms and brigades" to "familiarize themselves with the locality and conditions of settlement" at no cost to themselves. So, in the long history of resettlement, prospective peasant settlers managed to eke out a concession from the state, and the late Stalinist state at that, that permitted one of their own to take a preliminary look at where the state was proposing to send them and report back much as scouts did in Imperial Russia.[161]

This element of choice expanded as the resettlement regime underwent a transition from mandating to enticing resettlers. Competing with each other for the same pool of potential settlers, offices in different parts of the country produced brochures typically titled "Come settle with us in _____ oblast'/republic." Each brochure extolled its advertised region as a place to work and live, listed the benefits available to settlers, and often included glowing accounts by those who already had settled. Sakhalin, as described by L. Kheifets, was the "Jewel of the Far East" with a total area significantly exceeding such countries as Switzerland, Denmark, Belgium, and Holland. Kustanai oblast' in northern Kazakhstan, countered L. Shulgin, is larger than Portugal, Switzerland, and Denmark combined, not to mention all of Transcaucasia and the Baltic republics. But western Kazakhstan's climate "is dry and healthy. The steppe is always beautiful—in spring when it is covered by thick grasses, in summer when waves of grain resemble the sea, and in winter under a blanket of sparkling white snow."[162]

The testimonials are touching idealizations, variations on the theme of "how resettlement improved my life." "I send you fiery greetings from Sakhalin," wrote Fedor Sodovnik to his fellow countrymen back in Poltava oblast'. "It is very far from Poltava but my family and I do not regret where we are . . . We live well and in a cultured fashion on Sakhalin. Our collective farm is 6 kilometers from the district center next to a railroad. We have a club, a seven-year school, a medical station, and three stores. Our collective has electricity and

---

161. See "Postanovlenie Sovmina SSSR ot 21.12.1951 N 5263 o l'gotakh po pereseleniiu na 1952 god," http://www.lawrussia.ru/texts/legal_586/doc586a391x339.htm (accessed May 19, 2012); the 1953 version is in RGAE, f. 5675, op. 1, d. 670, ll. 167–79. For the 1973 version, see "Postanovlenie Sovmina SSSR ot 31.05.1973 N 364 o l'gotakh po pereseleniiu," http://bestpravo.ru/sssr/gn-normy/c6n.htm (accessed May 19, 2012).

162. L. Kheifets, *Pereseliates' k nam na Sakhalin* (Iuzhno-Sakhalinsk, 1954), 7; L. Shulgin, ed., *Pereseliates' v kustanaiskuiu oblast'* (Kustanai, 1960), 4; *Pereseliates' v zapadnyi Kazakhstan* (Ural'sk, 1960), 2.

radio." "We turn to you, our fellow countrymen from Ukraine," wrote some state farm workers from western Kazakhstan who also hailed from Poltava. "Dear comrades, come to us, to the Poltava sovkhoz. Here you will find everything to your liking. You will be at home, and at work you will earn a lot."[163]

Resettlement recruiters wooed potential settlers to Petrozavodsk, Kemerovo, Tomsk, Krasnoiarsk, and Khabarovsk—to name but a few offices that issued brochures during the 1950s. The pitch often proved deceptive, mainly, it seems, because collective and state farm directors failed to assign sufficient funds for home construction. They "systematically undermined" plans, for example, building only a little over 2,000 of the 3,500 farm houses in the Maritime krai in 1955. Subsequent resolutions, according to two local scholars, did not improve matters. Collective farms in Khabarovsk krai somehow managed to have an even worse rate of fulfillment over the years 1955–59.[164] The problem of housing newcomers would prove even more intractable for those heading to the city, as we shall see in chapter 3.

To track these less than impressive efforts is to help contextualize the Virgin Lands program of the late 1950s. Clearly, the recruitment of over three hundred thousand volunteers to settle the arid west Siberian and northern Kazakh steppe dwarfed other resettlement efforts in prestige and commitment of resources. The Virgin Lands program followed on previous efforts to settle the Kazakh steppe, beginning in the nineteenth century when Slavic peasants first displaced nomadic pastoralists. A succession of special settlers—ex-kulaks, Poles, Germans, and then during the Great Patriotic War Chechen and Ingush deportees—arrived before the appearance of the Virgin Landers. In recruiting settlers, the Komsomol reprised its role from the late 1930s when, prompted by Valentina Khetagurova's call, it sent twenty-five thousand youths to the Far East. Like those earlier enthusiasts, many who expected "a Kazakhstan that was empty of culture or people . . . were astonished and dismayed to find thousands of people whom they had been taught to think of as 'traitors' already living there."[165]

The comparison with the "Khetagurovites" also points to significant differences. The recruits for the Far East, four-fifths of whom were women, represented the most talented tenth of those who had volunteered to go. Recruiting commissions for the Virgin Lands,

163. Kheifets, *Pereseliates' k nam na Sakhalin*, 18; *Pereseliates' v zapadnyi Kazakhstan*, 19, 21. A memorandum from the Resettlement Administration's director, V. Volchkov, to all regional departments, "On Letters of Resettlers to their *Zemliaki*," emphasized that they could be "one of most effective forms of agitation," but only if they "correctly" described living conditions, the success and prospects for future development of kolkhozes, sovkhozes, and enterprises, [and] growth of material prosperity." USHMM, RG-22.027M, GARF, f. A-327, Reel 2, op. 1, d. 142, l. 71.

164. E. L. Motrich and S. A. Kravchuk, "Gosudarstvennaia politika khoziaistvennogo osvoeniia i zaseleniia Dal'nego Vostoka s kontsa XIX v. do serediny 1980-kh godov," *Vestnik SVO RAN*, no. 6 (2006): 123.

165. Michaela Pohl, "The 'Planet of One Hundred Languages': Ethnic Relations and Soviet Identity in the Virgin Lands," in Breyfogle, Schrader, and Sunderland, *Peopling the Russian Periphery*, 244.

according to Michaela Pohl, "tried to fill the total required of them, and sent anybody who would sign up." Consequently, a substantial proportion consisted of amnestied criminals or people with a "dark past." And whereas the departure in 1939 of approximately half of the 5,000 workers recruited by one of the main enterprises of Komsomolsk-on-Amur caused a scandal, turnover in the Virgin Lands reached far more massive proportions. "What started as a plan to permanently resettle 100,000 people turned into a *yearly* mobilization of that many workers," writes Pohl, and according to Viktor Perevedentsev, only 8 percent of those who came in 1954–55 remained by 1961.[166] Yet, between 1954 and 1957, the population of the Virgin Lands had increased by 350,000, indicating "resettlement on an unprecedented scale."[167]

Perevedentsev, who began studying the Virgin Landers within a few years of the campaign's inception, later recalled that the entire thrust of the state's migration policy—to redistribute population eastward via resettlement programs and other incentives—failed to match the flow of migrants in the opposite direction. Between the census years of 1959 and 1970, Siberia lost 924,000 people, mostly from the countryside.[168] This dismal (from the state's point of view) result points to the limitations of resettlement as a tool for manipulating population distribution, or at least to the limited funding devoted to the effort. A new Council of Ministers' resolution on benefits to resettlers, issued on May 31, 1973, seems generous on paper, but had little if any effect in counteracting the drain of population from rural to urban areas and from east to west, no doubt because of the same problems of enforcement and funding already discussed.[169]

But as if to demonstrate that there still was life in the state's veins, that authorities could still engage in social engineering, moving people around for the people's benefit, they occasionally did rouse themselves into action. Designating "settlements without a future" (*neperspektivnye derevny*) and moving inhabitants to centralized sovkhoz and kolkhoz farmsteads equipped with electricity and indoor plumbing represented the most ambitious resettlement project of the postwar decades. Propounded in a resolution of the party's Central Committee of March 1974, the scheme would sound the death knell to tens of thousands of communities throughout the Non-Black Earth region of the RSFSR.[170] The problem, as detailed in our chapter on migrants to the city, was that most new "viable" settlements

---

166. Shulman, *Stalinism on the Frontier*, 1, 69, 79; Pohl, " 'Planet of One Hundred Languages,' " 241, 244; Viktor Perevedentsev, "Migratsiia kak sud'ba," *Otechestvannye zapiski*, no. 4 (18) (2004), http://www.strana-oz.ru/2004/4/migraciya-kak-sudba (accessed May 19, 2009).

167. Verbitskaia, "Planovoe," 20.

168. Perevedentsev, "Migratsiia kak sud'ba." See also Prociuk, "Manpower Problem in Siberia," 190–210.

169. The resolution is at "Postanovlenie Sovmina SSSR ot 31.05.1973 N 364 o l'gotakh po pereseleniiu."

170. Kommunisticheskaia partiia Sovetskaia Soiuza, *KPSS v rezoliutsiiakh i resheniiakh s"ezdov, konferentsii i plenumov TsK*, 9th ed. (Moscow, 1986), 12: 405.

lacked the promised infrastructure, leaving the prospective migrants little choice but to flee to already-existing towns and cities. But this was not all. The basis on which authorities took decisions to close some settlements and reinforce others was faulty. How else to explain that in Perm oblast', for example, half of the communities identified as viable faded away in the course of the 1970s, whereas 47 percent of villages whose population increased had been among those declared nonviable?[171]

A number of factors—perhaps above all, its high degree of out-migration—made Non-Black Earth Russia particularly attractive to experimentation by authorities determined to raise agricultural productivity. But as suggested by the history of colonial projects elsewhere, more peripherally located and ethnically distinct areas of the country proved even more attractive. One such area was in northwestern Tajikistan where subsistence farmers in the Mastchah and Yoghnob valleys were relocated in the 1960s and 1970s to provide labor power for newly irrigated cotton fields. The authorities depicted the move largely in terms of providing better services and otherwise raising living standards. A more important objective, as John Schoeberlein argues, consisted of "a fundamental reorganization of communities which would . . . allow them only to function within the framework of institutions and practices imposed by the State," or in more concrete terms, "that people should not live in extended-family compounds, that streets should meet at right angles, and that at the heart of the community there should be offices of the Communist Party and local government."[172]

In the meantime, a rather inventive approach linking Central Asia to Non-Black Earth Russia appeared in the form of Uzbek-based construction trusts contracted by the RSFSR Ministry for Land Reclamation to improve land and construct housing for three fully functioning state farms ("Tashkent" and "Friendship" in Novgorod oblast', and "Uzbekistan" in Ivanovo oblast'). The project, an offshoot of the 1974 Central Committee resolution on revitalizing agriculture in the Non-Black Earth region, seemed to kill two birds with one stone: it would draw away underemployed rurals from Uzbekistan and supply badly needed agricultural workers to the Non-Black Earth region. These pilot programs spawned several others in Smolensk oblast', the Chuvash ASSR, and the oil and gas complex around Tiumen' in Siberia.[173] But for all the scheme's promise, for all the talk of a "reverse" or "second

---

171. L. N. Denisova, *Ischezaiushchaia derevnia Rossii: Nechernozem'e v 1960–1980-e gody* (Moscow, 1996), 122–25.

172. Schoeberlein, "Shifting Ground," 51–52. The relocations echoed the forced resettlement of the Gharmi people of central Tajikistan to the Qurgonteppa region in the republic's southwest and highland to lowland population transfers in that republic's northwest during the 1950s. See ibid., 62–63; and Ferrando, "Soviet Population Transfers," 41–43.

173. S. Enders Wimbush and Dmitry Ponomareff, *Alternatives for Mobilizing Soviet Central Asian Labor: Out-migration and Regional Development* (Santa Monica, 1979), 14–19.

virtgin lands," information about the fate of these trusts beyond the early 1980s is totally lacking.[174]

Attempts to relieve Central Asia of its "excess" labor supply precipitated other schemes in the last years before the breakup of the Soviet Union. Annual bonuses, free housing for the first two years, guaranteed apartments, extra vacation time, educational opportunities, and other incentives encouraged residents from Samarkand oblast' to relocate to the Far East, and Turkmenia's Komsomol members to work on the Perm Hydroelectric Power Station. But as with the reclamation trusts, these foundered on the unwillingness of many Central Asians to expose themselves to radically different cultures and ecologies, not to mention the real possibilities of interethnic hostility. Contrary to the expectations of some Western specialists that the forces of modernization would result in "considerable out-migration from the 'non-European' areas" of the Soviet Union, relatively few availed themselves of the opportunity.[175]

Resettlement emerges as one of the main arrows in the quiver that the Soviet state used to attack the maldistribution of people in relation to resources and enhance state security irrespective of historical associations and cultural practices. In this light, Jonathan L. Dekel-Chen's observation that "colonization did not transpire in a bubble [but] rather reflected contemporary conditions," takes on meaning well beyond its specific reference to Jewish farmers in Crimea and southern Ukraine in the 1920s.[176] Resettlement was a profoundly colonial project whether acknowledged as such by state authorities or not. Like colonization elsewhere in the world, it often followed deportation ("special settlement") and involved making previously unruly territories and their inhabitants more legible; it turned peasants and ex-soldiers into colonists by literally mobilizing them for a new life somewhere else; and it usually proceeded in conjunction with an ethos of pioneering.

Nevertheless, the arrow rarely hit its mark. Settlers blunted resettlement policy, some by demanding more than the state could provide and others by taking advantage of what was on offer to pursue alternative agendas. In the end, it was not only settlers who deviated from prescribed procedures, but also local authorities on whom settlers depended for housing,

---

174. See Anatolii Ivashchenko, "Polia tut belee khlopka," *Izvestiia*, March 27, 1981, 2. The last entry under "Uznovgorodvodstroi" in Eastview Data Bases search engine at http://dlib.eastview.com.proxy2.cl.msu.edu/search/simple is December 27, 1982. For a brief account of the Tashkent sovkhoz that survived until 1991, see Olga Kolotnecha, "Osobennaia fermerskaia zona," *Ekspert Severo-Zapad*, no. 37 (339): 2007, http://expert.ru/northwest/2007/37/derevnya_lesnaya/ (accessed December 5, 2012).

175. William Fierman, "Central Asian Youth and Migration," in *Soviet Central Asia: The Failed Transformation*, ed. William Fierman (Boulder, CO, 1991), 255–56, 277–82. For the optimistic forecast of migration, see Robert Lewis, Richard Rowland, and Ralph Clem, *Nationality and Population Change in Russia and the USSR: An Evaluation of Census Data, 1897–1970* (New York, 1976), 380–81.

176. Dekel-Chen, *Farming the Red Land*, 67.

work assignments, and much else. Settlers responded to unexpected difficulties as migrants have elsewhere—they moved on or they returned home, in either case emancipating themselves from this colonial regime.

Conclusion

The dissolution of the Soviet Union brought on another wave, albeit attenuated, of resettlement. When ethnic Russians, in the main, came from the former Soviet Republics (the "near abroad") to the Russian Federation, the government identified them as "forced migrants" (see chapter 6). Most would up in cities, but rural areas accommodated some of them. This was the post-Soviet version of resettlement, as testified by the fact that some locals referred to the forced migrants as resettlers. This proved to be an awkward arrangement because these families intruded on existing communities.

Elena Filippova characterized the feelings of resettlers toward host Russians in the eight oblasts where she studied their adaptability as follows: "These people are very fond of drinking; they are dissolute, lazy, unfriendly, rude, noisy, delight in scandal, irresponsible, [and] forgetful."[177] Locals repaid them in kind. "I'm already fed up with these resettlers," a personnel director was quoted in Literaturnaia gazeta in 2001. "When they ask for work they are all quiet and modest. But as soon as it is arranged for them, they begin to throw around rights. They write, complain, [and] demand continuously. Our lot work and keep quiet."[178]

Thus we see that the fit was often imperfect between people desiring to relocate with the aim of reproducing on a firmer footing their previous way of life and the state to which they often appealed for assistance to make this move possible. Many peasants in Imperial Russia resettled in Siberia only to face disappointment. Soviet settlers routinely lacked resources and other assistance promised by resettlement authorities. The Russians arriving in rural areas from the near abroad after the dissolution of the Soviet Union had more serious problems adjusting than did those accommodated in cities. But none of this is to deny that over the century millions of families succeeded in resettling far from their original homes, sometimes more than once. In these instances, resettlers' repertoires were congruent with state regimes to transform the landscape demographically and economically.

---

177. E. I. Filippova, "Rol' kul'turnykh razlichii v protsesse adaptatsii russkikh pereselentsev," in Identichnost' i konflikt v postsovetskikh gosudarstvakh: Sbornik statei, ed. Marta Brill Olkott, Valerii Tishkov, and Aleksei Malashenko (Moscow, 1997), 140.

178. Elena Korotkova, "V kholodnykh ob'iat'iakh. Provintsial'naia pressa o pereselentsakh," Literaturnaia gazeta, October 24, 2001, 4.

~ CHAPTER TWO ~

Seasonal Migrants

"Nobody seemed to consider my decision to earn extra money reprehensible. My parents looked on side earnings as a normal phenomenon."

—Viktor Gal'chenko, interviewed in 1986–87 for EKO

Seasonal and temporary migration animated the Russian landscape throughout the twentieth century in remarkably consistent forms. The constancy contradicts the images—and realities—of radical discontinuities of political system, the demographic shift in favor of urban populations, and changes in the technologies of transportation and rural life. Men and women continued to need an infusion of income not available at home, and yet also needed to maintain their household. Employers and enterprises required many more workers in some seasons—or in some years—than in others. Seasonal migration disrupted family hierarchies and took its toll on conjugal relations, but it also proved to be an effective coping strategy for cushioning the shocks of macroeconomic ruptures as well as more predictable periods of dearth.

What we demonstrate in this chapter is that while seasonal migration persisted throughout the century, those who engaged in it, the directionality and extent of their movements, and the nature of the work they performed changed. In Imperial Russia, the endemic seasonality of agriculture and limited opportunities for marketing crafts sent peasants to cities, mines, and large estates. This pattern did not disappear with the 1917 Revolution or even with the collectivization of agriculture, but new patterns began to make themselves apparent as city folk were mobilized and mobilized themselves for temporary work in construction and harvesting. By the end of the century, the economic sinews extended farther than before, crossing the new post-Soviet borders. Thanks to both technological advances in transport and telecommunications and widening income gaps between former Soviet republics, the traffic between the new nation-states of the Caucasus and Central Asia and

Russia's big cities thickened, with "unskilled" laborers and fruit, vegetable, and flower purveyors in some cases claiming more than one "home." Finally, although men continued to dominate construction work, changes in social norms stimulated and were stimulated by more seasonal employment of women in other fields. All these we understand as changes in seasonal migrants' repertoires as they interacted with alterations in the economic, legal, and political conditions constitutive of the regime of migration.

Seasonal Migrants in Imperial Russia

"As a rule," writes the social historian Gijs Kessler, "the historiography distinguishes between two forms of peasant migration in Russia in the second half of the nineteenth and first quarter of the twentieth century." One was resettlement of the entire peasant family to a new place of residence, from European Russia to weakly settled border regions beyond the Urals. The other was "going out," seasonal or temporary labor migration, "which quite possibly equaled resettlement in significance or even exceeded it." "All varieties of labor migration," Kessler points out, "expanded the economic base of the peasant household during the off-season of the agricultural cycle, thereby guaranteeing the peasant household's existence as an economic unit."[1] Hence, like those who resettled their households in the East, peasants who resorted to seasonal migration pursued a fundamentally conservative strategy. They were, to quote Jeffrey Burds, "soldiers of the village guard—sent out to defend the fiscal, organizational, and spiritual vitality of an institution under siege."[2]

Kessler's interpretation of the significance of seasonal labor migration (otkhodnichestvo) is only one of many tendered across more than a century. Perhaps the best known was Lenin's, which emphasized the opposite dimension, namely, its "diversion of the population from agriculture to industrial and commercial activity," and therefore—because "it raises people's literacy and their consciousness, developing their cultural habits and requirements"—its "progressive" nature.[3] The two actually are not necessarily incompatible. Intending to preserve the rural household, peasants who engaged in seasonal labor migration nevertheless might have transformed it, weakening, as Lenin put it, "the old patriarchal family."

Our point of departure is that seasonal migration was much more than a strategy. We do not deny that Russian peasants were rational actors who entered expanding labor markets

1. Khais [Gijs] Kessler, "Krest'ianskaia migratsiia v Rossiiskoi Imperii i Sovetskom Soiuze: Otkhodnichestvo i vykhod iz sela," in Sotsial'naia istoriia: Ezhegodnik 1998/99 (Moscow, 1999), 309–10.
2. Jeffrey Burds, Peasant Dreams and Market Politics: Labor Migration and the Russian Village, 1861–1905 (Pittsburgh, 1998), 13.
3. Lenin, Polnoe sobranie sochinenii, 3: 569–70, 576–77.

to maintain or increase their cash earnings in the face of inadequate income from their allotments, additional rented land, and various cottage industries and putting-out arrangements. We also are in essential agreement with Kessler's broad explanation of why peasants in certain parts of the country preferred seasonal labor migration to resettlement or the complete abandonment of an agrarian way of life. But we find ourselves in sympathy with Jeffrey Burds, who, reacting against the long-standing hegemony of economic interpretations going back to Lenin, asserted the necessity of restoring "the varying roles of politics, culture, kinship and religion to their rightful place alongside economic factors"—except that we do not think the rightful place of such practices belongs "alongside," but rather fully integrated with, economic factors.[4]

For example, pilgrimages, a form of seasonal migration that attracted mainly peasants, could not have assumed the mass character they did without both the expansion of the railroad network and the strenuous efforts of the Orthodox clergy to promote "spiritual travel." According to one recent estimate, at least one million pilgrims in the Central Black Earth region alone traveled every year by the end of the nineteenth century. Themselves a response to the secularizing trends of the age, these efforts and their reliance on modern forms of transportation paralleled the involvement of the Catholic Church in pilgrimages in France, Germany and elsewhere in Europe. They took thousands of parishioners by rail and steamship from the Tobol'sk seminary in western Siberia to the Solovki monastery on the White Sea and back, a distance of 5,600 miles covered in only five weeks; from Nizhny Novgorod to Murom, 101 miles to the southwest; and from Ekaterinburg to the Verkhoturskii monastery, located more than twice that distance to the north. Among those seeking miraculous benefits from the canonization of Serafim of Sarov (Tambov province) in 1903, nearly 40 percent came from beyond the Central Agricultural Region including one peasant from Astrakhan province who reported walking a thousand versts (over 650 miles). Unlike seasonal labor migrants, most of the parish pilgrims were women.[5]

Peasants went out for work in many regions of European Russia—going out meant traveling sufficient distances for earnings to require a passport from communal or township (volost') authorities. In the Central Industrial region (CIR), the provinces of Moscow, Tver, Yaroslavl', Kostroma, Kaluga, Nizhny Novgorod, Vladimir, Tula, and Riazan', they had done so at least since the eighteenth century in order to earn enough to pay quitrent to their masters. Although the emancipation freed peasants from this obligation as well as forced labor, the terms generally made it even less possible to survive solely on the basis of allotment land

---

4. Burds, *Peasant Dreams*, 6.

5. Robert H. Greene, "Bodies in Motion: Steam-Powered Pilgrimages in Late Imperial Russia," *Russian History* 39 (2012): 247–68; Christine Worobec, "Miraculous Healings," in *Sacred Stories: Religion and Spirituality in Modern Russia*, ed. Mark D. Steinberg and Heather J. Coleman (Bloomington, 2007), 24–25. For an example from Western Europe, see Ruth Harris, *Lourdes: Body and Spirit in the Secular Age* (New York, 1999).

held in communal tenure. In the CIR, redemption payments often exceeded the market value of the land. In the Central Agricultural region (CAR), the Black Earth provinces of Chernigov, Kursk, Orel, Tambov, and Voronezh, where the land was more productive, cutoffs at the time of the emancipation left peasant families with considerably less allotment land.

Peasant-migrants (otkhodniki) who sought employment in the CIR tended to find it in the region's major industries, located in Moscow, Ivanovo-Voznesensk, Serpukhov, or one of the smaller urban settlements. Both women and men found work in textiles, the largest industry by numbers hired and value of output. Those from Yaroslavl' and Tver, the northern and westernmost provinces of the region, were drawn more to St. Petersburg, where they comprised a third of all peasants resident in the city in 1910 and where they dominated the restaurant and transport trades.[6] Peasant migrants from the CAR gravitated southward. The vast majority sought work as hired laborers on the large grain-growing estates that extended across the New Russian steppe from Kherson, Tavrida, and Ekaterinoslav provinces in the west to Samara and Saratov provinces abutting the Volga. Toward the end of the nineteenth century, more than a million male peasants traveled annually by cart, railroad, and steamer, but mostly on foot, to large outdoor hiring markets located at important crossroads and railroad stations where they negotiated wages with agents of estate owners and grain merchants.[7]

Not all peasant-migrants who journeyed south worked in the fields. Substantial numbers—at least fifty thousand every year around the turn of the century—found work in the coal and iron mining and metallurgical enterprises of the Donets Basin (Donbas). Because of the seasonal nature of agricultural work and the insalubriousness of mining, some peasants included both forms of employment in their annual itinerary. Leaving their families behind in the CAR, they would work the harvest in the steppe in August and September, then head for the mines where they would be employed through the winter months, returning to their farms in March or April, typically at Easter. Some moved from one estate to the next or from one mine to another, depending on differential wages and conditions, as well as the state of their own health.[8] Peasant repertoires such as these brought in maximum

---

6. Evel G. Economakis, "Patterns of Migration and Settlement in Prerevolutionary St. Petersburg: Peasants from Iaroslavl' and Tver Provinces," The Russian Review 56, no. 1 (1997): 9–10. A. G. Rashin, Formirovanie rabochego klassa Rossii, istoriko-ekonomicheskie ocherki (Moscow, 1958), 438. Burds, Peasant Dreams, 116, notes that in 1890 60 percent of peasants with passports from Tver and almost 75 percent of those from Yaroslavl' went to St. Petersburg. For data from the 1897 census on province of origin for residents of St. Petersburg and Moscow, see Evel G. Economakis, From Peasant to Petersburger (Houndsmills, 1998), 165.

7. Tim Mixter, "The Hiring Market as Workers' Turf: Migrant Agricultural Laborers and the Mobilization of Collective Action in the Steppe Grainbelt of European Russia, 1853–1913," in Kingston-Mann and Mixter, Peasant Economy, 294–340; Gijs Kessler, "Russian and Ukrainian Seasonal Laborers in the Grain Belt of New Russia and the North Caucasus in the Late Nineteenth and Early Twentieth Centuries," in The Encyclopedia of Migration and Minorities in Europe, ed. Klaus J. Bade et al. (Cambridge, 2011), 658.

8. Theodore Friedgut, Iuzovka and Revolution, 2 vols. (Princeton, 1989), 1: 216–21. See also Charters Wynn, Workers, Strikes, and Pogroms: The Donbass-Dnepr Bend in Late Imperial Russia, 1870–1905 (Princeton, 1992), 45–59. According to the 1897 census, 74 percent of coal miners were ethnically Russian.

income and also allowed men to be home for planting in the spring and the most important religious festival of the year.

Kessler refers to the seasonal migration of agricultural workers to the south as a "transitional stage" between the development of export-oriented wheat cultivation and colonization of the region by peasants from densely populated provinces. The removal in 1906 of the commune's power to restrict resettlement reduced the supply of rural labor while increased mechanization of harvesting reduced the demand, at least for male workers.[9] By contrast, the mining industry's reliance on migrants remained strong; as it expanded to fuel late Imperial Russia's industrial boom, so did its migrant workforce. As late as March 1915, the minister of trade and industry V. N. Shakhovskoi complained that "a permanent cadre of mine workers has not been formed in the South, so the mines rely on workers from the northern provinces who come for the side earnings and are still hardly settled in the coal districts."[10] Shakhovskoi's discontent was founded in the peasant's own flexible repertoire.

Data compiled by the Russian historian Pavel Ryndziunskii show that between 1898 and 1900, 7.7 million people in European Russia received passports to travel out of their home district for up to a year and an additional 183,000 for up to five years. The great majority (5.3 million) came from the CIR, the CAR, and the left-bank Ukrainian provinces. Analyzing zemstvo household data for 1893–1903, Ryndziunskii lists Moscow province as having the highest percentage of seasonal migrants among its peasant population—nearly 38 percent of males. Moscow was followed by Yaroslavl', Kaluga, and Vladimir, each sending over a quarter of their male population.[11] Men vastly outnumbered women among labor migrants but the gap narrowed after 1890, particularly to destinations such as textile towns like Ivanovo-Voznesensk.[12] The trend was particularly evident among migrants leaving the province of Tver on the other side of Moscow from Ivanovo. In 1890, for every 1,000 men from this most impoverished of CIR provinces who found work in Petersburg, 408 women did so; by 1910, it was 825.[13]

Burds estimates from 1890s passport data that more than a third of adult peasant males "or at least one member of every peasant household" in the CIR was away from home.[14]

---

9. Kessler, "Russian and Ukrainian Seasonal Laborers," 658.

10. Iu. I. Kir'ianov, *Rabochie Iuga Rossii, 1914–fevral' 1917 g.* (Moscow, 1971), 32.

11. P. G. Ryndziunskii, *Krest'iane i gorod v kapitalisticheskoi Rossii vtoroi poloviny XIX veka* (Moscow, 1983), 106–8. Between 1906 and 1910 the average number had risen to 8.77 million per year, of whom 40–45 percent engaged in agricultural work and "not less than" 55 percent went outside agriculture. See V. P. Danilov, "Krest'ianskii otkhod na promysly v 1920-kh godakh," *Istoricheskie zapiski* 94 (1974): 71.

12. Susan Vorderer, *Migration Patterns, Occupational Strategies, and Work Experiences in a Large Textile Town: The Case of Ivanovo-Voznesensk*, Carl Beck Papers 1403 (Pittsburgh, 1999), 25.

13. Barbara Engel, *Between the Fields and the City: Women, Work, and Family in Russia, 1861–1914* (Cambridge, 1996), 69.

14. Burds, *Peasant Dreams*, 21–24.

Because they each wrote memoirs that were published after the October Revolution, Semën Kanatchikov and Fëdor Samoilov are among the very few individuals known to us.[15] Thanks to Reginald Zelnik's superb translation and annotation of his memoir, Kanatchikov has achieved posthumous celebrity among Anglophone readers.[16] Assiduously learning the patternmaking trade and urban ways, he eventually became a "conscious worker" and Bolshevik who turned his back on his peasant origins. Samoilov accompanied his entire family to Ivanovo-Voznesensk, where his father had gotten a job as a weaver. A few years later, the family returned to their native village, leaving the teenaged Fëdor alone as an apprentice. He too would become a Bolshevik, serving as a deputy in the State Duma.

These and a few other memoirists have played an outsized role in shaping the historiography for another reason: their trajectory from village-born peasants to urban factory workers is a synecdoche of what Soviet historians long defined as one of the key developments on the path to socialist revolution—a factory proletariat whose ties to the land weakened over time. Some who started out as migrant laborers eventually did become factory workers and even Bolsheviks, but this was only one among other trajectories. Joseph Bradley in his study of Moscow's urbanization in the late nineteenth and early twentieth century emphasizes that most factory workers did not sever their ties to the land even if they had followed their fathers into the factory. Among the memoirs he cites is that of Sergei Semenov, a peasant worker who, like Kanatchikov, hailed from Volokolamsk district, some 80 miles to the west of Moscow. Semenov was among those who did return home, in Bradley's words, "part of the small but growing peasant intelligentsia" that "bought up property with city earnings."[17]

Many otkhodniki from the CIR reached neither cities nor factories: they worked in peat cutting, brick making, stonecutting, or some other rural-based enterprise. Others, "a large number of peasants," according to Bradley, "made frequent moves in and out of the city."[18] Data from 1891 show that a grand total of over 750,000 people used the railroad to travel from (in descending order) Kiev, Poltava, Khar'kov, Chernigov, and Podol'sk provinces to work in the grain or sugar beet fields of Ukraine. Farther to the east in Samara province, an observer writing in 1898 noted "an enormous flood" of 400,000 workers arriving from Penza, Tambov, Saratov, and other provinces during harvest time.[19] If these and other agricultural workers ventured into cities at all, it was not for very long. And factories were not the major urban destination: the majority of Russian peasant-migrants to the cities worked

---

15. S. I. Kanatchikov, *Iz istorii moego bytiia* (Moscow-Leningrad, 1929); F. N. Samoilov, *Vospominaniia ob Ivanovo-Voznesenskom rabochem dvizhenii*, vol. 1, 1903–1905 gg. (Moscow, 1924).

16. Kanatchikov, *A Radical Worker in Tsarist Russia*.

17. Joseph Bradley, *Muzhik and Muscovite: Urbanization in Late Imperial Russia* (Berkeley, 1985), 112.

18. Ibid., 130.

19. Rashin, *Formirovanie*, 471–73; Mixter, "Hiring Market."

in construction, transportation, the retail trades, or, as was the case with most migrant women, domestic service.[20] Farther afield, Chinese migrants traveled by sea to Vladivostok or across the Amur between March and December to pan for gold, hunt for sable, collect ginseng, engage in construction (including along the Trans-Siberian Railroad), and supply Russian settlements with produce from market gardens. They represented a stream of peasant workers far removed from those of the CIR or elsewhere in European Russia, but no less essential to the economy of the Far East.[21]

Regardless of where or in what occupation peasant migrants labored, they relied on two institutions for mutual support. One was compatriot solidarity, the basis for loyalties enacted among villagers, people from the same township or district, in obtaining jobs and accommodation, defending reputations, and otherwise assisting people who were away from home. Bradley cites a statement by a St. Petersburg statistician at the turn of the century that sums up how it fostered chain migration: "It's enough just for one pioneer to come to the city before this pioneer drags along his fellow villagers and helps them get set up."[22] It would be fascinating but well beyond the scope of our study to inquire into what and who determined the geographic range of compatriot solidarity. Although province-wide data is characteristic for this period, Judith Pallot reminds us that "provinces are not the most appropriate scale for comparative research on the peasantry."[23]

The other institution was the *artel*, a voluntary association of workers in which members agreed to share wages and chose an elder to represent them.[24] The elder initially might have worked alongside those he represented, but over time became a more remote, impersonal figure who, as subcontractor, got the most out of the artel's members for his own benefit.[25] The two institutions dovetailed: both were well suited to itinerancy and many artels consisted of compatriots (*zemliaki*). Both served as regulators of migrant peasant behavior. How migrants did behave and how more generally they fared away from home are questions more properly addressed in another section. Here, we consider the effect of seasonal labor migration on those who remained behind.

---

20. Women servants in St. Petersburg at the turn of the century numbered over 92,000 compared with 57,848 who worked in all branches of industry. Engel, *Between the Fields*, 140.

21. Lewis H. Siegelbaum, "Another Yellow Peril: Chinese Migrants in the Russian Far East and the Russian Reaction before 1917," *Modern Asian Studies* 12, no. 2 (1978): 307–30; F. Solov'ev, *Kitaiskoe otkhodnichestvo na Dal'nom Vostoke Rossii v epokhu kapitalizma (1861–1917)* (Moscow, 1989); A. G. Larin, *Kitaiskie migranty v Rossii: Istoriia i sovremennost'* (Moscow, 2009), 20–34.

22. Bradley, *Muzhik and Muscovite*, 116.

23. Judith Pallot, "Review of *From Peasant to Petersburger* by Evel G. Economakis," *Slavic Review* 59, no. 2 (2000): 458–59.

24. Robert E. Johnson, *Peasant and Proletarian: The Working Class of Moscow in the Late Nineteenth Century* (New Brunswick, 1979), 69–74; Burds, *Peasant Dreams*, 114–17.

25. M. Sh. Shigabudinov, *Otkhodnichestvo v Dagestane v kontse XIX–nachale XX vv.* (Makhachkala, 2000), 67–68.

The consensus among historians who have studied labor migration's demographic effects is that it tended to reinforce the peasant practice of early marriage. In at least two districts of Kostroma province noted by Barbara Engel (Soligalich and Chukhloma), it seems to have hastened it. Where, however, tradesmen and craftsmen predominated among migrants, such as with those from Yaroslavl' province, marriage rates and age of marriage approximated urban middle-class patterns, suggesting that sons pursuing these trades waited to marry and establish their own household until after they had accumulated sufficient means.[26] Otherwise, early marriage "brought the migrant's parents a worker," namely, his wife, who "lived with them and labored in place of her migratory husband."[27] In some places, including those much-studied high migration districts of Kostroma province, the rhythm of migrants' comings and goings determined when gatherings would be held to show off prospective brides and the month of the nuptials.[28]

Indeed, seasonal migration shaped the most intimate aspects of peasant life, because it shaped family form and the timing of marriages and childbirth. According to Dmitri Zhbankov, the zemstvo physician from whom historians have obtained much information about peasant practices in Kostroma, "the entire family life" of some migrant peasants' brides—that is, their sexual activity—was limited to two or three months. For the rest of the year, the districts of high migration turned into "women's land."[29] In some villages, well over half of the adult men were away during the summer, leaving agricultural work and other chores up to their wives, children, and the aged. Their occasional presence did not necessarily make a difference in this respect, for they often lived "like guests" upon returning.[30] It would be interesting to know if the seasonal migrants in the Russian Far East, who originated mainly in Shandong and Zhili provinces south and southwest of Beijing, also lived like guests when they returned home. For, according to Russian official statistics from 1910, the gender imbalance among these migrants was even greater—a mere 4,000 or so women among a total of over 111,000 migrants.[31] This extreme imbalance was common for

---

26. Engel, Between the Fields, 38–40. See also Burds, Peasant Dreams, 71; Robert E. Johnson, "Family Relations and the Rural-Urban Nexus: Patterns in the Hinterland of Moscow, 1880–1900," in The Family in Imperial Russia, ed. David Ransel (Urbana, 1978), 268–69.

27. Engel, Between the Fields, 40.

28. Burds, Peasant Dreams, 71.

29. D. N. Zhbankov, Bab'ia storona: Statistiko-etnograficheskii ocherk (Kostroma, 1891), 82. Bradley, Muzhik and Muscovite, 26, refers to Zhbankov as "the leading contemporary authority on the phenomenon of seasonal labor in northern Russia." Engel (Between the Fields, 46–47, 55), who describes him as "the indefatigable chronicler of Kostroma life," cites one of his articles in a medical journal that refers to the "excessive indulgence" in which women engaged when men returned from the city.

30. Bradley, Muzhik and Muscovite, 28; Engel, Between the Fields, 41.

31. Larin, Kitaiskie migranty, 24.

Chinese migrant workers at the time, who also married young and left their wives at home with their in-laws, an arrangement widely practiced by Russian peasants as well.[32]

Seasonal labor migration changed what peasants ate, drank, and wore, thanks to what migrants brought back with them from their sojourns and also the money they sent while away. Among the few extant letters from a migrant's wife to her husband is one from Chukhloma, cited by both Burds and Engel, in which money is the main subject, but also mentioned is tea "and the presents that I wrote you about before."[33] Migrants brought back attitudes, too. Much as they might have missed their family and native village—Samoilov is particularly eloquent about this—their relative independence and exposure to outside influences tended to make them less obsequious to both the patriarchal authority of their fathers and the village priest. Burds devotes a whole chapter to the denunciation by religious authorities in Moscow province of some three hundred "deviants," 90 percent of whom were peasant-workers who migrated for side earnings.[34]

More independent too were wives of migrant laborers. Engel speaks of complementarity, mutual dependence, and partnership among such couples, as contrasted with the "oppressed pariahs of the black earth regions" of presumably lower out-migration. "In men's absence, women worked harder, but breathed more freely," she writes, qualifying the statement to refer to widows and wives of heads of households rather than younger women living in the household of their in-laws.[35] More independent still were widows, spinsters, and young single women who traveled outside the precincts of their commune to work. Their numbers varied a good deal from province to province and the jobs they found differed too. Generally, those who made it to the major cities did not arrive alone but in the company of married kinswomen or *zemliachki*. Yet Engel discovered that "an extraordinarily high proportion of working women (excluding servants) lived on their own"—86 percent in St. Petersburg and close to 93 percent in Moscow, according to the 1897 census.[36]

Here we will leave them for the time being, poised, like so many of their brothers, "between the fields and the city." The point needs emphasizing that most who got on one of the paths to the city returned to the village within a few years. Peasants, stereotypically the most sedentary of social categories, turn out to have been highly peripatetic, at least in those parts of the empire where outside earnings were available. But more than this, to quote Ryndziunskii, "otkhodnichestvo . . . for a large part of rural folk became the sole means of survival: unremunerative farming on allotment land actually was supported by

32. Leslie Page Moch, "Connecting Migration and World History, 1840–1940: Demographic Patterns, Family Systems, and Gender," *International Review of Social History* 52 (2007): 97–104.

33. Burds, *Peasant Dreams*, 63–64; Engel, *Between the Fields*, 42.

34. Burds, *Peasant Dreams*, 130, 186–218.

35. Engel, *Between the Fields*, 51. "Oppressed pariahs" is Zhbankov's term.

36. Engel, *Between the Fields*, 135.

these earnings. Thus was produced a contradictory situation: otkhodnichestvo undermined the patriarchal way of life in the village, at the same time that it supported its existence."[37] How viable was this contradiction? It is worth remembering that peasants had been laboring off the land for centuries. Moreover, long after they ceased doing so in Russia, peasants from such places as rural Anatolia, Central America, and the Maghreb continue to sustain their villages with migrant remittances.

Seasonal Migrants, 1917–41

Writing in 1927 from a town in the Galich district of Kostroma province, the peasant migrant I. Shcherbakov recalled that before the October Revolution all the men went to "Piter" for earnings. "Cooped up in dirty, crowded hovels, the otkhodniki fell under bad influences—heads or tails, card games, drinking bouts, prostitution." But how things had changed after the Revolution! These vices were almost unknown. At first one had to spend months looking for work, but year by year things got easier. "Pay got better, and in their free time instead of gambling, otkhodniki now read newspapers, go to the [workers'] club, to lectures, the theater, meetings. Youth are joining the Komsomol."[38]

Shcherbakov's letter, an early form of what Stephen Kotkin called "speaking Bolshevik," performed a useful propagandistic function at the time it was written. It continued to do so well into the 1970s when the Soviet historian Viktor Danilov, writing about the 1920s, cited it as evidence of how "the basic mass of otkhodniki . . . experienced not only new conditions of production but also principally different social conditions."[39] But although much might have changed in principle for seasonal migrants, thanks to the revolution, in practice much remained the same. The big changes came just before and just after the 1920s.

The First World War disrupted seasonal migration in Imperial Russia as it did so many other practices. The millions of peasant males mobilized for war no longer could set out for the mines, peat bogs, and factories to help make ends meet back on the farm. During the first three years of the war, according to the rural census conducted between May and October 1917, the army had called up 47 percent of all able-bodied males.[40] Coalmining, among the hardest hit of industries, lost between 25 and 30 percent of its workforce to wartime mobilizations. Moreover, workers who continued to leave the mines in summer for agricultural work back home tended to stay away longer, probably because food

37. Ryndziunskii, Krest'iane i gorod, 121.
38. N. N. Vladimirskii, Otkhod krest'ianstva kostromskoi gubernii na zarabotki (Kostroma, 1927), 172.
39. Danilov, "Krest'ianskii otkhod," 102.
40. Ekonomicheskoe polozhenie Rossii nakanune velikoi oktiabr'skoi sotsialisticheskoi revoliutsii, dokumenty i materialy, 3 vols. (Leningrad, 1967), 3: 72–73.

supplies were better there. Wartime exigencies demanded new sources of labor. Mining companies scrambled to make up the difference with Russian women, POWs, evacuees from the western front, Central Asians, and Chinese.[41] Farther to the south and east, the oil industry in Grozny, the second largest source in the empire after Baku, came to rely heavily on seasonal workers from the surrounding regions. Over 90 percent of Dagestanis employed in the industry between 1906 and 1921 were hired between 1915 and 1917.[42]

By this point, many soldiers had self-demobilized and were returning to their villages. The countryside was soon aflame with peasant seizures of estate land. Among the casualties of this agrarian revolution was seasonal work in agriculture. The market for harvest workers plummeted with the division of large grain-growing estates in the southern provinces. Elsewhere, the acquisition of land and relief from taxes among poor peasants narrowed the social base for seasonal labor migration everywhere. During the Civil War of 1918–21, food and fuel supplies to the major cities dwindled, leading to a flow of population from town to countryside. Although many miners continued to live and work under the Whites, Greens, and other anti-Bolshevik administrations, mining districts lost people too.[43] Sheila Fitzpatrick cites a complaint from "the peasant V." from a village in Smolensk province that "the miners have taken everything," by which he meant peasants who had worked in the mines in the Donbas but had returned to claim the same share of resources as his own. Fitzpatrick makes the interesting suggestion that the Bolsheviks' image of their allies in the village, an image central to their strategy of supporting poorer peasants against the kulaks, may have been informed by the returned politicized otkhodniki as well as peasant army veterans who were predominantly young and often armed.[44]

The best estimate of the scale of annual seasonal migration during the Civil War is no more than 250,000, a far cry from the nine million who earlier had tramped to work away from their home village.[45] Within a year or two of the introduction of the New Economic

---

41. Kir'ianov, *Rabochie Iuga Rossii*, 43–48. For other belligerents, see Ulrich Herbert, *A History of Foreign Labor in Germany, 1880–1980* (Ann Arbor, 1990), 87–108; Gary Cross, *Immigrant Workers in Industrial France* (Philadelphia, 1983), 33–42; Tyler Stovall, "Colour-Blind France? Colonial Workers during the First World War," *Race and Class* 35 (1993): 35–55.

42. Shigabudinov, *Otkhodnichestvo v Dagestane*, 58.

43. For these processes, see, respectively, Diane P. Koenker, "Urbanization and Deurbanization in the Russian Revolution and Civil War," *Journal of Modern History* 57, no. 3 (1985): 424–50; Hiroaki Kuromiya, "Donbas Miners in War, Revolution, and Civil War," in *Making Workers Soviet: Power, Class, and Identity*, ed. Lewis H. Siegelbaum and Ronald Grigor Suny (Ithaca, 1994), 138–58.

44. Sheila Fitzpatrick, *Stalin's Peasants: Resistance and Survival in the Russian Village after Collectivization* (New York, 1994), 32–33. The radicalization of seasonal peasant workers has been long observed in other contexts; see, for example, Alain Corbin, *Archaïsme et modernité en Limousin au XIXe siècle (1845–1880)*, 2 vols. (Paris, 1975).

45. Douglas R. Weiner, "*Razmychka*? Urban Unemployment and Peasant Migration as Sources of Social Conflict," in *Russia in the Era of NEP, Explorations in Soviet Society and Culture*, ed. Sheila Fitzpatrick, Alexander Rabinowitch, and Richard Stites (Bloomington, 1991), 147–48.

Table 2.1 Peasant migrant laborers in nonagricultural work, 1923–29 (in 000)

Year	1923–24	1924–25	1925–26	1926–27	1927–28	1928–29
Unskilled	512	1,063	746	665	683	443
Construction	237	453	557	582	754	936
Logging	196	127	555	579	889	1,409
Industry and crafts	164	266	398	323	366	341
Mining	62	64	168	136	132	174
Peat	82	65	86	123	116	127
Other	204	215	419	397	497	386
Total	1,457	2,253	2,930	2,805	3,437	3,817

Source: Derived from Gijs Kessler, "The Peasant and the Town: Rural-Urban Migration in the Soviet Union, 1929–40" (PhD diss., European University Institute, 2001), vol. 2, appendix B, table B-1.

Policy in 1921, opportunities for seasonal employment began to pick up. By 1923–24 Soviet authorities recorded only 215,000 seasonal migrants in agriculture, but nearly 1.4 million in nonagricultural pursuits such as construction and logging. Data compiled by Danilov for the years of "high NEP" (1925–27) show a return to the status quo ante for nonagricultural employment, but the persistence of far lower rates of employment in agriculture compared with the years before World War I. At about 350,000 per year, agriculture employed one in ten of all seasonal migrants, compared with nearly half before the war.[46]

But some crops continued to rely heavily on seasonal labor. Sugar beet production had expanded in the nineteenth century, concentrating seasonal labor power and feeding a demand for animal fodder and alcohol as well as sugar.[47] In the USSR, sugar beets grown in right-bank Ukraine attracted otkhodniki from Central Black Earth provinces such as Voronezh, Tambov, and Kursk. Indeed, as Danilov notes, particular districts and even townships specialized in harvesting and processing the crop. The closer to the plantations, the greater the numbers. Whereas Ternovsk township in Borisogleb district (Tambov province) supplied more than 3,700 seasonal migrants to the sugar beet fields, Dorogoshchansk township, situated in the same Kherson province as the plantations, sent nearly 8,200. Sheep and goat herding similarly continued to rely heavily on seasonal migrants from particular townships in Vladimir province.[48]

---

46. Danilov, "Krest'ianskii otkhod," 79–80.

47. Moch, Moving Europeans, 122; Brian R. Mitchell, European Historical Statistics, 1750–1970 (New York, 1978), table C2, 96–125; J. A. Perkins, "The Agricultural Revolution in Germany, 1850–1914," Journal of European Economic History 10 (1981): 106–7; Abel Chatelain, Les migrants temporaires en France de 1800 à 1914, vol. 2 (Lille, 1977), 704.

48. Danilov, "Krest'ianskii otkhod," 73, 80, 84.

As for nonagricultural seasonal workers, the best estimates, based on information from the Commissariat of Labor, are presented in table 2.1. Soviet economists at the time and thereafter tended to see the survival of seasonal labor as a continuation of economic backwardness, that is, as an indication of poor utilization of labor resources. More recent analyses have interpreted it as "a sign of economic dynamism and part of a process of diversification and modernisation."[49] The prodigious expansion toward the end of the decade of logging—an industry almost entirely dependent on wintertime seasonal labor—derived from both the construction boom occasioned by the upsurge in industrial activity and also the state's strategy of exporting timber to obtain foreign currency in order to import machinery.[50]

Although some of the overall increase reflected a broadening of the definition of otkhodnik after 1926–27 to include people employed and living outside their township (instead of district), the trend of expansion was clear.[51] It can be attributed to the persistence, perhaps even widening, of the gap between agricultural income and the demand for workers outside the agricultural sector. About the only difference, then, between seasonal labor migration in the 1920s and in the late Imperial period was its diminished scale. A little over four million agricultural and nonagricultural seasonal laborers by the end of the decade represented about half the number in the years just before World War I. As in agriculture, so in the nonagricultural trades Danilov discovered a "high degree of specialization from individual townships" that "indicates the long historical development of trades as one generation passed on skills to the next." For him, the seasonal migrants from Vladimir province who worked as warm-weather masons, plasterers, painters, and joiners "represent the direct descendants of the builders of the chapels and palaces of Vladimir, Suzdal, and Bogoliubov."[52]

A look at the contemporary press, however, reveals efforts by party activists and Commissariat of Labor personnel to break with the past. In a column from August 1926 headed "Among Seasonal Workers (*sezonniki*)," *Pravda* quoted a peat worker in a female team from Riazan' province who sought assistance: "We are waiting for someone to come and free us from our bitter 'baba' fate," she lamented. She and most other sezonniki were reported living in squalid conditions and deserving of more attention. The newspaper attributed their ills to subcontractors whom it variously described as kulaks, private intermediaries, and organizers of phony artels. Time to assist in forming new artels and "improving" (that is, replacing) their leaders, the Central Committee of the party instructed the Riazan'

49. Gijs Kessler, "The Peasant and the Town: Rural-Urban Migration in the Soviet Union, 1929–40," 2 vols. (PhD diss., European University Institute, 2001), 1: 66.

50. Ibid., 61.

51. Danilov, "Krest'ianskii otkhod, 71–72, 110.

52. Ibid., 90.

provincial committee.[53] Time, indeed, for the commissariat to set up "correspondence points" throughout the country that, staffed by "labor correspondents," could provide information about jobs and even arrange for hiring, thereby bypassing artels and their leaders altogether. These proved especially successful in placing workers in the peat industry, three out of four of whom used them during the mid-1920s. By contrast, most peasants who sought seasonal employment in construction continued to find it themselves. But how? An investigation of Moscow construction workers in 1928 revealed that 82 percent relied on compatriots and the practices of earlier years, 13 percent discovered the job accidentally, and 4 percent responded to newspaper advertisements. Less than 1 percent had learned about opportunities from correspondence points. Among construction workers, it seemed, artels and their elders proved more than a match for Soviet institutions, and the same was nearly so among miners, loggers, and unskilled seasonal workers.[54]

The party had a still tougher job in the Far East, where Chinese migrants continued to comprise a substantial proportion of seasonal workers, especially in the construction industry. Reporting from Khabarovsk, P. Eremievskii wrote in *Pravda* that the Chinese were much cheaper to hire than Russian workers, primarily because subcontractors mercilessly exploited them. Yet, because the Chinese knew neither Soviet laws nor the Russian language, they depended on their subcontractors even more than Russian peasants did.[55] This situation, essentially a continuation of pre-Soviet practices, differed little from how ethnically distinct seasonal migrants have been organized and employed in construction on other continents in other times.

All these attempts to eliminate the middleman between seasonal migrants and employers were part of a larger effort by the party to replace peasants' autonomy and associated loyalties with new institutions and dependencies. That effort, which targeted not only artels but also the village priesthood, the commune, and of course kulaks, greatly intensified with the collectivization of agriculture.[56] Collectivization, as Sheila Fitzpatrick noted, would stimulate "an enormous voluntary and involuntary outflow of peasants into the industrial labor force." But its "immediate impact was to disrupt the processes of peasant *otkhod* . . . and industrial labor recruitment."[57] In the spring of 1930, for example, the

---

53. *Pravda*, August 20, 1926, 5; June 18, 1927, 6; June 25, 1927, 6; November 28, 1927, 2.

54. *Pravda*, May 19, 1927, 5; A. M. Panfilova, *Formirovanie rabochego klassa SSSR v gody pervoi piatiletki* (Moscow, 1964), 18–19. Neither Panfilova nor any other source consulted explains the unusual degree of success that the correspondence points enjoyed in placing seasonal workers in the peat industry.

55. *Pravda*, August 23, 1926, 5.

56. Kotkin, "Peopling Magnitostroi," 77; Hiroaki Kuromiya, "Workers' Artels and Soviet Production Relations," in Fitzpatrick, Rabinowitch, and Stites, *Russia in the Era of NEP*, 75–82; Kessler, "Peasant and the Town," 1: 72–76.

57. Sheila Fitzpatrick, "The Great Departure: Rural-Urban Migration in the Soviet Union, 1929–33," in Rosenberg and Siegelbaum, *Social Dimensions of Soviet Industrialization*, 18.

Donbas coalmining industry experienced a shortage of labor when miner-otkhodniki, concerned about developments back home, left the mines earlier and in greater numbers than usual. Between March and August, the number of miners dropped by 27 percent, which, taking into account the recruitment of additional miners during this period, meant an even more dramatic exodus. Monthly output declined by 37 percent. The Komsomol's newspaper could proclaim "Flight from Coal Mines Is Treason to the Revolution," but neither the Komsomol nor any other organization was able to control departures. Collectivization also affected when otkhodniki returned to the mines, for whereas Pokrov (October 1) customarily marked the beginning of their stints, many waited until the kolkhozes had distributed the harvest, which could be as late as January.[58] Elsewhere, such as in Moscow, rumors about the "nationalization of wives in the kolkhozes" sent many otkhodniki scurrying back to their villages.[59]

Beyond these difficulties, kolkhoz administrators proved uncooperative in letting collective farmers go out for earnings even if the kolkhoz could claim between 3 and 10 percent of the earnings.[60] Contemporary reports cite concealment of recruitment announcements, deductions from the wages of otkhodniki that sometimes amounted to complete confiscation, expulsion from the kolkhoz of members of their family, and denunciations of seasonal laborers as deserters.[61] Nevertheless, there was no holding the peasants back. Otkhodnichestvo offered the security of a regular monetary income to complement a subsistence base from the family's garden plot and its share of what the kolkhoz administration deigned to distribute to members. Fitzpatrick refers to this strategy as based on a " 'maximization of advantages' attitude."[62] For those anticipating their own dekulakization, it may have been a lifesaver. For noncollectivized peasants (edinolichniki) such as Ivan Barabanov from a village in the Riazan' province, it helped to compensate for punitively high tax payments, buying them time while they sorted out the advantages and disadvantages of joining a collective farm. A bricklayer and stovemaker, Barabanov

58. Nobuaki Shiokawa, "The Collectivization of Agriculture and Otkhodnichestvo in the USSR, 1930," *Annals of the Institute of Social Science*, no. 24 (1982): 133–35; Hiroaki Kuromiya, "The Commander and the Rank and File: Managing the Soviet Coal-Mining Industry, 1928–33," in Rosenberg and Siegelbaum, *Social Dimensions of Soviet Industrialization*, 149.

59. *Pravda*, April 7, 1930, 4.

60. This is according to a resolution of the Kolkhoz Center of February 1930. Danilov, Manning, and Viola, *Tragediia sovetskoi derevni*, 2: 261.

61. *Izvestiia*, July 22, 1931, 3; August 8, 1931, 3; September 9, 1931, 3; Iu. V. Arutunian, "Kollektivizatsiia sel'skogo khoziaistva i vysvobozhdenie rabochei sily dlia promyshlennosti," in *Formirovanie i razvitie sovetskogo rabochego klassa (1917–1961 gg.)* (Moscow, 1964), 107–8.

62. Fitzpatrick, *Stalin's Peasants*, 165–66.

kept on going to Moscow to, as it was said, "tinker" in order to earn enough to feed his hard-pressed family.[63]

Kessler's analysis of the trade union census of 1932–33 shows that nearly three-quarters of peat-industry workers, and about 40 percent of transport, industrial, and civil construction workers, maintained an "involvement in agriculture," which meant they earned wages on a seasonal basis. Some kolkhoz members—as many as a quarter of the working population on dairy farms in Moscow province—worked outside the kolkhoz on a "permanent" basis, meaning more than nine months of the year. Kessler also points to the compulsory nature of much seasonal employment as well as instances of kolkhozes hiring outsiders to assist with the harvest, even though it was illegal to do so.[64] All this is to suggest that well before the end of the First Five-Year Plan, seasonal labor had integrated itself into the Soviet economy as an adaptive compensatory practice, compensating industry for what was fast becoming a congenital shortage of labor, and compensating rural dwellers for inadequate income from farm activity.

Beyond the functional and institutional lay the experiential dimension, few traces of which remain in the historical record. As often is the case with migration, we are afforded glimpses almost accidentally. Talking about his youth before the Great Patriotic War, Roman Evseevich Lazebnik, born in 1920 and raised in a Jewish settlement in Kherson province, recalled:

> In 1929 collectivization came to the Kalinindorf district. We turned in all our livestock to the kolkhoz . . . and were left with only one cow. Father knew immediately how this kolkhoz life would end, and left to work as a carpenter on the Dneprostroi project where workers were sent by contact to work for several months or half a year depending on how long they wanted to work on construction. In the spring, father returned to Krasnoslav to help us with the sowing, and again left for construction of the hydroelectric station.[65]

People took up one job after another with amazing frequency, some because they found the work too arduous or the living conditions unbearable, others in search of additional income, referred to—disapprovingly—as "the long ruble" (the Russian equivalent of "making a fast buck"). Stephen Kotkin, in reference to such labor fluidity, observed that

---

63. "Nikolai Barabanov," "Ia Pomniu/I Remember: Vospominaniia veteranov VOV," http://iremember.ru/tankisti/barabanov-nikolay-ivanovich.html (accessed January 14, 2012). Barabanov eventually capitulated to pressure to join a kolkhoz and ceased going to Moscow. He died in the "famine year" of 1938, according to his son, who was twelve at the time.

64. Kessler, "Peasant and the Town," 1: 83, 96–97, 99, 106; 2: table B-4b, table C-3.

65. "Roman Lazebnik," http://iremember.ru/partizani/lazebnik-roman-evseevich.html (accessed March 17, 2012), 1.

"the train, that ally of the Bolshevik leadership and its bureaucrats and planners, was being used against them: construction workers were using the trains to tour the country."[66] This was exactly what Soviet authorities feared—that otkhodniki who "had crowded the stations and are traveling to all ends of the Soviet Union, will head for secondary construction sites, leaving Dneprostroi, Magnitostroi, and Traktorstroi without workers." Such wandering or "drift" (*samotek*) was the bad kind of seasonal employment. The good kind was "organized enlistment" (*orgnabor*)—recruitment by agents of the Commissariat of Labor based on "control figures" of where and in what numbers seasonal workers would be needed. The numbers were huge and, of course, approximate—at least two million for construction, *Pravda* reported in March 1930. By October it was forecasting at least nine million for all the seasonal trades (such as construction, logging, oil, and fisheries), including whatever was needed by coal mining, which was determined to become nonseasonal.[67]

For a while, collective farm management succeeded in stymieing recruiters. Faced with the task of recruiting 120,000 kolkhoz peasants for seasonal work, commissariat agents in Ukraine enlisted a mere 5,300 by October 1930. "The commissariat," *Pravda* complained, "only knows where these workers are needed, not where to get them, and VSNKh [the Supreme Council on the National Economy] doesn't care."[68] But a lot of industrial enterprises and construction trusts did care, and by March 1931, they had gained the right to recruit directly. In June 1931 the Soviet government tilted the balance still more in favor of recruiters when it decreed that kolkhozes had to include provisions for otkhodniki in their annual plans and publicize opportunities, administrators could not deduct off-farm earnings from seasonal migrants or saddle them with additional responsibilities, and family members had equal rights to goods and services distributed by the kolkhoz. The decree also stipulated that once hired, otkhodniki could not return before the end of the contracted period without sacrificing all these benefits, but, tellingly, no penalty was assessed if they chose to remain beyond the expiration of the contract.[69]

Many kolkhoz administrators, eager to hold onto their labor force, violated these conditions by continuing to deduct earnings, persecute family members, and send out letters such as the following:

Reference. From Red Lightening Kolkhoz of Sukhodol'sk village soviet [Central Black Earth oblast'] to Citizen Volodin, I. K.: You are required to appear in person on July 1 [1931] because of an insufficiency of labor power. If you do not appear, you will be excluded from the kolkhoz with your family . . .[70]

66. Kotkin, "Peopling Magnitostroi," 85.
67. *Pravda*, March 26, 1930, 5; October 3, 1930, 4.
68. Ibid., March 16, 1930, 5; October 3, 1930, 4.
69. "Ob otkhodnichestve," *Pravda*, July 1, 1931, 1.
70. *Izvestiia*, July 22, 1931, 3; August 8, 1931, 3. See Panfilova, *Formirovanie*, 39, for other instances.

Many ordinary kolkhoz peasants supported these measures, if they did not instigate them. The reason is that living, as Fitzpatrick puts it, "on the margins," otkhodniki aroused a good deal of ill will among their neighbors. They had one foot in the kolkhoz and another outside. Throughout the 1930s and probably beyond, many kolkhozniki who did not go out for earnings thought of themselves as morally superior to otkhodniki, whom they considered "flitters." Rather than earning big money, they stuck it out, thereby, as one of them put it, "showing myself to be an exemplary builder of kolkhoz life."[71] Or maybe it was just envy.

The enterprises that hired seasonal migrants, though desperate for their labor, often did not fulfill their end of the bargain when it came to accommodations and money for travel.[72] Living conditions thus were hardly enviable. What is more, enterprises seemed to prefer to hire people who came on their own precisely to avoid committing themselves in advance to constructing housing and other complications associated with orgnabor.[73] Thus, at Magnitostroi, over half of the incoming population in 1931 consisted of people who arrived on their own. The region of origin for more than two-thirds of them—some 42,000 people—was listed as unknown.[74]

Toward the end of 1932, many grain-growing regions of the country including Ukraine, the North Caucasus, and the Volga began to experience famine. Literally millions abandoned the kolkhozes in search of food, more refugees than seasonal migrants. They included the Lazebnik family, whose paternal peregrinations we described above. This family returned to the village where Roman had been born, surviving the *Holodomor* only because of the *mamaliga* his mother prepared from the corn stored in their basement.[75] In December 1932 the Soviet government, alarmed that the refugees would overwhelm the resources of the towns to which they fled, announced the introduction of internal passports to permanent residents of cities and set about expelling those not engaged in socially useful labor as well as "kulaks, criminals, and other antisocial elements." A revision of the rationing system tied the ration cards more closely to employment and the imposition of a stricter regimen of labor discipline provided an additional weapon to purge the ranks of the unwanted. Finally, a decree of March 1933 revised the June 1931 resolution by requiring kolkhoz peasants to register contracts with prospective employers. Those "flitters" who left without a contract or had failed to receive the kolkhoz's authorization to depart faced expulsion.[76] Famine, like seasonal labor, disrupted Soviet plans to create a sedentary labor force.

---

71. Fitzpatrick, *Stalin's Peasants*, 170.

72. Panfilova, *Formirovanie*, 32–33.

73. Ibid., September 9, 1931, 3; September 10, 1931, 4; September 24, 1931, 3; May 16, 1932, 2.

74. *Pravda*, January 12, 1932, 4; Kotkin, "Peopling Magnitostroi," 73. See also Donald Filtzer, *Soviet Workers and Stalinist Industrialization: The Formation of Modern Soviet Production Relations, 1928–1941* (Armonk, 1986), 61.

75. "Roman Lazebnik," 1. *Mamaliga* is a porridge made from yellow corn flour traditional in Romania.

76. For a neat summary of these decrees see Fitzpatrick, "The Great Departure," 28–29. For revisions to the law in September 1934, see Kessler, "Peasant and the Town," 1:185.

Nobody seems to know exactly how many otkhodniki and members of their families actually were expelled. Fitzpatrick, relying on letters of complaint sent to the newspaper *Krest'ianskaia gazeta* (Peasants' newspaper) in 1938 and 1939, indicates they "were commonplace" and provides some juicy examples. However, she also indicates that higher authorities "almost always decided against the kolkhoz" when such cases were contested, at least in the mid-1930s.[77] Not all otkhodniki, of course, were keen to return to the kolkhoz. Exactly how many overstayed their visas (as it were) and settled into jobs at the factories they had just helped build as construction workers we do not know. But just as otkhodniki and refugees became indistinguishable during the famine of 1932–33, so seasonal migration often became a permanent rural-to-urban move, with children picking up where the parents left off. Take the parents of Vasilii Alekseevich Viktorov. They abandoned their village in the Tatar republic where he was born so that they could participate in the building of the Sverdlov factory in Dzerzhinsk, Gor'kii krai. From there, Vasilii was able to obtain a passport and a job at the Oka chemical factory as an apprentice electrician in 1939.[78] For other peasants, as Kessler points out, it was possible to commute to industrial enterprises and machine-tractor stations and thereby receive monetary earnings without engaging in migration at all.[79]

Despite the many circumventions and exceptions noted here, the state managed to gain a measure of control over the use of seasonal labor, largely at the expense of collective farm management. Forestry best illustrates this development. A decree of the Council of People's Commissars from November 1933 required kolkhozes in designated areas to include logging and rafting in their production plans, and assume full responsibility for their fulfillment. Subsequent resolutions from May 1935 and March 1936 forbade kolkhozes from recalling peasants from logging operations or preventing peasants from signing up for permanent work in forestry.[80]

Overall, however, the scale of seasonal migration declined during the latter half of the 1930s. If in 1935 approximately three million collective farmers were absent for a significant portion of the year other than for military service, then by 1939, only two million were away. This translates to somewhat less than one seasonal migrant for every four kolkhoz households. The reason adduced by Kessler is that an increasing proportion of households could make a go of it without needing to send someone out for earnings, or, in other

---

77. Fitzpatrick, *Stalin's Peasants*, 168.

78. "Vasilii Alekseevich Viktorov," http://iremember.ru/pekhotintsi/viktorov-vasiliy-alekseevich.html, 1 (accessed March 5, 2012). The link between seasonal and permanent migration is widely recognized. See Moch, *Moving Europeans*.

79. Kessler, "Peasant and the Town," 1:188.

80. M. A. Beznin, T. M. Dimoni, and L. V. Iziumova, *Povinnosti rossiiskogo krest'ianstva v 1930–1960-kh godakh* (Vologda, 2001), 76–77.

words, things were looking up on the kolkhozes. That is why, he argues, the government tried to "prune down" the garden plot and the household economy—to make it more necessary for peasants to send their able-bodied men to work in industry, then beginning to gear up for war.[81]

Seasonal Migrants, 1945–91

"The opportunity I had to travel with a 'wild' gang for earnings," Viktor Gal'chenko related in 1985–86, "arose after my second year at university, when I had decided to get married." Viktor had been working as a lab technician to support himself while at university, but was only earning 65 rubles a month, hardly enough to feed himself. "Nobody seemed to consider my decision to earn extra money reprehensible," he recalled. "My parents looked on side earnings as a normal phenomenon. I don't know how the family would have survived if mother hadn't been bringing in money from embroidery, as father was a drinker." So, it was no big deal when Viktor joined a group of guys from the same city who hadn't known each other before and became a shabashnik. They went north to Tiumen' oblast' in western Siberia to clear a forest plot, lay the first street of a new settlement, and build eight houses.[82]

By the time Viktor told his story to a Soviet journalist, he had been taking to the road nearly every year for some two decades. The most detailed account we have by a seasonal worker in the Soviet period, Viktor's tale represents a radical departure from the experiences of earlier generations of collective farmers out for earnings or dispatched via organized recruitment. Thus, we begin by mapping the postwar arc of seasonal migration, explaining similarities and differences between the new form that Viktor embodied and previous forms, and why and on what scale this new form emerged. We then return to Viktor's story, using it to assess the relationship between the personal, the familial, and governmental in shaping the conditions and consequences of this kind of work away from home.

As before the Great Patriotic War so in its aftermath seasonal work provided a source of supplementary income for collective farmers and flexibility for their employers. This symbiosis did not necessarily make for happy relations. During the immediate postwar years, much of the hiring for seasonal work occurred under the auspices of the Ministry of Labor Reserves.[83] Donald Filtzer notes the occurrence of "deliberate deception and fraud by

---

81. Kessler, "Peasant and the Town,"1: 206–8.

82. V. Gal'chenko with Nina Maksimova, "Zhitie odnogo shabashnika," EKO, no. 3 (1987): 104–8.

83. Formed in May 1946, the Ministry of Labor Reserves absorbed the functions of the Main Administration of Labor Reserves that had existed since 1940 under the Council of People's Commissars. It reverted to the status quo ante in 1954. See GARF, f. R-9507, op. 2, d. 1 (Polozhenie o glavnykh upravleniiakh, upravleniia, otdelakh i organizatsiiakh Ministerstva trudovykh rezervov, SSSR).

recruiting agents or enterprise managements," adding that within the context of orgnabor such abuses were nothing new. The data provided by Filtzer on workers recruited through this system refer for the most part to such nonseasonal industries as metallurgy, coal, oil, and electric power generation. But the ministry also oversaw recruitment of construction and forestry workers.[84]

Il'ia Bentsianovich Sheftel' (1920–76) was among those working in the ministry. Hired in 1947 as an inspector, Sheftel' assumed responsibilities that included issuing "announce-ments, posters, wall newspapers and sheets, and participating in the recruitment of work-ers in various branches of industry and construction work." During his three years at the job, he "familiarized himself with the forestry industry, the construction of mines and met-allurgical factories." While visiting work sites, he "collected material for placards that he would publish . . . telling about work and living conditions in the forestry and coal mining industries, and the construction of mines and factories." Is it possible that Sheftel', whose autobiography appears on a family history website, engaged in some of the deliberate de-ception and fraud to which Filtzer refers?[85]

One of the ways of attracting recruits after the war was to promise them access to con-sumer goods in short supply, which meant just about everything. During the 1945–46 sea-son, workers who completed their forestry assignments had the opportunity to purchase up to 6 meters of cotton cloth, one bar of soap, 100 grams of tobacco, three boxes of matches, 300 grams of sugar, 2 liters of kerosene, and 2 kilos of salt. Those who overful-filled their quotas could purchase an additional 4 meters of cotton cloth. Another incentive, particularly attractive to peasants from parts of the country lacking in timber, was the op-portunity to return home with this building material, the volume of which corresponded to their level of quota fulfillment. Kolkhoz bosses also received incentives for plan fulfillment by "their" seasonal workers. These took the form of both monetary bonuses and access to a "fund of valuable articles" that, in the 1947–48 season, included sewing machines, hunt-ing rifles, radios, phonographs, wrist and pocket watches, bicycles, and motorcycles.[86]

Some peasants, particularly those from poorer kolkhozes and with little opportunity to market produce from their garden plots, did not need much of an incentive to volunteer for seasonal work. Others from more prosperous kolkhozes avoided recruitment like the plague. In November 1951, the Council of Ministers issued a resolution critical of the

84. Donald Filtzer, *Soviet Workers and Late Stalinism: Labour and the Restoration of the Stalinist System after World War II* (Cambridge, 2002), 30–31.

85. "Sheftel', Il'ia Bentsianovich (1920–1976)," http://www.famhist.ru/famhist/sheftel/0002c21f.htm#00002f09.htm (accessed July 22, 2012). This is a manuscript of Sheftel's unpublished autobiography, entitled *Anketa moego sovremennika*.

86. Beznin, Dimoni, and Iziumova, *Povinnosti rossiiskogo krest'ianstva*, 90; Iu. V. Roshchin, *Migratsiia nasele-niia v sud'be Rossii* (Moscow, 2008), 166.

Ministry of Labor Reserves for its failure to exercise control over recruitment. Alleging that recruiters had taken the path of least resistance by concentrating on the economically weaker kolkhozes, it decreed that plans for both permanent and seasonal recruitment be developed down to the district level to correspond to labor resources. Once again, as in the early 1930s, it forbade individual enterprises from recruiting workers without written permission of the kolkhoz administration.[87] In other words, at least as far as the law was concerned, the pendulum had swung back toward control by collective farm management.

The labor reserve system continued to send peasants from collective farms to the forestry, peat cutting, and fishing industries for the remainder of the Stalin years. But, as a form of paid labor conscription, it proved to be an early casualty of the transition to less coercive forms characteristic of the post-Stalin era. Already in June 1953, the Council of Ministers issued a resolution calling for the introduction of individual contracts, albeit still under the rubric of orgnabor. All the while, the role of seasonal work in the forestry industry was declining. In 1946, over half the workers employed in the Komi peninsula, Karelian SSR, and Vologda oblast' forest trusts worked on a seasonal basis, but their proportion dropped dramatically. By 1956, only 13 percent of the forestry workforce in Vologda consisted of seasonal laborers.[88] This seems to have reflected increased mechanization that promoted greater reliance on "permanent" cadres.

Seasonal migration to the cities, by contrast, flourished during these years, serving as a major conduit for peasant youth to migrate on a more permanent basis out of the impoverished collective farms. The labor reserve system each year absorbed about sixty thousand people, of whom, during 1946–50, three-quarters consisted of rural youth. They alone probably were responsible for the absence of one-fifth to one-sixth of the rural population during annual population counts, which typically occurred in the fall and winter months. Additionally, girls left for the city, where they hoped to secure positions as maids and nannies and in the longer term, perhaps, a husband.[89]

Various state organs continued to rely on orgnabor as a method of redistributing labor to where planners determined it was needed, even after the elimination of the labor reserve system. Construction projects in the 1950s, ranging from the Bratsk High Dam to the building of new cities, and later the Baikal-Amur Mainline (BAM), drew on this method of

---

87. "Postanovlenie Sovmina SSSR ot 28.11.1951 N 4881 ob uporiadochenii provedeniia organizovannogo nabora rabochikh," http://pravo.levonevsky.org/baza/soviet/sssr6272.htm (accessed July 3, 2012). Over two decades later, in 1973, the Council of Ministers had to repeat this resolution. See "Postanovlenie Sovmina SSSR ot 19.06.1973 N 421 ob uporiadochenii otkhodnichestva kolkhoznikov na sezonnye raboty," http:// pravo.levonevsky.org/baza/soviet/sssr4652.htm (accessed July 3, 2012).

88. Beznin, Dimoni, and Iziumova, *Povinnosti rossiiskogo krest'ianstva*, 94–96; Roshchin, *Migratsiia naseleniia*, 165–67. Equivalent resolutions dated March 4, 1954 and January 5, 1955 applied to the peat and fishery industries.

89. O. M. Verbitskaia, "Migratsiia sel'skogo naseleniia," in *Naselenie Rossii v XX veke: Istoricheskie ocherki v. 3-kh t.*, tom 2, 1940–1959, ed. V. B. Zhiromskaia (Moscow, 2001), 280–81.

labor mobilization. But as the eligible rural population declined, especially in the Central, Industrial, Upper Volga, Central Black Earth, and other regions where organized recruitment had been particularly heavy, so did the scale of organized recruitment. From 2.8 million people between 1951 and 1955, it dropped to 1.6 million in 1956–60, even more sharply to 650,000 in 1961–65, and 570,000 in 1966–70.[90]

Many projects, including those mentioned in the previous paragraph, also tapped into a new form of seasonal labor from a quite different demographic source—student construction brigades (SSO—*studencheskie stroitel'nye otriady*). Sponsored by the Komsomol as a form of patronage, the initial SSOs exuded an enthusiasm and esprit de corps that imbued that organization in the late 1950s. Between 1956 and 1961, over eight hundred thousand young men and women participated in projects declared by the Komsomol to be "all-Union shock construction sites."[91] Eventually, earning some extra money, enhancing one's career prospects, and making sexual connections would weigh more among participants.

At the same time, unofficial informal hiring of seasonal construction brigades began to occur in the countryside. The practice harkened back to an earlier era when groups of peasants with time on their hands and hungry mouths to feed formed artels, hit the road, and parlayed their skills and brawn into temporary employment. Just as then, so in the 1960s and beyond one can find references in the Soviet press to artels, otkhodniki, and sezonniki. Sometimes these terms were used interchangeably with a new one—*shabashnik*. The first mention of shabashnik that we could find was in a speech given by Nikita Khrushchev in March 1957. Khrushchev used it as a synonym for loafer, do-nothing, a person without a definite occupation, or someone deriving income from dishonest means.[92] Etymologically, the term is distantly derived from the Russian word for Sabbath (*shabash*) but more closely comes from the noun *shabáshka*, meaning a "small item carried home from work," or "time free from work," and the corresponding verb *shabashnit'*, meaning "to finish work" or "to take a break from work."[93] It did not appear in any Soviet-era dictionary probably for the same reason that it is absent from Soviet economic and legal literature, namely, its unsavory connotations, or as the first (1992) post-Soviet edition of Ozhegov's dictionary noted, its "disapprobative" quality.[94]

90. Iu. A. Matveev, "Organizovannyi nabor kak odna iz osnovnykh form planovogo pereraspredeleniia rabochei sily," in *Migratsiia naseleniia RSFSR*, ed. A. Z. Maikov (Moscow, 1973), 67.

91. Roshchin, *Migratsiia naseleniia*, 171.

92. *Pravda* March 31, 1957, 2. Khrushchev used the term again in a speech that appears in *Pravda*, January 25, 1958, 2.

93. S. I. Ozhegov, *Slovar' russkogo iazyka*, 4th ed. (Moscow, 1961), 874; *Tolkovyi slovar'*, ed. B. M. Volin and D. N. Ushakov, 4 vols. (Moscow, 1935–1940), 4: 1310.

94. S. I. Ozhegov and N. Iu. Shvedova, *Tolkovyi slovar' russkogo iazyka* (Moscow, 1992), http://ozhegov. info/slovar/?q=%D0%A8*. As Hans Oversloot points out, an analogous term, kalymshchik (derived from the Turkic word for dowry but coming to mean "income received for an activity detrimental to society"), did appear in the 1978 edition of Ozhegov. Hans Oversloot, "Soviet Migrant Construction Workers (Shabashniki)," in Bade et al., *Encyclopedia of Migration*, 687.

If otkhodniki had their artels, shabashniki typically organized themselves into what they called "brigades." But because that term had a long and honorable Soviet pedigree, Soviet newspapers generally modified it by adding "hired," the more pejorative "on the side," and especially "wild," the word that Viktor Gal'chenko used. Ozhegov defined shabashnik as "a person who fulfills construction, repair, and other work, entering into private transactions at high prices." By Soviet standards this indeed was disapprobative. The private nature of the transactions involving shabashniki was no less problematic than the side deals otkhodniki engaged in during the 1920s and 1930s, or for that matter, when settlers went out to explore land on their own (samovol'no). Each by virtue of its self-organized, "on-the-side" nature, fundamentally violated the state's authority to govern labor activity via the mechanism of planning.

Disapproval of shabashniki often assumed a moralizing character. Echoing what some peasants said about otkhodniki decades earlier, Soviet newspapers characterized them as "going after the long ruble."[95] Pravda in its effort to discredit shabashniki reported in 1973 that Chechens were abandoning their villages to work far away "only for the sake of personal wealth." The "bacillus of acquisitiveness" was said to infect even some with party cards as well as school-aged youngsters who had not returned by the beginning of the school year.[96]

A decade later, the situation appeared to have gotten worse. "It is no secret," the newspaper opined, "that many people in the autonomous republics of the northern Caucasus are not involved in socially useful labor." "I know many young people," wrote a distraught nurse from the Chechen town of Gudermes, "who go for earnings for two-three years, and when they return walk around like kings." Such types were "depressingly vain." They "wear black trench coats, jeans, and imported shoes," their "houses are palaces . . . of ferroconcrete construction, with swimming pools, wine cellars, and garages."[97]

The Soviet press emphasized not just dissoluteness, for living in palaces with swimming pools and wine cellars probably appealed to many readers. The point was that shabashniki lived in limbo and were to be pitied. They were not much different from other highly mobile, essentially rootless groups—gypsies, beggars, bichi (down-and-outers), and bomzhi (an acronym derived from "without definite place of residence")—that we will discuss in our final chapter. "At home they are rare guests, and at the places where they work on construction they are total outsiders," a reporter for Komsomol'skaia pravda wrote. They "lead a cloistered and dull life. . . . Their undefined social status, and the mere fact that they have

---

95. Izvestiia, December 16, 1984, 2.

96. Pravda, November 11, 1973, 4.

97. Pravda, June 13, 1985, 3; October 29, 1985, 2. For the case of a school-aged sezonnik who turned up to school driving a Zhiguli he had purchased with the money earned from seasonal labor, see Izvestiia, April 23, 1984, 3.

dropped out of the orbit of the usual lifestyle, are hard on many of them."[98] Worse still, they existed in what one Western analyst called "a kind of legal twilight zone."[99] As independent contractors they were completely outside the system of labor legislation, including the benefits and protections provided therefrom. Or, as *Pravda* put it in 1966, "the seasonal worker does not receive a kopeck for [time off due to] illness, does not participate in socialist competition, and cannot count on a bonus."[100]

So much for the reputation of shabashniki and associated hazards. Who in reality became a shabashnik? Where did they come from and where did they find work? How were they paid and, perhaps most important, how was it possible that despite official opprobrium and the at best semi-legality of their transactions, they persisted in their ways probably on an increased scale in the Soviet Union's last decades? Little sociological data exist, but one article from 1981 refers to seasonal workers as men aged twenty to thirty-five ("the most able-bodied years"). They included party members, which another article described as "an alarming moral aspect."[101] Organizing themselves into teams of anywhere from five to twenty-five members, shabashniki spent from a few months during the summer to half a year away from home working as plasterers, plumbers, bricklayers, carpenters, and electricians. Working six days a week for twelve hours a day and sometimes longer, they built all manner of structures—from roads, sheds, and barns to apartment buildings and clubs on collective and state farms.

One source from 1985 indicates that "according to incomplete and approximate figures," some 350,000 seasonal migrants were so engaged. A more recent source provides a "very rough" higher estimate of between 500,000 and 2.3 million.[102] The areas of greatest demand included the Central Non-Black Earth region, the Urals, and Siberia, though the source for this information adds, "they may find work almost anywhere . . . someone with money wants something done faster than the normal government construction organizations would do it."[103] In the mid-1960s, tens of millions of rubles were said to change hands every year.[104] By the early 1980s, shabashniki and other moonlighters accounted for 70

98. "Seasonal Workers Outdo 'Official' Contractors," *Komsomol'skaia pravda*, April 14, 1981, 2, trans. in *Current Digest of the Soviet Press (CDSP)*, May 27, 1981, 7.

99. Patrick Murphy, "Soviet Shabashniki: Material Incentives at Work," *Problems of Communism* 34, no. 6 (1984): 57.

100. *Pravda*, November 20, 1966, 3.

101. "Seasonal Workers Outdo," 7; and "Who Will Stop the Private Construction Worker?" *Zaria Vostoka*, January 22, 1978, 3, trans. in *CDSP*, March 1, 1978, 15.

102. "The Road," *Izvestiia*, April 18, 1985, 3, trans. in *CDSP*, May 15, 1985, 20; Oversloot, "Soviet Migrant Construction Workers," 688.

103. Murphy, "Soviet Shabashniki," 49.

104. *Pravda*, October 20, 1966, 3.

million rubles' worth of construction and installation work in a single oblast', western Siberia's Kurgan.[105] Because payments sometimes were made in kind and for the most part under the table, the total amount undoubtedly was higher. Throughout the USSR, shabashniki accounted for at least 25 percent and as much as 40 percent of all rural construction, but in some places—Sverdlovsk oblast', Kazakhstan, and Saratov oblast'—more than half.[106] And in Siberia, according to an economist who studied a district of the Altai region in 1986, they were responsible for "not less than two-thirds."[107]

It is difficult to generalize about much else regarding shabashniki because of their bifurcated origins. Some—it is impossible to estimate proportions—hailed from the countryside. Articles in the press mentioned western Ukraine, Belarus, and especially the Caucasus (Armenia, Azerbaijan, Georgia, and the autonomous republics of the northern Caucasus).[108] These were areas where the rural population held more or less steady or increased between 1959 and 1979, and where in the case of the Caucasus, large families predominated.[109] These "professionals" tended to spend at least half a year away from home. They thus moved in an itinerary similar to the otkhodniki of the late nineteenth century who made the annual trek from their densely populated rural homelands to more sparsely settled regions, returning to take part in the harvest and recuperate.

The other source for wild brigades of shabashniki consisted of people like Viktor—urban residents, mostly students and those with higher education, whose income from their regular job did not cover expenses. "I moonlight," a graduate student told a reporter, "in order to come up with milk and stuff for the kids."[110] Some made arrangements with their regular employers to take time off, others simply quit "to go pick cherries," knowing that because of the pervasive labor shortage in the cities, they would be able to reclaim their jobs when they returned.[111] Urban-based shabashniki traveled varying distances. Some,

105. "Seasonal Workers Outdo," 6.

106. T. Ia. Valetov, "Mekhanizmy samoorganizatsii sezonnykh trudovykh migrantov v SSSR i na postsovetskom prostranstve," in "Sovetskoe nasledstvo": Otrazhenie proshlogo v sotsial'nykh i ekonomicheskikh praktikakh sovremennoi Rossii, ed. L. I. Borodkin, Kh. Kessler, and A. K. Sokolov (Moscow, 2010), 258–59. These proportions refer to the years 1976–81.

107. M. Shabanova, "Portret stroitelia-sezonnika," Nauka i zhizn', no. 9 (1986): 21.

108. See, for example, Pravda, May 24, 1960, 3; Komsomol'skaia pravda, June 1, 1966, 3; Pravda, November 11, 1973, 4; Izvestiia, December 16, 1983, 2; Izvestiia, December 16, 1984, 2.

109. On rural population, compare Tsentral'noe statisticheskoe upravlenie pri Sovete Ministrov SSSR, Itogi Vsesoiuznoi perepisi naseleniia 1959 goda RSFSR (Moscow, 1963), 26, and Tsentral'noe statisticheskoe upravlenie SSSR, Chislennost' i sostav naseleniia SSSR po dannym Vsesoiuznoi perepisi naseleniia 1979 goda (Moscow, 1984), 10.

110. "Seasonal Workers Outdo," 7.

111. "Discipline According to Conscience and the Law: He Quit 'to Go Pick Cherries,' " Sotsialisticheskaia industriia, September 6, 1983, 2, trans. in CDSP, November 9, 1983, 4.

like Oleg Kovriga, a "third-generation" intellectual who traveled from Moscow to Nizhne-vartovsk and Chukotka in the late 1970s, took long flights to remote parts of the Urals and Siberia, others restricted themselves to nearby rural areas.[112] A shabashnik from Nikolaev indicated that the first seasonal migrants to appear in that Ukrainian town were Koreans who arrived from Central Asia in the late 1960s to raise labor-intensive crops such as on-ions. Brigades from Nikolaev, Odessa, and Kherson soon followed in their wake and they too became known as "Koreans."[113] But whether growing crops or engaged in construc-tion, these urban-based seasonal migrants reversed the much older practice of otkhodniki who traveled to cities to supplement their meager rural incomes.

Indeed, what made it necessary or at least desirable for collective and state farm bosses to hire shabashniki was the major demographic shift of the post-Stalin decades—the exo-dus of young people and particularly males from the countryside to the cities. The resultant labor shortage in the countryside was at its most acute during the planting and harvesting seasons, which in Siberia significantly overlapped with the construction season. Unable to draw on their own personnel, employers could turn to a variety of state, cooperative, and interkolkhoz construction organizations. But these were notoriously top-heavy with ac-countants, supervisors, and foremen, and tended to stretch out projects for years. Failing that, Komsomol-organized student brigades patterned after the SSO and, if they were lo-cally available, military construction battalions (stroibaty) could fill in. Students from Central Asia, where high birth rates and low urbanization had left a lot of young people with not much to do, were particularly "well represented" among those engaged in sum-mer projects, mostly in construction. Nonstudent youths also took up opportunities for such work, responding to advertisements in newspapers such as Pravda Vostoka (Pravda of the East).[114] For getting the job done relatively quickly, there was no substitute for shabashniki.

Aside from the long hours they were willing to put in, unencumbered by family and most other responsibilities, these off-the-books workers had one other advantage to po-tential employers. They typically provided their own materials and supplies, obtaining them by barter, bribery, and theft.[115] Authorities would crack down on these operations—when they could find out about them—and the punishments meted out sometimes were severe. In one case, a "parasite" and "swindler" received a fifteen-year sentence from a

112. "Kovriga O.: Kak my shabashili," http://pro-shabashku.narod.ru/Part2_1.html (accessed December 8, 2013). See also "Tsoi K. A. Chukotskie meridian," http://pro-shabashku.narod.ru/Content.htm. We thank Alexandra Öberlander for drawing our attention to these sources.

113. "The Reader's Opinion—For, Against, or a Different View: A Police Officer and a Seasonal Worker Speak Frankly," Izvestiia, June 16, 1985, 2, trans. in CDSP, July 10, 1985, 1.

114. Fierman, "Central Asian Youth and Migration," 259–60.

115. Murphy, "Soviet Shabashniki," 54–55.

court in Rostov-on-Don for bilking collective and state farms. "He could do anything," farm managers (who also were prosecuted) explained in defense of their payment of advances to him.

> He went to work with his own building materials and no one had to worry about trying to obtain centrally allocated materials. [He] made deals with the head of the warehouses of . . . the Rostov Civil Construction Trust that enabled him to pilfer pipe, cement, crushed rock, and metal from its construction projects.[116]

He got caught, but many others like him successfully cut through the multilayered bureaucratic system. They were highly sought after by kolkhoz bosses anxious to complete projects and weary of cajoling collective farmers, but they must have irritated accountants, planners, law enforcement officers, and other elements of Soviet society responsible for checking up on what people did and at what cost they did it.

We can now give Viktor Gal'chenko the floor to explain what life was like in the gray zone of semi-legality inhabited by shabashniki. Gal'chenko (a pseudonym) volunteered to provide a Novosibirsk based journal his story at an opportune moment. In March 1987 when "The Life of One Shabashnik" appeared in print, many previously taboo subjects and views long restricted to private conversations were emerging in the media, the result of Mikhail Gorbachev's policy of glasnost'. "As the world is reflected in a drop of water, so the fate of this one man reveals several features characteristic of shabashnichestvo," wrote Nina Maksimova, the sympathetic journalist who edited Gal'chenko's story.[117]

For the fifty days of work that Gal'chenko put in building houses near Tiumen', he received 1,200 rubles. This represented more than he would have earned in a year working in the city eight hours a day, six days a week. After that initial experience of working with strangers, Gal'chenko decided to organize his own brigade. He chose among childhood companions, including his younger brother, and the group turned out to be "the healthiest collective I ever knew." They even registered themselves among the amateur societies and sports teams of the region. The group remained intact for several seasons, living in tents and wagons, buying and preparing food themselves like temporary workers everywhere.[118] The normal working day lasted ten to twelve hours with one half day off on Saturdays. Members of the brigade lived and breathed for their work. For this reason, they shunned

---

116. "Individual's Rights and Duties: At Someone Else's Expense," *Pravda*, October 5, 1984, 6, trans. in *CDSP*, October 31, 1984, 19–20.

117. Gal'chenko, "Zhitie odnogo shabashnika," 101. The remaining paragraphs are based on pp. 101–36 of the same source.

118. See Michael J. Piore, *Birds of Passage: Migrant Labor and Industrial Societies* (Cambridge, 1979).

alcohol and avoided contact with locals. They also reverted to a state of illiteracy and inaudibility, refraining from reading newspapers or listening to the radio.

The brigade found work primarily along the Enisei, the Angara, and in the Saian mountains in Siberia. "Of course, we didn't go just to smell the taiga," Gal'chenko insisted, "but we also didn't go only for the money." They yearned for new impressions, for self-affirmation, to test their endurance, to go to the limits. Wherever they went, they became the stuff of legends. "Why do you work like madmen?" the locals would ask. "Don't they feed you in the city?" When they entered a village store to buy provisions, they would be invited to jump the queue because people knew how they valued time.

The brigade worked as two teams of five men, each starting and finishing at different times but working about the same number of hours. Everyone received the same amount of money. Although Gal'chenko recruited members, assigned tasks, and instructed the novices, he did not accept a larger share. He also refused to deal with contractors, assigning that responsibility to "Valentin," a high school economics teacher and the oldest member of the brigade, who also arranged for supplies and kept all the accounts. Thanks to Valentin's contacts, the brigade occasionally masqueraded as a student construction brigade, thereby making it eligible for compensation for travel costs and exempt from income taxes. Because the majority of members had at least a high school education, and because the brigade was more productive than real student brigades, "we felt we had a moral right to those benefits not exactly conferred legally." This, according to Gal'chenko, was the only "compromise" they ever made. They neither asked for nor accepted bribes, for example, and to finish a job worked around the clock, on one occasion for thirty-six hours straight. Employers, by contrast, frequently violated contracts, which of course lacked the force of law. They commonly failed to deliver building materials on time or in the requisite quantities.

Gal'chenko writes that he first became a shabashnik to help support himself and his new bride. But he eventually realized that his summers away in the taiga were undermining his marriage. Rather than return to his "wild" brigade, he found another job in the city as a masseur, a skill he picked up while undergoing treatment for back pains suffered on construction sites. Unfortunately, the job paid almost nothing and his marriage collapsed the year after his son was born. There followed a second marriage that lasted four years, ending when his wife "grew tired of the romantic and philosopher earning next to nothing." "The instability of conjugal relations," he asserts, "is typical for shabashniki." By the time Gal'chenko met and married his third wife, Lida, he no longer was working for the psychology lab, which meant he was earning literally nothing. Ashamed to depend on Lida's income and still responsible for alimony payments to his first wife, he went "on shabashka," this time with a group of strangers.

They traveled to an unnamed island (perhaps Sakhalin) where "Kolia," a shady character with many contacts, "illegally recruited" them for construction work. They built houses and a banquet hall for a kolkhoz, each member receiving 1,000 rubles a month.

Freelancing, they built on the basis of their own blueprints a café, which they richly decorated, inspiring in Viktor the feeling that he was a missionary carrying to "this corner of the earth the culture of a European city." But they were swindled, receiving far less payment than agreed on. At this point, Gal'chenko's narrative becomes thick with the argot of this particular subculture. Sentences are full of references to "arrangers," moola, and the like, prompting the editor to liken Viktor to Ilf and Petrov's notorious trickster Ostap Bender and to observe that he seemed to have lost his moral compass. This is where we will leave him, teetering on the brink of the criminal underground and with the "first cracks" opening in his third marriage, while the entire country was in the process of descending into gangsterism.

In conclusion, these last incarnations of Soviet seasonal migrants reflect both how far the Soviet Union had come in accommodating an at best heterodox phenomenon and how it had not gone all that far after all. If the Viktor Gal'chenkos of the country could turn up every spring in some rural backwater to negotiate with prospective employers primarily off the books, it was only because they were fulfilling a practical need otherwise beyond local resources. The rest of the year, like Superman's alter ego Clark Kent, they led a relatively humdrum existence. So it was with the USSR. Outwardly regulated on the basis of the planning mechanism, labor laws, and the paternalistic oversight of police and other organs, workers could break away to work harder than their legitimate bosses could imagine. But then, they were not so removed from their seasonal migrant ancestors, the otkhodniki, in that both engaged in adaptive compensatory practices, compensating the Soviet economy for its congenital shortage of labor and compensating themselves for their inadequate incomes.

Post-Soviet Seasonal and Temporary Migrants

By the end of the century, a pattern of temporary migration emerged that would look familiar to migration scholars worldwide. Of all forms of migration we analyze in this study, post-Soviet labor migration to Russia most closely resembles contemporary or near contemporary practices in Europe and North America. We should not be surprised that the word *gastarbaitery*—from the German *gastarbeiter*—came into popular use in Russia at the end of the twentieth century.[119]

Among migrants registered as living in Russia, those from Central Asia increased in number by only 9 percent between 1989 and 2002. But the number of Central Asians who

---

119. Madeleine Reeves, "Black Work, Green Money: Remittances, Ritual and Domestic Economies in Southern Kyrgyzstan," *Slavic Review* 71, no. 1 (2012): 114.

are in Russia on a temporary basis has become much greater. "If illegal, temporary migration were added, the evidence would point to what could be termed a massive migration to Russia," writes Timothy Heleniak. Andrei Korobkov explains that the designation of illegality is questionable. Newcomers tend to arrive legally, but then register improperly, fail to undertake the activity listed on the visa, or gain entry through a tourist or student visa, for example. They thereby replicated repertoires practiced worldwide. The vast majority of migrants are employed, and might more properly be understood as undocumented or irregular migrants rather than illegals. In other words, temporary workers made the long trip to work in Russia to make a living that their homeland could not provide.[120]

The difficulty in clearly delineating temporary workers among contemporary labor migrants is that one cannot know—even migrants themselves do not know—whether or not they will ultimately stay at their destination. Workers plan to return home, and often do for vacations and visits, or in the case of market sellers, to replenish their supplies. Commonly, their earnings translate into remittances that underwrite new village homes, cell phones, and lavish weddings. Yet temporary migrants often gather the better part of a family or village to stay at one destination, creating the pattern of chain migration.[121] As a consequence, we often find tales of immigrant sellers or construction workers who arrive in a Russian city with a group of men but ultimately have parents, children, and wives join them.

The evolution of travels to Moscow from a cluster of villages in southwest Kyrgyzstan reveals one set of changes in cityward migration following the end of the USSR. Madeleine Reeves reports that men had traded rice and apricots from private plots and the kolkhoz in the markets of Nizhny Novgorod since the 1970s, but that the hard times of the 1990s, imposition of an international border, and policing of the route through Kazakhstan had altered this practice. Gradually, "going to town"—usually to Moscow, less often to Nizhny Novgorod—and working in construction became the dominant repertoire at the end of the century as, in the words of a villager, migration from the region "became a fashion."[122] In her survey of village households, Reeves found that nearly three-quarters obtained their most recent position in Russia through a relative, friend, or fellow villager; "relatives

120. Timothy Heleniak, "An Overview of Migration in the Post-Soviet Space," in *Migration, Homeland, and Belonging in Eurasia*, ed. Cynthia Buckley, Blair Ruble, and Erin Trouth Hofmann (Baltimore, 2008), 56; the number of people recorded as living in Russia permanently of Central Asian titular nationalities was 882,000 in 1989 and 963,000 in 2002; Andrei V. Korobkov, "Post-Soviet Migration: New Trends at the Beginning of the Twenty-First Century," in Buckley, Ruble, and Hofmann, *Migration, Homeland, and Belonging in Eurasia*, 77–78, 83–84.

121. There are examples of this phenomenon without number in anthropological, sociological, and historical studies; to cite two from Kyrgyzstan: Reeves, "Black Work, Green Money," 108–34; Matthias Schmidt and Lira Sagynbekova, "Migration Past and Present: Changing Patterns in Kyrgyzstan," *Central Asian Survey* 27, no. 2 (2008): 111–27.

122. Reeves, "Black Work, Green Money," 117, 121.

invited me" responded 45 percent, "friends/fellow villagers invited me," 27 percent. Intermediaries played a role for less than one in ten.[123] Advertisements for bus transportation to cities in European Russia and Siberia dotted local kiosks, and the majority of households had sent someone to Russia. This evolution echoes earlier migrations to the Imperial city, when the rhythm and values of village life were congruent with journeys to the city and yet were also threatened by what one might find there. The work, "black work," offered unprotected conditions to those who could move freely (but not necessarily legally) in the neoliberal labor market. This set of practices also reminds us of wider patterns, as family migrations emerged alongside male-only moves in the twenty-first century.[124]

But perhaps more often than the data suggest, migrants too undergo transformations. Take the Azerbaijani migrant Akhmed, who as of 2002 was forty-four years old. Akhmed came to Moscow several years previously from Nagorno-Karabakh, the contested territory within Azerbaijan populated mainly by Armenians, because "there is no place to trade there and no money." "Everyone," he added, wanted to leave. He found a job by word of mouth at the Danilevskii market helping to operate a dried fruit and nut stall. Before acquiring a residence permit, Akhmed had been "hassled" by the Moscow police, like so many other migrants from the Caucasus.[125] But by the time a reporter had caught up with him, he had his papers in order. He seems to have adapted to the ambivalent life of the migrant as a bird of passage, earning 200 to 300 dollars a month for four or five months, then going home to share his earnings with his family in Nagorno-Karabakh.[126]

---

123. Ibid., 125.

124. Ibid., 119.

125. Irina Sandul, "Time Runs Out for Russia's Foreign Workers," *The Russia Journal*, May 13, 2002, http://russiajournal.com/node/6205 (accessed November 23, 2012). See Meredith Roman, "Making Caucasians Black: Moscow since the Fall of Communism and the Racialization of Non-Russians," *Journal of Communist Studies and Transition Politics* 18, no. 2 (2002): 3: "The official reconceptualization of the capital from an inclusive multinational community to an exclusively white community has meant that the darker an individual's skin colour, the more abuse he or she is subjected to by police and city bureaucrats."

126. Sandul, "Time Runs Out."

~CHAPTER THREE~

Migrants to the City

"I just had to see the new cities . . . I didn't know if I would stay. But then I wanted to stay. There was something so light and bright and interesting about Magnitogorsk."

—Masha Scott as told to Pearl Buck, *Talk about Russia*

The city was the undisputed winner over the village in the twentieth century as rural areas ultimately emptied out in favor of the city. During a century that transformed urban areas and villages alike, cities drew migrants from their immediate hinterlands and far afield. The history of this migration is not uniform, either by kind of city, period, or region. It is rather a complex of attractions, repulsions, and coercions that at some points bound urban and rural areas in a symbiotic relationship and at others pitted the two against each other. Tsarist, Soviet, and post-Soviet Russian governments sought to control movement to the city: in the first instance, by legal strictures that kept peasants from definitively abandoning their village; in the second instance by restricting entry into urban areas, especially great cities; and in the third by continuing the Soviet-era residency permit system.[1] Spanning the tsarist and Soviet eras and continuing into the first decade of post-Soviet urbanism, we focus here on the migration experience of those people who moved to the city.

Considering Russia's twentieth century, we see the full range of conditions and motives for travel to urban areas. Three kinds of forces constitute the sources of urbanization (the growth of the proportion of people living in cities): net in-migration, natural increase from a

---

1. All three governments also took the defensive action of expelling citizens they deemed undesirable from the most important cities; we touch on this in chapters 7 and 8.

preponderance of births over deaths, and the reclassification by the state of rural areas. Generally speaking, mobility to the city was high at the end of the Imperial period, and that mobility accounted for the lion's share of urban growth. Indeed, about 80 percent of urban growth came from in-migration at the end of the nineteenth century (1885–97), partly because the balance of births and deaths did not work in the favor of growth. As cities became safer places for infants and children, natural increase contributed more to urban growth, but migration was still its primary engine, accounting for 62 percent of urban population increase (1926–39), and then 45 percent in the years 1959–70, when childbirth and child survival made a greater contribution to the postwar city.[2] These trends, calculated for all cities in the USSR on the basis of census data, give us only the barest impression of urbanward migration. We will fill out these generalities with evidence about the experience of newcomers.

In-migration created three periods of great urban growth in the twentieth century. Men and women took to the road or the railroad in the years before World War I as migration rates came to a peak. Their peregrinations resembled those of West Europeans.[3] The second wave of urban migration came in the 1930s after the country had recovered from war and revolution via the New Economic Policy (NEP). As urban migration in Western and much of Central Europe diminished with the Great Depression, it reached unprecedented proportions in the Soviet Union thanks to the push of rural collectivization and the pull of force-paced industrialization. Another great cohort of migrants headed for cities in the 1950s, when urban populations grew at a rate of over 4 percent per year.[4] The movement of industry to the Urals and farther East expanded cities in those regions especially during World War II, then an urban "great Siberian migration" expanded the cities devoted to natural resource extraction after the war. The emptying of villages after the Great Patriotic War again resembled postwar trends in other countries. Urban growth in Siberia and the Far North was reversed during the painful crisis years of the early 1990s and assumed a spotty pattern as the twentieth century drew to a close.

---

2. Robert Lewis and Richard Rowland report that 56 percent of the growth was due to migration in the 1926–70 period, as 27 percent was due to natural increase and 17 percent to the reclassification of rural areas as cities. After World War II, natural increase became more important. See Lewis and Rowland, "Urbanization in Russia and the USSR, 1897–1970," in *The City in Russian History*, ed. Michael Hamm (Lexington, 1976), 209–10. Calculations from B. Ts. Urlanis, *Problemy dinamiki naseleniia SSSR* (Moscow, 1974), yield about the same figures and same trends. We do not include figures for 1939–59 (when net migration was calculated to be responsible for 62 percent of city growth) because wartime displacements and the destruction of cities render the urbanization figures meaningless.

3. Steve Hochstadt, *Mobility and Modernity: Migration in Germany, 1820–1939* (Ann Arbor, 1999); James Jackson, Jr., *Migration and Urbanization in the Ruhr Valley, 1821–1914* (Humanities Press, 1997); Lucassen and Lucassen, "Mobility Transition Revisited," 347–77; Moch, *Moving Europeans*.

4. The average annual growth of the urban population was 4.6% in 1922–40, 0.95% in 1940–50, 4.1% in 1950–60, 2.8% in 1960–70, and 2.4% in 1970–75, according to James Bater, *The Soviet City: Ideal and Reality* (London, 1980), 60.

These population movements in Russian political space matched those of other regions of the world in the following ways: in the attraction of major cities, the expansions associated with industrialism, and the twentieth-century triumph of urban areas at the expense of the village. Yet there are also contrasts. From the beginning of the century to the end, the Russian state actively intervened, restricting who could reside in cities legally. It did its utmost from the early 1930s to manipulate urbanward movement. Second, only a handful of new cities were constructed in Western Europe after 1800 and the great industrial cities there expanded from a small-town base, whereas new cities built virtually from scratch comprise an important part of Russian urban history.[5] Magnitogorsk is only one of the best known of such cities, not all of which were erected in the Stalin era. These are the migration regimes that confronted potential city folk.

Studies correctly record the inhuman rush of workers and matériel to such sites and the urgency with which city building occurred, emphasizing the state's agenda. Likewise, state-sponsored educational programs—from the gymnasia and vocational institutions of provincial towns to the universities and higher technical schools of major cities—drew students and trainees. To this we add the repertoires of the newcomers themselves. The rural elites who came to take in the winter "season" operated as much in their culture as the itinerant workers hired for months or years at a time or the young women taking years to work in domestic service did in theirs. Connections from home villages and towns shaped urban work and living arrangements into and through the Soviet era.

It was work, in the main, that drew Russians to city life. The need for an educated bureaucracy expanded along with the demand for labor created by industrial growth and commercial expansion in Imperial cities. The exponential growth of extractive and heavy industries in Soviet times meant the demand for workers outstripped the considerable need for a literate bureaucracy and technical personnel. The post-Soviet labor force was diminished and less industrially oriented. Nonetheless, cities remained a magnet for aspiring workers.

Gender marked the labor force throughout Russia as deeply as elsewhere, so although both men and women moved to every kind of city, the balance between men and women depended on the local economy. Men worked in the mines and provided the vast majority of workers to steel mills, whereas women filled the textile mills, predominated in garment manufacturing, but in the Soviet period were more numerous in heavy industry than their sisters elsewhere. Although white-collar and bureaucratic employment was mixed, men generally prevailed in the upper levels and women provided the majority of teachers and physicians. Ideas about the pleasures and dangers of city life also varied by gender, since women were perceived to be more at risk in the city than men.

---

5. Jan de Vries, *European Urbanization, 1500–1800* (Cambridge, 1984).

Moving to the City in Late Imperial Russia

"To Moscow, to Moscow," intoned Chekhov's characters in *Three Sisters*.[6] Indeed, for Imperial Russians of means, Moscow and St. Petersburg held the same promise as Paris for the French and London for the English. They did so not only for people of means. The 1897 Imperial census reported that nearly 15 percent of the population was living away from its place of birth. One Russian statistician claimed in 1909 that the mobility of Russian peasants "is unequaled in Western Europe and perhaps can be compared only with the mobility of American workers."[7] In this most mobile of ages, Russians were settling distant landholdings as far away as the Far East and Central Asia, but they were also, like West Europeans, part of the broad trend of urbanization that expanded the city at the expense of rural habitation. This was especially the case in the northern and central provinces of European Russia where serfs had long ago been released seasonally to work in the city (as otkhodniki) and emigration had become built into village practices and family patterns; by the 1890s, two million peasants left home to work—one in seven of rural people, over one-third of adult men.[8]

In the years between 1860 and World War I, the urban population tripled, so that one of eight subjects of the Russian Empire lived in a city. Cities grew because they were swamped with newcomers whose living conditions horrified health officials and whose potential for solidarity and discontent horrified the forces of order. Moscow and St. Petersburg, long among the world's largest cities, joined the dozen with over a million residents by the turn of the twentieth century, while Warsaw, Odessa, and Kiev numbered over five hundred thousand.[9] Industrial and commercial cities such as Ekaterinoslav (now Dnepropetrovsk), Saratov on the middle Volga, and Baku on the Caspian Sea grew at a rapid clip.[10] People made their way to Tashkent in Russian Turkestan via the rail connection after 1906.[11] Like

6. Anne Lounsbery, "'To Moscow, I Beg You!': Chekhov's Vision of the Russian Provinces," *Toronto Slavic Quarterly*, http://www.utoronto.ca/tsq/09/lounsbery09.shtml (accessed March 19, 2011). Lounsbery adds: "Lovingly, obsessively, urgently, dreamily they repeat the name of the Russian capital, which ends up sounding like a talisman intended, it seems, to stave off the truth about their provincial lives."

7. B. P. Kadomtsev, *Professional'nyi i sotsial'nyi sostav naseleniia Evropeiskoi Rossii po dannym perepisi 1897 goda: Kritiko-statisticheskii etiud* (St. Petersburg, 1909), 67, quoted in Joseph Bradley, *Muzhik and Muscovite: Urbanization in Late Imperial Russia* (Berkeley, 1985), 28.

8. Barbara Engel, "The Woman's Side: Male Out-Migration and the Family Economy in Kostroma Province," *Slavic Review* 45, no. 2 (1986): 257–71; Bradley, *Muzhik and Muscovite*, 23–24; Jeffrey Burds, "The Social Control of Peasant Labor in Russia: The Response of Village Communities to Labor Migration in the Central Industrial Region, 1861–1905," in Kingston-Mann and Mixter, *Peasant Economy*, 55.

9. Hamm, *City in Late Imperial Russia*, 3.

10. Bradley, *Muzhik and Muscovite*, 31; Roger L. Thiede, "Industry and Urbanization in New Russia from 1860 to 1910," in Hamm, *City in Russian History*, 125–38; Jeff Sahadeo, *Russian Colonial Society in Tashkent, 1865–1923* (Bloomington, 2007), 111–13.

11. Paul Stronski, *Tashkent: Forging a Soviet City, 1930–1966* (Pittsburgh, 2010), 18, 28.

the other cities of Imperial Russia, Moscow was "a city of immigrants," and one in ten of all urban dwellers in Russia lived there.[12] The second largest city, after Petersburg, it housed 1.17 million people in 1902—73 percent of whom were born elsewhere and 67 percent of whom carried the legal status of peasant.[13]

Factory production and modern transportation set people in motion. The decline of cottage industry and labor surplus in the countryside, matched with an increase in urban jobs in industries, services, and construction, underwrote the push to urban life. In such a vast empire, as in smaller nations, the railroad was crucial to city growth, enabling, for example, grain to reach Odessa with dispatch and Tashkent cotton to find a market in faraway Moscow. The railroad complemented the system of waterways, which were energized by the steamers on the Volga and Dneper and transformed river cities like Saratov and Kazan into important centers of trade.[14] The textile town Ivanovo-Voznesensk, located some 200 miles northeast of Moscow, grew spectacularly from about 31,000 in 1883 to over 108,000 in 1909 and then 168,000 five years later. By 1897 the Russian Empire was home to fifty-eight of what have been called "migrant cities" in which over half the population had been born elsewhere.[15]

High mobility marked the age and the individual because new arrivals often moved on or returned home and many people moved repeatedly—as Prussian data reveal was also the case elsewhere. City growth in this period, then, was only one manifestation of roiling human movement. One-fifth of the people in Moscow who were counted in 1882 and again in 1902 had arrived within two years of the census dates; half the locally born enumerated in 1900 St. Petersburg had departed by 1910. Over half the men and women in the industrial district of Ivanovo had lived there less than five years.[16] Peasants like Andrei Petrovich Baidulin were not unusual. Baidulin left his home some 120 miles southeast of Moscow at age sixteen to work as a driver in the big city in a sanitation brigade. Three years later he continued to Kashira about 80 miles south of the city, where he worked in a brick factory for three years. After marriage in his home village, he returned to Moscow and another brick factory—and then six years in a market garden before moving on to Petersburg, where he found work as a coachman, then as a superintendent, and finally as a porter at the Moscow railroad station.[17]

---

12. Bradley, *Muzhik and Muscovite*, 33, 103.

13. Johnson, *Peasant and Proletarian*, 31.

14. Charlotte E. Henze, *Disease, Health Care, and Government in Late Imperial Russia: Life and Death on the Volga, 1823–1914* (London, 2011), 29.

15. Vorderer, *Migration Patterns*, 24; Daniel Brower, *The Russian City Between Tradition and Modernity* (Berkeley, 1990), 77–78.

16. Vorderer, *Migration Patterns*, 8, 24; Brower, *Russian City*, 80; Hochstadt, *Mobility and Modernity*; Bradley, *Muzhik and Muscovite*.

17. Bradley, *Muzhik and Muscovite*, 130.

Frequent moves did not mean easy moves, because despite the development of the rail-road, many people still made their way by horse and cart and on foot. The city health physi-cian of Saratov, one E. Ershov, took this testimony from a peasant who had come from Kazan, a good 400 miles south on the Volga:

> I left home on 7 January and went along the Volga all the time, sometimes alone, some-times in peasants' co-operatives (*artely*) with fellow-countrymen and other travelers. Ate whatever came into my hands. Spent the nights in the villages, they have nightshel-ters everywhere nowadays wherever you go. They are afraid of letting our brothers in peasant houses. It is dirty in the nightshelters, dark. . . . There you drag on the damp floor. In the morning you take your knapsack and again with the Lord to the next shel-ter. There, you see, again fifty people, some of whom sleep on the floor, and some up-stairs. Everybody driven by need. Well, so am I. I am going for the seventh time. . . . People are from all ends of the earth, from Saratov, from the north, and from Astra-khan', kalmyks, cossacks, other fellows, my brother—*Kazanets*—many of all of these. Up to 30,000, they say. We work until November, until the frost starts, up to the weather.[18]

Newcomers provided labor for the industry and commerce that built and expanded the great and lesser cities. Yet cities were distinct from one another in two important ways, the first being the language, ethnicity, and religion of those who moved in the vast Empire. Jews became much more urban during this period, actually constituting the majority of city dwellers in the Pale of Settlement provinces of Vitebsk, Grodno, Minsk, Mogilev, and Volhynia. The census of 1897—which categorized people by language and confession— yields additional insights into the ethnic mix wrought by late Imperial migrations. In Moscow, 97 percent of the residents spoke Russian and 93 percent were of the Ortho-dox faith; St. Petersburg was home to a more international population, of whom 87 per-cent spoke Russian and 85 percent were Orthodox. More significant ethnic and linguistic variations marked the south and east. In Odessa, where only 57 percent of the people spoke a Slavic language and 56 percent were Orthodox, a third of the population spoke Yiddish as its native tongue. Petroleum had made a boomtown of Baku, in which Russian and Armenian immigrants had diminished the proportion of Muslims, so that by 1897, 35 percent of the population was Russian, 17 percent Armenian, and only one-third identified as Muslims. In Central Asian cities like Tashkent, where Turkic and Persian languages dominated and the vast majority of people were not Slavs, just over a quarter of the people

---

18. A. Ershov, *Ocherk chernorabochego dvizheniia v saratovskom krae* (Saratov, 1909), 12; cited in Henze, *Disease*, 40–41.

spoke Russian. In the far reaches of the Empire, it is hard to read how much people mixed or intermarried, although it is clear that Russians depended on those who knew the climate, the water sources, and local markets.[19]

Second, distinct economies attracted distinct groups of people enumerated by their estate, or *soslovie*, the great majority of whom identified as peasants or *meshchane* (petite bourgeoisie). However, these labels do not denote a "castelike rigidity," as Daniel Brower noted some time ago; rather, they were themselves in flux, particularly so forty years after the end of serfdom at the dawn of the twentieth century. Moreover, they worked themselves out on the ground so that the lives of the urban and rural born overlapped. Peasants, indeed especially peasants, took on factory work and meshchane worked at nearly everything—as domestics, semi-skilled laborers, errand boys, and shop helpers.[20] Peasant *otkhodniki*, temporarily released from village life, often became industrial workers.[21] Commercial cities like Kiev, Saratov, and Odessa housed a minority of peasants because work for the meshchane—from shopkeepers to domestic servants—was more abundant; moreover, Jews inflated the proportion of meshchane, as did Armenians in the Caucasus.[22]

Two distinctions mark newcomers to the Russian city. The German adage "city air makes free" did not apply because one's legal relationship with urban life was defined by estate and passport status, even after serf emancipation in the 1860s.[23] For peasants, the vast majority of migrants, the legal bonds with the village were released only slowly. Serfdom survived in vestigial form with the requirement of passports that controlled legal movement; these allowed an absence of three or six months, a year or more. Passports empowered the head of the household, whose permission was required if one wished to depart. Fathers were not always willing to release their sons—much less their daughters—and could always threaten to force their return, as Semën Kanatchikov's father did at one point.[24] In addition, taxes and fees bound peasants to their village. However, redemption

19. Audrey Alstadt-Mirhady, "Baku: Transformation of a Muslim Town," in Hamm, *City in Late Imperial Russia*, 289; "Demoscope Weekly," http://demoscope.ru/weekly/ssp/rus_lan_97.php?reg=17 (accessed May 5, 2012); Patricia Herlihy, *Odessa: A History, 1794–1914* (Cambridge, MA, 1986), 242; Inge Blank, "A Vast Migratory Experience: Eastern Europe in the Pre- and Post-Emancipation Era (1780–1914)," in *Roots of the Transplanted*, vol. 1, ed. D. Hoerder and I. Blank (New York, 1994), 204.

20. Brower, *Russian City*, 26–27. Brower follows the pathbreaking article by Gregory Freeze, "The Soslovie (Estate) Paradigm and Russian Social History," *American Historical Review* 91, no. 1 (1986): 11–36. See also Robert Johnson, "Paradigms, Categories, or Fuzzy Algorithms? Making Sense of Soslovie and Class in Russia," *Cahiers du monde russe* 51, nos. 2–3 (2010): 461–66.

21. Brower, *Russian City*, 24; the proportion of peasantry in Ivanovo-Voznesensk was 68 percent in 1897, Vorderer, *Migration Patterns*, 28.

22. Herlihy, *Odessa*, 248; Hamm, *City in Late Imperial Russia*, 87; Vorderer, *Migration Patterns*, 28.

23. Reginald Zelnik, *Labor and Society in Tsarist Russia: The Factory Workers of St. Petersburg 1855–1870* (Stanford, 1971), 17.

24. Burds, "Social Control of Peasant Labor in Russia, 70–71; Kanatchikov, *A Radical Worker*, 94.

payments for former serfs were reduced in 1881 and tax reforms—the abolition of the poll tax in 1885 and redemption payments in 1905—eased debt. Collective responsibility for village taxes would end in 1903. Consequently, as Joseph Bradley observed, "the paths of peasant movement had become major thoroughfares" by the end of the nineteenth century, revealed in part by the mounting number of passports issued.[25] Once in the city, nonetheless, peasants retained the legal status of peasant, however they earned their bread. As a consequence, legal and financial practices, to say nothing of marriages and ties of friendship, kin, and culture, meant that the home village retained a stronger hold on the city dweller than in Western Europe.

Second, the Russian city was a male arena. In sharp contrast with cities to the west that were in the majority female, Russian cities offered work and dwelling space to men more than to women. Indeed, the settlements with over 15,000 people in 1897 Russia housed nearly 140 males for every 100 females.[26] The newcomers were young men, in the main; in Moscow, which did have a considerable need for women's work, there were only 677 immigrant women for every 1,000 male newcomers.[27] The male world was most exclusive in the heavy industries and construction that became so important in the late nineteenth century, although in the city, peasant men were "everywhere: carting loads of wood into town, selling wares, looking for work with their fellow villagers, and praying at the thousands of shrines and icons . . ."[28]

But not all cities were equally male, and distinct differences existed among different ethnic groups outside of Moscow and St. Petersburg. By 1897, Moscow housed 133 men for every 100 women; Petersburg 120. The differences among ethnic groups in the port city Odessa are telling. There were 120 Russian-speaking men for every 100 women; 159 for those who spoke Ukrainian; but the Jews of the city included more women than men by a slender margin because Jews were more likely to move as a family. In the cities of Central Asia, there were 128 men for every 100 women—about the same ratio for Russian speakers—whereas the larger Asian groups of Turkic and Tajik speakers had more balanced ratios of 117 or a bit more.[29]

In the central and northern provinces especially, women's place was in the village while husbands worked elsewhere, as we discussed in the previous chapter. The bifurcated family

---

25. Bradley, *Muzhik and Muscovite*, 24–25.

26. The exceptions to the West European pattern are Berlin in its days as a barracks city and Rome as a clerical center. Adna Weber, *The Growth of Cities in the Nineteenth Century* (Ithaca, 1965). The exact ratio is 139.6 men to 100 women, Richard Rowland, "Urban In-Migration in Late Nineteenth-Century Russia," in Hamm, *City in Russian History*, 115–18.

27. Bradley, *Muzhik and Muscovite*, 136.

28. Ibid., 63.

29. Herlihy, *Odessa*, 243–44; 1897 census for Central Asian Cities calculated from "Demoscope Weekly," http://demoscope.ru/weekly/ssp/rus_lan_97.php?reg = 17 (accessed May 2012).

achieved a special normality in the populous Central Industrial region of European Russia, where the factories and markets of Moscow and St. Petersburg attracted hundreds of thousands of migrants every year. Founded in village ties and prohibitive urban costs, the divided household meant that husbands without wives and parents without children populated the city. By 1902, twice as many married men as married women lived in Moscow.[30] Relatively few working-class men lived with their wives and children in urban Russia.

Like "birds of passage" that live apart from their families, village migrants shared space and lived sparely.[31] Promoted by the high costs of urban life, the collective living arrangements that characterize migrants in cities throughout the world were intensified in Russia by longstanding peasant practices of joint responsibility (krugovaia poruka).[32] Many countrymen (zemliaki) lived and worked together, like the employees of the Tsindel' cotton mill in Moscow, half of whose 1,500 workers came from a single province in 1899.[33] A quarter of the men in Moscow in 1902 lived in artels that pooled funds to pay rent and to hire someone to cook.[34]

The artel was hardly visible to observers, who were understandably distressed at the terrible housing, deplorable health conditions, and denigrated state of poor urban immigrants. They viewed more clearly the newcomers who overran the urban infrastructure, lived in sewage, drank polluted water, ate bad food and little of it.[35] Yet those who actually moved to the city followed their "best possibilities for income and endurance" and took the space they found, however foul, as their own. Most, particularly women, did not go far, and migration was part of what we can understand as a "spatial practice" of which they took ownership.[36] Susan Vorderer insists that in the denigrating and miserable environment of urban life at the turn of the twentieth century, "one must look to the resilience and courage displayed by ordinary men and women in attempting to overcome appalling conditions and financial hardships that were part and parcel of peasant-workers' situations . . ."[37] Migrant workers, in short, were the heroes of the Imperial city.

---

30. Engel, "Woman's Side"; Johnson, Peasant and Proletarian, 56–57; for comparison with Berlin household composition, see Bradley, Muzhik and Muscovite, 219–20.

31. Piore, Birds of Passage.

32. Timur Valetov, "Migration and the Household: Urban Living Arrangements in Late Nineteenth- to Early Twentieth-Century Russia," History of the Family 13, no. 2 (2008): 163–77.

33. Over one-fifth of the workers came from a single county; Johnson, Peasant and Proletarian, 69.

34. Only 4.4 percent of the women in Moscow lived in artels; Engel, Between the Fields, 151.

35. See, for example, Henze, Disease; and F. D. Nefedov's comments on "the Russian Manchester," Ivanovo, from P. M. Ekzempliarskii, Istoriia goroda Ivanova (Ivanovo, 1958), 1: 133–34, cited in Vorderer, Migration Patterns, 2.

36. See Joan Neuburger, Hooliganism: Crime, Culture, and Power in St. Petersburg, 1900–1914 (Berkeley, 1993); Michel de Certeau, The Practice of Everyday Life (Berkeley, 1988), 77–114.

37. Vorderer, Migration Patterns, 23.

Semën Kanatchikov's arrival in Moscow as a young man, vividly depicted in his autobi-ography, initiated his transition from peasant to urban worker, and then to revolutionary. His tale of arrival in the turn-of-the-century city is as emblematic for Russian history as is that of the stonemason Martin Nadaud, who arrived in Paris in the nineteenth century, for France.[38] Eager to leave home after the death of his mother, Kanatchikov was driven to Moscow in a cart by his father, himself a peasant who earlier had worked in St. Petersburg, living apart from his wife for most of each year until about age fifty. Upon arrival in Mos-cow, the young Semën was stunned by the brightly lit streets, multistory houses, stores, shops, and taverns. "All around us crowds of bustling people, rushing to unknown destina-tions for unknown reasons."[39] Given to the care of a fellow villager, and sharing a cot with Vanka, his guardian's son, Kanatchikov joined an artel of about fifteen men. He recalled being "awkward, sluggish, with long hair that had been cut under a round bowl, wearing heavy boots with horseshoes . . . a typical village youth." His urban colleagues pinched his ears, pulled his hair, and called him names—and so began his transformation into a worker who would dress better and differently, tucking his shirt into his pants, but not his pants into his boots.[40]

Kanatchikov may have chased after stocking-knitters in the Alexander Gardens by the Kremlin walls, and sought (in vain) the attention of milliners and dressmakers, but he seems otherwise to have lived in a world of fellow men—working, fighting, carousing, and exploring city life.[41] He managed to avoid marrying a village woman, despite his father's plea that "I want . . . to have you get married while I'm still alive, so that the house will mean more to you . . . "[42] By contrast, his original roommate Vanka entered into an arranged mar-riage with a woman from a well-off peasant family.[43]

Although less numerous or visible than men, thousands of immigrant women came to cities, particularly to Moscow and St. Petersburg, and as the nineteenth century drew to a close, their numbers grew in proportion to those of migrant men. Only 30 percent of the migrant population in Petersburg in 1869, they were nearly half by 1914. Although men remained in the majority in Moscow until the 1920s, the number of women per 1,000 men climbed to 839 by 1902 and the proportion increased more steeply for migrants of peasant

38. Kanatchikov, *A Radical Worker*; Martin Nadaud, *Mémoires de Léonard, ancien garçon maçon* (Paris, 1976), 79–84.

39. Reminiscent of the villager Emilie Carles' arrival in Paris and seeing people walk so fast, "as if they had just heard their houses were on fire," from Emilie Carles, *A Life of Her Own: A Countrywoman in Twentieth-Century France* (New Brunswick, 1991), 65-66.

40. Kanatchikov, *A Radical Worker*, 8–9.

41. Ibid., 10, 13, 25.

42. Ibid., 36.

43. Ibid., 52.

status.[44] As industrial work expanded, individual women as well as families pushed at the city gates and increasingly received passports to move together.[45]

The largest group of immigrant women was nearly invisible because they worked and lived behind closed doors—these were the domestic servants, the so-called white slaves, who made up about a quarter of the women workers in Moscow after 1900, over 70,700 in 1902 and 92,300 in 1912. Like newcomers to cities elsewhere on the Continent, peasant girls fresh from the countryside took this work out of the need for shelter and employers' preferences for pliable household help; unlike Western European servants, those in domestic work in Russia more often stayed into their middle age, having an average age of thirty-three to thirty-six at the end of the nineteenth century.[46] Indeed, domestic service in Russia, as elsewhere, is still today the quintessential female immigrant profession. It was even more important to the trading city of Odessa, where 45 percent of women workers were servants.[47]

Women immigrant workers, like men, tended to have access to the unskilled and semi-skilled avenues of work in contrast with the native city dweller who could dominate skilled positions in a segmented labor market that persists to this day. They worked especially in tobacco, textiles, and paper production; nearly a third of the factory labor force was female by 1913.[48] In addition, the needle trades occupied many women (about 8 percent of the female labor force in Moscow and St. Petersburg), who lived in dormitories and worked in sweatshops. Nonetheless, skilled tailors who required two to three years of training tended to be city women. Shop assistant and clerical worker positions usually came to the city native. City-born women and men had the inside track, training, and also the "standard of appearance and demeanor" desired by employers for white-collar jobs.[49]

There is no female Kanatchikov to relate her tale, but women's stories can be extracted from researchers' efforts to trace individual trajectories. The most common tale begins with an initial entry into domestic service. Thus began Evdokiia Kulikova's stay in St. Petersburg. After marriage, her husband left for the army, and an unbearable life with her in-laws compelled Kulikova to run away. Her first destination was a small provincial town, where she found work as a cook—then on to Petersburg, where she worked as a

44. Bradley, *Muzhik and Muscovite*, 34; Rose Glickman, *Russian Factory Women: Workplace and Society, 1880–1914* (Berkeley, 1984), 59.

45. In "Social Control of Peasant Labor in Russia," Burds reports whole families deserting village life in the 1890s for Moscow, 64; Engel, "Woman's Side," 361, 363, reports the increase in passports to women; Engel, *Between the Fields*, 67–72, reports the increase in the proportion of women migrants.

46. Glickman, *Russian Factory Women*, 60–61; Bradley, *Muzhik and Muscovite*, 165. Age information from David Ransel, *Mothers of Misery: Child Abandonment in Russia* (Princeton, 1988), 165.

47. Glickman, *Russian Factory Women*, 68–69.

48. Ibid., 75–82, 86.

49. Ibid., 66–67.

chambermaid. What sets Kulikova apart is her chance to receive advanced training and become a tailor, a graduate of Xavier Glodzinski's tailoring courses, where she mastered the creation of women's clothing and underclothes for both men and women. According to the elegant diploma in her file, Kulikova became a first-rate student as she completed "both 'the theoretical and practical course with great success.' "[50] Her sophisticated appearance opened a gap between herself and her erstwhile fellow villagers when she returned home and aroused their suspicion with her fashionable clothing and gold watch.

What does not set Kulikova apart, but rather puts her in the company of thousands, is that she bore a child out of wedlock while in St. Petersburg. She signals the vulnerability to pregnancy of newcomers to the city that has a proven association with the lack of a father or brother nearby.[51] At the turn of the century, about one-quarter of the babies born in Moscow and Petersburg were born out of wedlock—about the same rate as in Paris. Other continental cities had higher rates, but few children were born to single mothers in other Russian cities, towns, or villages; indeed, the rate of such births was usually under 2 percent.[52] Like foundlings everywhere, many of these babies had only a brief existence. Those sent to the Imperial foundling homes in Petersburg or Moscow had only slim chances for a long life.[53]

At the intersection of births to single mothers, the lack of protective parents, and work at low wages lay occasional, casual prostitution and the possibility of becoming a full-time registered prostitute.[54] Women who sold sex in Moscow and St. Petersburg numbered in the thousands at the turn of the century, as in other European cities: thirty to fifty thousand prostitutes worked in Petersburg in 1905.[55] Prostitution was not an ideal career, but a part-time possibility for the underpaid garment worker and the out-of-work domestic or chambermaid who could pick up some money on an evening walk.[56] It is impossible to

---

50. Barbara Engel, "Freedom and Its Limitations: A Peasant Wife Seeks to Escape Her Abusive Husband," in The Human Tradition in Imperial Russia, ed. Christine Worobec (Lanham, MD, 2009), 122. Her trajectory echoes that of many Western European women who managed to stay on in the city—including Jeanne Bouvier, brought to Paris by her mother to work as a servant, who then managed to become a skilled couturiere and thus open a gap between herself and her rural kin. See Jeanne Bouvier, Mes mémoires: Ou 59 années d'activité industrielle, sociale et intellectuelle d'une ouvrière, 1876–1935 (Paris, 1983), chap. 10.

51. Rachel Fuchs and Leslie Page Moch, "Pregnant, Single, and Far from Home: Migrant Women in Nineteenth-Century Paris," American Historical Review 95, no. 4 (1990): 1007–21.

52. Engel, Between the Fields, 126–27.

53. Ransel, Mothers of Misery, 8–30.

54. Barbara Engel, "St. Petersburg Prostitutes in the Late Nineteenth Century: A Personal and Social Profile," The Russian Review 48, no. 1 (1989): 32–33.

55. Glickman, Russian Factory Women, 68; see Laurie Bernstein, Sonia's Daughters: Prostitutes and Their Regulation in Imperial Russia (Berkeley, 1995); Richard Stites, The Women's Liberation Movement in Russia: Feminism, Nihilism, and Bolshevism, 1860–1930 (Princeton, 1978), 178–90.

56. Bradley, Muzhik and Muscovite, 185; Engel, "St. Petersburg Prostitutes," 30; Engel, Between the Fields, 166–67.

know how many hungry women took this option, because data exist only on the full-time card-carrying prostitutes of Petersburg. From them we learn that women did not enter prostitution when they arrived in the city, but rather had been in town for a few years. Nonetheless, they were disproportionately daughters of the peasantry. A large proportion had a background in that quintessential migrant occupation of domestic service—according to one 1890s survey, over 40 percent had worked as domestic servants, the vast majority as a lowly maid of all work. In these ways, they resembled their sisters in Western Europe.[57]

Both men and women operated insofar as possible in networks of contact and friendship as they did elsewhere in Europe. Semën Kanatchikov, like Martin Nadaud in Paris, was sponsored by his father and followed village practice when he arrived in Moscow; Evdokiia Kiseleva went to St. Petersburg, where she joined her sister, as did Juliette Sauget when she joined her sister in Paris.[58] And when an immediate tie was not available, some newcomers tested what the sociologist Mark Granovetter calls the strength of weak ties: just as Jeanne Bouvier, fired for the third time in a month and alone in Paris, remembered that her mother had a distant relative in the city, and then presented herself at the family door, so did Kanatchikov—newly arrived and absolutely friendless in St. Petersburg. Kanatchikov remembered that his "father used to talk of a distant relative who lived in Petersburg and who had once been married to his sister (my aunt) and who had remarried after she died . . . this relative too was a pattern-maker by profession. But I had never laid eyes on either my deceased aunt [or her husband] in my life." Nonetheless, he was greeted with great warmth and open arms and offered a place to stay until he found work.[59]

By the time World War I disrupted life in Petersburg and western Russia, Kanatchikov would be long gone—exiled to his home village, then sent to Saratov under police surveillance, and subsequently exiled to the Far North for three years before winding up in Irkutsk, where he lived until the Revolution. In his absence, the war and revolution would transform urban life. Petersburg, renamed Petrograd in 1914 as a patriotic gesture, experienced significant in-migration during the war from workers, on one hand, and refugees, on the other. The municipal census of 1915 showed a gain of 413,000 over 1910.[60] Workers came to support manufacturing once industry was adapted for war, and refugees from border regions sought safety behind the lines of conflict. In addition, some interior cities such as Moscow swelled with factory workers and their families relocated from more vulnerable cities, a case in point being the Provodnik rubber factory that brought from Riga the family of teenaged Eduard Dune, on whose memoirs we draw in chapter 5.

57. Engel, "St. Petersburg Prostitutes," 26–28, 39–40, 42; see also Bernstein, Sonia's Daughters.

58. Kanatchikov, A Radical Worker, 6; Nadaud, Mémoires de Léonard, x; Fuchs and Moch, "Pregnant," 1007; Engel, Between the Fields, 126.

59. Kanatchikov, A Radical Worker, 82–84.

60. Peter Gatrell, Russia's First World War: A Social and Economic History (London, 2005), 167.

While the country was at war, heavy industry and cities expanded. The number of met-alworkers recorded by the tsarist factory inspectorate rose from 347,000 at the beginning of 1915 to 546,100 at the beginning of 1917 (an increase of 66.5 percent). Inspectors' data for Moscow province show an increase in the number of factory workers from over 381,000 in 1914 to over 411,000 two years later. The tsarist Special Council on Fuel Supply tracked an increase of coal miners in the Donbas coal region from over 180,000 to over 280,000 during 1915 and 1916. Wartime shortages, the overthrow of the tsar in February 1917, unemployment, and the possibility of land reform would send working people back to the countryside, in a prelude to the further emptying of cities after the October Revolution.[61]

Urban Ebb and Flow, 1917–39

City people in northern food-importing areas fled during the Revolution and Civil War, driven out by the lack of foodstuffs and fuel. In a country where the elites had heralded the increase of urban population as a sign of progress and modernity, its reversal signified utter disaster. Moscow lost about half of its two million people between May 1917 and 1920 and Petersburg's population declined even more, from 2.5 million to about 700,000. Southern second-tier cities in more fertile regions like Odessa, Kiev, Saratov, and Ekaterinoslav lost proportionally fewer people.

Who left the cities? We learn from careful research by Diane Koenker that those who departed were in the majority working adult men and a good number of women, judging from the loss of over 56,000 female domestic servants from Moscow by 1920. The long-standing practice of service for country girls and women suggests that the workingwomen who departed were country people. This is also true of the men who had gone missing by 1920, so that those who returned to the countryside had the closest ties there—unskilled recent migrants, servants, and unemployed dependents. The Russians who left the cities in times of strife did so by a widely shared logic: they went to a more certain supply of food. Moreover, they went home in anticipation of the benefits of the division of large landhold-ings that may have come from the Revolution.[62] Connections with the countryside—maintained in tsarist Russia by custom and village obligations—paid off in this crisis.

---

61. L. S. Gaponenko, *Rabochii klass Rossii v 1917 godu* (Moscow, 1970), 47–51, 54–55, 68–69.

62. Koenker, "Urbanization and Deurbanization," 436–43. Some southern and eastern cities in less con-tested areas like Khar'kov, Rostov-on-Don, Baku, and Tbilisi actually gained population. Daniel R. Brower, " 'The City in Danger': The Civil War and the Russian Urban Population," in *Party, State, and Society in the Rus-sian Civil War: Explorations in Social History*, ed. Diane P. Koenker, William G. Rosenberg, and Ronald Grigor Suny (Bloomington, 1989), 61.

In the 1920s, people returned to the cities, expecting to find work. Some did and some did not. On the one hand, thanks to NEP, consumer goods industries rapidly expanded production—and their labor force—to meet the upsurge in consumer demand. On the other hand, the demobilization of several million soldiers and the return of rural folk to the cities in addition to the introduction of protective legislation put women and juveniles at a disadvantage in the labor force. "The combined effect . . . was to produce the paradox of unemployment rising at the same time as the number of workers employed also was increasing." Women accounted for 62 percent of unemployed workers who registered with the Moscow Labor Exchange in June 1922. Nationally the proportion of unemployed workers who were women—nearly 43 percent in January 1924—far exceeded their participation in the labor force.[63] For the remainder of the NEP period, 1924–28, landless peasants and seasonal workers comprised the main contingents of migrants to the city. This was exactly the moment, in 1927, when the peasant-born Aleksei Stakhanov left his native village in Orel province to try his luck as a coal miner in the Donbas. He would go on to become the most celebrated worker in the country, lending his name to a party-promoted movement to raise labor productivity among both workers and peasants.[64]

In the 1930s, when urbanward migration diminished in Western and much of Central Europe, it exploded in the Soviet Union. The movement that built and expanded cities broke all the records, and is perhaps the highest rate of urbanization in human history. Moscow's population doubled between 1926 and 1939. Newcomers spilled over into its suburbs, overwhelming the green belt surrounding the city. Most cities in industrial areas such as the Dnepr-Donbas region of the Ukrainian republic, the Urals, and the Kuzbas region of western Siberia more than trebled in population. No less prodigious was the expansion of cities along the Turkestan-Siberia Railroad. The industrial town of Novosibirsk, founded in 1893 as Novonikolaevsk, had three times the inhabitants as twelve years earlier. Khabarovsk, at the eastern end of the country 19 miles from the Chinese border, nearly quadrupled in population; the Black Sea resort town of Sochi increased fivefold.[65] In these cases, migration was responsible for almost all of city growth.

Between 1928 and 1932, the years of the First Five-Year Plan, nearly 12 million people, net, entered cities in the Soviet Union. In the peak year of 1931, 4.1 million added

63. Lewis H. Siegelbaum, *Soviet State and Society between Revolutions, 1918–1929* (Cambridge, 1992), 104–5.

64. See Lewis H. Siegelbaum, *Stakhanovism and the Politics of Productivity in the USSR, 1935–1941* (Cambridge, 1988).

65. The growth figures for specific cities are for 1926–37, from V. B. Zhiromskaia, *Demograficheskaia istoriia Rossii v 1930-e gody, vzgliad v neizvestnoe* (Moscow, 2001), 69–70; Robert Lewis and Richard Rowland, *Population Redistribution in the USSR* (New York, 1979), 216–17; Lewis and Rowland, "Urbanization in Russia," 207–8. Material on Moscow's suburbs is from Timothy Colton, *Moscow: Governing the Socialist Metropolis* (Cambridge, MA, 1998), 348.

themselves to urban populations—10.8 million arrived and 6.7 million departed.[66] They came from all over and went all over. Villagers from Uzbekistan and Tajikistan made their way by train to the Gorky automobile plant in Nizhny Novgorod; Bashkirs, Tatars, Kazakhs, and Ukrainians found work in Magnitogorsk and other industrial sites beyond the Urals; "hairy muzhiks," derided as bumpkins by urban workers, turned up everywhere.[67] Over a million Jews, long confined by the tsars to the little towns (shtetlach in Yiddish) of the Pale of Settlement, headed for the big cities of the Soviet interior—"not any less of a migration than the voyage from Odessa to Palestine or from Petrograd to New York," in Yuri Slezkine's words. Moscow boasted a quarter of a million Jews by 1939, up from 131,000 in 1926 and only a little over 15,000 in 1912.[68]

The New Industrial City

Powerful forces were at work to produce such unprecedented mobility, the first of which were the new projects for industrial expansion that fueled the First Five-Year Plan. In 1931, the metals city of Magnitogorsk had nearly 200,000 people, the coal center of Karaganda in Kazakhstan 96,000, and the coal town of Novokuznetsk in western Siberia nearly 46,000. By the end of that plan period, an estimated 305,000 labored on construction sites in the Urals, the privileged region for heavy industry.[69] This explosive city growth made for grand urbanization, but Moshe Lewin acutely characterized it as the "ruralization" (okrest'ianivanie) of the cities for the crush of new labor that was perceived, not without reason, as raw and undisciplined.[70]

Soviet industrialization has been labeled as "a chaos belied by the metaphors of planning and a discourse of order, camouflaged by the misleading regularity of statistics, and obscured by Western conceptions of 'totalitarian' control . . . containing within it a series of incompatible logics."[71] For the scholar of mobility, family and regional practices of migration, that is, repertoires, provide one of those logics, and migration regimes of the state another. The two were often, but not always, incompatible. In the words of Kate Brown,

66. Fitzpatrick, "Great Departure," 22.

67. Victor G. Reuther, The Brothers Reuther and the Story of the UAW: A Memoir (New York, 1976), 96–97; Kotkin, "Peopling Magnitostroi," 73–74; the insulting nickname "hairy muzhik" is from document 8 of Lewis Siegelbaum and Andrei Sokolov, eds., Stalinism as a Way of Life: A Narrative in Documents (New Haven, 2000), 34.

68. Yuri Slezkine, The Jewish Century (Princeton, 2004), 216–17.

69. Kotkin, "Peopling Magnitostroi," 81.

70. Moshe Lewin, The Making of the Soviet System: Essays in the Social History of Interwar Russia (New York, 1994), 218–21.

71. Rosenberg and Siegelbaum, Social Dimensions of Soviet Industrialization, xvii.

"motion took many forms—voluntary and involuntary, coerced and induced. People moved in vast, dense clouds or furtively and alone in the dark of night. They left their homes from fear and necessity or out of hope and ambition."[72] Men and women followed their own practices and plans when they were able, and these plans are not always visible to the historian.

Some cities were created from virtually nothing, most famously Magnitogorsk, to be the site of the largest blast furnace in existence. Stephen Kotkin relates that in March 1929 the first party of settlers arrived on horseback "to prepare the snow-covered site for the coming construction season."[73] When the railroad reached the site in June, workers began flooding in and in three years over 200,000 people lived there.[74] Recruiters—instruments of the state's migration regime—came to villages in search of workers, promising advances and free transportation, with mixed success. One peasant remembered, "The rumor that the biggest plant in the world would be built at Magnetic Mountain excited everyone, old and young. It was said that huge numbers of people were going there. Me and my cousin decided to go too."[75] Newcomers found personal contacts more trustworthy, including the young woman Masha Kalinovichka, who went in response to her sister's enthusiastic descriptions of Magnitogorsk; she traveled on borrowed money from another sister. "I could have gone to the employment bureau and got money for the trip," she explained, "but this I didn't want to do, because I didn't like to be under the obligation to stay, if I didn't wish it."[76] Most who came voluntarily to work in the new city eschewed official channels to pursue their own goals and travel by their own itineraries. Some came independently of any organized recruitment and others with compatriots following the longstanding repertoire of peasant seasonal labor. Even official statistics, meant to demonstrate the success of recruitment, could not disguise this because they reveal that recruits comprised only 48 percent of workers arriving in 1931 and less than 30 percent in the two subsequent years.[77] People came and went by the thousands—it seems that in 1930–33, for example, 293,000 workers arrived and 265,000 departed.[78]

Not every new city dweller left the countryside by choice, especially in the early years of the First Five-Year Plan. Hopes for control of one's land, nourished for a time by the

---

72. Kate Brown, A Biography of No Place: From Ethnic Borderland to Soviet Heartland (Cambridge, 2004), 117.

73. Kotkin, "Peopling Magnitostroi," 63

74. "Magnitogorsk, Russia," http://www.macalester.edu/courses/geog61/aritz/history.html (accessed July 18, 2012).

75. N. P. Sapozhnikov, "Kak ia stal domenshchikom," in Byli industrial'nye (Moscow, 1973), 280.

76. Pearl S. Buck, Talk about Russia with Masha Scott (New York, 1945), 91; Kotkin, "Peopling Magnitostroi," 68–69.

77. Kotkin, "Peopling Magnitostroi," 70.

78. Ibid., 83.

Revolution, were destroyed by collectivization. As a result, a spectrum of incentives to depart, from smelling trouble in 1929 or 1930—to use Sheila Fitzpatrick's evocative phrase—
to knowing that one might be persecuted as a kulak, inspired many a departure for urban
work. Other families identified as kulaks managed to move away before they were deported,
and many men found their way to construction sites that were too needy for labor to ask
questions. Like the father of Anna Dubova, who was labeled as a kulak and departed for a
construction site in Podolsk just south of Moscow, some fathers led the way to a worksite,
joined by their wife and children when they were able. Anna Dubova herself joined her married sister in Moscow and successfully hid her family's kulak stigma during her long life.[79]
She, along with the diarist Stepan Podlubnyi, were among the many children of kulaks who
"melted away" by fleeing to the towns, where they found work, concealed their past, and
became wage-earning workers.[80]

Some newcomers were unambiguously forced to arrive, traveling in boxcars and living
behind barbed wire. Desperate for labor, cities like Magnitogorsk claimed peasants assigned kulak status. They became "special settlers" upon arrival. The local official E. A.
Goncharov was told to prepare barracks for 25,000 of them. But, in his words, "they herded
in not 25,000 but 40,000. It was raining, children were crying, as you walked by, you didn't
want to look." They lived in tents.[81] Sheila Fitzpatrick estimates that in "the great departure" from the villages for towns, three to four million (up to a third) of the new arrivals
traveled involuntarily as the result of "dekulakization."[82]

This is not urbanization fueled by the eager city-bound, then, but rather a mixture of
those in search of work and a new life combined with people "squeezed" from the village,
to use Kotkin's verb, by famine or fear.[83] Rurals who in Western Europe experienced a sense
of no future at home also took to the road—but as a consequence of structural shifts in
landholding, employment demands, demographic patterns, and the deployment of capital.[84] Soviet peasants in the 1930s, by contrast, faced conditions that the state engineered.

The great forces that changed human mobility at the time of the First Five-Year Plan in-
tertwined with changes in the family and household. Family, of course, underpins migration repertoires; it provides the most basic ties for those who leave home, voluntarily or

---

79. Fitzpatrick, "Great Departure," 26–27; Barbara Engel and Anastasia Posadskaya-Vanderbeck, eds.,
A Revolution of Their Own: Voices of Women in Soviet History (Boulder, 1998), 28. For a tale of family dissolution
and reassembly with dekulakization, see that of Mariia Nikishova, "Krest'ianskaia sud'ba," in T. I. Slavko,
Kulatskaia ssylka na Urale, 1930–1936 (Moscow, 1995), 158–60.

80. Fitzpatrick, "Great Departure," 25; Jochen Hellbeck, "Fashioning the Stalinist Soul: The Diary of
Stepan Podlubnyi, 1931–39," in *Stalinism: New Directions*, ed. Sheila Fitzpatrick (London, 2000), 77–116.

81. Goncharov is quoted by Kotkin, "Peopling Magnitostroi," 70–71. See also chapter 7.

82. Fitzpatrick, "Great Departure," 33.

83. Kotkin, "Peopling Magnitostroi," 64; see also Kessler, "Peasant and the Town."

84. Moch, *Moving Europeans*, chap. 4.

Figure 2 Tents for newcomers in Magnitogorsk, Anri Vartanov et al., *Antologiia sovetskoi fotografii*, vol. 1, 1917–1940 (Moscow: Planeta, 1986), 98.

not, and historically determines who can depart—single or married, young or mature, male or female. Perhaps more important, families without ties to the land have been more mobile than peasants, so proletarianization has been a crucial force releasing people from their natal village.[85] The attractions of urban construction and industrialization projects in combination with collectivization and hardships in the village meant that millions of young men and women left home for the city. They were more likely than their ancestors in Imperial Russia to leave as single people, a phenomenon reflected in the rising age of marriage.[86] The dramatic legalization of divorce at the request of either partner that had come with the Revolution in 1917 cut people loose to depart as well.[87] The rural family, in short, lost much of its powers of retention.

Moreover, the conditions of housing in the cities discouraged marriage and the formation of extended families.[88] According to census data, the proportion of simple nuclear urban families reached a peak in 1939 when extended and multiple family households were at their nadir. "Migrants who had moved from village to town in the first half of the 1930s,"

85. Moch, *Moving Europeans*, 7; Kessler, "Migration and Family Systems," 144.

86. Kessler, "Migration and Family Systems," 144.

87. Sergey Afontsev et al., "The Urban Household in Russia and the Soviet Union, 1900–2000: Patterns of Family Formation in a Turbulent Century," *The History of the Family* 13 (2008): 187.

88. O. M. Verbitskaia, "Krest'ianskaia sem'ia v 1920–1930-e gody," in *Naselenie Rossii v XX veke: Istoricheskie ocherki v 3-kh t.*, vol. 1, 1900–1939, ed. V. B. Zhiromskaia (Moscow, 2000), 1: 195–97, 211–13.

notes a Russian research team, "had by the end of the decade married and founded families, but had not managed yet to sufficiently secure their position . . . to bring over their parents from the countryside."[89] Nonetheless, over time Soviet urban families managed to accommodate and depend on the helpful *babushka*.[90]

People bound for the cities in this period of intense migration relied on personal contacts in many cases, just as they had in the past. Some joined friends or relatives, sisters in the cases of young Masha Kalinovichka and Anna Dubova. Even official recruiters had the best results with local connections: when a Magnitogorsk recruiter made his pitch at the Frunze Artillery School in Odessa, every hand that went up was from a native of the Urals. Locally known recruiters often had much better luck than strangers because they were considered more trustworthy.[91] Artels redirected themselves to build the socialist city.

Yet artels and long-standing practices such as seasonal peasant work in construction (to say nothing of jumping on the train with one's friends to head for another construction site) indicated repertoires dependent on contacts, friendships, and loyalties. As discussed in the previous chapter, these loyalties irritated state officials who aspired to control the labor force. "We had to smash the artels," wrote one party member, explaining that they were unacceptable because their leadership and wage system were unacceptable: artels were led by old peasants who divided wages according to their own hierarchy. And so, Magnitogorsk introduced individual piece rates to encourage individual performance and brigades to offer new work organization with new leaders. Trade unions and the Komsomol pushed new loyalties. Indeed, the Komsomol became a mass organization in Magnitogorsk in 1930.[92] Fear of reprisal also diminished family and local loyalties. Anna Dubova recounts that no relatives would take in her mother and four dependent children after authorities had identified her father as a kulak and imprisoned him.[93] Their fear of punishment for harboring kulaks was a reasonable one.

The extraordinary turnover at construction site towns like Magnitogorsk suggests that it was so hard to retain workers that, as Stephen Kotkin concludes, "ordinary people seemed to hold all the cards."[94] They certainly voted with their feet by departing, so that while the arrival of labor was not a problem, massive departures crippled the effort to industrialize. In 1931, the site was 30 percent short of workers, and of the 116,703 people who left that year, 90 percent who complied with the required registration of their departure had lived in Magnitogorsk less than six months, 50 percent less than three months. And only

89. Afontsev, "Urban Household," 182, 185.
90. Ibid., 192.
91. Kotkin, "Peopling Magnitostroi," 68–69.
92. Ibid., 77.
93. Engel and Posadskaya-Vanderbeck, *A Revolution of Their Own*, 28.
94. Kotkin, "Peopling Magnitostroi," 86.

about 25 percent had bothered to register their exit.[95] Even Komsomol members fled, down from 11,000 to 5,400 in a year; by January 1934, over 3,500 of these had evaporated. Those who signed a pledge to stay to the end of the First Five-Year Plan left anyway.[96] They may have had the experience of the young man who, inspired by a Komsomol appeal, had gone off to Magnitogorsk in June of 1931. His letter to his uncle Fedia reached the archives:

> Hello, Uncle Fedia. Greetings from Magnitogorsk. Uncle Fedia, we arrived at the place here safe and sound. We sat and waited a very long time for the bus to take us to the place we were going. Toward evening the bus came for us. Brought us to open country and left us. They showed us a tent in which there was nothing except the tent itself . . . So began our camp life. [After four days] they finally gave us something to do: building temporary housing . . . We raised a fuss and handed to the employment office a request to have our agreement annulled, but they came back to us with time conditions: if by June 10 they didn't give us work by trade and did not lodge us in temporary housing and did not distribute overalls to us, then on the eleventh the agreement would be voided. We're waiting until June 15, and no mater what I'm coming back to Leningrad.[97]

This speaks of a dramatic push from the new city, despite the plentiful jobs it offered.

Such towns offered opportunities for work, but little else. At the beginning, they were sites void of infrastructure with filthy hastily built dormitories and scarce food, as reflected in the just-quoted letter that complained that "life here is impossible: first of all, there's no work by trade, they don't give you overalls, the chow is awful, we're living in tents, and the weather is cold and rainy all the time."[98] Yet some stayed on, seeing Magnitogorsk as a city that was bright and new, where people lived simply, but well, and with a mission.[99] When Central Asian cities like Tashkent were transformed into Soviet cities in the 1930s, an infrastructure was in place, albeit inadequate for this city that doubled in size to six hundred thousand by 1939. Moreover, Asian huts, *kibitki*, without windows or doors, housed many European Russians, much to their dismay; after all, they had come to build

95. Ibid., 82–83.

96. Ibid.," 84–86.

97. Document 3, personal letter by a young worker from Magnitogorsk, June 1931, GARF, f. 7952, p. 5, d. 172, ll. 59–60, in Siegelbaum and Sokolov, *Stalinism as a Way of Life*, 34–35.

98. Ibid., 35.

99. Buck, *Talk about Russia*, 91–93. See also John Scott, *Behind the Urals: An American Worker in Russia's City of Steel* (Bloomington, 1989; reprint of 1942 ed.). Scott lived on and off in Magnitogorsk from 1932 to 1938. The same was true of another "socialist city" (*sotsgorod*), Avtostroi, built next to the auto factory that would become GAZ.

socialism, civilize the Uzbeks, and expand the textile industry. European-style housing would have to wait.[100]

The Established City

Established cities like Moscow were another story. They burst their seams with newcomers during the First Five-Year Plan and on throughout the thirties. Moscow's numbers jumped from 2.2 to 3.7 million people during the First Five-Year Plan. These figures do not include its suburbs—counting them, Moscow grew to 4.5 million by 1939 and added 2 million peasants to its population in the process.[101] Industrial capacities mushroomed as heavy industry expanded, but because this was a city with a more varied economy the labor force was more heterogeneous than in the new industrial cities of the Urals and beyond. It was certainly young. Over half of Moscow's men and women in their twenties in the year 1933 had arrived since 1926.[102]

Moscow also attracted a larger proportion of women than the new industrial cities, and more than it had in the past; although the Imperial capital was a male city, Soviet Moscow would not be. Women in their early twenties (ages twenty to twenty-five) surpassed men their age by about ten thousand by mid-1933, and by the beginning of 1937, the city was nearly 54 percent female. Countrywomen continued to take the classic job for newcomers, domestic service, the occupation of over fifty thousand women in 1931 and again in 1933. Industrial jobs went first to the daughters of the urban proletariat, echoing the widespread and long-standing pattern of women's urban work. A few young peasant women went directly into factories, like Vera Ivanova, whose father worked in a steel plant where the plant manager was desperate for laborers.[103] Heavy industry offered the highest wages and most prestige.

Because Moscow had a longer history of human connections with migrating peasants than the new industrial towns, community and family ties played a larger role in its growth. Muscovites recalling their arrivals in the city recounted family tales to David Hoffmann. Many had a relative waiting—for Ivanova, her father; for the steelworker Aleksandr Korneev, his brother-in-law; and even for Evgenii Kostin, who came to Moscow in flight from collectivization, his uncle. Indeed, Anna Dubova, who joined her sister in Moscow when her family had to flee, chose that city because her sister was there. When Nadezhda Kuznetsova arrived at the age of sixteen in 1933, she not only lived with relatives but also

---

100. Stronski, *Tashkent*, 49–50.
101. Hoffmann, *Peasant Metropolis*, 7.
102. Ibid., 42.
103. Ibid., 43, 118, 119.

as in her home village, in a wooden house without electricity or plumbing, on a muddy street on the outskirts of the city, where the family grew much of its food in its own garden.[104]

Kuznetsova's situation reflects a more general phenomenon. Not only did long-standing practices of chain migration and gathering relatives in urban destinations continue in Soviet Russia, but they did so partly because the urban housing stock was completely inadequate. The most recent assessment of the urban household in twentieth-century Russia notes that the proportion of solitaries was lowest in the 1930s when housing was most scarce because of so many people moving to cities combined with "low investment in civil construction." The same conditions worked against forming extended families, despite the need to gather together because people had so little room.[105] New towns suffered from an almost complete lack of shelter in the beginning, before barracks sprang up; newly Soviet cities like Tashkent had almost nothing for settlers from European Russia. In the great, old city of Moscow 4 million square meters of housing were constructed in 1926–36, but the space per capita still dropped, from 5.9 square meters in 1928 to 4.2 in 1935.[106]

Where did newcomers live? Many families lived in communal apartments converted from the individual family apartments of prerevolutionary days, sharing a kitchen, bathroom, and sometimes their one room with other families. Others resided in factory-built housing because factories had the resources and the immediate need to accommodate newly arrived workers. Some of these were residences of rooms along a hallway, others were barracks, and they "generally," in Hoffmann's estimation, lacked plumbing. Shared kitchen facilities and shared rooms for sleeping were the norm, and inhumane squalor prevailed in these lodgings.[107]

Newcomers were often separated from established workers by policy and by social organization, especially during the early 1930s. Unincorporated suburbs, settlements, and shantytowns, known for their lack of infrastructure and for their lawlessness and lively social organization, typically accommodated new migrants. The outskirts of Moscow were no exception in the early 1930s; recently arrived peasants settled in the outer reaches of the city, so that while the population of the city center remained steady, the outlying industrial areas boomed and the suburbs beyond Moscow swelled. These regions housed a labor force and cultures that were marginal to the new Soviet ways since they largely sustained peasant loyalties, norms, values, and culture. Their denizens did not attend the theater or

---

104. Ibid., 32, 119, 107, 127.
105. Afontsev, "Urban Household," 190.
106. Hoffmann, *Peasant Metropolis.*
107. Ibid., 137–41.

ride in the metro, go to museums, or read much, particularly because it was a long way to work and there were no electric lights by which to read.[108]

The primary study of the formation of the Moscow working class in this period contends that artels of rural origins continued to have influence throughout the 1930s, whereas the primary study of the new city of Magnitogorsk contends that the political struggle to defeat the artels was largely successful.[109] Clearly the artels were of an "incompatible logic" with the goal of uniting Soviet workers on the basis of class rather than village or regional origin. Nonetheless, the different contentions of the two studies reflect the distinctions between the new industrial city, built from nothing and located in the Urals, and the centuries-old capital city. In one case, voluntary, recruited, and coerced workers were from a broad sweep of origins, largely from villages outside the Urals, all of whom were new arrivals; in the other, a more focused set of origins gave rise to newcomers set apart in housing and urban geography from their fellow workers. No wonder their identity was more difficult to erase.

The Passport and *Propiska*

The Soviet state reacted to the sheer, unprecedented—and uncontrollable—volume of human movement with an aggressively restrictive regime of migration containment. In the summer of 1931, the state introduced the practice of organized recruitment (*orgnabor*) to recruit peasant manpower for specific industrial and construction projects, especially in undesirable locations.[110] More sweepingly, the internal passport became the legal requirement for residence in border regions and an expanding list of important cities, labeled "regime cities," at the end of December 1932. Whereas in the tsarist era passports were distributed locally to enable peasants to move, in Soviet times they would be bestowed on urban adults. This hallmark of internal migration policy, as Gijs Kessler has pointed out, was essentially improvisational, responding to the famine that had peasants fleeing the villages by the hundreds of thousands in the winter of 1931–32.[111] In an effort to stop peasants from heading for the city and to police the urban population, the Central Executive Committee and

108. Ibid., 129–39. The vast historical and sociological literature on shantytowns may begin with Janice Perlman, *The Myth of Marginality: Urban Poverty and Politics in Rio de Janeiro* (Berkeley, 1976), and continue through *Paris-Banlieues: Conflits et solidarités: Historiographie, anthologie, chronologie, 1788–2006*, ed. Annie Four-caut, Emmanuel Bellanger, and Mathieu Flonneau (Paris, 2007).

109. Hoffmann, *Peasant Metropolis*; Kotkin, "Peopling Magnitostroi," 99, n. 93.

110. Orgnabor was the product of a resolution of TsIK and Sovnarkom of June 30, 1931. See Fitzpatrick, *Stalin's Peasants*, 97–99.

111. Gijs Kessler, "The Origins of Soviet Internal-Migration Policy: Industrialization and the 1930s Rural Exodus," in *Russia in Motion*, 76.

Council of People's Commissars introduced internal passports—available only to working urban citizens in possession of a residence permit (*propiska*).

The goal of the passport was exclusion—to keep certain kinds of people out of certain kinds of places. Passportization represented the Soviet equivalent of redlining, zoning, property covenants, gated communities, and other practices. These passport laws were subsequently modified to designate more "regime cities." Initially applied to only Moscow, Leningrad, and Khar′kov (the latter because of the heavy inundation of peasants from surrounding areas suffering from famine), the number increased to eleven by April 1933 and eventually to twenty-eight cities. Some twelve million residents of regime cities received passports by August 1934. The document showed the name of the bearer, along with age, nationality, social position, permanent residence, and place of employment. When first introduced, passport registration caused thousands of people to leave the "regime" cities because their social position rendered them ineligible or they anticipated being deported. Some indeed were deported as we discuss in chapter 7, others escaped beyond the 100-kilometer radius beyond which residence was permissible. Passports mark Russia to this day and privilege some citizens over others.[112]

Nonetheless, the passport was not entirely effective as a mechanism of control; that is, country people continued to find their way to the city. Many traveled as noncollectivized peasants (*edinolichniki*), not bound by kolkhoz rules, others by legally going out for temporary work, on otkhod. Still others obtained passports and urban registration "by informal means" after being hired at the gate by a new employer, leaving the collective farm without permission, or staying on in town after military service or education.[113] Where there was a will, there were many ways, and consequently, by 1934, peasants were increasingly finding their way to cities once again. Almost twelve million newcomers arrived in cities in that year, and cities showed a net gain of two to three million in 1934 and 1935. About 3.6 million kolkhozniki left the collective farms to work in towns, 1935–37, and in addition over four million workers aged sixteen to fifty-nine were on otkhod every year in the last half of the 1930s. Nonetheless, this was a stream of migrants to the city, no longer a flood.[114]

The Bogomolova sisters were among the kolkhozniki in the city in the late thirties. They arrived in Moscow in 1938 at ages ten and fourteen along with their mother and three brothers, once the kolkhoz assembly agreed to let them go, following their father, who had

---

112. Fitzpatrick, *Stalin's Peasants*, 92–96. On passportization, see Natalie Moine, "Passportisation, statistique des migrations et contrôle de l'identité sociale," *Cahiers du monde russe* 38, no. 4 (1997): 587–600; Paul M. Hagenloh, "'Socially Harmful Elements' and the Great Terror," in Fitzpatrick, *Stalinism*, 295–300; Paul Hagenloh, *Stalin's Police: Public Order and Mass Repression in the USSR, 1926–1941* (Washington, DC, 2009), 119–32; and David R. Shearer, *Policing Stalin's Socialism: Repression and Social Order in the Soviet Union, 1924–1953* (New Haven, 2009), 192–203.

113. Fitzpatrick, "Great Departure," 32.

114. Ibid., 31.

ceased his function as a brigade leader to take up work in the Moscow locomotive depot. Compared with rural life, they attested, "Moscow was like heaven on earth," despite the fact that the entire family lived first in a railroad car, then a barracks, because they did not go hungry.[115] About the same year, Aleksandr Pavlovich Zavadenko traveled to Leningrad at about age fifteen as a beneficiary of the Soviet educational system. He took the train from Crimea in order to attend mining school, leaving his family that had fled from famine first east then south. Zavadenko remembers being afraid of what city life might bring, but a woman on the train assured him that he would be all right. And he was: with free student passes to concerts and museums, he felt settled at the center of civilization. And he got by with a little help from his parents, a stipend, student cafeteria meals, and earning on the side by unloading at the Moscow station and packing at bakeries. "So," he concluded, "you could live there."[116]

The inflated movement to the cities in the early 1930s did not set the tone for the decade; rather, the exceptional pace of migration diminished after the first few years. Nonetheless, this mobility and the extreme steps of intervention taken by the state demonstrate that one feature of Soviet migration would endure: that is, the existence of two logics, side by side. On the one hand, the state, with some inconsistency, improvised to manipulate at least, control at most, its citizens with passports, labor policies, and official labor recruitment that together constituted its migration regimes. On the other hand, people sought to preserve their family groups, their lives, and their livelihoods by operating in long-standing or improvised practices and using the networks available to them to get to a city when it offered a higher standard of living, employment, personal contacts, the chance for advancement, or at least anonymity.

Rural-to-Urban Migration in Wartime and the Postwar Years

Russia's experience of World War II differed from that of the First World War at least in the fact that its cities not only did not swell with migrants from the countryside, eager to take advantage of increased demand for labor, but, on the contrary, shrank. Evacuation and flight, aerial and ground bombardment, occupation by the invader, and the systematic killing of Jews were the primary reasons for the almost complete destruction and massive depopulation of cities in the European part of the country. These included the Ukrainian cities

---

115. "Bogomolovy Polina Filippovna i Mariia Filippovna," http://iremember.ru/mediki/bogomolovi-polina-filippovna-i-mariya-filippovna.html, 1 (accessed August 31, 2012).

116. Aleksandr Pavlovich Zavadenko, http://iremember.ru/letchiki-istrebiteli/zavadenko-aleksandr-pavlovich.html, 1 (accessed October 22, 2012).

of Kiev, Khar'kov, L'vov, and Odessa; Minsk and Vitebsk in the Belorussian SSR; and Kalinin, Novgorod, Orel, Pskov, Rostov-on-Don, Smolensk, Voronezh and many smaller cities and towns in the RSFSR, to say nothing of besieged Leningrad and nearly obliterated Stalingrad.

To be sure, cities east of the Volga grew. "As Kiev, Minsk, and Stalingrad were leveled by bombs," writes Paul Stronski, "Tashkent ironically underwent unprecedented development."[117] It was not alone. Other cities in Uzbekistan, Kyrgyzstan, and Kazakhstan absorbed large numbers of evacuees, as did Novosibirsk, Cheliabinsk, Nizhny Tagil, and other cities in the Urals and Siberia.[118] Nevertheless, overall urban population declined sharply until 1943, after which some increase—at least in the RSFSR—is noticeable.

The end of the Great Patriotic War occasioned three distinct changes in patterns of rural to urban migration. First, it significantly reduced and then reversed the eastward flow of migrants. Second, it precipitated the return home of seven million demobilized soldiers by September 1946.[119] This, coupled with the simultaneous recruitment of young women from the countryside for work on reconstruction projects, reduced the rural gender imbalance, which had stood at 1.8 women for every man during the war. Third, it was accompanied by the reimposition of a policy of limiting collective farmers' garden plots that virtually guaranteed mass rural impoverishment and thus provided a major incentive for quitting collective farms altogether.[120]

Quitting is what substantial numbers of collective farmers did, including many who had just returned from the war. They took advantage of a trio of opportunities: enrollment in trade schools (FZO—fabrichno-zavodskoe obuchenie), whose graduates were assured of jobs in industry; organized recruitment that, although intended as temporary, often served as a one-way ticket out of the village; and resettlement to another part of the country, including the recently annexed territories of southern Sakhalin Island and Kaliningrad. According to recent Russian studies citing Ministry of Agriculture archival sources, recruitment predominated over self-departure. Of the 768,000 who left kolkhozes in the Russian republic in 1949 for permanent work in industry, 80 percent went through recruitment channels, a proportion that did not change appreciably in 1950. In the latter year, 1.3 million people were recorded as leaving rural regions, which, taking into account births, deaths, and the

---

117. Stronski, *Tashkent*, 96. Tashkent's population grew from approximately 600,000 before the war to as many as 750,000 by June 1942 and even more by 1944.

118. The urban population of the Urals rose by more than a million between 1941 and 1945, or roughly 20 percent; in Siberia the increase was a more modest 14 percent. V. A. Isupov, "Demograficheskie protsessy v tylovykh raionakh Rossii," in Zhiromskaia, *Naselenie Rossii v XX veke*, 2: 84.

119. See soldiers' trajectories in chapter 5.

120. O. M. Verbitskaia, "Migratsiia sel'skogo naseleniia," in Zhiromskaia, *Naselenie Rossii v XX veke*, 2: 277–78; L. N. Denisova, *Zhenshchiny russkikh selenii: Trudovye budni* (Moscow, 2003), 245–48.

few who arrived in the countryside, meant a decline in the rural population of some 540,000. In all, industry and other urban-based institutions recruited three million people from the countryside during the years 1945–50. Collective farms in the Central Economic region (the twelve oblasts around Moscow) lost proportionately more people than anywhere else in the country. In the Iur'ev-Pol'skii district of Vladimir oblast', for example, 40 percent of the able-bodied collective farm population left in the years 1949–51.[121]

Rarely do these people have the opportunity to relate their stories of migration other than to relatives and friends, but thanks to Piatachok (The gathering place), Aleksei Kha-niutin's documentary film from 1987, we get to hear a few. Vera Ivanovna Isaeva tells the camera that in June 1950 she and other girls were working in the fields clearing stumps when they saw a car approaching. By the time she arrived home, an older man ("patron") was already signing up recruits for a construction project in Moscow. Vera has fond memories of the dormitory room that she shared with three families upon her arrival in the capital. "It was like a fairy tale; there were no fights. Everyone was so friendly!" she recalls. "Muscovites," by contrast "hated us. They called us 'country girls' (niushki). . . . 'OK,' I would say, 'so you're not a niushka. What then do you eat? What do you live on that a niushka has not grown?' And they were silent." Similarly, no Muscovite would take up her invitation to join her construction brigade that worked "evenings and nights" building the twenty-five-story Leningrad Hotel next to the Kazan Station. It clearly still rankled with her that when she stood in line for provisions people would call her names like "niushka" and "dirty sow." "Go stand in another line," she would tell them, at least in her memory. Vera got her revenge, though, when one day she intentionally tipped over a bucket of wet cement onto a passerby who had been taunting her and others, and then stood up to the scolding she received from her foreman ("Ok, girls, which one of you has been hooliganizing?").[122]

The other migrant from these years who appears in the film, Anna Sergeevna Soboleva, seems far less resentful and combative. She recalls with amusement how much of a country bumpkin she felt when she first arrived at Moscow's Belorussian Station in 1946 with her husband and two children straight from her native village in Smolensk oblast'. "I had been told about things in the city, but I couldn't have imagined what the metro would look like, how tall the buildings would be and why people didn't fall from their great heights." Words she saw on the street such as "atelier" and "cable" were new to her. So too were the movies, of which she recalls seeing The Swineherd and the Shepherd (1941) and Six O'clock in the Evening after the War (1944). Like Vera Ivanovna, Anna Sergeevna lived in a crowded dormitory room.

121. Denisova, Zhenshchiny, 246–48; Verbitskaia, "Migratsiia sel'skogo naseleniia," 285.
122. Piatachok (Aleksei Khaniutin, dir., 1987). The film is available online at http://films.academic.ru/film.nsf/9498/Пятачок in six parts. The relevant sections are part 3 (2:20–3:20) and part 4 (4:00–7:00).

She eventually left her husband, but found love again at an advanced age when she met a man, also unhappily married, at the piatachok in the great glade of Ismailovskii Park.[123]

Leaving the Village after Stalin

The pace of out-migration from the countryside relented in the mid-1950s thanks to the Khrushchev reforms that somewhat lightened the burdens of collective farm members. In 1952 slightly more than a million people migrated to cities within the RSFSR, and 1.6 million arrived in 1953, but by 1956, only 610,000 did so. The majority fell within the ages of fifteen to twenty-nine and included those seeking technical and higher education as well as jobs in construction and industry. As a result of the privileging of men among recruits to industry, they exceeded women among migrants from the countryside, usually by 5 to 10 percent.[124] This only exacerbated the rural gender imbalance in this country devastated by war deaths. For every 100 men that the 1959 All-Union census recorded among the rural population of the Central Economic region, there were at least 127 (in Tula oblast') and as many as 141 (in Kalinin) women.[125]

Not all who left their homes traveled from village to city. As we indicated in connection with resettlement, many moved from one rural district to another, that is, from the central oblasts of the RSFSR to borderland territories or more locally. And as we discuss in chapter 4 on career migration, the "Thirty Thousanders" recruited to stimulate agricultural production in the mid-1950s embodied reverse migration from city to countryside. Moreover, during 1954–56 more than 460,000 people returned home to the countryside in "a number of oblasts of the RSFSR center."[126] Most probably they included students who had finished their courses and for one reason or another had failed to land jobs in the city, as well as young men who had completed military service. Nevertheless, as Ol'ga Verbitskaia notes, "in the Central and especially the Non-Black Earth oblasts, the loss of rural population had reached crisis proportions already by the late 1950s," with Riazan' and Yaroslavl' losing 40 percent of their rural inhabitants and Orel, Briansk, Vladimir, and Ivanovo more than 30 percent between 1939 and 1959.[127]

---

123. Ibid., part 3 (3:55–5:10) and part 6 (3:10–6:00).

124. Verbitskaia, "Migratsiia sel'skogo naseleniia," 282.

125. O. V. Gorbachev, *Na puti k gorodu: Sel'skaia migratsiia v Tsentral'noi Rossii (1946–1985 gg.) i sovetskaia model' urbanizatsii* (Moscow, 2002), 117. Women made up 55 percent of the urban population of the RSFSR according to the 1959 census. See I. P. Ostapenko, "Izmenenie demograficheskogo sostava gorodskogo naseleniia RSFSR v 1939–1959 gg.," in Zhiromskaia, *Naselenie Rossii v XX veke*, 2: 215.

126. Verbitskaia, "Migratsiia sel'skogo naseleniia," 285.

127. Ibid., 288–89. The Non-Black Earth region contains twenty-six oblasts divided among northern, northwestern, central, and Volga-Viatka zones.

Where did people go? They went near and they went far. They contributed to the replenishment of the populations of Moscow, Leningrad, and other European Russian cities depleted by starvation, evacuation, and destruction during the war, and they added to the already burgeoning populations of cities in the Urals, Siberia, and the Far East. They went to cities large and small, although within the RSFSR in the 1950s, the largest cities (those with more than 500,000 people) experienced the greatest influx *proportional* to their preexisting population. In 1951 alone, Moscow absorbed 51,800 new residents and even more the following year. Unfortunately, we do not know how many of them came from rural areas, for interurban migration also occurred. People came to study and to work. The three young women depicted in *Moskva slezam ne verit* (Moscow does not believe in tears, dir. A. Menshov, 1980) did both after arriving in 1956, but at least one of them, Liudmila, sought to enhance her chances of living there permanently by seeking a life partner: "Moscow is a big lottery," she tells Katia, one of her dormitory mates. The third roommate, Antonina, already has met her future husband, whereas Katia ensures her stay by hard work.

In Siberia and the Far East, in-migration—what Russian demographers refer to as "mechanical growth" as opposed to the "natural" kind through birth—drove up Novosibirsk's population by 28,209 and Cheliabinsk's by 15,300 in 1951 alone. In 1952, the urban population of Khabarovsk krai in the Far East rose by 38,900 because of migration, well above the increase of births over deaths. Siberia's cities experienced net in-migration of 1.4 million people during the 1950s, which accounted for roughly half of their population increase; throughout the RSFSR, the equivalent figure was 10.2 million.[128]

Rural areas leaked people over the next twenty years, during which they lost one-quarter of their total population. In just one year, 1974, 9.9 million people migrated to cities throughout the USSR, 1.7 million moved from cities to rural locations, and 4.0 million resettled from one rural location to another.[129] If in 1959 rural dwellers made up 48 percent of the total population of the RSFSR, by 1979 they comprised just 31 percent. Out-migration of youths, which deprived villages not only of their own presence but also their future offspring, contributed mightily to the decline. Viktor Perevedentsev, the dean of Soviet demographers, discerned three distinct age cohorts among youthful rural-to-urban migrants: 15–16 year olds who left after completing the eighth grade and were entering vocational programs and schools; 17–18 year olds who after finishing secondary school entered higher education or jobs in the city; and 20–21 year olds who, having completed military service, settled in the city either to study or begin working full time.[130]

128. Ostapenko, "Izmenenie demograficheskogo sotava," 209–10.
129. V. I. Perevedentsev, *Molodezh' i sotsial'no-demograficheskie problemy SSSR* (Moscow, 1990), 94.
130. Ibid., 98.

To Soviet planners, radical differences between one part of the country that was short of agricultural labor—say, the Central Economic region—and another such as Uzbekistan that had a surfeit seemed irrational.[131] We have mentioned in chapter 1 the launching of resettlement schemes in the 1970s and 1980s to entice Uzbek and other Central Asian workers to migrate to various regions in the RSFSR. But in contrast to its policy to eradicate unviable or "futureless" villages, which we shall take up below, the Soviet government did not undertake any precipitous or coercive action or even, as far as we know, contemplate it.[132] The state's relative passivity in this respect marks a pullback from the Stalin years and even under Khrushchev when it had enacted more forceful migration regimes.

The share of the urban population in large cities ("millionaire" agglomerations of over one million) continued to increase. If throughout the USSR they contained one in ten of all urban residents in 1959, then by 1987 their share had reached over one in five. By contrast, cities of less than fifty thousand contained 40 percent of the entire urban population of the country in 1959 but slightly under 30 percent by 1987. Since, as Perevedentsev points out, the data do not include residents formally living in rural locations but depending on jobs in cities—a situation common in Moscow oblast', for example—the degree of concentration was underestimated.[133] The agglomerative process occurred despite all efforts by Soviet officialdom to regulate urban growth via passports, residence permits, housing construction policy, and a host of other measures.

These macrolevel observations mask the great variety of situations that drove young people out of the village and into the city. They do not tell us what made one village more vulnerable to out-migration than another, why migrants chose to move to one city rather than another, or for that matter, whether they remained there, moved on, or returned home. Certain mesolevel considerations, however, can reveal important patterns. Verbitskaia notes the significance of proximity to urban areas. Settlements within a two-hour radius of cities lost considerably fewer people than those farther away. In Kalinin oblast', for example, the population of suburban settlements declined by 24 percent between 1959 and the

---

131. In 1974, the RSFSR had the highest rate of rural-to-urban migration in the Soviet Union (47 per 1,000 rural inhabitants) as well as a considerable rate of urban-to-rural migration (23 per 1,000), a combination of movements that bred city growth. The difference between migration to and from cities was greatest in the Belorussian SSR that year, followed by the Russian SSR and Lithuania. By contrast, Kazakhstan and the Central Asian republics had the lowest rates of migration. Ibid., 99. The data do not indicate cross-republic migration such as from the Urals and Siberia to urban-based enterprises in Central Asia. For some estimates, see I. Sh. Mazhinov, "Migratsionnyi obmen Rossii i stran Tsentral'noi Azii," in *Transformatsiia migratsionnykh protsessov na postsovetskom prostranstve*, ed. L. L. Rybakovskii (Moscow, 2009), 304.

132. See Nancy Lubin, *Labour and Nationality in Soviet Central Asia: An Uneasy Compromise* (London, 1984), 47: "Increased Soviet efforts to encourage migration to labour-short areas of the non-Asian USSR continue to meet with little response among Uzbekistan's Asian population."

133. Perevedentsev, *Molodezh'*, 105–6.

early 1980s, but more remote settlements lost 52 percent of their residents.[134] Villagers living within commuting distance of cities, we may surmise, benefitted from opportunities to sell produce from garden plots, work at wage-paying jobs to supplement earnings from agriculture, or vice versa.[135] In these cases, there seems to have been a symbiotic relation between urban and rural. From this observation comes another: garden plots in such locales may have acted as magnets for new arrivals.

There is no substitute for microlevel analysis that takes as its starting point the concrete experience of migrants and the sense they make of that experience. Although less encumbered by ideological strictures than their predecessors, Soviet scholars who studied migration during the post-Stalin period did not incorporate this dimension into their analyses. Even when grounding their work in specific localities and dealing with relatively small numbers of people, they cleaved to the positivistic notion that only by subjecting the complexities of human behavior to data analysis could they draw meaningful conclusions.[136] A case in point is a frequently cited monograph by Zhanna Zaionchkovskaia on new settlers in the cities of Siberia and their degree of rootedness. "Settling down is more easily defined quantitatively than by qualitative means," she affirms. Graced by forty-four tables and twenty-two diagrams among its 164 pages, Zaionchkovskaia's book offers detailed data about the comings and goings of migrants to and from eighty western Siberian towns (of which eight receive close attention). It correlates the longevity of new settlers' residence with their age and gender, level of education, family situation, and skill level upon arrival. It draws on questionnaire results, cross-tabulating them for new and old residents. It indicates that the rural population of western Siberia dropped by 22 percent from 1960 to 1972; moreover, those who moved were more likely to be from the kolkhoz because conditions were more attractive in the outlying agrarian-sovkhoz settlements. These were not black-and-white choices: although two-fifths of rural people agreed that city life is better than life in the countryside, only one-fifth said they would give up the natural environment and quiet life for the city.[137] The study contains not a single reference to, or quotation from, any individual.

One of the dimensions that Zaionchkovskaia does address and that featured even more prominently in the work of rural sociologists such as Tat'iana Zaslavskaia and Liudmila Korel' was gender. The migrants to the city in the 1960s and 1970s differed from their

134. O. M. Verbitskaia, "Demograficheskaia kharakteristika sel'skogo naseleniia v 1960–1979 gg.," in Zhiromskaia, *Naselenie Rossii v XX veke,* 3: bk. 1, 46.

135. See B. S. Khorev and V. N. Likhded, *Zhitel' sela—Rabotnik goroda* (Moscow, 1982).

136. Perhaps, as Jeff Sahadeo has suggested, the Soviet state's animus against informal migration militated against the publication of migrants' personal narratives. Sahadeo, "Accidental Traders," 524.

137. Zh. A. Zaionchkovskaia, *Novosely v gorodakh (metody izucheniia prizhivaemosti)* (Moscow, 1972), 19, quotation at 64, 119, 122–23. We could have chosen almost any sociological study. This one is among the best.

predecessors in the 1940s and 1950s in precisely these terms—they tended to be women. When in 1955 Nina Kozhevnikova of the village of Izmailovka south of Magnitogorsk espied her future husband at a dance, he had just arrived from a secret town to take up a position as tractor driver.[138] Such encounters would be the stuff of some of Vasilii Shukshin's most memorable short stories as well as popular songs of the era, but they are less characteristic of succeeding decades when rural Ninas left for cities, secret and otherwise.[139] The gender historian Liubov Denisova explains the change partly as a function of older women whose lives were marked by hunger and a heavy burden of labor advising their daughters to avoid the same fate—the notorious triple burden of job, housework, and garden.[140] There is undoubtedly something to this, though fathers could prod too. When Zinaida Ivanova was asked in 2010 how her parents regarded her departure for Saratov from a village where she had completed the ten-year school, she recalled that her father told her it was necessary "to acquire something, to study" because "in the kolkhoz you will perish."[141] The expansion of education that provided girls with a range of skills beyond those appropriate to farm work, the slim chances of finding a husband close at hand, and the easing of restrictions on departures also played a role.

Sixty percent of those leaving the villages during these two decades were women, the vast majority of whom were young.[142] In addition to factors already mentioned, long working days, low pay, and hard physical labor drove women away from rural life. In 1984, according to one study, 62 percent of girls who completed secondary school in rural areas indicated their intention of changing their place of residence (most often, leaving the village for the city). Only 20 percent of them cited an agricultural profession, compared with 48 percent of boys.[143] The 1989 census revealed the extent to which a great reversal in the

138. Nina Kozhevnikova, "Unhappy Wife," in *The Women of Izmaelovka, a Soviet Union Collective Farm in Siberia*, ed. Alexey Vinogradov and Albert Pleysier (Lanham, 2007), 72. We use the Library of Congress's transliterated version of the town's name in preference to Vinogradov and Pleysier's.

139. For some stories, see "Grin'ka Maliugin," in Vasilii Shukshin, *Sobranie sochinenii v trekh tomakh* (Moscow, 1985), 2: 108–20; "Styopka" and "Ignakha's Come Home," in Vasilii Shukshin, *Stories from a Siberian Village*, trans. Laura Michael and John Givens (DeKalb, 1996), 46–57, 58–67. For songs, see A. Denisenko, ed. *Sirenevyi tuman: Entsyklopediia zastol'nykh pesen, "blatnoi" i "ulichnoi" fol'klor* (Novosibirsk, 2001), 258–59, 459–61.

140. Denisova, *Zhenshchiny*, 262. On the triple burden, see Liubov Denisova, *Rural Women in the Soviet Union and Post-Soviet Russia*, ed. and trans. Irina Mukhina (London, 2010), 143–50. On its perpetuation into the post-Soviet years, see Hilary Pilkington, " 'For the Sake of the Children': Gender and Migration in the Former Soviet Union," in *Post-Soviet Women from the Baltic to Central Asia*, ed. Mary Buckley (Cambridge, 1997), 131.

141. Oxford Russian Life History Archive: http://www.ehrc.ox.ac.uk/lifehistory, at Oxf/AHRC P-10 DN PF3, Pskov, June 2010, 10. We thank Victoria Donovan for providing the interview transcript.

142. "Novaia informatsiia Goskomstata SSSR," *Vestnik statistiki*, no. 8 (1991): 52. During the years 1960–65 when seven million people left the countryside, six million (more than 85 percent) were in the age group seventeen to twenty-nine. Verbitskaia, "Demograficheskaia kharakteristika," 47.

143. "V pomoshch' agitatoru i propagandistu," *Vestnik statistiki*, no. 9 (1984): 65.

rural population's gender composition had occurred: for every 1,000 men between the ages of twenty and thirty-nine living in the countryside, there were 886 women. In some parts of the RSFSR such as Arkhangel'sk, Vologda, Pskov, and Mordovia, the ratio was more skewed still, falling below 800 women to every 1,000 men.[144] Long gone were the days when the village was "women's land."

The introduction in the early 1960s of compulsory education up to the eighth year (so-called incomplete secondary education) significantly expanded the number of children above grade five.[145] The greater the educational attainment, the less tolerable seemed conditions at home. M. Osipov, chair of the Land of Soviets kolkhoz in Tambov oblast', reported his unsuccessful attempt in 1970 to persuade the mother of a high-school graduate that her daughter should stay put "rather than leaving for some alien place." "Liuba did not finish the tenth class so that she could work on the kolkhoz," the mother categorically replied.[146] For girls, Denisova writes, "the beginning of an independent life was associated with moving to the city and entering a VUZ [higher educational institution]." She quotes one respondent as remarking ("with the pathos of a Chekhovian heroine"), "Yes, to flee, to flee. To Moscow, to Moscow, . . . Everyone would be more educated, there would be museums, and everything if I were to leave the provinces for the capital of our country."[147]

Among rural youth seeking higher education, only a tiny minority got to study in Moscow. Most, like the four children of Jiliana Selezneva, who were raised in Izmailovka, matriculated closer to home. But strikingly, once having left Izmailovka, they did not return. Jiliana's older son received his medical degree from the university in Cheliabinsk but practiced medicine in the Volga automobile city of Togliatti. Both daughters earned pedagogical degrees in Magnitogorsk. One remained there; the other, after briefly returning home, moved to the Orenburg region to take up a position as a principal. And the younger son, following in the footsteps of his older brother, studied in Cheliabinsk, where he worked as a physician.[148] The journeys of Selezneva's sons were reproduced by countless village boys. Writing to Sel'skaia molodezh (Rural youth) in the mid-1970s about a sheep-raising sovkhoz in the foothills of the Caucasus, Vadim Kuropatkin reported on the dearth of shepherds.

---

144. V. Brui and E. Mikhailov, "Nekotorye osobennosti demograficheskoi obstanovki v RSFSR," Vestnik statistiki, no. 7 (1991): 21; T. Levina, "Demograficheskaia situatsiia v sel'skoi mestnosti," Vestnik statistiki, no. 1 (1992): 15.

145. T. I. Zaslavskaia, ed., Migratsiia sel'skogo naseleniia (Moscow, 1970), 242.

146. Mikhail Osipov, "Ia smotriu na molodezh' nastoiashchuiu," Sel'skaia molodezh, no. 6 (1970): 1. Another mother put in more piquantly: "Her father and I spent our whole lives in muck and filth, let Zina do some other work. There's nothing for her to do in the country." Quoted in Susan Bridger, "Soviet Rural Women: Employment and Family Life," in Russian Peasant Women, ed. Beatrice Farnsworth and Lynne Viola (New York, 1992), 290.

147. Denisova, Zhenshchiny, 265.

148. Jiliana Selezneva, "Dedicated Nurse," in Vinogradov and Pleysier, Women of Izmaelovka, 39.

Over the previous five years, only one high-school graduate had signed up and he doubled as the veterinarian. As for the less well educated, "every year we hire two hundred, but two hundred leave by the end of the year."[149] Osipov, the struggling kolkhoz chair, tried his best to talk Valentin Grigor'skii, a high-school graduate, out of departing. "We need people desperately," he reports telling him. "There's more than enough work here." But Grigor'skii had been "hanging around with intelligent people" who made him ashamed of his job as a tractor driver, and so he requested a certificate (spravka) to leave. In the end, Osipov relented.[150]

The departure of young men such as Valentin meant fewer eligible bachelors for rural women, a situation the military draft exacerbated. "Many youths don't return to the kolkhoz from the army," wrote V. A. Shishliakov, chairperson of a kolkhoz in Vologda oblast', to the Communist Party's Central Committee in the mid-1960s. "They are seized by representatives of various construction projects, to where they are sent by the Komsomol and other organizations advertising the romance of any occupation except that of grain tiller on one's own kolkhoz."[151] Shishliakov actually began his letter by referring to the twenty milkmaids, aged eighteen to thirty, who worked on the kolkhoz's four farms. Only one, he reported, "lives with her husband," because "every normal person dreams of and prepares for family life, hoping to find personal happiness in conformity with social interests. But in our conditions such happiness doesn't smile on everyone." And just as "where there is a needle, there will be thread," girls will follow the boys to the city. "No passport regime or endless rhetoric," he concluded, "will stop young people whose personal lives are unsettled."[152]

Thus, it was not a matter of women leaving instead of men, or vice versa; the out-migration of the one made it more likely the other would leave too. As a popular ditty (chastushka) from the Russian republic's Non-Black Earth region had it,

Председателю сказала,	To the chairman I said,
Заместателю скажу:	To the deputy I will say:
«Если парня не найдете,	If a lad you don't find,
Из колхоза ухожу».	From the kolkhoz I will stray.[153]

Even when it was the "lad" who had stayed in the village, the woman was reluctant to return. Eighteen-year-old Valerii Kravchenko and his girlfriend, another Liuba, also eighteen,

149. Vadim Kuropatkin, "Duma o zolotom rune," Sel'skaia molodezh, no. 8 (1974): 3.
150. Osipov, "Ia smotriu," 1.
151. Rossiiskii Gosudarstvennyi Arkhiv Sotsial'no-Politicheskoi Istorii (RGASPI), f. 591, op. 1, d. 164, ll. 131–33.
152. Ibid., l. 133.
153. L. N. Denisova, Ischezaiushchaia derevnia Rossii: Nechernozem'e v 1960–1980-e gody (Moscow, 1996), 141.

are a case in point. As Valerii wrote in a despairing letter to *Sel'skaia molodezh*, he lived on a sovkhoz in southern Kazakhstan, while Liuba lived in the city. Although they saw each other often, they decided they couldn't live apart any longer. But when he proposed that she come live with him, she replied, "Better if you come to me in the city."[154]

From 1959 to 1973 the rural areas of the Central Economic region lost 4.1 million able-bodied people, of whom nearly two-thirds consisted of twenty to twenty-nine year olds.[155] Taking the thirty years between the censuses of 1959 and 1989, Kirov, at the northeastern edge of the region, led the way among sixteen oblasts with a loss of over 700,000 of its 1.2 million rural inhabitants, followed by Pskov, whose rural population dropped from nearly 700,000 to 312,000. The smallest decline was in Karelia, which "only" lost 40 percent of its rural population.[156]

Research on the rural depopulation of the Central Economic region should not obscure departures from elsewhere in the vastness of the Russian countryside, especially Siberia. Between 1959 and 1970, every oblast' in western Siberia except Tiumen' lost rural popula-tion, the decline ranging from 6.6 percent (Tomsk) to 21.2 percent (Kemerovo). To be sure, much of the efflux in the years 1959–62 consisted of former deportees returning to their homelands after the Khrushchev administration lifted Stalin-era prohibitions. But as one Western observer surmised in 1967, "the stream of returning settlers was swollen by many other inhabitants of Siberia who decided to take advantage of the opportunity to exchange the cold and unfriendly taiga for the rich sunny steppes of the North Caucasian region."[157] By 1979 the rural population had dropped a further 10.4 percent. At the same time, the proportion of urban residents rose from 61 to 68 percent, suggesting considerable intrare-gional migration from village to town. Eastern Siberia told much the same story. Between 1970 and 1979, while the urban population increased by 21.5 percent, rural population de-clined by 10.5 percent.[158]

Valentina Anoshina was among those who abandoned her native village in eastern Sibe-ria's Krasnoiarsk krai during the 1970s—in October 1973, as she recalled in an interview in 2010. At thirty-one years old, widowed and with a small child, Valentina traveled over 3,000

---

154. "Vam pis'mo," *Sel'skaia molodezh*, no. 8 (1970): 27.
155. Denisova, *Ischezaiushchaia derevnia*, 141; Gorbachev, *Na puti k gorodu*, 120.
156. Tsentral'noe statisticheskoe upravlenie pri Sovete Ministrov SSSR, *Itogi vsesoiuznoi perepisi naseleniia 1959 goda RSFSR* (Moscow, 1963), 24–27; Tsentral'noe statisticheskoe upravlenie pri Sovete ministrov RSFSR, *Narodnoe khoziaistvo RSFSR v 1989 g.: Statisticheskii ezhegodnik* (Moscow, 1990), 59–61. The decline reflects not only out-migration but also conversion of settlements from village to urban status.
157. Prociuk, "Manpower Problem in Siberia," 196. This theme is emphasized in Fiona Hill and Clifford G. Gaddy, *The Siberian Curse: How Communist Planners Left Russia Out in the Cold* (Washington, DC, 2003), 94–100.
158. V. B. Zhiromskaia, "Naselenie Rossii v 1970-e gg.: Chislennost', razmeshchenie, demograficheskie protsessy," in *Naselenie Rossii v XX veke: Istoricheskie ocherki v 3-kh t.*, vol. 3, 1960–1979, ed. V. B. Zhiromskaia and V. A. Isupov (Moscow, 2005), bk. 1, 257–60.

miles at the urging of a female friend who had gotten a job as a mechanic in a bus and truck depot in Pskov. Valentina became a dispatcher at the depot. At first she lived with her friend, but then moved to a suburb. She found Pskov, an ancient town about 125 miles south-southwest of St. Petersburg, "clean and with plenty of food," although no television. She married and had another child. From time to time, members of her family back in Krasnoiarsk krai visited her, and she once flew home to visit them, traveling from Pskov to Moscow, and thence to Novosibirsk, Krasnoiarsk, and finally North Eniseisk.[159]

Another Siberian, Igor Mitrofanov, wound up in Velikie Luki, the second largest town in Pskov oblast'. Not long after he was born in 1960, Igor and his parents moved to a small town in Kemerovo oblast' in western Siberia where his father oversaw construction of a cement factory. By 1971, however, the project was nearing completion and "we had to move." Did one have a choice where to go, he was asked? One did. Although his father received a position in Belgorod, just north of Khar'kov on the Russian side of the border with Ukraine, he turned it down in favor of Velikie Luki, where his friend had become a police officer. "Best to go where one has acquaintances," Igor remarked.[160]

Whether they had acquaintances or not, young people from all over Russia were drawn to cities because that is where the action was. Letters written to the journal *Sel'skaia zhizn'* (Rural life) in the 1960s by those left behind explained the departure of so many youths as a function not so much of the countryside's lack of well-paying jobs as of its relative poverty and dearth of amenities. "Youth live in boredom and want to leave," was how one letter writer summed up the situation on her kolkhoz in Kirov oblast'. "There is no spiritual life and daily life is primitive," wrote another from Krasnodar krai. The lack of electricity and telephones, badly supplied stores, the remoteness of medical facilities, and poor roads comprised some of the material elements about which letter writers complained. What there didn't appear to be a shortage of was alcohol. "It remains for youth to drink, hooliganize, and think about where they can escape to," wrote a villager in Saratov oblast'. "It is not surprising that we often have drinking bouts," stated a collectively written letter from Voronezh oblast'. "Vodka is the only form of 'entertainment.' "[161]

This litany of despair needs to be contextualized. First, relative to the Stalin era, individual happiness—the desire to lead a more comfortable and fulfilling life in a personal sense—seems to have counted for more. Education and the enhanced awareness it provided of how lives were lived elsewhere played a major role in this respect. Second, the Soviet project of overcoming "backwardness" proved to be a victim of its own success. People

159. Oxford Russian Life History Archive, at http://www.ehrc.ox.ac.uk/lifehistory, Oxf/AHRC P-10 DN PF4, Interview with Valentina Fedorovna Anoshina (July 2010), 1–7.

160. Ibid., Oxf/AHRC P-10 DN PF5, Interview with Igor Vladimirovich Mitrofanov (July 2010), 6–8.

161. RGASPI, f. 591, op. 1, d. 58, ll. 1, 3, 9, 15, 113 (February 11—April 12, 1969); d. 172, l. 8 (1966).

fled their home villages in the 1930s primarily as a means of physical survival, that is, to avoid starvation or being branded a kulak with the likelihood of deportation to a special settlement. From the 1950s onward, sheer physical survival was not nearly as difficult. It was then that people started to notice and complain about the lack of amenities. "One can speak of the formation of a mass consciousness," the historian Oleg Gorbachev has noted with reference to the early 1960s, whereby "without a club, youth leave the village."[162] But many people in the countryside—especially youth—soon adopted still higher standards. "We have attended to the material side of things," the beleaguered chairperson Shishliakov asserted somewhat self-servingly. "[We have] electricity, a radio in each house, ATS [automatic telephone dialing], internal roads, and two clubs."[163] Such items may earlier have signified the arrival of culture, but according to a veterinarian from Kirov oblast' writing in 1965, they no longer did so:

> We are used to talking about culture in the village with words like radios, electricity, clubs, libraries, television, and so forth. But this is now already little. They have become items of first necessity. Nowadays it is an everyday occurrence for a zoologist, agronomist, veterinarian, engineer, or teacher to have higher education. This doesn't surprise us, but try to find an artistic director of a House of Culture or the leader of a choir with higher education in the village. . . . I haven't heard of comrades after finishing the conservatory going to work as director of a club, say, in the village of Ardashi.[164]

Nevertheless, urban living did not fulfill every desire. Denisova cites the following lament uttered by a female migrant:

Эх, куда я залетела,	Where did I fly to,
Куда черт меня занес?	Where has the devil taken me?
Лучше б я жила в деревне	Better to have lived in the village
Работала на совхоз	And worked for the sovkhoz[165]

O. Lykhmanova, who had left her native village with her husband nine years earlier, might have identified with the lament. Writing to party officials, she complained of the lack of suitable accommodation, adding sarcastically that she expected to receive it "when our [yet

---

162. Gorbachev, *Na puti k gorodu*, 97.
163. RGASPI, f. 591, op. 1, d. 164, l. 133.
164. RGASPI, f. 591, op. 1, d. 22, l. 115 (October 1965). Ardashi is a village in Kirov oblast' located about 40 miles to the southeast of the city of Kirov.
165. Denisova, *Zhenshchiny*, 252.

to be born] children will be mamas and papas."[166] But aside from difficulties with housing or other material deprivation, the lament evoked a common feeling of longing (toska) or nostalgia among migrants. Writing to Sel'skaia molodezh in 1970, Neli Osipova, an eighteen-year-old student at a technical school, complained of a lack of friends that was in striking contrast to her former life in far away Yakutiia. "There, where I spent my childhood, [I] had bosom friends with whom I shared secrets and knew all of theirs. But now it is difficult to adjust to new people."[167] Even older people expressed this feeling. "Until the end of my days," wrote the novelist Viktor Astaf'ev (1924–2001), "I will never stop longing for the village. . . . It's like that as well for Rasputin, Nosov, and Belov—we never will stop being rooted in our hearts."[168] Perhaps this is why their fellow village poet Nikolai Rubtsov (1936–71) acknowledged in his poem "Boundaries" the desire to have it both ways—"to live somehow at once in the city and the village."[169]

It is certainly true that the volume of departures had alarmed kolkhoz officials, the rural party apparat, and editors of journals with a rural readership. Their concerns prompted economists, sociologists, and other social scientists to undertake numerous studies of the causes and dimensions of the problem and to suggest a variety of measures to alleviate it. Many recommendations revolved around increasing investment in rural infrastructure to raise the quality of life and expand opportunities for those with professional degrees to practice their professions on sovkhozes and kolkhozes.[170] But such efforts were swimming against a powerful ideological tide. The loss of rural population, far from being a cause for alarm, only confirmed that the country was heading in the right direction toward modernity, that it was overcoming what Marx and Engels had referred to as "the idiocy of rural life." Here, for example, is a typical statement from a collection of articles published by the State Committee on the Utilization of Labor Resources of the RSFSR Council of Ministers in 1973:

> The transfer of labor resources from the rural economy to other branches is the natural consequence of scientific-technical progress in agricultural production. Reduction in the absolute numbers of those working in agriculture and their share in the total number of those employed in the country's economy must be regarded as a progressive

---

166. RGASPI, f. 591, op. 1, d. 164, l. 174.

167. "Vam pis'mo," 27.

168. Cited in Denisova, Zhenshchiny, 252. These were all, like Astaf'ev, village prose writers (derevenshchiki) whose most active period was during the 1960s and 1970s.

169. N. Rubtsov, "Grani," cited and translated in Philippa Lewis, "Peasant Nostalgia in Contemporary Russian Literature," Soviet Studies 28, no. 4 (1976): 564.

170. See for example V. I. Perevedentsev, Migratsiia naseleniia i trudovye problemy Sibiri (Novosibirsk, 1966); Zaslavskaia, Migratsiia sel'skogo naseleniia; V. I. Staroverov, Sotsial'no-demograficheskie problemy derevni: Metodologiia, metodika, opyt analiza migratsii sel'skogo naseleniia (Moscow, 1975).

tendency, since it stimulates growth in labor productivity and raises the technical quotient in agricultural production.[171]

To be sure, the "released labor power from agriculture" was "not always realized in a sufficiently planned manner."[172] In Cynthia Buckley's judgment, the propiska and passport systems to control migration flows to the cities proved to be an "illusion," "a paper tiger of regulations that [officials] could not hope to completely enforce."[173] But at least rural migrants were helping to alleviate the shortage of (especially unskilled) factory and construction workers, a shortage endemic to the Soviet form of the planned economy.

Sometime in the late 1960s, authorities replaced the outright ban on new residents in "regime" cities with the system of time-restricted (usually three-year) residence permits. The system engendered limitchiki, that is, workers who crowded into dormitories that labor-starved enterprises provided along with the permits.[174] How many? Estimates understandably vary. In construction, they may have comprised as many as three of every four workers. They also worked in textiles, metallurgy, automobile production, and other industries performing "non-prestigious jobs which the Indigenous urban population considers undesirable."[175] Overwhelmingly ethnic Russians, limitchiki otherwise resembled immigrants in other countries in the ways they were perceived by locals, the conscientiousness and diligence of their labor, and the techniques they adopted (overstaying "visas," marrying "legals," and otherwise finagling the system) to become permanent residents. As the Russian expatriate sociologist Victor Zaslavsky observed, "any analysis of Soviet society and the Soviet working class which ignored the limitchiks would be as incomplete as an analysis of the German working class which failed to consider the role of the Gastarbeiter."[176]

Moscow and Leningrad of course could not absorb all migrants. Nonetheless, they had a decided preference for large cities (those with more than one hundred thousand people),

171. S. G. Gaiazova, "Nekotorye voprosy migratsii i estestvennogo dvizheniia sel'skogo naseleniia," in Migratsiia naseleniia RSFSR: Sbornik statei, ed. A. Z. Maikov (Moscow, 1973), 88.

172. Ibid., 89.

173. Cynthia Buckley, "The Myth of Managed Migration: Migration Control and Market in the Soviet Period," Slavic Review 54, no. 4 (1995): 911–14.

174. V. M. Moiseenko, "Migratsiia i emigratsiia v Rossii v 1960–1970-e gg.," in Zhiromskaia and Isupov, Naselenie Rossii v XX veke, 3: bk. 1, 115.

175. Victor Zaslavsky, The Neo-Stalinist State (Armonk, 1981), 144–46, 188–89; Ia. A. Davidovich, A. G. Kosaev, and M. N. Podol'naia, "Privlechenie i ratsional'noe ispol'zovanie inogorodnikh rabochikh," Sotsiologicheskie issledovaniia, no. 4 (1981): 123–28; Dietrich Andre Loeber, "Limitchiki: On the Legal Status of Migrant Workers in Large Soviet Cities," The Soviet and Post-Soviet Review 11, nos. 1–3 (1984): 301–8; quotation on 304.

176. Zaslavsky, Neo-Stalinist State, 144–45. For another case of internal migrants widely regarded as aliens, see Leslie Page Moch, The Pariahs of Yesterday: Breton Migrants in Paris (Durham, 2012).

and Moscow and Leningrad took 45 percent of them. Moreover, Moscow's pull extended well beyond its own region—46 percent of migrants to Moscow city and oblast' came from beyond the Central Economic region.[177] Many found homes in suburban towns and villages within commuting distance of Moscow and other large cities. Typically, males went off to the city while females tended to the garden plots and household chores.[178] Inhabitants of "settlements of an urban type" (*poselki gorodskogo tipa*), townlets of no more than three thousand residents dependent on a single factory or institution, straddled urban and rural-based economies in a somewhat different manner.

Soviet cities of the 1960s through the 1980s resembled each other in many ways, not least in the ubiquity of cranes engaged in erecting yet more high-rise, panel-clad, reinforced-concrete apartment buildings or standing idle waiting for the arrival of necessary workers and materials. Unlike in the Stalin era, few cities were entirely new. Even the motor cities of Togliatti and Naberezhnye Chelny, although widely advertised as such, expanded on preexisting towns. Other than cranes, the most characteristic feature of the urban landscape was the microdistrict—self-contained residential areas with educational, recreational, and commercial amenities. The high-rise buildings comprising the microdistricts, while anything but cozy, represented an enormous improvement over most rural housing (as well as the communal apartments of the Stalin era) primarily because they contained separate family apartments furnished with electricity, central heating, and indoor plumbing. The monotony of their appearance became legendary, though it is telling that *Ironiia sud'by, ili s legkim parom!* (Irony of fate, or enjoy the bath!, dir. E. Riazanov, 1975), the movie lampooning their sameness, is set in Moscow and Leningrad rather than mid-sized cities. Summing up Soviet analyses of migration patterns by the mid-1970s, the American economists Robert C. Stuart and Paul Gregory noted that "these studies . . . have tended to settle on the same variables found important in a market economy . . . standard of living differentials [such as] rural-urban wage differentials, availability of good quality housing, [and] the provision of services."[179]

For rural-based officials and others concerned about the depopulation of the countryside, the siren song of the city represented a challenge they could not meet. The fact that kolkhozniki did not have access to passports, which urban residents above the age of

---

177. Gorbachev, *Na puti k gorodu*, 127, 132.

178. See Khorev and Likhded, *Zhitel' sela*, 36–37.

179. Robert C. Stuart and Paul R. Gregory, "A Model of Soviet Rural-Urban Migration," *Economic Development and Cultural Change* 26, no. 1 (1977): 85–86. Stuart and Gregory assert that "males predominate especially in the younger age ranges." But according to the 1970 census, females outnumbered males in both the RSFSR and the USSR among those residing for less than two years in the place where the census was conducted. See Tsentral'noe statisticheskoe upravlenie pri Sovete Ministrov SSSR, *Itogi Vsesoiuznoi perepisi naseleniia 1970 goda*, vol. 7 (Moscow, 1974), 8; and n. 142 above.

fifteen were required to carry, did little to prevent rural-to-urban migration. The extension of internal passportization to collective farmers in 1976 made departures even simpler.[180] This proved to be the death knell for efforts to resuscitate village communities.

While some rural settlements eagerly awaited the clubs, asphalt, indoor plumbing, and other services promised to them, others were condemned as "settlements without a future (neperspektivnye derevny)," their residents correspondingly forced to leave. This is what happened to thousands of communities across the country but particularly in the Non-Black Earth region where, in deference to climate and topography, peasants typically lived in small settlements.[181] In a study devoted to the disappearing villages in that part of the country, Denisova cites the elimination of some 10,000 settlements in Kirov oblast' alone between 1950 and 1980, and the abandonment of 2,000 villages in Smolensk oblast' between 1973 and 1988.[182] Over all, of 142,500 rural settlements in the Non-Black Earth region, 43 percent were determined to have completely lost their productive functions and therefore as far as the state was concerned, their raison d'être.[183]

The policy of rationalizing the distribution of the rural population received the ideological imprimatur of the 1961 Communist Party program. The program projected that the kolkhoz would provide for all its members' needs, thereby obviating the need for private garden plots, and that villages would be "gradually transformed into reinforced population points of an urban type with comfortable housing, municipal services, consumer enterprises, cultural and medical institutions."[184] This came at the time of tremendous optimism in ruling circles about their ability to effectuate transformations that would catapult the USSR to the forefront of modern societies.

The vision survived Khrushchev's forced retirement in 1964 and actually gained new adherents in the 1970s when it seemed to represent an alternative to the total abandonment of the countryside by young people. The resolution of the party's Central Committee passed in March 1974 called for transferring 170,000 families to larger, newly built settlements by 1980.[185] The only problem was that many of the services associated with these

---

180. Mervyn Matthews, The Passport Society: Controlling Movement in Russia and the USSR (Boulder, 1993), 34: "A passport allowed immediate identification, the establishment of family status, etc., and could make travelling easier."

181. Denisova, Ischezaiushchaia derevnia Rossii, 121. According to the 1970 census, 1.5 percent of all villages in the Non-Black Earth region contained more than one thousand inhabitants and they comprised 20 percent of all rural inhabitants; the corresponding figures for the North Caucasus were 18 percent of all villages containing 70 percent of the rural population.

182. Ibid.,144.

183. Ibid., 123–24.

184. Kommunisticheskaia Partiia Sovetskaia Soiuza, Programma Kommunisticheskoi Partii Sovetskogo Soiuza priniata XXII s''ezdom KPSS (Moscow, 1961), 83, 85.

185. Kommunisticheskaia Partiia Sovetskaia Soiuza, KPSS v rezoliutsiiakh i resheniiakh s''ezdov, konferentsii i plenumov TsK (Moscow, 1986), 12: 405.

population points "of an urban type" remained overwhelmingly on the drawing boards of the RSFSR's State Committee for Construction, the Russian Institute of Land Management, and their subordinate oblast' offices. Consequently, when faced with having to leave their homes, many people chose to move to older and larger regional cities rather than some pie-in-the-sky agro-town. Sociologists on the ground found that of every hundred inhabitants below the age of twenty in villages declared unviable, thirty-one indicated a willingness to move to larger rural settlements including those "of an urban type," but fifty-six wanted the real thing—to move to a city.[186] After the initial hoopla surrounding the project, enthusiasm among officials waned. This migration regime never materialized, and by the early 1980s, the Soviet press was openly deriding it.[187] But the point is that nobody needed to tell the residents of small villages scattered across the country that they had no future. They could see it for themselves in the boarded up schools, libraries, and medical facilities, the lack of food deliveries, and even the shutting off of electricity. By the end of the 1970s the Non-Black Earth region had a third fewer rural settlements than in 1959.[188]

The village's loss was the city's gain. Peter ("Petia") Isakov, whom the viewer encounters at the piatachok playing the spoons and dancing in imitation of a rooster, left his native village in Tambov oblast' in 1970 because, he says, "everything was dull (sukhoi) and dying." Five of his ten siblings died, he claims, before he and his remaining brothers and sisters were packed off to Moscow to live with their grandfather. Never having gone to school, he is shown working as a housepainter, but proudly asserts that everyone in Moscow knows him for his exploits at the piatachok.[189] And while the rural culture embodied in the piatachok had migrated to and enriched the culture of the city, it died out where it originated. "I don't like to go back to play," says Viktor Alishin, a skilled accordionist who left the village in 1971 with his young bride and found work as a driver for an auto fleet. "When I go there, I feel like I am disturbing their peace."[190]

186. Denisova, *Ischezaiushchaia derevnia Rossii*, 125.

187. See, for example, "Inattention to 'Futureless' Villages Decried," *Izvestiia*, May 15, 1981, 2, trans. in *Current Digest of the Soviet Press (CDSP)*, June 17, 1981, 4–5; "Putting the Tiny Village's Case," *Komsomol'skaia Pravda*, April 29, 1981, 2, trans. in *CDSP*, June 17, 1981, 6; *Pravda*, March 5, 1982, 3.

188. Some of the decline can be attributed to the reclassification of large villages into towns. The remainder, however, occurred because small villages shrank owing to outmigration and the dying off of the remaining population. Denisova, *Ischezaiushchaia derevnia Rossii*, 125, 129. This downward trend would continue into the post-Soviet period. By the census year of 2002, 37,000 (24 percent) of the 155,000 villages within the Russian Federation contained fifty or fewer people and 13,000 "emptied out altogether." *The New York Times*, February 5, 2004, A9.

189. *Piatachok*, part 5 (6:00–9:40); part 6 (0:00–1:20).

190. *Piatachok*, part 5 (2:30–2:50).

The Northern Increment

Many cities in Russia's least accessible regions owed their origins to natural resource exploitation and dependence on Gulag labor. After the Great Patriotic War, however, the growth of these and newly established cities sprang from special measures to attract workers and their families with material incentives. These incentives, called the northern increment, did not apply to the entire region, but rather to cities and settlements favored for natural resource development. Among them were the string of towns along the Ob River in western Siberia rich in oil and gas—Nefteiugansk, Surgut, and Nizhnevartovsk—the arctic coal town of Vorkuta, and the far eastern island of Sakhalin. Some workers and managers stayed on after the expiration of their own sentences, like Vasilii Azhaev, whose story is told in the next chapter; others had arrived as special settlers or technical specialists. In some cases, newcomers took up residence in the very same places where camp inmates had toiled. As far as development strategy was concerned, the shift from dependence on coercion to a system of incentives occurred almost seamlessly.

In 1945 while the labor camp population was still rising, the Presidium of the Supreme Soviet decreed a system of benefits for individuals willing to work in the Far North and "equivalent" regions with extreme climatic conditions. The system functioned on the basis of regional coefficients that ranged from 1.0 to 2.0 of a standard wage depending on both geographic and climatic conditions and the economic importance of the region. Thus, whereas the coefficient for Sakhalin was 1.5, in remote northeastern Magadan oblast' it was 1.8, and in the Far North it varied between 1.8 and 2.0. The longer the period of work and residence in a particular region, the greater the increment. Other benefits included additional vacation time and coverage of travel expenses, provision of housing, and an accelerated pension schedule.[191] The system would be revised in 1955, 1960, and 1967, each time to adjust to changes in regional priorities and with the aim of making the incentives more attractive. For example, the 1967 version included a doubling of lump-sum payments to young specialists.[192]

One warm sunny day in July 2010, Irina Lukka explained how it came about that she grew up on Sakhalin Island, more than a continent away from her office in Helsinki at the National Library of Finland.[193] Irina is the daughter of Viktor and Nina, who met in the

---

191. Iu. V. Roshchin, *Migratsiia naseleniia v sud'be Rossii* (Moscow, 2008), 155–56.

192. Cf. "Decree of the Presidium of the U.S.S.R. Supreme Soviet: On Adjusting the System of Benefits for Persons Who Work in the Regions of the Far North and in Localities Equivalent to the Regions of the Far North," *Vedomosti Verkhovnogo Soveta SSSR*, no. 7 (1960): 70–72, trans. in *CDSP*, March 16, 1960, 26–27; and "Decree of the Presidium of the U.S.S.R. Supreme Soviet: On Expanding Benefits for Individuals Working in Regions of the Far North and in Localities Equivalent to Regions of the Far North," *Pravda*, September 27, 1967, 2, trans. in *CDSP*, October 18, 1967, 4.

193. Authors' interview with Irina Lukka, Helsinki, July 14–15, 2010.

mid-1950s in Iuzhno-Sakhalinsk, the oblast' capital, shortly after each had taken advantage of the regional coefficient to migrate there. According to Irina, her mother's brother, who had arrived on the island from the Maritime region, encouraged his sister to join him. Being a specialist in Russian literature and fine arts, Nina could practice her profession anywhere, he pointed out, and "here, it's paradise." Meanwhile, Viktor's older sister, Valentina, who had migrated with her three children from the city of Vladimir east of Moscow, wrote to him describing Sakhalin. After completing army service, Viktor decided to join her rather than returning to his job in Moscow. Viktor met Nina at a dance. Although he was not very well read, he started reading assiduously in order to woo her once he discovered that Nina taught literature.

"They were shocked by south Sakhalin's wildlife," remembers Irina. "So many fish! So inexpensive." Salmon was 1 ruble a kilo. Bread was in short supply, but seafood and berries were in abundance. The climate wasn't bad either—like Hokkaido's, -15 degrees Celsius in winter and rain in August. A lot of people came to Sakhalin from Khabarovsk and elsewhere in the Russian Far East but also from Moscow and Leningrad, primarily young people with degrees from pedagogical and other professional training institutions. But in 1959, the Soviet government lowered the regional coefficient for Sakhalin and otherwise reduced the incentives for settling on the island. Irina attributes the decision to Nikita Khrushchev's visit in August 1959 on his way back from the United States. "He saw how well everyone lived, materially, and decided to rescind or at least cut back on the wage coefficient. Almost immediately, there was a mass exodus from the island."[194] Indeed, out-migration exceeded arrivals by 32,200 in 1960, the sharpest drop in migration flows during the 1950s and 1960s. Only in 1964 did the government restore the coefficient. One wonders how much of a difference the restoration made, however, for between 1965 and 1980, departures outnumbered arrivals by slightly over 100,000.[195]

All the while, the cast of places made notorious by their association with the Gulag was changing as the camps were wound down or closed and the number of people taking advantage of the northern increment rose. At Noril'sk, the metallurgical city north of the Arctic Circle, the ratio of free laborers to prisoners that had been 1:5 in 1941 dropped to 1:2 by 1949. Most "free" laborers, however, were not entirely free but confined to the camps for one reason or another even after the expiration of their sentences, as we shall see in the case of Azhaev. Vasilii Romashkin, who spent the years 1939 to 1947 in camps at Noril'sk, called the years that followed his release "the best of my life." As he related to the American

194. Ibid.

195. A. N. Burykin, "Problemy formirovaniia postoiannogo naseleniia sakhalinskoi oblasti," *Nauka, obrazovanie, obshchestvo* (Iuzhno-Sakhalinsk), no. 3 (2005): 6–8.

journalist Andrew Meier, he continued to work at the *kombinat* "as a chief engineer, a man of stature." Two generations born and raised in Noril'sk followed.[196]

Only in the late 1940s did truly free workers—that is, not former prisoners, but those taking advantage of the northern increment—start coming to work there. By 1950, they accounted for some 20 percent of the twenty-five thousand workers employed in Noril'sk's production facilities.[197] The Soviet press celebrated the physical transformation of other former Gulag sites. *Pravda* reported in 1958 that Magadan, capital of the oblast' created in 1953, "has become a large city with modern improvements." Multistory apartment houses lined Leninskii Prospekt; children of young Russian, Ukrainian, and Belorussian miners working in outlying mines rubbed shoulders with young Chukchi and Evenki kids at boarding schools.[198] In 1955, the deputy chairman of Vorkuta's city soviet proudly informed readers of *Izvestiia* that his city "is full of construction scaffoldings." It already had "scores of streets, spacious squares, well-constructed apartment houses, and beautiful buildings housing cultural and service institutions."[199]

The expansion of population, if not urban infrastructure, continued at an accelerated pace over the next several decades. Between 1960 and 1985 the recorded population of the region nearly doubled from 4.7 million to 9.2 million.[200] Magadan oblast' recorded the highest proportion of migrants (78 percent) of any region within the RSFSR in the 1979 census, and at 80 percent, migrants comprised an even greater proportion of its urban population (essentially, the city of Magadan).[201] Driven by a boom in natural gas and oil production, new cities such as Surgut, Nefteiugansk in the Khanty-Mansi Autonomous okrug, and Novyi Urengoi in the Yamal-Nenets Autonomous okrug sprang up on the tundra like proverbial mushrooms after the rain. Hundreds of thousands of "mainlanders" (Soviet citizens from outside the Far North) poured into these boomtowns.

How, from where, and why? Three-quarters came on their own initiative. The largest proportion (more than 70 percent) came from the labor-deficit regions of the Urals, western and eastern Siberia, Kazakhstan, and the Far East. "This is unacceptable," wrote one researcher from Novosibirsk, "since these regions need more workers [and] the labor shortage in western Siberia's agriculture is critical." As for why migrants came, more than half cited their "desire for higher pay," though one suspects that some others also came for

196. Andrew Meier, *Black Earth: A Journey through Russia after the Fall* (New York, 2003), 227–28.

197. Leonid Borodkin and Simon Ertz, "Coercion versus Motivation: Forced Labor in Norilsk," in *The Economics of Forced Labor: The Soviet Gulag*, ed. Paul Gregory (Stanford, 2003), 80–83.

198. S. Morozov, "Na severe dal'nom," *Pravda*, January 12, 1958, 6.

199. *Izvestiia*, May 20, 1955, 2, trans. in CDSP, June 29, 1955, 32–33.

200. Perevedentsev, *Molodezh'*, 109–10. The region is the Far North and equivalent areas encompassing five territories in their entirety and parts of eleven others as defined by Tsentral'noe statisticheskoe upravlenie pri Sovete ministrov RSFSR, *Narodnoe khoziaistvo RSFSR v 1985 g.* (Moscow, 1986), 33.

201. Moiseenko, "Migratsiia i emigratsiia v Rossii," 116–17.

the pay but would not admit it. One-quarter of respondents who came on their own cited family circumstances (e.g., entering into marriage or joining one's spouse or relatives).[202] This was how "Sasha" arrived in Noril'sk. His mother had brought him with her in 1965 when she rejoined her truck-driving husband in the north.[203]

The average age of new arrivals—thirty-two years old—suggests that many had worked elsewhere previously. The Siberian timber and fishing industries, as well as agriculture, lost workers to the Far North. For them, higher pay was the major incentive. But while money could lure impoverished or footloose workers, it apparently could not keep them. A study from the mid-1980s indicated that more than half of all migrants to the natural gas town of Novyi Urgenoi departed within one year. Generally, the farther migrants had to travel to their destinations, the more likely they were to remain.[204] Among migrants who had declared their intention of leaving the Far North in 1969, the greatest proportion—46 percent—cited inadequate housing, followed by shortages of foodstuffs, manufactured goods, cultural amenities, and everyday services. The later Novyi Urengoi study produced the same findings. Once again, it appears that the state did not follow through with the implementation of a grand migration scheme, failing to provide the resources to underwrite it.[205]

Access to serial data on alcohol consumption, divorce, crime, environmental-related medical conditions, and other indices of social and familial dysfunction might show higher rates in these far northern towns than elsewhere in the country. Nevertheless, the region did become home to hundreds of thousands of newcomers. Some, like people throughout the world who move to a place that does not fulfill their expectations, were loathe to admit they had made a mistake and adapted as best they could. Others may simply have lacked the resources to leave. Evgenii Evtushenko's poem from 1977 titled—what else?—"Northern Increment" seems to have been dedicated to those who stuck it out. "What is the northern increment for?" asks Petr Shchepochkin (a play on the word for splinter—*shchepochka*), the

202. T. G. Gaponova, "Migration Studied in Soviet North, East," *Sotsiologicheskie issledovaniiia*, no. 2 (1976): 58–66, trans. in CDSP, October 13, 1976, 1–5. The study was undertaken by the Institute of Economics and Organization of Industrial Production under the Academy of Sciences' Siberian Division. For similar results from a later study of migrants to Novyi Urengoi, see G. F. Kutsev, *Chelovek na severe* (Moscow, 1989), 45–50.

203. Meier, *Black Earth*, 209.

204. Gaponova, "Migration Studied," 3; Ye. Gontmakher and N. Denisov, "Problem for Discussion: The Northern Pay Differential," *Sovetskaia Rossiia*, August 26, 1984, trans. in CDSP, November 14, 1984, 16.

205. Gaponova, "Migration Studied," 3; Kutsev, *Chelovek na severe*, 65. For an analysis of Soviet data from the early 1960s, see Prociuk, "Manpower Problem in Siberia," 198–99. This neglect hardly was unique to the Far North. For the argument that scant attention to social infrastructure was endemic to Soviet urban planning, see Lewis H. Siegelbaum, "Modernity Unbound: The New Soviet City of the Sixties," in *The Socialist Sixties: Crossing Borders in the Second World*, ed. Anne E. Gorsuch and Diane P. Koenker (Bloomington, 2013), 75–76.

poem's narrator, in the opening line. He answers his own question in sardonic fashion: "For a blizzard inside one's eyes / For such frost that the skin on one's face becomes a tarpaulin / For cargo dropped from a helicopter, containing no books except scientific brochures on 'The Poisonous Snakes of Soviet Deserts,' absolutely necessary for polar conditions." Paying an unannounced visit to his sister and brother-in-law outside Moscow, Shchepochkin confesses: "I am a convict! / I am in debt all around. / I will never get even." But his debt is not monetary; he has plenty of money that he is happy to lend or even give away. (It also is not to alcohol, although his consumption of nail polish, a cocktail "we Northerners" call "Shampuzo," and other concoctions is prodigious.) No, he is "chained to Russia—that's the debt." And Russia is in turn borrowing the lives of people who accept the northern increment. The poem ends in an orgy of things Shchepochkin intends to bring back with him—turquoise oil paint, smoked sausage, two volumes of Evtushenko, washable wallpaper, Alaska sheepskin boots, and "a can of beer, at least one."[206]

By the late 1980s, the damage to the environment and people's health caused by decades of intense mining and smelting in the Far North had reached alarming proportions.[207] This, coupled with the dislocations associated with perestroika and then the radical privatization of the economy in the immediate post-Soviet years, made the situation for residents—those who had stayed in the region after their terms in the camps had expired, recipients of the northern increment, and the indigenous population—immensely worse. While experienced and highly skilled personnel relocated elsewhere, inflation ate up the savings of those who remained. Rising prices of fuel and electricity also made it impossible for municipalities to support social infrastructure.

The cities, towns, and smaller settlements in the Far North and "equivalent areas" such as Sakhalin Island, Kamchatka, and the Amur basin suffered the most; they found themselves orphaned after 1991. They had been established and sustained by Soviet institutions whose dedication to natural resource development was matched only by their heedlessness to costs and damage to the ecosystem. By 1999, nearly a quarter of the able-bodied population in twenty-three of the twenty-seven regions of this part of the country "lacked steady employment" and, with production declining, had little chance of finding any.[208]

The situation had become so desperate that some were calling for an "evacuation" of hundreds of thousands of people to the mainland. "Logically," one reporter wrote in *Izvestiia* in January 1999, "the first to leave those latitudes should be pensioners, the disabled

---

206. Evgenii Evtushenko, "Severnaia nadbavka," *Pervoe sobranie sochinenii v vos'mi tomakh* (Moscow, 2002), 5: 114–46. The poem was originally published in *Iunost'*, no. 6 (1977).

207. See OECD, *Environment in the Transition to a Market Economy: Progress in Central and Eastern Europe and the New Independent States* (Paris, 1999), 172–74.

208. Semyon Novoprudsky, "Northern Take-Back," *Izvestiia*, August 6, 1999, 1, trans. in CDRP, September 1, 1999, 12.

and the unemployed, since it's absolutely clear that neither the state nor the local authorities are capable of providing them a decent existence." These people made up about a quarter of the population in the Komi republic in the northern Urals. Many had arrived in earlier decades as part the strategy for developing the far northern territories, a strategy that resulted in a density of population four times greater than in Alaska, Canada, and other countries sharing the same latitudes. Even in the Khanty-Mansi and Yamal-Nenets autonomous regions, where the discovery of oil and gas reserves once inspired comparisons with Norway and Kuwait, employment opportunities had become scarce and the cost of living double the national average. No wonder that the "great northern migration," once signifying the flood of people heading north via the northern increment, now referred to those moving in the opposite direction.[209]

And yet not everyone was keen to go. When the kombinat at Noril'sk introduced a resettlement program for the laid-off and retired replete with cash incentives, the recipients took the money but did not leave. The second attempt offered free apartments to lure them to the mainland, but after accepting the apartments, the topophilic northerners sold them. Finally, in June 2001 the World Bank loaned the Russian state funds to relocate people from Nor'ilsk, Vorkuta, and Magadan. By 2005 a mere 7,300 people had moved under this scheme. Those who stuck it out, the population lured there by the northern increment, doubtless stayed partly for the high salaries, but as Meier concludes, "the greater pull seemed the strange consolation, pride even, of inhabiting one of the world's most uninhabitable places."[210]

Finally, the area saw new arrivals in connection with natural resource exploitation and the relatively high wages paid by newly privatized companies. Turnover was great, making estimates of their numbers hazardous. Among the big gainers was Tiumen oblast', just north of Kazakhstan, where oil and natural gas extraction ruled. The city of Surgut stood out for its success: while other cities were fading, its population expanded from nearly 248,000 in 1989 to over 285,000 in 2002.[211]

Late-Century Cities

Even as the cities in the Far North and Siberia were shedding residents, migrants from the Caucasus and Central Asia were arriving in urban areas for the first time. Jeff Sahadeo

209. Valentina Kulakova, "The North: Outpost of Russia Struggles to Survive," *Segodnia*, November 2, 1994, 6, trans. in *CDSP*, December 7, 1994, 19; Vladimir Shmyganovsky, "The North Has Conquered Russia," *Izvestiia*, January 12, 1999, 7, trans. in *CDSP*, February 3, 1999, 2–4.
210. Meier, *Black Earth*, 229; Timothy Heleniak, "Growth Poles and Ghost Towns in the Russian Far North," in *Russia and the North*, ed. Elana Wilson Rowe (Ottawa, 2009), 155–57.
211. Goskomstat Rossii, *Chislennost'*, 172–73.

estimates that "thousands, likely tens of thousands" arrived in Leningrad and Moscow alone between 1964 and 1991 without official permission.[212] They had left their homes in search of economic, professional, and medical betterment, relying on informal, for the most part ethnically based networks that acted as surrogates for state services. They lived in crowded dormitories and private apartments. Lacking command of the Russian language upon arrival, they sold flowers at train stations and bazaars, peddled fruits and nuts, and traveled home periodically to stock up.[213]

Migrants to Soviet cities, like their counterparts elsewhere in the world, encountered various forms of coercion, especially from the police. As Sahadeo reminds us, "The idea of trade as at once dirty and also non-Russian extends back to the tsarist period."[214] As more and more traders from the Caucasus and Central Asia appeared on the streets and in the markets of Moscow and Leningrad, suspicions of criminal activity in connection with the marketing of flowers, citrus fruits, and other perishable items unavailable in state stores grew as well.[215] The fallout from the Afghan War, the unpredictability of supplies associated with perestroika, and the media's resort to sensationalist accounts about crime reinforced ethnic stereotyping, making life precarious for Central Asians and Caucasians alike during the Soviet Union's last years—and beyond.

In the post-Soviet period, as in the Soviet era, millions of people would experience big-city life for the first time. Interviewed recently as part of the Oxford Russian Life History project, Dmitri Mukhin, a twenty-six-year-old PhD student born in Vologda, admitted he was "scared stiff" the first time he went down a metro escalator in St. Petersburg. "I mean, I couldn't bring myself to make the first step off that moving staircase and back onto firm land. . . . In the end some local women [sic] just grabs me . . . and we take the last step together."[216] Mukhin was not unique. One day in May 2011, a pedestrian was about to enter the Kaluga station on the Moscow metro's Kaluzhskaia-Rizhskaia line when a woman of about forty approached to ask how to get to Rechnoi vokzal. "Oh," he replied, "that's quite far but it's not that difficult," and as he pointed to the small metro map she was carrying, he suggested she get off at one station, then take another train to the last stop. But she didn't seem to understand these directions. He thereupon offered to accompany her at least

212. Jeff Sahadeo, "Black Snouts Go Home! Racism and Reaction in Late Soviet Leningrad and Moscow" (unpublished paper), 5, cited with permission of author.

213. Sahadeo, "Accidental Traders," 524–35.

214. Sahadeo, "Black Snouts Go Home," 17.

215. S. Bablumyan, "Face to Face with the Law: Flowers of Evil," *Izvestiia*, March 11, 1982, trans. in *CDSP*, April 7, 1982, 19.

216. Victoria Donovan, "Being 'Civil': Narrative Constructions of Provincialism in the Russian North West," paper presented at AAASS Convention, Boston, November 2009, 1 (Interview Oxf/AHRC-SPb-07 PF 32). For the Oxford project, see www.ehrc.ox.ac.uk/lifehistory.

until he had reached his destination. As they entered the metro, it became clear that she had no idea what to do. After he ushered her through the turnstile, they approached the escalator and, as fear gripped her, she gripped his arm.[217]

We can conclude that some things do not change; provincial people continue to be bowled over by the urban features of Moscow or Petersburg much as was Semën Kanatchikov in 1895. Nonetheless the years directly after the end of the USSR produced a crisis that induced extreme shifts in mobility. The initial shocks of dissolution had the same effect on large cities like Moscow and Petersburg as did the Bolshevik Revolution of 1917: people left the city for nearby rural areas. The motive was also the same because people moved to a more certain food supply.[218] The initiation of new, longer-lasting patterns became visible by the end of the twentieth century, patterns in a state that no longer aspired to engineer the mobility of its citizens. Henceforth, migration regimes would be more inspired by the economy than by the bureaucracy.

Of course, charting continuities and discontinuities in migration patterns before and after 1991 is fraught with difficulties. The problem is not the absence of data. With only a brief hiatus, the State Committee of the Russian Federation on Statistics (Goskomstat) took up where the Soviet Central Statistical Administration left off, and turned out a steady stream of annual volumes on population. The problem is knowing how to assess the significance of a host of shifts: the vast expansion of market relations; the opening up of enormous gaps in price structures and cost of living between urban and rural areas, and between Moscow and Petersburg on the one hand and smaller cities on the other; the dramatic reconfiguration of political space that left people previously inhabiting the same country scattered among fifteen independent states; changes in Russian migration policy and variations in the degree of its application; ethnic and civil strife that set into motion refugees; and, finally, popular association of migrant labor with ethnic "others."

Migration to cities in the post-Soviet era followed distinct regional patterns within what G. Lappo describes as "centrifugal compression of the population in certain areas."[219] That is, particular cities and regions became attractive to newcomers, especially Moscow, Petersburg, and their respective oblasts. The boom in minerals, natural gas, and oil extraction attracted newcomers to cities servicing these industries, although on a far smaller scale. Other cities shrank because of out-migration: monofunctional cities that ran almost exclusively on mining, textiles, heavy industry, the military, or research were particularly hard-hit

---

217. The pedestrian in question was Lewis Siegelbaum.

218. Irina Molodikova and Alla Makhrova, "Urbanization Patterns in Russia in the Post-Soviet Era," in *The Post-Soviet City: Urban Form and Space Transformations in Central and Eastern Europe after Socialism*, ed. K. Stanilov (Dordrecht, 2007), 56–57.

219. G. Lappo, Urbanization in European Russia: The Process and Its Results," in *Gorod i derevnia v Evropeiskoi Rossii: Sto let peremen*, ed. T. G. Nefedova et al. (Moscow, 2001), cited in Molodikova and Makhrova, "Urbanization," 54.

in the early post-Soviet years.[220] Overall, whereas for several centuries Russia had exhibited a population drift toward the north and east, the drift began to reverse itself in the mid-1980s. Not all this population movement was from rural to urban areas. Many who had been attracted to cities in the north and Far East by the northern increment and other incentives fled when not only the incentives but also basic supplies became difficult to obtain. What emerges, then, is a complex series of migrations since the mid-1990s, the outlines of which were captured by the 2002 census.

In the aggregate, cities did not lose population by migration after 1992, for migration from rural areas to cities once again outpaced movement in the reverse direction. Russia was as much a country of big cities in 2002 as in 1989; indeed the share of people living in a city of over one hundred thousand increased from 37 to 40 percent in those thirteen years. But some cities were more attractive than others—only 5 of the 13 cities with over a million people increased in size—Moscow, Kazan, Rostov-on-Don, Novosibirsk, and Volgograd. Of the 155 cities with a population of between one hundred thousand and one million, 91 lost population, but 18 increased by over 10 percent.[221] Many cities decreased in size, but in the aggregate, that was due to natural decrease—the predominance of deaths over births—rather than out-migration.[222]

Moscow saw the greatest growth of any large city, both proportionally and in absolute numbers. After losing citizens in the first half of the 1990s, the city swelled by over 1.5 million people by 2002.[223] Net growth due to migration during roughly the same period (1991–2003) came to 616,000.[224] Most new arrivals to both Moscow and St. Petersburg came from within the Russian Federation, although newcomers from the Caucasus and Central Asia were more visible.[225]

220. Molodikova and Makhrova, "Urbanization," 62–63; Barbara Engel, "Public Space in the 'Blue Cities' of Russia," in Stanilov, Post-Soviet City, 285.

221. Molodikova and Makhrova, "Urbanization," 58–59.

222. See the opening of this chapter for the three elements of urbanization: migration, natural increase, and reclassification; and Molodikova and Makhrova, "Urbanization," 55.

223. For 1989, see "Vsesoiuznaia perepis' naseleniia 1989 g. Chislennost' gorodskogo naseleniia RSFSR, ee territorial'nykh edinits, gorodskikh poselenii i gorodskikh raionov po polu," in "Demoscope Weekly," http://demoscope.ru/weekly/ssp/rus89_reg2.php.html (accessed November 21, 2012); for 2002, see Goskomstat Rossii, Chislennost' i migratsiia naseleniia Rossiiskoi Federatsii v 2002 godu (Statisticheskii biulleten') (Moscow, 2003), 9.

224. Nikita Mkrtchian, "'Zapadnyi dreif' vnutrirossiiskoi migratsii," Otechestvennye zapiski, no. 4 (18) (2004), at http://www.strana-oz.ru/2004/4/zapadnyy-dreyf-vnutrirossiyskoy-migracii#t1 (accessed November 21, 2012).

225. Molodikova and Makhrova, "Urbanization," 56–58. In the year 2000, Russia began using the unit of federal district (federal'nyi okrug), distributing the eighty-nine (now eighty-three) "federal subjects" (e.g., republics, oblasts, autonomous okrugs, autonomous oblast', and two federal cities) among seven federal districts: Central, Northwestern, Southern, Volga, Urals, Siberian, and Far Eastern. In 2010, the North Caucasus federal district was subdivided from the Southern federal district.

People gravitated to other towns as well, especially within the Central and Southern Federal districts. These, in fact, were the only districts in which the population actually became more urban between 1989 and 2002.[226] The general "western drift" did not help relatively rural oblasts in the Central and Volga federal districts such as Riazan', Kursk, Tambov, Orenburg, and Penza, which lost population. Nor was it apparent in the Northwestern federal district where, despite significant migration to St. Petersburg, the population declined by some 10 percent between 1991 and 2003.[227] In the southern regions of the USSR (including the North Caucasian federal district), the shabashniki who migrated seasonally during the Soviet period paved the way for out-migration in the 1990s intensified by ethnic conflicts and war in the Chechen republic. Migrants settled in Krasnodar and Stavropol', the administrative centers of neighboring territories, as well as Rostov-on-Don and Volgograd, where they constituted substantial if impermanent diasporic communities.[228]

We thus far have concentrated on migration flows within the Russian Federation. But one of the most characteristic features of post-Soviet Russia has been the influx of people from the "near abroad," that is, other former Soviet republics. They included both ethnic Russians and other national groups "returning" for one reason or another to their "homeland," and those indigenous to the other former SSRs. During the third quarter of the last century the RSFSR lost some 2.5 million people to the other Soviet republics because of migration; in the last fifteen years of the Soviet Union's existence, that flow was reversed: 2.53 million people migrated to the Russian republic from the other SSRs. The breakup of the Soviet Union into fifteen independent republics only intensified the migration of people across new borders into the Russian Federation: it is estimated that between 1991 and 2000, net in-migrants to Russia from the near abroad totaled 4.1 million.[229] Annual data show that beginning in 1992 net in-migration to Russia from its near abroad exceeded 200,000 people every year until 2003. It rose sharply in 1993 to 526,000 and remained above the half-million mark until 1998. Initially between 1989 and 1991, Ukraine supplied the greatest number of migrants. In 1992 and 1993 the newly independent Central Asian states supplanted Ukraine, after which Kazakhstan outdid them.[230]

Out-migration from Russia totaled slightly more than 4 million people, of whom nearly 2 million went to Ukraine and 750,000 to Kazakhstan.[231] The outflow of former Soviet citizens to the "old" or "far" abroad—primarily Germany, Israel, and the United States—is

---

226. Ibid., 54.

227. Mkrtchian, " 'Zapadnyi dreif,' " 4–5.

228. Ibid.

229. Roshchin, *Migratsiia naseleniia v sud'be Rossii*, 196.

230. Iu. Iu. Karpova, "Migratsionnyi obmen mezhdu Rossiei i Ukrainoi," in Rybakovskii, *Transformatsiia migratsionnykh protsessov*, 58–59.

231. Ibid., 60.

beyond the scope of our study. It was particularly heavy in the 1990s, when it averaged over 100,000 per year, vastly reducing the number of ethnic Germans and Jews in Russia, Kazakhstan, and Ukraine and raising the specter of a "brain drain."[232] We also do not address immigration from outside the former Soviet Union. Negligible at first, Chinese and Korean commuter migrants, small-scale traders, workers, and students became a real presence in many Siberian and Russian Far Eastern cities before the end of the century.[233] Migrants from Vietnam and Afghanistan, working primarily in retail trades, also have established communities in these cities as well as in Moscow and St. Petersburg.

Russia became the destination of so many migrants from the other former Soviet republics for two fundamental reasons. First, the breakup of the USSR meant that twenty-five million ethnic Russians and four million people of other nationalities native to Russia became foreigners "as they slept in their beds," and the insecurities associated with this status sent many fleeing "back" to their native countries.[234] This impetus conforms to Rogers Brubaker's observation that, in contrast to Western Europe, "In Eastern Europe, much migration—not only in the last fifteen years, but over the last century—has involved unmixing, reducing rather than increasing [ethnic] heterogeneity." Second, the lack of opportunities for employment at home and the rapid growth of an income gap between Russia and other republics stimulated labor migration. We will have occasion to consider Russian repatriation in connection with the legal category of "forced migration" in chapter 6. Here, we focus on the less privileged labor migrants, those who began coming to Russia's cities in the latter half of the 1990s primarily from Central Asian and Caucasian states to work, either legally or illegally, at jobs increasingly targeted for them. Their growing presence in the Russian Federation, *pace* Brubaker, echoes the "new forms and degrees of ethnic, racial, linguistic, and religious heterogeneity" characteristic of Western Europe.[235]

An Azeri peddler whom Sahadeo interviewed was the "first swallow" of the many who would follow. They increased, thanks to stark inequalities of income, access to relatively cheap air and rail tickets, and the security of telephone contact with loved ones at home. Estimates of illegal Azeri migrants in Russia number between one and two million, of whom some eight hundred thousand reputedly live in Moscow and work in markets and

232. Vladimir Mukomel', *Migratsionnaia politika Rossii: Postsovetskie konteksty* (Moscow, 2005), 58; Leonid Rybakovsky and Sergei Ryazantsev, *International Migration in the Russian Federation* (New York, 2005), 9–12; Schmidt and Sagynbekova, "Migration Past and Present," 111–27.

233. See Vladimir Datsyshen, "Historical and Contemporary Trends of Chinese Labor Migration into Siberia," in *Chinese Migrants in Russia, Central Asia, and Eastern Europe*, ed. Felix B. Chang and Sunnie T. Rucker-Chang (London, 2012), 29–37.

234. Lidiia Grafova, "Kak pereselentsy pytalis' spasti Rossiiu ot demograficheskoi katastrofy," *Otechestvennye zapiski*, no. 4 (18) (2004), at http://www.strana-oz.ru/2004/4/zapadnyy-dreyf-vnutrirossiyskoy-migracii#t1 (accessed November 27, 2012), 1.

235. Rogers Brubaker, *Ethnicity without Groups* (Cambridge, MA, 2004), 153.

services.[236] Those who came resembled the Africans, Asians, and the West Indians in France, Britain, and the Netherlands; the Turks and East Europeans in Germany; and the Central and South Americans in the United States.[237] The inequalities may not have been quite as extreme as in these other places, but at the equivalent of US$31 in the case of Kyrgyzstan and US$13 in Tajikistan, the average monthly income as of 2001 was well below the figure of US$147 in Russia. Moreover, as the late demographer Elena Tiuriukanova noted a few years ago,

> Russia's demographic and geopolitical situation, as well as its more stable economic position compared to other CIS and Southeast Asian countries, the weakness of Russian migration legislation, porous borders with the CIS countries and the presence of a great number of ethnic diasporas in Russia, are indicators that Russia will remain a receiving country for a long period.[238]

Most migrants, according to Tiuriukanova, found employment in the "shadow sectors of the economy where they are exposed to fierce exploitation." Goskomstat estimated that this sector employed ten million people (not only migrants) in 2001 and accounted for over a fifth of Russia's entire gross domestic product. In a study conducted under the auspices of the International Labour Organization between 2003 and 2005, Tiuriukanova surveyed 442 migrant laborers in Omsk, Stavropol', and Moscow oblasts. Of her interviewees, only 3 to 5 percent had learned about the possibility of working in Russia through official channels. Only 1 in 5 knew before departing where and for whom they would be working in Russia. They relied for the most part on advertisements in the mass media and recruiters at railroad stations. For example, when thirty-seven-year-old N. from Tajikistan, a roofer by trade, alighted from a train, he saw a man holding a sign that read "Workers for construction required." This contractor assembled 10 men from different countries for a variety of construction sites. He showed up on the first payday to collect twenty dollars from each for his services.[239]

Not all workers were men and not all who found jobs worked in construction. Tiuriukanova reports that agents could recruit girls in the villages of Central Asia and Kazakhstan

---

236. O. D. Vorob'eva and O. N. Lezhenkina, "Integratsiia migrantov v novuiu sredu v ekonomicheskie izderzhki migratsionnovo obmena," in Rybakovskii, *Transformatsiia migratsionnykh protsessov*, 248–50.

237. For an entrée to the vast literature on these migration patterns, see Klaus Bade, *Migration in European History* (Malden, 2003); Stephen Castles and Mark Miller, *The Age of Migration: International Population Movements in the Modern World* (New York, 2009); and Moch, *Moving Europeans*.

238. Elena Tyuryukanova, *Forced Labour in the Russian Federation Today: Irregular Migration and Trafficking in Human Beings* (Geneva, 2005), 4.

239. Elena Tiuriukanova, "Trudovaia migratsiia v Rossii," *Otechestvennye zapiski*, no. 4 (18) (2004), at http://www.strana-oz.ru/2004/4/zapadnyy-dreyf-vnutrirossiyskoy-migracii#t1 (accessed November 27, 2012), 1, 2, 4.

for domestic service and sex work in Russia, typically paying the most vulnerable parents one hundred to two hundred dollars and promising to arrange study and accommodation, with regular payments in the future by the daughters themselves.[240] One of Tiuriukanova's informants, a sixteen-year-old girl from Kazakhstan, described her family background and recruitment in an interview conducted in Omsk:

> There were six children in our family. I am the second. There [in Kazakhstan] people live in poverty, lacking electricity and water. Sometimes we didn't even have bread at home. My mother made ends meet by occasional earnings, and my father spent everything on drink. I was thinking about how to get out of this situation, to help my brothers and sisters and do something for myself. And I met a man by chance. He proposed that I could earn money at market. He came to my parents—I am underage—and proposed that I work at a market in Smara [sic]. He paid money to my parents so that they would let me go to Samara.

She also reported that her "documents were forged and she was subsequently a victim of fraud, physical and sexual coercion, physical restraint and threats." Because she had no documents, she was totally dependent on her abductors—until she seized the opportunity presented by an auto accident to run away.[241] Traffic of young girls into sex work attracts the most journalistic and scholarly attention, but the survey also cited complaints by adult women, men, and boys about various forms of coercion, sexual and otherwise.

Migrants' vulnerability to coercion had multiple causes. One of every five migrants in the survey reported that employers took possession of passports and other documents, and a slightly lower percentage cited debt bondage, that is, the necessity of paying off debts in excess of a month's earnings. Less than 20 percent had signed (as opposed to orally agreed to) contracts with employers, and nearly three-quarters received wages in the form of "black cash," that is, off the books. The very illegality of migrants' presence in the country made it virtually impossible to estimate their numbers. In 2000 the Federal Migration Service registered 213,000 migrants from the near abroad—working in descending numbers in construction, trade and public catering, industry, agriculture and forestry, and the remainder in supplies, services, and transportation. But it estimated anywhere from 1.5 to three million "illegals" in the country. One encounters other estimates of five and even fifteen million.[242]

---

240. Ibid., 5.

241. Tyuryukanova, *Forced Labour*, 108–9.

242. Anastasia Naryshkina, "Ob'edinenie rabodatelei vystupaet protiv trudovykh migrantov," *Izvestiia*, March 7, 2003, 2; Svetlana Alikina, "15 Million Illegal Migrants Staying in Russia," *Itar-Tass Weekly News*, September 11, 2003; Mukomel', *Migratsionnaia politika*, 194; Irina Ivakhnyuk, *The Russian Migration Policy and its Impact on Human Development: The Historical Perspective* (New York, 2009), 16, 32–33.

Illegality stemmed indirectly from the recoding of the Russian territory as Slavic or white, a popular reaction to the breakup of the Soviet Union into ethnically defined independent states. Whereas Soviet official discourse had emphasized the equality and brotherhood of the peoples, post-Soviet media renderings of people from the Caucasus and Central Asia stressed their unruliness, ingratitude, and criminality. Little wonder that in Moscow, where it was most coveted, residential registration was "often an unsuccessful ordeal for a person of colour . . . much in the same way that officials in the southern United States had frightened blacks into not registering to vote." "Black" criminality thus became a "self-fulfilling prophecy. Denying dark-skinned individuals registration encourage[d] many of them to turn to criminal activity because without a *propiska* they are unable to gain lawful employment."[243]

As the Russian economy heated up, its demand for migrant labor increased. But Russia's was hardly a unitary economy. The sociologist Vladimir Mukomel' employs a typology that distinguishes three "leading" regions—Moscow, the Khanty-Mansii Autonomous okrug, and the Yamalo-Nenets Autonomous okrug. These three alone had attracted more illegal migrants than all of the twenty-one regions he considered economically vibrant (e.g., St. Petersburg, Samara, Moscow oblast', etc.) and almost as many as the forty-three "average or below average" (Rostov, Stavropol', Saratov, Kaliningrad oblasts, etc.).[244] Within the leading regions the two autonomous okrugs are home to the natural gas and metals boomtowns of Surgut and Noril'sk. Moscow, which by the twenty-first century had joined the ranks of world cities, is in a class by itself.[245] Its attractiveness for migrant laborers is not only the large number but also the range of jobs increasingly "reserved" for migrants—construction, domestic service, and petty trade for sure, but also office and apartment repair, courtyard cleaning, window washing, street cleaning, car washing and repair, child care, sick care, elderly care, and certain forms of entertainment including the sex trade.[246] As Tiuriukanova points out, "the systematic use of migrants' labor creates serious transformations not only in the economy but in social relations." Just as in developed countries, she adds, "thanks to female migrants looking after children, the aged, and the sick, middle-class women are freed from such work, raise the level of their activeness in the public sphere, and demand more socially prestigious work."[247] Indeed the immigrant labor force underwrites the same kinds of social change as it does elsewhere in the world.

---

243. Meredith Roman, "Making Caucasians Black: Moscow since the Fall of Communism and the Racialization of Non-Russians," *Journal of Communist Studies and Transition Politics* 18, no. 2 (2002): 3, 12–13.

244. Mukomel' defines the economically vibrant regions as those "anticipating income" (*Migratsionnaia politika*, 194, 326–27).

245. The world city status of Moscow is contested in Sarah Hudspith, ed., "Moscow: A Global City," *Slavic Review* 72, no. 3 (2013): 453–527.

246. Tiuriukanova, "Trudovaia migratsiia," 8.

247. Ibid. For a fictional account of this relationship in the Soviet sixties, see Iurii Trifonov, "Vera i Zoika," *Novyi Mir*, no. 12 (1966): 75–85. We thank Mihaela Pacurar for drawing our attention to the story.

Conclusion

Once the shock of the break with the Soviet past had worn off, migration to the city dramatically accelerated trends that had been developing for some time. The city was triumphant over the village in twentieth-century Russia, and late-century patterns of arrivals resembled those elsewhere. In what is awkwardly called this "globalized world" newcomers arrived from afar—from China, for example, but also often from near-abroad states like Kazakhstan and Kyrgyzstan. Ties among former Soviet republics echoed the strong links between some Western European states and their former colonies, but not in a precise way because Soviet republics were integral to the Union and shared a continuous land mass. Most new immigrants to the post-Soviet city, like many newcomers in Western Europe, operated without legal papers; many appeared ethnically and linguistically distinct from residents and were subject to discriminatory treatment as a consequence. Finally, although migrants tended to take unskilled jobs, they did not necessarily hail from villages but in many cases came from a distant city. Migration patterns are more distinct to post-Soviet cities that owe their existence to the extraordinarily rich natural resources of the country's least hospitable zones. The most successful of these cities   or those with the most valuable resources—continue to attract residents of the Russian Federation and from the near abroad.

The thread of continuity throughout this chapter is the perception of the city as a site of opportunity and interest, albeit in dramatically different forms since Semën Kanatchikov descended from his father's cart in 1895 or Evdokiia Kulikova arrived to work as a chambermaid. The industrializing Soviet city offered work and a chance to blend in for those under suspicion, and culture to aspiring students. The operations of minerals extraction made careers, and with the development of the service sector at the end of the century, business students, market vendors, construction workers, and caregivers alike flocked to prosperous towns and cities. Kazakh parents allowed their daughter to be taken to Samara out of the belief that this city of over a million people offered opportunity; market vendors traveled from Azerbaijan to Moscow because the city offered the chance to trade. Yet for all the observations about wage differentials and economic rationality, migrants' own repertoires mattered. Networks of kin and friendship continue to lead most migrants like the Kyrgyz interviewed by Madeleine Reeves to their destination; people seek out destinations that their compatriots have chosen, and find their way along a path taken by others whom they trust.[248]

Distinctions among regimes stand out in this portrait of migration to cities across the twentieth century. In the early years, when rates of mobility were particularly high, village

---

248. Madeleine Reeves, "Black Work, Green Money: Remittances, Ritual, and Domestic Economies in Southern Kyrgyzstan," *Slavic Review* 71 (2012), 125.

legal and family structures forged ties that kept village people going home in certain seasons and for their later years. Early Soviet divorce legislation and collectivization significantly frayed familial and legal bonds with the village, as urbanization jump-started with the First Five-Year Plan and continued thereafter. Soviet authorities recruited workers and specialists alike to the new towns of the Far North and the resource-rich areas of Siberia, where earlier prisoners had labored. With the end of the USSR, mobility meant the crossing of international borders for many who had been at home in the multinational state. Once a neoliberal regime allowed labor to be recruited in an unregulated market, newcomers in the city could be hired, fired, and exploited at will, whether citizens or not. The end of the century found the cities of the Russian Federation in a state that was recognizable to denizens in most developed countries—the native-born held most of the cards in a segmented labor market.

~CHAPTER FOUR~

Career Migrants

Pursuing a career often has caused a departure from home, either temporary or permanent. As one of us noted in reference to Western Europe, the bureaucratization of the state in the nineteenth century meant that the majority of career migrants were white-collar functionaries.[1] The employer, in this case the state, typically not only hired the functionary but also designated the location of his or her work. As in Western Europe so in Russia, the state sent schoolteachers and agronomists to far-flung villages, engineers and other technical personnel to resource-extractive enterprises, and officials of all ranks to regional capitals. This institutional determination of where the work is performed, on the face of it irrespective of employee desire, is what makes career migration distinct. Thus the study of career migration nudges us away from the more self-determined movements that pioneered settlements, harvested crops, built cities, and populated them. Within this particular regime of migration, however, migrants could deploy repertoires to maximize possibilities for making the state's agendas compatible with their own. Here we emphasize those who were called on to control others' mobility. Even as they took up their positions in destinations prescribed by their employers, career migrants used networks of affinity and familial loyalties to affect where they were assigned, the conditions under which they lived, and how long they would remain. Geographic hierarchies—being near or far from the favored cities, in an obscure or key location—had important implications for access to goods and services, cutting across occupational, class, and other distinctions.

Of course, many peripatetic careers existed beyond state employment, especially in Imperial Russia and again as a result of privatization during the 1990s. Our focus on

---

1. Moch, *Moving Europeans*, 17. Of course, the culture of capitalist corporations also demands career migration from its managerial strata. For the founding observations on this phenomenon, see William H. Whyte, *The Organization Man* (New York, 1956).

state-employed professionals fleshes out John Randolph and Eugene Avrutin's observation that "governance *of* mobility created the tools to attempt governance *through* mobility."[2] The tsarist state, as we saw in the case of resettlement, had a great interest in controlling where settlers went and the conditions under which they traveled. We begin this chapter by discussing administrators—and closely follow one—deployed by the state to that end.

The Soviet state had greater ambitions and from the 1930s onward sought a monopoly over employment and deployment. The apex of state ambition came with the First Five-Year Plan. The uprooting of peasants by a state intent on redistributing them according to its lights has attracted a great deal of attention from scholars, and justifiably so. But as Kate Brown observes, "the first people roused into motion were the 'cadres' . . . people who knew statistics, agronomy, veterinary sciences, engineering, and mechanics."[3] And, one might add, the security forces that rounded up kulaks and led them out of the villages to the special settlements. Here, we concentrate on personnel in two major state institutions: the agricultural and resettlement administrations and the security apparatus. We follow them from the late nineteenth century across the Imperial-Soviet divide. We then consider the assignment of young specialists in general and their efforts to shape their own future, concluding with post-Soviet retrospective views of this system.

Agricultural Administrators

Aleksei Alekseevich Tatishchev served as a midlevel bureaucrat in the resettlement department of the Main Administration of Land Management and Agriculture (itself part of the Ministry of Agriculture and State Domains) from 1906 until the Bolshevik Revolution. Tatishchev's memoirs, completed in 1924 but only published in 2001, have served as a window into the "technocratic ideology" that, so it is argued, reigned supreme in the Resettlement Administration.[4] But more important for our purposes, they document the career of an official who preferred the relative independence of fieldwork to remaining in Petersburg "composing inquiries and notes for some superior maybe to notice or maybe not in

---

2. John Randolph and Eugene M. Avrutin, eds., *Russia in Motion: Cultures of Human Mobility since 1850* (Urbana, 2012), 7–8.

3. Brown, *A Biography of No Place*, 115–16.

4. Holquist, " 'In Accord with State Interests,' " 151–79. After the Revolution, Tatishchev worked for the Hetmanate government in Kiev as a secretary to the Council of Ministers, and more briefly for Semën Petliiura's Directorate. He then served as an assistant director in the Union of Agricultural Cooperatives in Khar'kov, and eventually became involved in implementing agrarian reform measures under General Wrangel in Crimea and southern Ukraine.

deciding some matter of great significance."[5] Even while based in the capital between 1906 and 1911, he seized the opportunity to make two extended trips to Siberia and the Russian Far East: in 1906, immediately upon his appointment, he accompanied Grigorii Glinka, the Resettlement Administration's director, on an inspection tour of resettlement stations; two years later, he accompanied an expedition of botanists and geologists to identify land appropriate for settlement in the Amur basin, extending his sojourn from three to six months in order to visit Khabarovsk and Vladivostok.

Tatishchev returned to Vladivostok in the spring of 1911 to serve as the administration's field director for the Maritime province. He was all of twenty-five and, to mollify his mother, promised not to refuse the offer of an appointment closer to Petersburg should one be made in the future. He reports that the workday in his office began at nine o'clock, but Tatishchev, like many migrants, adhered to routines he had acquired back home and so arrived at ten. He liked the city well enough, though its demographic stratification meant that his "extreme youth" relative to other civil servants and, we might add, his bachelor status limited his social life. The military and naval officers lived by themselves and the world of merchants and lawyers held no attraction for him. In any case, he spent much time traveling—to Khabarovsk, Sakhalin, settlements along the Iman and Malinovka-Vaka rivers, and even Japan.[6]

In November 1912, his patron Glinka offered him the position in Tashkent as head of the Turkestan Department of Agriculture and State Domains, and although resettlement did not have much of a presence in the region, he accepted. Here too the working day began at nine in winter and an hour earlier in the summer, but our hero persisted in his ways, arriving at ten and staying after others had departed. "As in other cities in Turkestan," he writes, " 'Russian Tashkent' arose alongside the native town," which "for us, hardly existed." He did rely, however, on two "Sarts" (the term used in Imperial Russia for Turkic-speaking urban residents)—a servant who lived in a building behind the house Tatishchev occupied and a footman who spoke Russian "fluently and almost correctly."[7]

At first, the Great War scarcely affected Tatishchev's responsibilities, but in the fall of 1915 Governor-General Martson assigned him the task of determining the capacity of Turkestan's cities to receive refugees. Then, in December, the Resettlement Administration transferred him back to Petrograd for reassignment. Sent to the Caucasian front to assess possibilities for colonizing lands conquered from the Turks, Tatishchev returned to the capital, where he passed the summer writing reports that went nowhere.[8] Then he was off

5. A. A. Tatishchev, *Zemli i liudi: V gushche pereselencheskogo dvizheniia (1906–1921)* (Moscow, 2001), 99.
6. Ibid., 65–70, 98, 102, 108–9, 117–18, 125.
7. Ibid., 141, 157–58.
8. One such report is discussed by Holquist, "In Accord with State Interests," 171.

Career Migration of A.A. Tatishchev, 1906-1920

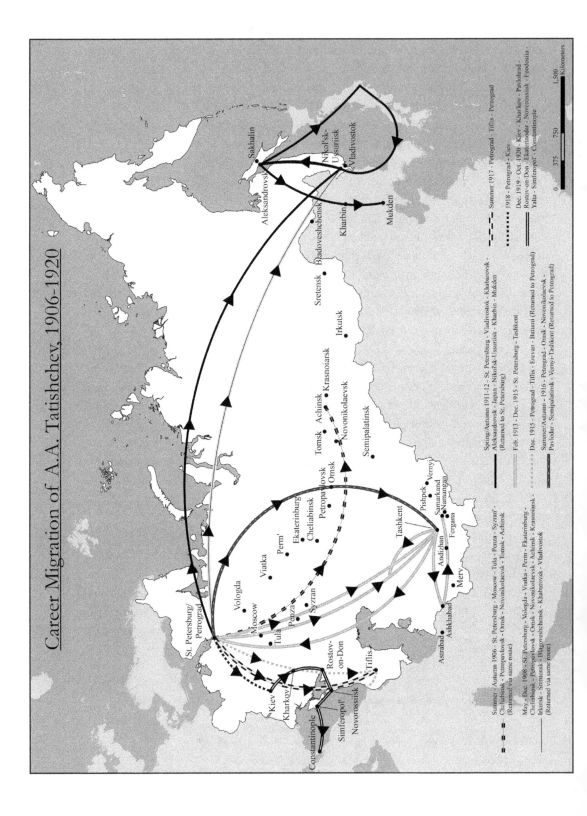

Summer - Autumn 1906 - St. Petersburg - Moscow - Tula - Penza - Syzran' - Cheliabinsk - Petropavlovsk - Omsk - Novonikolaevsk - Tomsk - Achinsk (Returned via same route)

May - Dec. 1906 - St. Petersburg - Vologda - Viatka - Perm - Ekaterinburg - Cheliabinsk - Petropavlovsk - Omsk - Novonikolaevsk - Achinsk - Krasnoiarsk - Irkutsk - Sretensk - Blagoveshchensk - Khabarovsk - Vladivostok (Returned via same route)

Spring/Autumn 1911-12 - St. Petersburg - Vladivostok - Khabarovsk - Aleksandrovsk - Japan - Nikol'sk-Ussuriisk - Kharbin - Mukden (Returned to St. Petersburg)

Feb 1913 - Dec. 1915 - St. Petersburg - Tashkent

Dec. 1915 - Petrograd - Tiflis - Erevan - Batumi (Returned to Petrograd)

Summer/Autumn - 1916 - Petrograd - Omsk - Novonikolaevsk - Pavlodar - Semipalatinsk - Vernyi-Tashkent (Returned to Petrograd)

Summer 1917 - Petrograd - Tiflis - Petrograd

1918 - Petrograd - Kiev

Dec. 1919 - Oct. 1920 - Kiev - Kharkov - Pavlohrad - Rostov-on-Don - Ekaterinodar - Novorossiisk - Feodosiia - Yalta - Simferopol' - Constantinople

0   375   750   1,500
Kilometers

again, this time to Siberia and eastern Kazakhstan, site of the violent rebellion sparked by the extension of conscription to ethnic Kazakhs. He spent most of 1917 in Petrograd, but in October traveled to Tiflis as the Resettlement Administration's representative on a commission investigating a dispute among Russian settlers and Turks ("Tatars") over water rights.[9]

Tatishchev's career demonstrates how individual proclivities dovetailed with structural forces. As a member of the nobility and the son of a governor (of Poltava), he seemed destined for state service, a destiny reinforced by his matriculation at St. Petersburg's prestigious Alexander Lycée. "By established order," he writes, "one of the privileges of the lycée was that upon completion, its students automatically were enrolled in state service."[10] But not all who entered state service had Tatishchev's yen to serve in the provinces. Moreover, his interest in resettlement—the subject of his prizewinning student essay—increased the likelihood that the provinces would be remote (see map 4.1).

Bonds formed at school aided Tatishchev's career, and family and class ties helped him adjust to new environments, serving as an upper-class equivalent of *zemliachestvo*. When Tatishchev arrived in Tashkent, he discovered that one of his colleagues had attended the same school as his uncle. When he went to Erevan during the war, he paid a visit to the governor, Lachinov, a former guardsman and classmate of his brother Nikita. Lachinov's assistant turned out to be first cousin of one Saburov, whom Aleksei had known at the lycée. When later in 1916 he journeyed to Semipalatinsk, he met that province's governor, Fedia Cherntsov, who had grown up on the estate next to Tatishchev's in Tver' province. Also present was Cherntsov's wife, Olga Alekseevna, "with whom we had been close from time immemorial."[11] Even the uniform with its insignia could facilitate bonding, such as when General Nikolai Iudenich, commander of the Caucasian Army, noticed the Turkestan badge that Tatishchev was wearing. Iudenich thereupon recalled his service as a young man in that part of the empire, a memory "he would cherish for the rest of his life."[12] So although in Jane Burbank's words, "collectivity . . . was not a quality easily come by for imperial officials," they nonetheless had a society of their own, even—or especially—in the Far East, Central Asia, and the Caucasus.[13]

Russia's service elite, like that of other empires, was multiethnic. Men of German, Tatar, Polish, Georgian, Armenian, Finnish, and other ethnic origins figured among its military officers and civil officials. The Empire also provided opportunities for non-Russians to

---

9. Tatishchev, *Zemli i liudi*, 198–202, 216–52. Tbilisi was known in Russian as Tiflis until 1936.
10. Ibid., 31.
11. Tatishchev, *Zemli i liudi*, 151, 235–36, 244.
12. Ibid., 160, 237.
13. Jane Burbank, "The Rights of Difference: Law and Citizenship in the Russian Empire," in *Imperial Formations*, ed. Ann Laura Stoler, Carole McGranahan, and Peter C. Perdue (Santa Fe, 2007), 93–94.

obtain land in the colonies, which in the case of Stanislaw V. Poniatowski, became the basis of his expertise in the Resettlement Administration. Tatishchev, his colleague, describes Poniatowski as a "long-time resident of Turkestan" who "knew local conditions well, not only theoretically but from . . . having bought land not far from Tashkent which he farmed."[14]

Tatishchev was most expansive about the multitalented "self-made man," Nikolai L'vovich Gondatti (1860–1946), the son of an Italian sculptor. Gondatti's more brilliant career helps to contextualize Tatishchev's. Educated in the Alexander Institute in Nizhny Novgorod and then at Moscow University, Gondatti traveled to Turkestan and China as a member of the Imperial Geographic Society to study tea and silk production. His state service began in 1894 when he accepted an appointment as chief of the Anadyr okrug in the extreme northeast of the Eurasian continent. During his two years' stay, he conducted a census of the indigenous Chukchi and used his training in anthropology to study their language and customs. He then worked for the Resettlement Administration in the Ussuri krai, a little more than a decade before Tatishchev arrived in the region. A series of appointments as governor in Siberia and the Far East followed—to Tobol'sk, Tomsk, and finally, in 1911, the Priamur krai, where Tatishchev encountered him and where he served until the February Revolution.

Until then the Russian nobility had demonstrated great flexibility in adapting to institutional change.[15] Tatishchev's memoirs suggest that affinities formed earlier in life or while on the job facilitated such adaptation by the state's peripatetic officials. War and revolution took their toll, however. Iudenich had success against Turkish forces, but, relieved of his post by the Provisional Government, threw in his lot with the failed putsch attempt of General Lavr Kornilov. His subsequent assault as head of the Northwestern Army on Red Petrograd also failed, and he departed for exile in France. Gondatti went into exile in Harbin, the Russian enclave in Manchuria. Tatishchev left Crimea for Constantinople and eventually settled in France.

Others stayed on to work for the Soviet government.[16] According to a Soviet census of the state bureaucracy from 1928, "holdovers" from the tsarist era comprised slightly more than one-quarter of all administrative personnel, although no more than 6 percent of the total—about forty thousand individuals—had worked in state (as opposed to municipal,

---

14. Tatishchev, *Zemli i liudi*, 149–51.

15. Don Karl Rowney, "Organizational Change and Social Adaptation: The Pre-Revolutionary Ministry of Internal Affairs," in *Russian Officialdom: The Bureaucratization of Russian Society from the Seventeenth to the Twentieth Century*, ed. Walter McKenzie Pintner and Don Karl Rowney (Chapel Hill, 1980), 303.

16. For some of the officials from the Resettlement Administration and the work they did for the Soviet government, see Holquist, "In Accord with State Interests," 171–79.

zemstvo, or private) institutions.[17] But percentages varied considerably among different branches of government. Of the Soviet commissariats, agriculture had the highest proportion of holdover employees—63 percent in 1923. As late as January 1928, over half of those working on the provincial level and slightly under half on the county level had begun their careers doing essentially the same thing for the tsarist government. As one Communist Party secretary complained with respect to the Gomel provincial land section in the Belorussian SSR, "The real bosses were not the communists sitting there but specialists of doubtful character."[18]

George Yaney has argued that what most of these fellows did was to continue to consolidate the land that the peasant commune had subdivided into narrow strips. This process of land consolidation had been at the core of the Stolypin reforms. The work, he concludes, "seems to have gone forward at a much faster pace in the 1920s than it did in 1906–1914." The substantial increase in the number of specialists assigned to the county level no doubt facilitated it. As part of the Bolsheviks' effort to expand the Soviet state's presence in the countryside, the number of Narkomzem personnel at this level rose from less than 14,000 to 23,500 between 1925 and 1928, an increase of almost 70 percent. Meanwhile, republic-level organs of the commissariat lost one-third of their staff.[19]

Many of these rusticated officials, it has been surmised, "were probably loathe to leave comfortable urban posts" and "did so with great reluctance." To make matters worse, their salaries, according to James Heinzen, "were miserly in comparison with specialists with similar training employed in industry and transport," about which they "voiced their resentment openly." Those who did not leave for jobs in these other more prestigious fields shifted from one district to another in search of more remunerative work.[20] In one case that Heinzen cites from the commissariat's journal, a surveyor worked successively in Odessa, Kharkov, the Caucasus, Arkhangel'sk, Tver, Perm, Omsk, Biisk, Blagoveshchensk, Kustanai, and Samarkand, "never spen[ding] more than six months in any one place because he could always find a land section desperate for experienced surveyors."[21]

---

17. *Gosudarstvennyi apparat SSSR, 1924–1928* (Moscow, 1929), 59–62, cited in Stephen Sternheimer, "Administration for Development: The Emerging Bureaucratic Elite, 1920–1930," in Pintner and Rowney, *Russian Officialdom*, 343. See also E. H. Carr, *Foundations of a Planned Economy, 1926–1929* (Harmondsworth: Penguin, 1971), 2: 320–21.

18. James Heinzen, *Inventing a Soviet Countryside: State Power and the Transformation of Rural Russia, 1917–1929* (Pittsburgh, 2004), 97–98; George L. Yaney, "Agricultural Administration in Russia from the Stolypin Land Reform to Forced Collectivization: An Interpretive Study," in *The Soviet Rural Community: A Symposium*, ed. James R. Millar (Urbana, 1971), 6.

19. Yaney, "Agricultural Administration," 7; Sternheimer, "Administration for Development," 323, 326–27.

20. Sternheimer, "Administration for Development," 326–27; Heinzen, *Inventing a Soviet Countryside*, 174.

21. Heinzen, *Inventing a Soviet Countryside*, 175.

Salary aside, living conditions in the depths of the provinces and the absence of means of transport tried even the most dedicated of agricultural specialists. So did the adherence among peasants to their own methods of farming and suspiciousness of agronomists' advice. No wonder graduates of agricultural technical institutes, including Moscow's prestigious Timiriazev Academy, refused to accept postings outside major cities. By 1929, the head of Narkomzem's agronomic section was characterizing this as a mass phenomenon.[22] Their attitude was hardly unique. Following the abolition of the provincial administrative level in 1930, "officials in a number of organizations," we read in a summary report by the Central Control Commission, "experienced feelings of panic and a reluctance to go to the *raiony* [districts]." "The wife won't go," one official in the Urals claimed. "There're a lot of sick people there, she says." To avoid being sent to district offices, officials in Vladivostok themselves "showered the party committee with petitions with all sorts of certificates attached about ailments."[23]

These officials' reluctance to relocate to the countryside contrasts most strikingly with the enormous success of mobilizing the Twenty-Five Thousanders recruited from the ranks of the party and trade unions to put backbone in the collectivization movement. By the time the party's Central Committee had announced in November 1929 the necessity of mobilizing "not less than twenty-five thousand workers with sufficient organizational-political experience," many of the representatives of state authority in the countryside had been relieved of their responsibilities. Prominent among the targets of what was a general purge of the state bureaucracy were holdovers from the tsarist administration, also known as "formers" whose "alien" class origin was enough in the new circumstances of Stalin's Great Turn to have them removed.[24] Thus the "cadres" mentioned by Brown were not those with experience dating back before the Bolshevik Revolution, but over two hundred thousand "new people"—the Twenty-Five Thousanders, political activists, and demobilized Red Army soldiers—who, having received crash-course training, fanned out among the machine-tractor stations (MTS) and the collective and state farms.[25]

These groups represented an offshoot of the accelerated promotion program that in the course of the 1930s created the new Soviet elite.[26] What distinguished them from workers

---

22. Ibid., 176–77.

23. Siegelbaum and Sokolov, *Stalinism as a Way of Life*, 114 (document 39).

24. For mention of the Twenty-Five Thousanders in the November 1929 decree, see *Kommunisticheskaia partiia sovetskogo soiuza v rezoliutsiiakh i resheniiakh s"ezdov, konferentsii i plenumov TsK (1898–1986)*, 9th ed., vol. 5, 34. For the purge of Narkomzem, see Heinzen, *Inventing a Soviet Countryside*, 198–208. For Siberia, see S. A. Krasil'nikov, ed., *Marginaly v sotsiume: Marginaly kak sotsium: Sibir' (1920–1930-e gody)* (Novosibirsk, 2004), 186–99.

25. Yaney, "Agricultural Administration," 29.

26. The classic study of this phenomenon is Sheila Fitzpatrick, *Education and Social Mobility in the Soviet Union, 1921–1934* (Cambridge, 1979).

sent to higher educational institutions or promoted from the bench directly into administrative positions was that their promotion contradicted conventional practice. They typically moved from city to village, from institutions such as factories and army barracks that
had become symbols of Soviet progress to rural areas stereotypically mired in backwardness. Their career trajectories, of course, did not necessarily stop with this move, although
for many it would be difficult, if not impossible, to return whence they came.

Demobilized soldiers comprised the largest contingent of the cadres. The defense commissar Kliment Voroshilov announced in January 1930 the goal of sending 100,000 to the
countryside, three-quarters of whom would be trained to manage collective farms and service tractors and other machinery. By the end of the year, the army had overfulfilled its goal,
training 103,000. But what about the goals of the soldiers? Some, upon arriving back in the
countryside, evidently got carried away with identifying members of soldiers' and officers'
families as kulaks. Were these young men, the majority of whom had been day laborers and
poor peasants when they entered the army, seeking to exercise their political muscle as the
embodiment of the worker-peasant alliance? Whatever the case, the conjoining of agendas—
state and demobilized soldiers—was brief. After 1930, the army's Political Administration
(PU RKKA) limited its program to training tractor drivers, most of whom wound up in the
MTS, established to supply collective farms with equipment and technical assistance.[27]

The Twenty-Five Thousanders had more staying power. Lynne Viola sums up the criteria
established by the party's Central Committee for recruiting them as class consciousness,
political literacy, factory experience of at least five years, and a lack of residual ties to the
village. Seventy percent of recruits were to be party or Komsomol members; 15 percent
were to be women. Over 70,000 workers volunteered, of whom over 27,500 were selected.
They included Civil War veterans and hereditary proletarians, some with several decades of
experience on the shop floor. Among them were men like I. V. Vasil'ev, a Red Guard in 1917
and a commissar in the Civil War who had earned shock worker status; A. V. Gruzdev, the
editor of the factory wall newspaper who had propagandized against religion in Baptist
villages and joined the party during its Lenin Levy of 1924; and the crew leader Cherednichenko, from Moscow's Hammer and Sickle Factory, a veteran of the Soviet-Polish War
of 1919–20 whom Lev Kopelev memorably described as the "one-eyed commissar." As it
turned out, over nine in ten of all Twenty-Five Thousanders were male—overfulfilling the
target for men. Moscow and Leningrad provided over 40 percent of all recruits, which made
for quite an urban contingent heading for rural life.[28]

---

27. Mark von Hagen, *Soldiers in the Proletarian Dictatorship: The Red Army and the Soviet Socialist State, 1917–1930* (Ithaca, 1990), 312–25.

28. Lynne Viola, *The Best Sons of the Fatherland: Workers in the Vanguard of Soviet Collectivization* (New York, 1987), 37–46; Lev Kopelev, *The Education of a True Believer* (New York, 1978), 184. Shock workers typically engaged in "socialist competition" with other workers to meet or exceed quotas.

Unresolved issues like salary, expected length of service, and the reluctance of factory organizations to part with valued members hindered the recruitment drive, but Viola insists that evidence of the use of coercion or subterfuge to fulfill quotas is scant. "Some workers may have volunteered with expectations of future educational opportunities," she adds. "Yet it is more than likely that the skilled workers who volunteered to go to the countryside could, by exerting much less effort, have secured the opportunity to study had they simply remained at the factory." Rather than materialistic or self-interested motives, Soviet patriotism—the desire to overcome backwardness and defeat the country's enemies—was "the primary leaven of the campaign" and the most powerful reason for volunteering.[29]

The Twenty-Five Thousanders represented the vanguard of a revolution in the countryside, embodying a leap of faith that the ways of the factory could be applied to agricultural production and that peasants would eventually appreciate their imposition. They would serve as the eyes and ears of Kolkhoztsentr (the Union of Agricultural Collectives), the Moscow-based institution that had sent them, and act as troubleshooters in relations between local cadres and collective farmers.[30] But, leaving the cities "with a triumphal march," at least one enthusiastic participant described his arrival in the village as "a funeral dirge." His experience thus repeated a pattern dating back at least to the 1870s when populists went to the countryside with high expectations of bringing socialism to the peasants, only to be met with suspicion.[31]

Most Twenty-Five Thousanders became collective farm chairmen or deputy chairmen, but because of what Viola calls the "famine" in rural leadership, they took on additional responsibilities such as accounting, bookkeeping, agronomy, and political education. They rarely met with a warm reception. According to Kopelev, the above-mentioned Cherednichenko, sent to a Russian village on the Ukrainian side of the border, felt "it was like the Civil War all over again," and "became an absolute dictator." The peasants, at first cowed, eventually rioted and Cherednichenko barely escaped with his life. Indeed, some Twenty-Five Thousander collective farm chairmen—at least fifty by one count—were murdered. Many more were transferred repeatedly by district officials, or simply ignored. "I am a victim of the class struggle," wrote one to his trade union after district officials had expelled him from the party. "I was slandered. I am a victim of the delusions of the district officials who don't want to admit their own mistakes. . . . I am desperate . . . help, help me!" Others wrote to the newspapers or their factory

---

29. Viola, *Best Sons of the Fatherland*, 58–59.

30. Ibid., 132, 136.

31. Ibid., 76. It also paralleled the experience of many demobilized Red Army soldiers—festive sendoffs by the army and "indifference or hostility" back in their home villages. Von Hagen, *Soldiers in the Proletarian Dictatorship*, 300. This refers to the mid-1920s.

committees complaining of neglect, if not betrayal.[32] Long workdays, near constant dousing of bureaucratic fires, lack of supplies, lateness in receiving their salaries, and stupendous exhaustion were the rule.

Like other sorts of migrants, not all stuck it out. Of the original 27,519 who had arrived in the countryside in January–February 1930, some 22,000 remained by the summer. The rest had taken ill or died, received orders to return to their factories, or "deserted," that is, departed of their own free will.[33] Those who came from factories that engaged in patron-client relations with villages or went to areas from which their factories recruited seasonal labor tended to have an easier time than where no such contacts existed. Those sent to Central Asia, particularly where relations between Slavic settlers and indigenous people were fraught with conflict, experienced the most danger. Relief came for thousands in the form of promotions to higher positions, including to district offices that officials at the provincial level had avoided like the plague. But the majority stuck it out on the collective farms, holding steadfast through the two years to which they had committed themselves. About 7,000 workers left after 1932, most to return to their respective factories or enter an educational institution. Some 11,000 remained in the countryside.[34]

In subsequent decades, the Twenty-Five Thousanders became talismans of a sort, symbols of commitment to the ideals of Soviet socialism. As part of his "voluntarist" approach to raising agricultural productivity, Khrushchev ordered the mobilization of an even larger number of cadres—the "Thirty Thousanders"—in 1955, and frequently invoked their predecessors. Some of the original contingent survived in the collective farm system long enough to advise the neophytes.[35] The longer-term legacy is more ambiguous. When interviewed more than seventy years later, Vera Prokof'eva, who had grown up in a village in Yaroslavl' oblast', could still remember the two young men who came from the city after collectivization, one to be chairman and the other to be accountant of the collective farm. "And in a short time they transformed the economy. . . . We had five breeding ponds for big fish, so they organized the catch, and took the fish to the city where they sold them and got money for clothes, soap, and other household items for everyone. And soon everything was hunky-dory (v azhure) in Ivashkova."[36] But, as someone put it in response to a query about

32. Kopelev, Education of a True Believer, 185, 188–89; Viola, Best Sons of the Fatherland, 145, 159, 186–92. For the estimate of fifty murders based on "far from complete information," see V. M. Selunskaia, Rabochie-dvadtsatipiatitysiachniki (Moscow, 1964), 145. Viola considers this an underestimation and notes that most murders occurred in national minority areas.

33. Viola, Best Sons of the Fatherland, 118.

34. Ibid., 174, 196, 206–7; Selunskaia, Rabochie-dvadtsatipiatitysiachniki, 149–50.

35. Viola, Best Sons of the Fatherland, 207.

36. "Vera Prokof'eva," http://iremember.ru/mediki/prokofeva-vera-aleksandrovna.html (accessed August 26, 2012).

the meaning of "twenty five thousanders" sent to an online information site in Russia in 2009, "This long word says nothing to today's youth."[37]

And then there are the descendants. In March 2010, someone wrote to the chat forum "Our Viatka" inquiring about the Twenty-Five Thousanders because "grandpa Pavlov Aleksandr Pavlovich, born 1903, was sent from the Kirov Factory [in Leningrad] to build up the collective farms. He reached Khakasiia [central Siberia]." This prompted "ksenia" two months later to write, "I too seek information about this. From the words of my grandmother, my great grandfather, Kolesnov, Mikhail Ivanovich, worked at the Kirov Factory and was sent from Leningrad to build up the collective farms. From Leningrad twelve people were sent to Krasnoiarsk, and then two of them left for Khakasiia. My great grandfather was chairman of the Mal Khadari collective farm." We know that Kolesnov was still chairman of the kolkhoz ten years later, for he is mentioned by Stanislaw Puchlik in his account, solicited by the Krasnoiarsk branch of Memorial, of having been deported along with his family and other Poles in June 1941 to this very kolkhoz. "The chairman Kolesnov didn't like us," he writes, "because he considered us enemies of the Soviet Union. But we didn't ask to be sent to Siberia."[38] And so one form of migration yet again crashed into another, albeit with a delay of ten years.

The broader history of collective farm chairmen, as analyzed from more than three hundred published biographies from the years 1930–70, shows that the proportion who came from outside the kolkhoz fluctuated a great deal. As evident in the case of the Twenty-Five Thousanders, the initial cohort was "composed chiefly of persons alien to rural life and without knowledge of local conditions."[39] By the late 1930s, however, this was less likely to be the case. The typical kolkhoz chairman of those years, as described by a Soviet newspaper decades later, "was an intelligent, not very literate peasant, who knew, however, how to count centners [hundredweight, equal to 100 kg.] and rubles."[40]

The immediate postwar years saw a reversion to the earlier pattern of most kolkhoz chairmen appointed from the outside. They weren't necessarily from urban areas, though, and few, it seems, had been industrial workers. The backgrounds mentioned in available biographies—accounting-finance, teaching, the trade network, village soviet leadership—suggested that counting "centners and rubles" remained an important criterion.[41] The data

---

37. ["Kto takie dvadtsati piati tysiachniki??? Zaranee spasibo!" Otvet.mail.ru] http://otvet.mail.ru/question/32775128/ (accessed August 26, 2012).

38. "Kniga pamiati zhertv politicheskikh represii Respubliki Khakasiia. Tom 3," http://www.memorial.krsk.ru/Articles/XKP/3/18.htm (accessed August 26, 2012).

39. Gregory Bienstock, Solomon M. Schwarz, and Aaron Yugow, *Management in Russian Industry and Agriculture* (New York, 1944), 179, cited in Jerry F. Hough, "The Changing Nature of the Kolkhoz Chairman," in Millar, *Soviet Rural Community*, 104.

40. *Sovetskaia Rossiia*, February 6, 1968, 1, cited in Hough, "Changing Nature," 106.

41. Hough, "Changing Nature," 107–10.

compiled in 1947 during an inspection of the twenty-four kolkhozes in a district in Crimea suggest that whatever their qualifications or desired characteristics, chairmen did not remain in their positions for very long. In 1945, seventeen of the twenty-four kolkhozes had replaced their chairman; in 1946, thirty-five did so, meaning that as many as eleven kolkhozes had removed more than one incumbent; and in 1947, thirteen were removed. The Red October kolkhoz won the competition for the highest turnover by changing its chairman eight times in the three years.[42]

With the 1955 call for thirty thousand "progressive and highly qualified people of the socialist city" to take up positions as collective farm chairmen, the pendulum swung even further in the direction of recruiting from outside agriculture.[43] Over one hundred thousand responded, at least some probably attracted by the cash bonuses promised for the first three years paid on a sliding scale. Some who were chosen had backgrounds that resembled their First Five-Year Plan predecessors. For example, the seventy volunteers from Rostelmash, the giant agricultural machine factory in Rostov-on-Don, included a foreman and secretary of one of the factory's party organizations with twenty-five years of work experience, and a Hero of Socialist Labor. Their general level of education was higher, though, as one might expect given the expansion of educational opportunities and attainments in intervening decades.[44]

Accompanied by their families, the Thirty Thousanders took up their positions in the collective farms on what they assumed was a permanent basis. Of the original cohort of some twenty thousand dispatched to collective farms in the summer of 1955, thirteen thousand were still working as chairmen three years later.[45] A few years further on, however, Jerry Hough detected "an apparent reversal" of Khrushchev's policy. Once more, as during the late 1930s, it appeared that local boys were preferred.[46] This lack of consistency suggests a restless search by political authorities to overcome the accursed contradictions between town and country, or in less highfalutin terms, technical competence and local trust. Here, we also find a complexity of migratory patterns, even in the case of career migration. We use several biographies to illustrate.

The first is that of Polikarp Sergeev as described in his letter of January 1938 to Krest'ianskaia gazeta. Born in 1887 to a middle peasant family, Sergeev became a farmhand

---

42. USHMM RG-22.027M, GARF, f. A-327, Reel 340, op. 2, d. 626, l. 180. These were all kolkhozes of settlers recruited to replace the Crimean Tatars who had been deported in 1944.

43. The directive, dated March 25, 1955, can be found in Direktivy KPSS i Sovetskogo pravitel'stva po khoziaistvennym voprosam, sbornik dokumentov, vol. 4 (Moscow, 1958), 373–98.

44. Of the eighteen thousand sent to collective farms in the RSFSR, Ukraine, Belarus, and Kazakhstan, 55 percent had completed a higher or specialized secondary education degree. A. N. Karamelev, "Dvizhenie tridtsadtitysiachnikov i ukreplenie kolkhozov," Voprosy istorii KPSS, no. 1 (1962): 118–22.

45. Ibid., 125. The twenty thousand comprised approximately 23 percent of all kolkhoz chairmen.

46. Hough, "Changing Nature," 111–16.

at age eleven. In 1900 he moved to Moscow. Called up for military service in 1909, he served in the town of Blagoveshchensk on the Amur. There he encountered a Tolstoyan who converted him. After the completion of his military service, he alternately worked in a "farming artel" outside Tula and at a vegetarian cafeteria in Moscow until the outbreak of the First World War, when he fled to Siberia to avoid conscription. He returned to Moscow after the Revolution, but "some time later" left for the countryside with his whole family. In 1931, he was elected chairman of the Lenin kolkhoz and to a village soviet in Orel oblast'. But in December 1937 he was ousted as chairman and soon thereafter expelled from the kolkhoz as a sectarian, wrecker, and enemy of the people.[47] Neither a Twenty-Five Thousander nor "alien to rural life," Sergeev had considerable experience of urban life, to say nothing of extensive travel within the country. He definitely exemplifies career migration, although it is hard to say which career was paramount.

Our second kolkhoz chairman, Petr Abovin-Egides, seems to be even more of an outlier. Born in the revolutionary year of 1917 in Kiev, he taught in a village before studying philosophy in Moscow. He completed his university degree in 1941 and immediately left for the front. Wounded and taken prisoner, he escaped, only to be sent to a Gulag camp in Vorkuta in 1943 for having betrayed the Motherland. After his release in 1949, he taught for a few years in Ukraine. His stint as chairman of the "Dawn" collective farm—which he described as "the most typical kolkhoz of the most provincial district of the most central oblast' of the Russian Federation (Penza)"—coincided with the Khrushchev "Thaw" from 1956 to 1959. Throughout the 1960s, he taught philosophy in Irkutsk, Briansk, and Rostov-on-Don. In 1970 his involvement in the human rights movement landed him in a psychiatric hospital for two years, and in 1980 he emigrated.[48]

Abovin-Egides, the self-described "philosopher in the kolkhoz," explains in his memoirs that he decided to become a kolkhoz chairman to determine if "it would be possible to build real . . . socialism with our people." This quixotic experiment inevitably fails, but not before he had encouraged the demand for equality of job opportunity, caused the removal of several overbearing party members from their positions, and seriously embarrassed the party obkom secretary.[49] Clearly, Abovin-Egides would never be mistaken for one of those Thirty Thousanders who made a career in kolkhoz administration. But we have no way of knowing what had moved those kolkhoz chairmen, or for that matter, where they had moved, how often, or why.

We can only know that kolkhoz chairmen numbered in the thousands and that like many Soviet officials, some led peripatetic lives. How far they had traveled to arrive at their

47. Siegelbaum and Sokolov, *Stalinism as a Way of Life*, 318–20 (document 116)
48. Petr Abovin-Egides, "Filosof v kolkhze (Fragmenty iz knigi)," *Kontinent*, no. 42 (1984): 200, 239.
49. Ibid., 204, 214–16, 221, 228.

positions could be measured in kilometers but also in cultural terms. Abovin-Egides' account suggests that neither he nor those with whom he hoped to build "real" socialism were psychologically prepared for each other. His was an extreme case, but that the encounter happened at all is telling. To come full circle, our memoirist Tatishchev represented the Resettlement Administration in the far-flung corners of the Empire, where he ministered to the needs of Russian peasant settlers. Yet his closest encounter with "the actual life of the peasants" occurred in 1920 in southern Ukraine, where he "spent the nights and took meals with one or the other members of the county soviet" while working for Baron Petr Wrangel's short-lived Ministry of Agriculture.[50]

Prison Personnel

Soldiers on the move are most visible in wartime, "a million regimental assassins," as Voltaire wrote, perpetrators of killings in Tolstoy's words.[51] But not all soldiers were called to fight in wars. Nameless thousands served as guards. To "see" them in Imperial Russia's prison system, we sometimes need to read the sources from the side if not against the grain. At the end of October 1885, the American George Kennan visited a snowy site at one of the convict mines of Kará in the far east of Siberia. Thirty to forty convicts were hacking at the earth, surrounded by "a cordon of Cossacks." "There was little or no conversation," observed Kennan, "except that around a small camp-fire a few yards away, where half a dozen soldiers were crouching on the snowy ground watching a refractory tea-kettle, and trying to warm their benumbed hands over a sullen, fitful blaze."[52] Rarely mentioned explicitly, soldiers working as guards appear in drawings and photos that depict incarceration in Imperial Russia, marching alongside, in front of, and behind prisoners heading East or out to work. Their presence was noted by Kennan in 1885, by Harry de Windt in 1894, and by James Simpson two years later.[53] Former prisoners mention them too. To cite only one example, Semën Kanatchikov, sentenced to exile as a political prisoner in 1901, journeyed under military guard for two weeks by rail and coach from Saratov to Moscow,

50. Tatishchev, Zemli i liudi, 350.

51. Voltaire, Candide, or The Optimist (London, 1888), 75; Leo Tolstoi, War and Peace, 3 vols., trans. (London, 1911), 3: 346.

52. George Kennan, Siberia and the Exile System, vol. 2 (New York, 1891), 162.

53. Harry de Windt, The New Siberia: Being an Account of a Visit to the Penal Island of Sakhalin, and Political Prison and Mines of the Trans-Baikal District, Eastern Siberia (London, 1896); Kennan, Siberia and the Exile System; James Young Simpson, Side-Lights on Siberia: Some Account of the Great Siberian Railroad, the Prisons and Exile System (Edinburgh, 1898).

from Moscow to Arkhangel'sk, then on foot, traveling 20 to 30 miles a day to the remote settlement of Pinega with a small group of prisoners.[54]

In 1890, the American Caleb Randell heard "Demetrius" (undoubtedly Dmitri) Komorsky, the inspector-general of the prisons of Siberia, speak in Paris at the Société Générale des Prisons. Because the American had been impressed by Komorsky's organization of the Fourth International Penal and Prison Congress held earlier in the year in St. Petersburg, he reported his words in detail. Komorsky was explicit only in his mention of Sakhalin, called by some the "new Siberia" because it was perceived to have a bright future as a site of incarceration. For one thing, Siberia already had enough former-convict settlers and escapees; for another, escape from Sakhalin was nearly impossible. On an island the size of Bulgaria or Greece, he mentioned, home to nearly 6,000 prisoners and about 3,200 discharged prisoners, 960 soldiers served, organized in four companies.[55]

The hierarchy of incarceration personnel seems to have been short: governor, prison director, director's assistant, and guards make a brief list. With few office employees available, convicts did the clerical work in some places.[56] Governors seem to have lived well and were in contact with Moscow and St. Petersburg, judging from the impressions of visitors who were dazzled by their accommodation, furniture, grand pianos, and invariably gracious wives.[57] Both governors and prison directors lived close to their work because they lived among convicts who worked in their offices and in their homes as servants—a director could not be cruel to the convicts, reported Komorsky, because he "would be murdered in three days."[58] Careers in the prison administration, then, put men and their families at risk of separation from the comforts and culture of the European Russian cities and placed them in surroundings that were often dismal.

But not all prison personnel were men. Although we do not know the gender of those who guarded the women prisoners—20 to 30 percent of those transported to Sakhalin in 1890—we do know about other women associated with the prison system. Because schools for the children of prisoners needed instructors, there was work for women, such as the wife of a prisoner who had chosen to accompany her husband and together found a household at the end of his term. At the Aleksandrovsky prison for convicts, the largest in Sakhalin, Harry de Windt met a Mme Taskine who supervised the school for 48 students where the boys would learn a trade and the girls would train as domestics; she would soon be joined by a Mlle Elnikoff, who would serve as schoolmistress while her husband served his

54. Kanatchikov, A Radical Worker, 548–60.
55. Caleb Dwinell Randell, The Fourth International Penal and Prison Congress, St. Petersburg, Russia (Washington, DC, 1891), 244, 247.
56. Randell, Penal and Prison Congress, 251.
57. See, for example, de Windt, New Siberia, 56.
58. Randell, Penal and Prison Congress, 248.

term of five years. The inland school at the Rykovskaia prison site had 127 students led by a political exile and his wife.[59] In the administration of prisons and attached communities the lines between prisoner, exile, and settler could be, and were, crossed by some individuals.

The Soviet state vastly expanded and transformed the carceral system as a means to extract natural resources for industrial production and national defense. Whether the resources were such prosaic but essential materials as timber, coal, and oil or more exotic, "rare" metals as palladium, nickel, cobalt, and gold, Siberia and the Far North had them. To a much greater extent than under the tsars, the Soviet Union had the capacity to extract them. Doing so involved massive feats of technology; it also presupposed getting people in sufficient numbers to very sparsely populated or previously uninhabited areas, indeed to migrate to some of the most inhospitable territory in the world.

Soviet authorities employed two approaches: coercion via the establishment of camps administered by the Gulag and material incentives systematized according to a sliding scale of regional coefficients.[60] The coercive approach, the default mechanism of Stalinism, predominated from the 1930s through the early 1950s, after which material incentives prevailed. The distinction is somewhat blurred by the fact that carceral institutions established to develop resources in remote parts of the country partly relied on enticing free individuals with incentives. Not only prisoners but also NKVD (after 1946, MVD) personnel and "freely hired" employees populated Kolyma and Magadan, Noril'sk and Vorkuta-Pechora, to cite only the most notorious of the camps within the Gulag.[61]

The workings of the Gulag system were assured by the proletarians of the security apparatus—the guards who manned watchtowers, escorted prisoners to and from worksites, and otherwise kept an eye on them. Aleksandr Solzhenitsyn describes the MVD recruits of the early 1950s as "robust youngsters born during the First Five-Year Plan, who had seen no war service when they took their nice Tommy guns and set about guarding us." Vladilen Zadorny, born in 1933, was among them. From the age of eighteen to twenty, he served unhappily at a camp in north-central Kazakhstan, reporting later that even though separated by barbed wire from the prisoners and dressed in a greatcoat, he felt a prisoner himself. However, MVD troops did receive higher pay than soldiers of the same rank in the regular army, and in polar regions considerably more.[62]

---

59. Ibid., 244; de Windt, New Siberia, 48, 108–9, 127.

60. We discuss material incentives in the northern increment section of chapter 3.

61. The official names of these camps were, respectively, the Far Northern Construction Trust (abbreviated to Dal'stroi), the Noril'sk Corrective Labor Camp (Norillag), and the Vorkuta-Pechora Corrective Labor Camp.

62. Aleksandr Solzhenitsyn, The Gulag Archipelago, 1918–1956: An Experiment in Literary Investigation V VII, trans. Harry Willetts (New York, 1978), 219, 222, 224–25.

Others had lengthier careers in the Gulag system. We present the career migrations of four emblematic individuals. According to an interview conducted not long before his death in 2008, Iurii Maksimovich Gallat was born in Irkutsk oblast', the son of a political exile killed by the Whites a few months after Iurii's birth in 1918. He completed seven-year school in the town of Kirensk, northwest of Lake Baikal, and high school in Irkutsk, and then worked for two years in an office attached to the Baikal-Amur Mainline (BAM) construction project. Called up in 1938, he fought against the Japanese at Khalkin-Gol, was wounded, and demobilized in 1939. Along with two friends from his unit, he traveled to Vladivostok where, as he later recalled, "they were recruiting with all their might for Far Eastern Fisheries, Far Eastern Administration, Far Northern Construction (Dal'stroi)."

"Come to Kolyma, you'll work in the camps," the recruiter for Dal'stroi urged them.
"What's a camp?"
"That's where prisoners sit."
"But how are we to understand what prisoners are?"
"They're the ones who are arrested and sentenced . . ."

The dialogue should not to be taken too literally. It is inconceivable that Red Army veterans in 1940 did not know something about prisoners and camps. Earlier in the interview, Iurii had described the job he held at BAM as "inspector for the release of prisoners" at its Corrective Labor Camp (BAMLAG), providing laborers for construction of the main line. Rather, as generally with recalled speech, the point is about the meaning attached to it retrospectively. Whatever Iurii and his mates knew or had heard about the camps did not prepare them for what they experienced at Kolyma, or so he would want us to believe and perhaps may have come to believe himself. The recalled naïveté continued after a stormy passage by sea and arrival at Kolyma:

"Do you want to work in the organs?"
"I do!"
"Here, fill out this questionnaire!"
I had no idea what "the organs" were. I thought it was the police. I asked:
 "Is this to get into the police?"
"No, the organs!"
"So, the police are not the organs?"

Assigned to the Economic Department of the NKVD's State Security Office within Dal'stroi, Iurii earned his sergeant's stripes within six months. Beginning in April 1941, he accompanied twice-weekly gold transshipments by plane to Khabarovsk and Novosibirsk—seventy-five boxes of 25 kg each—for four years, basically, the war years. He described this task as "very complicated" and "dangerous," and clearly was proud that no accident or mishap ever occurred. His first "independent" position after the war was running the NKVD's district office at the Ten'kin mining facility. He subsequently served at several other facilities within Dal'stroi, and as chief investigator for the Charsk Valley facilities in Eastern Siberia before holding positions in Bashkiria, Udmurtiia, and Central Asia. "Never! Never in my twenty-three years of service did I lay a finger on a suspect," he asserted with what seems even in print like exaggerated defensiveness.[63]

Aleksandr Pavlovich Zavadenko, born in Ukraine in 1923, worked as a measurement specialist at the Kolyma gold mining facility within the Dal'stroi complex. He started working at Kolyma after his release from the army in 1945. He spent the rest of his working life at Kolyma, where he married and had two children. Zavadenko retired in 1976 and moved to Moldavia. In a recent interview, he described an incident shortly after he started working with prisoners in which one of them stabbed him in the back in revenge for his refusal to doctor the prisoner's results. Only the thickness of the coat he wore saved him. Despite the incident, he characterized his time there as "not so much life, as a fairy tale" full of "interesting work, friends, and oh what hunting and fishing." "I still miss the north," he added.[64]

The only information we have about Zavadenko's decision to work at Kolyma is his laconic comment that "someone told me they needed specialists in the north." By contrast, Fedor Vasilevich Mochulsky, born in the Belorussian town of Slutsk in 1918, provides a full account of his recruitment by the NKVD. The account appears in his memoir, written in the late 1980s, about working at Pechorlag in the arctic Vorkuta camp complex.[65] Having graduated in 1940 from the Railroad Transport Engineering Institute of the Commissariat of Railroad Transport, Mochulsky, a candidate member of the Communist Party, was summoned to one of the buildings of the party's Central Committee in Moscow. There, "an elderly grey-haired man" laid out the dangers facing the country's fuel supply in the event of war and the necessity of developing its coal resources in the Pechora basin in the far north of the Urals. He also indicated that the railroad institute had recommended Mochulsky "to strengthen the staff at both prison labor camps, especially Pechorlag."[66]

Persuaded by the patriotic pitch, Mochulsky accepted his "mandatory work assignment" as a young specialist (see below). After forty-five days of traveling by train,

---

63. "Iurii Gallat," http://iremember.ru/nkvd-i-smersh/gallat-uriy-maksimovich.html, 1, 6–10 (accessed October 22, 2012). On Dal'stroi, see I. D. Batsaev, Dal'stroi i sevvostlag OGPU-NKVD SSSR v tsifrakh i dokumentakh, 2 vols. (Magadan, 2002); on the mining operations specifically, see V. G. Zeliak, Piat' metallov Dal'stroia: Istoriia gornodobyvaiushchei promyshlennosti Severo-Vostoka Rossii v 30–50-kh gg. XX v. (Magadan, 2004).

64. "Aleksandr Pavlovich Zavadenko," http://iremember.ru/letchiki-istrebiteli/zavadenko-aleksandr-pavlovich.html, 1, 9 (accessed October 22, 2012).

65. Fedor Vasilevich Mochulsky, Gulag Boss: A Soviet Memoir, ed. and trans. Deborah Kaple (Oxford, 2011). Kaple indicates that Mochulsky wrote his reminiscences "during the late 1990s," but this is a misprint.

66. Mochulsky, Gulag Boss, 6–9.

steamship, and horseback, he arrived at the camp administration headquarters, where he received an initial assignment as unit foreman at the northern edge of the camp complex. Over the next several years Mochulsky held a variety of other positions from section boss to railroad division boss and secretary of the regional Komsomol committee. Deborah Kaple, who edited and translated Mochulsky's memoir, describes it as "straightforward and work-oriented," the story of "a fairly low-level boss" who thought of himself as " 'a good man in a bad place.' " She faults him for his lack of "compassion or sadness at his role in perpetuating the 'big Soviet lie' to its citizens."[67] We might regret his silence about his personal life and why he decided to leave the camp administration for a career in diplomacy. Indeed, throughout the memoir, he denies making decisions at all. "As I recall those years in the Gulag, I see that so many things in my life happened by chance," he writes near the end, absolving himself not only of responsibility but also agency.[68]

We know a lot more about the life trajectory of Muscovite Vasilii Azhaev, author of the Stalin Prize-winning novel *Far from Moscow* (1948), thanks to Thomas Lahusen's assiduous mining of Azhaev's literary archive. Azhaev traversed the experiential divide between coerced and voluntary migration in that he arrived in the Russian Far East in 1935 as a prisoner, sentenced for "counterrevolutionary agitation" for four years, of which he served two in BAMLAG. Upon his release in March 1937, he worked in camp administration, from October 1940 serving as senior inspector at a camp on the outskirts of the new town of Komsomol'sk-on-Amur. Lahusen describes Azhaev writing "endless reports, orders, accounts . . . about almost everything on earth, from timber exploitation to increased ventilation, from sanitary services to a speech for a rally," all on behalf of the building of an underground pipeline from Komsomol'sk along the Amur to the Pacific coast.[69]

Lahusen notes that despite his heavy workload, Azhaev's "passion for belles lettres" never flagged. While still a prisoner, he produced a large number of stories, essays, and plays for the camp's newspaper and literary journal. By 1937 he had become the journal's editor-in-chief, and in 1939 enrolled in a correspondence course offered by Moscow's Gorky Literary Institute. In a long letter to an old friend, Azhaev wrote in 1941 that he had "become an eternal student" (he was twenty-six years old at the time) but that "if the construction lets me go, if the authorities in Moscow will not object," he would come to

---

67. Ibid., xxxvi, 13–21, 99–117, 166.

68. Ibid., 177–78. In the preface (xxxvi), Mochulsky uses the following locution: "I, Fyodor Vasilevich Mochulsky, as fate would have it, found myself in a different situation."

69. Thomas Lahusen, *How Life Writes the Book: Real Socialism and Socialist Realism in Stalin's Russia* (Ithaca, 1997), 15, 42–53. This is the town that figures centrally in Elena Shulman's account of the *Khetagurovites* discussed in chapter 1.

Moscow to take his exams. His boss did grant permission, and Azhaev made the trip, exulting in his diary about being back in "my Moscow." During his visit, Nazi Germany invaded the Soviet Union, but blind in one eye, Azhaev was declared unfit for military service. Also while in Moscow, he received word that the Special Board of the NKVD had expunged his conviction of 1934 "with all its attendant restrictions."[70]

The restrictions would explain why Azhaev had not returned to Moscow after he served his sentence, but why didn't he stay in Moscow after learning of their removal? Lahusen indicates that Azhaev had given his word to his NKVD boss that he would return, and surmises that marital ties also played a role. These are both plausible reasons, but Lahusen also suggests another: it was not enough to have his crime expunged. Driven by his Soviet subjectivity, his desire to be accepted as a loyal Soviet citizen, he had to continue working "polyphonically"—serving the NKVD as an administrator and writing the novel that would varnish the reality of the pipeline project by transforming its actual dependence on slave labor into a fictive reliance on volunteers. Until May 1943 he remained in Komsomol'sk; he then was reassigned to another facility in Khabarovsk. Released from his service to the NKVD in April 1946, he spent the next two years editing the journal Dal'nii Vostok (Far East), in which his novel appeared serially. The success the novel enjoyed after its publication in 1948 enabled its author not only to return to Moscow permanently, but also to move into a well-located apartment opposite the Tret'iakov Gallery. There he spent the rest of his life as a member of the Writers' Union working not terribly productively. His only other novel, The Boxcar, which concerned the dolorous experiences of a young man sent to a labor camp in the Far East, was published in 1988, twenty years after his death and well after it would have come as a revelation to most readers.[71]

Carceral institutions continued to play a role in the post-Soviet era in isolating convicted criminals from their homes and loved ones. Indeed, as two British scholars point out, even as conditions of confinement improved in Russia, the role of distance in the punitive regime "moved to the foreground." At the same time, such institutions provided relatively stable sources of employment to both locals in the "penal heartland" of the Arkhangel'sk, Komi, Mordovian, Perm', Sverdlovsk, and Krasnoiarsk oblasts and professionals brought from other parts of the country. Such institutions even came to inspire a degree of pride and esprit de corps as the interface between the prison colonies and local communities has thickened and the educational attainments of the staff have risen.[72]

---

70. Ibid., 83, 85, 89, 96–97.

71. Ibid., 14, 65, 68, 98–101, 189–90.

72. Judith Pallot and Laura Piacentini, *Gender, Geography, and Punishment: The Experience of Women in Carceral Russia* (Oxford, 2012), 64–69, 74–92.

Assignment of Young Specialists

In *Education and Social Mobility in the Soviet Union*, Sheila Fitzpatrick emphasized the radical transformation in the social composition of the Soviet intelligentsia occasioned by the accelerated promotion of workers and peasants through vocational training. "Intelligentsia," she notes, "was often very broadly defined in the 1930s," and, we would add, continued to be so in subsequent decades. In identifying the "new Soviet elite," she refers to qualified specialists—"graduates of higher and secondary specialized educational institutions"—as a "key group" within the intelligentsia. Their numbers grew "spectacularly" between 1928 and 1937—from under half a million to 2.2 million, excluding the military.[73]

What Fitzpatrick did not address and what remains rather obscure is the transition from study to work, and specifically the geographical relocations that accompanied the transformation of students into "young specialists." We are concerned in the first instance with the 170,000 specialists who graduated from all-Soviet institutions of higher education during the First Five-Year Plan (1928–32) and the 370,000 graduating in the years of the Second Five-Year Plan (1932–37). We know that most of them became "leading cadres."[74] But how did they get their start? How did their career trajectories carry them from training to other locations? What role did the migration regime, officially inaugurated in 1933 for "the improvement of the use of young specialists," play? And what of the regime's evolution beyond the interwar period and Stalin's rule?

We begin with the law of September 15, 1933 that set the regime in motion. Observing that "a significant proportion of young specialists upon finishing their degrees do not proceed to production," the law stipulated that all such graduates work in their field at positions assigned by respective commissariats for a term of five years. These positions were to be staffed by those among lower administrative-technical personnel in accordance with their specialty. Prospective graduates would be informed of their assignment a year before the end of their studies so as to be able to relate their diploma project to their future employment, be it in medicine, mining, metallurgical production, or whatever field. Finally, the law assigned responsibility to the directors of the assigned enterprises for provision of graduates with appropriate technical material, accommodation, "and so forth."[75]

To what did the law owe its existence? First, it stemmed from Soviet authorities' determination to overcome the antipathy among higher technical school graduates to working

---

73. Fitzpatrick, *Education and Social Mobility*, 240.
74. Ibid., 245.
75. "Postanovlenie TsIK SSSR, SNK SSSR ot 15.09.1933 ob uluchshenii ispol'zovaniia molodykh spetsialistov," in *Resheniia partii i pravitel'stva po khoziaistvennym voprosam: Sbornik dokumentov za 50 let v piati tomakh,* ed. K. U. Chernenko and M. S. Smertiukov (Moscow, 1967), 2: 436–38.

directly in production. Kendall Bailes attributed their attitude to the legacy of the "white glove," symbolic of engineers' status anxiety before the Revolution about being associated with manual labor, and the desire of production engineers to avoid the conflicts and harassment of the pressure-cooked atmosphere in Soviet industrial plants.[76] It also reflected the enormous expansion of production facilities during the first two five-year plans and recognition that skilled workers promoted to positions as engineers (so-called *praktiki*) were not up to the job. Finally, it was part of the proliferation of attempts to centralize and expand control over human resources.[77] On the face of it, the law imposed onerous conditions for graduates, postponing any plans for graduate study and depriving them of agency in determining where they would work. What we need to elucidate is the application of the law, that is, the process of determining where graduates would be sent, their experiences at destination, or, if they avoided assignment, how they did so.

Information about the workings of the migration regime, even of the anecdotal kind, is difficult to come by for the first few years after the 1933 law took effect. It seems likely that the same problems frequently discussed in the press toward the end of the 1930s were occurring earlier. These were of two kinds: those relating to the commissariats' lack of seriousness in making assignments and graduates' own manipulation of the system. Of course, given that institutions of higher education were graduating well in excess of fifty thousand people every year, complete compliance with the law was out of the question.[78] It was not even expected. Like many other decrees from this time, it provided higher authorities with a club should subordinates' noncompliance get out of hand, which indeed it did.

The most common complaints against officials responsible for placing graduates was that assignments were inappropriate: they had failed to determine the needs of enterprises, had not sufficiently familiarized themselves with the qualifications of graduates, and were overstaffing administrative offices in major cities at the expense of more remote production facilities. Andrei Zhdanov, Leningrad party boss and soon-to-be Politburo member, combined all these complaints in his speech to the Eighteenth Party Congress in March 1939. "The commissariats don't know what their requirements are in terms of cadres," he contended. They operated "on the basis of *samotek* and casual requests, via secondary people, with neither plan nor system." Consequently, enterprises most in need of cadres— those in far off regions and rural clinics—didn't get them, while young specialists were

76. Kendall E. Bailes, *Technology and Society under Lenin and Stalin: Origins of the Soviet Technical Intelligentsia, 1917–1941* (Princeton, 1978), 297–304.

77. This included investigations and political purges in institutions of higher education. For some examples, see Siegelbaum and Sokolov, *Stalinism as a Way of Life*, 134–47.

78. In the first three years of the Third Five-Year Plan (1938–40), a reported 328,000 specialists graduated from institutions of higher education. L. A. Komarov, *Planirovanie podgotovki i raspredeleniia spetsialistov v SSSR* (Moscow, 1961), 16.

being sent to places where they were not needed.[79] *Pravda* repeated these complaints in an editorial several months later, citing such absurdities as a Leningrad institute that used the alphabet as a basis for assignments—students with last names beginning with one letter were sent to one commissariat's institutes and enterprises, and those with another to a different commissariat. The proportion of graduates assigned to line production positions not only failed to increase over succeeding years, but at 31 percent in April 1941, was lower than in the previous two years.[80]

As for the graduates, most probably considered it reasonable to repay or "work off" their debt to the state—which is how the state encouraged them to view their mandatory placement. Working in the provinces to bring the benefits of their training to people in real need undoubtedly evoked patriotic feelings among some. Indeed, those sent to remote locations and into harm's way were showered with praise, serving as models in the manner of Stakhanovites. They included A. Belousov, a graduate of one of Moscow's medical institutes, who assumed the position of People's Commissar of Health in the autonomous republic of Iakutiia located in the vastness of eastern Siberia; and Evgeniia Ampeevna, who accepted "without hesitation" the position of military doctor on the western Ukrainian front—"doubly difficult for a woman"—and reportedly was "happy" to be there.[81]

But there also existed what *Pravda* described as "deserters," young graduates who responded to the regime of assignments with their own repertoires. Take Matveev, who after completion of his history degree from the Karl Liebknecht Pedagogic Institute in Moscow took up an assignment to teach in the Maritime krai but "fled" back to Moscow not long thereafter. Or, "G. B.," a graduate of the Odessa Medical Institute. When asked by an official from the Commissariat of Health in Moscow why she had abandoned her assigned position in the Western Kazakh oblast', she replied that she had not received an apartment there, as promised. When it was discovered that none other than the Kazakhstan party secretary had signed an order for the apartment, she "tried another trick." Five days later, her "husband," a mining engineer, appeared in the commissariat's office with a request to have his "wife" assigned to Moscow oblast'. This marriage ploy was popular, or at least well known, according to *Pravda*. Still others simply refused assignments, never showed up, or went missing.[82]

Although not subjected to the ultimate penalty, as military deserters were, graduates who failed to report to their assigned positions or abandoned them without due cause did face criminal prosecution. So did employers who rigged the system by accommodating people who had not been assigned to their enterprises. Yet, because the number of

79. *Pravda*, March 5, 1939, 2.
80. *Pravda*, June 22, 1939, 1; April 29, 1941, 4.
81. *Pravda*, October 4, 1939, 4.
82. *Pravda*, March 29, 1941, 1; April 29, 1941, 4.

positions generally exceeded the number of graduates, adjustments by informal negotiation were commonplace—and continued to be so into the postwar years. It is otherwise
difficult to explain why in 1948 the Council of Ministers issued a modified version of the
1933 law, which it justified on the grounds that "many ministries and departments frequently send young specialists to functioning enterprises . . . located in large city centers
with a large saturation of engineering-technical cadres, at a time when no less important
enterprises and construction sites located in the periphery experience a severe shortage."
The resolution accompanying the law also placed blame on the educational institutions for
their failure to "inculcate among students the spirit of duty to the state."[83]

The new regulations modified the assignment regime. Prospective employers would
send requests for a certain number of graduates to their respective ministries. The ministries would forward the requests via the State Planning Commission to the Ministry of
Higher and Secondary Specialized Education, which would distribute placement orders to
specific institutions of higher education. At this point, in the spring, placement commissions would examine the records of prospective graduates in each field, inform them about
jobs they considered appropriate, and take into account (but not be obliged to satisfy) the
students' preferences. They then would assign students for a term of three years, a reduc-
tion from the original five. Students dissatisfied with their placement could petition the
decision. The only exceptions to these cumbersome procedures applied to physically disabled students, students supporting disabled parents, wives of military personnel, women
who were pregnant or with infants, and husbands and wives graduating simultaneously.
These people received diplomas entitling them to "self-placement."[84]

As we have seen in the case of Mochulsky, trained in transportation but recruited for
prison work, the system of assigning young specialists came in handy to the security organs. It also served them well during the late 1940s and early 1950s when Jewish students
experienced extreme difficulty in proceeding to graduate study as a consequence of the
anticosmopolitan and anti-Zionist campaigns of those years. What happened to Viktor
Mikhailovich Sinaiskii, who graduated from Voronezh University in 1951, well illustrates
the tweaking of the regime to serve multiple purposes. "On August 30, 1951, a hot day, my
wife and I left Moscow for Vorkuta," Sinaiskii wrote many years later.

> Until the last moment, I thought there must be some mistake. After finishing university
> with high marks, I was recommended by the examination commission for graduate

---

83. "Postanovlenie ot 29 maia 1948 g. N 1840 ob uporiadochenii raspredeleniia i ispol'zovaniia molodykh spetsialistov, okanchivaiushchikh vysshie i srednie spetsial'nye uchebnye zavedeniia," http://best
pravo.ru/sssr/gn-gosudarstvo/jor.htm (accessed September 7, 2012).

84. Ibid. Nicholas De Witt, *Education and Professional Employment in the U.S.S.R.* (Washington, DC, 1961),
361–62. In 1956, 15 percent of the 2,027 graduates of Moscow State University received "free" diplomas.

work. Why then did the placement commission direct me to the NKVD complex at Vor-kuta Coal? Every attempt I made to escape from the clutches of the NKVD had failed. This occurred before the Doctors' Plot and we still did not understand that the anti-Semitic campaign already had taken an open character.

When they arrived three days later, snow was on the ground. As Viktor would discover when he attended his first meeting of young specialists at Vorkuta Coal, he was far from alone. Jews predominated among the specialists hired from the outside, many of whom, like Vik-tor, were assigned to laboratories that had nothing to do with their training. Still, long after leaving in 1955 for a successful career in Moscow, he could appreciate the "rich practical experience" he gained, experience that "turned out to be quite useful in later life and work."[85]

It is hard to say whether in general the new rules improved compliance. On the one hand, the press continued to publish articles and letters extolling young specialists who were willing to accept positions in out-of-the-way places. Typical of them was a young en-gineer who wrote from the Donbas that in the year since his graduation he had come to love his work and become friends with local people, adding that the fear expressed by some specialists of ending up in some "forgotten" area was "not right." One of the fullest reports about civic-minded youth appeared in *Literaturnaia gazeta* in 1963. Similar in intent to arti-cles about Belousov and Ampeevna cited above, "Ballad of a Young Specialist" followed Nikolai Tyn'kov, a young doctor from Smolensk. After he had graduated from the medical institute, he proceeded to his assigned post in a remote corner of the Altai, "indisputably in the backwoods." Once settled in the village whose name translates as "Farewell, Trees," he discovered he had to do it all—deliver babies, perform surgeries, cure pneumonia, an-gina, and catarrh. He meets and marries an eighteen-year-old paramedic. He eventually learns to adjust his expectations about working as a doctor, overcoming the difficulties he could overcome and tolerating "without hysterics" those he could not. After a year, he is transferred as per a "gentleman's agreement" to the district capital, but a letter arrives from the village requesting his return because nobody had replaced him in the interim. He re-turns. Tyn'kov clearly had "repaid his debt to the state that gave him an education." He is working "where he is needed because he is needed."[86] Other graduates, it was reported in 1962, were fanning out across the country—especially to the Far North—to contribute to the Motherland. Overall, the Minister of Higher and Secondary Specialized Education

85. Viktor Sinaiskii, "Vorkuta glazami molodogo spetsialista," in *Gulagovskie tainy osvoeniia severa*, ed. E. V. Markova et al. (Moscow, 2001), 200–220. Sinaiskii's references to the NKVD are anachronistic, as it had become the MVD in 1946.

86. "Letters of Young Specialists," *Pravda*, April 6, 1950, 3, trans. in *CDSP*, May 20, 1950, 56; "Motherland Awaits Young Specialists," *Pravda*, June 23, 1954, 2, trans. in *CDSP*, August 4, 1954, 4; *Literaturnaia gazeta*, August 23, 1963, 2.

could claim that the placement rate in the RSFSR had risen to 96.8 percent, meaning that the number of young specialists not arriving at their assigned jobs had declined to nearly nothing.[87]

On the other hand, just as before 1948, "certain students" reportedly were declining appointments and otherwise "refusing to go where they are needed." In 1954, a certain female student by the name of Pasternak was "trying with the aid of influential friends to stay in Moscow," while comrades Makarova and Dimitrov, graduates of Leningrad University's history department, were "resorting to various tricks in order to remain in Leningrad." That same year, the father of a Moscow teacher's college graduate admitted that his daughter's marriage was "just make-believe. As soon as she gets an assignment to one of the schools in Moscow, she will get a divorce." Four years later in 1958, "some" young people were shunning positions where they were likely to face difficulties, and others had pretentions to senior positions right out of school. In 1961, the satirical magazine Krokodil published a cartoon of a modishly dressed youthful couple under the title "Facing Production Practice," with the girl saying to the guy, "Spring always rattles me. . . . What if they send me to the Virgin Lands to work?" Among the fifty-four graduates placed by a Moscow economics institute the following year, none made it to such "important" (but remote) districts of the country as Magadan, Chita, Tiumen' and the Maritime krai.[88]

Anecdotal in nature, these reports do not necessarily denote a pattern. However, according to Soviet engineering exchange students in the United States who spoke with Nicholas De Witt, those in the know employed classic migrant repertoires to obtain desirable posts. "There was a real choice of jobs but . . . it took brains to get a better one," they said. The brainy ones did not wait until they were placed, but rather established "good contacts while taking their industrial practice" and "solicited letters from plant directors or officials from research institutes recommending them for employment to the placement committees." Disappointing as it probably was to higher authorities, directors of enterprises and higher education institutions turned out to be no more willing to follow the rules than they had been earlier. They were said to "scorn the young engineers and technicians," trying "in every way to avoid employing them" or assigning them to jobs that unskilled laborers could perform. Even when all other procedures had been observed, graduates could still experience real hardships because enterprise directors did little to provide or arrange for accommodation, despite admonitions from the government.[89]

87. Pravda, July 20, 1962, 1, 3.
88. "Motherland Awaits Young Specialists," 4; N. I. Boldyrev, O moral'nom oblike sovetskoi molodezhi (Moscow, 1954), 27; Pravda, June 11, 1958, 1; Pravda, July 20, 1962, 3.
89. "Employ Young Specialists Correctly," Pravda, October 21, 1954, 1, trans. in CDSP, December 1, 1954, 27; Pravda, July 5, 1960, 1; De Witt, Education and Professional Employment, 362.

Still, graduates had the upper hand in structural terms because, with the exception of a few fields, their numbers did not keep pace with the expansion in the number of jobs. In 1964, eight years after the stick of criminal prosecution had been removed, a new statute threatened the withdrawal of diplomas from those who rejected assignments or failed to serve the entire three years.[90] The sanction does not appear to have changed behavior. In fields reflective of the much-touted Scientific-Technological Revolution (NTR, in Russian), ratios cited by De Witt of eight jobs for every graduate in petroleum engineering, seven for one in electronics, and twenty for one in nuclear technology were the norm.[91] The massive expansion of higher education in the late 1960s and early 1970s somewhat reduced those ratios, but not by much.[92] Scientists in the most prestigious of these fields could aspire to appointments in special complexes built just for them (and their families) such as Akademgorodok outside Novosibirsk, Dubna at the northern edge of Moscow oblast', Korolev and Zelenograd just beyond the Moscow city limits, and several others that in post-Soviet times would become known as "science cities." These were essentially settlements or colonies for the elite, urban living as comfortable as it got in Soviet times.[93]

What about the less fortunate, though? In 1969, *Krokodil*, ever the sardonic commentator on Soviet life, published a cartoon of two "packages" talking to each other in a post office. One, addressed "*Glubinka* [backwoods] Village Middle School," asks another labeled "Kolkhoz Vigilant," "Are you also a teacher?" to which the Vigilant-bound package replies, "No, I'm a livestock specialist." The implication is that the teacher is among the unfortunates whose assignment is to the back of the beyond, whereas the livestock specialist is going to a destination appropriate to his training. But, in a country where the standard of living was far lower in rural areas than in cities, but where cities hungered for labor, graduates seeking urban-based employment had little difficulty persuading employers to take them on. Even livestock specialists could be accommodated by employers eager to pad the rolls in anticipation of higher production norms. Thus, the news that "many graduates of agricultural schools are not going to work on farms but are staying in the cities and working outside their specialty" should not have shocked Soviet readers in 1976.[94] Even in Orel oblast',

90. Only a few fields such as secondary school teaching in history and Russian had plenty of personnel. "Postanovlenie TsK KPSS, Sovmina SSSR ot 21.54.1964 N 499 o srokakh podgotovki i uluchshenii ispol'zovaniia spetsialistov s vysshim i srednim spetsial'nym obrazovaniem," http://www.libussr.ru/doc_ussr/usr_6082.htm (accessed September 1, 2012).

91. De Witt, *Education and Professional Employment*, 362.

92. Kendall E. Bailes, "The Technical Specialists: Social Composition and Attitudes," in *The Social Context of Soviet Science*, ed. Linda L. Lubrano and Susan Gross Solomon (Boulder, CO, 1980), 154–55.

93. Paul R. Josephson, *New Atlantis Revisited: Akademgorodok, the Siberian City of Science* (Princeton, 1997).

94. "Taking Care of Young Specialists," *Pravda*, January 8, 1976, 2, trans. in CDSP, February 4, 1976, 20. The *Krokodil* cartoon is accessible at http://sovietdetstvo.livejournal.com/259782.html (accessed July 23, 2012).

Figure 3 Young specialists unwillingly go to the village, "Molodye spetsialisty neokhotno edut na selo," *Krokodil*, no. 2 (1969).

which remained predominantly rural in population, 169 specialists with diplomas from agricultural institutes and over 500 agronomists, animal husbandry specialists, and veterinarians with secondary education found employment in industry, transport, communications, trade, and insurance. State and collective farms meanwhile went begging for specialists.[95]

Nevertheless, specialists trained in agronomy did go to the countryside, albeit never in the numbers required.[96] But, as the agrarian historian Liubov Denisova piquantly put it, they "did not linger." During the 1970s kolhozes and sovkhozes in Vologda oblast' received an average of 150 specialists with higher education every year, and every year 200 of them returned. Huge tasks, long working hours, low pay, and the lack of creature comforts sent them back to the city. As one who worked in Novgorod oblast' wrote to the journal *Sel'skaia zhizn'* (Rural life) in 1963, "After I finished the institute, I worked as chief engineer on a sovkhoz. Together with me many graduates were sent there. But after a couple of years, only a few remained." So, those without specialized education took up the slack.[97]

---

95. "Concerning the Teshchiny Bliny Café," *Pravda*, November 16, 1975, 6, trans. in CDSP, December 10, 1975, 24.

96. As of the mid-1970s, the Non-Black Earth region's need for 200,000 specialists went only half met. Denisova, *Izchezaiushchaia derevnia Rossii*, 53.

97. Ibid., 53–56.

Judging by the web-based chat room "sovietdetstvo" (Soviet childhood), post-Soviet Russians have somewhat contradictory recollections of compulsory placement during the Soviet era. To one contributor's assertion that "absolutely all graduates received an obligatory placement and had to work off this term at a designated place," another stated, "By far not everyone and not obligatorily. It was possible to refuse, but then one deprived oneself of the possibility of receiving a job, living space, and other associated benefits." Still another, who graduated in 1985, questioned whether anyone actually received these benefits, while someone else affirmed that the only people who avoided placement were those with Moscow residence permits (propiski). Finally, a contributor entertained readers with what she obviously intended as a horror story about one of her cousin's female friends who, having graduated from an institute of technology in Dnepropetrovsk, was sent to teach chemistry in a small village near Navoi in south-central Uzbekistan between Bukhara and Samarkand and could not get transferred at all.[98]

This contributor, too young to have experienced the Soviet system of compulsory placement, probably would not be in favor of its restoration. That would put her in the minority. In April 2012, one month before the expiration of his term as President of the Russian Federation, Dmitri Medvedev suggested that students seeking a degree in either medicine or engineering at a state-run institution of higher education sign a contract upon matriculating that would commit them to accepting assignments in their field "for a certain number of years" after graduation. If they refused the assignment, they would have to pay back the state for the cost of their education. "When you pay for your own education," Medvedev explained, "you are the master of your own fate. But if the state or a business pays for you, according to this agreement, you must be on the job for, say, three years in a position the state considers important and to which it has directed you."[99]

When the "recruiting portal" SuperJob.ru invited visitors to its website to vote on Medvedev's suggestion, a clear majority voted in favor, 29 percent were opposed, and the rest could not make up their minds. An earlier survey from July 2010 cited proportions even more strongly in favor of returning to the Soviet practice of assigning young specialists.[100] The appeal of the system might stem from the difficulties students and their parents were having in paying for higher education at private institutions and finding jobs in their

---

98. "O raspredelenii vypusknikov i o posylkakh," http://sovietdetstvo.livejournal.com/259782.html (accessed July 23, 2012).

99. "Medvedev khochet vernut' v VUZy sovetskuiu sistemu raspredeleniia," April 7, 2012, http://www.66.ru/news/society/114824/ (accessed September 11, 2012).

100. "Rossiiskie studenty odobriaiut trudovoe raspredelenie posle vuza," May 17, 2012, http://www.1obl.ru/news/o-lyudyakh/rossijskije-studenty-odobrajut-trudovoje-raspredelenije-posle-vuza-111617052012/ (accessed August 6, 2012); "68% rossiian za trudovoe raspredelenie vypusknikov vuzov," July 28, 2010, http://www.glavbyh.ru/n/1/68-rossijan-za-trudovoe-raspredelenie-vypusknikov-vuzov/ (accessed August 6, 2012).

specialties after graduation. Evidently unnoticed by Russians was the fact that in 2007 Belarus—that most Soviet of post-Soviet successor states—had reinstituted the Soviet system of graduate placement, albeit for a shorter term.[101]

Part of the constitutional guarantee to employment, the system of mandatory placement for graduates of higher educational institutions basically dictated career migration for hundreds of thousands and eventually millions of people. Like so much else that had to do with what the state demanded of its citizens, the provisions softened over time. It is difficult to assess the degree to which compliance with those provisions correspondingly weakened, for so much is based on anecdote and hearsay. Little wonder that young people in post-Soviet Russia appear both attracted to and fearful of the revival of this regime of geographical assignment.

101. "Polozhenie o raspredelenii vypusknikov uchrezhdenii obrazovaniia, poluchivshikh professional'no-tekhnicheskoe, srednee spetsial'noc ili vysshee obrazovanie," December 10, 2007, http://job.bseu.by/help/assignment.htm (accessed August 6, 2012).

~CHAPTER FIVE~

Military Migrants

"They say it is a wide road that leads to war and only a narrow path that leads home again."

—A Russian heavy artillery soldier, August 1914, Alfred Knox,
With the Russian Army, 1914–1917

Armies imply movement. They presuppose the "mobilization" of human resources and supplies, and conscription takes men away from home. Yet as Joshua Sanborn has observed, "historians of migration have been even less receptive to the notion that soldiers can be analyzed as migrants than historians of armies have been to the idea that soldiers can be analyzed as murderers."[1] Fortunately, historians of migration are coming to their senses, and in a pathbreaking survey of European migration, Jan Lucassen and Leo Lucassen considered soldiers' and sailors' movements as one of the primary types of human mobility. They estimate that over five million soldiers and sailors left home between 1850 and 1900 while serving the Imperial army and navy in European Russia alone.[2]

Sanborn's key article from 2005 argued for "treating the Russian battle zones of World War I as a social and temporal space of 'violent migrations.'" He observed that both perpetrators and recipients of violence lived within "a radically new social and political ecosystem that shaped their behavior in important ways" and "progressively unsettled the Russian Empire." We would like to suggest that just as during the First World War, so in subsequent conflicts Russian/Soviet battle zones were sites of violent migrations. It thus follows that

---

1. Joshua A. Sanborn, "Unsettling the Empire: Violent Migrations and Social Disaster in Russia during World War I," *The Journal of Modern History* 77 (2005): 291.
2. Lucassen and Lucassen, "Mobility Transition Revisited," 372.

as in the years 1914–18 (or 1921, if we extend the migrations of World War I through the Russian Civil War), so again in 1939–45 and at the end of the century soldiers can be analyzed as militarized migrant communities that interacted with one another, the enemy, officialdom, and the local populations they encountered.[3]

Our extension of Sanborn's analysis to soldiers of the Soviet and post-Soviet armies rests on their individual and collective experience. As in other armies, including the Russian Imperial forces during World War I, they experienced not only geographical displacement associated with conscription but also social dislocation and relocation. Their training, like that received by soldiers elsewhere and previously, was intended to replace previous norms of behavior with a new set of militarized values—unquestioning obedience to authority, capacity to murder on command, and fortitude under fire. Reinforced by the replacement of their civilian garb by uniforms, new forms of address and rituals, and a predominantly homosocial environment, this shift had both psychological (that is, internalized) and cultural dimensions pointing in the direction of brutalization. Yet, as with other forms of migration, military migrants employed a variety of repertoires to mitigate the negative effects of the regimes to which they were subjected, and these often had life-saving consequences.

Military Service in War and Revolution

Beginning in 1874, all men age twenty-one were subject to universal conscription for six years of active service and a further nine years as reservists. The term of service was much more humane than it had been previously, when it called for twenty-five years of a life and recruits were mourned by their family members as if they had been condemned to death, then plied with vodka and delivered to the recruiting officer in the district capital.[4] Exemptions for certain occupations, poor health, family considerations, and education together excused nearly half of the eligible males from peacetime service. This conscription statute, with modifications for Cossacks and ethnic minority groups, prevailed until 1917. Since troops were increasingly concentrated on the western borderlands, the army dislocated recruits from their home military district. By 1910, troop assignments so poorly matched soldiers to their home district that the Warsaw military district drew 99 percent of its annual contingent from other districts and the St. Petersburg military district well over half—no wonder Russians called this distribution system dislokatsiia. Some 450,000 men per year

---

3. Sanborn, "Unsettling the Empire," 291, 295.
4. Allan Wildman, *The End of the Russian Imperial Army: The Old Army and the Soldiers' Revolt (March–April 1917)* (Princeton, 1980), 25.

left home as new conscripts, to be gone for six years. Although the term of active service would be reduced to four, then to three years, the reserve period would be extended. Russia was thus assured a peacetime force and a growing trained reserve of millions.[5]

The departure of soldiers, as they were harvested annually when village men turned twenty-one, could have devastating consequences for the village they left behind. Each soldier gone was a peasant lost to the fields and the winter labor force in village or city. The possibility of conscription was a source of anxiety for each man and his family. Indeed, mothers went to village healers to foresee if their sons would be drafted, and young men sought help in contracting a disease so that they could be declared exempt. Because Russian peasants married young, many conscripted soldiers had wives and children. Wives went to the same source to hear how their husband was doing, if he missed his wife and children, and if he was faithful.[6] Like the wives of seasonal migrants, soldiers' wives were rendered especially vulnerable by their husband's departure. Unprotected from their in-laws, other villagers, or slander, many became quite marginal, like widows and spinsters.[7] Sometimes they had to leave, which could bring on more hardships, like those suffered by the soldiers' wives "on tour" as prostitutes in market towns.[8] The story of Evdokiia Kulikova, who escaped to St. Petersburg via domestic service, where she trained to become an accomplished seamstress in the 1890s, is rooted in her husband's conscription that left her as a miserable dependent in the home of her widowed father-in-law. Her court case, elucidated by Barbara Engel, demonstrates the narrow range of possibilities for soldiers' wives.[9]

Men went to extreme measures to avoid conscription, along with the indignities, departures, and lost years that came with it. The lottery system and exemptions meant that peasants felt that they had "either escaped from or fallen victim to an onerous form of involuntary servitude," and many were determined to escape.[10] As Sanborn has pointed out, at the top

5. Bruce W. Menning, *Bayonets before Bullets: The Imperial Russian Army, 1861—1914* (Bloomington, 1992), 23, 222–26; Wildman, *End of the Russian Imperial Army*, 26.

6. Samuel Ramer, "Traditional Healers and Peasant Culture in Russia, 1861–1917," in Kingston-Mann and Mixter, *Peasant Economy*, 223.

7. Engel, *Between the Fields*, 20–21, 54–60; Robert McNeal, *Tsar and Cossack, 1855–1914* (New York, 1987), 41–42; Christine Worobec, "Victims or Actors? Russian Peasant Women and Patriarchy," in Kingston-Mann and Mixter, *Peasant Economy*, 179–80.

8. Timothy Mixter, "The Hiring Market as Workers' Turf: Migrant Agricultural Laborers and the Mobilization of Collective Action in the Steppe Grainbelt of European Russia, 1853–1913," in Kingston-Mann and Mixter, *Peasant Economy*, 314.

9. Evdokiia Kulikova's father-in-law, she attested, was conducting an affair with another daughter-in-law and showing sexual interest in her after her husband's departure. Engel, "Freedom and Its Limitations," 115–27; this case and many others are analyzed by Barbara Engel, *Breaking the Ties That Bound: The Politics of Marital Strife in Late Imperial Russia* (Ithaca, 2011). In 1912 the state mandated benefits to soldiers' wives (*soldatki*).

10. Wildman, *End of the Russian Imperial Army*, 27.

of Russian authority, institutional struggles took place over control of the draft, but at the village level the stakes were at least as high in "the struggle to determine which young men would leave their villages and towns for a few years or forever." The language of peasant and bureaucratic petitions was the same—state interest, equality, and justice. Nonetheless, the difference between the two levels was fundamental because, while bureaucracies fought over numbers, "the struggles at the local level involved men with first names, families, farms, and sweethearts."[11] Working within a draft lottery from which certain professions and men with certain family responsibilities were exempt, the more eligible were called and submitted to a medical examination. A large proportion failed this initial physical exam—42 percent in 1909. Some were genuinely too weak or ill to serve, but others starved themselves before the exam, cut off their trigger finger, or damaged their hearing or vision in order to fail. Those who had the money resorted to bribery and approached officials in the local military commissariat for an entitlement; those who lacked the funds simply did not show up for the draft, over 9 percent of the pool of young men in 1913.[12]

Soldiers were on the move throughout the year, first to training sites and field exercises at summer encampments in May, June, and July. Afterward, they did not return to barracks until October or November, but rather the regiment shrank, for example, from 1,800 to 300 men while soldiers went off to make money in the civilian economy on "free work." This necessity was rooted in the expectation that regiments be economically self-sufficient. As one officer noted, "his men needed blankets, the blankets had to be paid for and the only recourse was to collect the money soldiers earned at their civilian work."[13] What was the work? One general noted that in July soldiers would "fan out in hay-mowing, in forests, along railway lines, in town for building." In other words, soldiers performed the same seasonal work that peasants engaged in, and because they were with recruits from their home military district, zemliaki worked together and formed artels.[14] Peasant seasonal work patterns were built into the military economy, then, and the tsarist regiment's annual labor cycle was, at least in part, familiar to the peasant.[15]

The Imperial army recruited unevenly: some ethnic minorities—most famously the Kazakhs ("Kirgiz") of Central Asia, as well as people of Finland and most tribal peoples of the Caucasus and Siberia—went unregistered and unconscripted, whereas Jews were disproportionately called to serve.[16] Although Jews were reputed to be brazen draft-dodgers and

11. Joshua Sanborn, Drafting the Russian Nation: Military Conscription, Total War, and Mass Politics, 1905–1925 (DeKalb, 2003), 25.

12. Sanborn, Drafting the Russian Nation, 21–24. This amounted to 144,271 men.

13. John Bushnell, "Peasants in Uniform: The Tsarist Army as a Peasant Society," Journal of Social History 13, no. 4 (1980): 567.

14. Ibid., 569.

15. Ibid., 567–68.

16. Wildman, End of the Russian Imperial Army, 103.

bad patriots, Yohanan Petrovsky-Shtern's careful analysis of conscription data shows quite the reverse.[17] Indeed the exemptions for family entitlements that protected so many peasant soldiers from conscription offered less protection to Jews, who were treated as a distinct group.[18] Jews also could not enter the General Staff Academy or serve as officers.[19]

Cossacks, also treated as distinct, constituted an important and heralded part of the armed forces with a history and migration patterns all their own.[20] Cossacks emerged in previous centuries as a kind of border vocation among both Slavic and non-Slavic peoples. Ranged in self-governing communities (Hosts) along the southeast steppe provinces, they engaged in agriculture, trade, banditry, and warfare.[21] Their privileges and military autonomy were curbed in the last quarter of the nineteenth century as their tax and recruitment liabilities came to resemble those of other subjects. Nonetheless, they continued to have a military vocation and to serve in elite guard units and in the army primarily as cavalry. In 1900, 67,000 Cossacks served in the active army, ready to expand to 109,000 in wartime.[22]

War came early in the century, but not where the Russian mobilization plans anticipated. The way troops were moved during the Russo-Japanese War helps us understand their reactions. On the one hand, the soldiers mobilized from the Siberian and Far Eastern military districts were, as Allan Wildman reminds us, "veterans of the expeditionary force to China during the Boxer Rebellion and could be more easily persuaded that they were defending their homeland against a tangible foe."[23] On the other hand, reservists from the Kiev and Moscow districts grew antagonistic and demoralized as they endured a five-week journey by train across Siberia. The situation deteriorated for them at the end of this short and disastrous war. Not only had they traveled thousands of miles from home for a fruitless campaign, but also they could not get home. Three months after the signing of the peace in Portsmouth, New Hampshire, "very few of their million-odd number" were en route home; the poor condition of the railroad compounded by railroad strikes blocked repatriation.

17. Yohanan Petrovsky-Shtern, *Jews in the Russian Army, 1827–1917: Drafted into Modernity* (Cambridge, 2009), 133, 136–43.

18. Sanborn, *Drafting the Russian Nation*, 22, 28–29.

19. Ibid., 69.

20. For entrées into the rich histories of the Cossacks, see Brian Boeck, *Imperial Boundaries: Cossack Communities and Empire-Building in the Age of Peter the Great* (Cambridge, 2009); Brian Boeck, "Containment vs. Colonization: Muscovite Approaches to Settling the Steppe," in Breyfogle, Schrader, and Sunderland, *Peopling the Russian Periphery*, 41–60; McNeal, *Tsar and Cossack*.

21. See Thomas M. Barrett, *At the Edge of Empire: The Terek Cossacks and the North Caucasus Frontier, 1700–1860* (Boulder, 1999); Boeck, *Imperial Boundaries*.

22. Menning, *Bayonets before Bullets*, 28, 115.

23. Wildman, *End of the Russian Imperial Army*, 44–45.

Propaganda from railroad workers and political exiles added to discontent and ignited soldiers' revolts in overcrowded transit points such as Vladivostok, Harbin, and Chita.[24] As the winter of 1905–6 faded, soldiers got home, the revolts in Siberia were squelched, and Cossacks had shown themselves to be a counterrevolutionary police in the revolution at home.[25]

The declaration of war in July 1914 produced a much more successful and massive mobilization.[26] Like other European states, Russia had been planning this operation for years, and as elsewhere, troops were mustered effectively in the summer. Because the size of the fighting force was Russia's strength, the dimensions of mobilization challenge the imagination. The active army of 1.4 million men was joined by auxiliary forces such as medical personnel and officer wives, and most important by an unprecedented number of reservists: in two weeks in the summer of 1914, over 3.9 million men left their homes for military units. This is a greater movement than the well-studied emigration from the western regions of the Empire between 1880 and 1914. By the end of the war, nearly 15 million men had been mobilized into the active army, a figure that overshadows even the mass of peasant settlers who made out for Siberia.[27] The army of migrants would be away from home, on the move, and confronting strangers for months or years to come, engaged in a war, or wars, in contrast with the dug-in stalemate on the western front.[28]

An enllsted man wrote that the conditions "in constant proximity to the enemy, with equal chances for life and death, brought individuals together into a tight and friendly family" that he likened to "a primitive tribe on the hunt."[29] This statement evokes soldiers as a migrant group—separated from home, desocialized, then resocialized into new norms within their own community. Like the temporary migrants evoked by Michael Piore, soldiers undertook tasks and exhibited behaviors they would shun at home.[30] Soldiers learn to be violent and to kill, lessons that are not easily contained. As primitive and as violent as Russian peasant men were reputed to be, village life did not demand the kind of violence called for by war.[31] One of the few soldiers to leave an account, Fedor Stepun, saw fields of

24. Ibid., 52–53.

25. Ibid., 60, 64; McNeal, *Tsar and Cossack*, 222.

26. Sanborn, *Drafting the Russian Nation*, 25–29.

27. Sanborn, "Unsettling the Empire," 296. More precisely, the two figures compare the mobilization of 3,915,000 men with 3,715,000 emigrants; the total mobilized was 14,923,000. For emigration from the western parts of the empire, see Hoerder, *Cultures in Contact*, 322–28.

28. Sanborn, "Unsettling the Empire," 292.

29. Ibid., 298, quotes Vladimir Paduchev, *Zapiski nizhnego china 1916 god* (Moscow, 1931), 14.

30. Piore, *Birds of Passage*.

31. Nicholas Werth, "Les déserteurs en Russie: Violence de guerre, violence révolutionnaire et violence paysanne, 1916–1921," in Stéphane Audoin-Rouzeau et al., *La violence de guerre, 1914–1945: Approches comparées des deux conflits mondiaux* (Brussels, 2002), 99.

corpses—mutilated and whole, freshly killed and some days old—after only a few days at the front and wrote:

> In the name of God, tell me, is it really possible to see all of this and not go out of your mind? It turns out that it is possible and not only is it possible not to go out of your mind, but much more, it is possible to eat, drink, and sleep on the very same day, and possible even not to dream about it afterward.[32]

A fledgling movement of civic pacifists, Tolstoians, and members of religious groups such as Dukhobors, Baptists, and Mennonites objected to the brutality of armed conflict in growing numbers after 1914. They found little sympathy or tolerance, however, and were in many cases the victims of brutal punishments.[33]

Letters from home gave soldiers a connection with their peacetime life and personae, and like other emigrants, soldiers wrote home—but more so, since their correspondence set records on every front.[34] World War I came on the heels of a great move forward in literacy, most pointedly among recruits, over two-thirds of whom were literate in the case of Russia.[35] Soldiers needed to hear from home, to learn about their farms and families; they were anxious particularly because in addition to men, requisitions of livestock had taken their toll on the production of food and fodder. Otherwise, they felt as if they were, in the words of one soldier, "cut off from the whole world."[36] Letters to home reveal the high cost of separation. As one censor wrote about a year into the war, aside from farms, both officers and soldiers' "expressions of love for their wives also occupies an important place. . . . Jealousy is also noticeably growing; the fear that wives will betray their long-absent husbands plays a large role in the growing war weariness."[37] The need for letters drove a relatively effective system of postal delivery under mobile and adverse circumstances because armies needed to boost the morale of their troops.[38]

32. Fedor Stepun, *Iz pisem praporshchika artillerista* (Prague, n.d.), 19–20, quoted by Sanborn, *Drafting the Russian Nation*, 171.

33. Sanborn, *Drafting the Russian Nation*, 183–99.

34. See, for example, Martha Hanna, "A Republic of Letters: The Epistolary Tradition in France during World War I," *American Historical Review* 108 (2003): 1338–61; and Martha Hanna, *Your Death Would Be Mine: Paul and Marie Pireaud in the Great War* (Cambridge, MA, 2006).

35. Although this proportion was smaller than for troops to the west, it was a record high for Russian recruits. See Hanna, "A Republic of Letters"; Sanborn, *Drafting the Russian Nation*, 144; Sanborn, "Unsettling the Empire," 299.

36. From report of military censors in Sanborn, "Unsettling the Empire," 299.

37. Ibid., 299–300; for the impact on village production, see Alessandro Stanziani, "The First World War and the Disintegration of Economic Spaces in Russia," in *Transforming Peasants: Society, State, and the Peasantry, 1861–1930*, ed. Judith Pallot (New York, 1998), 183–85.

38. For Russia, see Holquist, *Making War*, 208.

At the beginning of the war, "a gigantic wave came from inner Russia and flowed beyond the 'watershed' " that marked the usual geographic division between peoples who moved West and those who moved East. In this case, the watery metaphor used by Eugene Kulischer may be apt because soldiers on the move had little agency.[39] The results of this first offensive were promising as the army conquered nearly all of Galicia and Austrian Poland. However, fatalities were high even in these first few months, when well over a million casualities resulted, surprising "even the men whose job it was to consider worst-case scenarios."[40] In the months to come, the limits on trained manpower, munitions, and arms would reduce the path home to a narrow track, and 1915 would be worse in terms of human loss. The offensive became the Great Retreat of April 1915, when German and Austro-Hungarian troops broke through Russian lines and proved to be unstoppable. By August the army had lost four million men, and by the end of the year, had backed up to a line it would manage to hold until the Treaty of Brest-Litovsk in March 1918.

After the nadir of the 1915 retreat, more soldiers were called for, but none were available by the standing practices of recruitment. Not only the regular conscripts but also the untrained reservists up to age thirty-two, and then to age thirty-six, had been "frittered away" by the summer. Only a change of law could implement the call-up of men who were the sole support of their family; this law was passed in August, allowing reservists age twenty to twenty-four to be taken from home. What followed made earlier attempts to avoid conscription pale, because "villages were suddenly made aware that the last barrier had been removed against the disruption of their economies and the extermination of their menfolk," including men with small children and supporters of widowed mothers and young siblings.[41] Soldiers' wives and inductees took collective and individual action, writing letters of protest, rioting, arguing, and deserting during troop transfers.

Draftees used every sort of strategy to stay home or get home. The conscript Aleksandr Dneprovskii was surrounded by men who had inflicted wounds on themselves, given themselves hernias, or paid bribes to avoid conscription, some with success. But self-starvation did not have the desired effect for him. Weakened by his effort, he slipped away from training in central Ukraine with a group of ill soldiers and took to spending days in the local library, where he could be anonymous, and nights in hiding. Eventually, his company moved out and he purchased a false passport and made his way home.[42] Men were especially reluctant to leave home when others—like the police—continued to be exempt.

39. Eugene Kulischer, *Europe on the Move: War and Population Changes, 1917–47* (New York, 1948), 28, 30.

40. Sanborn, *Drafting the Russian Nation*, 31; Wildman, *End of the Russian Imperial Army*, 85–86.

41. Wildman, *End of the Russian Imperial Army*, 96.

42. Sanborn relates the story from Aleksandr Dneprovskii, *Zapiski dezertira, voina 1914–1918 gg.* (New York, 1931), 39–54, in *Drafting the Russian Nation*, 36.

"Bloodsuckers! Pharaohs!" were among the taunts delivered to these guardians of order by conscripts in Petrograd in one of the many actions that targeted police.[43] Nonetheless, over two million men in all categories of reserves found themselves in uniform in 1916, even those whom officers found to be a liability because they balked at induction, jumped off troop trains, and refused to follow training exercises.[44] Men were desperate to stay at home in wartime, and the army was desperate for soldiers.

Indeed, so desperate was the army for fresh recruits that in the spring of 1916, the decision was made to recruit Muslim subjects in Central Asia who were not "legible" to the state, to use James Scott's word, because there were no lists of any kind of eligible men.[45] For these reasons alone, Russian military and civilian officials objected to this conscription, even for support and labor services. Moreover, the Kazakhs and Kyrgyz certainly had no stake in the tsar's battle. In addition to wishing to stay home, they had no interest in serving the government that had taken so much of their land for use by settlers. As a consequence, the attempt to recruit them immediately created a ruinous uprising in the summer of 1916 that distracted Imperial troops rather than creating a useful force: tens of thousands of Central Asians and over thirty-five hundred Russian settlers were killed, some nine thousand Russian homesteads were destroyed, fourteen battalions of troops and thirty-three "hundreds" of Cossacks were taken out of battle and sent to Turkestan. The fighting ended in brutal massacres, making this the least successful conscription in the war.[46]

By the fall of 1916, the demoralized state of soldiers at the front was the army's most severe problem. On the one hand, censors' reports reveal despair that the bloodletting would never end and that victory was impossible; on the other hand, soldiers feared for their families as they heard that inflation had made life at home impossible. Socialized into violence, soldiers began to form communities of disorder. Kremenchug, a city on the Dnepr in central Ukraine that served as a collection point for soldiers returning to the front, attracted deserters and became a stewpot for disturbances. For two days in the fall, several thousand men broke out of the barracks, drank, rioted, plundered the stores, complained about conditions, and sharply asked about army exemptions for the police. The acuteness of

---

43. Wildman, *End of the Russian Imperial Army*, 97. See also Viktor Shklovsky, *A Sentimental Journey: Memoirs, 1917–1922*, trans. Richard Sheldon (Ithaca, 1984), 10. Shklovsky, who worked as an instructor in a reserve armored division stationed in Petrograd, remembers his unit "marching along, hooting at a squad of policemen and shouting, 'Dirty cops, dirty cops.'"

44. The total number of *ratniki* drafted in 1916 is 2,075,000; Wildman, *End of the Russian Imperial Army*, 98–99.

45. Scott described legibility as "a central problem in statecraft" in *Seeing Like a State: How Certain Schemes to Improve the Human Condition Have Failed* (New Haven, 1998), 2.

46. Sanborn, *Drafting the Russian Nation*, 35–36; Wildman, *End of the Russian Imperial Army*, 104–5.

this situation lay in the fact that soldiers brought in to quell the riot refused to fire on their compatriots.[47] Violent disorder, much worse than Kremenchug, would proliferate in the spring and reverberate thereafter.

Soldiers deserted, some to see to their family's welfare and then return, but for most the goal was a permanent return home. As an agitated soldier exclaimed to Fedor Stepun, "What's the use of invading Galicia anyway, when back home they're going to divide up the land?!"[48] In 1917 desertions were understood to be the most alarming part of the apparent anarchy that threatened the army, with disobedience, mutinies, and lynching of officers. The point of tension was often on the means to get home, the railroad. In the spring 1,000 deserters a day were reported to arrive at the Kiev railway station.[49] By the summer, a peasant veteran from some 130 miles southeast of Moscow pleaded with Prime Minister Kerensky to arrest the "masses of runaway soldiers and deserters" who were "introducing degeneracy and decay into the countryside."[50] The best estimate from published tables gives nearly 170,000 deserters from the six months from March to August. Desertion visibly threatened the country because it seemed to leave Russia undefended and because soldiers appeared everywhere, reportedly fomenting crime and disorder.[51] Wildman insists that almost all deserters left not the front, but rather units in the rear and urban garrisons, and many men simply went home. Nonetheless, lawless "deserter colonies" animated the cities and underwrote the impression of wholesale desertion.[52] This large-scale emigration from war is the "soldiers' plebiscite" that spelled withdrawal for Russia and assisted the Bolsheviks' rise to power.[53]

Other soldiers, prisoners of war, could not return home until after peace was declared, and not even then, in some cases. In the great retreat of the spring and summer of 1915, the Central Powers took more than a million Russian prisoners. By the end of 1916, the figure reached 2.1 million and would grow to 2.4 million in 1917. Prisoners found themselves at the receiving end of German propaganda in instruments such as the prisoner paper *Russkii vestnik* (Russian news). Whatever the German powers of persuasion, it is impossible to know whether some prisoners used capture as the opportunity to escape the war, but some soldiers—or entire units—did surrender in hopeless situations.[54] Surviving sons,

---

47. Wildman, *End of the Russian Imperial Army*, 106, 114, 119.

48. Fedor Stepun, *Byvshee i nesbyvsheesia*, 2 vols. (New York, 1956), 2: 10.

49. Wildman, *End of the Russian Imperial Army*, 235. See also Orlando Figes, *A People's Tragedy: The Russian Revolution, 1891–1924* (Harmondsworth, 1996), 80.

50. Letter to Kerensky from Ivan Shabrov, Riazan' province, July 13, 1917, in Mark Steinberg, *Voices of Revolution, 1917* (New Haven, 2001), 236–38.

51. Werth, "Déserteurs en Russie," 99–100; Wildman, *End of the Russian Imperial Army*, 230–32.

52. Wildman, *End of the Russian Imperial Army*, 364–66.

53. Sanborn, *Drafting the Russian Nation*, 34.

54. Wildman, *End of the Russian Imperial Army*, 89, 95, 347, 363; Karen Petrone, *The Great War in Russian Memory* (Bloomington, 2011), 104–5.

interviewed about their own experience in the Great Patriotic War, related their fathers' World War I POW experience in neutral terms, simply commenting that father came home in 1918 after a year, or returned home to Samara after the Revolution, was released in 1917, or had four years in German coal mines, 1914–17. But Il'ia Zakharovich Frenklakh stated that his father remembered the Germans as good people from his years of incarceration that began in 1916.[55] In Peter Gatrell's assessment, POWs who worked in agriculture were impressed by farming methods, and those in camps were by contrast radicalized by exposure to Bolshevik propaganda.[56] Konrad Zielinski estimates that 300,000 Russian POWs were on German soil at the war's end, when they began passing through Poland with the help of relief agencies. Many were unable to continue on home, however, because the Polish-Soviet War that began in February 1919 generated new waves of Russian POWs, these from the Red Army. By the end of that war in 1921, a total of about 110,000 Red Army POWs remained in Poland. Anti-Bolshevik émigrés and Polish authorities recruited some to their cause, but others returned home.[57] The total number of imprisoned men reached an estimated 5 million overall, of whom 1.8 million perished in captivity. Nearly half the prisoners were captured in 1914 and 1915, and an estimated 3.4 million were still in captivity on January 1, 1918.[58]

The war situation shifted drastically in 1917 as the revolution intensified in Petrograd. The offensive that Russia's allies insisted on and Minister of War Kerensky vociferously defended proved a bust when inestimable but significant numbers of soldiers sabotaged, deserted, and mutinied. Most soldiers had had enough and most officers grew leery of crossing them lest they wind up eviscerated, strung up, or beaten to death. The loss of deference to those in command proved fatal to Russia's continued participation in the war and the provisional government that insisted on prosecuting it. The Bolsheviks' seizure of power, otherwise known as the October Revolution, is unimaginable apart from the old army's effective demobilization. Their own armies wracked by supply shortages and war weariness, the Central Powers took advantage of the implosion of Russian political power to advance deep into the Baltics, Belarus, and Ukraine. The Treaty of Brest-Litovsk, signed in March 1918, removed Russia from the Great War. Less than two weeks later, the Soviet

---

55. [Interviews with sons of WWI Russian POWs] http://iremember.ru/tankisti/karasik-ilya-isaakovich. html (accessed October 10, 2012); http://iremember.ru/razvedchiki/krasilschikov-zakhar-evseevich.html (accessed October 10, 2012); http://iremember.ru/razvedchiki/shinder-mikhail-lvovich.html (accessed October 10, 2012); http://iremember.ru/razvedchiki/frenklakh-ilya-zakharovich.html (accessed October 10, 2012); http://iremember.ru/artilleristi/shvartsshteyn-leonid-abramovich.html (accessed October 10, 2012).

56. Peter Gatrell, Russia's First World War: A Social and Economic History (London, 2005), 66.

57. Konrad Zielinski, "Population Displacement and Citizenship in Poland, 1918–24," in Homelands: War, Population, and Statehood in Eastern Europe and Russia, 1918–1924, ed. Nick Baron and Peter Gatrell (London, 2004), 113–14.

58. Gatrell, Russia's First World War, 66, 248.

government, still fearing for Petrograd's vulnerability to German attack, moved the capital to Moscow. Already by this time, it had decreed a new army—a "Workers' and Peasants' Red Army"—and rumblings of civil war were evident.

Fighting in the Civil War

Recent historiography has stressed quite correctly the continuity of war across a "continuum of crisis" that stretched at least from the beginning of World War I until the end of 1921 when the Bolsheviks had become the "indisputable masters" of Russia.[59] For our purposes, though, it is important to note the singularity of that part of the continuum represented by the Civil War (1918–21). Unique to it was the multiplicity of contenders for state power within Russian-dominated political space and their rival claims over the population to supply the military and serve in it. Serving the military included the reorientation of the economy toward the war effort via a series of measures that Lenin retrospectively would call War Communism. But it meant much more than that: not only a conflation of military and civilian functions—what in other contexts has been known as the militarization of society— but also, as Peter Holquist argues, a transformation of "the parameters and substance of both military and civilian realms . . . to produce a specific civilian-military hybrid."[60]

The career of Eduard Dune, related in his well-known memoir, illustrates the cumulative effect of war, revolution, and civil war on an individual identifying with the Soviet project. It also exemplifies a kind of military migration previously unimaginable. A native of Latvia, Dune was fifteen when he left Riga with the rest of his family for Moscow, where the Provodnik rubber factory that employed his father was relocated. Wartime Moscow converted him to bolshevism, so that he became part of a workers' militia that in turn became a Red Guard unit. The signing of the Brest-Litovsk Treaty found him in the Don Cossack territory (the Vendée of the Russian Revolution) combating the Volunteer Army that former tsarist officers had mustered. With the formation of the Red Army, Dune became a political commissar, sent to join troops in Saratov province along the Volga. Captured by the "Greens" (independent guerillas), he was handed over to the White Army, then hospitalized with "the second scourge of the civil war," typhus. By late 1919, he was in a military hospital— still a prisoner—on the northeast coast of the Black Sea to witness the flight of the White Army and the arrival of a strengthened and more professional Red Army unit than the one he had joined. After his recovery and return to military service, he spent 1920 on the Kuban

59. See especially Peter Holquist, "Violent Russia, Deadly Marxism? Russia in the Epoch of Violence, 1905–21," Kritika 4, no. 3 (2003): 627–52; Holquist, Making War; Sanborn, Drafting the Russian Nation.

60. Holquist, Making War, 286. See also Werth, "Déserteurs en Russie," 99.

in the northern Caucasus as the White Army retreated from Crimea. Then at the year's end he was sent to Dagestan to put down an Islamist rebellion. "In Dagestan," he explained, "lived 1.2 million people belonging to thirty-four ethnic groups, speaking thirty-four different languages."[61]

Not every soldier had Dune's wide-ranging peregrinations, but few did not see a different part of the country as a result of their service and some traveled even farther than he. As previously with the Imperial army, we begin our analysis of migration in the Red Army with recruitment. We start with the formation of the Red Army's officer corps and its recruitment of soldiers. We then consider the ambiguities of the bandit-partisan binary, and conclude with some observations about the Russian-Polish War through the lens of Isaac Babel's diary and short stories.

Many Bolsheviks worried about the reliability of officers in the former tsarist army who came over to the Reds. The Red Army's employment of these "military specialists," initially numbering about 8,000, quickly became its most controversial feature. Trotsky, as Commissar of War, plumped for them, insisting against the Left Communists and later the Military Opposition within the party that until a sufficient number of Red commanders could graduate from military training courses, the army had to rely on the specialists' expertise.[62] To placate critics, Sovnarkom extended the system of commissars introduced by the Provisional Government as a check on tsarist bureaucratic holdovers. Thus was institutionalized dual command (*dvoenachalie*) whereby commissars countersigned all commanders' orders. But during 1918, commissars were few—no more than 6,500 by December—and Red commanders were fewer still, whereas the Red Army employed as many as 165,000 military specialists.[63]

Dune, who was highly suspicious of the military specialists, also had a low assessment of the peasant draftees in this unit: "There were very many among them who . . . could barely read. . . . They talked among themselves only about their villages, their streams, their sweethearts. They were obsessed with land." They also regarded him with a barely disguised hatred that made him fear for his life. Such were the difficulties of finding the right balance in recruitment policy between quality and quantity, or as the Bolsheviks conceived of the problem, as a Red rather than a "people's army."[64] In July 1918, the Central

---

61. Eduard M. Dune, *Notes of a Red Guard* (Urbana, 1993), xiii–xviii, 154, 217–22.

62. Lenin argued on much the same basis of expediency for the employment of technical specialists in industry. See Kendall E. Bailes, *Technology and Society under Lenin and Stalin: Origins of the Soviet Technical Intelligentsia, 1917–1941* (Princeton, 1978), 47–50.

63. Mark von Hagen, *Soldiers in the Proletarian Dictatorship: The Red Army and the Soviet Socialist State, 1917–1930* (Ithaca, 1990) 28, 40. This figure evidently includes staff and medical personnel. For a much lower figure, see S. S. Khromov, ed., *Grazhdanskaia voina i voennaia interventsiia v SSSR: Entsiklopediia* (Moscow, 1983), 106.

64. Dune, *Notes of a Red Guard*, 128–29; von Hagen, *Soldiers of the Proletarian Dictatorship*, 57.

Committee of the Communist Party embarked on the mobilization of party members with combat experience. These shock troops helped turn the tide on the eastern front, recapturing the city of Kazan from the Czechoslovak Legion in September.[65] But the Red Army needed many more soldiers than there were available Communists. In the largest recruitment drive of the entire war, it called up over a million men between October and December 1918 to counter the new anti-Bolshevik Armed Forces of South Russia formed by the merger of the Volunteer Army with the Don Army under General Anton Denikin. This was followed by a call-up of poor and middle peasant volunteers by township executive committees, but instead of an anticipated 140,000, only some 25,000 reported. Mobilization by age groups—the traditional tsarist method that the Red Army used in its late 1918 call-up—had better results. By this system, the army inducted over half a million in the first half of 1919, and by the end of the year its numbers stood at nearly three million men.[66]

This figure evidently does not include deserters. They numbered 1.7 million by the end of 1919. Most, about three-quarters, simply had failed to appear for induction. Another 18–20 percent fled from conscription points and rear units, which meant that, similar to World War I, only 5–7 percent deserted from frontline combat units.[67] Some deserters returned home to rejoin their families and assist with farm tasks, but men conscripted by one side sometimes defected to the other. At least as often, they engaged in "violent migrations" of their own by forming or joining freelance groups, sometimes identifying themselves as "anarchist" and sometimes as "Green." The extent and importance of such groups tended to be overshadowed in Soviet times by the ideologically more palatable conflict between Reds and Whites. When Soviet historians did refer to them, the two most common terms they employed were "partisans" and "bandits." Partisans were, by definition, groups allied with the Red Army; bandits lent themselves to "use by enemies of Soviet power to undermine civil and military measures of the Soviet government [and] disorganize the Red Army's rear as expressed in . . . mass disorders, arson, killing of party and soviet employees, sabotaging of railroad lines, etc." Such was the protean nature of loyalties, though, that bandits could become partisans, or, as was more common after the defeat of the Whites, partisans could become bandits.[68]

---

65. N. E. Kakurin and I. I. Vatsetis, *Grazhdanskaia voina, 1918–21* (St. Petersburg, 2002), 71–85. The Czechoslovak Legion consisted of volunteers and former POWs who rebelled when the Soviet government tried to disarm them during their slow exit from Russia eastward via the Trans-Siberian Railroad.

66. von Hagen, *Soldiers of the Proletarian Dictatorship*, 39, 68, 79. For other figures see Orlando Figes, "The Red Army and Mass Mobilization during the Russian Civil War," *Past and Present* 129 (1990): 184–87.

67. von Hagen, *Soldiers of the Proletarian Dictatorship*, 69.

68. *Grazhdanskaia voina i voennaia interventsiia*, 53, 424–25; quotation from 53. For insight into the shifting loyalties in the civil war, see Werth, "Déserteurs en Russie," 112–14.

Hardly any area did not see partisan-bandit activity, but south-central Ukraine, the Tambov province of the central agricultural region, and western Siberia (including parts of the Urals and current Kazakhstan) saw the most. Here, we concentrate on the dislocations in just one part of western Siberia, the Altai.[69] Home to hundreds of thousands of descendants of peasants who had resettled from the Russian interior, the Altai was an area sufficiently rural, remote from the citadels of Soviet power, and, like the other two regions just mentioned, capable of producing agricultural surpluses to generate strong autonomist sentiment.[70] Throughout 1919, bands of partisans gained strength in members and weapons, seizing large swathes of territory and increasingly isolating the White Kolchak government based outside the area in Omsk. "As long as the Omsk government remained a more or less viable operation," writes Norman Pereira, "most Siberian partisans were not disposed to judge the Bolsheviks too critically."[71] The falling out came in 1920 when the Bolsheviks applied grain requisition quotas (*prodrazverstki*) and sought to subordinate to the revolutionary committees (*revkomy*) and Red Army command partisan detachments that prized their independence and claimed legitimacy from the local soviets.

Most members of these groups were peasants, although a smattering of village *intelligenty* also participated. Among the leaders, Efim Mamontov (1889–1922) had left Voronezh province with his parents to resettle 4,000 kilometers away in the Altai in 1893, received a primary school education there, and served at the front in World War I. Before he turned against the Bolsheviks, he led a volunteer rifle brigade against Wrangel's army in southern Ukraine. Grigorii Rogov (1883–1920), born to poor peasants in the Altai's Barnaul uezd, was a veteran of the Russo-Japanese War and the First World War. By 1919, he was jointly commanding with the anarchist Ivan Novoselov up to five thousand guerillas who repeatedly bested Kolchak's army, seized several towns including the mining settlements of Kuznetsk (today, Novokuznetsk) and Shcheglovsk (the future Kemerovo) hundreds of kilometers to the northeast of Barnaul, where they laid waste to stores, warehouses, and much other property, and slew scores of townsfolk. Twice he fell out with the Bolsheviks, the second time leading to his death in a village some 60 kilometers from home. Novoselov, from a poor peasant family in Tomsk province, had served as an orderly at the front during the First World War. During the uprisings of 1919–20 in the Altai and the neighboring

---

69. For Ukraine, see *Nestor Makhno: Krest'ianskoe dvizhenie na Ukraine, 1918–1921: Dokumenty i materialy*, ed. V. Danilov et al. (Moscow, 2006); for Tambov, *Krest'ianskoe vosstanie v tambovskoi gubernii v 1919–1921 gg., "Antonovshchina": Dokumenty i materialy*, ed. V. Danilov, T. Shanin et al. (Tambov, 1994); and Erik C. Landis, *Bandits and Partisans: The Antonov Movement in the Russian Civil War* (Pittsburgh, 2008).

70. According to the 1897 census, 86 percent of the population of the Altai okrug consisted of peasants by estate (soslovie) and 85.8 percent of the population was involved in agriculture. See N. A. Troinitskii, *Pervaia vseobshchaia perepis' naseleniia rossiiskoi imperii, 1897 g.*, 89 vols. (St. Petersburg, 1899–1904), 79: 2, 148–51.

71. N. G. O. Pereira, *White Siberia: The Politics of Civil War* (Montreal, 1996), 145.

Kuzbas, he articulated the program of the Federation of Altai Anarchists ("Soviets without Communists") and flew the black flag. Finally, Filipp Plotnikov (1874–1920), one of the leaders of the People's Insurgent Army that fielded thousands against the Red Army in the "steppe Altai uprising" of the summer of 1920, had a background similar to Rogov's—a poor peasant from Barnaul.[72]

So these were World War I veterans who either hailed from the Altai or were brought there as children. They returned from the war, armed and prepared to do battle again, this time against internal enemies. None appears to have deserted but they recruited plenty of deserters from both Kolchak's army and the Red Army. Their violent migrations during the Civil War did not take them all that far, although several hundred kilometers on horseback or wagon could take weeks. They represented extensions and adaptations of military service in times that were anything but conventional. One more point is in order: we can only track their movements so far, beyond which all seems chaos. But chaos is perspectival and largely a function of our distance.

The publication of documents in recent years brings us somewhat closer, although the usual caveats of partiality and indeed partisanship certainly apply. Here is part of the protocol of an interrogation dated June 20, 1920. The interrogator is identified not by name but as "the director of intelligence of the 228th regiment of the 26th rifle division"; the person being interrogated is Nikolai Nazarenko, "grain cultivator from the village of Korobeinikovo, Zerkal'sk township, Barnaul uezd, Altai province, [who] earlier served in the army of Kolchak, the third Barnaul regiment." He also served in the Red Army under the commandant of the city of Barnaul. "On June 15 of this year," Nazarenko's testimony begins,

> the former partisan Plotnikov appeared with a detachment in Korobeinikovo, [and] demanded from the chairman of the soviet a list of former Kolchakites and announced the mobilization of those whose names appeared. The detachment had about three hundred men . . . eighty to one hundred rifles, little ammunition, and one Lewis machine gun. Plotnikov mobilized about thirty former Kolchakites in addition to whom ten to fifteen partisans voluntarily joined the detachment.

From Korobeinikovo, he and his now enlarged detachment moved the next day to the village of Krest'ianskoe ("Peasant") where he mobilized an additional forty former

72. V. I. Shishkin, ed., *Sibirskaia vandeia*, 2 vols. (Moscow, 2000), 1: 61–130; V. I. Shishkin, "Antikommunisticheskoe vooruzhennoe soprotivlenie v Sibiri v 1920 g. (chislennost' i sostav povstantsev)," in *Iz istorii revoliutsii v Rossii (pervaia chetvert' XX v.)*, ed. L. I. Bozhenko (Tomsk, 1996), 2: 94; Shishkin, "Narodnaia povstancheskaia armiia Stepnogo Altaia (leto 1920 goda)," at http://zaimka.ru/power/shishkin6.shtml (accessed October 15, 2012).

Kolchakites. From there it was on to Mel'nikovo, where everyone eligible for mobilization during the years 1908–22 was called up. However, in the next village, "the citizens refused to go with him," after which those mobilized turned back and dispersed.[73]

Not before, according to another report, skirmishing with the 5th Red Army's Petrograd regiment. Four days later, Plotnikov was reported to have left the pine forest to which he and his troops had repaired, intending to reach a destination some 80 kilometers to the east. The following day he was sighted; a Communist detachment sought to apprehend his family in the village of Belovo, but found nobody at home. Similar to the "Antonovshchina" in Tambov province and reminiscent of guerilla wars fought elsewhere and in other times, this cat-and-mouse game continued for several months more. Toward August, there were numerous sightings of Plotnikov's forces along the Irtysh River in present-day northeastern Kazakhstan far to the west of where he had been reported previously. Authorities downstream in Pavlodar became sufficiently nervous to order that town's evacuation. Plotnikov issued orders throughout August and September to a number of villages urging peasants to resist the grain requisitions by Communist authorities, calling on them to turn over their weapons to his insurgent army, and announcing the draft of all able-bodied twenty- to forty-year-old males, evasion of which was punishable by "the highest measure." But by October, supplies and the ardor of locals were diminishing. Finally, on the twentieth, in the little settlement of Peschanaia ("Sandy") about 60 kilometers north of the district seat of Aleisk, the 26th Rifle Division that had been tracking the insurgents for months caught up with Plotnikov and killed him along with ten others.[74]

Meanwhile in the spring of 1920, at the southwestern end of the country, the army of independent Poland, assisted by guerilla forces loyal to the erstwhile Ukrainian hetman Simon Petliura, took advantage of Soviet Russia's internal turmoil to launch an offensive. They occupied Kiev, but only for several weeks before a Red Army counterattack threw them back. In combating the "Polish bourgeois-landowning regime" and its "Ukrainian petty-bourgeois chauvinist" ally, Soviet authorities drew not only on the already overstretched and exhausted Red Army units but also several hundred thousand new recruits and thousands of former tsarist officers, many of whom responded to an appeal from General Aleksei Brusilov that *Pravda* published at the end of May 1920.[75] Thanks to Isaac Babel's stories published as *Konarmiia* (1926; *Red Cavalry*, 1929), we know best the First Cavalry Army under Semën Budënnyi. Formed in 1918 as a guerilla unit among Don and Kuban Cossacks, the

73. Shishkin, *Sibiskaia vandeia*, 1: 149.

74. Ibid., 150–57, 236–41, 246–47, 259–67; Shishkin, "Antikommunisticheskoe vooruzhennoe soprotivlenie," 88–89. The name of the settlement is also given as Peschanoe.

75. For this language, see entries on the "Petliuraists" and the Soviet-Polish war of 1920 in *Grazhdanskaia voina i voennaia interventsiia*, 452, 550–51.

cavalry played an important role in routing Denikin's army during the fall of 1919. After its participation in the war against Poland, its violent migrations included action against the remnants of Wrangel's White army in southern Ukraine and Crimea, and operations in Siberia, Central Asia, and the Russian Far East. Here we use Babel's diary to examine the multiple dislocations and fractured identities of these Cossacks as well as Babel himself, a Jew from Odessa, as the horse army fought, squabbled, and plundered its way back and forth across the provinces of Volhynia and Galicia in the summer of 1920.

Babel generally wrote his diary while lodging with townspeople who had no choice about putting him up, or while on the road. We do not know exactly when the diary began, for the first fifty-four pages of the notebook containing his entries have not survived. The dates encompassed are July 3 to September 15, but the latter date is unlikely to have been the last. Descriptions of battles occupy only a small portion of the diary, though the threat and consequences of violence are nearly ubiquitous. They are captured brilliantly within the series of contradictory images that, he writes, his mind rather than his eyes received.

Off the Lesznjów highway, for instance, he encounters a "dreadful field, sown with mangled men, inhuman cruelty, unbelievable wounds, fractured skulls, naked young bodies gleaming white in the sun, jettisoned notebooks, leaflets, soldiers' books, Bibles, bodies amid the wheat." Later, he summarizes five days of having been "on the move the whole time" as "endless roads, the squadron's pennant, Apanasenko's horses, skirmishes, farms, corpses." The poignancy of being among the perpetrators of violence against "a settled way of life" is captured in yet another series occasioned by the plundering of a Polish estate: "gymnastic equipment, good books, tables, jars containing medicines, everything sacrilegiously mutilated. An unbearable feeling, I want to run away from these vandals, but . . . describe their gait, their faces, their hats, their foul language, as they drag sheaves of oats through the clinging mud." Actually, despite this unflattering characterization, Babel was not unsympathetic to the Cossacks with whom he rode as a war correspondent. While to him "all peasants look alike," he perceives the Cossacks as "many-layered: looting, reckless daring, professionalism, revolutionary spirit, bestial cruelty."[76]

Much has been written on Babel's own ambiguous identity.[77] In places he used the first-person plural to refer to Cossacks, but elsewhere described himself as an "outsider." He admires but at the same time is repelled by their decisiveness and physicality. His relationship with the Volhynian and Galician Jews is even more complicated. "We are an ancient people, exhausted, but we still have some strength left," he writes after his encounter with a cluster of ghetto Jews, then, "an old Jew—I like talking with my own kind—they

76. Isaac Babel, 1920 Diary, ed. Carol J. Avins, trans. H. T. Willetts (New Haven, 1995), 50, 68, 86.
77. See Carol J. Avins, "Kinship and Concealment in Red Cavalry and Babel's 1920 Diary," Slavic Review 53, no. 2 (1994): 694–710.

understand me." Yet, sometimes in the presence of Jews he conceals his kinship, distinguishing "our type" (that is, Odessite, Soviet, assimilated, secular) from "these Jews." He also repeatedly expresses the migrant's most common plaint—homesickness. He misses his wife, his father, and more generally, Odessa.[78]

In the end, the emancipatory thrust of the Red Cossacks' movement through these Ukrainian-Polish-Jewish towns is thwarted by their rapine ways, surrenders and defections to the Polish side, and eventual military withdrawal. As the troop train departs from a station in central Volhynia, the wounded, deserters, and other stragglers clamber aboard only to be thrown off at the next stop. "Shameful panic," Babel observes, "an army incapable of fighting." The long arc of Russia's continuum of crisis that had paved the way for the Bolsheviks to come to power and both facilitated and complicated their transformational agenda was coming to a close, and with it the violent migrations of its soldiers. Babel's judgment about the Russian Red Army infantryman at this point was harsh: "not just unmodernized, but the personification of 'pauper Russia,' wayfaring tramps, unhealthily swollen, bug-ridden, scrubby, half-starved peasants."[79] More beggar than liberator.

Military Service—Great Patriotic War and Beyond

Approximately 30 million people, all but 820,000 of them men, entered the Soviet armed forces between 1939 and 1945. Most had had some prior exposure to the Workers' and Peasants' Red Army through lectures in school, newspaper and newsreel accounts, and training offered by the voluntary organization Osoaviakhim (Society for Air and Chemical Defense) that enrolled 3 million new members every year. Between 1939 and 1941 the army engaged enemy forces on widely scattered fronts—from the border between Mongolia and the Japanese "puppet state" of Manchukuo, to Galicia west of what had been the border with Poland, and on the forested terrain along the border with Finland. In addition, it occupied the Romanian provinces of Northern Bukovina and Bessarabia, and the former Baltic states of Latvia, Estonia, and Lithuania. Despite considerable casualties—an estimated 200,000 during the 1939–40 Winter War against Finland, for example—the number of active soldiers in the Red Army increased from about 1.8 million in 1939 to 3 million by the time of the German invasion in June 1941.

We return to Sanborn's argument that soldiers should be considered migrants, which pertains even more specifically to the years 1939–45, when movement was endemic to their "job" and very often to their survival.[80] Some, but not much, of this movement conformed

---

78. Babel, 1920 Diary, 28, 38, 41, 55, 56, 63–64, 69, 78, 94.
79. Ibid., 97.
80. Sanborn, "Unsettling the Empire."

to the lines of prewar planning. Some emanated from military strategists who, huddled together over maps in Moscow, redrew vectors on a frequent basis. Much of it involved ad hoc decision making and wandering. As in the case of the Red Army infantrymen described by Babel, soldiers in the Great Patriotic War sometimes resembled migrants who feature in other chapters of this book.

Second, while many soldiers remained entirely within Soviet territory, very few remained within the region from which they had come. Most, whether separated from their territorially based units or traveling together with others from their home districts, crossed into unfamiliar territory that may or may not have been Soviet before the war, but that often was inhabited by people speaking a language other than their own. In this sense, our understanding of soldiers as migrants conforms to Jan and Leo Lucassen's rationale for including them in their analysis of "cross-community migration."[81] Actually, millions of Soviet soldiers went farther, temporarily *emigrating* either as prisoners of war or as liberators and occupiers. Third and finally, we need to incorporate demobilization and reintegration into civilian society as part of soldiers' migratory experience.

We begin with recruitment, which for the soldiers of the Great Patriotic War proceeded according to quotas determined by the General Staff for each military district. These were then passed down to local district and town military councils that evaluated claims for exemption and weeded out the infirm, the insane, and known "enemies of the people." "Joining up," notes Catherine Merridale in her evocative social history of the ordinary "Ivans" of the Great Patriotic War, "was part of life, as traditional in Russian villages as wife beating and painted eggs." Those called up in the villages behaved in ways that their fathers and grandfathers would have recognized. They got drunk.[82] Parents too responded as in pre-Soviet times. Sergei Priadko, a tank driver, recalled that when he was called up his mother gave him little crosses, icons, and amulets, which he kept throughout his eight years of military service.[83] Aleksei Ivanov, who had just graduated from the district high school in Degtianka, Tambov oblast', when the war began, remembers accordion music, men singing and drinking, and women crying.[84]

Scenes like this were repeated throughout the war as successive waves of youth—not only in the Russian republic and not only in the villages—received call-up notices. Lazar' Tsents, born in 1923 in the town of Polotsk (Belorussian SSR), grew up in Kazakhstan because his father, a veteran of the Civil War and the war against Poland, had gone there to help build the Turksib railroad in 1928. "I dreamed of becoming a naval officer," he told an

81. Lucassen and Lucassen, "Mobility Transition Revisited," 351. The Lucassens get "cross-community migration" from Patrick Manning, *Migration in World History* (London, 2005), 7.

82. Catherine Merridale, *Ivan's War: Life and Death in the Red Army, 1939–1945* (New York, 2006), 55–56.

83. "Sergei Priadko," http://iremember.ru/tankisti/pryadko-sergey-terentevich.html, 3 (accessed September 17, 2012).

84. "Aleksei Ivanov," http://iremember.ru/samokhodchiki/ivanov-aleksey-petrovich.html, 1 (accessed September 17, 2012).

interviewer in 2009, "and in the spring of 1941 filled out a form to enter the Dzerzhinskii Naval Engineering School in Leningrad." The day after his high-school graduation, he boarded a train to Moscow to take the entrance exams. The train arrived on June 22, 1941, the very day of the German invasion. Lazar' had to return to Alma-Ata, where, because he was still too young for the draft, he entered the mining and metallurgical institute. A year later, in December 1942, he was drafted and sent to the Riazan' Artillery School, which had been evacuated to Talgar, a Kazakh village located some 20 kilometers from his home.[85] So the war had a way of pulling people in on its terms rather than their own.

Lazar' Tsents waited until he was called, but not everyone was so patient. Merridale describes the loyal Soviet masses throwing themselves "into a surge of volunteering."[86] In Moscow, "recruitment centers were jammed round the clock," with more than 3,500 applicants in the first thirty-six hours after the war began. Workers, after assembling to hear patriotic speeches, trooped off "like boy scouts" to recruiting stations.[87] Among those clamoring to be accepted were women—thousands "begging, demanding and crying" to be sent to the front flocked to meetings and jammed recruiting stations within twenty-four hours of the invasion. By the end of the first week of war, 20,000 had volunteered.[88] In Leningrad, Zinovii Merkin remembers people greeting the war by gathering on street corners to listen to announcements on loudspeakers, some shedding tears in apprehension and others grimly shouting, "We'll show those bastards!" He and his friends went to the local military office to volunteer only to discover it was closed. They returned the next day hoping to sign up.

> Standing alongside me was my classmate Andrei Brylev. He was older than me by a month. Someone asked him the year of his birth. He said 1924. "Well, then we'll call you," he was told. So I am thinking, "Yeah, well, that won't do!" So I said 1923. Andrei looked at me, with bulging eyes—he knows that he is older than me. The captain said to me: "Write an application." I wrote a statement and on the third of July, I was summoned to the Novocherkassk barracks on the right bank of the Neva, where the Alexander Nevsky Bridge now stands.[89]

By war's end, 20 million Soviet citizens had applied to join the Red Army or Navy.

---

85. "Lazar' Rafael'evich Tsents," http://iremember.ru/artilleristi/tsents-lazar-rafaelevich.html, 1 (accessed September 18, 2012).

86. Merridale, Ivan's War, 92.

87. Ibid.

88. S. Aleksievich, ed., U voiny—ne zhenskoe litso (Moscow, 2004), cited in Roger Markwick and Euridice Charon Cardona, Soviet Women on the Frontline in the Second World War (Houndmills, 2012), 33; see also 36.

89. "Zinovii Merkin," http://iremember.ru/razvedchiki/merkin-zinoviy-leonidovich.html, 1 (accessed September 17, 2012). For a strikingly similar account by another Leningrader, Albina Gantimurova, who eventually became a senior commander of a naval infantry reconnaissance unit, see Markwick and Cardona, Soviet Women on the Frontline, 35.

The starting point for most Red Army soldiers, though, was a letter from the local military commissariat (*voenkomat*). But in the strained circumstances of war, neither receipt of the letter nor compliance with it could be assured. Two days after the invasion, Mikhail Volkov, a reservist working in Kiev's metals industry, received notice to report to a unit in L'vov. After a harrowing journey by train, he arrived in a city already "in complete chaos" and discovered that his unit had fled toward the east. With fellow reserve officers, he reversed direction, this time traveling by foot to Tarnopol, where they found the remnants of their unit.[90]

Recruitment continued throughout the war, sometimes coming at odd conjunctures. In the case of Vasilii Borodin, a Cossack raised near the town of Kalach-on-Don (Stalingrad oblast'), a burst appendix coincided with the liberation of the town from enemy occupation in 1943 and the receipt of his draft notice. Borodin remembers going straight from the hospital where he was recuperating to Nal'chik, 800 kilometers to the south. The draft board looked at him in astonishment and told him to go home. Two days later, he claims, he received instructions to report to the Red Barracks in Stalingrad (which was in ruins and still not entirely free of the invading German forces), but there too he was rejected. On the third occasion, now in Mozdok, North Ossetia, 100 kilometers to the east of Nal'chik, recruiters whom he refers to as "buyers" bid for his and his friend's services because everyone else from his year already had been sent to the Far East. Artillery, infantry or intelligence? The friends chose intelligence.[91]

As for the women who enlisted, Anna Krylova argues that the 120,000 who volunteered for combat units did not so much erase as transform gender differences. For these women steeled by paramilitary training, Komsomol activism, and the school curriculum, the front line became "a place of accelerated development of prewar unconventional discourses on womanhood and soldierhood into novel military cultures and new gendered landscapes."[92] Used by Krylova in the metaphoric sense, geography had a literal dimension too. The front, after all, consisted of more than "spaces" for "the articulation and acting out of pre-war gender contradictions." It was where pillaging, rape, maiming, and death occurred on a daily basis.[93]

Many years later, Mariia Galyshkina, who had served as a sniper during the Red Army's advance through Ukraine and into Romania, could respond to an interviewer's question

90. Merridale, *Ivan's War*, 94–95.

91. "Vasilii Borodin," http://iremember.ru/razvedchiki/borodin-vasiliy-parfenovich.html, 1 (accessed September 18, 2012).

92. Anna Krylova, *Soviet Women in Combat: A History of Violence on the Eastern Front* (Cambridge, 2010), 18, 25, 30.

93. Ibid., 203. For the critical comment on Krylova's book, see Roger Markwick's review in *The Russian Review* 70, no. 1 (2011): 160–61.

about whether she thought a woman's "place" was at the front by asserting, "Women have more strength than men. Women are needed in war."[94] But as Krylova herself acknowledges, female mobilizations "created several gendered landscapes for the army."[95] The considerably larger number of women—five hundred thousand—who also served at the front but in the noncombat roles of medical personnel, clerks, typists, signalers, laundresses, drivers, and cooks had less opportunity to demonstrate their strength through mastering mechanized violence. They also seem to have been subjected to greater pressure from male officers to serve as "mobile field wives" (*polevaia pokhodnaia zhena* or *pokhodno-polevaia zhena*, both abbreviated as PPZh, a pun on mobile field guns, PPSh).[96] Judging from Krylova's account, women in combat and especially pilots (the so-called night witches) experienced more equal "comradely bonding," romance, and longer-lasting marriages.[97]

Finally, some who were called up never showed up or deserted. Reliable information on the number who fled service in the armed forces is lacking, but it is likely to have exceeded a million.[98] Less than three weeks into the war, the head of political propaganda on the southwest front wrote to his boss Lev Mekhlis of the "masses of soldiers and officers, singly and in groups, with arms and without, mov[ing] along the roads to the rear, wreaking havoc" with their "panic, cowardice, desertion, and indiscipline." Five days later he referred to the "exceptionally large number of deserters," citing 5,000 in one rifle corps alone who had been apprehended and returned to the front.[99] A military judge in Yaroslavl' oblast' reported in November 1941 that 81 of the 270 draftees sent from Borisogleb district to Antropovo in neighboring Kostroma oblast' never made it because they deserted.[100] Soldiers during this, the most devastating, period of the war had many reasons to desert—shortages of food and other supplies, the overwhelming superiority of the enemy's

94. "Mariia (Kleimenova) Galyshkina," http://iremember.ru/snayperi/galishkina-mariya-aleksandrovna.html, 4 (accessed September 26, 2012).

95. Krylova, *Soviet Women in Combat*, 29; see also the chapter "By State Order: Old and New Gender Landscapes for the Military," 149–56.

96. Markwick and Cardona, *Soviet Women on the Frontline*, 239–40; Merridale, *Ivan's War*, 239–41.

97. Krylova, *Soviet Women in Combat*, 236–89. But for quite a few long-lasting marriages between women who had served as nurses and soldiers they met during the war, see "Mediki," http://iremember.ru/mediki/blog.html, 1–5.

98. According to a recent estimate, deserters from the Red Army totaled at least 1.7 million soldiers by the end of the war, of whom 376,000 were arrested and punished and 212,000 evaded search parties. Mikhail Zefirov and D. M. Dëgtev, *Vse dlia fronta? Kak na samom dele kovalas' pobeda* (Moscow, 2009), 378.

99. TsAMO SSSR, f. 229, op. 213, d. 12, l. 13, cited in P. N. Knyshevskii, *Skrytaia pravda voiny: 1941 god* (Moscow, 1992), 264.

100. D. V. Tumakov, "Prestupnost' v periferiinykh raionakh SSSR v gody velikoi otechestvennoi voiny, 1941–1945 gg. (po materialam iaroslavskoi oblasti)," www.gvw-rggu.narod.ru/section/section3/stati2012/tumakov.htm (accessed September 24, 2013).

Figure 4 Soldiers on foot, 1944, Anri Vartanov et al., *Antologiia sovetskoi fotografii*, vol. 2, 1941–1945 (Moscow: Planeta, 1987), 185.

firepower, maltreatment by commanding officers. As their units retreated, some conscripts peeled off to return to their homes, trying to melt into the civilian population and survive under occupation.[101]

Among deserters, those who lived in the countryside generally stood a better chance of evasion than residents of cities, where papers were checked more frequently. But by forging documents or purchasing them under an assumed name even urbanites could escape the

---

101. In 1943–44, the NKVD arrested over five hundred thousand soldiers who had left the field of battle, gone AWOL, did not hold proper documents, or deserted. See Mark Edele and Michael Geyer, "States of Exception: The Nazi-Soviet War as a System of Violence, 1939–1945," in *Beyond Totalitarianism: Stalinism and Nazism Compared*, ed. Michael Geyer and Sheila Fitzpatrick (New York, 2009), 385–86.

clutches of authorities or at least extend the period of their freedom. After deserting in December 1941, I. S. Sidorov turned up in his home village in Gor'kii oblast' telling friends and other acquaintances that the authorities had released him owing to illness. "Nobody checked my papers," he told his interrogators after his apprehension in May 1942. "On the contrary, the kolkhoz administration offered me work, which I accepted. The village soviet knew that I lived at home and worked on the kolkhoz but nobody discussed with me the reasons for my return from the front."[102] Labor-hungry kolkhoz administrations asked no questions.

Nonetheless, even as the Red Army suffered heavily in one disastrous battle after another, millions of Soviet soldiers followed orders. Their violent migrations took them eastward deep into the Soviet interior. After Stalin's Order No. 227 ("not one step back") of July 28, 1942, retreating was no longer an option and the balance of the violent migratory movements subsequently pointed westward. Thus was realized Eugene Kulischer's prediction from early 1940 (more than a year before Operation Barbarossa) that "in their attempt to expand towards the East . . . the German[s] will finally precipitate the fatal Russian advance towards the West. . . . A policy which aims to reverse the peoples' movements may reinforce its violence and even pile up corpses and ruins."[103] Some soldiers, like Ivan Cherpukha, a Cossack who joined the cavalry as a nineteen year old in 1932 and later received artillery training, endured both eastward and westward migrations. A participant in the battle at Khalkin-Gol against the Japanese in 1939, Cherpukha fought in the catastrophically unsuccessful defense of Kiev in 1941, in Stalingrad and Kursk in 1942–43, moved on to Moldavia in 1944, and eventually Budapest and Vienna, where he remained stationed as a captain until 1951.[104]

How different from Mikhail Il'chenko's migrations! In October 1941, he and others from his Khar'kov-based unit were surrounded by German soldiers and taken prisoner near Kaluga, 100 miles southwest of Moscow. They marched to a transit camp in the town of Roslavl', another 200 miles to the southwest in Smolensk oblast'. In May 1942, he was transferred to a POW camp in Lithuania where he worked on nearby peat farms alongside local farmhands. Perhaps because conditions in the camp were so tolerable, he rejected efforts to recruit him to the Russian Liberation Army. In May 1944, he and eleven others were sent to Norway, where they handled freight in the ports, cut timber, and did construction work. At the end of the war, he did not hesitate (he says) to answer in the affirmative

102. Zefirov and Dëgtev, *Vse dlia fronta?* 370–71, 378.
103. Kulischer, *Europe on the Move*, v–vi.
104. "Ivan Cherpukha," http://iremember.ru/artilleristi/chernukha-ivan-danilovich.html, 1–4 (accessed January 21, 2012). For an interview conducted in April 2012 by the teacher and students of a fourth-grade class in Volgograd with the ninety-nine-year old Ivan Danilovich Chernukha, see "Nasha obshchaia pobeda," http://4145.su/archive/one/12329 (accessed September 18, 2012).

when asked if he wanted to return to the USSR. Boarding a steamer, he and other returnees belted out the popular song "Katiusha" in celebration. After a long journey through Finland, Leningrad, and Moscow, their train turned east. Eventually, they reached their destination—a reserve military formation near Ioshkar-Ola, the capital of the Mari ASSR lying north of the Volga, where the NKVD checked and provisionally cleared him for return to active duty. Il'chenko's odyssey recommenced when his reconstituted regiment entrained for the Far East. But with the Japanese surrender, Il'chenko, the Ukrainian farm boy, spent a few weeks mowing rye on a kolkhoz in the Urals where he met and married a local girl and where, after further interrogation, he was demobilized.[105]

These two soldiers—Cherpukha and Il'chenko—took almost diametrically opposed routes through the war. Cherpukha began in the Far East, saw action outside Kiev, retreated to Stalingrad, and then victoriously moved west all the way to Vienna. Il'chenko's wartime service began in Vitebsk and ended soon after in Kaluga. His westward travel was as a POW and after liberation he headed east, bound for Japan until the war in Asia ended. Of the two, Il'chenko's survival was the more improbable. Even if we take as more accurate the figure of 6.9 million deaths among Soviet military personnel resulting from combat, accidents, and illness, rather than earlier and somewhat lower estimates, the chances of surviving in a German POW camp must be considered slimmer, especially if the period of captivity included 1941–42.[106] According to German records cited by John Barber and Mark Harrison, a total of 5.8 million Soviet officers and soldiers were taken prisoner, of whom 3.3 million, or 57 percent, died by May 1944.[107] The fatality rate peaked in October–December 1941, the

105. "Mikhail Il'chenko," http://iremember.ru/letno-tekh-sostav/ilchenko-mikhail-alekseevich.html, 1–25 (accessed September 18, 2012). See also Robert Dale, "Re-Adjusting to Life after War: The Demobilization of Red Army Veterans in Leningrad and the Leningrad Region, 1944–1950" (PhD diss., University of London, 2010), 52–53: "Filtration camp inmates were forced labourers in all but name. Whilst undergoing the humiliation of interrogation and investigation at night, former POWs were expected to work exhausting eleven hour days."

106. For earlier estimates of 3–5 million, see Kulischer, Europe on the Move, 276; Frank Lorimer, The Population of the Soviet Union: History and Prospects (Geneva, 1946), 181–83. A good guide to Soviet and Russian historiography up to 2000 is L. L. Rybakovskii, "Liudskie poteri SSSR v velikoi otechestvennoi voine," Sotsiologicheskie issledovaniia, no. 6 (2000): 108–18, and no. 8 (2000): 89–97; and Rybakovskii, "Velikaia otechestvennaia: Liudskie poteri Rossii," Sotsiologicheskie issledovaniia, no. 6 (2001): 85–95. Much of the earlier estimates were superseded by G. F. Krivosheev et al., Rossiia i SSSR v voinakh XX veka, poteri vooruzhennykh sil: Statisticheskoe issledovanie (Moscow, 2003), 229–37.

107. John Barber and Mark Harrison, "Patriotic War, 1941–1945," in The Cambridge History of Russia, vol. 3, The Twentieth Century, ed. Ronald Grigor Suny (Cambridge, 2006), 225. For other estimates based on German sources, see A. A. Sheviakov, "Repatriatsiia sovetskogo mirnogo naseleniia i voennoplennykh, okazavshikhsia v okkupatsionnykh zonakh gosudarstv antigitlerovskoi koalitsii," in Naselenie Rossii v 1920–1950-e gody: Chislennost', poteri, migratsii, sbornik nauchnykh trudov, ed. Iu. A. Poliakov (Moscow, 1994), 199; V. B. Zhiromskaia et al., "Liudskie poteri v gody velikoi otechestvennoi voiny: Territoriia i naselenie posle voiny," in Zhiromskaia, Naselenie Rossii v XX veke, 2: 143.

Ivan Cherpukha and Mikhail Il'chenko's Military Migrations, 1939-1945

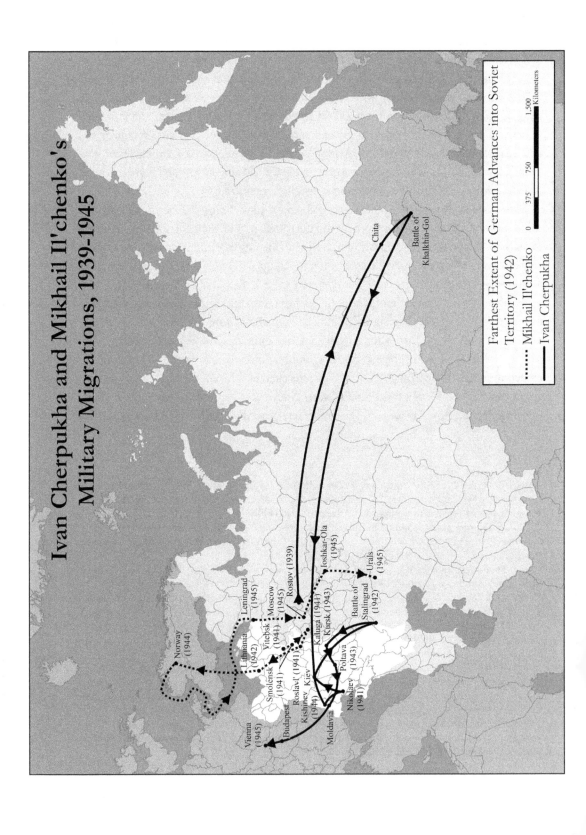

Farthest Extent of German Advances into Soviet Territory (1942)

· · · · · Mikhail Il'chenko

——— Ivan Cherpukha

0   375   750   1,500
Kilometers

Chita

Battle of Khalkhin-Gol

Rostov (1939)

Ioshkar-Ola (1945)

Urals (1945)

Leningrad (1945)

Moscow (1945)

Vitebsk (1941)

Kaluga (1941)

Kursk (1943)

Battle of Stalingrad (1942)

Lithuania (1942)

Smolensk (1941)

Roslavl' (1941)

Kiev (1941)

Poltava (1943)

Nikolaev (1941)

Norway (1944)

Kishinev (1944)

Budapest

Moldavia

Vienna (1945)

first three months of Il'chenko's incarceration, when between 900,000 and 1.5 million deaths occurred.[108]

Stalin's infamous Order No. 270 of August 1941 equated Soviet soldiers who had "allowed themselves to be captured" with traitors, and for decades thereafter much calumny was heaped on prisoners of war. Nonetheless, I Remember/Ia Pomniu, the web-based project founded in 2000 to collect and make available information from and about veterans of the Great Patriotic War, contains interviews with 52 who survived German captivity and lived to an advanced age.[109] Among them is Aleksandr Moiseevich Slutskii. Taken prisoner during the battle of Kerch in 1942, Slutskii probably would have been among the 140,000–165,000 Soviet Jewish POWs exterminated by the Germans had he not escaped, first by dismantling the floorboards of a railroad car in Dnepropetrovsk, then after his recapture by pretending to be Aleksandr Pavlovich Suslov, an ethnic Russian from Kamenets-Ural'sk, and finally by escaping with other POWs from a camp in Vinnitsa oblast', whereupon he entered counterintelligence.[110] Roman Lazebnik, whom we have encountered elsewhere, similarly reinvented himself as a Ukrainian, Roman Oleksievich Labzenko, after his capture near Tartu, Estonia, in July 1941. Lazebnik/Labzenko escaped while in transit in December 1942 and joined the 2nd Kalinin partisan brigade in Pskov oblast' in March 1943. Wounded in July 1944, he underwent nightly interrogations at an NKVD filtration camp near Podol'sk, 25 miles south of Moscow, and ended the war serving in a territorial defense squadron (TOR) guarding against intrusions by guerillas from western Ukraine.[111]

Joshua Sanborn reminds us that POWs in World War I performed "crucial tasks" in agriculture but also "in the battle zones working on 'front' and 'other' projects."[112] Vasilii

---

108. Christian Gerlach, *Krieg, Ernährung, Völkermord* (Hamburg, 1998), 33. See also Pavel Polian, *Zhertvy dvukh diktatur: Ostarbeitery i voennoplennye v Tretyem Reikhe i ikh repatriatsia* (Moscow, 1996). For a collection of memoirs by surviving POWs, see Pavel Polian, *Skvoz' dve voiny, skvoz' dva arkhipelaga: Vospominaniia sovetskikh voennoplennykh i ostrovtsev* (Moscow, 2007). For a lengthy memoir about surviving for more than three and a half years ("1,338 days and nights") in "Stalag 17" (the same camp that served as the setting for a 1951 Broadway play and the more famous 1953 Hollywood film), see D. T. Chirov, *Sred' bez vesti propavshikh: Vospominaniia sovetskogo voennoplennogo o Shtalage XVII "B" Krems-Gnaiksendorf, 1941–1945 gg.* (Moscow, 2010).

109. On the "indelible stain" of POW status, see Markwick and Cardona, *Soviet Women on the Frontline*, 243–44; and V. P. Naumov, "Sud'ba voennoplennykh i deportirovannykh grazhdan SSSR: Materialy komissii po reabilitatsii zhertv politicheskikh repressi," *Novaia i noveishaia istoriia*, no. 2 (2008): 91–112. For the list, see "Plen," http://iremember.ru/plen.html.

110. "Aleksandr Moiseevich Slutskii," http://iremember.ru/razvedchiki/slutskiy-aleksandr-moiseevich.html, 4–9 (accessed September 19, 2012). Slutskii endured a brief period in a punishment unit after rejoining the Red Army.

111. "Roman Lazebnik," http://iremember.ru/partizani/lazebnik-roman-evseevich.html, 3–6 (accessed March 15, 2012). For the case of a Soviet Jewish soldier who joined the partisans in his native Zhitomir oblast' but continued to identify himself as a Ukrainian (Margulis became Ostapenko), see "Iosif Margulis," http://iremember.ru/partizani/margulis-iosif-ilich.html, 3, 8 (accessed September 30, 2012).

112. Sanborn, "Unsettling the Empire," 318.

Viktorov, taken prisoner outside Rostov in the autumn of 1942, could relate to such precedents. "The Germans took some of us on jobs: clearing airfields, dragging ammunition, wherever physical labor was needed." Transferred to a camp in Opole, Poland, he worked in a paper factory with Poles, Croatians, and British POWs.[113] Leonid Lashkov also worked on an aerodrome until, as guards escorted him through the streets of Riga on his way to work, he tried to escape. Transferred to Osnabrück, he helped construct the camp from which he made another unsuccessful escape attempt. Nikolai Berdnikov, captured on the Volkhov front in June 1942, spent the next three years in a total of fourteen camps cultivating vegetables; loading and unloading peat, logs, and plywood; cutting coal in the Ruhr; and winding up in Buchenwald, from which he escaped in the waning weeks of the war.[114]

So at least for these POWs, confinement did not signify an end to movement across borders or contact with different civilian communities. Nor did it mean a lack of choices, daunting as those choices were. We need to remember, however, that our informants counted among the fortunate minority who because of strong constitutions, sympathetic doctors, the right choices, comrades with whom they shared their food and thoughts, and lots of good fortune, survived the ordeal. And then? Like Il'chenko and Lazebnik, other former POWs had to undergo interrogations at filtration points and camps, most often more than once. Those who could not convince authorities that they had tried to resist capture and had done their best to escape faced the same treatment as civilians suspected of having collaborated while living under occupation or working as *Ostarbeiter*. They were liable for service either in military labor battalions or punishment battalions, sent to so-called Verification-Filtration Camps for further investigation, or sentenced to a Gulag corrective labor camp, after which their settlement was restricted.[115]

Even those who passed through filtration without punitive assignment or confinement had to undergo repeated interrogations after the war. Berdnikov, who returned to his native Tomsk, reports that the local military authorities called him "often" for the first three postwar years. "I understood it was necessary," he recollected. "I wasn't offended." The last

---

113. "Vasilii Viktorov," http://iremember.ru/pekhotintsi/viktorov-vasiliy-alekseevich.html, 1–3 (accessed September 20, 2012).

114. "Leonid Iashkov," http://iremember.ru/partizani/lashkov-leonid-efimovich.html, 1–2 (accessed September 20, 2012); "Nikolai Berdnikov," http://iremember.ru/artilleristi/berdnikov-nikolay-vasilevich.html, 1–2 (accessed September 20, 2012).

115. Nick Baron, "Remaking Soviet Society: The Filtration of Returnees from Nazi Germany, 1944–49," in *Warlands: Population Resettlement and State Reconstruction in the Soviet-East European Borderlands, 1945–50*, ed. Peter Gatrell and Nick Baron (Houndmills, 2009), 91–93, 115; Zhiromskaia, "Liudskie poteri," 142–45. Of approximately 1.5 million former POWs who passed through filtration points by March 1946, 18.3 percent were dispatched to residences, 42.8 percent were reinstated in the military, 22.3 percent were assigned to military labor battalions, 14.6 percent were transferred to NKVD's administration, and 1.8 percent remained at the disposition of military authorities for future assignment (Zhiromskaia, "Liudskie poteri," 154).

time he was called, in 1953, was to receive an Order of the Red Star, "your reward for perseverance and courage in the German camps," a commissar told him. But more than half a century later, the psychological trauma associated with prisoner-of-war status was still evident:

> And now—now life is completely different. My daughter lives in Sakhalin. I used to visit her every year on vacation. Now I don't fly anymore—no pension is enough for a ticket. My wife has died. I live alone. I do social work. I don't like barking dogs. Now, though, the dogs are behind fences, where the houses are worth a lot.[116]

Between June 1945 and the end of 1948, over 8.5 million veterans received their discharge from the armed forces. Among the first two groups released by the end of September 1945 were men thirty years and older; veterans with higher, technical, or agricultural degrees and those with seven years of continuous military service; students who had interrupted their studies; those wounded at least three times; and women. People in these categories numbered 3.5 million.[117] The youngest veterans had to wait the longest, in some cases more than three years. "As so often in Soviet history," Mark Edele notes, "the logistics of demobilization of the wartime army were insufficiently worked out, and the infrastructure not extensive enough to cope with such an enormous population movement."[118] For the officially declared 2.5 million surviving invalids—the actual number was probably much higher—difficulties obtaining medical treatment, prosthetic devices, and, perhaps surprisingly, the sympathy of their fellow citizens compounded other problems.[119] "But everyone," writes Merridale, "even the first back, would have trouble finding their feet."[120]

Yet another problem—for the authorities—had to do with soldiers' temporary residence in Germany and other parts of Central Europe during and immediately after the war. The fortunate few, overwhelmingly officers, came back with trophies of victory, in some cases even automobiles.[121] But the subversive effect of witnessing the standard of living among

116. "Nikolai Berdnikov," 2.

117. For the initial decree, "Zakon—O demobilizatsii starshikh vozrastov lichnogo sostava Deistvuiushchei Armii," see *Pravda*, June 24, 1945, 1. For overviews of the process, see Merridale, *Ivan's War*, 355–71; Dale, "Re-Adjusting to Life after War," 10, 35–56; Robert Dale, "Rats and Resentment: The Demobilization of the Red Army in Postwar Leningrad, 1945–50," *Journal of Contemporary History* 45, no. 1 (2010): 113–33.

118. Mark Edele, *Soviet Veterans of the Second World War: A Popular Movement in an Authoritarian Society, 1941–1991* (Oxford, 2008), 38.

119. Beate Fieseler, "The Bitter Legacy of the 'Great Patriotic War': Red Army Disabled Soldiers under Late Stalinism," in *Late Stalinist Russia: Society between Reconstruction and Reinvention*, ed. Juliane Fürst (London, 2006), 46–61. The number "was the result of . . . regulations from above, which stipulated strict limits on who could be recognised as an invalid" (47).

120. Merridale, *Ivan's War*, 361.

121. See Siegelbaum, *Cars for Comrades*, 216–17.

noncollectivized peasants could be greater.[122] Here, for example, is what Vasilii Krysov, an artillerist who fought his way through Poland to East Prussia had to say to an interviewer many decades later:

> The civilization is higher. Look, . . . we talked to the peasants. They farmed with diesel engines that did everything—cut the grain, ground the flour, and prepared the fodder. That's number one. Secondly, while we portrayed Michurin almost as a god, over there every peasant is a Michurinist: the wheat stalks are highest and strongest; simple peasants cross cherries with currants; asphalt roads are everywhere so that you can ride to any populated point on asphalt.[123]

Peasants made up the vast majority of soldiers, and so it is not surprising that among those discharged, most wound up in the countryside, returning, in Merridale's words, "to mud and cockroaches again."[124] Data reproduced by Edele from local reports sent to the Labor Reserves Administration show that of a total demobilized population of 7.5 million as of January 1947, just over 5 million returned to the countryside. Among cities, Moscow and Leningrad were each the destination of about 212,000, Kiev was a long way behind at 44,500, followed by Gor'kii at 32,500, Rostov, Novosibirsk, Kuibyshev, and so forth. In light of the penury of rural life, why did veterans from the countryside return to the village?[125]

Edele points to several factors governing veterans' decisions: preference for the known, rumors of a relaxation of the kolkhoz regime, promises of material assistance by military authorities to rebuild homes damaged during the war. He also notes that "living on the kolkhoz did not necessarily mean *working* there," for no sooner had they returned than many were off on *otkhodnichestvo* while others worked their private plots and sold or bartered the produce.[126] Furthermore, not all who returned to the countryside came home. Instead they scouted out or were recruited to settle in other parts of the country that had been depopulated, repeating a pattern from the 1930s, discussed in our chapter on resettlement.

---

122. Merridale, *Ivan's War*, 356: "But from the government's point of view the real problems were inside the soldiers' minds."

123. "Vasilii Krysov," http://iremember.ru/samokhodchiki/krisov-vasiliy-semenovich.html, 7 (accessed September 25, 2012). Ivan Michurin (1855–1935) was a botanist whose "productive" approach to selection of plants for propagation and hybridization was lauded by propagandists as characteristically Soviet.

124. Merridale, *Ivan's War*, 362.

125. Mark Edele, "Veterans and the Village: The Impact of Red Army Demobilization on Soviet Urbanization, 1945–1955," *Russian History* 36 (2009): 159–67.

126. Ibid., 167; Jean Lévesque, " 'Into the Grey Zone:' Sham Peasants and the Limits of the Kolkhoz Order in the Post-war Russian Village," in Fürst, *Late Stalinist Russia*, 112–16.

In the longer term, after demobilized soldiers had "found their feet," they got itchy to leave and many did. Some had purely personal reasons such as incompatibility with spouses from whom they had grown apart during the war, or no spouses at all. But the reinforcement of the collective farm regime in 1946, the famine of 1946–47 that hit much of Ukraine and southern Russia, and the campaign of 1948 against "freeloaders" and other rural dwellers taking advantage of access to collective farm property and services undoubtedly convinced many that remaining on the kolkhoz was unviable. In fact, after 1947, rural population growth in the Russian republic went into reverse and would continue declining for the remainder of the Stalin era. Edele cites several reports from central and northern Russia indicating veterans' departures, but what proportion of the total loss can be attributed to their out-migration is hard to say.[127]

Where did they go? Leningrad, which suffered enormous population loss but proportionally less physical destruction than many towns and villages in the surrounding oblast', proved a popular destination. Unfortunately, as Robert Dale notes, it is impossible to determine how many Red Army veterans chose it, for lacking permission to migrate there, they were "reluctant to make themselves too visible to local administrators."[128] The city was also temporary residence for veterans who for one reason or another could not stay. Sergei Otroshchenkov, commander of a tank battalion, had worked at several Leningrad factories (Marti, Mikoian) before the war. Surviving the battle of Stalingrad, he advanced with the 170th tank brigade through the whole of Ukraine, Romania, and Hungary and ended up in Linz, Austria. In October 1945 he was reassigned to the Molotov Higher Officers' Armored Tank Academy in Leningrad, but before his course ended, he received word of his demobilization. "So, I went to the Marti factory, where I worked before the war, and ran into some old friends. The personnel officer said to me. 'Come join us. You can start work tomorrow; we'll find you housing, and get you married. We have lots of girls. We'll give you the apartment straight away.' They really lacked workers, especially skilled workers."[129] But Otroshchenkov didn't have the chance to accept the personnel officer's offer because the army recalled him.

Like Otroshchenkov, Il'ia Karasik was twenty years old and in Leningrad when the war broke out. He too became a tank commander, and was abroad—in Hungary—when the war ended. However, his entry into an armored tank academy in Moscow was blocked, he claims, because of his Jewish nationality. So he returned to Leningrad instead, picking up

127. Edele, "Veterans and the Village," 174–75. On the famine, see V. F. Zima, *Golod v SSSR 1946–1947 godov: Proiskhozhdenie i posledstviia* (Moscow, 1996).
128. Dale, "Re-Adjusting to Life after War," 55.
129. "Sergei Otroshchenkov," http://iremember.ru/tankisti/otroschenkov-sergey-andreevich.html, 17 (accessed September 29, 2012). Otroshchenkov reenlisted and was posted to the Zabaikal region.

where he left off as a student at the Leningrad Polytechnic Institute, and upon completion of his engineering degree worked at the Baltic Factory. The "anticosmopolitan" campaign eventually caught up to him there too, and in 1953 he was released. After failing to find work in Leningrad "even as a simple welder," he moved to Minsk, where eventually he was hired as head of a laboratory at the giant tractor factory. A few months later, a personal representative from Baltic's director came to offer him his old job back with an apartment thrown into the bargain, but he "decided not to step into the same river twice," and so remained in Minsk, where he retired.[130]

These two examples illustrate the interplay of state policies and individual choices. Just as with Edele's veterans who returned to their villages only to leave them after a few years, neither Otroshchenkov nor Karasik remained in Leningrad, despite the enticement of an apartment in each case. Toivo Kattonen, who grew up only 20 kilometers from the city, also did not stay in Leningrad, although he really had no choice in the matter. An ethnic Finn, Kattonen already had been expelled twice—once from his native village in 1936 because the authorities came to regard Finns as a security risk, and the second time from Leningrad in 1942, presumably for the same reason. He was deported for a third time shortly after his demobilization in 1945 and lost his job at one of the city's power stations. "Such were the long paths I took," he added laconically.[131] The agenda of demobilization thus collided with that of state security, as one form of migration—deportation—overwhelmed another.

A few other trends concerning demobilization are evident from interviews conducted with veterans for the I Remember/ Ia Pomniu project. One is that it did not affect ablebodied career officers. Some remained with the Soviet occupation forces in Europe, while others moved seamlessly from fighting Nazi Germany to the war against Japan. Anatolii Bordun, a fighter pilot, had his first combat experience in June 1944 in Belorussia; later, he was to see action in China and Korea, participating in the first jet-propelled aerial combat. Viktor Koliadin, also a fighter pilot, went to Mukden in 1950 to train Chinese pilots on MIG-15s. After graduating from an aeronautical engineering school in Riga, Boris Gol'dinov embarked on a career of teaching aerodynamics first in Tashkent and then in Frunze to students from Africa and Asia. And Anatolii Lilin, an artillery crewman during the war, served afterward in seventeen different places within the USSR, from Sakhalin to

130. "Il'ia Karasik," http://iremember.ru/tankisti/karasik-ilya-isaakovich.html, 4 (accessed September 29, 2012).

131. "Toivo Kattonen," http://iremember.ru/pulemetchiki/kattonen-toyvo-matveevich.html, 1 (accessed September 29, 2012).

Kaliningrad, each time accompanied by his wife and children. "Wherever the Motherland sent me, I took my family, along with two or three suitcases."[132]

When military men did retire or were demobilized, quite a few headed to Narva on Estonia's northeastern border with the Russian republic. Some received assistance in obtaining jobs and housing by friends they had made while serving or relatives who had settled there already. The town, although devastated by Soviet aerial bombardment in 1944, accommodated a large influx of ethnic Russian migrants. The giant Kreenholm Textile Mill that dated back to the middle of the nineteenth century, and the Baltiets metalworks factory, founded in 1947, crop up in several interviews. So, especially among veterans who came from collective farms in the Russian interior, does the area's higher standard of living.[133]

Reliance on the knowledge and pull of relatives and friends—migrants' capital the world over—guided demobilized soldiers to other cities. Semën Zadlav, from the town of Khmel'nik in Vinnitsa oblast', Ukraine, returned home to find none of his relatives had survived, a not uncommon occurrence among Jews. He headed to Vinnitsa city, where he had a cousin who gave him shelter. He helped to rebuild the city's phosphate plant and spent the next forty-six years working there as a crane operator. Surviving relatives beckoned others to frontline cities such as Kishinev, capital of the new Moldavian SSR, and Minsk.[134] Yet another cluster of demobilized soldiers either had no relatives on whom they could rely, lacked a home to return to, or had other reasons for making a clean sweep of things. Iakub Faizullaev, a Crimean Tatar who fought in the infantry, was demobilized in 1946 as a lieutenant. As he told a Tajik friend and fellow officer at the time, "My parents were deported where I don't know, somewhere in Central Asia, and where I will go I also don't know." "Come to us," his friend replied. "You can stay with us, we will find your parents' address." Faizullaev accepted his friend's offer. They traveled to Namangan and Chust in Uzbekistan, with Faizullaev settling in the latter city, but he never found his parents. Server Akimov, another Crimean Tatar, was more fortunate in his search for his

132. "Anatolii Bordun," http://iremember.ru/letchiki-istrebiteli/bordun-anatoliy-zinovevich.html, 1 (accessed September 30, 2012); "Viktor Koliadin," http://iremember.ru/letchiki-istrebiteli/kolyadin-viktor-ivanovich.html, 4 (accessed September 30, 2012); "Boris Gol'dinov," http://iremember.ru/letchiki-bombardirov/goldinov-boris-bentsion-yakovlevich.html, 3 (accessed September 30, 2012); "Anatolii Lilin," http://iremember.ru/letchiki-bombardirov/lilin-anatoliy-vasilevich.html, 13 (accessed September 30, 2012).

133. See, for example, http://iremember.ru/pekhotintsi/raevskiy-vasiliy-vasilevich.html, 3 (accessed September 30, 2012); and http://iremember.ru/artilleristi/alekseev-viktor-aleksandrovich.html, 1 (accessed September 30, 2012). Baltiets is now Balti ES, a subsidiary of Odense Steel Shipyard Ltd.

134. "Semën Zadlav," http://iremember.ru/razvedchiki/zaslav-semen-iosifovich.html, 1, 4 (accessed October 30, 2012). See also http://iremember.ru/tankisti/kalinenok-marat-aleksandrovich/stranitsa-12.html, Zadlav hid his Jewish identity at the front and in fact right up to 1953.

parents because his friend's father gave them his address and they, living in Andizhan, Uzbekistan, found him.[135]

Finally, Roman Lazebnik, he of the Ukrainian pseudonym, calls attention to himself. When we last left Roman he was serving in a territorial defense unit in western Ukraine. Having turned down an offer of a commission as lieutenant, he left the army, but "I didn't know where to go." He dared not return to his native village in Ukraine because, although he had hidden from the authorities his unfortunate experience as a POW, his mother (who somehow had survived the Holocaust) "blabbed" to several acquaintances. An Uzbek by the name of Mukhtar came to the rescue. "Rationing, hunger, and destruction did not visit Tashkent," Mukhtar told Roman. "It's warm, there is plenty of fruit, and work. Come with me to Uzbekistan. If you like it, stay." Roman "decided to give it a try," did like it, and stayed working in cinema administration.[136] So, not only demobilized peasant-soldiers moved around. Lots of other demobilized soldiers did as well, often more than once. They searched for better jobs or a higher standard of living; they sought to escape stigmas from wartime; or they had befriended someone who extended a hand to them, sometimes across ethnic barriers.

What about in subsequent decades? According to Western students of Soviet military practice, the branch of armed forces to which conscripts would be assigned and the part of the country where they would perform their service depended heavily on their nationality. It had been different in the early years of the Red Army. Until the mid-1930s, territorial-based units prevailed. Abandoned during the years of the Great Terror (1935–38), the territorial principle made a comeback during the war only to be phased out in the 1950s. Interviewed in the West during the late 1970s, former Soviet soldiers explained the adoption of extraterritoriality as principally motivated by security concerns. It would not do, they surmised, for too many Uzbeks to be stationed in Uzbekistan, especially as internal policing numbered among the army's potential responsibilities. "The clear policy is to send minorities as far from home as possible," said one respondent. Or, as another put it, "If you are an Uzbek, you go to Russia. If you are a Balt, you serve in Uzbekistan." Variations on this theme included assigning mostly Russians, Ukrainians, and Belorussians to the border guards (*pogranichniki*) but not permitting Ukrainians and Belorussians to serve on the borders of their own republic. Likewise, nationality-based criteria were evident in other branches of the service—disproportionate representation of Slavs in the high-technology services such as the Strategic Rocket Forces, the Air Force, and Navy; higher percentages of non-Slavic nationalities in the artillery and infantry; and "sizeable" representation of

135. "Iakub Faizullaev," http://iremember.ru/pekhotintsi/fayzullaev-yakub-akhmetovich.html, 3 (accessed September 30, 2012); "Server Akimov," http://iremember.ru/partizani/akimov-server/stranitsa-2.html, 2 (accessed September 30, 2012).
136. "Roman Lazebnik," 8.

Central Asians in particular in the two low-prestige noncombat units, the construction battalions (*stroibat*) and the internal security forces of the Ministry of Internal Affairs, which also contained the uneducated and those with criminal records.[137]

Another peculiarly Soviet institution—the military buyer—often determined exactly where and in which unit a recruit would serve. Buyers would "claim" conscripts at military commissariat assembly points after examining their files. As with young specialists, connections and payoffs could assure an assignment in a unit close to home or to a desired branch of the armed forces. In one instance, a recruit persuaded the local commander to assign him to a construction battalion within walking distance of his home in Azerbaijan by paying him ten sheep. In the absence of such deals, more desperate conscripts would bolt from commissariat offices or even the trains taking them to their designated units. "Relatives took recruits from the railway cars and ran away with them . . . in[to] the mountains [or] head for the taiga," reported one former political officer. Other respondents mentioned interethnic fights among soldiers, the casual racism experienced by Central Asians serving in Russian or Ukrainian areas, and the hostility, also tinged with racism, of the resident Baltic and western Ukrainian populations toward Russians stationed nearby. Describing the situation in Riga, a Russian officer observed, "You are better off staying in the barracks because you may get beaten up by the locals."[138]

Interviews with former conscripts demonstrate continuity in the ethnic segregation of soldiers across the decades. Josief Jankielajc, born in eastern Poland in 1935, had never been beyond his native village (which became part of the Lithuanian SSR) until he entered the army in 1954. Put in a cattle car in Vilnius, he spent what might have been a week or a month ("I don't remember—we traveled a long time") moving east through Cheliabinsk, Omsk, and Tomsk, before finally arriving at a station on the Angara River, 80 kilometers from Irkutsk. Not once, he claims, did he have the chance to disembark along the route. Were recruits divided up according to whether they hailed from the city or the countryside? "No," he replied, "only the blacks were separated from us. They were Uzbeks. . . . They formed their own group; they ate together." When asked what sort of groups existed within his construction battalion, Vitalii, a self-described Cossack from Krasnodar krai who entered the army in the late 1980s and was assigned to a unit in the Urals, responded, "Only national ones—Russians, non-Russians, you know . . ." "This played a role?" his interviewer asked. "Yes, it's normal," he replied.[139]

137. S. Enders Wimbush and Alex Alexiev, *The Ethnic Factor in the Soviet Armed Forces* (Santa Monica, 1982), 12–16.

138. Ibid., 8–10, 44–46.

139. Oxford Russian Life History Archive, interview Oxf/AHRC SPb-10 DN PF1, June 15, 2010, 4–6; ibid., Oxf/AHRC SPb-10 DN PF2, June 20, 2010, 4. We are grateful to Victoria Donovan for providing the full transcripts of these interviews.

Intervention in Afghanistan seriously disrupted Soviet normality. From an initial 40,000, Soviet troop strength in Afghanistan rose to 90,000 in 1981, 105,000 in 1982, and 115,000 in 1984. This meant that over the first five years, roughly 400,000 soldiers had rotated in and out of the country. Sending minorities as far from home as possible may have made sense in the context of Soviet domestic concerns, but military strategists thought otherwise when it came to deciding whom to send across the long southern border with Afghanistan. Logistical and economic considerations as well as the belief that shared ethnic, linguistic, and/or religious affinities would solidify relations with Afghans, led to the assignment of between 30 and 40 percent of soldiers from the Central Asian republics. According to a Soviet soldier who had defected, the policy failed because Central Asians "showed little interest in fighting 'their neighbors.' "[140] Quite possibly, but, as we have indicated, few soldiers from Central Asia had any combat training and few were assigned to combat units. The intervention that ended only in 1989 failed to sustain a friendly government in Kabul and undermined Soviet military morale. It also spewed veterans (known as *afgantsy*) onto the streets and into the metro stations of the country's major cities. Many of them drug or alcohol addicted, they served as a daily reminder of the debt owed to these often physically and psychologically maimed individuals.[141]

Post-Soviet Military Service

The breakup of the Soviet Union into fifteen independent republics alleviated at least one problem associated with the multiethnicity of the Soviet armed forces. Military authorities in Moscow no longer needed to worry about Ukrainians guarding the country's western borders, or where Uzbeks would do their military service. This, though, may have been the only advantage. Intervention in Afghanistan proved to be the beginning of a downward spiral not only for the morale of Soviet officers and soldiers but also the army's reputation and, perhaps most important, its funding. Privileges previously accorded to officers failed to survive the dissolution of the Soviet Union not so much as a result of a change of policy

---

140. J. Bruce Amstutz, *Afghanistan: The First Five Years of Soviet Occupation* (Washington, DC, 1986), 165–70. See also S. Enders Wimbush and Alex Alexiev, "Soviet Central Asian Soldiers in Afghanistan," *A Rand Note*, N-1634/1 (1981), www.rand.org/content/dam/rand/pubs/notes/2009/N1634.1pdf (accessed June 30, 2013); Geoffrey Jukes, "The Soviet Armed Forces and the Afghan War," in *The Soviet Withdrawal from Afghanistan*, ed. Amin Sakal and William Maley (Cambridge, 1989), 82–100. For the entire ten years of the Soviet intervention, up to 730,000 served, of whom an estimated 14,453 died and nearly 50,000 suffered wounds. Maya Eichler, *Militarizing Men: Gender, Conscription, and War in Post-Soviet Russia* (Stanford, 2012), 28.

141. A. Manyshkin, "Komu nuzhdy oni, eti 'afgantsy'?" *Krasnaia zvezda*, April 25, 1992; Aleksei Tarasov, "Glaverem bandyubits nazyvaiut podpolkovnika afgantsa," *Izvestiia*, November 19, 1996; Viktor Smirnov, "Ubit lider sverdlovskikh 'afgantsev,' " *Kommersant-Daily*, August 21, 1998, all via East View Information Services Universal Databases. See also Mark Galeotti, *Afghanistan: The Soviet Union's Last War* (London, 1995).

as a collapse of the Ministry of Defense's budget. Moreover, the demands on soldiers' violent migrations intensified. Between the end of the Second World War and the war in Afghanistan, Soviet armed forces had intervened in East Germany in 1953, in Hungary in 1956, and in Czechoslovakia in 1968. But less than a year after the last troops had exited Afghanistan in February 1989, some 20,000 soldiers arrived in Baku to restore order in the wake of pogroms against Armenians. There followed in rapid succession interventions in Osh, Kyrgyzstan (June 1990), Vilnius, Lithuania (January 1991), South Ossetia (June 1992), Transnistria (June–July 1992), and Abkhazia (August 1992), all within what had been Soviet territory. Then the troops came to Chechnya.

They did so to crush the separatist regime that had installed itself in Grozny under the leadership of Djokhar Dudaev. Born in 1944 just days before his family's deportation to Kazakhstan, Dudaev returned to Chechnya in 1957. His military migrations took him from air force training schools in Tambov and Moscow oblast' to strategic bombing units in Ukraine and Siberia, service in Afghanistan, and, as major general (the only Chechen to hold that rank in the Soviet army), the command of an air force base in Tartu, Estonia. In 1990 he again returned to Chechnya and emerged as head of the de facto independent Chechen Republic of Ichkeria in November 1991. The Russian government under Boris Yeltsin responded by sending forty thousand troops to Chechnya in December 1994. Setting themselves up at checkpoints and in fortified headquarters around the outskirts of Grozny, they bombarded the city into submission. A British journalist visiting the war zone in February 1995 later reported that the Russians rarely ventured on foot patrol, "clung to their armoured vehicles with limpet-like strength," and "huddled behind their barricades" so that "even in the immediate aftermath of . . . victory . . . it was hard to tell who was besieging whom."[142]

The precarious Russian victory turned into defeat when in August 1996 Chechen irregulars recaptured their devastated capital. The career officers and members of the (Spetsnaz) "special purpose units," most of whom were afgantsy, found this turnabout particularly humiliating and tended to blame it on the low pay, poor provisioning (including of food), and lack of motivation among conscripts, all the consequence of corruption in Moscow.[143] Indeed, as many scholars have pointed out, the 1990s saw massive draft evasion by those who could bribe their way out of serving and desertion by inductees. "The losers in the process of Russia's economic transition," wrote one, "are more likely to find themselves serving in the army . . . which has contributed to the negative societal image of the military and of conscripts."[144]

---

142. Anatol Lieven, Chechnya Tombstone of Russian Power (New Haven, 1998), 47, 58.
143. See for example Gennadi Troshev, Moia voina: Chechenskii dnevnik okopnogo generala (Moscow, 2001), 13, 28–30.
144. Eichler, Militarizing Men, 71. See also Lieven, Chechnya Tombstone, 49–55, 224, 269, 280; Serguei Alex. Oushakine, The Patriotism of Despair: Nation, War, and Loss in Russia (Ithaca, 2009), 144–48.

The two Chechen campaigns—that of 1994–96 and the more brutal Second Chechen War of 1999–2009—subjected conscripts to the geographic dislocation, resocialization, and cross-community migration similar to what their predecessors in the Soviet and Imperial Russian armies experienced. The most notorious departure was the *dedovshchina*. Originating sometime before the Afghan War and evidently derived like much army culture from the Gulag, *dedovshchina* ("the grandfather system") consisted of ritualized violence against new recruits ("spirits") by senior conscripts ("granddads") about to finish their eighteen months to two years of service. Arkady Babchenko, drafted as a second-year law student from Moscow in November 1995, has provided the most graphic and extensive account of the practice. He writes of numerous beatings he suffered while stationed in the town of Mozdok, over the border from Chechnya in North Ossetia. But then, "everyone beats everyone," he writes. "The *dembels* [soon to be demobilized], with three month's service to go, the officers, the warrant officers. They get stinking drunk and then hammer the ones below them . . ." "It's good for a spirit to have his personal granddad," he adds sardonically. "First of all, only one person beats you. Then you can always complain to him if someone else makes claims on you . . ."[145]

The practice served to disconnect recruits from their pasts, humiliating (or, in the view of one scholar, feminizing) them as a means of inculcating subordination within the "total institution" of the army.[146] But several sources cite the deleterious effects on new recruits—lasting and in some cases permanent physical injuries, lowered self-esteem, even suicides—to say nothing of provoking high rates of absences without leave and occasionally, murder. Babchenko, for reasons he doesn't quite understand himself, nevertheless re-upped for the second Chechen campaign after finishing law school in 1999. "I just couldn't help it," he writes. "It was as if only my body had returned from that first war, but not my soul."[147]

Other veterans, especially the officers and noncoms in the Spetsnaz, seem to take comfort in regimental loyalties. "In recent years," we read in a collection of stories by such folks, "the 104th regiment, as well as the entire Pskov division, has appeared more and more often 'on the front lines' in the hottest places."

When the country fell apart, the Pskov paratroopers appeared on the fault lines, trying with their arms, and often with their bodies, to bind up the disintegrating state. They put a stop to the enmity and bloodletting, defended the people from bandits and political maniacs, and stood like walls on the borders.

---

145. Arkady Babchenko, *One Soldier's War*, trans. Nick Allen (New York, 2006), 82–83.
146. Eichler, *Militarizing Men*, 65.
147. Lieven, *Chechnya Tombstone*, 290–93; Babchenko, *One Soldier's War*, x.

In this manner, they could be linked to past sacrifices and glories going all the way back to "Aleksandr Nevskii and Prince Dovmont (the monk Timofei), who in thirty-three years on the throne never lost a single battle."[148] Such associations undoubtedly have helped to salve the wounds of defeat and despair. Others have had different associations. The 1996 film *Prisoner of the Mountains* (*Kavkazskii plennik*), is an updating of the short story by Leo Tolstoy that bore the same name and was itself derived from a poem by Aleksandr Pushkin from 1820–21. These connections inadvertently point to the perpetuation of the colonial relationship—replete with certain orientalist tropes—that Russians have had with peoples indigenous to the Caucasus, a relationship frequently involving capture narratives.[149] They also serve to remind us that military migration within Russian political space continued to involve crossing cultural boundaries right up to the end of the century and beyond.

---

148. Vladislav Shurygin, "Sniskali bessmertic," in *Rasskazy o chechenskoi voine* (Moscow, 2004), 25–26, 38–39.

149. Bruce Grant, *The Captive and the Gift: Cultural Histories of Sovereignty in Russia and the Caucasus* (Ithaca, 2009), 120–23.

~CHAPTER SIX~

Refugees and Evacuees

"I have an eighty-four-year-old mother, in bad health . . . and a son in school. I expect
to be called [to the army] and therefore need to get my family out of Moscow. . . .
I therefore ask permission to evacuate my family to Kuibyshev, where my close
relatives live, from whom I have received an invitation, and herewith attach their
telegram. The district and city evacuation offices did not grant permission."
                    —Request from I. V. Ivashin to the Chairman of the Evacuation
                                        Council of the USSR, August 19, 1941

War serves as the backdrop for this chapter as it did for Russia's twentieth century. If
soldiers engaged in violent migrations, many civilians faced by an invading enemy
abandoned their homes either on their own or with the encouragement and assistance of the
state. Authorities not only in Russia but everywhere call those who flee refugees. The word in
Russian, *bezhentsy*, literally means people on the run. It served as the main identifier of the millions displaced by the invasion of Imperial Russian territory during World War I. The term of
choice in World War II—the Great Patriotic War in Soviet parlance—was "evacuee." The Soviet
state's preference for "evacuee" reflected its massive effort to take its people and production
facilities out of harm's way in times of war and disaster, a manifestation of its extraordinary
ambition to control the movement of its citizens. The terms rarely were interchangeable, but
the experience of many evacuees seemed—to them—indistinguishable from that of refugees.

Refugees in World War I

The Great War of 1914–18 set in motion the first refugee crisis of the century as unprecedented numbers of people attempted to "escape from violence."[1] Refugees loom large as a

---

1. Aristide Zolberg et al., *Escape from Violence: Conflict and the Refugee Crisis in the Developing World* (New York,
1989), 18; Violetta Thurstan, *People Who Run: Being the Tragedy of the Refugees in Russia* (London, 1916), 1.

harvest of war in the history of the twentieth century, but rarely do they receive their due as anything more than victims. Here we aspire to contribute to a history that, in the words of Peter Gatrell, "seeks to explain the circumstances, practices and possibilities of population displacement [and] examines structures and networks of power, social experience and human agency . . ."[2]

People who write about refugees, from wartime relief workers and railroad personnel to scholars working decades later, use natural disaster metaphors to describe this unmanageable human movement. Violetta Thurstan recalled in 1916 the previous summer, when "refugees poured in like a submerging tidal wave by road and by rail" to Moscow; much later, Michael Marrus opened the Russian section of his general history of refugees by referring to them as an "avalanche" brought on by the war.[3] In our terms, this language implies that the repertoires and goals of the refugees counted for little in the face of wartime circumstances and the armed force of contending states.

The floods, tidal waves, and avalanches of refugees can be imputed to the helplessness of those who tried to feed, house, clothe, count, control, or even describe them. As he studied refugees in the Urals from World War I through the Civil War and famine of the early 1920s, Gennadii Kornilov wisely observed,

> The more authorities attempted to impose control, the more they complained of "spontaneity" on the part of refugees. The choice of words was not, of course, accidental. The rhetoric of Soviet officialdom was strikingly reminiscent of the vocabulary used by tsarist officials. It drew attention to the metaphorical distance, as it were, between a settled bureaucracy, [and] . . . vast, unsettled populations.[4]

Not all observers were part of a "settled bureaucracy," but refugees did inspire discomfort, pity, hostility, and unease on the part of those who saw them.[5] In this chapter, we aspire to avoid the overwhelming sense of helplessness that came with observing the chaos of war and refugee movements in order to trace the major tracks of refugees and to capture the range of their experiences.

In a few years after 1914, a record number of people fled their homes in Imperial Russia. Eugene Kulischer observed decades ago that as many people became refugees in the war as had moved to Siberia over the twenty-five years before 1910.[6] To begin with the "heat of cold numbers," the best estimate of the refugee population lies at 2.897 million for January 1916

2. Peter Gatrell, *The Making of the Modern Refugee* (Oxford, 2013), 9–10, 35.

3. Thurstan, *People Who Run*, 89; Michael Marrus, *The Unwanted: European Refugees in the Twentieth Century* (New York, 2003), 53, 55.

4. Gennadii Kornilov, "Refugees in the Urals Region, 1917–25," in Baron and Gatrell, *Homelands*, 178.

5. Views of refugees are a major theme in Peter Gatrell, *A Whole Empire Walking: Refugees in Russia during World War I* (Bloomington, 1999).

6. Kulischer, *Europe on the Move*, 32.

and 5.256 million a year later, culminating in 6.391 million in July 1917.[7] By 1916, the largest group, nearly one-third, had come from the province of Grodno, and about one-fourth from Volhynia province. Two-thirds of the refugees at the beginning of that year were Russian, Ukrainian, or Belorussian, another 11 percent Poles, and the rest Latvians, Armenians, Lithuanians, and Estonians.[8]

As Gatrell indicates, "the search for the archetypal refugee will be fruitless" because, though massed and seemingly faceless to many observers, refugees saw themselves as, and were, distinct from one another in outlook, origin, and identity. Nonetheless they constitute a demographically distinct group because wartime refugees were primarily women and children—indeed, Gatrell notes that an estimate of adult men at 22 percent is high. Adult women (age seventeen to fifty-five) constituted the largest single category, according to a 1917 survey, followed by boys, then girls fourteen and under.[9] It is difficult to generalize refugee destinations, not only because they shifted in wartime but also because information is scarce. Kulischer wrote that a quarter of refugees remained near the front lines, while about 40 percent moved to central Russia and the rest to Siberia and Central Asia. A survey of over a half million refugees in the spring of 1916 reveals that "Russians" (meaning ethnic Russians, Ukrainians, and Belorussians) usually found themselves in rural areas, while Jews and Poles were disproportionately likely to be in an urban area.[10] The mass deportations of ethnic minorities to behind the lines, particularly Jews and Germans, will appear in the next chapter although these forced migrations are in some cases strikingly similar to the many refugee movements that the military ordered or compelled.

From the first German victories in August through December 1914, refugees fled East Prussia and the Baltic coastal region so that some hundred thousand Polish and Jewish refugees had crowded into Warsaw by the year's end. Some Jews in the Polish provinces fled eastward in advance of the Germans' arrival, fearing not so much the Germans themselves as retribution from local Poles and returning Russian soldiers who suspected them of being predisposed to collaborate with the enemy. In Suwałki, a town about 100 miles north of Bialystok, retribution in the form of a pogrom visited those who had remained during the three-week occupation.[11] To the north, Lithuanian farmers sought refuge in Vilnius. During the spring and summer of 1915 German troops advanced again, this time taking all

---

7. Gatrell, A Whole Empire Walking, 211–12, quotes Aleksandr Blok and furnishes the figures of the Soviet demographer Evgenii Volkov; we use the figures that exclude the forcibly displaced populations, mostly Germans and Jews, who will appear in chapter 7.

8. Gatrell, A Whole Empire Walking, 213.

9. Ibid., 205, 214 (quotation on 205).

10. Kulischer, Europe on the Move, 32; Gatrell, A Whole Empire Walking, 214.

11. Details can be found in USHHM RG-22.018M, Personal Archives of Meer [Khaimovich] Bomash, member of State Duma, 1908–1917, GARF, f. 9458, op. 1, d. 169, ll. 65–72, 113. This is a report, dated October 24, 1914, to the Petrograd-based Jewish Committee for Assistance to Victims of War from one of its plenipotentiaries.

of Poland, Lithuania, and much of Belorussia. The Empire's third largest city, Warsaw, fell in July and the fourth largest, Riga, was threatened. At the same time, Austrian troops re-conquered Galicia. Thus in a year, the Russian army had retreated some 300 miles and with it, or in its wake, came civilians—Poles, Jews, Latvians, Ukrainians, Lithuanians, and Russians. They comprised "the whole empire walking," to which Gatrell's study refers.[12]

To focus on Latvia alone for the moment, the rural population south of Riga took to the road before the German advance, heading for that city and Dvinsk. An estimated two-thirds of the population of northwestern Latvia crossed the Dvina River to settle on the Vidzeme plateau to the northwest, or to move on. As many as five hundred thousand people were on the move from three provinces that had been home to 1.3 million Latvians in 1897.[13] By midsummer, they included the workers of Riga, among whom the most fortunate possessed skills that made them worthy of evacuation along with factory and family. This is how a highly skilled worker from the Provodnik rubber factory wound up in Moscow along with his fifteen-year-old memoirist son Eduard Dune.[14] The Imperial government saw that this entire family was moved, and housed, in the city; in this case the regime and desired repertoire for this Latvian family made a good match. Other urban workers, like rural people, left spontaneously to make their way east.[15]

Photos show Latvians traveling in wagon trains, walking alongside their horse-drawn carts of household goods en route to the Russian interior. The majority of adults are women, although men are present. Those who traveled by cart had some power to determine their own route, but the advantages ended there because the roads were jammed with retreating troops and carts became mired in the mud that came with autumn rain.[16] Refugees boarded boxcars in a rail system already stretched to the limit by the demands of battle and factory evacuations.

The experience of train travel proved dangerous, unhealthy, and unpredictable, since food and water were scarce and travel itself undependable, with long stops when refugee wagons were shunted aside or uncoupled. Under these circumstances, refugees lost family members. People died on the trains, so their fellow passengers traveled with corpses, or themselves caught cholera, dysentery, pneumonia, tuberculosis, and typhus in what became the biggest health crisis in Russia since 1848.[17] During the succeeding Civil War, "the louse thrived" because "sanitary and epidemiological control over the migrating people, even in the railroad network, was practically nonexistent." In Robert Argenbright's view, the determination of the new Soviet regime to keep the railroads running but its failure to

12. Gatrell, A Whole Empire Walking, 19–20.
13. Ibid., 25 and n. 95, p. 230
14. Dune, Notes of a Red Guard, xiii–xiv.
15. Gatrell, A Whole Empire Walking, 25.
16. Ibid., 29, 100 103.
17. Ibid., 58.

control what he too calls "the waves of migrants" fostered "ideal conditions for the spread of typhus."[18] People consequently regarded refugees as a "hungry and angry flock," so stymied were they by their dismal circumstances and lack of control over their destination, health, or food supply. Indeed, when refugees heading for the Urals in an unheated boxcar were warned against using the boiler they had installed because it was a fire hazard, they replied that it did not matter whether they died of frostbite or by fire.[19]

Nonetheless, the trains successfully moved hundreds of thousands of people away from the war zone, most dramatically in 1915, when refugees began to arrive in the interior. Their numbers peaked in the fall—by mid-September, about 750,000 refugees had arrived and two million more would join them by the end of the year, if we count scheduled trains alone. Fifty-four of the registration points in European Russia saw 148,900 in the second half of September, 111,800 in October, 8,600 in November, and 1,700 in December.[20] This rhythm helps us to understand why railroad officials would give up trying to count people and turn to phrases such as "waves" of refugees.

As helpless as they may have been under enemy fire, refugees had their own agendas and ideas of what to do. Some did not want to leave home at all: "I was born in this khata; here I was born and here I thought I'd die," stated an elderly Ukrainian.[21] Once displaced behind the lines by opening battles, others wanted to go no farther: " 'We've already come far enough'; 'It can't get any worse than this'; 'Where is there for an old woman to go?' "[22] Most crucial: to keep with one's family, yet thousands of children and parents were separated while moving, sometimes when children were too young to know their names or identify themselves. This was the case for the Latvian refugee Olga Stengel whose three-year-old son Karl went missing on September 23, 1915 while she was at a train station barracks some 125 miles west of Saratov, deep in the Russian interior. "He is wearing dark blue clothes," Sputnik bezhentsa (The Refugee's Companion) reported. "He speaks no Russian. His mother asks all well-meaning people to let her know where her child can be found and to return him to the barracks where she is living, at 2, Balashovsk railway station." Gatrell asks, "Was he whisked off to an orphanage or a 'children's colony' in the countryside? Was he able to give his name to those who found him? Did he become 'Russian'?" Perhaps the mother searched in vain, like the husband of Iuliania Romanova Bychuk from the western provinces who sought his wife and three children after they had been taken aboard a military transport because their horse had collapsed and died en route to the family's planned

---

18. Robert Argenbright, "Lethal Mobilities: Bodies and Lice on Soviet Railroads, 1918–1922," *The Journal of Transport History* 29, no. 2 (2008): 269, 272.

19. Gatrell, *A Whole Empire Walking*, 28, 29, n. 126, p. 232.

20. A. N. Kurtsev, "Bezhentsy pervoi mirovoi voiny v Rossii (1914–17)," *Voprosy istorii*, no. 8 (1999): 104.

21. Gatrell, *A Whole Empire Walking*, 20.

22. Ibid., 50.

meeting place.[23] Refugees had plans, then, to meet, to stay together with family and compatriots, and to survive.

Two different images of refugees emerge—one of helpless people without energy or resources, the other of angry and demanding displaced persons. On no front is the image of helplessness, ill health, and degradation more stark than in the south, where Armenian refugees fled the Ottoman empire in the face of slaughter and forced marches. Perhaps 250,000 survived to flee into Russian territory in August 1915. They expanded the population of Erevan from its 1914 level of 30,000 to over 125,000 by January 1916, then the refugee population tripled during that year. Just as the property of German farmers in Russia would be given to other peasants when they were expelled, the Ottomans gave the farms of Armenians to Turks.[24]

The presence of relatives often determined where refugees would wind up. After Kalmon Izrailovich Bliumberg and his family left Kovno in May 1915, they found themselves "at the mercy of fate, traveling from one city to the next" until they moved in with his sister, who lived in Moscow and taught at a gymnasium. We know about Kalmon and his family because he wrote to Meer Khaimovich Bomash, a Jewish Duma deputy from Lodz, seeking support for his request to remain in Moscow until the end of the war. Other refugees lamenting their fate wrote from Sychevka in Smolensk province, from Khar'kov, from Tula, and elsewhere asking Bomash to intercede on their behalf or simply to lend them money. They also relied on networks of friends and charitable institutions.[25]

It is difficult for scholars to wrap their minds around the obdurate fact that people who move usually move more than once—they rarely leave one home to settle permanently in another. This is even more the case in the study of refugees, for whom continued displacement is common because they were not, generally speaking, welcomed, nor did they wish to stay. Indeed, the refugees in Russia who made attempts to settle were rare, limited to cases in Siberia where land was available in the Tomsk oblast', for example, and on the island of Sakhalin where several hundred refugees "praise the local climate, the abundance of timber, the fertility of the soil, and the opportunity to hunt and fish"—at least according to the *Iugobezhenets* (The Southern Refugee) of July 1916.[26]

More were like the family from Grodno in today's Belarus who had reached Kazan, some 1,100 miles to the east, where they were fortunate enough to have survived, to be in the company of each other and compatriots, and to have shelter with a peasant family outside the city. Anna Panotocheek had walked with her two children, age two and five. "My

---

23. Ibid., 76.
24. Ibid., 26.
25. USHMM RG-22.018M, GARF, f. 9458, op. 1, d. 44, ll. 2–4; d. 39, ll. 3–4, 6–8, 16–20,
26. Gatrell, *A Whole Empire Walking*, 55; *Iugobezhenets*, July 20, 1916, 2, cited in ibid., 244, n. 44.

husband had gone to dig trenches, so we left everything behind, I not being able to carry anything besides the children. . . . At times, people used to help me carry them, but almost all the way I had to carry one or other of them myself. It was very difficult because they were so heavy. At times I wanted to leave them behind on the roadside," she confessed. At a Red Cross station, they got a train for the small town of Stonin and from there north to Baranovichi, where she found her husband. After several days in that Belorussian town, they were advised to go to Minsk, and from there "the officials put us in the train for Kazan."[27] They had survived because others sometimes carried the children, they had managed to be reunited, helping agencies had intervened, and they were able to avoid the epidemic illnesses. In this case, the state's migration regime aided the migration repertoire of the family.

However, refugees, like other migrants, often attempt to follow their own itineraries in spite of the fact that they are supposed to be under the authority and care of the state and/or charities. Indeed, the seeming spontaneity of refugees has frustrated officials and continues to frustrate researchers. The historian Kornilov explains that "these migrations were largely spontaneous and disorganized, so that in a majority of cases it was impossible to register origins, numbers and destinations of displaced persons."[28] As usual, in other words, the archives can only suggest the volume and intent of human mobility.

A. N. Kertsev has calculated that by the summer of 1917, 3.8 million people had registered as refugees. Nearly one in five remained in the war zone of European Russia, most in the northwest around Livonia and Minsk provinces or in the southwestern front. Nearly one in ten refugees reached the Caucasus and Transcaucasia, and only about 3 percent traveled as far as Siberia, the Far East, or Central Asia. The vast majority—over two-thirds—were behind the lines in European Russia, where the city of Moscow counted nearly 171,000 refugees and a total of 212,000 in its province. Samara province absorbed 173,000 and the province of Ekaterinoslav nearly 235,000.[29] From this point through the Civil War and succeeding famine years (1918–22), it becomes impossible to keep track of the numbers of refugees, their peregrinations, and even the causes of their displacement. Did they take to the road to evade impressment into Red and White armies, locate lost family members, stave off hunger, or return to their homes abandoned during the Great War? The sources contain evidence of all these itineraries, but they are incomplete, more so than for any other period. Their incompleteness was a function of the unusual haphazardness of data collection, the frequency with which territories changed hands, and the elusiveness of the

---

27. Thurstan, *People Who Run*, 142–43.
28. Kornilov, "Refugees in the Urals Region," 156.
29. Kurtsev, "Bezhentsy pervoi mirovoi voiny," 108. Kornilov, "Refugees in the Urals Region," 160, mistakenly substitutes Ekaterinburg for Ekaterinoslav.

refugees themselves.[30] One could have fled the advancing enemy in 1914–15, settled in the interior for a couple of years, only to have had to pick up stakes again because of armed conflict within Russia, and then once more owing to the Mid-Volga famine in 1921–22.[31]

Beginning in 1918 what had been a vast movement of people toward the east reversed itself, as "reevacuation" of refugees gathered steam. The Lithuanians, Poles, Latvians, and other borderland peoples who had arrived in the Urals and other parts of the Russian interior in droves started going home. Many crowded around the Narva railway junction southwest of Petrograd on the new international border with Estonia. The intent to return home could not be stopped by the formulated instructions and procedures of the new Soviet government that had replaced those of Imperial refugee relief. The office in charge, *Tsentrevak*, registered its frustration with the situation, betraying what would become a characteristic Soviet hostility toward spontaneity (*stikhiinost'*). "As a rule," it claimed, "any spontaneous movement of human masses grievously undermines the territorial evacuation plan."[32] When refugees heard there was to be a reevacuation, they would simply begin to leave on their own—and local authorities would give them travel permits without orders from above in order to get rid of the persistent, demanding refugees. The trips west were not a great deal easier than those to the east in wartime because returnees were stopped to wait their turn to depart—and as before, lodging, food, and sanitary conditions were wanting.

Finally, requirements for registration and reregistration, identification, and documentation from the Soviets slowed movement, as did the demands from the new homeland nations of Poland, Latvia, and Lithuania complicated by diplomatic mistrust.[33] A complex of new regimes of migration slowed homeward journeys. People without documents, like

---

30. For a history of everyday life in the Urals as catastrophe, see Igor' Narskii, *Zhizn' v katastrofe: Budni naseleniia Urala v 1917–1922 gg.* (Moscow, 2001). Narskii notes that the "weakness of state services and the extraordinary scale of the human catastrophe was reflected . . . in the imprecision and lack of coordination of data by which the authorities operated" (128).

31. The paucity of reliable data raises a question that speaks to the discursive nature of the term "refugee." It had opposite connotations: carriers of panic and disease on the one hand, helpless victims on the other. See Gatrell, *Making of the Modern Refugee*, 14, 29. Who gets to designate someone as a refugee? Is displacement from one's home with no immediate prospect of returning sufficient? Or does it require some state or nongovernmental authority to identify the refugee and treat him or her accordingly? But what if authorities failed to see displaced people as refugees, either because of their capacity for blending in or because authorities lacked interest in seeing them? For the argument that, decades before UN definitions, conationals heading and participating in relief agencies "saw" refugees better than Russian authorities and relief agencies, and sought to redeem them as part of nation-building projects, see Baron and Gatrell, *Homelands*.

32. Kornilov, "Refugees in the Urals Region," 167; 163 draws on GARF, f. 3333 [Tsentroplenbezh], op. 2, d. 236, ll. 93, 93ob.

33. Kornilov, "Refugees in the Urals Region," 164–65. See also Tomas Balkelis, "In Search of a Native Realm: The Return of World War One Refugees to Lithuania, 1918–24," and Kateryna Stadnik, "The Repatriation of Polish Citizens from Soviet Ukraine to Poland in 1921–22," in *Homelands*, 74–137.

the refugee from Grodno province living in a town 200 miles north of Ekaterinburg, suffered infinite delays. He wrote that the uezd evacuation committee had lost his family's papers seven months before and without news or documentation, "It's impossible to get work. . . . We ask you, as refugees of the German war, to evacuate us to our homeland."[34] Thousands of displaced people did succeed in departing Ekaterinburg, home to 19,000 foreign refugees in 1920, 16,500 in 1921, but only about 3,000 in 1922.[35]

Civil War and Famine Refugees

Historians speak of three waves of refugees—those from World War I, the Civil War, and the famine of 1921–22—but it is important to realize that the waves were not just successive; they were cumulative and "from 1921 . . . began to merge." The regional offices of Moscow's *Tsentrevak* attended to not only world war and Civil War refugees but also local industrial workers, agricultural settlers, former prisoners of war, and deserting and demobilized soldiers. The numbers and proportions were bound to vary from one region to another depending on the intensity of fighting, the availability of foodstuffs, and whether rail lines functioned. So overwhelmed was Ukraine's regional office that *Tsentrevak* requested the cooperation of the Commissariat of Agriculture (Narkomzem) in shipping three thousand people back to Siberia.[36]

The Volga region from Kazan to Samara and Saratov was another crossroads for those trying to escape devastation and starvation. But as early as October 1918 the forces of the anti-Bolshevik Komuch (Committee of Members of the Constituent Assembly) destroyed many of the railway bridges that crossed the river as they retreated to Ufa to join with Siberian anti-Bolsheviks. Refugees congregated in railroad stations, along sidings, or by riverbanks where they mingled with soldiers, local townspeople, and hungry peasants from the surrounding countryside. Also mingling thereby were the microbes that these desperate and physiologically weakened groups carried with them. Four in ten refugees in Saratov became ill in December 1918 and January of the next year, when troops would become the main carriers, so that the Red Army had 522,000 typhus cases in 1919–20.[37] Saratov province reported over 16,000 refugees in the summer of 1917 but as many as 150,000 a year

---

34. Kornilov, "Refugees in the Urals Region," 177.
35. Ibid., 167–68.
36. RGAE, f. 478, op. 7, d. 704, ll. 25–26. Narkomzem refused, pointing to a Sovnarkom resolution of July 1922 that banned settlement in Siberia for the remainder of the year.
37. Kulischer, *Europe on the Move*, 62–63.

later. It is not clear whether this much more expanded—or better-reported—group was in flight from the Civil War, from World War I, or from the Ottoman empire.[38]

The citizens Logina, Tserkina, and Mikulin, who sent an appeal to the Commissar of Agriculture in August 1922, embodied the overlapping nature of refugeedom. The "old tsarist government," they wrote, had forced them to live in poverty (bedstvovat') and in the midst of the First World War to abandon their native village in Vilna province for Siberia. They settled in Tomsk province, where they spent the next six years. In 1921, a (unspecified) "White attack" caused them to flee back home. However, home now was under Polish rule, and sure enough, they found Polish families living in the houses they used to inhabit. They took up temporary residence in tents, but wrote to request assistance to return to Siberia. How do we categorize this trio of unfortunate families? As resettler-returnees who had second (or third?) thoughts? As refugees who after reevacuating themselves turned out to be refugees again? The commissariat did not want to touch this one and simply abandoned the supplicants to their fate.[39]

With the famine of 1921–22, a third wave of refugees took to the road in flight from hunger on the heels of a disastrous crop—especially in the Volga and parts of the Urals, but also southern Ukraine, the Don provinces, and the North Caucasus. Although the failed harvest was the immediate cause, hunger struck a population already weakened by years of warfare and caloric deprivation. This would be the final blow to strike the country since 1914, starving an estimated three million people, scattering refugees in its wake, and shredding families without number.[40] Railroads registered over nine hundred thousand refugees, and as many people probably traveled by road. Where did victims go? Although the American Relief Administration (ARA) provided a tidy map with the account of its history, reality was more complex, and in the words of Kulischer, "the refugees went anywhere and stayed wherever they could. A considerable number long remained in a state of vagabondage."[41] A very large group from the Volga traveled beyond the Urals. Another sought refuge in the Kuban province to the south, where they had such little success that the local statistical office reported "the Volga came to die on the Kuban." "But the main current," according to Kulischer, was toward Moscow, Petrograd, and the other cities of the northwest that would recoup their wartime losses from times that "saw a flight from the cities to the countryside. In 1921–22 the reverse occurred: the population fled from the famine-stricken

38. Orlando Figes, *Peasant Russia, Civil War: The Volga Countryside in Revolution (1917–1921)* (Oxford, 1989), 138–39.

39. RGAE, f. 478, op. 7, d. 700, l. 118.

40. Kulischer, *Europe on the Move*, 69–70; this is a minimal estimation because deaths from starvation are confounded with deaths from typhus and other diseases that were rampant during the famine.

41. Harold H. Fisher, *The Famine in Soviet Russia, 1919–1923* (New York, 1927), 107; Kulischer, *Europe on the Move*, 71–72.

countryside, and a reflux from the village to urban centers took place." Between 1920 and 1923, the population of Moscow increased by over 40 percent, that of Petrograd by greater than 35 percent, and in other towns in the Non-Black Earth area, 15 percent. In contrast, the urban population of the stricken areas decreased.[42]

By the time Herbert Hoover's ARA arrived to provide relief, peasants from villages in Kazan province were fleeing eastward.[43] A reporter for *Izhevsk Pravda* caught up with some of them, describing in August 1921 the "dreadful" sight of "a string of passing wagons . . . from which could be heard children's squeals and cries," while their "pale [and] emaciated" parents stared ahead with "dull gazes."[44] Far more numerous than those displaced by the Civil War, these "famine refugees" also were the most "stricken," in Kornilov's word, burdened not only by hunger but also various strains of typhus.[45] The official historian of the ARA, Harold Fisher, quoted a horrified Russian observer's description of the station at Simbirsk on the Volga, where starving refugees gathered, uncounted and unregistered. "It has proved to be impossible to clear them out, although *thirty-six decrees* ordering it have been issued," the witness declared. "It is impossible to close the railway station. *There is no way to stop this great wave of starving peasants who come to the city to die.*"[46]

By the mid-1920s, the decade of trauma that began with the outbreak of war in 1914 had come to an end, and for a brief period there would be few refugees in the Soviet Union. Then, with war-like ferocity, agents of Soviet power descended on the villages to "assist" in collectivizing agriculture and driving out—or rather, "liquidating"—the kulaks. Millions of peasants fled, becoming refugees in their own country. Nomadic herdsmen from Kazakhstan escaped sedentarization (largely without their herds) by crossing into China or heading north into Siberia and the Urals. Many eventually would return home to be absorbed within livestock sovkhozes and kolkhozes; others, like the peasants who fled collectivization in Russia and Ukraine, "ruralized" the cities and burgeoning industrial sites.[47] Unaided and uncounted by the state, they are hard to get at as refugees; we address their trajectories in our chapters on seasonal migrants, rural-to-urban migrants, and itinerants.

---

42. Kulischer, *Europe on the Move*, 72–73, uses the figures of L. I. Lubny-Gertsyk, *Dvizhenie naseleniia na territorii SSSR za vremia mirovoi voiny i revoliutsii* (Moscow, 1926), 49.

43. Bertrand Patenaude, *The Big Show in Bololand: The American Relief Expedition to Soviet Russia in the Famine of 1921* (Stanford, 2002), 54.

44. Cited in Narskii, *Zhizn' v katastrofe*, 365.

45. Kornilov, "Refugees in the Urals Region," 157–58.

46. Fisher, *Famine in Soviet Russia*, 90 (italics in the original); for other descriptions of the station at Kazan, see Patenaude, *Big Show in Bololand*, 54–55.

47. Niccolò Pianciola, "Famine in the Steppe: The Collectivization of Agriculture and the Kazak Herdsmen 1928–1934," *Cahiers du monde russe* 45, nos. 1–2 (2004): 171–84.

Evacuees in World War II

Two days after the German invasion of June 22, 1941, the USSR Council of People's Commissars and the All-Union Communist Party's Central Committee created the Council for Evacuation (*Sovet po evakuatsii*) that set to work removing Soviet citizens from harm's way.[48] By December 25, the Director of the Civilian Evacuation Administration reported having successfully moved 10 million citizens to the east.[49] Movement occurred first, to match the initial German advance in the last half of 1941, and then in response to the German occupation of the North Caucasus in the summer of 1942.[50] Soviet historians claimed that as many as 25 million people were evacuated. More recent estimates have tended to range between 10 and 17 million. Even these more modest estimates are excessively high, according to Vadim Dubson, who has calculated fewer than 6.5 million evacuees by the end of 1941 and no more than 7.5 million by December 1942.[51] The radical differences among these estimates are a tribute both to the difficulty of tracking people who moved with such urgency and to the energy with which evacuation authorities reported their successes.

Whether the state moved 20 million or half that, the feat of relocating so many citizens in such a short period of time had no precedent. Even if we take the lowest estimates, it surpassed the number of settlers transported to Siberia at the end of the nineteenth and beginning of the twentieth centuries; it also exceeded the number of prisoners sent to the Gulag in the prewar years and the number of deportees and exiles over the same period. Moreover, the whole evacuation regime was carried out in a mere eighteen months—from the German invasion to the end of 1942. Finally, despite the very different associations we

---

48. For the decree, see *Izvestiia TsK KPSS*, no. 6 (1990): 201. Our thanks to Roger Markwick for sharing this document. On the absence of prior planning, see I. Grinberg, G. Karataev, and N. Kropivnitskii, eds., *Evakuatsiia v Kazakhstan: Iz istorii evakuatsii naseleniia zapadnykh raionov SSSR v Kazakhstan, 1941–1942* (Almaty, 2008), 11; Rebecca Manley, *To the Tashkent Station: Evacuation and Survival in the Soviet Union at War* (Ithaca, 2009), 24–25.

49. Kiril Feferman, "A Soviet Humanitarian Action? Centre, Periphery, and the Evacuation of Refugees to the North Caucasus, 1941–1942," *Europe-Asia Studies* 61, no. 5 (2009): 816.

50. For an alternative periodization with specific reference to Jews and their differential rate of survival, see Mordechai Altshuler, "Escape and Evacuation of Soviet Jews at the Time of the Nazi Invasion: Policies and Realities," in *The Holocaust in the Soviet Union and the Sources on the Destruction of the Jews in the Nazi-Occupied Territories of the USSR, 1941–1945*, ed. Lucjan Dobroszycki and Jeffrey S. Gurock (New York, 1993), 77–104.

51. For useful summaries of the estimates, see Manley, *To the Tashkent Station*, 1, 50, who gives a figure of 12 million by the end of 1941 and 16.5 million by the fall of 1942; and M. N. Potemkina, "Evakonaselenie v ural'skom tylu: Opyt vyzhivaniia," *Otechestvennaia istoriia*, no. 2 (2005): 86–87. See also Vadim Dubson, "Toward a Central Database of Evacuated Soviet Jews' Names, for the Study of the Holocaust in the Occupied Soviet Territories," Research Note, *Holocaust and Genocide Studies* 26, no. 1 (2012): 96, 99–101. Dubson argues that administrators systematically inflated the numbers; on the other hand, Kristen Edwards explains why the Resettlement Administration figures are low in "Fleeing to Siberia: The Wartime Relocation of Evacuees to Novosibirsk, 1941–1945" (PhD diss., Stanford University, 1996), 50.

may have with these other state-organized displacements, their logistics, procedures, and vocabulary shared an essential similarity. Indeed, at times evacuees could not distinguish their treatment from that of political exiles and deportees.

In what follows, we take a qualitative approach, tracing the evacuation of Soviet citizens from their departures through their journeys, relocation, and eventual return. We are attentive not only to the circumstances that made people evacuees but also to how they navigated within those circumstances, that is, their repertoires. These involved expressing needs to those who had life-and-death decision-making power. To articulate their needs, potential and actual evacuees often had to identify themselves and explain why they were so deserving of the state's attention.

Our primary argument is that both Soviet authorities and evacuees depended on the institution of the family to provide sinews of survival. We demonstrate this reliance by using three kinds of sources—letters to authority, typically requests or appeals (zaiavleniia); the myriad forms employed in intrabureaucratic communication detailing the provision of transportation, food, accommodation, and employment; and recollections—in the form of interviews and memoirs—by people who survived not only evacuation but in many cases the Soviet period. None of these sources can bear the weight of reliability; each is partial and otherwise problematic as representative. Nonetheless, taken together and put in conversation with one another, they allow us to analyze crucial dimensions of the evacuee experience.

Departures

Because Soviet authorities considered evacuation a key component of wartime strategy, its guiding principles were those that would most effectively underwrite the military effort. The June 27, 1941 decree on evacuation gave first place to the machinery and factory equipment essential for the military struggle. Among civilians, priority went to those who could supply materiel, arms, and personnel: "qualified workers, engineers, and employees with enterprises evacuated from the front; the population, in the first place youth fit for military service; Soviet and party leadership cadres."[52] A week later, an additional decree authorized the evacuation of the families of ranking officials and military officers. In practice, women and children were targeted for evacuation—or to be more specific, women with children, women whose worker status was crucial for the war effort, or women whose husbands were elite officials or military officers. Members of the intelligentsia also had priority, along with institutions ranging from the Bolshoi and Moscow State University to

---

52. Manley, To the Tashkent Station, 34, quotes the decree in "Iz istorii velikoi otechestvennoi voiny: Nachalo voiny," Izvestiia TsK KPSS, no. 6 (1990): 208.

pedagogical institutes. Just as the families of persecuted groups such as kulaks or deported nationalities were punished, so would the families of the Soviet elite be privileged by the wartime migration regimes.[53]

In response to the German invasion, the Soviet state possessed more than the will for such an enormous undertaking. Ordinary civilians, bureaucrats, and the military remembered the suffering of refugees in the Imperialist War of 1914–17 and aspired to avoid it. Since that war, the state had geared up its capacity to move large numbers of people such as kulaks and minority nationalities. This capacity was seated in the great Soviet zeal for redistributing the population, previously to bring it closer to the location of resources, now to keep both people and resources out of enemy hands.[54] As a consequence, refugees became evacuees (evakuirovannye)—a new term for the many Soviet citizens displaced in wartime—their movement organized and executed by central authorities who imposed their will on local authorities and resources behind the lines.[55]

Authorities were determined to avoid chaotic flight from war by establishing a migration regime that would organize the orderly removal of population—or at least certain categories of people. Yet such an organized evacuation proved impossible, especially at the war's outset. For one thing, the German invasion caught many people away from home: students in the midst of taking entrance exams, the L'vov Philharmonic on tour in Ukraine, and the nineteen-year-old Kievan student Anna Dashevskaia on a geological expedition to Crimea.[56] For another, nobody knew the price of leaving or staying. As Abram Tseitlin remembered many years later, "in the first days of the war, nobody knew or could know how such a terrible fate was being prepared for those who remained in places occupied by the Germans, knew or could know how such suffering would befall those who chose evacuation." In the case of his father, Tseitlin recalls great puzzlement about what to do. When a retreating Red Army unit passed through his native town in Ukraine's Vinnitsa oblast', he told the commanding officer, "nobody—neither the raikom nor the raisoviet tells us

53. Manley, To the Tashkent Station, 36–38.

54. For Soviet zeal to control and redistribute population, see Brown, A Biography of No Place; Fitzpatrick, "Great Departure"; Kotkin, "Peopling Magnitostroi."

55. Although Rebecca Manley cites Soviet citizens on the novelty of the term evakuatsiia, it had been used in World War I by regional authorities seeking to relocate refugees under Tsentroplenbezh (Central Committee for Prisoners of War and Refugees), formed in April 1918. Regional bodies, in Ekaterinburg for example, included a Committee for Prisoners of War and Refugees, and a Regional Administration for Evacuation (Ekaterinburgskoe gubernskoe upravlenie po evakuatsii naseleniia, or gubevak). Kornilov, "Refugees in the Urals Region," 163, 251; Manley, To the Tashkent Station, 7–8.

56. USHMM RG-31.053, Memoirs of Abram Tseitlin, "Evacuation," 15; USHMM RG-31.113, Diary of Anna Dashevskaia, 6; "Lazar' Rafael'evich Tsents." For families separated because one or more members had been traveling to distant locations when the war broke out, see US HMM 22.027M, GARF, f. A-327, Reel 48, op. 2, d. 70, l. 70; d. 73, l. 29. We will follow Dashevskaia's journey below.

anything—stay or leave?" and then asked, "if you were in my place, what would you do? I have a wife and three children, the youngest of whom is three years old. One more thing. I am a Jew and most of the people you see in the square are Jewish. I have heard that the Germans don't particularly like Jews." The officer replied, "I don't need to be in your place; I know what the Germans do to Communist officers. I don't know what my family has done, whether they have been evacuated, but if I were with them, I would have left. . . . Leave immediately."[57]

Complicating the decision to leave was that despite what people had heard or read about the "Hitlerites" and "German fascists," some had positive associations with Germans from the earlier war. Mikhail Shinder's father, who had been a POW in Germany from 1915 to 1917, refused his son's entreaties to be evacuated from Kiev, telling him that not all Germans are bad. Il'ia Frenklakh's father, also a World War I POW, thought likewise and decided to return to his native village in Belorussia's Gomel oblast' after fleeing with Il'ia's mother to a nearby railroad station. It wasn't only former POWs. Despite the horrific stories of Nazi atrocities that Jewish refugees from western Poland told after their arrival in the part of Poland the USSR had annexed in 1939, Grigorii Isers remembers, "We didn't believe [them] because in World War I Germans protected Jews from pogroms." He also blamed "Soviet propaganda" that "had drummed into our heads that Germany was a friend of the USSR while the British were the real enemy."[58] Within days of their appearance in Kiev, Berdichev, and other cities and towns, the Germans announced that all Jews had to assemble at such-and-such town square, intersection, or railroad station for "resettlement." The term—so ambiguous from its varied employment by Soviet authorities in the 1930s—may not have deceived anyone. But not everyone had heard about the fate of Jews in Poland

---

57. Memoirs of Abram Tseitlin, "Evacuation," 14, 17.

58. "Mikhail Shinder," http://iremember.ru/razvedchiki/shinder-mikhail-lvovich.html, 1; Il'ia Frenklakh," http://iremember.ru/razvedchiki/frenklakh-ilya-zakharovich.html, 12; Mark Gabinskii," http://iremember.ru/grazhdanskie/gabinskiy-mark-aleksandrovich.html, 4; "Grigorii Isers," http://iremember.ru/partizani/isers-grigoriy-izrailevich.html, 1 (accessed March 1, 2013) See also Anna Shternshis, "The Role of Ethnic Identity in the Survival of Soviet Jewish Civilians in 1941" (paper presented at "Russian Jewish Migration Across Borders, Across Time," Harriman Institute Conference, Columbia University, October 2012), 5, 12–14. Memories of invading Germans from World War I proved doubly deceptive. In Belgium and northern France the memory of Germans' harshness ("barbarity") provoked millions to take to the road in the *exode* of May–June 1940; in the East, recollections of their correct behavior dissuaded many from leaving. See Richard Vinen, *The Unfree French: Life under the Occupation* (New Haven, 2006), 23–25. For a contrary case of brutality by the German army on the eastern front in World War I and Russian and Polish outrage, see Laura Engelstein, "'A Belgium of Our Own': The Sack of Russian Kalisz, August 1914," in *Fascination and Enmity: Russia and Germany as Entangled Histories, 1914–1945*, ed. Michael David-Fox, Peter Holquist, and Alexander M. Martin (Pittsburgh, 2012), 13–38.

or in other towns within Nazi-occupied Soviet territory, and many of those who did know realized that it was too late to resist or escape.[59]

Personal experience and recollections from the previous war, rumor and propaganda, one's own nationality—these constituted only part of the "complex web of reasons" that went into each family's decision to stay or leave.[60] Yet another factor was social geography. Residents of major cities had difficulty imagining how evacuation to some unknown, god-forsaken kolkhoz could be preferable to staying put in the relative comfort, or at least familiarity, of one's own apartment. As Rebecca Manley notes, "in a state in which residence rights were strictly controlled, return to the country's major cities could easily be denied by the state." Moreover, only a few years had passed since "the same state that now proclaimed its desire to protect" members of the intelligentsia had whisked large numbers of urban dwellers away in the dead of night.[61]

But even those most determined to leave needed the means to do so, and in the first months of the war not much functioned as it was supposed to. "Please send convoy," a local official from the Leningrad oblast' town of Staraia Russa wrote in a telegram to Stalin on July 10. People had abandoned work to crowd the railroad station in hopes of escaping from enemy aerial bombardment. Meanwhile, someone from the oblast' executive committee was telegraphing another official in Staraia Russa to "use what transport you have" to evacuate children brought to the town from elsewhere, including Leningrad, and left pretty much to their own devices.[62] Staraia Russa, located a good distance from the border that the Germans had crossed, was only one of thousands of towns and settlements suddenly made vulnerable to bombardment and occupation.

Those who did not have access to the railways tried to escape on foot. Peasants from a livestock kolkhoz north of Staraia Russa drove 104 cattle to a location assigned to them in conformity with Stalin's speech of July 3 instructing authorities not to leave anything in the way of livestock, crops, or movable property to the invading enemy. But as the official in charge despairingly wrote to the Leningrad party boss Andrei Zhdanov, "when we arrived, there was nobody there. Where to go, we don't know." According to a letter to Stalin from a soil scientist on assignment in Saratov oblast', his wife walked 100 kilometers with their

---

59. For testimony to this effect by a survivor from Kiev, see Tat'iana Evstaf'eva and Vitalii Nakhmanovich, eds., *Babii Iar: Chelovek, vlast', istoriia: Dokumenty i materialy v 5 knigakh* (Kiev, 2004), 1: 256–58.

60. Shternshis, "Role of Ethnic Identity," 10.

61. Rebecca Manley, "The Perils of Displacement: The Soviet Evacuee between Refugee and Deportee," *Contemporary European History* 16, no. 2 (2007): 498.

62. USHMM RG-22.030, TsGA SPb, f. 7179, op. 11, d. 814, ll. 3, 74, 76. For a letter sent to *Leningradskaia pravda* by forty-seven distraught parents claiming the children were hungry, unsupervised, full of lice, and suffering from diarrhea and other diseases, see V. M. Koval'chuk, "Evakuatsiia naseleniia Leningrada letom 1941 goda," *Otechestvennaia istoriia*, no. 3 (2000): 17–18.

two young children. She initially had gone to Staraia Russa but fled south to Beglovo to catch a train. But there was no train. She proceeded on to a village with the picturesque name of Pustynia ("wilderness"), from where "the district executive committee and evacuation troika ha[d] left long ago."[63]

Thus, contrary to the image of discipline and solicitude for the population that the Soviet state liked to project of itself, many people were left to their own devices. Those with the means and the intent cleared out much as the previous generation's wealthier inhabitants had done during World War I, but sometimes the German *Blitzkrieg* moved east more rapidly than they could. Thanks to his father's contacts with the river transport authorities, Dmitri Mironenko's family was among the first to depart from Cherkassy in central Ukraine. They traveled 80 miles down the Dnieper to his maternal grandmother's home and thence to Poltava, another 60 miles or so to the northeast to take refuge with an uncle. Two months later, the Germans arrived, and, exhausted by their journeys, family members started to believe they could survive under occupation.[64]

Others had to consider themselves fortunate if they got away. Misha, a Jewish boy of nineteen, asked if he could hitch a ride with a truck full of Soviet soldiers retreating from Vilna, but the officer in charge turned him down. Fortunately for him, the peasant conscripts were more accommodating. With a wink, they helped him clamber aboard. Never again seeing his parents, Misha made it to the Urals, joined the Red Army, and as an officer witnessed the Victory Day parade on Moscow's Red Square. We know him as the great historian of Soviet Russia, Moshe Lewin.[65] Efim Gol'braikh's retrospective account of his family's escape from Vitebsk is worth citing too. On July 8, shortly after "refugees" started passing through the city, twenty-year-old Efim led his mother, little sister, and brother to the train station.

> On the platform stood a passenger train, a Red Army convoy, while in the square in front of the station, officers' families waited to board the train. Nobody else was permitted to board. Suddenly there appeared a no longer young major, unknown to us, who took our bags and said, "Follow me." He led us past the guards, opened the door to the railway carriage and literally pushed us inside. "Do not get off this train anywhere," he told us. I don't know the name of this gentleman, but my family and I owe our lives to him; he saved us from certain death. Until the end of her days, my mother prayed for this man.[66]

---

63. USHMM RG-22.030, TsGA SPb, f. 7179, op. 11, d. 814, l. 74; USHMM RG-22.027M, GARF, f. A-327, Reel 48, op. 2, d. 73, ll. 9–10; For Stalin's speech, see K. I. Bukov, M. M. Gorinov, and A. N. Ponomorev, eds., *Moskva voennaia, 1941–1945: Memuary i arkhivnye dokumenty* (Moscow, 1995), 63.

64. USHMM RG-50.226.0024, Oral History interview with Dimitri Vasilievich Mironyenko (August 1994), 8:40–13:50.

65. Ronald Grigor Suny, "Living in the Soviet Century: Moshe Lewin, 1921–2010," *History Workshop Journal*, no. 74 (autumn 2012): 194.

66. "Efim Gol'braikh," http://iremember.ru/pekhotintsi/golbraykh-efim-abelevich.html, 1 (accessed February 18, 2013).

Figure 5 Self-evacuation, Dnepropetrovsk region, 1941, Anri Vartanov et al., *Antologiia sovetskoi fotografii*, vol. 2, 1941–1945 (Moscow, 1987), 58.

Whether by truck, thanks to peasant conscripts, or by train, owing to the compassion of a "no longer young major," these narrow escapes do not qualify as evacuation. Beyond official usage, the term "refugee" survived as a reality. According to a recent study, the "great majority" of civilians who made it to the North Caucasus in the fall of 1941—primarily Jews from Ukraine—were not part of the organized evacuation process but rather were "wild," that is, essentially refugees who had self-evacuated.[67] The term "refugee" survived in other respects as well—as a linguistic tic and a form of self-representation. When evacuees arrived in Kazakhstan, state farm workers in Kustanai oblast' allegedly greeted them as "refugees" and "exiles." The distressed inspector from the evacuation and relocation office who reported this assumed that the term indicated hostility toward or at least denigration of the evacuees, but it may just have been ignorance of political correctness.[68] Petitioners could self-identify as refugees to indicate their abject state. Long after he had tried in vain to obtain the assistance of local authorities, the Chuvash ASSR's government, and even the

---

67. Feferman, "A Soviet Humanitarian Action?" 823.

68. USHMM RG 74.002 Tsentral'nyi Gosudarstvennyi Arkhiv g. Almaty (TsGA Almaty), f. R-1137, op. 6, d. 1278a, ll. 20–21.

Council of People's Commissars, Isaak Shil'kron (evacuated to a kolkhoz) described himself and his family in a desperate letter as "refugees."[69]

To appreciate the complexity of the evacuation effort, it is necessary to read the correspondence of both regional and central party and state authorities; to assess the effectiveness of these efforts, one also needs to familiarize oneself with evacuees' accounts. From the center's perspective, regional officials congenitally dragged their feet at preparing evacuation stations and institutions receiving evacuees. Regional officials meanwhile fumed over their lack of sufficient staff and funds while extolling their own accomplishments. The methodological challenge of putting these documents into conversation is compounded by the difficulty of assessing the veracity of evacuees' complaints and the urgency of their requests for assistance. Conversely, many parents of sick children and sick adults concealed illness from medical and other authorities lest they be left behind in quarantine or otherwise separated from loved ones.[70] But it is often impossible to know how to interpret silence.

There is no gainsaying the scale of the state's evacuation effort. Manley describes it as "an operation of gargantuan proportions."[71] Between June 29 and August 14, 1941, authorities in Leningrad reported that they had evacuated 469,029 people.[72] Most evacuees left by train for cities to the east. Cherepovets, Vologda, and Yaroslavl' served both as destinations and temporary evacuation points where those in need of medical attention could receive it. Yaroslavl' (barely) accommodated almost 80,000 children evacuated from orphanages during August. In October, when the German advance threatened the Yaroslavl' region with occupation, most of the children who had not been reclaimed by parents or sent somewhere else in the meantime were reevacuated farther to the east to the Tatar ASSR, Molotov, Cheliabinsk, and Omsk oblasts. After the Germans cut the last rail connection with the rest of unoccupied Soviet territory in early September, evacuations from Leningrad dwindled but picked up again in November with the opening of the ice road across Lake Ladoga. From January 21 through April 20, 1942, another 550,000 people were thus evacuated from the besieged city. Having endured the first winter of the siege, many were so weak that they did not survive the journey and even more died in evacuation hospitals in Vologda—up to 40 percent of all admitted, according to one source.[73]

---

69. USHMM RG-22.020, GIAChR, f. 1263, op. 1, d. 44, l. 42. His last desperate letter was to the Council on Evacuation.

70. Mikhail Frolov, "Evacuation from Leningrad to Kostroma in 1941–42," in *Life and Death in Besieged Leningrad, 1941–44*, ed. John Barber and Andrei Dzeniskevich (Houndmills, 2005), 72.

71. Manley, *To the Tashkent Station*, 28.

72. [Aleksandr Mikhailovich Tiranin], "Nedavno rassekrechennye dokumenty blokadnogo Leningrada," TsGA SPb, f. 7179, op. 53, d. 58, l. 30, http://artofwar.ru/t/tiranin_a_m/text_0190.shtml (accessed March 3, 2013).

73. Frolov, "Evacuation from Leningrad to Kostroma," 73, 79.

Later that year, with the renewal of the Germans' drive to the southeast, the flow of evacuees from Voroshilovgrad, Rostov, and Voronezh oblasts into Stalingrad and beyond increased, as did the number of evacuation stations set up by oblast' departments. In early August, these departments began evacuating women and children *from* Stalingrad, and by the end of that month fifty to sixty thousand were arriving on the eastern bank of the Volga *every day.*[74] On a much smaller scale but one more typical of efforts throughout the shifting frontal zone, about fifty party and government personnel, supplemented by more than three hundred individuals from the NKVD and police, prepared to evacuate two thousand families from Kursk to Novosibirsk oblast' in November 1942. They set up medical facilities, pried away trucks from the army to transport people, and somehow obtained the petrol to fuel them.[75]

Evacuation depended on the establishment of a migration regime by administrators drawn from military, party, and civilian government bodies. Both the Resettlement Administration and the NKVD had extensive experience in moving people en masse and both organizations not surprisingly played significant roles in the evacuation process. Policy decisions concerning the implementation of the above-mentioned principles resided with the supreme wartime organ of government, the six-man State Defense Committee (GKO), and the Evacuation Council. The latter body drew its membership from the Council of People's Commissars, commissariats at the all-Union and RSFSR levels, Gosplan, and the trade unions' central council. But it was the evacuation commissions formed by party and state organizations in the affected areas that bore the brunt of day-to-day decision making. The commissions identified and contacted evacuees, determined where and when to send them, and tried to obtain the necessary transport, food, and other provisions. Procedures varied from one city to another and to a certain degree over time, but all evacuation commissions generally understood that civilian institutions' *nachsostav* (from *nachal'stvuiushchii sostav*, or leading staff) and the army's *komsostav* (from *komandnyi sostav*, or officer staff) had priority.

For a few remarkable days in mid-October 1941, Moscow, which had been directing the entire evacuation effort, itself succumbed to an unseemly scramble among elites who hitherto had stayed put. Once Stalin ordered the evacuation of government offices to the Volga town of Kuibyshev on October 15, the public "fear[ed] that the government had abandoned the population to its fate," and the city "was in the grip of mass panic verging on anarchy." Party and state officials commandeered available transport, and roads out of the city heading east were clogged with vehicles bearing them and their precious household items, barrels of fuel, and cash. Nearly a thousand railway cars left the city's stations during the days

74. USHMM RG-22.027M, GARF, f. A-327, Reels 46, 42, op. 2, d. 50, l. 1; d. 26, ll. 40–45.
75. USHMM RG-22.027M, GARF, f. A-327, Reel 40, op. 2, d. 2, ll. 1–6.

of flight.[76] On board were leading personnel of key industries and scientific institutions. October 14–15 saw the exodus of 404 individuals from twenty-four scientific institutes for Kazan, Sverdlovsk, Alma-Ata, Samarkand, Frunze, and Ashkhabad. The cream of Moscow's theatrical world from ten different companies left on the latter day, some for these cities and others for Magnitogorsk, Karaganda, Tashkent, and Irkutsk.[77]

As the siege deprived many Leningrad enterprises of their raw materials and individuals of sufficient nutrition, war-related factories were dismantled, packed up, and sent to the east. Their engineering staff—42 from a rubber factory that produced compressed molds for tank and artillery pieces, 16 from a cellulose nitrate plant essential for gunpowder production, and many others—accompanied the machinery. In July and August 1941, the Leningrad armaments plant OKB-43 sent its top staff on two convoys to Ioshkar-Ola, the Marii ASSR's capital on the upper Volga. In October, the factory's director, citing an order from the Commissariat of Defense, requested permission to dispatch an additional 40 "highly skilled workers." Permission was granted.[78] Evacuations of staff from Leningrad continued throughout the winter. Between January and April 1942, hundreds made it out thanks to institutional connections—34 from the Architectural-Planning Administration of the city executive committee; 25 from the Murmansk Ship Repair Yard; 58 from the Baltic Fleet's administrative offices; 44 from Leningrad State University; 35 from the Leningrad City Soviet; 207 from the Northern Sea Route Administration; and 152 from various cultural organizations ranging from the famed Kirov Ballet to the Hermitage and Russian museums, the State Conservatory, and the Pushkin Theater.[79]

Bosses could request passes for individuals too. This was how two employees of the Leningrad Oblast' Statistical Administration, including the recipient of a Badge of Honor awarded for his work on the 1939 census, exited the besieged city in December 1941. We don't know if Ivan Simonov, an engineer employed by the Northern Energy Construction Trust made it to Sverdlovsk, but at least his boss was willing to seek passage for him and twelve family members (his wife, two teenaged sons, his mother, two sisters, three nephews, and three aunts). Even the relatives of drivers working for the NKVD could garner the recommendation of their boss, though the drivers themselves presumably remained behind in the besieged city.[80]

---

76. Quotation from John Barber and Mark Harrison, *The Soviet Home Front, 1941–1945: A Social and Economic History of the USSR in World War II* (London, 1991), 64. See also Manley, *To the Tashkent Station*, 59–63; Gennady Andreev-Khomiakov, *Bitter Waters: Life and Work in Stalin's Russia* (Boulder, CO, 1997), 163–82.

77. *Moskva prifrontovaia 1941–1942: Arkhivnye dokumenty i materialy*, ed. M. M. Gorinov (Moscow, 2001), 254–57, 260.

78. USHMM RG-22.033, TsGA SPb, f. 330, op. 1, d. 4, ll. 4–6, 24, 31–33.

79. USHMM RG-22.033, TsGA SPb, f. 330, op. 2, d. 81, ll. 2–4, 6; d. 82, ll. 21–24, 26, 37, 136, 199–205; d. 83, ll. 227–40. Some of these numbers included family members, a point to which we will return.

80. USHMM RG-22.033, TsGA SPb, f. 330, op. 2, d. 81, l. 47, 89; op. 2, d. 83, ll. 23.

Many people seeking to leave Leningrad had no sponsors and had to make cases for themselves. Others had received approval for evacuation but illness—either their own or that of a close family member—had prevented them from departing.[81] As time passed and hunger became more pervasive, illness began to play the opposite role; people increasingly referred to it to underscore the urgency of their evacuation. Marta Raud's story combined both illness and death. The daughter of a military engineer evacuated from Moscow to Tashkent, she lived with her mother and brother in Leningrad until her brother volunteered for the front. She and her mother had received the necessary documents for evacuation in August 1941 but could not go because her mother's health was failing. In the petition for her own evacuation, Marta reported that her mother had died and she had not heard from her brother since his induction. She was fifteen years old.[82]

As one memoirist wrote of the hungriest months of the siege—the winter of 1941/42—"Everyone wants to be evacuated. To leave Leningrad for anywhere, if only to receive a piece of real bread. . . . People sweetly dream of this, sitting in the darkness of their frozen rooms, shuffling along the dead, snow-covered streets, standing in lines before the empty shelves of the stores, at work, in the cafeterias."[83] Among them undoubtedly were those who wrote to authorities directly. "If in the next few days I am not able to leave, I will die," wrote a forty-nine-year-old male factory worker in February 1942. Thirty-two-year-old Pelageia Samoilova, employed as a forewoman in a shipyard, reported that her powers were failing and she could not survive on a daily ration of 125 grams of bread. "Help me decide the question of life," she wrote to Leningrad city committee secretary Kuznetsov. "I want to live! I want to work!" These are examples of resorting to a kind of moral blackmail—putting the onus for one's survival or that of one's relatives on the recipient of the appeal. So urgent did Samoilova make her condition seem that she provided Kuznetsov with a telephone number "because the post takes time."[84]

Other repertoires competed for the attention of authorities. One emphasized past contributions and/or the importance of the individual seeking evacuation. The fourteen single-spaced typewritten pages that A. A. Novoselov used to describe the "about one hundred inventions" and rationalization schemes he had made—"unfortunately, not many

81. See for example USHMM RG-22.033, TsGA SPb, f. 330, op. 2, d. 81, ll. 78, 108; d. 82, l. 39; d. 83, l. 170; USHMM RG-22.030, TsGA SPb, f. 7179, op. 11, d. 814, l. 217.

82. USHMM RG-22.033, TsGA SPb, f. 330, op. 2, d. 83, l. 182.

83. D. A. Granin and A. A. Adamovich, eds., Blokadnaia kniga (Moscow, 1982), quoted in Mariia Shardakova, "'Svoi ili chuzhie?' Evakuirovannye leningradtsy v Cheliabinske, 1941–1948," in Puti sledovaniia: Rossiiskie shkol'niki o migratsiiakh, evakuatsiiakh i deportatsiiakh XX veka, ed. Irina Shcherbakova (Moscow, 2011), 151.

84. USHMM RG-22.033, TsGA SPb, f. 330, op. 2, d. 83, ll. 11, 13; op. 2, d. 81, ll. 128–30. For an interpretation of "narratives of appeal" from earlier Soviet decades, see Golfo Alexopoulos, "The Ritual Lament: A Narrative of Appeal in the 1920s and 1930s," Russian History/Histoire russe 24, nos. 1–2 (1997): 117–29.

realized"—represented an extreme version of this strategy.[85] Others combined it with descriptions of the parlous state of their health or that of loved ones. A father serving as battalion commissar asked that his twenty-three-year-old son be evacuated because he suffered from multiple sclerosis and was "one of the most talented young poets of Leningrad." A member of the party since 1919 who "died" at Pulkovo Heights defending Soviet power against the Whites contrasted his own desperate condition with the three healthy, well-fed women whose evacuation "thanks to contacts" had "offended" him. And after reminding the Leningrad city soviet chairman Popkov of her late husband's numerous contributions to the defense of the Soviet Union, O. I. Averichkina requested evacuation by air for herself and her two children because of her daughter's weak health and the fact that she was "experiencing hunger in the full sense of the word." The file contains not only Averichkina's request but also the certificate issued a month later by a district evacuation commission for all three of them to be evacuated by air. This was a privilege, as Manley notes, "generally reserved for the political and cultural elite."[86] (See figure 6 for a more typical permission.)

Then there was Leopold Langfellner, a twenty-seven-year-old native of Vienna who had gone into exile in the Soviet Union after the defeat and persecution of Austrian Social Democrats by fascists in February 1934. Langfellner went on to serve in the XI International Brigade in Spain and after his return to the USSR had worked as a driver. His letter to Zhdanov, written in German but translated into Russian, contained elements of still other repertoires. One was utilitarian: as a driver, he would be more useful somewhere else because Leningrad was running out of petrol. The somewhere else turned out to be Minusinsk, 250 miles south of Krasnoiarsk along the Enisei River, where the NKVD had sent his wife, also Austrian, after arresting her in 1937. Langfellner explained that since her arrest, their son, who remained with Leopold but did not accompany him to Spain, had become "a hooligan."[87] The family as a unit of security and welfare anchored yet another repertoire.

It figured in the appeal from the Muscovite I. V. Ivashin to Evacuation Council chairman Shvernik. Ivashin, soon to be drafted as a political commissar, requested that his eighty-four-year-old mother and student son be permitted to travel to Kuibyshev to join close relatives whose invitation he enclosed. It was employed by Zinaida Postnikova to have her aged mother sent from Leningrad to join her in Moscow, or, failing that, to live with relatives in Chkalov oblast.'[88] It was among the reasons that A. Rogozin, whose parents had just starved to death, gave to travel to Sverdlovsk, where his brother lived. Rogozin also mentioned his ailment—as an invalid of the Third Group (90 percent sightless)—and the award

85. USHMM RG-22.033, TsGA SPb, f. 330, op. 2, d. 22, ll. 36–47.
86. USHMM RG-22.033, TsGA SPb, f. 330, op. 2, d. 82, l. 95; op. 2, d. 21, l. 51; op. 2, d. 81, ll. 60–62, 76–77; Manley, To the Tashkent Station, 56.
87. USHMM RG-22.033, TsGA SPb, f. 330, op. 1, d. 4, l. 178–79.
88. USHMM RG-22.027, GARF, f. A-327, Reels 46, 48, op. 2, d. 50, l. 135; op. 2, d. 73, l. 1.

Figure 6 Evacuation permission document for Anna Iakovlevna Generalova, February 4, 1942, TsGA SPb, f. 330, op. 2, d. 82, l. 192.

his brother, evacuated earlier with others from the Kirov Factory, had once received "from the hands of Kirov himself."[89] These and many other requests cited family connections because family connections disburdened authorities, relieving them of much of the responsibility of providing evacuees with food and accommodation. Such requests therefore had a decent chance of being approved.

89. USHMM RG-22.033, TsGA SPb, f. 330, op. 1, d. 36, l. 14; op. 2. d. 81, ll. 16–17.

But what if as a result of the hastiness and inefficiency of evacuation, people got separated from family members? What if some wound up in one city or collective farm and a close relative had been evacuated to another place, perhaps even to another Soviet republic? This was the very question that the assistant director of evacuation for Kazakhstan received from a provincial official in November 1941. "Every day evacuees turn to us with requests for train tickets to various places—Fergana, Kokand, Tashkent, Chkalov, etc.—where they have relatives," the official wrote. "Do we have the right to give them?" The answer—"If there is documented proof of relatives living there, then you can distribute tickets"— implicitly endorsed the state's reliance on the family.[90]

In instances where the war found children in summer camps or boarding schools or where no family connections existed, as with orphans, the state assumed responsibility for evacuation without prompting.[91] But the growing numbers of orphans during the war strained the resources and resolve of evacuation and child welfare personnel. Government officials from areas near the front claimed they lacked sufficient food for orphans and pleaded with central authorities to permit their evacuation to the east. Absent the voices of the orphans themselves, we must rely on these officials' letters to convey the dire condition of the "very many children whose parents either were killed by the fascists or died of hunger under occupation." According to one account from Kalinin oblast', they were found to be "exhausted to the extreme, completely disheveled, louse-ridden, [and] living in cellars and holes in the ground of destroyed villages." Of the 1,750 orphans identified within the oblast', 500 were of preschool age and 250 were infants.[92]

Journeys

Lydia Chukovskaia, daughter of the famous children's writer Kornei Chukovskii and herself a poet and novelist, kept a diary that, as she explained decades later, "became less and less a re-creation of my own life, turning into episodes in the life of [the poet] Anna Akhmatova."[93] In late July 1941, Lydia traveled from Moscow by steamer with her daughter, nanny, and nephew to Chistopol, a port town on the Kama River. The journey, arranged for her and the families of several Moscow writers, took them north via the recently completed

90. USHMM RG-74.002, TsGA Almaty, f. R-1137, op. 6, d. 1284, ll. 134–35.

91. *Moskva prifrontovaia*, 251. See also Natalie Belsky, "New Types of Communities: The Role of Women's Organizations in Helping Evacuees," paper presented at Midwest Russian Historians' Workshop, Urbana, March 2014; Lena Jedwab Rozenberg, *The Girl with Two Landscapes: The Wartime Diary of Lena Jedwab, 1941–1945* (New York, 2002).

92. USHMM RG-22.027, GARF, f. A-327, Reel 45, op. 2, d. 43, ll. 112, 114, 122. These letters and memoranda date from July to October 1942.

93. Lydia Chukovskaya, *The Akhmatova Journals*, vol. 1, 1938–41, trans. Milena Michalski and Sylva Rubashova (New York, 1994), 6.

Moscow-Volga Canal, east along the Volga past Gor'kii, Cheboksary, and Kazan, then south for a short distance to the mouth of the Kama and east again to Chistopol. She found accommodation as an evacuee at 20 Rosa Luxemburg Street, and that was where one evening in mid-October Akhmatova appeared at the gate, having arrived by airplane from Leningrad. By this time, Lydia's father had arranged for her and his grandchildren to travel by train from Kazan to Tashkent, whence he had been evacuated, and Akhmatova announced a few days after her arrival that she had made up her mind to join them.

In Kazan, the traveling party, which included the writers Aleksandr Fadeev and Samuil Marshak, waited silently "like in a prison queue" for four hours on the platform in total darkness. When the train finally arrived, the two carriages reserved for writers and their families barely accommodated everyone. "I'm glad to be seeing so much of Russia," Akhmatova exclaimed gazing out of the window. Indeed, if not but for the evacuation, she and many others from Leningrad and Moscow probably would never have traveled so far into the interior of the country. In Novosibirsk, Akhmatova spotted some blue carriages from the Moscow metro. A few days later they encountered a trainload of Volga Germans—that is, deportees—that also was heading east. Desert, camels, mountains—finally two weeks after departing, the train arrived in Tashkent, where Kornei Chukovskii met them with a car. It was November 9, but everything was in bloom.[94]

As arduous as Lydia's and Akhmatova's journey was, others had a much more difficult time. On June 6, 1942 Aleksei Kosygin, then deputy chairman of the Evacuation Council, received a telegram from Petr Popkov, chairman of Leningrad's executive committee—in effect its mayor—informing him that a convoy of evacuees had been standing for three days at a station in Kadui, about 310 miles east of Leningrad. For some reason, the evacuees had not received any food or water during this time, and Popkov referred to "much death among them."[95] Intended to preserve life, the journeys that evacuees took could have the opposite effect. The reason could have been bureaucratic disconnect—evacuation personnel failing to communicate the needs of evacuees to appropriate officials in the commissariats of transport and trade or the regional soviet government through whose territory the train passed. Sometimes the inadequacy of food or other supplies had to do with the unexpectedly large number of people in need. For example, in August 1942, it was reported from recently liberated Smolensk oblast' that two hundred to five hundred people arrived daily, on foot, from occupied territories, crowding the little Toropets station on the Kalinin rail line.[96]

94. Ibid., 184–93.

95. USHMM RG-22.027, GARF, f. A-327, Reel 46, op. 2, d. 50, l. 14. Kosygin was Popkov's immediate predecessor as Leningrad executive committee chairman.

96. USHMM RG-22.027, GARF, f. A-327, Reel 40, op. 2, d. 2, l. 78.

The extraordinarily privileged, like Akhmatova, were flown to safety, but although tedious, railroad journeys also could be lifesaving, even life affirming. Among the detailed accounts by evacuees that have survived, several reveal instances of cooperation and mutual aid aboard such trains. For example, after Genya Batasheva and her friend Manya had survived the massacre of Jews at Babi Yar, they walked all the way to unoccupied territory, where they encountered a Soviet army officer who took them under his wing and provided truck transport. In Voronezh, they joined a convoy bound for Tashkent. Traveling in a *teplushka*, they went without food for three days until the songs of their fellow passengers moved the two young women to tears. At this point, the evacuees offered them both food and companionship. Genya discovered among them an elderly Kievan who had worked with her cousin in a printing shop. Abram Tseitlin, whom we left with his father wondering whether to flee or to stay, recounts companionable conversation and traditional road food (bread and butter, onions, hard-boiled eggs, pickles, and boiled chicken) on the train that took his family to Central Asia. On the month-long journey that ended at Kagan near Bukhara, Tseitlin reports that the *teplushka* became a sort of communal apartment "where each family had its own corner." And, "like every communal apartment, we had our difficulties with each other—over whose turn it was to dispose of garbage and prepare food."[97] Finally, for the above-mentioned Anna Dashevskaia, who kept a diary of her journey from Kiev to the Urals via Alma-Ata, the train teemed with human emotion. "On the convoy," she wrote, "a lot of people were arguing, women crying, and men chatting, wiping back tears. As the train slowly pulled away from the station, a great noise went up from our wagon filled with children. Husbands ran after the train car, waving caps, tears fell uncontrollably on their cheeks—women wailed, pulled at their hair . . . then descended into deathly silence, each thought about herself and quietly wiped away tears . . ."[98]

At stops along the way, Dashevskaia and her sisters kept on bumping into acquaintances—a cousin with his wife and children, a neighbor of their aunt Eva, several classmates—who had been evacuated earlier. At the procurator's office in Alma-Ata, the convoy's last stop, her sister Marusia secured a work assignment to Ural'sk. And so on September 22, 1941, more than a month after they had left Kiev, the four sisters and their brother boarded a train for the 1,200-mile journey back across the vast Kazakh steppe. Missing her parents terribly, Anna imagined seeing them at every stop. A week later, she and her siblings arrived at their "temporarily-permanent place of residence."[99]

---

97. USHMM RG-50.226.0008 Oral History Interview with Genya Batasheva, part 6, 3:30–27:00; Tseitlin, "Evacuation," 21, "Kermine," 26. Batasheva and her friend survived by telling a German soldier that they were not Jewish and had wandered to Babi Yar out of curiosity. They were driven back to Kiev and released. For testimony Batasheva gave in 1980, see Evstaf'eva and Nakhmanovich, *Babii Iar*, 106–8, 321–22.

98. Diary of Anna Dashevskaia, 7–8.

99. Ibid., 18–22.

The Routes of Three Evacuees during the Great Patriotic War

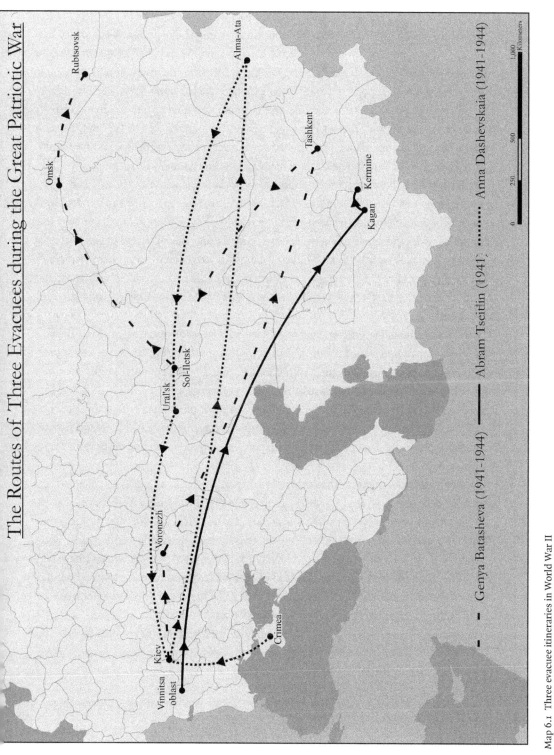

- - - Genya Batasheva (1941-1944) ———— Abram Tseitlin (1941 ⋯⋯⋯⋯ Anna Dashevskaia (1941-1944)

Map 6.1 Three evacuee itineraries in World War II

Destinations

Our three Jewish informants all left Ukraine in the late summer and early autumn of 1941 to escape what years later would be called the Holocaust. Many other Jews from Ukraine evacuated themselves to the North Caucasus, the territories of Krasnodar and Stavropol', where they comprised about 70 percent of the total evacuated population. In these territories, only 9 to 12 percent of evacuees claimed Russian nationality, and 14 percent claimed Ukrainian.[100] The region proved to be a doomed destination, especially for Jews, not only because the indigenous population reacted to so many needy evacuees with anti-Semitic hostility but also because it would fall to the Nazis in the summer of 1942.

Russian-nationality evacuees, by contrast, were the clear majority (64 percent) in the Molotov/Perm territory in the Urals as of October 1941. Farther east, in Novosibirsk oblast', 41 percent of evacuees were Russian and 11 percent were Jews—suggesting that many other nationalities were present among evacuees in Siberia that fall. In Kazakhstan, where 45 percent of evacuees were Russian, slightly over a third were Jews, and 11 percent claimed Ukrainian nationality.[101] The registered evacuees had shifted in number and nationality by the time of the next count six weeks later; this was a fluid, moving, and growing population.

Jews predominated among evacuees in the North Caucasus because, as Kiril Feferman points out, "the region was on a natural escape route from Ukraine into the Soviet interior." Naturalness may not have weighed with officials, but, as we have noted, most incomers were self-evacuated, or in other words, refugees. Contrarily, evacuees from besieged Leningrad could only leave through official channels. In principle, the advantage that the organized removal of the population had over the spontaneous flight of individuals and families lay in the opportunity it gave to prepare transport, accommodation, and other resources at destination.

However, this distinction often broke down in practice. Many evacuees assigned to a particular destination wound up somewhere else either through their own doing or because of what frustrated higher authorities referred to as "irregular" (samovol'nye) reassignments by regional personnel. Counting on the strategy of family connections, some evacuees reportedly insisted on being deposited at places where they claimed to have relatives rather than proceeding on to the Altai or Novosibirsk—even when it turned out they did not have any relatives where they claimed they did. One instance of irregular reassignments occurred in January 1942 when Sverdlovsk oblast' officials "readdressed" a convoy of 750 Leningraders to Omsk; it happened again when authorities in Omsk readdressed the

100. Feferman, "A Soviet Humanitarian Action?" 820. Feferman uses resettlement department data.
101. Ibid.; Grinberg, *Evakuatsiia v Kazakhstan*, 100.

same convoy to Petropavlovsk, 150 miles away in northern Kazakhstan. The Germans' offensive of the summer of 1942 precipitated massive reassignments of convoys away from Stalingrad, Saratov, and Kuibyshev oblasts toward the Altai territory, Novosibirsk, and Omsk oblasts.[102] These were more legitimate, but legitimate or not, they left authorities at the receiving end unprepared and evacuees ill served.

Correspondence between the central resettlement office and regional evacuation authorities reveals the extent to which the placement (razmeshchenie) of evacuees resulted from negotiation. For example, in May 1942 a resettlement official reported on his attempts to persuade oblast' personnel via telephone to accept evacuees from Leningrad. Four of seven individuals contacted agreed to accept some, although only Novosibirsk would accommodate the full complement of forty thousand. Two (Gor'kii and Ivanovo) refused to take any, pleading food shortages, and in Ivanovo's case, an epidemic. Nobody answered the phone at the Mari republic's headquarters, and Ufa, capital of the Bashkir ASSR, had no telephone connection.[103] Throughout the latter half of 1942, Leningraders were the great majority (numbering eighty thousand or 85 percent of all evacuees) arriving in Novosibirsk. This oblast' may not have been the nearest safe place for Leningraders, but it could absorb many more than the overflowing destinations in between that in some cases refused to take more evacuees.[104]

If they survived the journey, millions of evacuees found or were assigned places to live. They usually disembarked in unfamiliar territory. Tseitlin's first impression of Kermine, a dusty town roughly midway between Bukhara and Samarkand, was that "everything was different—the language . . . the scorching sun, the mud-brick homes and outbuildings, the colorful market, the fruits I had never seen before, the Uzbeks . . ." Arriving in Ural'sk with three sisters, an infant, and her brother, Anna Dashevskaia recognized that as "refugees," their choices of accommodation were limited to the street, the squalor of the train station, or the henhouse offered by the neighbor of a distant contact. Fortunately, they met great kindness, even though they were not among their own people (zemliaki).[105]

Evacuees accompanying institutions and privileged individuals could count on being accommodated in a city. For example, in Novosibirsk oblast', over 93 percent who had arrived with employing institutions and their families were accommodated in an urban

---

102. USHMM RG-22.027, GARF, f. A-327, Reels 48, 46, op. 2, d. 68, l. 15; op. 2, d. 50, ll. 33, 103–6. Reassignments occurred from the beginning: in early October 1941, Kazakhstan had steeled itself for over sixty thousand evacuees from Moscow, but less than nine thousand arrived because "evacuation stations in Novosibirsk, Chkalov, Kuibyshev, Saratov, and elsewhere irregularly reassigned evacuees." USHMM RG.74.002, TsGA Almaty, f. 1137, op. 9, d. 141, ll. 75–76.

103. USHMM RG-22.027, GARF, f. A-327, Reel 46, op. 2, d. 50, ll. 24–25.

104. Edwards, "Fleeing to Siberia," 109–10.

105. Tseitlin, "Kermine," 8; Diary of Anna Dashevskaia, 22–23.

area.[106] Manley notes that Muscovites and Leningraders as well as the families of party, state, and military elites enjoyed the additional privilege of settling in any city where relatives or friends were willing to share living space.[107] One such city, Alma-Ata, the Kazakh republic's capital, accommodated scientific and cultural luminaries, leading members of Kiev's Theater of Musical Comedy, the prizewinning Stakhanovite combine driver and Supreme Soviet deputy Maria Demchenko, and the wife of the well-known poet Aleksandr Bezymenskii. When the time came to evacuate from Moscow the family of the Stalin Prize-winning author Sergei Mikhalkov, Lazar Kaganovich, a member of the Politburo and the Evacuation Council, informed the chairman of the Kazakh Council of Ministers. He in turn instructed the city's mayor to provide a suitable apartment.[108] Mikhalkov's wife and two sons flew to Alma-Ata, where, in addition to the families of cultural figures, "those able-bodied men who did not want to fight sat out the war thanks to 'handy' certificates," as Mikhalkov sardonically recalled in his memoirs.[109] For these people, the evacuation regime worked hard to minimize the pain of dislocation.

Others did not fare so well in urban destinations. Of the eleven institutes evacuated from Moscow to Kazakhstan by early November 1941, the Evacuation Council assigned only four to Alma-Ata (including the cinematographic institute where Sergei Eisenstein continued working on "Ivan the Terrible"). The others found homes in lesser Kazakh cities.[110] The unexpected arrival in Alma-Ata of 104 students from the Nikolaev Shipbuilding Institute upset this delicate balancing act. Kazakh officials let Grigorii Kaplun, the acting Commissar of Shipbuilding, know of their displeasure in no uncertain terms. "We have been forced to support them for two days," wrote Koishigulov, the deputy chairman of the Kazakh Council of People's Commissars. "Your silence . . . is incomprehensible to us." Kaplun, who had been evacuated to Gor'kii, replied that he too had been taken unawares and was trying to get authorization to transfer the wayward students to Omsk. Two days later, Koishigulov wrote to Shvernik of the Evacuation Council begging him to order the rerouting of the students. "It is no longer possible to keep the wagons at the station in Alma-Ata," he added. Eventually, the students joined their classmates and faculty in Frunze, the extremely landlocked capital of the Kyrgyz SSR.[111]

Less fortunate still were people at institutes displaced by the placement of others in their premises. To cite but two examples, the evacuation of the all-Union and RSFSR

---

106. The figure for "organized" evacuees was 93 percent in March 1942 and 96 percent in January 1943; see Edwards, "Fleeing to Siberia," 229, 231.

107. Manley, *To the Tashkent Station*, 151.

108. USHMM RG.74.002, TsGA Almaty, f. 1137, op. 6, d. 1279, l. 18; d. 1280, ll. 13, 42–43.

109. S. V. Mikhalkov, *Ot i do . . .* (Moscow, 1997), 134.

110. USHMM RG.74.002, TsGA Almaty, f. 1137, op. 9, d. 142, l. 66.

111. Ibid., ll. 302–5; op. 6, d. 1279, l. 175.

commissariats of forestry to Kirov sent that city's pedagogical institute—including several hundred students and dozens of faculty members—to comparatively "isolated and primitive" Iaransk, over 125 miles to the southwest of the oblast's capital. By Larry Holmes's calculation, it was one of seventy-two higher-educational institutions throughout the country displaced by the evacuation of more prestigious bodies.[112] Second, someone in the evacuation bureaucracy had decided that the Moscow Power Engineering Institute belonged in the extreme eastern Kazakh city of Leninogorsk. Not only did the assignment disappoint the students and faculty of the engineering institute who had been looking forward to residing in Alma-Ata and had totally exhausted their funds to get there, but it also required the transfer of the Leninogorsk mining and metallurgical college to Chimkent in the extreme south. This would have been fine except that the lack of available transport tripped up the operation. The Muscovites arrived in Leninogorsk but had to wait at the station until the college students departed, only then to discover that a hospital was occupying part of the college's premises and could not be converted to classrooms or living space.[113]

Some of these institutions functioned during the war so that they could allow children and students a near-normal life. This proved to be the case for children in a Young Pioneer summer camp on the Neman River in southern Lithuania who were evacuated more than 1,400 miles east to a children's home in Udmurtia. A sort of triage followed: the camp counselors went home, the students born in 1924 and 1925 were mobilized, and 55 parents came to fetch their children, so that of the 215 children in camp, 160 remained in February 1942. "Did I ever dream that I would be so far from home, in a remote village in Udmurtia? That I would be the ward of a children's home?" asked Lena Jedwab.[114] Uprooted first from Bialystok and then the Young Pioneer camp, Jedwab replaced the camp counselors for awhile along with two friends, gradually realizing that as much deprivation as she suffered, it was mild compared to what she heard of through letters and visits from people like the children's home director's wife, who arrived from Leningrad in the fall of 1942. Lena's friends applied to schools in the spring, one entering the faculty of philology that had been evacuated from Moscow to Saratov. Lena herself stayed on at the children's home through tenth grade in order to qualify for higher-educational institutions. She then applied to schools in Kazan, Sverdlovsk, Moscow, and nearby Izhevsk in the summer of 1943. In the fall, she started at the Bauman Technical Institute in Moscow, and then went on to enter the faculty of philology at Moscow University. It was at this time she learned from other Polish

112. Larry E. Holmes, *War, Evacuation, and the Exercise of Power: The Center, Periphery, and Kirov's Pedagogical Institute, 1941–1952* (Lanham, 2012), 11–15, 23.
113. USHMM RG.74.002, TsGA Almaty, f. 1137, op. 9, d. 142, ll. 97, 130, 163, 201, 315, 318; op. 6, d. 1279, ll. 62–63.
114. Rozenberg, *Girl with Two Landscapes*, 15, 70, 75 (quotation on 15).

Jews that her entire family—mother, father, brother, and sister—had been killed early in the war; but thanks to the Soviet state's evacuation regime, she had survived.[115]

Fortunate indeed were the children who, unlike Lena Jedwab, experienced the years of evacuation with parents or other close relatives. Fathers might have been at the front or already deceased, but mothers, aunts, grandmothers, and siblings—especially heroic mothers—perpetuated family life. The family gave these children a way of coping with traumatic circumstances much as it had during the 1930s.[116] Evgenii Dolgov never saw his father after evacuation from Riga in June 1941 when he was eleven. He, his mother, older brother, and grandmother first traveled to Ivanovo, where his mother's sister lived, then to Khabarovsk, where she had an older brother. However, the threat of Japanese invasion sent them to Uzbekistan, and they came to live in Samarkand. "I simply don't understand how mother managed to sustain us," he declared decades later. With difficulty they survived, helped by military rations, rising early to wait in queues for food and attending school with evacuees from all over the country.[117]

School attendance was more likely in the city. The countryside did not have the resources to enforce it and, in any case, many mothers complained that their children lacked the necessary footwear and warm clothing.[118] Indeed, for rural evacuees, everything was more difficult. Investigatory reports filed by labor inspectors largely confirmed evacuees' complaints, many penned on used paper, to local and regional authorities as well as the Supreme Soviet and its chairman, Mikhail Kalinin.[119] They tell a sorry tale of acute material deprivation. "We have received nothing, not even salt," wrote a group of Leningrad evacuees from the Chuvash republic to Kalinin in January 1943. "We are very seriously hungry," complained the Muscovite mother of three children from the republic's Toretskii district in March 1942. "Our situation is not bad, it is desperate," a group of soldiers' wives wrote.[120] Aside from food, petitioners pleaded for dresses, coats, shoes, and cloth. Many simply described themselves or their children as "barefoot and naked" (golaia bosaia).[121] Kolkhoz administrators bore part of the blame: labor-day calculations, the basis for access to

---

115. Ibid., 85, 87, 92, 103, 145, 169.

116. See Cathy Frierson, Children of the Gulag (New Haven, 2010), chaps. 2–4; Catriona Kelly, Children's World: Growing Up in Russia, 1890–1991 (New Haven, 2007), 221–42, 372–86; Orlando Figes, The Whisperers: Private Life in Stalin's Russia (London, 2007), 160–64, 540–41, and chap. 7 below.

117. "Evgenii Dolgov," http://iremember.ru/drugie-voyska/dolgov-evgeniy-aleksandrovich.html (accessed February 27, 2013).

118. USHMM RG-22.020, GIAChR, f. 1263, op. 1, d. 51, ll. 153, 230–31, 301.

119. For such reports from the Chuvash republic, see US HMM RG-22.020, GIAChR, f. 835, op. 1, d. 354, l. 37; f. 1263, op. 1, d. 51, ll. 73–75, 153, 179–80; d. 78, ll. 2–3.

120. USHMM RG-22.020, GIAChR, f. 827, op. 1, d. 599, l. 19; f. 1041, d. 599, l. 46; f. 1263, op. 1, d. 51, l. 180.

121. USHMM RG-22.020, GIAChR, f. 835, op. 1, d. 354, ll. 3, 9, 11, 13, 14, 17–170bv, 20, 22, 37, 45, 113, 125, 134, 205, 217, 261, 302.

resources, allegedly slighted evacuees; ordinary kolkhozniki including host families were at best unwelcoming and at worst aggressively hostile.[122] To be fair, already stretched rural dwellers had to share finite resources with many more people. They needed able-bodied agricultural workers but that rarely was what they got.

The least privileged evacuees found themselves in the countryside—on kolkhozes and sovkhozes—even if they had no experience of farm work. They mostly consisted of women, children, the elderly, and the handicapped—predominantly people who came without a sponsoring employer.[123] In fact, the majority of evacuees lived in rural areas: at the end of the first quarter of 1943, roughly two-thirds of 663,290 evacuees in the oblasts of Saratov, Gor'kii, and Kirov went to villages. In the predominantly black-earth Penza oblast', 84 percent of the evacuees lived outside cities, but in the more urbanized Novosibirsk oblast', only 38 percent did so.[124]

Many people, like Evgenii Dolgov's family, moved more than once. In some cases, the wartime fronts changed with German advances; in others, evacuees sought better conditions elsewhere; in still others, they reunited with family members. Often, travel was interrupted by long waits at evacuation stations, and the final destination was unknown. Novosibirsk served as an important node for evacuees. Civilians who had come to the Donets basin, for example, continued their journey eastward as the Germans approached. Some fourteen thousand arrived in Novosibirsk in November and December 1941.[125] Among the Leningraders who arrived in Novosibirsk in the latter half of 1942, some continued their journeys to the Altai krai, Kazakhstan, the Krasnoiarsk krai, Irkutsk oblast', and Kyrgyzstan.[126]

Itineraries are lost in the aggregated data. We learn about the possibilities from the family of Abram Zakharovich Shteingol'ts. In charge of the bakeries of Minsk, Shteingol'ts was evacuated to Tambov. His wife, son, and two daughters followed by truck and by train—"so we were refugees," remembers his daughter—and found him working and living in a bakery. In November 1941 the family relocated to a small village in the northeast corner of Kazakhstan, after an arduous trip during which food "ran out." Abram was

---

122. USHMM RG-22.020, GIAChR, f. 1263, op. 1, d. 51, ll. 18, 53, 101, 128, 212, 237obv, 243.

123. Edwards, "Fleeing to Siberia," 5. Of 6.9 million evacuees registered as of January 1942, 3.4 million (48 percent) were sent to rural areas, compared with 2.7 million (39 percent) sent to cities. The remaining 13 percent are not accounted for. See Natalie Belsky, " 'Hiding Behind the Name of Evacuee One Cannot Sit and Remain Idle in the Soviet Union': The Struggle for Employment of 'Unorganized' Evacuees," paper presented at Midwest Russian Historians Workshop, Evanston, March 16, 2013.

124. The figures for all oblasts are for April 1, 1943, but those for the Novosibirsk oblast' are for January 1943. USHMM RG-22.027, GARF, f. 327, Reel 42, op. 2, d. 26, ll. 25, 35, 49, 73; Edwards, "Fleeing to Siberia," 231.

125. Edwards, "Fleeing to Siberia," 108.

126. Ibid.,108–11.

called to the front only to return in 1942 because of a stomach ulcer. Thereafter, he worked in the rationing administration for the district, and then became a factory director in Alma-Ata. The family joined him in 1944 along with relatives from Leningrad who had survived the blockade.[127] Despite their many moves, this family found a way to reunite and stay together.

High mobility and regathering family also serves as a theme in the story of Genya Batasheva. When we last left her, Genya was en route to Tashkent with her girlfriend Manya. There, the evacuation station assigned them as minors (Genya was eighteen years old at the time) to an artel southwest of the city. But, having been told of rampant typhus in the area, the girls boarded the first convoy that came along. They wound up over 1,500 miles to the northwest in Chkalov oblast', at a former Cossack settlement on the steppe called Sol-Iletsk. Genya did indeed take ill but was nursed back to health on a kolkhoz where she helped the director with correspondence and learned how to harvest grain. Eventually, she established written contact with an aunt who had been evacuated to Omsk and who invited her to come. Another journey of over 1,000 miles brought her and Manya to that southern Siberian city where they got jobs at a shipbuilding factory evacuated from Leningrad. It was there that they learned from the radio that their native Kiev had been liberated. Unusually, both girls' fathers survived the war, but not their mothers. Manya joined her father in Kiev; Genya reunited with hers in Rubtsovsk, a town in the southern Altai where the Khar'kov Tractor Factory that employed her father had been evacuated in 1941.[128]

Returns

Soviet evacuees—like most people displaced during the war elsewhere in Europe— wanted to go home. However, for them, as well as for citizens everywhere displaced by the conflict, going home was not a simple matter. All across Europe, the war had destroyed villages and homes and made it difficult for tenants to reoccupy their apartments.[129] In the Soviet Union, the fierce competition for the right to return home and its refusal in certain cases has given rise to suspicions among some historians of official anti-Semitism.[130] City dwellers were especially eager to return home in this country where the urban place of residence was privileged and permission to live in a major city was not easy to come by.

---

127. Grinberg, *Evakuatsiia v Kazakhstan*, 43–47.

128. USHMM RG-50.226.0008, Batasheva, part 6, 28:00–49:00.

129. See for example Leora Auslander, "Coming Home? Jews of Postwar Paris," *Journal of Contemporary History* 40, no. 2 (2005): 37–59; Annette Wieviorka and Floriane Azoulay, *Le pillage des appartements et son indemnisation* (Paris, 2000).

130. For a discussion of this issue, see Manley, *To the Tashkent Station*, 249–51.

Here none outdid Muscovites, seized by "suitcase moods" early on, as denizens of the most privileged city.[131] Already in December 1941, after the worst of the battle for the capital city was over, some started on the return journey despite the fact that the railroad administration was forbidden to issue tickets. Plenipotentiaries in Penza in central Russia reported in January 1942 that Muscovites had heard from relatives that they could come home, and so they filled the stations. Without permission, came a report from Riazan', one thousand people showed up at the railroad station every day trying to get to Moscow, 125 miles away. Similar reports came from cities both near and far—from central Russia's Yaroslavl' and Kalinin to Molotov and Sverdlovsk in the Urals.[132]

Even before the Red Army had pushed the German invaders out of Soviet territory, authorities began to allow "reevacuation," as returns were called, but insisted on controlling the process. First, the RSFSR Council of People's Commissars decreed that "only citizens organized to return" would receive a free ticket home.[133] Second, although villagers could reclaim their homes without obtaining a residence permit, restrictions applied to city dwellers. These could be quite stringent. In one case cited by Manley, the Voronezh city soviet "simply abolished all rights to previously occupied living space." Authorities elsewhere, faced with the prospect of a flood of returnees and a reduced housing stock, tried to impose expiration dates on tenants' rights or distribute living space to them from the pool of less-than-full accommodations.[134] As for Moscow, the city council decreed on June 2, 1944 that only those who had paid rent all along—in absentia, in wartime—and who could find their way back to the city within sixty days of receiving notice could reoccupy their former apartment.[135]

Urbanites expressed their desire to return in no uncertain terms. Take the indignant Dr. Roman Shakhnovich, a Kremlin physician, who until his evacuation to the Chuvash republic had lived in an apartment on the highly desirable Gork'ii Street. Shakhnovich wrote in November 1942 that his wife and sons had vacated the apartment to join him in evacuation. Sometime thereafter, he reports, his neighbor illegally (samovol'no) took over his apartment even though he had paid rent continually. When he sought to move home, city authorities asserted that he was still on assignment.[136] Reoccupying the family's

131. Manley, To the Tashkent Station, 240. According to G. A. Kumanev, forty-six of the sixty-five resolutions about reevacuation that the State Defense Committee and the USSR Council of People's Commissars adopted between January 3 and March 9, 1942 concerned Moscow. See Kumanev, "Evakuatsiia naseleniia iz ugrozhaemykh raionov SSSR v 1941–1942 gg.," in Zhiromskaia, Naselenie Rossii v XX veke, 2: 77.

132. USHMM RG-22.027, GARF, f. A-327, op. 2, d. 68, ll. 10, 13.

133. As cited in USHMM RG-22.020, GIAChR, f. 1263, op. 1, d. 81, l. 39.

134. Manley, To the Tashkent Station, 256–60.

135. USHMM RG-22.020, GIAChR, f. 1263, op. 1, d. 81, ll. 47, 52, 55.

136. USHMM RG-22.020, GIAChR, f. 1041, op. 1, d. 599, l. 206.

apartment proved difficult too for Esther Sigal, who returned to Kiev in September 1944 after spending three years in Kazakhstan. First she lived with someone named Kuik, then after two months she moved in with her sister Sheindl. Her son, Abram, who wrote regularly from his army unit in Tashkent and after November 1944 Hungary, urged her to invoke a "special decree" in her attempts to reacquire the apartment, adding that "I in my turn will try through my commanding officer." But four days short of 1945, he was still sending his letters to her c/o Kuik.[137]

Not everyone went home. Some had difficulty obtaining permission from their employers in evacuation. Others, such as the nearly 2,500 families of evacuees in Ulianovsk, continued to depend on the material assistance of resettlement authorities as late as 1947.[138] Many had no home to go to and, like the demobilized soldiers in the previous chapter, no surviving relatives. But some—it is impossible to determine how many—preferred to make a go of it where they were. After the war, the assistant director of the resettlement administration in the Bashkir ASSR reported that nearly 1,500 evacuees expressed a desire to remain on the kolkhozes (albeit out of nearly 30,000 originally sent there).[139] Enina Shteingol'ts and her parents, whom we left in Alma-Ata during the war, were called back to Minsk but refused to return to Belorussia because all their relatives had died. Her father became director of the bakeries of Alma-Ata. Enina's mother, having learned Kazakh and gotten on very well in their new place, became head of a school. She retired in 1968 and passed away in Alma-Ata in 1999.[140]

Thanks to the war and their evacuation, many Soviet citizens experienced their country in a new way. Although nerve-racking at the time, the experience could take on a romantic hue in retrospect. For those who were children, the wondrousness of the Soviet Orient created lasting images. Tseitlin's description cited above goes on at some length and includes aural as well as visual recollections—the rumbling of passing trains and the whistles of their locomotives, the measured roar of the cotton mill, the "mournful singing" of the muezzin calling the faithful to prayer, "the penetrating cries" of the donkeys, the nocturnal howling of jackals. Together the sounds "produced a peculiar symphony that no composer could have re-created," nor any impressionable youngster likely to forget.[141]

Whether evacuees perished, found new homes, or returned at the war's end, they confirm our observation that World War II is the central event of migration history in the twentieth century. When we add to them their military compatriots and the deportees to whom we turn in the next chapter, we see an entire nation on the move, and a state struggling

137. USHMM RG-31.089 Sigal Family Papers, 1920–1947, items 4–21.
138. USHMM RG-22.027, GARF, f. A-327, op. 2, d. 440, l. 229.
139. USHMM RG-22.027, GARF, f. A-327, op. 2, d. 441, l. 34.
140. Grinberg, Evakuatsiia v Kazakhstan, 46–47.
141. Tseitlin, "Kermine," 8

to fulfill myriad goals: protect the citizenry from occupation, salvage its productive capacity, and defeat the invading enemy.

Postwar Evacuees

Between 1948 and 1952, well over two hundred thousand convicts from the Gulag labored to build the Volga-Don Canal, one of the grandiose projects among the many that inundated farmland to expand water transportation and power generation in the postwar years. For over two centuries, Russia's rulers had dreamed of linking these two mighty rivers. Stalin made that dream a reality by drawing on a source of labor never more plentiful than in the immediate postwar years—prisoners in the camps and colonies of the Ministry of Internal Affairs (MVD)—supplementing them with laborers borrowed from kolkhozes.[142] Compared with earlier hydraulic feats, such as the notorious White Sea-Baltic Canal of the mid-1930s, the construction of the Volga-Don Canal did not cost many lives. Perhaps this is why it is far less well known.[143]

It did, however, displace whole villages, and the story of this displacement   evacuation by another name—can be pieced together from relevant documents. In July 1950, two years into the project, the director of the RSFSR's Resettlement Administration received a progress report from its Stalingrad office. Local authorities had fulfilled the target of moving some three thousand households by 100.2 percent, the report said. That was the good news. The bad news was that the construction of new housing lagged such that more than half of the householders were living in "summer kitchens" and temporary housing. Funds promised to the householders as compensation for the inconvenience of having to move "had been slow" in arriving, and, with six weeks to go before the beginning of the school year, eighty-four school buildings had yet to be erected. The report from Rostov oblast' two months later indicated a considerably higher proportion of families housed in new locations (88 percent) and only eleven school buildings unreconstructed. However, only 67 of 190 wells had been dug. By October, 80 percent of the six thousand families evacuated from Stalingrad oblast' had found new homes, but the quality of the homes was "poor"; as in Rostov, the construction of wells lagged behind ostensibly because the contractor lacked

---

142. Klaus Gestwa, "Auf Wasser und Blut gebaut: Der hydrotechnische Archipel Gulag," *Osteuropa* 57, no. 6 (2007): 255–56; A. I. Kokurin and N. V. Petrov, eds., *Gulag (Glavnoe upravlenie lagerei), 1918–1960* (Moscow, 2000), 447.

143. For a recent, full-blown account of the entire project, see Nikolai Ivanovich Buslenko, *Volgo-Don: Sliianie vod. istoriko-ekonomicheskie, sotsial'no-politicheskie ocherki stroitel'stva volgo-donskogo kanala, tsimlianskogo gidrouzla i irrigatsionnykh sistem Iugo-Vostoka Rossii: Dokumenty, kommentarii, memuary, belletristika v piati knigakh* (Rostov-on-Don, 2011).

funds to pay its workers, and merging with existing collective farms was proving more difficult than anticipated.[144]

Whether or not this story pleased higher authorities, it says nothing about the experience of the evacuees—Cossack families for the most part who had lived and farmed in the area for generations. State archives are not particularly rich in the voices of ordinary citizens, and so we have to rely on what local historians have been able to turn up. Nikolai Buslenko, who has put together a collection of "documents, commentaries, memoirs, and belles-lettres" on the project, quotes an old Cossack woman from a village perched on the shore of the Tsimliansk reservoir in Rostov oblast': "I stood on the bank and saw how the water rose to our garden—first the trunks of the trees went under the water, then their tops disappeared. . . . I'm not leaving, I am standing there and looking . . . and tears are flowing . . ." Buslenko adds, "The cemetery and the church sank beneath the surface. On a calm day, one of the churches is clearly visible under the water. It is said that priests conduct services on this spot; people gather in boats."[145] Reversing the practice of American developers who name housing estates after the natural features they have destroyed, the reservoir created by the dam bore the name of one of the Cossack villages that sank beneath its waters.

Even before the completion of the Volga-Don project, other dams were transforming the mighty Volga farther upstream. One of them, the Kuibyshev Hydroelectric Station (GES) required moving about ten thousand households from six districts containing 131 "populated points" including the city of Stavropol'.[146] Documents similar to those for the Volga-Don Canal can be found among the papers of the Resettlement Administration, but again to gain access to the topophilic response of residents, we must look elsewhere. In this case, we find at least an echo in *Avtograd*, a novel from 1994. Raised in a shoreline village that disappeared under the rising waters, the protagonist pays a visit in the early 1980s to his parents, who have been living in a ramshackle dwelling. During a stroll before dinner, his father, who worked on the dam project, unburdens himself by expressing deep regret for his failure to appreciate what the dam had destroyed: "the fish, the meadows . . . the old river beds, even towns." He then asks for forgiveness from the river ("*Matushka*") and the people displaced from their homes.[147] As at Tsimliansk, it is believed that a church is visible under water.

Between the time of Stalin's hydraulic projects and Mikhail Gorbachev's efforts to revitalize the Soviet system, Soviet citizens experienced relatively little displacement. The refugees and evacuees they encountered tended to be victims of war and famine that they saw

144. USHMM RG-22.027, GARF, f. A-327, Reel 1, op. 1, d. 76, ll. 5–6, 47–49, 58, 60, 79–87.
145. Buslenko, *Volgo-Don*, bk. 4: 383.
146. USHMM RG-22.027, GARF, f. A-327, Reel 1, op. 1, d. 91, ll. 29–30, 170–73.
147. V. P. Volochilov, *Avtograd: Roman* (Samara, 1994), 61–62. We owe to Kate Brown the observation that topophilia is an underappreciated sentiment in Russian history.

on television or read about from the Middle East, Africa, and Asia. Natural disasters, however, did unseat Soviet citizens during these decades. The 1966 earthquake in Tashkent temporarily displaced approximately fifteen thousand families to other cities in Uzbekistan and many children to Young Pioneer camps throughout the USSR.[148] In this instance as well as in northern Armenia, where an earthquake devastated the republic's second largest city in December 1988, most survivors remained within the immediate area, albeit in makeshift housing. The explosion of nuclear power reactor no. 4 at Chernobyl on April 26, 1986, by contrast, necessitated permanent evacuation.

The accident produced few victims in the short run.[149] That is because below a few hundred rems (roentgen equivalent in man), iodizing radiation takes time to work its way into the tissue and cells of the human body. Thousands of people in the affected region spanning today's Belarus and Ukraine thus carried the radioactive danger with them in their bodies when they were evacuated. An official government report from 1990 cited a figure of 116,000 evacuees. The Canadian scholar David Marples wrote that this figure did not include children, who were evacuated from a broader area than adults, so that the total number probably reached in excess of 500,000. A team of Belorussian scholars wrote in 2011 that 117,058 persons were evacuated from Belarus alone, with some regions far more affected than others.[150]

Evacuations began with the town of Pripiat', closest to the explosion and home to the nuclear-reactor workers, thirty-six hours afterward, and then included the rest of the villages and towns in a 30-kilometer radius. According to "testimony" cited by the nuclear power expert Grigori Medvedev, people being evacuated were told they "would be returning within three days."[151] Authorities ordered plant operators, farmers, and their families to pack up to leave, and city buses from Kiev carried them to regional villages, Young Pioneer camps, and Kiev.[152] Some, diagnosed with severe radiation poisoning, were sent on to sanatoria—in the case of one nuclear engineer and his family from Pripiat', traveling to

148. *Tashkent entsiklopediia*, ed. S. K. Ziiadullaev (Tashkent, 1983), 132–34.

149. Svetlana Alexievich, *Voices from Chernobyl* (Normal, IL, 2005), vii. According to a 1990 Soviet government report submitted to the United Nations, only thirty people died "as a result of the accident or of their work in dealing with its immediate consequences." However, it acknowledged many others "received high doses of radiation." International Atomic Energy Agency, Information Circular, INFCIRC/383, 24 July 1990, cited in "Seventeen Moments in Soviet History," www.soviethistory.macalester.edu (accessed April 10, 2014).

150. Dmitri Grigor'evich Lin, S. V. Sevdalev, and N. A. Baburova, eds., *Demograficheskie i sotsial'no-meditsinskie posledstviia chernobyl'skoi avarii na territorii Belarusi* (Gomel', 2011), 13; David Marples, *Social Impact of the Chernobyl Disaster* (New York, 1988), 31. For an assessment of the social consequences of the accident, see E. M. Babosov, *Chernobyl'skaia tragediia v ee sotsial'nykh izmereniiakh* (Minsk, 1996).

151. Gregori Medvedev, *The Truth about Chernobyl* (New York, 1991), 181–82.

152. Glenn Alan Cheney, *Chernobyl: The Ongoing Story of the World's Deadliest Nuclear Disaster* (New York, 1993), 79–80; Marples, *Social Impact*, 114–15.

Leningrad in a bus with lead plates over the windows.[153] Generally speaking, although clearly many people, especially villagers, were not cognizant of the dangers of radiation poisoning, the explosion and forced evacuation was ruinous for residents. In the months that followed, many in Belarus and Ukraine looked for children, relatives, and friends from whom they had been separated.[154]

People with children demonstrated a willingness—even an eagerness—to leave in order to protect their offspring. Indeed, some parents in Kiev (about 100 miles away by automobile) telephoned Pripiat' to have their children inscribed on the list of young people from that stricken town so that they could get to a Young Pioneer camp at a distance. Aneliya Perkovska, the secretary of the Pripiat' City Komsomol Committee, had the grim task of deciding which children could go to Young Pioneer camps and of assigning them to Camp Artek on the Black Sea or the less popular Young Guard camp. Because only children aged seven to fifteen could go, having finished grade two to grade nine, Perkovska was faced with parents who asked, "And the tenth graders—are they not children? And what do we do with the first grade?" She reported to *Komsomol'skoe znamia* the following year, "Naturally, I go ahead and write, without a twinge of conscience, a different year of birth for this boy."[155] In late May, all children from Kiev and northern Ukraine were evacuated to camps for the summer.[156]

The people of Pripiat', exposed to the most virulent levels of radiation (only outdone by the so-called liquidators who worked to destroy the buildings of uninhabitable areas), became pariahs. Until the disaster, these people considered themselves, and were looked upon by others, as privileged participants in a project of Soviet modernity.[157] Resettled in Kiev, the aforementioned nuclear engineer and his family got an apartment in a building set aside for refugees from Pripiat'—yet in the city they found that Kievans did not want to ride in the same elevator with them and that mothers warned their children that playing with a child from Pripiat' would cause them to go bald.[158] When Perkovska of the Pripiat' Komsomol collapsed from radiation sickness and went to the hospital, the staff warned against saying where she was from and advised her to name the more benign Taganrog or Kishinev. When she revealed her origins to two women, her tablemates in the hospital

---

153. Cheney, *Chernobyl*, 81.

154. *Molod Ukrainy*, January 1, 1987, reported "endless lines of people" searching for loved ones, Marples, *Social Impact*, 144.

155. Marples, *Social Impact*, 143, from *Komsomol'skoe znamia*, March 11, 1987.

156. Cheney, *Chernobyl*, 92.

157. Anna Veronika Wendland, "Visions and Foundations of the Atomograd Nuclear Technology, Urban Utopia, and (post-) Soviet Social Identities," unpublished paper presented at Second World Cities conference, Washington, D.C., April 2014, 6-8; see also Politik und Gesellschaft nach Tschernobyl, ed. Melanie Arndt (Köln-Wien, forthcoming).

158. Ibid., 82.

cafeteria, they fled and were replaced by women from the contaminated town of Chernigov, whom she called her "comrades in misfortune."[159]

The villagers who moved to another farm in the region had the least difficulty in finding work and a familiar routine, but some—especially the elderly—resisted evacuation. They demonstrate the love of home, as well as the importance of the Great Patriotic War in regional memory. Svetlana Alexievich writes that the Nazis destroyed 619 Belorussian villages, along with their inhabitants, and that after Chernobyl, 485 villages and settlements were lost, 70 of them buried. Her elderly interviewee Zinaida Evdokimovna Kovalenko recalled a couple who would "take their cow and go into the forest. They'd wait there. Like during the war, when they were burning down the villages."[160] Locals like the elderly survivor of the Battle of Stalingrad who got a respirator and stayed at home, turning off his lights at night to hide, were called partisans; this one was reported by his son only after the water supply was turned off. "I took one pensioner out on 20 May," reported one Komsomol instructor—over three weeks after the explosion.[161] The Estonian journalist Tonis Avikson reported in 1987 that "during the evacuation, many old women and men . . . fled to their home forest, concealed themselves in cellar nooks, lofts, cucumber salt water barrels, and even under firewood." Even when found and taken away, they left again in two or three days to be found, "sitting like a pair of cuckoos on a bench in front of their cottage," because they knew how to slip by control posts. They would implore the soldiers "do not take us away, sons. We are already old, and have seen everything in life. Even the Germans were unable to take us. . . . Let us at least die at home."[162] Years later, they would be joined by refugees from dangers more visible than radiation.

The Refugee Returns

"Refugees! That seemingly forgotten concept has become an everyday reality in Azerbaijan and Armenia," wrote a Soviet journalist in early 1989.[163] They would reappear with depressing frequency in the coming decade. The conflict over the sovereignty of the Nagorno-Karabakh Autonomous oblast', a region within the Azerbaijan SSR but with a majority of

---

159. Marples, *Social Impact*, 145.

160. Alexievich, *Voices from Chernobyl*, 1, 29.

161. Marples, *Social Impact*, 141.

162. Tonis Avikson, *Noorte haal*, August 13, 1986, quoted in Marples, *Social Impact*, 141–42. See also Brown, *A Biography of No Place*, 226–38; and Kate Brown, *Plutopia: Nuclear Families, Atomic Cities, and the Great Soviet and American Plutonium Disasters* (Oxford, 2013), 282–86.

163. Konstantin Mikhailov, "The Epicenter: Alarming Days in Apsheron," *Sobesednik*, no. 3 (1989): 6–7, trans. in *CDSP*, February 8, 1989, 4.

Armenians, marks the beginning of the return of refugees to Soviet space and the introduction to the ethnic homogenization of post-Soviet states. The conflict precipitated the mass exodus of Azerbaijanis to safer areas within Azerbaijan; that in turn led to pogroms against resident Armenians, which in turn sparked Armenian flight. The hundreds of thousands of Azerbaijani refugees went by military helicopters, airplanes, buses, trains, horseback, and on foot, sometimes over snowy mountain passes; the Armenians fleeing from Baku, the Azerbaijani capital, and other cities boarded ferries and airplanes.[164] Together they recapitulated the means of transportation that refugees and evacuees had used throughout the century.

These refugees and those who followed distinguished themselves from earlier wartime refugees in the century in two ways. First, they fled conflicts that were much more acutely defined by ethnicity than those of the great wars, although ethnicity did play a role in earlier displacements. Second, whole families fled, so that, unlike in wartime, women were not disproportionate among the refugees.[165] However, the displacements of the late 1980s and early 1990s resembled pre-Soviet movements in one crucial respect. Whereas the Soviet state earlier had claimed responsibility for identifying, transporting, and caring for evacuees— however poorly it executed these functions—people in harm's way now found no such protection. They, like their predecessors of the early twentieth century, were refugees.

Historians are still debating whether the incapacitation of the late Soviet state stemmed from rising nationalist fervor in the constituent republics or whether perceptions of a weakening central authority encouraged nationalistic fervor.[166] In our view, the best way to understand the interethnic clashes of this period is to recognize their interactive relationship with the decline of any supranational cohesive force. At first, the most vulnerable people in this respect were non-Russians living outside their titular territory, such as the above-mentioned Azerbaijanis and Armenians, and minority peoples in larger nationalizing states, like the Meskhetian Turks of Uzbekistan and the Ossetians of Georgia. In the scramble for political power and resources during the late 1980s, even the distribution of refugees became a volatile issue. For example, the rumor that thousands of refugees from Azerbaijan would be accommodated in Soviet Kyrgyzstan was sufficient to provoke disorder in its capital, Frunze.[167]

---

164. Ibid.; C. Litovkin and S. Mostovshchikov, "The Road to Nowhere," *Izvestiia*, January 17, 1989, 6, trans. in CDSP, February 13, 1989, 1. For the figures of 200,000 Azerbaijani and 350,000 Armenian refugees, see *Pravda*, September 20, 1991, 1–2.

165. Hilary Pilkington, *Migration, Displacement, and Identity in Post-Soviet Russia* (New York, 1998), 121–22; Moya Flynn, *Migrant Resettlement in the Russian Federation: Reconstructing "Homes" and "Homelands"* (London, 2004), 79.

166. Cf. Ronald Grigor Suny, *The Revenge of the Past: Nationalism, Revolution, and the Collapse of the Soviet Union* (Stanford, 1993); Mark R. Beissinger, *Nationalist Mobilization and the Collapse of the Soviet State* (Cambridge, 2002).

167. "Echo of Baku," *Komsomol'skaia Pravda*, February 13, 1989, 1, trans. in CDSP, March 21, 1990, 15.

Russians, too, became vulnerable. Numbering in excess of 20 million, the Russians out-side the RSFSR had already begun reducing their numbers before the dissolution of the Soviet Union. In the case of Armenia, a third had departed, and in Azerbaijan and Georgia a somewhat smaller proportion by 1988.[168] By 2005, at least half of the remaining Russians had departed from these three south Caucasian states as well as Tajikistan, while a quarter had left Uzbekistan, Turkmenistan, and Kyrgyzstan.[169] This increasing ethnic homogeni-zation put those of mixed nationality in an especially awkward position, forcing them ei-ther to change nationality or move.

With the dissolution of the Soviet Union, the borders of Soviet republics became interna-tional borders, complicating migration to the newly constituted Russian Federation. In Feb-ruary 1993, the Russian government distinguished among those leaving their homes involuntarily by passing two laws, one "On Refugees" and the other "On Forced Migrants" (*vynuzhdennye pereselentsy*), the latter referring to people of Russian nationality in possession of Soviet passports who could exchange them for Russian passports. In addition to mi-grants from what came to be called the "near abroad," refugees fled Chechnya, plagued by war beginning in 1994. By January 1998, registered refugees and forced migrants numbered almost 1.2 million but estimates of the total in-migrant population were as high as ten million.[170]

Russian migrants themselves relate a variety of pressures from the subtle to the overt. The sociologist Valentina Gritsenko, herself a forced migrant from Kazakhstan, sums up the shared experience of departure, reporting that neighbors helped them to pack and wished them a good trip, but nonetheless made no attempt to deter them. "They didn't drive us out; they didn't, thank goodness, shoot us in the back; but they didn't try to hold us back." Some reported mundane slights, like the single mother who arrived in Samara from Kazakhstan in 1998; nobody offered her a seat on public transportation when she was pregnant or later when she held a small baby.[171] A forty-five-year-old man who left Kyrgyz-stan in 1993 summed up the accumulating fatigue from such incidents:

I grew tired of proving to myself and others that people should be respected for their personal or professional qualities independent of the shape of their eyes, the length of

---

168. Korobkov, "Post-Soviet Migration," 71.

169. Heleniak, "An Overview of Migration," 53.

170. Korobkov, "Post-Soviet Migration," 70; Flynn, *Migrant Resettlement in the Russian Federation*, 1, gives the figure as 1.5 million as of 2001; Vladimir Nikitin, chairman of the Duma subcommittee on relations with compatriots and migration policy, gave a figure of 717,000 "officially registered" forced migrants in February 2002, in Elena Goliakova, "Zakonoproekt vynuzhdennykh pereselentsev stanet men'she?" *Rossiiskaia gazeta*, February 13, 2002, 6.

171. V. V. Gritsenko, *Russkie sredi russkikh: Problemy adaptatsii vynuzhdennykh migrantov i bezhentsev iz stran blizhnego zarubezh'ia v Rossii* (Moscow, 1999), 40; Flynn, *Migrant Resettlement in the Russian Federation*, 64.

their skulls, the color of their skin and hair; *I was tired of never forgetting that I am Russian, tired of constantly being on guard against offending anyone. . . . Stay for what?* Constantly feeling that not only was I not needed, but I felt like a leper.[172]

Russian psychologist Nadezhda Lebedeva theorized migration among those who "felt like a leper" as "above all, an attempt to escape from a 'zone of disrespect.' "[173]

Scholars have referred variously to these migrants as "children of empire," an "imperial minority," or a "stranded minority." Once avatars of empire, they embodied what the migration historian Leo Lucassen calls the "reversal of fate principle," similar to the *pieds noirs* of postcolonial France and the Hungarians left outside Hungary after the collapse of the Dual Monarchy.[174] Language became an important tool for excluding such intruding minorities. A middle-aged graduate from Kyrgyzstan attributed the "gradual squeezing out of management" and the replacement of Russians to the designation of Kyrgyz as the state language, for "at our age you can't learn the state language." Among eighty-three forced migrants surveyed in Orel oblast' in the mid-1990s, 45 percent cited the law on state language as a motivating ("push") factor. They named "poor ethnic relations," "everyday nationalism," and "personal safety" slightly less often. Concern about the "future of the children," mentioned by 72 percent of respondents, topped the list of factors.[175]

Overwhelmingly from urban areas in the former Soviet republics, most newcomers wound up in cities, notwithstanding the difficulties of obtaining the propiski that would allow them to work, reside, and establish citizenship in Russia.[176] As the bureaucratic bar to full fledged citizenship rose and fell, they utilized those longstanding migrant repertoires of joining kin who had moved before them, and of sending family members ahead to scout out opportunities for residence and employment. Some achieved remarkable

---

172. Gritsenko, *Russkie sredi russkikh*, 41 (italics in the original).

173. N. M. Lebedeva, *Novaia russkaia diaspora: Sotsial'no-psikhologicheskii analiz* (Moscow, 1995), cited in Gritsenko, *Russkie sredi russkikh*, 44.

174. Sergei Panarin, "Etnicheskaia migratsiia v postsovetskom prostranstve," in *V dvizhenii dobrovol'nom i vynuzhdennom: Postsovetskie migratsii v Evrazii*, ed. A. V. Viatkin, N. P. Kostomarskaia, and S. A. Panarin (Moscow, 1999), 62; Emil Payin, "The Disintegration of the Empire and the Fate of the 'Imperial Minority,'" in *The New Russian Diaspora: Russian Minorities in the Former Soviet Republics*, ed. Vladimir Shlapentokh, Munir Sendich, and Emil Payin (Armonk, 1994), 21–36; Robin Cohen, *Global Diasporas: An Introduction* (London, 1997), 190–95. Leo Lucassen in correspondence with the authors, August 8, 2013.

175. Pilkington, *Migration, Displacement, and Identity*, 129, 136. Cf. Panarin, "Etnicheskaia migratsiia v postsovetskom prostranstve," 41–43.

176. The Russian government abolished the propiska on October 1, 1993, but it survived in other forms established by regional authorities, or as Hilary Pilkington quipped, "The propiska is dead, long live the propiska" (*Migration, Displacement, and Identity*, 40).

success, and were profiled in the local and even national media as subjects with "happy endings . . . in the American style."[177]

At the same time, generally surpassing the host population in educational attainments, they often found it difficult to get along with the locals. Gritsenko, who surveyed them in Saratov and Volgograd oblasts, is not alone in citing evidence of their superior attitudes, rooted in their experiences in the near abroad and the conviction that "in Russia, family ties are less strong, family relations are less warm."[178] Those who, for whatever reason, wound up in rural areas had the hardest time adjusting, as one might have predicted. Natalia Kosmarskaia's fieldwork, conducted in 1994–95 in rural areas of Orel oblast', turned up a deep well of despair among forced migrants from the Caucasus, Kazakhstan, and Central Asia. "We never lived here [in Russia] before, and now we don't live—we exist," she was told by one. "Here, only the language is the same, everything else is different," said another. As for locals, they had had such limited contact with outsiders that their main point of reference toward these newcomers was the Great Patriotic War. To them, the migrants were "non-Russians" (nerusi), "refugees," "emigrants," and even "black assholes" (chernozhopia), an ugly racist term usually applied to people of color.[179]

As the century came to a close, the second Chechen war bred new refugees who poured over the border into Ingushetia, Dagestan, Stavropol' krai and beyond, trying the patience of local residents and stretching the resources of relief agencies. These were wartime refugees: primarily women, children, and the elderly. It was estimated in August 1999 that over 120,000 people had left Chechnya in search of safety. Neighboring Ingushetia initially absorbed most of them, many spending nights in cars, railroad stations, and under the stars because of a lack of housing. Outside Narzan, the capital (until 2002), "tens of thousands" resided in camps where the accommodation consisted of tents, train cars, and old Soviet automobiles. There, children attended makeshift schools learning adat, the Chechen customary law, and Shari'a, Islamic law imported by bearded young men recently arrived from abroad.[180]

Data from the 2002 census can be used to sum up a decade of the Russian Federation's absorption of forced migrants from the near abroad and its own internal refugees, primarily from the wars in Chechnya. Just over 20,000 forced migrants entered Russia in 2002, less than half the number who had arrived the previous year. That brought the total number

177. "V kholodnykh ob'iat'iakh: Provintsial'naia pressa o pereselentsakh," *Literaturnaia gazeta*, October 24, 2001, 4.

178. Gritsenko, *Russkie sredi russkikh*, 31.

179. N. Kosmarskaia, "Trudnosti adaptatsii pereselentsev v sel'skoi Rossii: Popytka kontseptualizatsii," in Viatkin, Kostomarskaia, and Panarin, *V dvizhenii dobrovol'nom i vynuzhdennom*, 223–31.

180. "Potok bezhentsev narastaet," *Nezavisimaia gazeta*, September 29, 1999; "Gumanitarnaia katastrofa?" *Moskovskaia Pravda*, October 8, 1999; Meier, *Black Earth*, 83–84.

of people registered in this category since July 1992 to a little over a half million. Kazakhstan accounted for 43 percent of the total, 24 percent came from the Central Asian states, and Chechnya sent another 13 percent. The remaining 20 percent originated in Georgia, Azerbaijan, North Ossetia, and the former Soviet republics in the Baltic. The Southern federal district contained more forced migrants and refugees—some 135,000—than any other, with North Ossetia and Ingushetia the most popular destinations. Both Orenburg oblast' (in the Volga federal district) and Omsk oblast' (in the Siberian federal district) accommodated over 20,000 forced migrants, overwhelmingly from neighboring Kazakhstan. At 4,500 and 7,800 respectively, Moscow and Leningrad oblasts were far behind.[181]

One of the great lessons of the twentieth century is the value that refugees and forced migrants might offer host societies. At least in some instances, local authorities were alert to the lesson. Take Tamara Khakimova Rasulova. Of Uzbek-Russian parentage, she was forced out of Tajikistan with her husband and took up residence in the town of Mikhailovka in Volgograd oblast'. Khakimova is an allergist—the only one in Mikhailovka. Indeed, according to the head of the local employment agency, "the city is filling up with such specialists who often are in short supply in big cities and never existed before in district centers such as our Mikhailovka—gastroenterologist, chest specialist, cardiologist, allergist, rhythmic dance instructor, philosopher, . . . and many other specialists." Refugees without higher education made other contributions. "Guys!" a local tractor driver cried out in vain to two mechanics recently arrived in Saratov oblast' from Kazakhstan, "Enough! Let's have a smoke!" But they were bent on plowing all night long, lest the field dry. The local then observed, "They're not normal. I don't know what to call it."[182]

---

181. Goskomstat Rossii, *Chislennost' i migratsiia naseleniia Rossiiskoi Federatsii v 2002 godu* (Statisticheskii biulleten') (Moscow, 2003), 138–41.

182. Gritsenko, *Russkie sredi russkikh*, 150, 154.

~CHAPTER SEVEN~

Deportees

"The feeling for my native land helped me endure any difficulty."
—N. N. Pavlov recalling his escape from "kulak exile" and
journey home as a thirteen-year-old boy

The act of deporting—literally, carrying off or away—is among the oldest, most widespread, and decisive measures a state can take against a group or an individual. As part of their "democratic revolution," the ancient Greeks developed the practice of ostracism (*ostrakophoria*) to eliminate the threat that prominent individuals posed to the stability of the polis.[1] The Romans preferred exile (*exsilium*), which could be either temporary or permanent. In the early modern era, overseas colonies provided the opportunity for authorities to disburden the metropole of the indigent, religious dissenters, criminals, and other unwanted individuals of both sexes. The British populated several of their North American colonies and, after 1783, Australia with such types; after 1848, the French exiled revolutionaries to Algeria and convicts to Guiana and New Caledonia. Convict transport also exported thousands across the Indian Ocean.[2] In the nineteenth century, the federal government in the United States took advantage of vast stretches of territory at its disposal to remove

---

1. Sara Forsdyke, *Exile, Ostracism, and Democracy: The Politics of Expulsion in Ancient Greece* (Princeton, 2005).

2. For an entrée into this literature see, for example, Clare Anderson, *Convicts in the Indian Ocean: Transportation from South Asia to Mauritius, 1815–1853* (Basingstoke, 2000); Anderson, "Gender, Subalternity, and Silence: Recovering Convict Women's Experiences from Histories of Transportation," in *Behind the Veil: Resistance, Women, and the Everyday in Colonial South Asia*, ed. Anindita Ghosh (New York, 2008); Emma Christopher, Cassandra Pybus, Marcus Rediker, *Many Middle Passages: Transportation and the Making of the Modern World* (Berkeley, 2007); Kristy Reid, *Gender, Crime, and Empire: Convicts, Settlers, and the State in Early Colonial Australia* (Manchester, 2007); Alan G. L. Shaw, *Convicts and the Colonies: A Study of Penal Transportation from Great Britain and Ireland to Australia and Other Parts of the British Empire* (Victoria, 1977); Stephen Toth, *Beyond Papillon: The French Overseas Penal Colonies, 1854–1952* (Lincoln, 2006).

Native American tribes from their homelands. Local police and vigilantes, acting at the behest of corporate executives, occasionally rounded up striking workers and their leaders for relocation, and during World War II, federal authorities infamously interned Japanese Americans in specially organized camps.

Deportation could mean, as it did in antique Greece, expulsion beyond the boundaries of the polity; but if the state is of sufficient size, as was Russia, people could be banished to peripheral areas, remote from the centers of power, privilege, and prestige. Political space in that case acquired hierarchical dimensions. Within Russian political space, as in all empires, deportees' destinations defined the bottom of the spatial hierarchy.[3] From its absorption into the empire in the seventeenth century onward, Siberia occupied this position. It served as an effective means of isolating and punishing obstreperous or merely unproductive serfs, religious heretics, common thieves, and political criminals. It was, in Andrew Gentes's phrase, Russia's "multi-purpose prison."[4] The Far North also saw its share of both common and political prisoners.

Later, in Soviet times, Kazakhstan and parts of Central Asia accommodated class enemies and entire nationalities forcibly resettled as punishment for betraying the socialist Motherland. Conversely, cities from which criminalized "elements" of the population were banned "occupied first place (with Moscow the supreme center) while rural areas and distant peripheries were relegated to lower status."[5] Part and parcel of what Judith Pallot and Laura Piacentini have identified as Russia's unusually well-developed "spatial exclusionary processes," these distinctions persisted beyond the 1917 Revolution and in fact were strengthened in Soviet times as a tool of social control.[6] Like their predecessors before the Revolution, individuals sentenced to terms of exile remained excluded from certain areas upon completion of their sentence. Exiled national groups required formal nullification of deportation orders. These came in the latter half of the 1950s for some, but not until the last years of Soviet power for others.

In this chapter, we focus on the process by which state authorities compelled both individuals and entire groups in Imperial Russia and the Soviet republics to abandon their homes and homelands to take up residence in exile, their movements, and their return. We confine ourselves to isolated places of exile in Imperial Russia and special settlements and colonies in the USSR rather than the entire prison system, and to their physically dislocative

---

3. Nick Baron and Peter Gatrell, "Population Displacement, State-Building, and Social Identity in the Lands of the Former Russian Empire, 1917–23," *Kritika: Explorations in Russian and Eurasian History* 4, no. 1 (2003): 97.

4. Andrew Gentes, *Exile to Siberia, 1590–1822* (Basingstoke, 2008), 167.

5. Baron and Gatrell, "Population Displacement," 95.

6. Judith Pallot and Laura Piacentini, *Gender, Geography, and Punishment: The Experience of Women in Carceral Russia* (Oxford, 2012), 49.

dimensions as opposed to the quotidian experiences of the labor camps about which both memoirists and scholars have written a great deal. Like the United States and Argentina, Russia had contiguous space to continue this practice well after other states had let go of it. But Russia deported more of its subjects and citizens over a longer period of time than any other state. We examine the reasons and the consequences.

Coercion shapes the deportee experience. Since coerced migrations are designed to separate the migrant from home—often definitively—this chapter emphasizes the tension between deportation and the desire to return.[7] Instances of escape, sending children home, or rejoining relatives illustrate deportees' understandably greater desire to recover agency than any of our other migrants. Topophilia, that fondness for a particular place or home-land, runs rampant among those whose departure is forced.[8] We will emphasize the jour-neys into exile and repertoires of return beginning with those who were sent to remote parts of the Russian Empire at the turn of the twentieth century and conclude with the last of the deported peoples to obtain official permission to return to their homeland, the Crimean Tatars, at the end of the Soviet era.

Deportees in Late Imperial Russia

Exile was a longstanding practice of the Imperial Russian state that Catherine the Great expanded to entrap tens of thousands of convicts and deportees in Siberia, New Russia, and the Far North. Punishment by exile sought to remove political opponents and criminals and to settle and secure the vast Empire and its borderlands. Unlike expulsion, where re-moval is the primary goal, the destination is key to the practice of deportation and exile.[9] By the beginning of the twentieth century, the fate of exiles had been well chronicled by both Russia's finest writers and by the Western press—from Fyodor Dostoyevsky and An-ton Chekhov to George Kennan, to signal the most famous.[10]

7. Charles Tilly defines coerced migration as "obligatory departure, forced severing of most or all ties at the origin, and little or no personal connection between the migrants and people at the destination." Charles Tilly, "Transplanted Networks," in *Immigration Reconsidered: History, Sociology, and Politics*, ed. Virginia Yans-McLaughlin (New York, 1990), 88.

8. Yi-fu Tuan, *Topophilia: A Study of Environmental Perception, Attitudes, and Values* (Englewood Cliffs, NJ, 1974), esp. 92–100, 113–28.

9. See, for example, Gentes, *Exile to Siberia*, 120, 174; and Nicholas Breyfogle, *Heretics and Colonizers: Forging Russia's Empire in the South Caucasus* (Ithaca, 2005).

10. Fyodor Dostoyevsky, *House of the Dead*, trans. H. Sutherland Edwards (New York, 1962). Chekhov vis-ited Sakhalin Island as an observant physician; see Anton Chekhov, *Sakhalin Island*, trans. Brian Reeve (Rich-mond, 2007). The best-known and most thorough English-language account is George Kennan, *Siberia and the Exile System*, 2 vols. (New York, 1891).

When Russia hosted the Fourth International Penal and Prison Congress in 1890, the US delegate expressed surprise because "alleged cases of cruel treatment of criminals and politicals" had been published (an allusion especially to George Kennan's widely read reports about his tour of the exile system and Siberia). Many delegates labeled transportation "inexcusable" as part of a punishment regime, while recognizing that France, like Russia, was still attached to exporting the citizens it understood to be dangerous. Nonetheless, delegates saw that there was great interest in prison reform in Russia—although there was no end in sight for exile.[11]

Several categories of deportees and exiles existed at the end of the nineteenth century. Most hard-labor convicts, judged by sovereign courts, worked far from home; penal colonists made their way where they were allowed, which was most often Siberia; exiles included people arrested for vagrancy (many recidivists and escapees among them) and large numbers banished by their village commune. Political offenders were relatively few in number but found in all the above categories. A large crowd of "voluntaries" consisting of accompanying spouses, children, and some parents joined the convicts, colonists, and exiles, who were primarily adult men.[12] Penal colonists lived with their family, and so could convicts once they had served their time.[13] It also was possible to settle under one roof with a new partner, but the location of that roof was up to authorities. Most important for our purposes: most prisoners and exiles were not allowed to return to their home region; rather, they were to stay and settle, colonizing the hinterlands of the Empire.

In 1882–85, nearly 73,000 exiles were counted, over 30 percent of them women and children who had accompanied the head of household. Kennan's count of the 15,776 exiles from 1885 tells us something about their demographic composition. Over 9 in 10 of hard-labor convicts, penal colonists, vagrants, and people exiled by their village commune were men. Women made up 1 in 7 of those exiled by judicial sentence or executive order, but were the clear majority of "voluntaries."[14] After the 1905 revolution, the number of

---

11. Caleb Randell, *The Fourth International Penal and Prison Congress, St. Petersburg, Russia* (Washington, DC, 1890), 12, 14; Galina Mikhailovna Ivanova, *Labor Camp Socialism: The Gulag in the Soviet Totalitarian System* (Armonk, 2000), 7. Bruce Adams observes that Western visitors to Siberian prisons were concerned with conditions for political prisoners, with whom they were sympathetic, rather than with the criminal population, and that they were ignorant of the condition of prisons in their home country and of the standard of living or travel conditions for most people in Russia. See Adams, *The Politics of Punishment: Prison Reform in Russia, 1863–1917* (DeKalb, 1996), 5–6.

12. Randell, *Fourth International*, 21; Ivanova, *Labor Camp Socialism*, 7; Kennan, *Siberia and the Exile System*, 1: 79.

13. For an 1897 case of the workings of convict status evolution, see Andrew Gentes, " 'Beat the Devil!' Prison Society and Anarchy in Tsarist Siberia," *Ab Imperio*, no. 2 (2009): 201–33.

14. Kennan, *Siberia and the Exile System*, 79–80. The figures for exile to Siberia are in about the same proportion for 1894, but 1894 figures are less useful here because they are not broken down by sex; there were that year 935 hard-labor convicts, 2,300 penal colonists, 1,111 vagrants, 2,674 exiled by village commune, 427 exiled by judicial sentence or executive order, 1,979 refused reentry to their commune, and 6,772 "voluntaries," for a total of 16,198; see James Simpson, *Side-Lights on Siberia: Some Account of the Great Siberian Railroad, the Prisons and Exile System* (Edinburgh, 1895), 198–99.

Figure 7   Exiles at work on the Amur railroad, *Aziatskaia Rossiia*, vol. 2 (St. Petersburg: A. F. Marks, 1914), 539.

subjects exiled to hard labor increased dramatically and continued to rise, reaching 21,000 by 1909.[15]

Arduous journeys took Russian subjects into exile. For those heading for the carceral spaces of Siberia, and especially beyond Lake Baikal, a voyage of at least three months by barge, railroad, and on foot was broken by stays in notoriously dirty and dangerous transfer prisons and stations called *étapes*. The completion of the Trans-Siberian Railroad as far as Irkutsk in 1898 considerably reduced exiles' exposure to disease and the elements as they journeyed to nearby Alexandrovsky, the penal settlement at Nerchinsk, and the gold mines at Kara.[16]

Sakhalin Island off the Pacific coast ranked as the most dreaded destination for prisoners because it was the most remote.[17] For that very reason, it had a promising future in penal terms. Officials saw Sakhalin as a more secure holding place for the exiled and criminal population, one that could reduce the presence of escapees that plagued Siberia. Russia had been sending convicts to Sakhalin since the 1860s and possessed the entire island by 1875, but plans for expansion would be interrupted by the 1904–5 Russo-Japanese War, when Russia was forced to cede the southern half of the island.

15. Ivanova, *Labor Camp Socialism*, 7–8.

16. Simpson, *Side-Lights on Siberia*, chap. 6.

17. See Gentes, " 'Beat the Devil' "; Gentes, "Sakhalin's Women: The Convergence of Sexuality and Penology in Late Imperial Russia," *Ab Imperio*, no. 2 (2003): 115–38; Kennan, *Exile to Siberia*. See also Benjamin Howard, *Prisoners of Russia: A Personal Study of Convict Life in Sakhalin and Siberia* (New York, 1902), esp. chap. 4, "The Reputation of Sakhalin," 57–68.

Nonetheless, this was such a promising location, yet so remote, that 800 prisoners at a time made the long journey. Convict ships picked up prisoners in Odessa, where they had been delivered by train, then sailed through the Suez Canal past Colombo on the west coast of Sri Lanka, Singapore, Nagasaki, and Vladivostok—the same route with the same ports of call as carried settlers to the Far East.[18] Male convicts traveled on a separate ship from female convicts, women "voluntaries," and children on this journey that required about two months—and had to be completed before October, when ice made the trip impossible. In March 1894, for example, the *Yaroslavl'* departed Odessa with 802 male convicts, arrived in Sakhalin in mid-May, and turned back to make another voyage between August and October. That summer, the steamship *Moskva* brought to Sakhalin women convicts and voluntaries in about equal number, along with their children. These 1,334 people (about 70 percent convicts, 10 percent women voluntaries, and 20 percent children) represent the total number of newcomers to Sakhalin that year.[19] At the beginning of 1896, the Russian population on the island consisted of about one-third free persons, nearly one-third convicts, and over a third exiled settlers and freed exiles.[20]

The journey of Semën Kanatchikov into exile may tell us more than any set of statistics. We left him as a young man who had been embraced by the community of patternmakers and distant relatives when he departed from Moscow for St. Petersburg in 1898. The next four years found him in prison for his political activities, exiled back in his home village, then in Moscow, and finally ordered to Saratov under police surveillance. After a hunger strike in Tsaritsyn over prison conditions, Kanatchikov was exiled in 1902 to the Far North for three years and began the long journey to an obscure village northeast of Arkhangel'sk. We are interested in the journey because, an integral part of the punishment regime, it exemplifies what so many other convicts would experience.

Kanatchikov's journey began without the political prisoner's privilege of books and other possessions, but rather in a locked railroad car with common criminals. The wagon would occasionally be uncoupled and pushed aside, then reconnected to another train in the night. It included two stops in prisons, then six days in the Yaroslavl'4 transit prison, where he shared a cell with common criminals and got to know how his fellow prisoners acted out their power, loves, and hatreds. By August, he was in Arkhangel'sk and in the

---

18. Harry de Windt, *New Siberia: Being an Account of a Visit to the Penal Island of Sakhalin, and Political Prison and Mines of the Trans-Baikal District, Eastern Siberia* (London, 1896), 9; Simpson states that the truth "lies between" messieurs Kennan and de Windt, in *Side-Lights on Siberia*, 195; the history of de Windt's rosy account discourages its use beyond a description of the shipping route. See Adams, *Politics of Punishment*, 6.

19. This total represents 942 convicts, 131 women voluntaries, and 261 children; Simpson, *Side-Lights on Siberia*, 143.

20. About 4,500 natives—Gilyaks, Tunguses, Orochons, and Ainus—lived on the island as well. Simpson, *Side-Lights on Siberia*, 273–74.

company of fellow political prisoners. Still a few hundred miles from his final destination, Kanatchikov and his small party departed on foot, accompanied by soldiers. Crossing rivers by ferry or fishing boat, they pressed on some 120 miles to Pinega. The police guard "apparently grew tired of this long, tedious task (in any case there was nowhere for us to flee)," so he gave the prisoners their papers and had them go on along with the driver in the "wildness and stillness." They eventually reached a village on the Pechora River founded by fugitives and religious schismatics, where political exiles made him welcome.

But the journey was not over: Kanatchikov pressed on in a covered mail boat for lack of land routes, with a village policeman pulling the boat and using the oars when the wind was right. He arrived at his destination on September 5, with the first snowfall, to live with a peasant family, having for company a few other political exiles. After two dark winters and heading into a third, Kanatchikov was freed in November 1904 and found his way by sled to Arkhangel'sk, to the railroad, and back to Saratov.[21]

As Kanatchikov's narrative illustrates, prisoners and political exiles were scattered in the least populated areas. Political opponents to the tsar faced repeated deportation, best recorded in the carceral careers of the Russian Social Democratic leadership. Julius Martov (Iulii Osipovich Tsederbaum), who would become leader of the Menshevik wing of Russian Social Democracy, served a five-month sentence in Petersburg's Kresty Prison (1893), then two years of administrative exile in Vilna. In January 1896 he was again arrested, held for a year in prison, and then sentenced to three years of exile in Siberia. Martov served this sentence in Turukhansk, a settlement of 250 inhabitants on the Enisei River, described by his biographer as "at the end of nowhere." Martov himself characterized the town as "God-forsaken in all respects." He shared his misfortune with three other political exiles, two of whom he found congenial.[22]

Lev Davidovich Bronshtein, who would become known as Leon Trotsky, received in 1900 a sentence of four years' exile to eastern Siberia with fellow leaders of the South Russian Workers' Union. The prisoners traveled to Irkutsk by rail, then drifted down the river Lena, "the great water route of the exiled," with barges of convicts and a convoy of soldiers, heading for the small settlement of Ust-Kut. After a few months he, along with his wife and first child, was able to relocate to a marginally better town where, he wrote, "we had friends." Thanks to sympathetic peasants and friends he escaped in 1902, carrying a passport bearing the name by which history knows him.[23] Seven years later, Trotsky

21. Kanatchikov, A Radical Worker in Tsarist Russia, 347–79.

22. Israel Getzler, Martov: A Political Biography of a Russian Social Democrat (Cambridge, 1967), 37; Iu. V. Martov i A. N. Potresov: Pis'ma 1898–1913, ed. I. Kh. Urilov (Moscow, 2007), 27.

23. Leon Trotsky, My Life: An Attempt at an Autobiography (New York, 1970), 123–25; Isaac Deutscher, The Prophet Armed: Trotsky, 1879–1921 (New York, 1965), 55.

received the more severe penalty of exile in perpetuity to a settlement near the mouth of the Ob River within the Arctic Circle. Describing the month's journey, he wrote "every day we descend one degree farther into the kingdom of cold and barbarism." The destination—a thousand miles from the nearest railroad and with spotty postal communication—was sufficiently foreboding to inspire escape. Informed by knowledgeable locals, he took off due west over roadless terrain to arrive at a rail connection in the Urals, and thence to St. Petersburg.[24]

Josef Stalin's carceral travels are well known: exile north of Irkutsk in 1903, a journey that took over a month; deportation in 1908 to Solvychegodsk, a little settlement in northern Vologda, a three-month trip, and a return visit in 1910 to the same hellhole; and then in 1913 consignment to northern Siberia.[25] Like many other travelers in constrained conditions, Stalin contracted typhus. He also escaped repeatedly. The February Revolution liberated Stalin. He went west with the waves of political exiles and released prisoners, "fêted all the way."[26] Thousands of people joined this wave. On March 17, the Provisional Government declared an amnesty that freed over 88,000 prisoners, of whom 1 in 15 was a political prisoner. An additional 14,000 prisoners found their way out without proper authorization. In April 1917 the Provisional Government abolished exile and granted to released prisoners the right to choose their place of residence.[27] It seemed that exile was at an end.

Deportees from World War I to Collectivization

From the outbreak of World War I in 1914, forced migrations served as a blunt instrument for state authorities to round up aliens from enemy nations. Not only did France, Germany, Austria, and Britain all incarcerate and restrict enemy nationals, but faraway Australia did too, and with their entry into the war in 1917, so did Brazil and the United States. Whatever plans foreign nationals may have had, regimes took the lead. Among these regimes, Russia deported over 255,000 enemy subjects from cities and strategically sensitive areas,

---

24. Trotsky, My Life, 190–97.

25. In one of many cruel ironies of history associated with Stalin, peasants branded as kulaks would be deported to this little settlement in 1930 as the Soviet state prosecuted collectivization. For the case of one family, ethnic Germans from the Volga German Autonomous Soviet Socialist Republic, see Anna Molchanova and Anna Novkova, " 'Vse bylo, bylo, bylo . . .': Sud'ba sem'i spetspereselentsev iz Nizhnego Povolzh'ia," in Puti sledovaniia: Rossiiskie shkol'niki o migratsiiakh, evakuatsiiakh i deportatsiiakh XX veka, ed. Irina Shcherbakova (Moscow, 2011), 79.

26. Isaac Deutscher, Stalin: A Political Biography (Oxford, 1972), 56–58, 102–3, 108–11, 122–25, 129–31; quotation on 131.

27. Ivanova, Labor Camp Socialism, 10.

assigning them to internment camps and other faraway locations.[28] Eric Lohr argues that Russia's deportations differed from others because enemy nationals, while marginal elsewhere, played crucial roles in the prewar economy, so "the stakes and potential impact of a campaign against enemy aliens were much greater in Russia." Moreover, the campaign against enemy aliens quickly became much more—a movement to expel and expropriate the property of naturalized immigrants and members of certain ethnic groups who had been born within the Empire.[29] Fueled by the perceived economic dominance of Germans and Jews, the campaigns began with the first battles in Galicia.

Subjects of Germany were first in line as forced migrants (*vyselentsy*). From the beginning of the war, the army's Chief of Staff N. N. Ianushkevich concerned himself with deportation, issuing orders "to clear all enemy subjects *without exception* from areas near the front."[30] In 1914 alone, 68,000 enemy subjects were deported eastward by train to camps and other locales in Penza, Simbirsk, Kazan, and Viatka provinces. By early 1915, even women and children were cleared from Volhynia and the Baltic provinces, and by the summer not only from areas under military administration but also from a broader set of exclusion zones.[31] Poles and other Slavs also could be categorized as enemy aliens, but their requests for exemptions often had more success than those of Germans, Jews, Turks, or Hungarians.[32]

With 1915 came a shift in focus: Germans who were subjects of Imperial Russia became targets, less as security risks than as property owners. According to a decree from June 1915, "German colonists owning land and other immovable property as well as landless, urban residents registered with colonist communities are subject to obligatory deportation *at their own expense* to locations outside the theater of war."[33] Over 420,000 Germans in the Polish provinces and at least 100,000 urban Germans faced deportations. Rural and urban

28. This minimal figure is from the railroad administration; it does not include people who traveled on their own to avoid traveling under guard or those deported from areas occupied by Russia in wartime; the number of enemy subjects deported or expelled is roughly 300,000. Eric Lohr, *Nationalizing the Russian Empire: The Campaign against Enemy Aliens during World War I* (Cambridge, 2003), 127–28. For a local case of Germans in England, see Laura Tabili, *Global Migrants, Local Culture: Natives and Newcomers in Provincial England, 1841–1939* (Houndmills, 2011).

29. Lohr, *Nationalizing the Russian Empire*, 3.

30. Ibid., 124.

31. Ibid., 124–25, 127–28. For the establishment of the zone extending as much as 150 versts (160 km) from the borders with Germany and Austria-Hungary, see the decree of February 2, 1915, in Istoriia rossiiskikh Nemtsev v dokumentakh (1763–1992 gg.), ed. V. A. Auman and V. G. Chebotareva (Moscow, 1993), 38–40.

32. Lohr, *Nationalizing the Russian Empire*, 127.

33. V. F. Dizendorf, ed., *Nemtsy v istorii Rossii: Dokumenty vysshikh organov vlasti i voennogo komandovaniia, 1652–1917* (Moscow, 2006), 573 (emphasis added). An internal military communication from October 1915 indicated that the decree applied only to able-bodied males of draft age in areas threatened with invasion (575).

Germans submitted a flood of petitions for exemption—along with requests to define the "German colonist"—and received only vague replies that these were people of "German descent."[34] Persistence and determination in the face of rail shortages and war marked the effort to clear Germans from the western front, an effort that lasted until the February Revolution of 1917. Imperial authorities settled refugees on land vacated by German deportees, requiring them to share their harvest with the state. Some 40,000 newcomers took advantage of this arrangement in Volhynia province after the deportation of "in excess of 200,000 German settlers" in 1915.[35]

One resident of Volhynia recalled his village being awakened about midnight as armed police stormed homes, three entering his house and ordering his family out of bed to leave for Siberia. "While the police were crowding us to finish packing, they ransacked our cupboards, chests, bins—and even the sacks and bags we already had packed. They took anything that pleased them. . . . They even seized our wedding rings." Everyone, including children, pregnant women, and old people, was herded into cattle cars without heat, toilets, or water.[36]

Although denied choice of destination as of summer 1915, deportees from the Polish provinces, the Baltic region, Ukraine, and Bessarabia sought out German communities in the Volga and elsewhere. Others, like the nearly 12,000 residents of the Girshengof farming community in Eastern Livonia (the Estonian province of Kurland), found themselves farther east—in Perm in the Urals.[37] And some "were unceremoniously shipped to Siberia or central Asia, in a brutal foretaste of the horrors inflicted upon the next generation under the Stalin regime."[38]

The violent expulsions of Jews from the western front regions stemmed from the prevailing belief in the army that Jews, Russian subjects or not, were fundamentally disloyal. This attitude went unchecked by civilian authorities as Jews faced persecution and expulsion from the Pale of Settlement through which the army passed in attack and then retreat in the spring of 1915. At first, the expulsions had a sporadic character, but in April 1915 a mass operation began emptying out whole districts and provinces. The 150,000 Jews of Kovno province, for example, departed within two weeks. Because authorities only counted those boarding trains and because the period of mass deportations was relatively brief, we can only guess at how many Jews left the region. Estimates vary from a half million to a million.[39]

----

34. Lohr, *Nationalizing the Russian Empire*, 130–32.

35. Gatrell, *A Whole Empire Walking*, 24; Lohr, *Nationalizing the Russian Empire*, 130–32.

36. M—r, in *Heimatbuch des Deutschen aus Russland* (1962), 35–36, cited by Fred Koch, *The Volga Germans in Russia and the Americas, from 1763 to the Present* (University Park, PA, 1977) 243–44; Lohr, *Nationalizing the Russian Empire*, 135–37.

37. Lohr, *Nationalizing the Russian Empire*, 135–37, 155.

38. Gatrell, *A Whole Empire Walking*, 24.

39. Lohr, *Nationalizing the Russian Empire*, 137, 138, 143.

Where did these displaced Russian subjects go? They left the Pale of Settlement (which would be abolished in August 1915) and moved east to a string of provinces from Mogilev and Chernigov in the north to Poltava, Ekaterinoslav, and finally Taurida on the northern Black Sea coast.[40] From Poltava, according to an account from October 1914,

> Several groups of Jews have been incarcerated and expelled in stages to Siberia. The Governor requested that the military send all those who had been administratively exiled, appeared unreliable, or were suspected of spying. This order was interpreted loosely to include even those who had rights of passage or who voluntarily had arrived in Poltava province to join the heads of their families.[41]

So we see the replacement of "the old-style anti-Judaism . . . seeking to keep Jews isolated in the Pale of Settlement" by "the new-style anti-Semitism" identifying Jews "as *politically and militarily unreliable.*"[42]

How to understand these developments? Peter Holquist argues for their modernity, made possible by the mid-nincteenth-century invention of military statistics. People thereby became "elements"—some more reliable than others, some more expendable than others. This approach found broad application in the Russian Empire's expanding colonial territories, but Russia was no exception. The French in Algeria and the British in South Africa also practiced this brand of population politics with Russian observers observing. "The First World War," Holquist notes, "re-imported colonial practices of violence back to their homeland, Europe. . . . The emergence of total war mobilization, breaking down the traditional barrier between the military and the civilian realms, vastly extended preexisting practices of violence into domestic civilian spheres."[43] Indeed, the deportation of every German colonist, including children and invalids, from some areas testifies to the uncompromising determination to define people on the basis of ethnicity and to separate them from their property and livelihoods. Many other groups, in addition to Germans and Jews, would be defined in this way and forcibly removed in the years to come.

The Russian Civil War provided ample opportunity to perpetuate these practices. Both Reds and Whites at least contemplated mass expulsions. In 1920, Soviet military units cleared about nine thousand Terek Cossack families from nine settlements to punish them

---

40. Ibid., 137–42.

41. USHMM RG-22.018M Personal Archives of Meer [Khaimovich] Bomash, member of State Duma, 1908–1917, GARF, f. 9458, op. 1, d. 169, l. 49. This is a long letter from N. Shtif to the Petrograd-based Jewish Committee for Assistance to Victims of War, dated October 24, 1914.

42. Peter Holquist, "To Count, to Extract, and to Exterminate: Population Statistics and Population Politics in Late Imperial and Soviet Russia," in *A State of Nations: Empire and Nation-Making in the Age of Lenin and Stalin*, ed. Ronald Grigor Suny and Terry Martin (Oxford, 2001), 124.

43. Holquist, "To Count, to Extract," 112, 123.

for throwing in their lot with the Whites and to enable some twenty thousand Chechens to return to the region from which the Cossacks had deported them some fifty years earlier—in short, "a form of anticolonial reparation" as Terry Martin has described it. Grigorii Ordzhonikidze, then of the Military Revolutionary Committee and head of the Bolsheviks' Caucasian Bureau, issued an order "to load onto convoys and send to the north the entire male population from eighteen to fifty years old." Judging from the sources we consulted, "the north" turned out to be Arkhangel'sk province for some and the Donbas coal mines for others. In subsequent years local authorities reported periodic attempts by the Cossacks to move back, prompting additional expulsions.[44]

We should distinguish between expulsions and deportations, for in this early period Soviet authorities concerned themselves far more with the removal of people from a particular area—expulsions—than their settlement somewhere else. Whether Cossacks in the Caucasus or Russian peasant settlers in Turkestan and Kazakhstan, the main point was getting them out so that previous occupants of the land could reoccupy it. Where the expellees went was of secondary importance. It remained so throughout the rest of the decade. Pavel Polian's handy list of "repressive forced migrations in the USSR" contains only two additional entries for the 1920s. One refers to the "philosophy steamer" carrying 160 anti-Bolshevik intellectuals to Germany in 1922. The other, from the middle of the decade, concerns former noble estate owners.[45]

The exiling of former landlords was a curious affair. Discussion in the Central Executive Committee's Presidium of the draft law in 1925 reveals considerable disagreement. When Valerian Kuibyshev began describing how the operation would proceed (first near the borders, then those occupying important administrative positions, then those residing illegally), Petr Smidovich interrupted him to say,

> We already have started doing this. . . . We have 10,000 to 12,000 families, the majority of which are regulated. In cases where they have been expelled, they are bereft, and sit at railroad stations with nothing but the clothes on their backs. . . . The economic

44. N. F. Bugai, "20–40-e gody: Deportatsiia naseleniia s territorii Evropeiskoi Rossii," *Otechestvennaia istoriia*, no. 4 (1992): 37–41; N. F. Bugai and A. M. Gonov, *Kavkaz: Narody v eshelonakh (20–60-e gody)* (Moscow, 1998), 83–88; Terry Martin, *The Affirmative Action Empire: Nations and Nationalism in the Soviet Union, 1923–1939* (Ithaca, 2001), 61; Pavel Polian, *Against Their Will: The History and Geography of Forced Migrations in the USSR* (Budapest, 2004), 59–60.

45. Polian, *Against Their Will*, 327. The expulsion of landlords did not appear in the earlier Russian edition. See also the more elaborate list in N. L. Pobol' and P. M. Polian, eds., *Stalinskie deportatsii, 1928–1953* (Moscow, 2005), 789–98. On the philosophers' expulsion, see V. G. Makarov and V. S. Khristoforov, eds., *Vysylka vmesto rasstrela: Deportatsiia intelligentsii v dokumentakh VChK-GPU, 1921–1923* (Moscow, 2005); Lesley Chamberlain, *Lenin's Private War: The Voyage of the Philosophy Steamer and the Exile of the Intelligentsia* (New York, 2007).

significance of these measures is minimal and the political effect is negative. Why sow panic? All this plundering and confiscation will pervert our authority. Let us turn the matter over to the GPU, which has lists of the most harmful elements and expels them without simply throwing them out on the street.

Another member of the presidium disagreed with Smidovich, contending that the adoption of the law would reassure peasants that the restoration of landlords' authority is impossible. Still another presidium member argued for the exemption of those who had fought on the side of the Bolsheviks during the Civil War.[46]

It is difficult to get a handle on how many landlords were expelled according to the law because central authorities did not collect such data, and, it seems, nobody has had the perseverance to examine all the relevant provincial files. Nor is it clear if expropriation—which clearly was of greater importance to the authorities—necessarily meant the departure of the former landlord. Some moved out as intended by the legislation; some appealed, postponing their departures; and some apparently transformed themselves into game and forest wardens, horse breeders, or whatever was required to stay on. In comparison to what kulaks would face in just a few years, the whole process seems gentle and humane. In the Moscow region, landlords were given a month's notice and if they could not find lodging in that time, the period was extended. In some cases, local peasants petitioned successfully to allow a landlord to remain. Among the 220 liable for expulsion in Moscow province before 1927, only 45 in fact were expelled, while in Smolensk only 215 of 665 families departed.[47] When the campaign concluded at the end of 1928, it had removed only about a third of the more than 10,000 families liable to expulsion.[48]

We also should mention the expansion of the security apparatus's powers—OGPU—in 1928 to expel speculators and currency traders from Moscow. This included banishing such individuals to specific locations after they completed their sentences in labor camps if the security police still considered them "socially dangerous." Both the regular police and the security forces exercised surveillance of individuals expelled from urban areas or deported to a particular locale, but did not dictate the nature of these people's employment or source of livelihood. That power would only come with the establishment of the system of special

46. RGAE, f. 478, op. 7, d. 3176, ll. 2–5.

47. I. N. Lozbenev, "Vyselenie byvshikh pomeshchikov iz mest ikh prozhivaniia v regionakh tsentral'noi Rossii v 1925–1927 godakh," *Rossiiskaia istoriia*, no. 1 (2009): 83; John Channon, "Tsarist Landowners after the Revolution: Former *Pomeshchiki* in Rural Russia During NEP," *Soviet Studies*, no. 4 (1987): 575–98. Channon claims that "almost all the former pomeshchiki designated for expulsion by the guberniya [provincial—LS/LM] commissions lodged complaints . . . during 1926" (588).

48. See also V. A. Sablin, "Sud'ba pomeshchikov v vologodskoi derevne v 1920-e gody," *Vologda: Krae-vedcheskii al'manakh* 4 (Vologda, 2003), http://www.booksite.ru/fulltext/4vo/log/da/8.htm (accessed March 17, 2013).

settlements and the power of the security organs to send large numbers of both rural and urban inhabitants to them during the First Five-Year Plan.[49]

Soviet authorities did not rely on compulsory migration otherwise during the 1920s because they were optimistic about recruiting voluntary settlers to fill the empty spaces they saw as essential to developing the country's abundant resources. Potential recruits included peasants from overpopulated regions, demobilized soldiers, the urban unemployed, and "political emigrants" from abroad. Immigrants, however, represented a threat as much as an opportunity. Koreans, who by 1926 numbered over a quarter of all rural inhabitants in the Vladivostok region, are a case in point. In Terry Martin's analysis, Soviet military weakness in the Far East plus concern about Japanese influence on Korean immigrants caused a distinct loss of optimism. Prompted as well by expressions of concern from the regional party apparatus, central authorities issued a decree in December 1926 to resettle the majority of Koreans who rented rather than owned land north of Khabarovsk and to replace them with presumably more reliable Slavic peasants from central regions.[50]

The plan remained secret and dormant, however, partly as a result of intense opposition from Korean Communists. The Council of People's Commissars revived it in April 1928, this time beginning with "voluntary resettlement of individual Korean families" to prepare the ground for "mass processing of resettled Koreans in 1929."[51] Another problem reared its head—the difficulty of finding replacements. In fact, according to Nick Baron and Peter Gatrell, the entire approach to colonizing remote regions suffered from a shortage of recruits. Baron notes in his own work on Soviet Karelia that "the most significant constraint on the region's development plans was its critical shortage of labor." Perhaps more housing and other infrastructure at destination would have persuaded more people to move, but without sufficient numbers of people to build these structures, this was not going to happen. In this context, "plans for the coercive colonization of the North" formulated by the OGPU gained adherents.[52]

49. Paul Hagenloh, *Stalin's Police: Public Order and Mass Repression in the USSR, 1926–1941* (Washington, DC, 2009), 51–52, 143–45.

50. Martin, *Affirmative Action Empire*, 318–19; Michael Gelb, "An Early Soviet Ethnic Deportation: The Far-Eastern Koreans," *The Russian Review* 54, no. 3 (1995): 394–95.

51. See Pobol' and Polian, *Stalinskie deportatsii*, 37–38; Lohr, *Russian Citizenship*, 166 emphasizes the law's application only to non-citizens. A draft resolution of July 1930 calling for the development of a general plan to move all Korean families into the interior "within the next few years" implies that little had been done up to this point (Pobol' and Polian, 38). After resettling about 1,300 families (including 431 by force) in 1930, authorities abandoned this plan. See Terry Martin, "The Origin of Soviet Ethnic Cleansing," *The Journal of Modern History* 70, no. 4 (1998): 841.

52. Baron and Gatrell, "Population Displacement," 97; Nick Baron, *Soviet Karelia: Politics, Planning, and Terror in Stalin's Russia, 1920–1939* (London, 2007), 52, 74; Brown, *A Biography of No Place*, 91. The OGPU (1923–34) was absorbed within the Commissariat of Internal Affairs (NKVD) in July 1934.

Meanwhile, the Ukrainian Council of Ministers had decided that the western border-lands needed "the fastest possible economic recovery," and that this would require the re-moval of "citizens identified as socially dangerous" within 14 miles of the border. This resolution from November 1929 and others soon to follow played a crucial role in the tran-sition from the relatively voluntary migration of the 1920s to the dominance of coercive migration regimes during the 1930s. On the one hand, the resolution stipulated that re-settlement contingents should be formed "on a voluntary basis." It also instructed Ukraine's Commissariat of Agriculture to provide loans and other assistance to poor fami-lies to help them settle in the Siberian taiga. On the other, it called on the commissariat to "adopt the necessary measures to stimulate applications by these families to resettle (im-pact of taxes, etc.)."[53]

The hybrid character of this demographic displacement reminds us of the untidiness of any migration typology. We might just as well have included it in our chapter on "resettlers"—the term, after all, used by this resolution and subsequent directives. But, as Kate Brown has argued, plans for economic and cultural improvement on the one hand and for mass deportation on the other formed part of the same axis. Having failed to dislodge "back-wardness" from the people inhabiting this particular borderland once known (in Polish) as the kresy, Soviet authorities decided, in her words, that "the people who inhabit the place of rural, backward persistence must be moved instead."[54] The Politburo's decision in March 1930 to deport 3,000 to 3,500 "kulak families in the first instance of Polish nationality" from Belorussia and 10,000 to 15,000 such families from Ukraine already indicated which way the axis had tilted.[55]

Special Settlers: Dekulakized Peasants

Even during the 1920s when the Soviet government relied primarily on the recruitment of settlers to colonize and develop the resources of remote regions, it was laying the founda-tions for an alternative migration regime. This included legislation in 1922 permitting ad-ministrative exile for terms up to three years and the drafting of plans to use penal labor in mining operations in Siberia, Sakhalin Island, and Kazakhstan. In 1928, the commissar of justice, N. M. Ianson, recommended the expansion of the OGPU's labor camps to accom-modate much larger numbers of prisoners, especially for the northern timber industry.

---

53. See RGAE, f. 5675, op. 1, d. 23a, ll. 41–42, cited in Pobol' and Polian, *Stalinskie deportatsii*, 39–40. For a communication from the Ukrainian agriculture commissariat to the central commissariat in Moscow from April 1930 that maintained the voluntary principle, see ll. 43–44, cited in *Stalinskie deportatsii*, 43–44.

54. Brown, *A Biography of No Place*, 83, 91.

55. Pobol' and Polian, *Stalinskie deportatsii*, 41–42.

These recommendations formed the basis for a joint report (by the Commissariats of Justice and Internal Affairs as well as the OGPU) that the Politburo used in its decree of June 1929 calling for an expanded camp system.[56]

Yet, that large numbers of peasant families would wind up in special settlements (spetsposëlki) was not part of any plan. Peasants labeled as "kulaks" filled these scttlements, supposedly because they had hired labor or otherwise exploited their fellow villagers. "The timing of dekulakization was . . . fortuitous," notes Lynn Viola.[57] The process of dekulakization followed from decisions made in late 1929 and early 1930 to frighten peasants into compliance with collectivization by having some within their midst identified as kulaks, confiscating their property, and banning them from collective farms. This strategy of promoting collectivization via dekulakization rested on the ostracism—the physical removal—of a portion of each community. Also part of the strategy was holding local authorities responsible for meeting quotas and making those with the courage to oppose the persecution of individual families liable for exile themselves as kulak supporters. But this in turn presupposed having places to send the ostracized, places to which nobody would voluntarily go but that held promise as sites to develop in the service of the national economy.

The places these millions would inhabit and initially build themselves, called special settlements, remained "unchartered territory" until the 1990s when survivors began to come forward to tell their stories and historians began to piece them together with archival sources.[58] Many accounts emphasize the haste and arbitrariness of the process of identifying and deporting kulaks. The historian Tat'iana Slavko, for example, provides an excerpt from the protocols of a general assembly held in the Urals village of Kostyleva in January 1930 that contained the following reasons for deporting five residents: "intentional destruction of livestock," "impeded ongoing activities of the soviet," "was a policeman," "agitated against kolkhozes, grain and hay procurements, and milk contracts," "organized troops against the Soviets." There is no mention whatsoever of the standard Soviet criteria for identifying kulaks. No less significantly, the only one of the five the assembly considered "socially not dangerous" and exempted from deportation was the organizer of troops against the Soviets. Generally, to fulfill quotas mandated from above, to

---

56. Ivanova, *Labor Camp Socialism*, 18; Viola, *Unknown Gulag*, 58–59.

57. Viola, *Unknown Gulag*, 59.

58. Ibid., 3–4. Viola points out that even Aleksandr Solzhenitsyn "was unable to document that other part of the Gulag archipelago that housed the special settlers." "Special settlements" first appeared as an official category in a resolution of the RSFSR Council of People's Commissars of December 16, 1930. Documents before this date refer to "kulak settlements" or "labor colonies." For one of the first publications of archival documents, see N. V. Teptsov, "Ssyl'nye muzhiki: Pravda o spetsposelkakh," in *Neizvestnaia Rossiia, XX vek* (Moscow, 1992), 1: 184–268.

get rid of unpopular villagers, or to avoid any whiff of liberalism, such assemblies applied the kulak label so generously that they inevitably included middle and even poor peasant families.[59]

It is not hard to find such instances in other sources, and even the occasional oddity such as in the village of Topki in the Central Black Earth oblast' where reportedly only kulak families signed up to join collective farms.[60] Collectivizers may have thought that dekulakization would drive those they spared into the collective farms, but it is now generally accepted that the overall effect of linking dekulakization to collectivization was counterproductive in economic terms. The expulsion of a lot of competent and hard-working farmers sabotaged whatever chances there were of making the collective farms work. At the same time, we recognize that the greatest injustice was not that the wrong people were sent packing, but that any family had to endure the trauma of expulsion from their home, dispossession of their property, and an arduous journey aboard sealed and overcrowded trains to some wretched location in the middle of nowhere.

The Politburo resolution of January 30, 1930 mandated deportations of family members of first-category kulaks ("counterrevolutionary kulak activists") who were either incarcerated in GULAG camps or executed, and the more numerous second-category "kulak activists" with their families. Third-category kulaks, deemed relatively harmless, were dislodged but not deported. Authorities targeted a total of some 150,000 families in the second category—30,000 to 35,000 from Ukraine; 25,000 from Siberia; 20,000 from the North Caucasus; 10,000 to 15,000 from the Central Black Earth, Lower Volga, Urals, and Kazakhstan each; and slightly lower figures for the Middle Volga and Belorussia. The Northern krai, rich in timber but poor in lumberjacks, would get 70,000, nearly half of all the exiled families; Siberia, the Urals, and Kazakhstan would absorb 20,000 to 25,000 each.[61] An exception, notable for its portent of actions later in the decade, was made by the Politburo in a special directive ordering the clearance of 15,000 "counterrevolutionary and kulak elements" from the region bordering on Poland. In this case, deportation applied to

59. T. I. Slavko, *Kulatskaia ssylka na Urale, 1930–1936* (Moscow, 1995), 55–56. For a typical report about "leftist excesses" in the form of exiling middle and even poor peasants (in western Siberia), see Danilov, Manning, and Viola, *Tragediia sovetskoi derevni*, 2: 360–64. For changing criteria in identifying kulaks, see I. I. Klimin, *Rossiiskoe krest'ianstvo v zavershaiushchii period sploshnoi kollektivizatsii sel'skogo khoziaistva (1933–1937 gg.)* (St. Petersburg, 2012), 340–42.

60. See the compilation of letters from peasants to the newspaper *Sotsialisticheskoe zemledelie* from the end of March 1931 in Danilov, Manning, and Viola, *Tragediia sovetskoi derevni*, 3: 106–7. See also letters in Teptsov, "Ssyl'nye muzhiki," 218, 222, and the excerpt from the diary of a teacher and Komsomolets sent to guard some dekulakized peasants about to be deported: "By what they said it emerged that they were middle peasants. . . . What was this? Bungling, a distortion of the class line, or had there been some kind of directive?" N. A. Ivnitskii, *Sud'ba raskulachennykh v SSSR* (Moscow, 2004), 39–40.

61. Viola, *Unknown Gulag*, 22–23.

all three categories of kulaks and those of Polish nationality were to receive special attention.[62]

Just as with "kulak," so Soviet authorities ascribed ethnic identity. Scholars have been emphasizing for some time now that the Soviet state assigned nationality as a means of rendering populations legible, ascribing to them different degrees of political reliability irrespective of people's own sense of belonging or "national indifference." The inhabitants of the kresy in the western borderland often discovered their Polishness when told by officials they were Poles; similarly, Tajiks brought to the lowlands because authorities thought these Persian speakers could best represent Sovietness vis-à-vis Iranians on the other side of the border were among many groups in Central Asia who "did not know their own nationality."[63]

Between January and early May 1930, slightly less than 100,000 families (with a total of more than 500,000 members) were exiled—two-thirds beyond their native region. By the end of 1930, some 46,000 families had been sent to the Northern krai, a little over 30,000 ended up in the Urals, and 27,000 were received by Siberia. A second and larger wave of kulak exile occurred in the summer of 1931. This time, the North took fewer families compared with the Urals, Kazakhstan, and especially western Siberia. Approximately a quarter of a million families—over a million people—were deported to special settlements all told, with, again, two-thirds traveling beyond their native region. Thus, the totals of peasants exiled for the two years reached in excess of 380,000 families (1.8 million people).[64]

How did they get to their prescribed destinations? "They came with two sledges in the middle of the night," wrote A. M. Cherkasova in 1989, referring to the "purge" of her family from a recently formed kolkhoz in eastern Ukraine in 1930 when she was nine. "They threw all of us out of the hut, loaded us up, and took us away from the village." They lived for six months in a hut with two other families a few miles from the village, but then carts arrived to take everyone to the station. N. N. Pavlov, exiled as a thirteen-year-old boy from Belorussia to the Urals, recalled being taken with his parents on a cart "with two armed policemen for our guards" to a collection point at a railroad station. On the way, they came across

---

62. Brown, *A Biography of No Place*, 106–7. See also Martin, *Affirmative Action Empire*, 320–21, for evidence of the popular identification of Poles with kulaks and the embarrassment of "hundreds of Poles, including many communists . . . fleeing across the Polish-Soviet border."

63. "National indifference" is from Tara Zahra, "Imagined Noncommunities: National Indifference as a Category of Analysis," *Slavic Review* 69, no. 1 (2010): 93–119; Brown, *A Biography of No Place*, 21–23; Botakoz Kassymbekova, "Humans as Territory: Forced Resettlement and the Making of Soviet Tajikistan, 1920–38," *Central Asian Survey* 30, nos. 3–4 (2011): 361. For "did not know their 'true' nationality," see Francine Hirsch, "Toward an Empire of Nations: Border-Making and the Formation of Soviet National Identities," *The Russian Review* 59, no. 2 (2000): 210.

64. Cf. Danilov, Manning, and Viola, *Tragediia sovetskoi derevni*, 2: 415, 747; Viola, *Unknown Gulag*, 32; Ivnitskii, *Sud'ba raskulachennykh*, 42, 71.

other carts carrying "unfortunates like us."[65] In these and most other cases when special settlers traveled beyond their own region, authorities sent them on convoys of converted boxcars equipped with primitive stoves. Known as teplushki, these were the same vehicles that transported both voluntary settlers and labor-camp-bound prisoners to their respective destinations in the 1930s. In the succeeding decade teplushki also conveyed both evacuees and national contingents of special settlers. Indeed, it is hard to imagine any of these operations occurring without such means of transportation.

The standard convoy transporting dekulakized peasants to the special settlements in the early 1930s consisted of 44 cars, each accommodating forty people, eight goods wagons, and one fourth-class wagon for OGPU personnel. Each car had an appointed elder and an assistant, the only ones permitted to leave the train at stations to obtain food and water. The doors of the cars had to be shut tightly when the convoy was stationery; otherwise, they could be open five to six inches for ventilation. "When and how we were loaded into the wagons, I don't know," wrote V. T. Slipchenko, another who experienced deportation as a child. "We traveled for a long time, endlessly. It was always dark in the wagon. . . . Everyone slept sitting on the floor. We ate bitter-tasting bread that was green with mold and disgusting cabbage, poured water from a common bucket, and draped a cloth in the corner for a latrine. The pain, the stuffiness, and the stench often threw us into oblivion."[66]

Oblivion, as Michel Foucault famously pointed out with respect to carceral practices derived from late eighteenth-century penal reforms, is exactly where state authorities wanted their charges to be. The intent of incorporating transportation into the regime of generalized punishment—of using "geography as punishment"—seems obvious.[67] Sensory deprivation and disorientation thus emerge as the stock in trade of Benthamite-inspired techniques for inducing detachment from one's previous self and the beginning of a new identity. Such a motivation may have inspired the system of penality that functioned during the heyday of the GULAG with its emphasis on the individualization of punishment. The problem with assuming it also applied to the exiling of kulaks and for other groups of class- or nationally defined deportees is that the very same conditions also existed for groups whose geographic displacement the authorities did not consider punitive, such as wartime evacuees.

Most letters sent by deportees during their journeys into exile that authorities intercepted were merely informational—"I hasten to inform you that we are all by the grace of God alive and well," wrote someone named Kurman; "We have been on the road for six days," wrote Marusia, "and everything so far is all right, twice a day we are given hot water and at each

65. Teptsov, "Ssyl'nye muzhiki," 214; Slavko, Kulatskaia ssylka, 154.
66. Slavko, Kulatskaia ssylka, 71.
67. For the use of geography as punishment, see Pallot and Piacentini, Gender, Geography, and Punishment.

station they check the wagons to see who is ill and once a day hand out borshch." Shakhva-rotov, writing back to the northern Caucasus, even urged his Polina to give all her property to the kolkhoz in the name of "building the collective life." These authors may well have suspected their letters would be read by authorities. Others nevertheless poured out worry and bitterness. "We still don't know where they are taking us," wrote an unidentified deportee. "I am sorry that I don't know for what our family is being exiled." "They keep us in the wagon like animals," wrote Grigorii Shkaruba, "not letting us look out and always crying 'close the doors.' "[68] This sounds a lot like what Slipchenko recollected.

In this manner, 715 convoys transported over a million people plus thousands of horses, wagons, plows, and harrows to sites in the Far North, the Urals, Siberia, and Kazakhstan during the years 1930–31. Typically, upon disembarking exiles found themselves in remote locations, "pencil points on a map," as Viola calls them.[69] In the Northern krai alone, 189 such points, each presided over by an autocratic commandant, became settlements by the end of 1930. "People . . . here turn into wild animals," wrote an anonymous "settler" from a settlement near (but probably not very near) the northern town of Kotlas in 1930. "A person cannot remain a person in such conditions."[70] Cherkasova described the place where she was deposited—in the Urals near the Chusovoi River—as "wild, uninhabited, surrounded by taiga, mosquitoes, [and] midges, where a few, poor quality goods were distributed by list." They cut timber and floated the logs downstream but first had to use what they cut to build the "special" settlement. For food they collected linden leaves and baked cakes, supplementing their diet with what they could obtain from begging at nearby settlements.[71]

Data from October 1931 indicate the regional division of labor among special settlers. Forestry predominated in two areas—the Northern krai, where nearly all of the approximately 143,000 settlers serviced that industry; and the Urals, in which 293,000 people, or slightly over half, did so. Agricultural "colonization" claimed 176,000 or over 60 percent of the special settlers in western Siberia, with the remainder distributed among forestry, coal mining, and metallurgical enterprises. Forestry pulled in a third of the special settler population in eastern Siberia, and nonferrous metallurgy about a quarter, while in the Far East the proportions were nearly two-thirds in nonferrous metallurgy and slightly over one-third in forestry. Finally, in northern Kazakhstan just under half were involved in railroad construction and a little over a third were associated with coal mining.[72]

68. N. N. Pokrovskii, ed., *Politbiuro i krest'ianstvo: Vysylka, spetsposelenie 1930–1940*, 2 vols. (Moscow, 2006), 2: 887–88.

69. Viola, *Unknown Gulag*, 75.

70. Ivnitskii, *Sud'ba raskulachennykh*, 62; Teptsov, "Ssyl'nye muzhiki," 211.

71. Teptsov, "Ssyl'nye muzhiki," 215.

72. Pokrovskii, *Politbiuro i krest'ianstvo*, 2: 320–23.

Special settlers evidently moved around quite a bit from one village to another, both to alleviate isolation and boredom and to engage in sometimes life-saving exchanges of goods. The existence of hybrid settlements in which men commuted to mines and other industrial sites while women, children, and the elderly remained behind to cultivate garden plots complicates the neat distinctions between economic sectors we have just noted. Kapitalina Ogloblina's family, exiled from the outskirts of Briansk to a special settlement in Perm oblast', exhibited a variation on this theme. While her two older brothers went off to fell timber, her father worked as a bookkeeper and her mother taught in a primary school.[73]

Transfers of settlers within this "other archipelago" and between camps in the GULAG system and special settlements also occurred, in effect, a second coerced migration. In 1935, for example, the NKVD boss Genrikh Iagoda informed officials in Tajikistan of the impending arrival of two thousand special settler families to supplement the settlers recruited within the republic to expand cotton cultivation. About a quarter would be coming from camps in Central Asia, another quarter from Karaganda in Kazakhstan, and half from locations yet to be determined. The settlers would constitute "nonstatutory agricultural artels"—an intermediate category between special/labor settlements and collective farms that was becoming increasingly popular with security officials. A later communication from February 1936 indicated that the least economically viable settlements in Stalingrad krai would provide the other thousand families.[74]

Some special settlers—sources at our disposal do not yield precise numbers—wound up at large construction sites. Stephen Kotkin describes one such special labor settlement located about 435 miles south of Cherkasova's wild, uninhabited locale. Set up in 1931 behind barbed wire, the settlement became a largely self-contained district of Magnitogorsk. By 1933 four other such settlements, all together inhabited by some thirty thousand dekulakized peasants, existed within the expanding town limits. Eventually, the barbed wire was removed and some exiles, apparently with official permission, moved outside the boundaries of the settlements to live with relatives.[75] The White Sea-Baltic Canal, built largely by Gulag inmates during the First Five-Year Plan, relied heavily on special settlers to colonize the region and construct new ports, shipbuilding facilities, lumber mills,

---

73. Kseniia Zviagina and Margarita Lavrova, "Zhivaia istoriia: Stranitsy zhizni Kapitaliny Petrovny Oglovlinoi-Aksenovoi," in Shcherbakova, Puti sledovaniia, 41.

74. Pokrovskii, Politbiuro i krest'ianstvo, 2: 45–46, 431–32, 444. On the development of cotton production in the Vakhsh Valley, see Sh. I. Kurbanova, Pereselenie: Kak eto bylo (Dushanbe, 1993), 76–77. See also Kassymbekova, "Humans as Territory," 360. A decree of the Council of People's Commissars in September 1938 transformed all nonstatutory artels into regular kolkhozes. See V. N. Zemskov, Spetsposelentsy v SSSR, 1930–1960 (Moscow, 2003), 53. "Other archipelago" comes from Lynne Viola, "The Other Archipelago: Kulak Deportations to the North in 1930," Slavic Review 60, no. 4 (2001): 730–55.

75. Kotkin, Magnetic Mountain, 133.

Table 7.1 Population of special settlements

Region	Jan. 1, 1932	Jan. 1, 1933	Jan. 1, 1934
Urals	484,380	365,539	300,313
Siberia	357,566	319,473	362,987
Kazakhstan	180,708	140,383	134,579
Northern krai	120,509	112,266	79,537
Other*	173,859	204,423	195,130
Total	1,317,022	1,142,084	1,072,546

Source: N. A. Ivnitskii, *Sud'ba raskulachennykh v SSSR* (Moscow: Sobranie, 2004), 75.
*Far Eastern krai, Central Asia, Ukraine, Nizhegorod krai, North Caucasus, Leningrad oblast', Middle Volga, Bashkiria, Belomorsk-Baltic Canal

and railroad lines. About twenty settlements accommodated dekulakized peasants from as far away as Ukraine and Azerbaijan.[76]

In July 1931, the Politburo resolved to halt mass deportations of peasants.[77] Although, as we discuss below, substantial numbers of coerced migrants would continue to arrive, the population of the settlements declined from one year to the next (See table 7.1). The excess of deaths over births—an average of 78,000 for the years 1932–34—explains only some of the decline. After 1934, recorded births actually surpassed deaths for each year of the remainder of the decade. Transfers of minors and the elderly to relatives back home, the provision after 1938 of passports to enable those reaching the age of sixteen to work and study elsewhere, and other ameliorative acts contributed. But far more significant was the excess of escapees over those caught and returned—nearly 125,000 on average during 1932–34. Although after 1937 returned runaways exceeded those escaping, the numbers were relatively small and the differences slight.[78] These trends, which continued through the 1940s, suggest improvement in the living conditions of the special settlements and a stabilization of their population after 1933.

The extraordinary extent of flight—over half a million people during the years 1932–34, or about one in six of all special settlers—hints at the intolerable conditions in the

76. See V. Ia. Shashkov, *Spetspereselentsy v istorii murmanskoi oblasti* (Murmansk, 2004), 120–24; Pokrovskii, *Politbiuro i krest'ianstvo*, 2: 95–96, 426–29, 430–31. For a history of the canal project, see Cynthia Ruder, *Making History for Stalin: The Story of the Belomor Canal* (Gainsville, 1998).

77. Oleg V. Khlevniuk, *The History of the Gulag: From Collectivization to the Great Terror*, trans. Vadim A. Staklo (New Haven, 2004), 19.

78. Zemskov, *Spetsposelentsy v SSSR*, 20–21, 71–72. The figures for returned runaways include those who "returned voluntarily" as well as those who were caught.

settlements.[79] It also implies that escape was not that difficult. As in the case of Siberian exiles during the tsarist era, authorities counted on the settlements' isolation rather than carceral structures or the presence of guards to deter runaways. But so determined were many of the condemned not to succumb to the state's coercive migration regime that they pursued their own repertoires.

People escaped from the special settlements early and often. They escaped individually and in groups. Able-bodied young people predominated among escapees. Some who were caught and sent into exile a second time found a way to escape again. According to one report from the assistant director of the OGPU in the Urals, kulaks intending to escape obtained false documents from relatives and the local population, or fashioned them themselves, forging the signatures of commandants.[80] "The flight of kulaks is our main scourge," admitted Rudolf Austrin, the head of the OGPU in the Northern krai, in a report from September 1930. Figures from October show that more than 29,000 had escaped from settlements in his region, although more than half had been caught. This was a significantly higher rate of apprehensions than in western Siberia, where of 12,000 runaways only 30 percent were caught. In some districts, one almost wonders why anyone remained in the settlements at all. Of the nearly 9,000 people who had arrived in the spring of 1930 in one police district about 250 miles northeast of Omsk, only 1,246 were left by August. So unpopular was the Narym territory, some 250 miles up the Ob River from Tomsk, that 23,400 of the 28,400 sent there had escaped by the autumn of 1930. The OGPU offered bounties to informers and punished escapees with penalties up to confinement in labor camps, but the hemorrhaging remained heavy until conditions in the settlements improved toward the middle of the decade.[81]

Where did they go? In most cases it is not possible to answer this question because runaways tried to avoid detection by authorities, and we depend heavily on official sources. Heavily, but fortunately not entirely. In recent years, individuals and civic societies have published accounts of deportees who escaped and survived. Among them is Tat'iana Timofeevna Malakhveeva, whose odyssey back to her village in Voronezh oblast' followed four years of exile in the Northern krai. Only sixteen, Tat'iana traveled alone through the taiga, covering hundreds of miles on foot and by boat. Reaching Kotlas, she was approached by two policemen on the docks. She grabbed her knapsack and fled. When she returned to

79. For a discussion of the settlements' living conditions and their gradual improvement during the 1930s, see Slavko, Kulatskaia ssylka, 88–114; Klimin, Rossiiskoe krest'ianstvo, 426–49.

80. Pokrovskii, Politbiuro i krest'ianstvo, 2: 943. The report was from August 1930.

81. Klimin, Rossiiskoe krest'ianstvo, 530–45; Sergei Krasil'nikov, Serp i molokh: Krest'ianskaia ssylka v zapadnoi Sibiri v 1930-e gody (Moscow, 2003), 161, 163; (from April 1932) Pokrovskii, Politbiuro i krest'ianstvo, 2: 551–53. Klimin argues that the figures for runaways are likely to be lower than the true numbers because commandants whose reports are the main sources had an incentive to underreport escapes.

the harbor, they were gone, and she boarded a steamer for Vologda, 300 miles to the south-west. Although the police did not check documents at embarkation, they did during the journey. Tat'iana leapt from the upper to lower deck, hiding among the ship's cargo and then in the toilet until the coast was clear. Her luck seemed to run out in Vologda, though. Seized by the authorities, she was taken to an orphanage. Fortunately for her, it only accepted small children. She once again escaped the clutches of the police, bought a ticket on the train to Moscow, and again hid in the toilet to avoid the authorities. In Moscow she spent a night sleeping on a park bench—it was August—then took a train to Riazan'. Her money ran out, but two peasant women gave her the necessary amount for a ticket to Voronezh; after another night on another bench, and the intercession of a kindly cashier, she boarded the train, the last leg of her journey. Malakhveeva found work feeding rabbits in a sovkhoz, obtained a residency permit in 1935, and married several years later. She lost her husband to the Soviet-Finnish War, spent most of the Great Patriotic War living about 50 miles east of Voronezh in evacuation, and only several years after the war ended, began to experience something like a normal life with her second husband. Her peregrinations remind us once more of the multiplicity and variety of individuals' migratory repertoires.[82]

Mikhail Akimov wanted to go home too, but did not succeed. His is a story of the long-term, adverse consequences of defying the special settler regime. Exiled in 1931 from Rostov oblast' to a special settlement in the Urals, nineteen-year-old Mikhail worked with his father Artëm at logging. In 1933 both his father and mother, Dar'ia, died. Alone, he escaped from the settlement in January 1934, "because," as he later told the authorities, "I wanted to go home, as I had received a letter [telling me] that things were good at home and I would be accepted into the kolkhoz." He made it to a town north of Perm, from where he took a train to Sverdlovsk, winding up in a village south of the city. He "escaped again" (from what is not clear), but was caught at a railroad station almost 200 miles south of Sverdlovsk. All in all, he had been on the run for three months. The records show that Mikhail was sent to a mining settlement in Kirov oblast', where he married and had a son in 1937. Viktor Berdinskikh, the historian who found the Akimov file, reproduces another document from it: a letter dated January 27, 1941 that Mikhail's mother—who did not die after all in 1933 but returned home that year—wrote to Soviet president Mikhail Kalinin. Describing herself as "an old woman of sixty-six and without any family," she requested that her son be permitted to return home to look after her. This request went unfulfilled because the authorities back in Rostov oblast' assured the NKVD that as a "member of the family of a kulak," Mikhail had been "exiled correctly." Moreover, the NKVD wondered why his mother had been allowed to leave the special settlement in the first place.[83]

82. Alina Kartavtseva, "Dolgoe vozvrashchenie domoi," in Shcherbakova, *Puti sledovaniia*, 61–73.
83. V. A. Berdinskikh, *Spetsposelentsy: Politicheskaia ssylka narodov Sovetskoi Rossii* (Moscow, 2005), 244–47. Mikhail Akimov was freed from the special settlement in 1947.

The pull of home is undeniable in these accounts as it is A. L. Zaerko's edited collection of stories by thirty-four Belorussian peasants who also escaped from special settlements during the 1930s. Their journeys by train started out in towns in the Far North and Urals like Arkhangel'sk, Kotlas, Syktyvkar, and Molotov; passed through Vologda, Kirov, Gor'kii, Leningrad, and Moscow; and terminated in the Belorussian cities of Vitebsk, Minsk, and Orsha. All headed in the same direction and that direction was toward home. Their reasons for escaping—the hunger, the cold, the begging, the deaths of others including in the im-mediate family—are depressingly similar. They express gratitude to the strangers who fed them, gave them shelter, drove them in carts, ferried them across rivers, and hid them when local activists, the police, or the OGPU came around. But when they did reach their own district or village, they more often than not did not return to their own home—which they found either occupied by another family or too dangerous—and so they moved in with rela-tives or merciful neighbors.[84] As Viktor Zemtsov points out, readjusting to life outside the special settlements was not easy, and nostalgia for those left behind in exile was not the only reason why during the 1930s "tens of thousands" eventually turned around and went back.[85]

We can conclude with N. N. Pavlov, also from Belorussia. When we last left young Pav-lov, he was in a cart on his way to the railroad station with his family soon to be deported to a special settlement in Sverdlovsk oblast' on the Siberian side of the Urals. While his par-ents grew weak with fatigue and illness, he traveled from one village to another within the region of his family's confinement begging and doing odd jobs. He sometimes heard peo-ple singing "pessimistic songs" such as the one with the words:

From my native land I am deprived	Стороны родной лишился
From honest peasant labor.	За крестьянский труд честной.
Oh, I will die, and they will bury me,	Ох, умру, похоронят меня,
And my family will not know	И родные не узнают,
Where my grave will be.	Где могилка моя.[86]

But Pavlov's parents did not want their youngest child to die far from home and so ar-ranged for him to escape with a woman who had been deported from a village a mere 4 miles from his own. Because "patrols operated at all the train stations of the northern

84. A. L. Zaerko, *Pobegi iz ada* (St. Petersburg, 2003). We thank Andrey Shlyakhter for recommending this source.

85. Zemskov, *Spetsposelentsy v SSSR*, 67.

86. Slavko, *Kulatskaia ssylka*, 156–57. The song "Akh, ty, dolia moia, dolia" is attributed to Sergei Sinegub, a revolutionary populist who went to the people in 1874 as part of the Chaikovskii movement. For three vari-ants, see http://a-pesni.org/popular20/ahtydola.htm (accessed March 27, 2013).

railroads" to catch runaways, the two escapees chose a southern route. They hired a coachman to drive them to Tiumen', a distance of about 75 miles. From there they headed by train
not west but east toward Omsk; only after reaching that city did they turn west, passing
through Kurgan, Cheliabinsk, Ufa, and Kuibyshev. Their money eventually ran out and so
they took to begging. Upon reaching the city of Bobruisk in Belorussia, less than 45 miles
from home, Pavlov's traveling companion abandoned him, claiming his parents had not
given her enough money. For a while, he carried luggage for railroad passengers to earn
enough to hire a driver. With still some 12 miles to go, the driver learned where he had been
and why, and drove him the rest of the way for nothing.[87]

Labor Settlers: "Déclassé Elements" and Ethnic "Kulaks"

The special settlements, fruits of collectivization, began to resemble collective farms especially after the Politburo's decision to end the mass deportation of kulaks in July 1931 led to
efforts to sustain and stabilize the existing population. These included the provision of
substantial plots of land, seed, and tools for vegetable gardens; the right to purchase draft
animals and to build individual housing; and tax relief.[88] At the same time, the population
of the corrective labor camps run by the Gulag swelled, doubling between 1930 and 1933.[89]
Earlier, in 1930, the OGPU Special Department head Iagoda had advocated converting
camps into "colonization settlements" to lower costs and improve labor output. In late
1932, he and Matvei Berman, director of the Gulag administration, returned to this idea,
envisioning a new system of labor settlements in western Siberia and Kazakhstan that
could accommodate as many as two million new settlers engaged in agriculture, fishing,
and craft production.[90]

Intended as a practical solution to a crisis, the plan also bore the stamp of an ideologically inspired flight of fancy whereby the state assumed the authority to move people wherever it thought appropriate and under whatever conditions it deemed necessary. The final
version of the plan, approved by the Politburo in March 1933, scaled down the number of
settlers by half, largely, it seems, because of practical objections raised by the western Siberian territorial party leader Robert Eikhe. Ultimately, 268,000 people were deported. Camp
and prison inmates, transferred to relieve pressure on those institutions, constituted half

---

87. Slavko, *Kulatskaia ssylka*, 157.

88. Khlevniuk, *History of the Gulag*, 20–21.

89. For the law of August 7, 1932, see Danilov, Manning, and Viola, *Tragediia sovetskoi derevni*, 3: 453–54.
On the increase in prison and labor camp population, see Khlevniuk, *History of the Gulag*, 37.

90. V. P. Danilov and S. A. Krasil'nikov, eds., *Spetspereselentsy v zapadnoi Sibiri, 1930–1945*, 4 vols. (Novosibirsk, 1994), 3: 264–65.

of the new settlers.[91] "Kulaks and other saboteurs of grain procurement," essentially collectivized peasants and independent farmers who had avoided exile in previous years, represented another category. In addition, two new categories appeared in the crosshairs of the police and security forces: "déclassé elements" in urban areas and people from western border regions considered unreliable on the basis of imputed class or nationality.

Let us look into these groups further. Déclassé elements emerged from the requirement of passports for residence in "regime cities." Passportization had the twin objectives of halting in-migration to these cities and cleansing them of undesirable, socially marginal, or harmful "elements." Individuals "not carrying out socially useful labor," kulaks who had fled from the countryside, and a variety of disenfranchised groups known as lishentsy (former tsarist police and White Army officers, private traders, clerics) were barred. They had to leave for a nonregime city or the countryside within ten days or face a fine and possible deportation.[92] The proliferation of regulations, in other words, engendered a proliferation of outlaws.

Deportees from Moscow and Leningrad began arriving by train in Tomsk in April 1933 as part of a contingent totaling some twenty-five thousand people. More came in May. What happened to them provoked a scandal that led to a series of investigations and a large paper trail of depositions. The historical society and civil rights organization Memorial, which began its own investigation in the late 1980s, as well as several document collections and historical monographs published since then have shed much light on "the Nazino affair."[93] It is indeed among the best known of Gulag-related events, since it indicates the extent to which the Stalinist state would go in disposing of unwanted "urban déclassé and socially harmful elements" via the most coercive of migration regimes.

Briefly, a convoy of four barges normally used to transport wood left Tomsk on May 14 for the most northerly of labor settlements in the Narym territory's Aleksandro-Vakhov district. They traveled along the Tom and Ob rivers toward the Arctic Ocean about 560 miles downstream. Aboard was a human cargo of a little more than 5,000 deportees, kept below deck and fed a daily ration of 200 grams of bread per person. The journey took four days. Fearing that the "urban déclassé elements" would "steal everything, pillage everything, and massacre the local people," the local OGPU commandant ordered disembarkation on an uninhabited island in the middle of the river opposite the village of Nazino. A second

91. Khlevniuk, History of the Gulag, 56, 68; Hagenloh, Stalin's Police, 143. By the end of the year, however, only 116,653 remained in exile. The rest died, escaped, or were transferred to labor camps.

92. On lishentsy, see Golfo Alexopoulos, Stalin's Outcasts: Aliens, Citizens, and the Soviet State, 1926–1936 (Ithaca, 2003). See also Tat'iana Smirnova, "Byvshie liudi" Sovetskoi Rossii: Strategii vyzhivaniia i puti integratsii 1917–1936 gody (Moscow, 2003).

93. Danilov and Krasil'nilov, Spetspereselentsy v zapadnoi Sibiri, 3: 76–119; V. N. Maksheev, Narymskaia khronika: Tragediia spetspereselentsev, dokumenty i vospominaniia (Moscow, 1997); S. A. Krasil'nikov, ed., Nazinskaia tragediia: Dokumental'noe nauchnoe izdanie (Tomsk, 2002); Nicholas Werth, Cannibal Island: Death in a Siberian Gulag, trans. Steven Rendell (Princeton, 2007).

convoy arrived on the island on May 27 with about 1,200 additional deportees whose condition was described as even more "degraded" than the first. Exposed to the elements and with nothing to eat but flour, approximately 1,500 of the deportees died on the island; others tried to escape by building rafts and floating across the river, but many were shot by guards, or drowned; still others later succumbed to typhus. Reports of cannibalism add to the gruesomeness of this incident.[94]

Within the context of coerced migration, it does not get much worse than this. A major part of the responsibility for the disaster must lie with the OGPU and its regional agents who vastly undersupplied the convoys with everything including competent guards. Iagoda and Berman also contributed by their determination to rid the cities of certain "elements," and to use those elements to colonize vast stretches of sparsely settled territory. All these officials seem to have shared a fearfulness of people of no fixed address, occupation, or, for that matter, name, as if such "deindividualized 'masses to be processed'" would spread their influence, like a disease, among others.[95] Thanks to Vasilii Velichko, a twenty-five-year-old propagandist within the Narym okrug party committee who listened to the survivors, we know the names of thirty of them and a bit about their biographies. Some were longtime urban residents; others were on their way to visit relatives, go shopping, or take in a cultural event. Many were students, Komsomol, and party members and had relatives in the party, the police, or the OGPU. Some carried passports with them.[96] But again, as in the case of people wrongly identified as kulaks, this misses the point: nobody ever should be subjected to such a heartless and indeed lethal regime of deportation.

Yet it continued. Several convoys of "déclassé elements" from Leningrad and Moscow—many of them aged and infirm—arrived in the Aleksandro-Vakhov district in July. They were among a larger group of mostly peasants from Ukraine, the North Caucasus, and the Volga basin sent to labor settlements during the spring and summer of 1933.[97] These actions were much harsher than the treatment of "socially alien elements" in the aftermath of

94. Werth, Cannibal Island, 105–25 (quotation on 123). See also the contemporary account contained in the letter by V. A. Velichko, a regional party activist, to Stalin and Eikhe, in Danilov and Krasil'nilov, Spetspereselentsy v zapadnoi Sibiri, 3: 89–100. Velichko's letter, read by members of the Politburo, provoked the initial investigation.

95. See the report by Izrael' Pliner, chief official of the OGPU's Special Settlements Department, to Iagoda in July 1933, which advocated sending "socially harmful elements" not to labor settlements but to camps "in order not to contaminate, through their pernicious, demoralizing influence, other contingents of deportees." GARF, f. 9479, op. 1, d. 19, l. 9, cited in Werth, Cannibal Island, 158. Pliner would lead the removal of Koreans from border areas in the Russian Far East in 1937. For "deindividualized 'masses to be processed,'" see Werth, Cannibal Island, 173.

96. Velichko letter, in Danilov and Krasil'nilov, Spetspereselentsy v zapadnoi Sibiri, 3: 96–99. Velichko also provides a few lyrics to songs he heard the settlers sing—viz., "Mother does not come with a fervent prayer over the grave of her son to cry/ Only the forest above will sing forever its song of Narym" ("In the Boggy Marshes"). See also Berman's reference to "individual members of the party, Komsomolites, workers, employees" in his report to the OGPU leadership in early July 1933 in Pokrovskii, Politbiuro i krest'ianstvo, 2: 425.

97. Werth, Cannibal Island, 156.

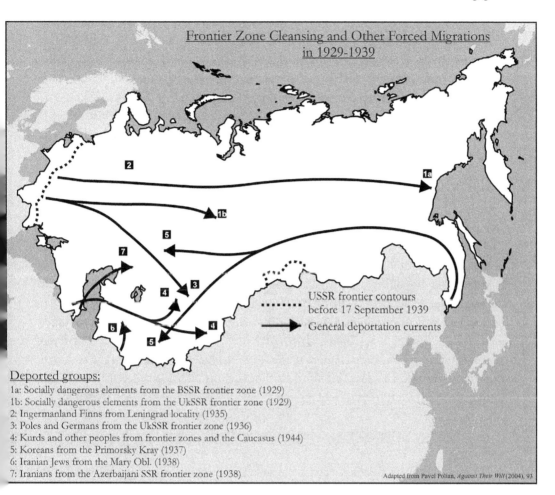

Map 7.1 Frontier zone cleansing and other forced migrations in 1929–1939

the assassination of the Leningrad party boss Sergei Kirov in December 1934. An NKVD decree in February 1935 "On the expulsion of the counter-revolutionary element from Leningrad and its suburban districts," gave former nobles and other lishentsy a month to leave. This "Kirov stream" of ten thousand to twelve thousand individuals had to relocate but were not confined to any particular region. They, like the expropriated landlords of the 1920s, were banished rather than deported.[98]

---

98. Polian, *Against Their Will*, 94; Katerina Gerasimova and Sof'ia Chuikina, "Ot kapitalisticheskogo Peterburga k sotsialisticheskomu Leningradu: Izmenenie sotsial'no-prostranstvennoi struktury goroda v 30-e gody," in *Normy i tsennosti povsednevnoi zhizni: Stanovlenie sotsialisticheskogo obraza zhizni v Rossii, 1920–1930-e gody*, ed. Timo Vikhavainin [Vihavainin] (St. Petersburg, 2000), 37–38. Many wound up in Kuibyshev but were deported from there to the Altai krai in December 1941 to make room for evacuees from Moscow. Zemskov, *Spetspereselentsy v SSSR*, 77–78.

In the meantime, the rise of Hitler to power significantly altered the migration regime imposed on Soviet Germans. Less than three months after Hitler became chancellor, an officer within the secret political department of the OGPU noted that about sixty ethnic German special settlers in the Urals had requested material assistance from abroad. They also allegedly had contacted the International Red Cross office in Moscow requesting foreign passports. Special settlers in the Russian Far East and the Northern krai also initiated such contacts, the purpose of which, the officer reported, was to *"prepare an insurrection as well as terrorist and diversionary acts timed to coincide with the outbreak of war."*[99]

This, of course, was just one report among many routinely filed every week, but war talk was becoming rife. Another report sent a few days later, on "C[ounter] R[evolutionary] rebellious activity of A[nti-] S[oviet] E[lements] among Exiled Kulaks," cited statements about the inevitability of war and specifically the prospect of Japan attacking the Soviet Union from the east while Poland attacked from the west.[100] The statements might have been imagined or fabricated, but our point is not the causal significance of these reports, but rather that they illustrate a particular mentality—an insecurity derived from a sense of the fragility of Soviet power—that foreign events intensified.[101] The insecurity extended beyond concern about nationalities living near international borders to include other groups: in December 1934 Iagoda, now NKVD head, ordered the deportation of 1,500 "kulak families" from national regions of the North Caucasus to Uzbekistan and southern Kazakhstan; in February 1935, as already mentioned, the NKVD expelled lishentsy from Leningrad; and in April 1935, it sent dozens of Mennonite families that had settled in Uzbekistan to Tajikistan, and a smaller number of religious sectarian families living in the Altai to the Narym territory as punishment for their noncompliance with military service.[102]

Large-scale ethnic cleansing began in the western border regions in 1935 and continued on and off for nearly three years. It resulted in the removal of a third to a half of all those defined as ethnic Finns, Poles, Germans, and other nationalities from the special zone originally defined as 22 kilometers but eventually encompassing territory up to 100 kilometers from the border. It culminated in the wholesale deportation of Koreans from Far

---

99. Pokrovskii, *Politbiuro i krest'ianstvo*, 2: 992–94 (emphasis in original). For independent evidence of ethnic German special settlers contacting Germans abroad and receiving marks through the mail, see Molchanova and Noskova, " 'Vse eto bylo, bylo, bylo,' " 81–82. The German government sent food aid to ethnic Germans (*Volksdeutsche*) in the Soviet Union as part of its "Brothers In Need" program. See Wendy Lower, *Nazi Empire-Building and the Holocaust in Ukraine* (Chapel Hill, 2005), 16.

100. Pokrovskii, *Politbiuro i krest'ianstvo*, 2: 995.

101. For the prevalence of rumors among Soviet peasants during the 1930s and an interpretation, see Fitzpatrick, *Stalin's Peasants*, 67–69, 75–76, 286–96.

102. Pokrovskii, *Politbiuro i krest'ianstvo*, 2: 429, 439; Polian, *Against Their Will*, 94.

Eastern borders in late 1937.[103] Borderland clearances continued into 1938 with smaller-scale operations repatriating Iranian and Chinese nationals, and deporting to Kazakhstan those with Soviet passports. Soviet authorities repeatedly used the metaphor of cleansing in reference to the forcible removal from a given territory of groups they identified as kulak, anti-Soviet, counterrevolutionary, and antikolkhoz, but also "unreliable," which almost always bore an ethnic specificity.[104]

The conditions of deportation prescribed in the NKVD's memoranda were nearly identical for all of these groups. The regional NKVD apparatus, assisted by local "sovpartkomsomol" activists, would select families; they were to avoid including former Red partisans, families of Red Army soldiers, reservists, and foreign citizens. Only families having at least one able-bodied member were liable for deportation. They had to have a two-month's supply of food as well as sufficient clothes and footwear. A horse and, "if possible," a cow were to accompany every five families. Each family could bring up to 30 puds (72 pounds) of domestic items and an unlimited quantity of money. They would travel by convoy, each containing two cars devoted to food preparation. To prevent flight, the authorities would take into custody the heads of deported families a week or more before departure. Assigned destinations ranged from the White Sea-Baltic Canal and the "most remote northern districts of Krasnoiarsk krai," south to the Vakhsh Valley of Tajikistan.[105]

So these peasant families—"kulaks" of a national flavor—were to be deported with supplies that would enable them to survive deep within the interior of the country. They thereby would occupy a circle of hell somewhat higher than where most labor camp inmates dwelt. But how did deportees actually experience their putatively well-supplied displacement? According to the field notes of Adolf Zborovskii, who was in charge of deporting families from the Markhlevsk Polish Autonomous Region of western Ukraine in the spring of 1935, some were convinced or had persuaded themselves that the move was necessary and not a punishment but rather for their own good. Others resented having been chosen and tried to appeal the decision. What threw Zborovskii, though, was how little the standard provisions cited in the previous paragraph resembled reality. Several families lacked an adult male because he had been arrested or had fled (Kate Brown calls this the "missing man" syndrome of the "Soviet rural underclass"), many children lacked warm clothes and shoes, lack of wagons prevented deportees from bringing their possessions, and regional

103. Martin, *Affirmative Action Empire*, 328–35. For the relevant NKVD memoranda, see Pokrovskii, *Politbiuro i krest'ianstvo*, 2: 432–43.

104. For a discussion of the term "ethnic cleansing" and its appropriateness to this context, see Martin, "Origins of Ethnic Cleansing," 817.

105. Danilov, Manning, and Viola, *Tragediia sovetskoi derevni*, 4: 510, 550–51; Zemskov, *Spetsposelentsy v SSSR*, 78.

authorities had difficulty fulfilling the assigned quota of deportees for lack of obvious enemies.[106]

Among the families deported by Zborovskii from the village of Ol'shanka was Edward Guzovskii's. The account he gave to Brown more than sixty years later is reminiscent of others we already have encountered from earlier deportations—the abruptness of the announcement, the boxcars, the ignorance of the destination, and the intensity of nostalgia for home. In the case of the three hundred families from the Markhlevsk district, including Guzovskii's, the destination proved to be eastern Ukraine. There they joined over eight thousand other families from western Ukraine—but few stayed for long. While peasants exiled to "the most remote northern districts of Krasnoiarsk krai" may have found escape a daunting prospect, eastern Ukraine could not hold these deportees. Most returned home during the summer and fall of 1935. This may be why the Council of People's Commissars decreed another round of deportations in 1936—this time not of eight thousand but of fifteen thousand German and Polish households, not as labor settlers but as less autonomous special settlers, and not to eastern Ukraine but to farther-off Kazakhstan.[107]

Martin uses the term "ethnic cleansing" somewhat liberally to apply to both the deportation of borderland "diaspora" nationalities and the 1937–38 national operations—that is, the arrest and either imprisonment or execution of hundreds of thousands of Poles, Germans, Finns, Latvians, Estonians, Greeks, and other national groups. The differences between the two processes are not only in the degree of lethality. Deportation, as Brown astutely points out, "only heightened allegiance to the imagined group and the conviction among deportees that the soviet state unfairly persecuted them." The act of arrest, by contrast, isolated defendants.[108] It also did not so much displace them geographically as radically confine their immediate physical environment.

Before we proceed to other groups, we should follow the German and Polish households deported from western Ukraine to their destinations in northern Kazakhstan. As with departures, the NKVD went to no little trouble planning arrivals. In late May 1936, shortly before the first party of deportees arrived, Berman wrote to Iagoda and other NKVD officials about preparations, which included transferring skilled construction workers and tractors from Karaganda labor settlements to accelerate the provision of housing for the newcomers. His report to Iagoda noted that the first parties of deportees, some 10,500 individuals, had arrived by train on June 10; that it took 75 trucks eight to ten hours to transport them and their belongings to the new settlement sites; and that food, medical, and

---

106. Brown, *A Biography of No Place*, 135–38.

107. Ibid., 142–46; Martin, *Affirmative Action Empire*, 330. For the resolution see Pobol' and Polian, *Stalinskie deportatsii*, 56–59.

108. Brown, *A Biography of No Place*, 163–64.

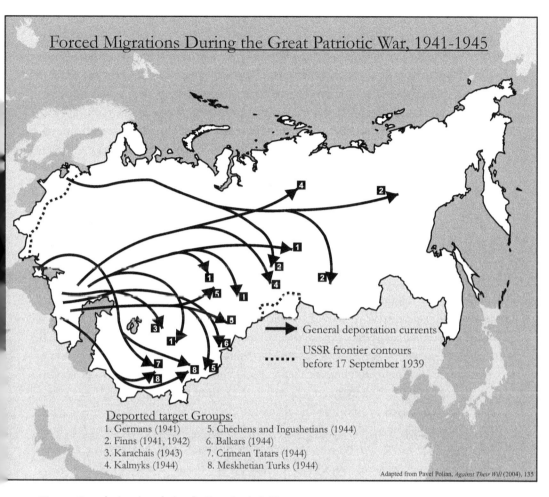

Map 7.2 Forced migrations during the Great Patriotic War, 1941–1945

sanitation stations performed as required. He added that the Karaganda health authorities were organizing two hospitals, each with one hundred beds and a "complete" medical staff; Tsentrosoiuz, the consumer cooperative society, had set up seven "trading points" containing food, manufactured goods, and firewood; the NKVD had obtained tents and barracks capable of temporarily accommodating 20,000 people, and it also had assembled building materials, some of which already were "on site."[109]

109. Pobol' and Polian, *Stalinskie deportatsii*, 59–63.

It is a good thing that the building materials were being gathered because when Julia Sorokina and her sister Valentina arrived with their parents in late September as part of the second and larger party of households, they discovered, as Julia told Kate Brown, "there was nothing there at all, no houses, no tents." This was only partly due to the fact that instead of a planned forty-five thousand special settlers, nearly seventy thousand had arrived, apparently because the NKVD had underestimated the average size of the families it was deporting. Irrespective of numbers, after spending weeks traveling in those inevitable box-cars, many newcomers found the Kazakh steppe "bare" and "naked," adding to their sense of disorientation and vulnerability. They named their settlements after their home villages—a sure sign of topophilia—but this hardly helped accustom them to such a radically different environment.[110] One indication of the needs of deportees during their first weeks and months in Kazakhstan comes from what the Gulag official Izrael Pliner listed as on order in a report to his bosses: from Tsentrosoiuz, more warm clothing, shoes, heating fuel, and vegetables; from the Commissariat of Health, more doctors and medical assistants; and from the education commissariat, more teachers.[111]

As for housing, Pliner reported that each of the 64,319 new residents occupied an average of 2.18 square meters. We don't have information about how much living space these Polish and German families occupied back home. We also lack comparative data for rural inhabitants elsewhere, but 2.18 meters was far below Muscovites' average of just over 4 square meters (in 1940), and even residents of the new industrializing towns of Magnitogorsk and Irkutsk had almost 4 square meters.[112] So things were cramped. Whether the deportees felt deprived by shortages of vegetables, clothing, and shoes is another matter, as these items likely were not plentiful back home either. Ultimately, their attitudes about where they lived had less to do with the lack of living space or the scarcity of consumer goods than with the coerced nature of their departure and the unfamiliarity of the topography. Some deportees adjusted quite well, according to the Gulag boss Berman, especially recently demobilized Red Army soldiers who became kolkhoz activists. Others, however, chose from among the repertoires of migration a form characteristic of people subjected to coercive regimes—they fled. Berman, citing instances of passports and other documents obtained through the mail, reported "massive flight of the deportees to various places in the USSR."[113]

---

110. Brown, *A Biography of No Place*, 174.

111. Pobol' and Polian, *Stalinskie deportatsii*, 69–72. The report was dated October 11, 1936.

112. Sheila Fitzpatrick, *Everyday Stalinism: Ordinary Life in Extraordinary Times: Soviet Russia in the 1930s* (Oxford, 1999), 46. Six weeks later, Pliner was proud to report that the construction targets had been fulfilled by an average of 100.6 percent, that "all resettlers have been accommodated in newly built houses," and that their average living space had risen to 2.26 square meters. Pobol' and Polian, *Stalinskie deportatsii*, 73.

113. GARF, f. 9479, op. 1, d. 38, ll. 1–2. Thanks to Kate Brown for providing this document. There is some dispute about the prevalence of flight. See Brown, *A Biography of No Place*, 282.

No matter how many left, more kept on arriving. As the Kremlin's anxiety about "unreliable elements" intensified, the list of national groups subjected to deportation grew: in November 1936, 1,000 so-called kulak households from Dagestan and Chechnya; in July 1937, 1,121 Kurdish, Armenian, and Meskhetian Turkish "counterrevolutionary elements . . . contrabandists, bandits, and members of their families" from the southern border zones of Armenia and Azerbaijan; and then in September–October 1937, the nearly complete displacement of Koreans, over 170,000—some to the same steppe region of northern Kazakhstan and others to southern Kazakhstan, Kyrgyzstan, and Uzbekistan. So poorly organized was the deportation of the Kurds, Armenians, and Meskhetian Turks that Lieutenant Konradov, a Gulag official in charge of labor settlements, had to admit that the deportees were left to their own devices without any commandant to whom they had to report. They thus engaged in "self-arrangement," which meant that at least some of them (he could not estimate how many) escaped.[114] As for the Koreans, their journeys into exile took a month on average. Most wound up in Uzbekistan; some four thousand, though, arrived on December 31, 1937 at the Kustanai railroad station in Kazakhstan, where they spent an absolutely frigid week unsupervised and without any accommodation, water, or bread.[115]

We have seen the repressive organs of the state acting with a heavy hand but also, as in cases such as this, hardly present at all. Hitherto, we have stressed escape as the only alternative to deportees' abject dependence on the state, a dependence that, especially in the early going, often proved fatal. But an analysis that goes no further than this is an impoverished one. For every special or labor settler who escaped, others stuck it out by adapting. A far less spectacular response, adaptation is nevertheless what enabled the former deportees interviewed by Brown to speak with pride about their accomplishments, even those who spoke with bitterness about what the state had done to them.[116] In Kazakhstan, Polish and German deportees adapted their skills in animal husbandry and in grain cultivation to a different climate and topography; in Uzbekistan, Korean deportees built an irrigation system that enabled them to adapt their skills in rice and vegetable cultivation. Over the long haul, as a report from the United Nations High Commissioner for Refugees observed in 1999, "Koreans have been among the most successful out of all deported peoples, adapt[ing] most successfully to their new area of settlement."[117]

114. Pobol' and Polian, Stalinskie deportatsii, 77–78. The report is from April 1939.
115. Ibid., 82.
116. Brown, A Biography of No Place, 185–86.
117. The report, published originally in November 1999, has been reproduced by Refworld, a service of the Immigration and Refugee Board of Canada, and is available at http://www.unhcr.org/refworld/topic,463 af2212,488edfby6e38,3ae6ad805a,0,IRBC,,.html (accessed April 12, 2013).

Deportees during World War II

In September 1939, the Soviet Union annexed eastern Poland, distributing its eleven provinces between the Ukrainian and Belorussian Soviet Republics. The following year, it absorbed Latvia, Lithuania, Estonia, Finland's Karelian Isthmus, and the Romanian provinces of Bessarabia and Northern Bukovina. Policies dictated by security considerations have a way of deepening insecurity, and these actions proved no exception. It is impossible to know how many of the approximately twenty-two million new citizens were ill disposed toward the Soviet Union, and that is just the point.[118] Before 1939, Soviet authorities had worried about the reliability of those living in the border zones. Now, the officer corps; the intellectual, legal, and political elites; the clergy; the well-to-do farmers, industrialists, and other large property owners—all provoked concern. Between September 1939 and June 1941, organs of state security in the newly acquired western territories applied methods honed in the 1930s by imprisoning over one hundred thousand people "with a compromised social and political past."[119] In April–May 1940, the NKVD executed some twenty-two thousand Polish prisoners of war and other "fifth-column" elements, the overwhelming majority of whom were Poles by nationality.[120] It also arrested and executed former elites in the Baltic republics and what had become the Soviet republic of Moldavia.

Many more new Soviet citizens were deported in 1940. The painstaking research of A. E. Gur'ianov has turned up evidence of a total of 211 convoys transporting some 270,000 people in three different operations—on February 10, April 9–13, and June 29. Each targeted a different subset of former citizens of Poland: osadniki (in Polish osadnicy), that is, army veterans and their families granted homesteads in the eastern Polish provinces plus a smaller contingent of forest rangers; a second eclectic group consisting of wives and children of army and police officers executed at Katyn and elsewhere, refugees refused permission to settle in German-occupied Polish territory, and registered prostitutes; and refugees who had fled east to escape the German invaders and who were overwhelmingly Jewish (See table 7.2).[121] The ability of the security organs to mobilize and coordinate transportation, food, and other logistics and move such large numbers of people in a single day is as

---

118. For the breakdown of populations, see L. S. Rogachevskaia, "Naselenie i territoriia SSSR i RSFSR nakanune velikoi otechestvennoi voiny," in Zhiromskaia, Naselenie Rossii, 2: 10.

119. O. A. Gorlanov and A. B. Roginskii, "Ob arestakh v zapadnykh oblastiakh Belorussii i Ukrainy v 1939–1941 gg.," in Repressii protiv poliakov i pol'skikh grazhdan, ed. A. E. Gur'ianov (Moscow, 1997), 87, 105.

120. On the executions of Poles at Katyn Forest and other NKVD sites, see Timothy Snyder, Bloodlands: Europe between Hitler and Stalin (New York, 2010), 135–41; and for documents, see Anna M. Cienciala, Natalia S. Lebedeva, and Wojciech Materski, eds., Katyn: A Crime Without Punishment (New Haven, 2007).

121. A. E. Gur'ianov, "Pol'skie spetspereselentsy v SSSR v 1940–1941 gg.," in Gur'ianov, Repressii protiv poliakov, 114–16.

Table 7.2 Deportees from western Belorussian and Ukrainian SSRs, 1940

	Number of deportees			Number of convoys
	Western Belorussian	Western Ukrainian	Total	
Osadniki	50,683	88,385	139,068	101
Families of repressed	27,279	29,012	56,291	52
Refugees	23,764	51,503	75,267	58
Total	101,726	168,900	270,626	211

Source: A. E. Gur'ianov, ed., *Repressii protiv pol'iakov i pol'skikh grazhdan* (Moscow: Zven'ia, 1997), 119.

impressive as it is appalling. It would set a precedent for future actions during the Great Patriotic War.

The first of these deportations—of osadniki and forest rangers—was the largest of the three operations, and also the most elaborately planned. The plan approved for L'vov oblast', for example, included the number of households and occupants to be deported and the "troika" assigned to lead operations: the NKVD's own servicemen, soviet and party activists, and rural activists. Here and there acts of resistance accompanied embarkation. In Belorussia's Belostok oblast' an exchange of gunfire left one osadnik dead; in a Brest oblast' village, two sons of an osadnik tried to escape and one succeeded; in Ukraine's Drogobych oblast', crowds of locals that had gathered at several embarkation points to prevent the loading of deportees were dispersed by force. Still, a report from the head of the Drogobych oblast' troika could claim, "the operation went off in an organized manner without any serious excesses." Perhaps the subzero temperatures, which caused frostbite to some of the soldiers (and doubtless deportees too), hindered resistance.[122]

Less sanguine was a report from March 1940 about the arrival of the osadniki and their distribution among 115 special settlements in the Russian North and Siberia. It cited instances of lists of deportees failing to tally with the number of people counted as they disembarked; of families dispersed among several oblasts, husbands being separated from wives; and of parents arriving without children, and children, including a two year old, without parents. Some people had in their possession instructions from district executive committees indicating that they were "not subject to deportation." A "significant number of osadniki arrived without any personal documents."[123]

At least some of these bureaucratic hitches would be overcome in time. Overcoming the bitterness provoked by deportation would take longer. Although Siberia had been a

---

122. Pobol' and Polian, *Stalinskie deportatsii*, 107–27.
123. Ibid., 128–30.

destination of Polish deportees since the 1830s, many of these Poles had no previous experience of Russian rule. Nor did it help that living conditions in the 563 special settlements they occupied had only marginally improved since the disaster at Nazino Island.[124] Fortunately for the osadniki, the Nazi invasion of the USSR prompted an agreement between the Soviet government and the London-based Polish government that resulted in their amnesty and release from the special settlements, prisons, and labor colonies. Perhaps as many as ten thousand from the special settlements volunteered for Anders's army (the Polish Armed Forces in the East under General Władysław Anders); they were evacuated with their families in 1942 through Iran to Palestine and placed under British command.[125] The majority, however, were granted Soviet passports and took up residence elsewhere in the country—except in border regions or first- and second-category regime cities from which they were barred.[126]

No sooner had the NKVD dispatched the osadniki to the East than Commissar Lavrentii Beriia initiated preparations for deporting families of Polish officers who, already in the NKVD's custody, soon would be executed. As in the previous operation, the eighty-one convoys were longer—fifty-five instead of forty-four cars—but, at thirty instead of forty people per wagon, less crowded than those of earlier in the decade. Beriia decided to send the wives and children of officers to Kazakhstan for ten years, the stranded refugees to the lumber settlements in the North, and the prostitutes to Kazakhstan and Uzbekistan. Respective commissariats (Forestry, Finance, Trade, Health, Railroads, Non-Ferrous Metallurgy) were informed what they needed to do upon the arrival of the deportees. The collection of documents concerning these operations also contains a letter, originally published in the Soviet journal *Novyi mir* in 1991, from four children of Polish prisoners of war. Written in Polonized Russian, it reads in part:

> We are small children with a big request for the Great Father Stalin from our hearts we want you to return our fathers. . . . We are being sent from western Belorussia to Siberia and are not being allowed to take anything with us. . . . We ask father Stalin not to forget about us. . . . We always in the Soviet Union will be good workers, only life is hard without our fathers.[127]

---

124. See the reports in Khlevniuk, *History of the Gulag*, 274–79. On the number of settlements, see Zemskov, *Spetsposelentsy v SSSR*, 86.

125. The amnestied Poles produced a rich set of testimonies about deportation. From classic memoir, to personal recollections, to analysis of identity, see Joseph Czapski, *The Inhuman Land* (New York, 1952); Tadeusz Piotrowski, ed., *The Polish Deportees of World War II: Recollections of Removal to the Soviet Union and Dispersal throughout the World* (London, 2004); Katherine R. Jolluck, *Exile and Identity: Polish Women in the Soviet Union during World War II* (Pittsburgh, 2002).

126. Polian, *Against Their Will*, 119; N. S. Lebedeva, "Armiia Andersa v dokumentakh rossiiskikh arkhivov," in Gur'ianov, *Repressii protiv poliakov*, 176–96. In all, the amnesty freed some 389,000 Polish citizens.

127. Pobol' and Polian, *Stalinskie deportatsii*, 137–49.

These women and children contended with the loss of their former identities. Absent husbands and fathers, they sought "to impose the coherence of home and community in the image of the traditional family." They also would become more conscious of their Polish nationality away from their native Poland. Indeed, one historian asks, "Could one imagine a person from the *kresy* still identifying him- or herself as simply 'from here' after 1945?"[128]

The deportation in June 1940 of refugees from Nazi-occupied Poland—85 percent of whom were Jews—used the two earlier deportations as models. Two things precipitated this action: the refusal of the German occupiers to accommodate these people, and the fact that at least some had been—in the words of a Ukrainian NKVD official—"wandering around from oblast' to oblast'." Their relocation to the forests of the Russian North and Siberia solved whatever security threat these "interned emigrants" posed, but in other respects was an utter disaster. Teachers, tradesmen, and shopkeepers back home, most of the men were ill suited to forestry. A November 1940 report contrasted the osadniki and forest rangers, who "in the vast majority work well," with the refugees, who adjusted "painfully" and who "don't know how to work, fear work, don't want to work," in short, had "suitcase attitudes." By April 1941, Beriia was reporting to Stalin that "the NKVD considers it advantageous to transfer specialists and tradesmen, physically useless for work in forestry and mining, to cities and populated points . . ."[129]

April 1941 brings us nearly to the German invasion of the USSR, but there still was time for two more NKVD operations. On May 14, the Soviet government and Communist Party issued a joint resolution to "remove counterrevolutionary organizations" (primarily members of the Organization of Ukrainian Nationalists) from Ukraine's western oblasts. This and an analogous order for western Belorussia produced a plethora of executions but also the ugly Soviet acronym of *admssyl'nyi* ("administratively exiled"), used just for this purpose. Numbering over thirty thousand, the *admssyl'nye* were distributed among special settlements in Novosibirsk and Omsk oblasts, and the Altai and Krasnoiarsk krais, with the same degree of efficiency and solicitude for their welfare as the NKVD exhibited in previous operations. And for a longer period of time—twenty years.[130]

Cleansing Moldavia and the three Baltic republics annexed by the Soviet Union in June 1940 also appeared on the NKVD's agenda. The social backgrounds of the deportees—primarily former officers, large landowners, and businessmen—resembled the Leningraders expelled in 1935. But because the ever-tighter security regime had made those imposing it

128. Jolluck, *Exile and Identity*, xxi, 283.

129. Pobol' and Polian, *Stalinskie deportatsii*, 151–62.

130. Ibid., 194–97; Zemskov, *Spetsposelentsy v SSSR*, 90–91. The category "exiled settler" (*ssyl'noposelenets*) replaced "administratively exiled" in June.

even more insecure in the interim, these people were treated like the nationalists from Ukraine and Belorussia. Hilja Lill, a schoolteacher in a small town not far from Tartu, Estonia, remembers how "strangely quiet" it was on June 13, 1941 when a truck pulled up to the gate of her neighbor's house and disgorged soldiers. Half an hour later August Tilk and his wife emerged carrying bundles wrapped in bedsheets—all they would take into exile.[131]

In most cases, the NKVD arrested male heads of households and sent other family members to settlements as "exiled settlers." Sometimes, however, women and children traveled in convoys that proceeded in parallel fashion to those transporting men until Sverdlovsk, where the men's trains turned north toward "concentration camps" while the women and children continued eastward. In yet another variant, Ligita Dreifelde, a Latvian girl, was fourteen when she and both parents went into exile on June 14, 1941. But her father, Jānis, was separated from her and her mother on the journey somewhere in Kaluga oblast' southwest of Moscow, and they never saw or heard from him again.[132] Women, children, and the elderly were sent to some of the same parts of the country as the Ukrainians and Belorussians, but also to some different locations (see table 7.3). These deportees, distributed among state and collective farms as well as other enterprises, had the same complaints about the separation of families, lack of sufficient clothing, and overcrowded living conditions as other forced migrants we have encountered and will encounter again.[133]

Some did more than complain. When a contingent of 1,400 from Belostok oblast' arrived at the Omsk railroad station on July 7, they initiated what a local NKVD official called an "openly nationalist anti-Soviet demonstration." At first, they refused to receive food and money for the rest of the journey, and then demanded to be returned home. When it was explained to them that the outbreak of war made this impossible, they offered to go to the front and risk their lives. Two days later, as the deportees were being transferred from train to boat, a group of about 120 women engaged in a regular *bab'i bunt*—a women's rebellion.[134] They started yelling that they were being bullied just like the fascists had bullied them, and announced they weren't going any farther. They then surrounded "in a tight ring" the cars that were supposed to take them to the harbor. Only the intervention of the police who made several arrests got things moving again.[135]

---

131. Tiina Kirss and Rutt Hinrikus, ed. and trans., *Estonian Life Stories* (Budapest, 2009), 41–46.

132. Sandra Kalniete, *With Dance Shoes in Siberian Snows* (London, 2009), front matter. The KGB of the Latvian SSR informed Ligita in 1990 that her father had died on December 31, 1941. See V. N. Maksheev, *Spetsy: Issledovanie* (Tomsk, 2007), 69, for the claim that women and children traveled in separate convoys from men as far as Sverdlovsk.

133. Pobol' and Polian, *Stalinskie deportatsii*, 227–34. Among those sent to Novosibirsk oblast' were 762 assigned to the Aleksandrov district of the Narym okrug, the location of Nazino Island (246).

134. For the classic work on this form of protest, see Lynne Viola, "Bab'i Bunty and Peasant Women's Protest during Collectivization," *Russian Review* 45, no. 1 (1986): 189–205.

135. Pobol' and Polian, *Stalinskie deportatsii*, 248–49.

Table 7.3 Destinations of "exiled settlers" from Latvia, Lithuania, Estonia, and Moldavia, 1941

	Latvia	Lithuania	Estonia	Moldavia
Altai krai		7,462		
Kirov oblast'			2,049	470
Komi ASSR		1,549		352
Krasnoiarsk krai	6,000	164		470
Novosibirsk oblast'	2,580	3,507	1,619	5,787
Omsk oblast'	656			6,085
Total	9,236	12,682	3,668	13,164

Source: GARF, f. 9479, op. 1, d. 87, l. 15, cited in Zemskov, *Spetspereselentsy v SSSR, 1930–1960* (Moscow: Nauka, 2003), 91; GARF, f. 9479, op. 1, d. 87, l. 238, reproduced in N. L. Pobol' and P. M. Polian, eds., *Stalinskie deportatsii, 1928–1953 gg.* (Moscow: Materik, 2005), 259.

The war really had broken out by this point—not the lopsided affairs against Poland in 1939 and Finland in 1939–40, but the real thing, the war against the German fascist invaders and their allies. That, however, did not stop the NKVD from deporting people. On the contrary, mandated by a whole host of decrees and directives issued in 1941–42, the security organs rounded up and deported to the Far North, Siberia, and Kazakhstan Soviet Germans, Finns, and a variety of other "diaspora nations" in what it described as preventative actions. In 1943–44 after the Red Army had driven back the invading forces, Soviet security organs engaged in the retributive deportation of six entire national groups indigenous to the country plus assorted diaspora groups.[136] By war's end these actions directly affected about 1.8 million people.

They demonstrate, among other things, that Soviet authorities operated during the war according to the principle that nationality trumped all other identity markers including class and professions of political loyalty. Anticipated in their deportation of Koreans in 1937, this principle gained traction early in the war and remained dominant at least until the end of the Stalin era. The principle's enactment represented an admission of defeat, an implicit acknowledgment of ethnicity's high capacity for not only resisting political homogenization but also "ethnicizing" Soviet institutions such as the kolkhoz and the party chain of command. The intolerability of paramount ethnic loyalties in time of war required the geographic dispersion of the ethnicity's social medium, that is, the ethnic community.[137]

136. Polian, *Against Their Will*, 140.
137. V. A. Kozlov and M. E. Kozlova, "Paternalistskaia utopiia i etnicheskaia real'nost'," in *Vainakhi i imperskaia vlast': Problema Chechni i Ingushetii vo vnutrennei politike Rossii i SSSR (nachalo XIX–seredina XX v.)*, ed. V. A. Kozlov et al. (Moscow, 2011), 679–710.

We do not wish to imply that other groups were exempted from deportation during the war or that other principles had no bearing. Beriia, pending Stalin's approval, was an equal opportunity deporter: if given the opportunity, he found a way to deport. In June 1944, for example, the NKVD decided to deport from central Russia 537 families belonging to the True Orthodox Christian sect. According to Beriia's explanation to Stalin, these families had led "a parasitical way of life, did not pay taxes, refused to fulfill their military obligations, and prevented their children from attending school." The security organs located space for these families in several Siberian territories including the Khanty-Mansi national okrug of Tomsk, where most refused to do any work because, in the words of one of them, "it is better to die for Christ than work for the anti-Christ."[138]

The Vlasovites, Soviet POWs who joined the Russian Liberation Army under the command of Lieutenant-General Andrei Vlasov, were another nonnationally defined category listed in tables of deportees. Some, if found by filtration commissions to have committed crimes against the USSR, faced long sentences in the Gulag, but many wound up assigned for terms of six years to special settlements along with family members. Nikolai Bugai, whose painstaking research on deportees is unparalleled, cites Ministry of Internal Affairs (MVD) data from 1951 showing nearly eighteen thousand in settlements in western Siberia's Kemerovo oblast', nearly thirty thousand more widely distributed in eastern Siberia, and a few hundred in Uzbekistan. Unlike the True Orthodox Christians, they worked—mainly in construction, forestry, and the mining of coal, gold, and mica. Viktor Berdinskikh traces the paths of a few Vlasovites. One, Ivan Al-ov, can be followed from his first interrogation in May 1945 to an initial assignment to a camp, transfer to a special settlement in the Kandalaksha district of Murmansk oblast', confinement in a hospital following an unsuccessful attempt at suicide, contraction of Parkinson's disease, and finally, a second, this time successful, attempt at suicide in June 1952, after the expiration of his six years.[139]

Soviet Germans constituted the largest group of deportees. Of the 1.4 million counted in the 1939 census, just under 950,000, or a little over two-thirds, were deported, about half to Kazakhstan and the other half to Siberia. The RSFSR supplied 3 out of 4 ethnic German deportees, of whom nearly a half million came from the Volga German Autonomous SSR. Beriia assigned thousands of Red Army soldiers, police, and his NKVD colleagues to this operation. This substantial wartime commitment of military and security forces, rolling stock, and other resources to deport Soviet citizens is a measure of the Stalinist

---

138. A. S. Ivanov, " 'Istinno-pravoslavnye khristiane' na spetsposelenii v Khanty-Mansiiskom natsional'nom okruge v gody voiny (1944–1945 gg.)," *Istoricheskii ezhegodnik* (Novosibirsk, 2009), 147.

139. N. F. Bugai, L. *Beriia–I. Stalinu: "Soglasno Vashemu ukazaniiu . . ."* (Moscow, 1995), 246–48; Berdinskikh, *Spetsposelentsy*, 664–69.

leadership's mordant suspiciousness. Beriia's instructions on August 27, 1941 made it plain that "all inhabitants of German nationality living in the cities and towns" of a particular region were to be deported in one action. The vast majority of these people undoubtedly considered themselves loyal, their families having lived in the country for generations. Deportees included families of Red Army soldiers and officers, although they were to receive preference in work assignments and living conditions. Couples in which the wife was German but the husband was of another nationality were exempted.[140]

Evgenii Miller, who was ten years old when his Volga German family learned of the impending deportation, recalls thinking that it was "completely unbelievable and absolutely unforeseen." He also guiltily remembers having felt excited by the journey, as "carts, carts, carts in front and behind as far as the eye could see" took the deportees to the Volga, where they boarded barges. By late September the family was ensconced in their new home in a small village in the Altai. Evgenii's father taught in school, his older brother worked in accounting, and he attended the fifth grade in a Russian school. An incident in his history class sticks out in Evgenii's memory. One day, the teacher began their lesson with the normal question, "Whose turn is it to be monitor today?" "Hitler's!" came a cry from the back of the room, meaning it was Evgenii's turn. "I burst into tears," he writes, "and could not be consoled for a long time." However, after "an oppressive silence," the teacher came to Evgenii's defense and "with a sharp feeling of his own powerlessness, said to the class, 'Lads, you should not offend Miller. It seems to me they are not guilty of anything. Someday, people will learn how it was.' "[141]

The urgency of deporting ethnic Germans east of the Urals guaranteed substandard accommodation, inadvertent separations among some families, and inattention to their requests for reunification. After long, rough train journeys the shock of arrival was palpable. In the case of Berta Bachmann, her mother, and two younger brothers, a friendly young Kazakh escorted them to their lodgings in a village of some thirty huts. "Greater yet was our disenchantment when we stepped into the low-beamed mud hut! Is it possible that people live like this, like cattle in a stall?!" They would stay in Kazakhstan until long after the war, and would never again see her father and older brother, who had been drafted into forced labor months before their own departure.[142] But such problems hardly distinguished these deportees from others or, for that matter, from evacuees heading in the same direction and sometimes to the same destination.

140. Zemskov, *Spetsposelentsy v SSSR*, 92; Pobol' and Polian, *Stalinskie deportatsii*, 284–85; Berdinskikh, *Spetsposelentsy*, 313–14. In all, the NKVD had at its disposal 16,950 troops and police as compared with over 100,000 for the similarly sized Chechen-Ingush operation (see below).

141. E. Miller, "Veter v litso," *Volga*, no. 7 (1990), reproduced in Berdinskikh, *Spetsposelentsy*, 464–65.

142. Berta Bachmann, *Memories of Kazakhstan: A Report on the Life Experiences of a German Woman in Russia* (Lincoln, 1983), 8, 20. Bachmann left Ukraine October 8, 1941; her brother and father left in August of the same year.

Indeed, when authorities first began to discuss among themselves moving Soviet Germans, they referred to their "evacuation" rather than deportation.[143] And when two policemen came to tell Berta Bachmann's mother that they would be collecting her and Berta the next day from their house in a Donbas village, they too spoke of evacuation.[144] They may have engaged in an intentional deception—Berta thought so, at least in retrospect—but evacuation personnel in Kazakhstan, if not elsewhere, tended to treat German "settlers" no differently from evacuees. They—the Germans—had their own column in tables devised by evacuation officials indicating how many people had arrived along with Leningraders, Muscovites, and people evacuated from the front. Individual Soviet Germans could even request "places of settlement" from evacuation officials and receive their support. No wonder untutored locals got confused about whether the newcomers were evacuees, refugees, or deportees.[145]

Even some deportees themselves were confused. Wolfgang Leonhard was thirteen when he arrived in the Soviet Union from Germany in 1935 with his mother, a political refugee. He writes in his memoirs that in mid-September 1941 he received a summons to report to the district police office in Moscow. There, the chief of police told him he had received instructions to remove all Germans living in Moscow to Kzyl-orda, Kazakhstan, for the duration of the war as a "necessary precaution." A student at the Foreign Languages Academy and a member of the Komsomol, Leonhard let himself be convinced that once in Kazakhstan he could rejoin the academy, then about to be evacuated to Alma-Ata. This proved impossible, although Leonhard did make it to the Karaganda Educational Institute, received a posting a year later to the Comintern School in Ufa, and by July 1943 was back in Moscow.[146]

It would not do, however, to overlook the differences between deportees and evacuees. Leonhard reports that while in Karaganda he attended a conference among German émigrés at which speakers told "appalling" stories of receiving abuse and ridicule at the hands of kolkhoz authorities, inferior rations, and the worst accommodation as a matter of course owing to their German nationality.[147] Moreover, according to decrees issued by the State Defense Committee in January and February 1942, Soviet German males between ages seventeen and fifty and capable of physical work had to serve in worker colonies,

---

143. Pobol' and Polian, *Stalinskie deportatsii*, 323–25.

144. Bachmann, *Memories of Kazakhstan*, 9.

145. See for example USHMM RG.74.002, TsGA Almaty, f. 1137, Reel 4, op. 9, d. 141, l. 93; op. 6, d. 1279, l. 191; op. 6, d. 1278a, ll. 20–21. An evacuation official explained the confusion as the result of a "lack of political work" and "unfriendly attitudes" toward the newcomers.

146. Wolfgang Leonhard, *Child of the Revolution*, trans. C. W. Woodhouse (Chicago, 1958), 126–62. Leonhard left the Soviet Union in 1949 and had a long career as an expert on communism and Eastern Europe.

147. Ibid., 151–52.

essentially a form of militarized labor popularly known as the labor army. A subsequent decree of October 1942 extended the compulsory service to men aged fifteen to fifty-five and women from sixteen to forty-five, except those who were pregnant or had children less than three years old.[148] More than three hundred thousand recruits engaged in logging, factory, and railroad construction, and later, mining. For those already deported—the vast majority—labor army service represented yet another deportation. They included Evgenii Miller's father, who died while serving, his mother, who did not return until 1946, and his brother. Historians have found evidence of both a grim determination to demonstrate loyalty through overfulfillment of work quotas and efforts to escape, most of which were unsuccessful.[149]

Finally, German deportees were confined to exile for decades (Leonhard being among the exceptions), whereas evacuees had the right to return home and most did within a few years of the war's end, if not sooner. Most remained in Kazakhstan and Siberia until they emigrated in the late 1980s and early 1990s. The Volga German ASSR and other administrative territories created for Germans in the 1920s and 1930s did not survive the first months of the Great Patriotic War. Later, it was as if they and their inhabitants had never existed. The petitions submitted by Soviet Germans and the demonstrations they mounted in the 1970s to emigrate went unreported in the USSR. Their stories are both astonishing and moving.[150]

Already culled by border clearances in 1935–36, Finns living in the Leningrad area—so-called Ingrians (in Russian, *Ingermanlandtsy*; in Finnish, *Inkeriläiset*)—were subjected to the same deportation decree as Soviet Germans and shared the same fate. The blockade around Leningrad, imposed by the Nazis on September 8, 1941, ended deportation by train, but barges continued to carry some deportees across Lake Ladoga, undoubtedly saving many from starvation. A second, smaller deportation occurred in March 1942, that is, even as Leningraders were clamoring to be evacuated after the first siege winter.[151] According to

148. Auman and Chebotareva, *Istoriia rossiiskikh Nemtsev v dokumentakh*, 168–69, 172–73. See also N. F. Bugai, ed., "*Mobilizovat' Nemtsev v rabochie kolonny . . . I. Stalin*," *sbornik dokumentov (1940-e gody)* (Moscow, 1998).

149. Berdinskikh, *Spetsposelentsy*, 466–70. A. A. German and A. N. Kurochkin, *Nemtsy v SSSR v "Trudovoi armii": 1941–1945* (Moscow, 1998), 136–42.

150. See, aside from those already cited, Nelly Däs, ed., *Alle Spuren sind verweht: Rußlanddeutsche Frauen in der Verbannung* (Stuttgart, 1997); Wolfgang Ruge, *Gelobtes Land: Meine Jahre in Stalins Sowjetunion* (Reinbeck bei Hamburg, 2012); and the website devoted to Karbushevka, founded as a community of German deportees, at http://www.karbushevka.de/14101.html.

151. Pobol' and Polian, *Stalinskie deportatsii*, 326–30, 386–87. The plan sent by assistant commissar Merkulov to Beriia on August 30 included provision of 190 barges, each with a capacity of 500 people. In all, 88,700 Finns and 6,500 Germans were subject to "evacuation."

Vladimir Zemskov, nearly forty-five thousand Ingrian Finns were deported as special settlers—primarily to Krasnoiarsk krai and Irkutsk oblast'.[152] They had an easier time after the war leaving their places of exile than did the deported Germans. But in attempting to return to Leningrad oblast', they faced a maze of restrictions (see chapter 1) and, after Stalin's death, the opposition and hostility of settlers who had taken up residence in the meantime.

"Due to the fact that during the period of occupation of the Karachai Autonomous oblast' by the German fascist aggressors many Karachais behaved traitorously . . ." So began the Supreme Soviet's decree of October 1943 regarding these Turkic-speaking people of the North Caucasus. The decree banished "all Karachais residing on the territory . . . to other regions" of the country, and liquidated the Karachai Autonomous oblast'. The legal foundation for retributively deporting the Karachais, this decree served as the model for the same treatment of the Kalmyks in November 1943, the Chechens, Ingush, and Balkars in March 1944, and, last but by no means least, the Tatars and other peoples of Crimea in the spring and summer of 1944.[153]

Thirty-four convoys transported the nearly sixteen thousand Karachai families to the Dzhambul and South Kazakh oblasts of Kazakhstan and Kyrgyzstan's Frunze oblast'. They were distributed among already existing state and collective farms and placed under the rule of commandants, each of whom would be responsible for between ten and fifteen farming communities. In the case of the South Kazakh oblast', accommodation consisted of newly built "standard type" two-room houses, plus apartments made available through the "consolidation" of resident families. One wonders how well the latter—possibly ethnic Kazakhs, but conceivably deportees or evacuees who had arrived earlier in the war—got along with the newcomers. This deportation included snafus endemic to this particular kind of migration regime. But occurring relatively late in the war, it was particularly cruel in that it seemed to mock the sacrifices made by individual Karachai on behalf of the Soviet war effort. Among the deportees were war invalids, families of Red Army servicemen including officers, and members of partisan bands who had earned medals from the Soviet government for their actions against the German occupiers. These people collectively petitioned the Kazakh NKVD and that republic's Communist Party to release them from deportation, but as the responsible NKVD official in Alma-Ata wrote to his superiors in Moscow, "Lacking your instructions on how to review these complaints . . . we provisionally rejected them."[154]

---

152. Zemskov, Spetsposelentsy v SSSR, 95. A larger number of Ingrians lived under German occupation until their deportation to Finland in 1943–44, repatriation to the USSR, and administrative exile outside Leningrad oblast' after the war. For details see Ian M. Mately, "The Dispersal of the Ingrian Finns," Slavic Review 38, no. 1 (1979): 10–16.

153. Pobol' and Polian, Stalinskie deportatsii, 393, 412, 458, 489, 497. The relevant decree pertaining to the Crimean Tatars emanated from the State Defense Committee rather than the Supreme Soviet.

154. Ibid., 409.

The Supreme Soviet's decree on the deportation of all Kalmyks and the liquidation of the autonomous republic that bore their name reads similarly to the earlier decree on the Karachai. It claimed that "many Kalmyks had betrayed the Motherland," but it would be more accurate to say that merely living under German occupation for five months (August 1942–January 1943) doomed the Kalmyk people to deportation. Many Russians and Ukrainians lived under occupation too, and some who ardently collaborated paid for it dearly after liberation. But Russians and Ukrainians were too numerous to deport as a whole. With a total population of 134,402 in 1939, the Kalmyks, steppe-dwelling pasturalists living on the right bank of the lower Volga, were moveable. Zemskov may also be right when he surmises that Stalin intended deportation to serve as a mechanism for accelerated assimilation into Soviet society of insufficiently sovietized "small peoples."[155]

Thus, about 93,000 Kalmyks were moved in the teeth of the winter of 1943/44 to Siberia and in smaller numbers to Kazakhstan. According to Beriia, writing in November 1944, the Kalmyks had had a hard time adjusting to their new environment, and were facing another winter without adequate supplies of soap, tea, wool, and cotton fabric. He also indicated that the majority lacked shoes; a year later in October 1945, he wrote that "an absolute majority . . . lack clothes and shoes."[156]

Zemskov's small-people theory would hold for the Balkars deported in March 1944, but not the more numerous Chechens and Ingush. Moreover, the Chechen-Ingush titular autonomous republic did not fall under occupation, except for a small portion in the northwest. A better explanation of the events of February 1943 lies in the territory's historical unruliness—evident in low military recruitment and high desertion rates—combined with the NKVD's confidence derived from the expertise it had gained from other operations.[157] The deportation of Chechens and Ingush, accomplished in one week, dwarfed all other operations in the Caucasus in terms of the number of deportees (nearly 500,000), the strength of the forces used to carry it out (well over 100,000 NKVD troops, 70 percent of whom had previous experience), and the extent of resistance and brutality (slaughter of whole communities, arbitrary executions of children and the elderly). Pobol' and Polian consider it the "culmination of the USSR's entire deportation policy."[158]

---

155. Zemskov, *Spetsposelentsy v SSSR*, 107.

156. Pobol' and Polian, *Stalinskie deportatsii*, 425, 432–34.

157. On Chechen resistance to Soviet authority, particularly among draft-age men, see Aleksandr M. Nekrich, *The Punished Peoples: The Deportation and Fate of Soviet minorities at the End of the Second World War*, trans. George Saunders (New York, 1978), 50–57; N. F. Bugai, *Iosif Stalin–Lavrentiiu Berii: "Ikh nado deportirovat": Dokumenty, fakty, kommentarii* (Moscow, 1992), 98; P. M. Polian, "Operatsiia 'Chechevitsa': Nemtsy na Kavkaze i deportatsiia vainakhov v marte 1944 g.," in Kozlov et al., *Vainakhi i imperskaia vlast'*, 642, 663–67.

158. Pobol' and Polian, *Stalinskie deportatsii*, 436–42, 473.

Crammed into boxcars and suffering from the usual shortages, Chechens and Ingush experienced the full range of horrors to which deportees could be subjected both en route and in the years to follow. More than 100,000 deportees from the North Caucasus died between 1945 and 1950, according to NKVD-MGB data cited by Zemskov and others. By far the worst was the first year, when nearly 45,000 people died and only 2,230 were born.[159] Kazakhstan, that veritable sponge for soaking up deportees, received over three-quarters of the survivors, with the rest going to Kyrgyzstan. After fourteen years, in January 1957, a decree of the Supreme Soviet's Presidium restored to the Balkars, the Chechens and Ingush, the Kalmyks and Karachai their territorial homelands. The actual physical return of deportees, which had begun surreptitiously in the preceding years, varied in length of time and degree of orderliness. It appears to have been smoothest for the Balkars and most drawn out and complicated for the Chechens and Ingush. Clashes—sometimes violent—occurred between them and the settlers occupying their houses and land. Still, by 1961, 384,000 Chechens and 84,000 Ingush had returned from Kazakhstan and Kyrgyzstan.[160]

As a place of exile, perhaps even Kazakhstan was reaching a point of saturation after absorbing nearly half a million Ingush and Chechens. When it became the Crimean Tatars' turn in May 1944, most were sent to Uzbekistan with the remainder winding up in the Urals and European Russia. Rasmie Chelokhaeva was ten years old when that "awful moment" she never will forget occurred. At 4:00 a.m. on May 18, 1944, soldiers banged on the door of her house in the village of Tuak, crying, "Open up!" and then proceeded to bundle her off with her four siblings. "Everyone was shouting and crying," she remembers, "even the sheep and cows were bleating and bellowing."[161] Rasmie, whose father was killed at the front defending the Motherland and whose mother took six months to locate her children in an Uzbek orphanage, went on to study at a teachers college in the eastern Uzbek city of Kokand. In 1954 she graduated, married a fellow deportee, and began teaching in school. Free to travel and settle anywhere in the country—except Crimea—she remained in Uzbekistan for the next forty years. "All the time," she told an interviewer, "I wanted to return to Crimea," and by way of explanation cited the proverb, "Better to live like a pauper in your own land than like a tsar in a foreign land." In 1994 she and her husband did return.[162]

---

159. Zemskov, *Spetsposelentsy v SSSR*, 194. The MGB (Ministry of State Security) took over responsibilities for special settlements from the NKVD in 1946.

160. Robert Conquest, *The Nation Killers: The Soviet Deportation of Nationalities* (London, 1970), 141–63; Bugai, *Iosif Stalin–Lavrentiiu Berii*, 281–82.

161. Berta Bachmann also recalls the "howl of anguish from our dog" (whom the police shot) as she, her mother, and two sisters were led away from their house. Bachmann, *Memories of Kazakhstan*, 11.

162. "Rasmie Chelokhaeva," http://iremember.ru/grazhdanskie/chelokhaeva-rasmie-akimovna.html, 1–2 (accessed April 20, 2013).

The knock on Chelokhaeva's door repeated itself throughout the Crimean peninsula as some thirty-two thousand NKVD servicemen roused and rounded up the entire Tatar population. By 4:00 p.m. on May 20, approximately forty-five thousand families were on their way into exile. They were followed a month later by smaller contingents of Soviet Greeks, Bulgarians, and Armenians whose presence in Crimea the NKVD could no longer tolerate. Rasmie's journey to Fergana oblast' aboard a convoy seems absolutely typical—the boxcars lacking windows and toilets, the guards opening the doors for only five minutes at the stations, the ignorance of the passengers about their destination. She remembers that the trip took twenty-two days, the cabbage given to them had worms, and three people in their carriage died. Although Nariman Kazenbash's journey into exile took only eighteen days, he remembers seven of the forty-six in his carriage dying; two of whom were thrown into a river as the convoy rolled on. By contrast, nobody died in the carriage carrying Leilia Izmailova and thirty-five other passengers who also took eighteen days to reach their destination in Central Asia. Leilia attributes their relative good fortune to the fact that their departure on May 20 gave the authorities time to provide more food and water.[163]

Rasmie's experience was typical in one other respect: according to a Soviet dissertation from the mid-1960s cited by Aleksandr Nekrich, children comprised 53 percent of Crimean Tatars in the special settlements of Uzbekistan, women made up 32 percent, and men only 15 percent.[164] Where were the men? Some had died at the hands of the occupying Germans; some, like Rasmie's father, had fallen at the front; and others were in Red Army uniforms, but still very much alive. Alim Bekirov and Server Akimov were among them. While still in the service, Bekirov received a letter his brother had sent "from the shores of the Volga" as the family was on its way to Central Asia. Demobilized in 1946, he rejoined his family in the newly created town of Begovat on the Uzbek-Tajik border. Upon obtaining his passport at the local police station, Alim was shocked to discover he had to register with the commandant as a special settler. "Nobody resettled me," he told the commandant, "I came from the army—here are my papers!" Alim resolved to leave rather than subject himself to the humiliation of reporting once a month to the commandant, but in the end succumbed to his father's wish that he stay.[165] Akimov, whose first thought upon hearing about the deportation was that it only applied to collaborators, found his parents in Uzbekistan's Andizhan

---

163. "Nariman Kazenbash," http://iremember.ru/partizani/kazenbash-nariman-osmanovich.html, 4 (accessed April 21, 2013); "Leilia Izmailova," http://iremember.ru/grazhdanskie/izmaylova-salieva-leylya-ametovna.html, 2 (accessed April 21, 2013). For similar accounts, see Nekrich, *Punished Peoples*, 110–11.

164. The dissertation by Kh. I. Khutuev, "Balkarskii narod v gody velikoi otechestvennoi voiny i poslevoennyi period (Vosstanovlenie avtonomii balkarskogo naroda)," is cited in Nekrich, *Punished Peoples*, 115. Unfortunately, Nekrich does not indicate a date.

165. "Alim Bekirov," http://iremember.ru/zenitchiki/bekirov-alim-useinovich.html, 5–6 (accessed April 22, 2013). Begovat is now Bekovod.

oblast′. He settled there as well, getting a job repairing oil wells, and he too registered once a month and had a certain proportion of his pay subtracted to support the commandant.[166] Some soldiers never did reconnect with their parents. We already have encountered Iakub Faizullaev's fruitless search for his parents.[167] It is even possible they never made it to Uzbekistan, for as we already know, many died along the way.

Trying to sort out the fatality rate among the deportees—not only during their "middle passage" to Central Asia but even more so during the first two years when disorientation and despair compounded the effects of material shortages—is a tricky business. Claims of 46 percent made during the 1960s by the movement for the return and compensation of deported Crimean Tatars seem exaggerated. Nekrich cites a figure of 17.7 percent but admits to its incompleteness. Comparing "normally expected" and actual population increases between the censuses of 1939 and 1959, even allowing for losses due to war, is trickier still.[168]

We are more concerned with the meanings of such migrations for those experiencing them than with the extent of their casualties, which we cannot know.[169] One of those meanings is rooted in the chance encounters with childhood friends or lost relatives that survivors relate about their years in exile. People who know each other unexpectedly cross paths all the time; what made such encounters among deported people so meaningful was that both parties had experienced forced dispersion. The other person literally embodied the homeland. Server Akimov's encounter, for example, came in 1957 when his cousin recognized him as they were about to board a ship on Ukraine's Black Sea coast.[170] The utter unexpectedness of the meeting seems to have been profoundly comforting, diminishing their feelings of aloneness and perhaps reducing their sense of victimization.

We acknowledge as well that deportees' misfortune could make others indifferent, if not hostile. Galina Tat′kova, born in the Altai region in 1927, moved to Crimea in March 1941 after her mother's niece had written urging them to come because it was warm all year round. During the war, Galina joined the partisan movement and was nearly captured several times. In an interview about her wartime experiences, she mentions Tatars only twice, once as guards working for the Germans, and the second time when, in reply to the question of whether any had been part of her unit, said, "No, and not only that, but they even made a stand at Baksan, where a wealthy German lived . . . they basically were at war

---

166. "Server Akimov," http://iremember.ru/partizani/akimov-server.html, 1–2 (accessed April 23, 2013).

167. "Iakub Faizullaev," http://iremember.ru/pekhotintsi/fayzullaev-yakub-akhmetovich.html, 2–3 (accessed April 22, 2013). See chapter 5.

168. Nekrich, Punished Peoples, 112–14, 138.

169. At the same time, we recognize that survivors' accounts are only authoritative about their own recollections and the emotions they evoked.

170. "Server Akimov," 2.

with us."[171] She exults at the memory of liberation and the end of war and recalls the hunger of 1946 but has nothing to say about deportation. As for hostility, when an interviewer asked Efim Rybakov, a Kievan Jew who worked from 1942 to 1945 as an explosives expert in a wolfram mine near Samarkand, what kind of people worked at the mine, he replied, "Mostly Koreans, Uzbeks, and many Tatars, probably Crimean, because they were especially not liked, and they hated us. The Koreans were regular guys, we got along with them, but those Tatars were like beasts, and openly hated the Soviet regime."[172] The "because" is particularly revealing.

Borderland Deportees Redux

The machine continued to churn out deportees almost as if acting automatically. During 1944–45, as the Red Army drove the invading military forces out of the country and pursued them all the way to Berlin, the NKVD launched two new operations that targeted national groups. One, essentially prophylactic, harkened back to prewar border clearances of ethnic groups considered unreliable, only this time along the southern border with Turkey. The other returned to the sites of earlier actions in western Ukraine and the Baltic region, but now as retribution for collaboration with the Nazis and, after the Nazis' defeat, for taking up arms against the reassertion of Soviet power.

During the autumn of 1944, the Soviet government made deportees of three ethnic groups living in the southern part of Georgia: Meskhetian Turks, Kurds, and Hamshens (Armenian-speaking Sunni Muslims, also known as Hamshils, and in Russian as *Khemshiny*). Once the authorities had determined their portability, the next step, as usual, was to find space for them to occupy. The Kyrgyz and Uzbek government and party organizations did what central authorities expected of them by agreeing to absorb the requisite number of special settlers. Although at first their Kazakh counterparts caviled, claiming they needed more time, they accepted a slightly reduced number of families in the interests of concluding the operation before winter.[173]

Bugai and Gonov write that "nothing special distinguished the campaign to resettle these peoples of Georgia from earlier ones." However they do mention the participation of Studebaker trucks that the United States provided via the Lend Lease agreement, the fact that between 1941 and 1944 some of the deportees had helped build the local railroad line

---

171. "Galina Tat'kova," http://iremember.ru/grazhdanskie/tatkova-galina-petrovna.html, 3–4 (accessed April 23, 2013).

172. "Efim Rybakov," http://iremember.ru/grazhdanskie/ribakov-efim-yakovlevich-khaim-yankelevich.html, 3 (accessed April 23, 2013).

173. Bugai and Gonov, *Kavkaz*, 214–15.

that transported them away from their homeland, and that "many of those departing carried in their hands the works of J. Stalin, including his essay on 'Marxism and the National Question' (1912)." They also refer to documents indicating that "many considered the resettlement to be a rescue mission, because of the possibility of war with Turkey and Stalin's desire to protect civilians." One Meskhetian Turk, cited elsewhere by Bugai, recalled being told by the soldiers loading him and others into trucks that they had only a half hour to clear out of the village because "the Germans were near and we had to hurry so that everyone could be saved." Like Rasmie Chelokhaeva who recalled noises of animals, he could still hear the howling of dogs, the bellowing of cows, and the cries of children. But it would be many years later before he became aware of "that terrible word—deportation."[174]

Of over 90,000 deportees from Georgia, 50,000 were dispatched to Uzbekistan, 29,000 to Kazakhstan, and 10,500 to Kyrgyzstan. What certainly did not distinguish this operation from others was the inadequacy of supplies both during the journey and at its end. Writing to Beriia in January 1945, the head of the Uzbek NKVD reported that some 8,000 of the arriving "settlers" lacked food, clothing, and shoes.[175] Things do not seem to have gotten much better thereafter. In the longer term, despite the absence of any official accusations of collaboration with the enemy during the war and their release in 1956 from the special settlements, the Meskhetian Turks failed to secure their return to Georgia. Most remained in Uzbekistan until June 1989 when, in the midst of economic crisis, pogroms perpetrated by Uzbeks caused many to be evacuated to Azerbaijan and Russia, making them not deportees but refugees.[176]

Vitalii Petrenko, who was scarcely eighteen when his artillery unit crossed the Oder in pursuit of the retreating German army, greeted the end of the war in Prague. The respite was short. Three days later, his unit left the Czechoslovak capital for western Ukraine to combat the forces of the Ukrainian Insurgent Army (UPA), the military wing of the Organization of Ukrainian Nationalists (OUN). "It was worse than at the front," he recalled in an interview. "There, at least, you knew that ahead of you are the trenches and gun emplacements. But the 'Banderas' always shot at you from just around the corner." The task the Soviet government had set—"seeking out and destroying the bandits and sending their accomplices to Siberia"—required not standing on ceremony. So, at least for this soldier, the war did not end; it just took a different form. Actually, that war had been going on for at least a year. The first convoys of "accomplices" (that is, family members of known or

174. Ibid., 215–16; N. F. Bugai and M. I. Mamaev, *Turki-Meskhetintsy: Gruziia, Uzbekistan, Rossiia, SShA* (Moscow, 2009), 112.

175. Bugai and Gonov, *Kavkaz*, 219. See also Pobol' and Polian, *Stalinskie deportatsii*, 536.

176. On the failure of efforts to return to Georgia, see Conquest, *Nation Killers*, 187–89; Bugai and Mamaev, *Turki-Meskhetintsy*, 197–207; and Helsinki Watch, *"Punished Peoples" of the Soviet Union: The Continuing Legacy of Stalin's Deportations* (New York, 1991), 51–59.

suspected OUN-UPA members) left for Krasnoiarsk krai in April 1944. By October, western Ukraine's seven oblasts had coughed up over ten thousand deportees, and by April of the following year, just before Petrenko's unit arrived, Siberia had swallowed an additional thirteen thousand.[177]

The Soviet government deported members of its enemies' families both as a prophylactic measure to deprive what amounted to a guerilla movement of support and as retribution. Its extension of agricultural collectivization to western Ukraine contributed to this dynamic, producing deportees independent of families' political affinities, much like collectivization had done in the early 1930s in the rest of the country. The trains therefore continued to rumble eastward bearing their unhappy travelers. By November 1949, nearly 75,000 western Ukrainians had become residents of Siberian special settlements in Kemerovo oblast', Omsk, Cheliabinsk, and elsewhere. Between 1950 and 1952, nearly 56,000 additional deportees arrived from the same region. They comprised half of all new special settlers during these years. By January 1953, two months before the driver of this great locomotive engine died, the settlements contained over 170,000 western Ukrainians known officially as "OUNites" and known to Vitalii Petrenko as "Banderas."[178]

The same story can be told about Moldavia and the three Baltic republics. In each, armed bands previously allied with the Nazis and unreconciled to the restoration of Soviet power, the old economic and political elites, and farmers opposed to collectivization provided obvious targets for elimination. But tracking them down could take years, and in the meantime, their families could be deported. Lithuania, the most unruly of the three, gave up the most deportees. On May 22–23, 1948 under the code name "Spring," the MVD gathered together and entrained nearly fifty thousand individuals. The trains delivered them to settlements, mostly devoted to timber cutting, all over Irkutsk oblast', Krasnoiarsk krai, and the Buriat-Mongol ASSR.[179] This was just a prelude, though, to a far larger operation, code named "Surf," encompassing the entire Baltic region. Sanctioned by the Council of Ministers in late January 1949, the operation was conducted in late March by seventy-six thousand MGB soldiers and party activists, both local and from outside the region. More than thirty thousand families (nearly ninety-five thousand individuals) were transported to Siberia and the Russian Far East. The authorities in Moldavia took a little longer, but in April 1949 they received the go-ahead to launch "South," the operation to deport and resettle over forty thousand "kulaks, former landowners, major merchants, active collaborators with

---

177. "Vitalii Petrenko," http://iremember.ru/artilleristi/petrenko-vitaliy-mikhaylovich.html, 3 (accessed April 24, 2013). Stepan Bandera was the head of the OUN and from 1940 of the OUN-B, the more militant of the two factions into which that movement split; Pobol' and Polian, *Stalinskie deportatsii*, 568, 576, 579.

178. Bugai, *L. Beriia–I. Stalinu*, 209; Zemskov, *Spetsposelentsy v SSSR*, 198, 210; Amir Weiner, *Making Sense of War: The Second World War and the Fate of the Bolshevik Revolution* (Princeton, 2001), 173.

179. Bugai, *L. Beriia–I. Stalinu*, 229.

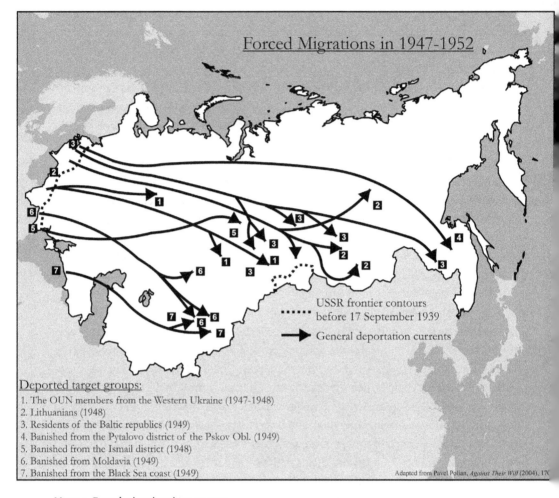

Map 7.3 Forced migrations in 1947–1952

German occupying forces and activists of pro-fascist parties." By the evening of July 7 they had completed the operation.[180]

This recitation of numbers risks dehumanizing the people whose lives deportation radically altered. Information we have provided in other cases about where deportees went, what they did when they got there, and how long they remained helps to envision life trajectories, but fails to convey the repertoires these forced migrants employed and the meanings they derived from their experiences. Despite the great variety in the experiences of

---

180. Polian, *Against Their Will*, 167–68.

coerced migrants, some patterns can be discerned. Some were so embittered they never recovered; and some, like Ivan Al-ov, the Vlasovite cited above, never made it out of the special settlement alive. Some decided to remain in their place of exile, blending in with other former *spetsposelentsy* as their pre-deportation selves retreated into an unrecoverable past; some settled down elsewhere seeking to establish new identities; and some returned home, making the necessary adjustments, albeit painfully.

The nine years that Aili Valdrand, an Estonian woman, spent in a special settlement occupied only a small portion of the sixty-four years she had accumulated when she wrote her life story just as the millennium drew to a close.[181] Nevertheless, her identity clearly revolved around those nine years. This is one reason we choose to dwell on her narrative. Another is its extraordinary self-reflectiveness. Born in 1936, Aili was the youngest of three surviving children of a farming couple on the island of Saaremaa. In 1944, as the "Russians" were about to return to Estonia, Aili's father and older brother "fled across the sea" to Sweden, leaving her and her mother to run the farm. "Thus my carefree childhood ended," she writes. Listed as kulaks in 1947, they were deported "from our homeland—permanently and forever" on March 25, 1949. Their new home was a dairy sovkhoz near Tatarsk, at the western edge of Novosibirsk oblast' about 125 miles east of Omsk.

Life on the sovkhoz made Valdrand tough. She did not go to school, but stayed home to work. "Work was required, but . . . I learned how to shirk . . . I found life at the tail end of a cow very boring. When they swore at me, I returned the favor." She picked up some attitudes of Russian children but "did not become completely russified, since the level of culture in my home was higher." Then again, she "blended in with the locals" and spoke Russian without an accent. Characterized by her mother as " 'Quick to cry, quick to laugh, even quicker to get angry,' " Aili recalled that she once had "to box the ears of two Russian women one right after the other to protect my mother. She was too submissive . . ."

In 1958, she and her mother were allowed to return home. Although at first elated by the news, she noticed already on the trip back that people behaved toward one another with less friendliness: "It was in Pskov that people with gloomy faces began boarding the train. No one shouted 'Hello, friend, how's it going?' as we had heard in Russian all those years in Siberia." At age twenty-two, Valdrand began her adult life among her own people, where she "felt stupid and backward," working as a field brigadier at a sovkhoz, as a machine knitter, and finally, in a day care center. Characteristic of people released from long-term incarceration, she tried "to make one day count for several, in order to make up for the time I had lost in Siberia." But material life remained difficult. It was from the day care center,

---

181. Kirss and Hinrikus, *Estonian Life Stories*, 439–55. Valdrand's story was one of several hundred submitted in a 1999 competition, "One Hundred Lives of a Century," and originally appeared in *Eesti rahva elulood*, an Estonian publication of 2000.

from the "scraps from other people's tables," that she was able to feed the son born to her after she met another former exile from Siberia. Although he refused to marry or live with her, we note that her most significant relationship was with a fellow deportee.

By the 1990s, her son was in the Technical School for Economics in Tallinn and Aili had retired and began to write her memoirs, as she finally was able to rest. Estonian deportees gathered every March 25. Relatives came from abroad, including her brother. By then it was "clearer than clear that the people from over there cannot understand us [Siberial exiles]." For all the decades that she lived in her home country, it is striking that Valdrand still considered it "a different planet":

> The old Estonian proverb says that everyone is the blacksmith of her own happiness. But if you have spent most of your life on a different planet, when you don't know the word "urine" and think it means something much thicker, and people smile over you at the polyclinic, then understandably, you skip over many things that a local person would do without thinking . . .

The impossibility of fitting in resonates with Valdrand's identification with Russia, as illustrated by her rescue of Russian-language books thrown out by the daycare center during the explosion of Baltic national hostility toward the Soviet Union in 1989. The rescue also testifies to her feistiness as does her offhand remark, "life has never quite been successful at flattening me."

The last deportations listed by Polian in his book on forced migrations date from 1951 and early 1952. They involved not a large but quite eclectic group of people—Jehovah's Witnesses from Moldavia, the Baltic republics, and western Ukraine; kulaks from the same areas who somehow had avoided earlier deportations; Adventists and Innokentevites from Moldavia and southern Ukraine.[182] Rumors of a plan to deport Soviet Jews to the Jewish Autonomous oblast' surfaced in connection with the Doctors' Plot of 1952–53 and have swirled ever since, but Stalin's death on March 5 led to the release of the accused doctors and the end of mass deportations.

The number of deportees and special settlers had continued to climb in the postwar years: in July 1949 it stood at 2.55 million and by July 1952 it reached 2.77 million. But as Zemskov notes, the material and living conditions of the special settlers was improving such that "the newly born became the main source of growth in [their] numbers" rather than newly arrived "settlers."[183] All the while, the legal differences between these and other

---

182. Polian, *Against Their Will*, 333; Pobol' and Polian, *Stalinskie deportatsii*, 798.

183. Pobol' and Polian, *Stalinskie deportatsii*, 762; Zemskov, *Spetsposelentsy v SSSR*, 198, 203 (quotation on 198).

Soviet citizens were diminishing. First, deportees' children who married someone from the outside could leave their places of confinement; then, graduation from an institution of higher learning released them. In the aftermath of Stalin's death, the highest organs of the Soviet government and Communist Party began to adopt measures proposed by the MVD to release different categories of special settlers such as former kulaks deported before 1933 and Soviet Germans from certain parts of the country. Supreme Soviets in Moldavia and the Baltic republics reviewed and overturned decisions from the late 1940s and early 1950s to deport thousands of peasants on the grounds that the designation of "kulak" was inaccurate. Yet because the subjects of these measures received no compensation and were forbidden from returning to their previous places of residence, the freedom they received was most often theoretical.

The legislation was sufficiently encouraging, however, to embolden some families to pick up stakes and try their luck at returning to their old homes. Some historians suggest that these "irregular" returns hastened the formal granting of the right of return and the restoration of territorial administrative autonomy to the peoples of the North Caucasus in 1957–58. Given the territorial adjustments and extent of demographic replacement that had occurred in the intervening years, homecomings could only have been bittersweet, if not in some cases provoking of interethnic violence. That, though, is a story that would take us well beyond the limits of this chapter. All but the hard core of anti-Soviet partisans ("bandits") could join the exodus from the special settlements. For example, Ligita Dreif-elde, the Latvian woman who had accompanied her mother into Siberian exile at age fourteen, returned at long last to Latvia in May 1957 with her husband—a March 1949 deportee—and their four-year-old daughter.[184] For some groups of deportees—notably, the Crimean Tatars, Meskhetian Turks, and Germans—administrative exile rather than homecoming replaced special settler status. A legally formulated right of return remained elusive for decades to come.[185]

The special settlements themselves dwindled in population from nearly 150,000 at the beginning of 1958 to less than 50,000 a year later. The toughest nuts to crack from the state's point of view were the OUNites: they far outnumbered any other group, comprising 70 percent of all special settlers at the beginning of 1959. Officially classified as bandits and

---

184. Kalniete, *With Dance Shoes*, front matter.

185. Nekrich, *Punished Peoples*, 137–66; Polian, *Against Their Will*, 194–223. Between the censuses of 1989 and 2001, over two hundred thousand Crimean Tatars returned to Crimea. Their percentage of the total population in Crimea increased from 1.9 to 12.1 percent. Nearly seven of ten respondents in 1998 claimed their material situation worsened after returning. See A. Viatkin, "Krymskie Tatary: Vozvrashchenie na rodinu i problem adaptatsii," in Viatkin, Kostomarskaia, and Panarin, *V dvizhenii dobrovol'nom i vynuzhden-nom*, 272–75. For official census data, see "Glavnoe upravlenie statistiki v Avtonomnoi respublike Krym," http://sf.ukrstat.gov.ua/perepis.htm (accessed April 29, 2013).

nationalists, accomplices, or kulak-nationalists, they, along with their Baltic counterparts, received a reprieve from the USSR Supreme Soviet only in 1960, thus bringing to a close this sorry chapter in Soviet history.[186]

Or almost. As Pobol' and Polian indicate, "relapses" of forced resettlement occurred as late as the mid-1960s when authorities in the Tajik SSR abandoned attempts to persuade mountain-dwelling ethnic minority groups to voluntarily resettle in the valleys next to irrigated cotton fields and resorted to forced resettlement. In some cases, after piling the villagers into trucks, police destroyed their homes and irrigation ditches. Motivated by the necessity of bringing in the all-important cotton crop, the transplantation of these people exposed them to unfamiliar microbes, thus making them vulnerable to dysentery, diphtheria, and tuberculosis. Similar actions in Dagestan are alleged, though we have no information on their extent.[187]

We have argued that the animus for mass deportation came from a combination of revolutionary ambitiousness and insecurity, the latter stemming in part from the recognition of extensive popular hostility to the state's transformative agenda. After Stalin, the Soviet state grew less ambitious, but also less insecure, and consequently, mass deportation as one of the state's main regimes of migration became a thing of the past. However, insecurity, born of new political and economic configurations, returned to the former Soviet Union in the 1990s. In some places it fueled popular antipathies, resulting in interethnic violence and the production of refugees. In Moscow, the expanded presence of Caucasians—among them, refugees—and their much-sensationalized association with crime and the antics of petty capitalism produced popular insecurity and demands for order. Moscow's mayor Iurii Luzhkov evidently saw this situation as an opportunity to assert his leadership by endorsing crackdowns by the regular police and the OMON (Special Purpose Mobile Unit) against darker-skinned people whose papers were not in order.[188]

Expulsion figured as a weapon in the Moscow city government's arsenal. During and immediately following the showdown between President Yeltsin and the legislature, the police declared a state of emergency (October 3–18, 1993). In the course of those days, they expelled between nine thousand and twelve thousand "immigrants," 90 percent of whom reportedly hailed from Azerbaijan, Armenia, and Georgia. Another ten thousand or so left voluntarily, fearing random and sometimes brutal police searches. *Plus ça change, plus c'est la même chose.* Almost exactly a century earlier, the Moscow and St. Petersburg city administrations saw fit to expel an estimated twenty thousand people "of other origin" (*inorodtsy*)— their origin being not in the Caucasus but of the Mosaic faith. Chechen refugees and Central

---

186. Zemskov, *Spetsposelentsy v SSSR*, 263–77.

187. Pobol' and Polian, *Stalinskie deportatsii*, 776.

188. Meredith L. Roman, "Making Caucasians Black: Moscow since the Fall of Communism and the Racialization of Non-Russians," *Journal of Communist Studies and Transition Politics* 18, no. 2 (2002): 1–27.

Asian immigrants would receive similar treatment as the twentieth century drew to a close.[189]

But, as we noted at the outset, expulsion is not identical to deportation. "Escorted by police officers," the victims of the state of emergency operation "were sent home by rail" rather than deported from their homelands.[190] True, as in earlier Soviet times, authorities were quick to employ the same hygienic metaphor of "cleansing," and they distinguished native or "our" folk from "aliens," now with clear racial overtones.[191] Yet the echo of deportation was faint. When in years to come people faced expulsion, it more likely had to do with the application of the new capitalist regime of gentrification in the central districts of Moscow and other major cities than any impulse for social engineering or sense of insecurity.[192]

---

189. Lidiia Osheverova and Anton Bulanov, "'Kazaki-razboiniki' na stolichnykh rynkakh," *Izvestiia*, October 14, 1993, 5; Gillian Tett, "Moscow Slated over Rights: 'Campaign Against Ethnic Minorities' Criticised by Helsinki Group," *Financial Times*, October 16, 1993, 2; Carlotta Gall, "Moscow's Refugees Face 'Second Deportation,'" *The Moscow Times*, March 1, 1996; Keith Gessen, "From the Caucasus to Moscow," *The Moscow Times*, July 19, 1997.

190. Tett, "Moscow Slated over Rights," 2.

191. Roman, "Making Caucasians Black," passim.

192. Natal'ia Rogozina, "Zhdite nasil'stvennogo vyseleniia," *Nezavisimaia gazeta*, September 30, 1997.

~CHAPTER EIGHT~

Itinerants

"There is no life without movement," Kazakh saying
—Mukhamet Shayakhmetov, *The Silent Steppe*

This chapter does not fit the typology of migration that has framed our study, nor did the denizens of this chapter fit snugly into the categories employed by respective Russian states to make their populations legible.[1] It is about people who did not seek to be part of a sedentary society, but who rather sought to remain on the margins, or whose lifeways were rooted in migrations. The first group consisted of escapees, tramps, beggars, and orphans fending for themselves, whose ambition it was to fall through the cracks or to begin a new life under a new identity. The second were the mobile people for whom being on the move was central to their life routines, at least at the beginning of the twentieth century: the Roma, the reindeer herders of the Far North, and the livestock-herding pastoralists of Kazakhstan. Both groups found themselves contending with a state that wished them to settle down and be counted—or at least identified. That is, the dominant regime the state wished to impose was not one of migration, but rather settlement. This is the story, then, of the stormy relationship between migrants and an antimigration regime; it is also the story of the ambitions and repertoires of fugitives, wanderers, and nomads.

Writing about these people who either shunned detection or attached themselves to regular migration itineraries presents a considerable challenge. Even more than with other categories of migrants, we find their voices muted and evidence of their intentions and agency scarce. Aside from a few conversations recorded by travelers from abroad and the

---

1. Our typology of migrations distinguishes among kinds of movement, that is, the connections (or lack of connections) between home and destination, the permanence of the move, and degree of coercion (see introduction, 13).

odd memoir or two—sources that contain their own limitations—we are dependent on the word of contemporary officials, sojourners, and social commentators as well as scholars' retrospective insights. Yet, if we lack confirmation of aspirations and motives, we are not entirely clueless. We assume that prevarication and camouflage are part of these people's repertoires, we read sources at our disposal against the grain, and we legitimately draw inferences from studies of people in similar situations elsewhere.

Fugitives

We have threaded fugitives throughout this book because every carceral—and many a welfare—regime had its escapees. Conscripted men disappeared. Children slipped away from state orphanages. Special settlers who managed to escape took to the road. Migrants from Central Asia and the Caucasus on the worksites and in the markets of large post-Soviet Russian cities spent much energy avoiding harassment and deportation by police who considered them illegals. We have discussed these people previously because they were engaged in one form or another of migration before they chose the repertoire of flight or evasion. Others avoided incarceration, deportation, or just social opprobrium via self-reinvention and imposture.[2]

Laying low was another strategy. For many families the dekulakization efforts of the late 1920s and early 1930s made laying low a way of life. Here, we cite but one instance, that of Mariia Nikishova's family from a village in Ul'ianovsk oblast' bordering on the Volga. When, in late 1929, the burden of increased taxes became crushing, Mariia's father obtained false documents identifying him as a middle peasant and left for the city of Frunze in Central Asia. By the time he returned home a year later, someone had denounced him and he "fled into the fields." Mariia's mother was sent to prison but the rest of the family scattered: her older brother to Leningrad, where he became a dockworker; her sister Nina to another town, where she found work in a clothing factory; and Mariia, the youngest of four siblings, and her other brother to live with their maternal grandmother. In the summer of 1931, her father turned up in the town where Nina was working, found work himself, and was joined by her mother, who had escaped from prison. By 1933 the entire family was together again and living in a 14-square meter room in a barracks 30 miles west of Sverdlovsk. The father and younger brother worked as bricklayers, but were often cheated and did not earn much because, like illegals everywhere, they "were afraid to stand up for themselves."

---

2. See Sheila Fitzpatrick, *Tear Off the Masks! Identity and Imposture in Twentieth-Century Russia* (Princeton, 2005). See also the fascinating "Case of Kiril Korenev" in David R. Shearer, *Policing Stalin's Socialism: Repression and Social Order in the Soviet Union, 1924–1953* (New Haven, 2009), 371–404. We discuss this case below.

The older brother worked at a potassium bi-chromate factory. In 1935, he received an induction notice from the army and reported for service. The rest of the family fled to Kazan, fearing the authorities would be on to the parents. That is where Mariia finished high school, graduating just before the war. Thus for a decade, Mariia's family led a precarious existence on the lam, earning just enough to get by.[3]

Fugitives *from* carceral institutions also populated Russian territory in the twentieth century. Men and women who escaped from the Imperial Russian system of prison and exile settlement had the greatest presence in Siberia as *brodiagi*. Usually translated as vagrants, the term *brodiagi* comprised a broad legal category of people without institutional connections, police authorization, or a way to prove the legitimacy of their status.[4] To read contemporary sources, Siberia was crawling with them. In 1894, James Simpson reported that captured brodiagi made up 20 percent of prisoners in the trans-Baikal territories—and the most troublesome during the trek to prison because they were inflated by a superior sense of experience and "their marvelous *esprit de corps*."[5] The Amur's governor-general in the 1890s put the proportion of brodiagi among exile-settlers as up to half.[6] Brodiagi on the loose—fugitive exiles—were thick on the ground because men especially found it easy to escape remote prisons and exile assignments. For example, reports Andrew Gentes, "depending on the exilic category, Siberian administrators could not account for the whereabouts of between 10 and 50 percent of those exiled between 1887 and 1898."[7]

Those outside the prison system saw fugitive exiles as a threat. "He who has not lived long in Siberia cannot understand how terrible the reverberations of exile have been on its inhabitants," the Irkutsk newspaper *Siberia* complained in the 1880s, "how much innocent blood has been shed thanks to the wandering masses of drunken, embittered, unsheltered people here; how much moral evil these wretches have spread and how many unbearable hardships have been imposed on local inhabitants by exiles' actions!"[8] They were, indeed, active in the theft and murder that plagued Siberia and the rural empire; in Irkutsk province, for example, exiles and brodiagi accounted for 44 percent of the convictions for crimes in 1886.[9]

---

    3. Slavko, *Kulatskaia ssylka na Urale*, 158–60.

    4. "Brodiazhnichestvo," in *Entsiklopedicheskii slovar'*, F. A. Brokgauz, I. A. Efron (St. Petersburg, 1891), vol. 4, 695.

    5. Simpson, *Side-Lights on Siberia*, 176.

    6. Rossiiskii gosudarstvennyi istoricheskii arkhiv dal'nego vostoka, f. 1, op. 1, d.1383, ll. 4–37 [l.7], cited in Andrew Gentes, "Vagabondage and Siberia: Disciplinary Modernism in Tsarist Russia," in *Cast Out: Vagrancy and Homelessness in Global and Historical Perspective*, ed. A. L. Beier and Paul Ocobock (Athens, OH, 2008), 185.

    7. Gentes, "Vagabondage and Siberia," 195.

    8. Translated from *Sibir'* (Irkutsk), April 5, 1887, by Gentes, "Vagabondage and Siberia," 196.

    9. Gentes, "Vagabondage and Siberia," 197; for rural crime, see Stephen P. Frank, *Crime, Cultural Conflict, and Justice in Rural Russia, 1856–1914* (Berkeley, 1999), 115–44.

What ambitions did these elusive people harbor? Most fundamentally, to escape prison and exile life—to choose their own place and perhaps return home. Although many begged and threatened their fellow subjects, and some were doubtless the hardened criminals they were feared to be, they did seek employment in order to live. Nikolai Iadrintsev noted in the 1870s that brodiagi worked as "sentries, beekeepers, herdsmen, millers . . . tailors, cobblers, glassblowers, brewers, saddlers, locksmiths, and joiners." But they were perhaps more likely to be engaged in summertime work as harvesters.[10] As Trotsky observed years later, remembering his days in exile, "The police in Siberia were as helpless as we were. The vastness of the country was an ally, but an enemy as well. It was very hard to catch a runaway, but the chances were that he would be drowned in the river or frozen to death in the primeval forests."[11] In other words, Siberia was dangerous for a fugitive, and especially so in the winter, and for this reason, many brodiagi followed an annual rhythm.

Prison escapes followed the seasons. In the spring, "when the ice mantle begins to disappear, and the snow weeps off the prison roof to the black earth beneath, and the trees come out of bondage, casting away their chilly fetters, and the song-birds rejoice," as Simpson so poetically put it in 1894, prisoners found ways to escape. In the language of the peasantry, they were following the call of the cuckoo, joining General Kukushka's army.[12] Peasants who were sympathetic (or fearful of reprisals) left some stores of food for brodiagi in their own summer pastures and some villagers left food out on a windowsill or doorstep for these people.[13] The imagined life on the lam is well recorded, but aside from court records of convicted murderers, the reality is more elusive. Nonetheless, "Russia's substantial population of underemployed and unemployed, indigents, drifters, and escapees from prison or exile" was most visible in the summer months.[14] Provincial records show that the inmate population expanded in fall and winter. "Along with thousands of Russia's wandering vagabonds who had fled their places of exile," affirms Stephen Frank, "it was common practice to turn oneself over to authorities with the onset of winter, hoping for a warm prison cell until spring."[15] As they entered or reentered prison, a remarkable proportion of brodiagi effectively disguised their identity by claiming fantastic surnames, but most often chose the name Nepomniashchii—not remembering/don't remember.[16]

10. Nikolai M. Iadrintsev, Russkaia obshchina v tiur'me i ssylke (St. Petersburg, 1872), 434, cited in Gentes, "Vagabondage and Siberia," 199.

11. Leon Trotsky, My Life: An Attempt at an Autobiography, 3 vols. (New York, 1930), 1: 132.

12. Simpson, Side-Lights on Siberia, 177–78.

13. Ibid., 178.

14. Frank, Crime, 140.

15. Ibid., 142.

16. Most visitors to the camps and prisons noted this, as did Anton Chekhov in his 1890 survey of Sakhalin; Gentes, "Vagabondage and Siberia," 196.

People continued to be incarcerated and to escape from prisons and prison camps throughout the last years of tsarism and again in the early Soviet period. We have decided to revisit fugitives at the apex of incarceration—the period from the formation of the labor camp system (the Gulag) in 1930 until the death of Stalin in 1953. Before the opening of the archives, information about escapes came in anecdotal form from ex-camp inmates who published their accounts after emigrating or had them smuggled abroad. Virtually all of these authors were educated people. In *Gulag Archipelago*, Aleksandr Solzhenitsyn amplified their voices, most notably that of Georgi Tenno, who contributed an entire chapter. Solzhenitsyn himself concluded that escape from the camps was "an enterprise for giants among men—but for doomed giants," and other former inmates corroborate this contention.[17]

But as Anne Applebaum has noted, "both attempted and successful escapes were more common than most memoirists concede," numbering in the tens of thousands every year. This makes sense, for during the period of the Gulag population's rapid expansion, camp administrators lagged behind in tightening the noose of security. In 1933 the Gulag logged nearly 46,000 people as having escaped, of whom 38 percent got away without capture. The following year, 1934, was an all-time high, with the NKVD reporting over 83,000 escapees. Thereafter, even as the camp population swelled, the number escaping tailed off, suggesting not improved conditions—as in the case of the special settlements discussed in the previous chapter—but rather an increasingly strict regimen that made escapes harder to pull off and successful ones rarer still. By 1941, escapes were down to about 10,500.[18] Their numbers dropped further still during the war. Postwar fugitives, some of whom had been toughened for escape by service in the Soviet armed forces and time in German POW camps, had greater success remaining at large—in 1947, for example, nearly three-quarters got away.[19]

This doesn't mean it was easy. Solzhenitsyn contrasts the extravagant lengths to which the Soviet state would go to bring in fugitives, including payments to those who turned in prisoners, with the situation in tsarist times when

> surveillance was poor, there were no secret police posts along the roads, you were not tied to your work day in and day out by police supervision; you had money (or it could be sent to you), and places of banishment were not remote from the great rivers and

17. Solzhenitsyn, *Gulag Archipelago*, 154–92 (quotation on 97).

18. Anne Applebaum, *GULAG, A History* (New York, 2003), 393–94; Steven Barnes, *Death and Redemption: The Gulag and the Shaping of Soviet Society* (Princeton, 2011), 139; Oleg Khlevniuk, *The History of the Gulag from Collectivization to the Great Terror* (New Haven, 2004), 308.

19. Applebaum, *GULAG*, 395; Solzhenitsyn, *Gulag Archipelago*, 126, 193–94.

roads; again, no threat hung over anyone who helped a runaway, nor indeed was the runaway himself in danger of being shot by his pursuer, or savagely beaten, or sentenced to twenty-five years' hard labor . . .[20]

The Soviet state's pursuit was especially intense for fugitives from the Special Camps designed in the postwar period for "especially dangerous state [political] criminals," whereas those imprisoned for lesser political crimes, and ordinary criminals, remained in Corrective Labor Camps.

Any escape was too many for the security authorities.[21] Georgi Tenno escaped from the Special Camp of Ekibastuz in northeastern Kazakhstan. When captured, he and his fellow escapee were informed that the state had spent 102,000 rubles on their recapture: some work had been discontinued so that guards could go out on the hunt; 23 vehicles had searched the steppe, spending their annual allotment of fuel; search groups had been dispatched to neighboring towns and settlements; and a nationwide search had begun with the distribution of four hundred photographs of Tenno and his companion. This information was meant to shame the fugitives, but instead it made them proud of their survival during weeks on the lam.[22]

Professional criminals (urki)—denizens of the burgeoning underworld of the Soviet period—engendered less elaborate attempts at recapture. We know little about criminals escaping because many of them were illiterate and in any case not prone to write memoirs. We only hear second hand about escapes like that of three criminal prisoners from Cape Lazarev near Sakhalin Island—in the tank of the truck that came weekly to empty camp latrines. The toughness and networks of the urki enabled them to have greater success than political prisoners. It is no accident, speculates Solzhenitsyn, that Georgi Tenno, the "committed escaper," had learned a thing or two from the underworld in his past life as a sailor and circus worker—then from his cohabitation with urki in disciplinary barracks of several prisons.[23]

---

20. Solzhenitsyn, *Gulag Archipelago*, 96. The rewards for turning in a fugitive were substantial enough to motivate some men to earn their living as bounty hunters, like Yegor of Lazarev, who reportedly was paid 5,000 rubles, alcohol, white flour, meat, and tea for each murder of a confirmed escapee. See A. P. Butskovsky, "The Fate of a Sailor," in *Voices from the Gulag*, ed. Aleksandr Solzhenitsyn (Evanston, 2010), 190–91.

21. Barnes, *Death and Redemption*, 164–68, 199–200. For measures taken to eliminate escapes, see A. B. Bezborodov and V. M. Khrustalev, eds., *Istoriia stalinskogo Gulaga: Konets 1920-kh–pervaia polovina 1950-kh godov: Sobranie dokumentov v 7-mi tomakh*, t. 4, *Naselenie Gulaga: Chislennost' i usloviia soderzhaniia* (Moscow, 2004), no. 75 (188), no. 84 (199–202).

22. Applebaum, *GULAG*, 280–92; Khlevniuk, *History of the Gulag*, doc. 39, 119–23; Solzhenitsyn, *Gulag Archipelago*, 191.

23. Among the many observations of the differences between the underworld and the so-called politicals, see Barnes, *Death and Redemption*, 164; Solzhenitsyn, *Gulag Archipelago*, 127. For the escape, see Butskovsky, "Fate of a Sailor," 190–92.

Thanks to David Shearer's painstaking work of assembling the story of Kiril Kirilovich Korenev from the USSR Procuracy (*Prokuratura*) files, we have an example of an expert fugitive who often defied the NKVD and police. Although the son of Socialist Revolutionaries, he was not exactly a political but rather was repeatedly arrested for hooliganism and petty theft. He was sufficiently adept at writing to forge passports and identity papers, and after release from the White Sea NKVD camp administration, practiced journalism as a corresponding staff writer for *Komsomol'skaia Pravda*. Precisely during the years when escapes were on the decline in the late 1930s, Korenev used every trick in the book to escape: he slipped away from a transfer point, swapped identities with a fellow prisoner, assumed the identity of a dockside acquaintance, and managed to walk away from several camps. He experienced camp life from one end of the country to another, from the White Sea to Vladivostok and Khabarovsk. The record encompasses eight years of his life, from 1933 until the commutation of his death sentence in May 1941. Shearer considers Korenev's story far from unique, "repeated not in the thousands but in the millions."[24] This does not do justice to Korenev's unusual skill and will to remain at large again and again.

Escape stories have a tripartite structure: the planning, the flight from the camp, and the journey. Although some escapes were spontaneous, most prisoners relate meticulous planning and preparation. They fashioned or managed to steal weapons, such as knives and the essential wire-cutter and compass, to set aside food and to scrounge supplies such as civilian clothing. How and when to depart required a plan that matched guard routines and prisoner visibility. For example, before his escape from Ekibastuz, Tenno and his partner established the routine of playing chess outdoors near the guard tower—eccentrically carrying a briefcase that could later be filled with supplies—and cutting their way out so near to the tower that they could not easily be seen by guards.[25] Seasonality still prevailed, as it had in Imperial Russia: men (for most fugitives were men) escaped into the taiga in spring and summer, in Kazakhstan in the cooler seasons, and in the frozen north in winter, before thaws turned the terrain to swamps.

Tension surrounded the moment of departure, when planning would pay off or fugitives would be sighted and caught. The great tasks of cutting and getting through barbed wire fences and eluding guards and guard dogs were only possible if nothing were suspected. Slavomir Rawicz's detailed description of cutting through barbed wire on a snowy night, scaling two 12-foot fences, and leaping over rolled wire with six fellow escapees while listening for guard dogs illustrates the importance attached to this brief episode.[26] Tenno

---

24. Shearer, *Policing Stalin's Socialism*, 371–404 (quotation on 404).

25. Solzhenitsyn, *Gulag Archipelago*, 191, 150–54. Vladimir Chernavin and Tat'iana Chernavina, *Zapiski "Vreditelia": Pobeg iz GULAGa* (St. Petersburg, 1999), 312–28, 441–45; this is the Russian-language edition of two memoirs originally published in English in 1934.

26. Slavomir Rawicz, *The Long Walk* (New York, 1956), 93–97. Other elements of this memoir defy credibility, as Applebaum observes in *GULAG*, 399.

relates in equally vivid detail his crawl through boundary wire and the main wire fence, hoist over the wooden fence and, last, over rolled wire, all under the expectation of machine-gun fire. Once "beyond the wire," fugitives scarcely had time to absorb the sweetness of freedom; they kept moving, exposed to enormous physical and psychological strain. It is not surprising that those who have left accounts of their escapes refer to overworked imaginations and hallucinations.[27]

The journeys themselves delineate itineraries of avoidance. At least in the beginning, they were undertaken entirely on foot. The danger of being turned in meant that fugitives tried to be self-sufficient, but hunger and thirst drove them to threaten, cajole, or lie to those they encountered.[28] The Chernavins, traversing the dense Karelian forests and swamps in the summer of 1932 to reach nearby Finland, had no worries on this score, for water was plentiful and they did not see a soul. But fugitives who traveled near settlements, such as the Polish escapees from northeastern Siberia who encountered some settlers as they skirted the eastern shore of Lake Baikal, and Tenno, who saw villagers, river buoy keepers, and a leisure cruise ship on the Irtysh River, had to be more wary.[29] "People moved to escape disaster," writes Mark Edele. In the case of fugitives from the Gulag, they were not guided by their "long and deep histories," but rather by the impulse to stay out of sight.[30]

Wanderers

Roma

In August 1952, Boris Chernousov, the chairman of the RSFSR Council of Ministers, drafted a request to Georgii Malenkov, widely regarded at the time as Stalin's most likely successor as Communist Party leader. Chernousov wanted the USSR's Ministry of Internal Affairs to settle "nomadic Gypsies" at construction sites under its authority—meaning the Gulag—where they could be employed and receive assistance in obtaining skills. At a time when the Gulag had reached its maximum population of some 2.6 million inmates, the chances of Chernousov's request being fulfilled were slight. It is not even certain that he sent it.[31] For our

---

27. Solzhenitsyn, *Gulag Archipelago*, 154–55, 162.

28. For an example of all three, see Tenno's story in Solzhenitsyn, *Gulag Archipelago*, 154–92.

29. Rawicz, *Long Walk*, 125–35; Solzhenitsyn, *Gulag Archipelago*, 159–79.

30. Mark Edele, *Stalinist Society, 1928–1953* (Oxford, 2011), 72–73.

31. USHMM 22.027M, GARF, f. A-327, Reel 48, op. 1, d. 90, ll. 89–90. This is an unsigned draft. Chernousov uses the Russian word *tsygane*, linguistically related to the German *zigeuner*, the Romance languages' *gitano/gitan*, and the English *gypsy*. Alaina Lemon reported in 1991 "at least ten groups classified as 'Tsygane' that differ in dialect, language and culture." See Lemon, "Roma (Gypsies) in the Soviet Union and the Moscow Teatr 'Romen,'" *Nationalities Papers* 19, no. 3 (1991): 367. We follow her lead in using the word "Roma" (or the adjectival "Romani") when speaking in our voices and "Gypsies" when reproducing contemporary speech and perspectives.

purposes, its main importance lies in what provoked it—the persistence of at least some Roma in pursuing a way of life in defiance of Soviet norms and previous attempts to sedentarize and civilize them.

Roma long represented the antithesis to settled agriculture and law-abiding society. Stereotypical itinerants, they often went unregistered, rarely paid taxes, and crossed both internal and international borders at will. Their association with certain trades but especially peddling, repair work, theft, and smuggling dates back at least several centuries.[32] In Russia, where the state historically used confession as the main criterion for distinguishing among peoples of the Empire, Roma were anomalous: those in Crimea and Central Asia practiced Islam, whereas the Roma of Ukraine, the Polish provinces, the Baltic region, and the Russian heartland adhered to different denominations of Christianity.[33] They also were extremely hard to count. The 1897 census recorded 44,582 Roma, of whom 85 percent lived in the countryside. The New Russian provinces of the south contained the largest concentration, followed by Bessarabia in the southwest, and Siberia. David Crowe, who has written extensively on Roma in Eastern Europe and Russia, has difficulty explaining why the census figure is several thousands lower than estimates from the 1830s and 1860s: was it the cholera epidemic of 1891–92, Romani adoption of alternative (Tatar and Turkmen) identities, or some other factor?[34] The suspicion is that because of their unusually high degree of itinerancy, Roma tend to be undercounted, but by how much?

Did Romani mobility disrupt or paradoxically support the immobile structures of Russian society? It could be argued that much like the noble savage or the small peoples of the north, the imputation of certain qualities to "the Gypsy"—exoticness, obliviousness to restraints of all kinds, but especially legal and sexual—helped to define the moral and legal boundaries for others, especially in educated society. Students of Pushkin and Tolstoy, both of whom helped to romanticize the Gypsy for generations to come, are familiar with this argument.[35] Perhaps, then, Romani mobility depended on immobile structures.

---

32. For Western Europe, see Leo Lucassen, Wim Willems, and Annemarie Cottaar, eds., *Gypsies and Other Itinerant Groups: A Social-Historical Approach* (New York, 1999). Lucassen argues that police in Germany from the eighteenth century onward considered vagrants and Roma almost indistinguishable. See Lucassen, *Zigeuner: Die Geschichte eines polizeilichen Ordnungsgegriffes im Deutschland, 1700–1945* (Weimar, 1996).

33. For evidence of syncretic practices among Crimean Roma combining elements of Islam and Christianity, see Lev Tcherenkov and Stéphane Laederich, *The Roma: Otherwise Known as Gypsies, Gitanos, Gyphtoi, Tsiganes . . .*, 2 vols. (Basel, 2004), 2: 567–79.

34. David M. Crowe, *A History of the Gypsies of Eastern Europe and Russia* (New York, 1994), 170–71.

35. On the persistence of this image see Alaina Lemon, *Between Two Fires: Gypsy Performance and Romani Memory from Pushkin to Postsocialism* (Durham, 2000), 31–55.

The role of the Roma in the circulation of certain goods outside legal strictures suggests an economic synergy at work. Among these goods, horses occupy much space in legal records and ethnographic accounts. Settlers in Siberia's Tobol'sk province, for example, reported the loss of their horses to Gypsies, some of whom they identified as "exiles." One report from a settlement of sixty-eight households in Serebriansk volost' describes the operation as an "organized trade" with Gypsies, Kirgiz [Kazakhs], and settlers (presumably from elsewhere) themselves making off with about forty every year.[36] Of course, owners of such property had little appreciation for this form of circulation. When, as in two cases cited by Stephen Frank from Riazan' province, peasants caught Roma in the act, they imposed frontier justice on the malefactors replete with whips that "fell generously upon their backs" and "such beatings . . . that one died."[37] On the other hand, rurals in need of pots, pans, and horseshoes could rely on Romani tinkers, the Kalderash (in Russian kotliary), who comprised an entire subethnic group that originated in Romania.[38]

Just as not all who were itinerant in Imperial Russia were Roma, so not all who identified themselves as Roma employed a repertoire of itinerancy. The Gypsy choirs heavily patronized by the Russian nobility were among the urban-based Roma. In Moscow, they gravitated toward Mar'ina Roshcha and Petrovskii Park in the northwestern part of the city because these were the locations of the restaurants where they performed. There too could be found Kalderash who occupied themselves with tinkering and cutlery making as well as, in the case of women, fortune-telling.[39] Imperial Petersburg at the turn of the century exhibited a similar ethno-occupational division of labor with Russian Roma oriented toward music making and the more recently arrived Kalderash pursuing the metal trades. Both groups lived in Bol'shaia Okhta (today, Krasnogvardeiskii district), between the Neva and Okhta rivers.[40]

We know far more about the urban-based Roma than the majority who pursued an itinerant repertoire and lived in camps (tabori) scattered across the countryside. This reflects the greater degree of literacy and involvement in broader political and cultural affairs among the urbanites. For the young and progressive-minded among them, the October

36. Stankevich, Materialy dlia izucheniia byta pereselentsev tobol'skoi gubernii, 1: 394.

37. Frank, Crime, 252, 261.

38. Donald Kenrick, Historical Dictionary of the Gypsies (Romanies), 2nd ed. (Lantham, MD, 2007), 136–37. See also Tcherenkov and Laederich "Roma Trades," in, Roma, 1: 532–53.

39. Brigid O'Keeffe, " 'Backward Gypsies,' Soviet Citizens: The All-Russian Gypsy Union, 1925–28," Kritika: Explorations in Russian and Eurasian History 11, no. 2 (2010): 286; Lev Nikolaevich Cherenkov, "Tsygane Moskvy i Podmoskov'ia," http://gypsy-life.net/history26htm, 3–4 (accessed June 3, 2013). Cherenkov indicates that Eldorado Lane (a name derived from one of the restaurants), which is located two blocks north of Petrovskii Park, bore the name "Gypsy Corner" until 1951.

40. N. V. Bessonov, "Tsygane," in Mnogonatsional'nyi Peterburg: Istoriia, religii, narody, ed. I. I. Shangina (St. Petersburg, 2002), 810–15.

Revolution presented an opportunity to save their "backward" brethren, backwardness being defined as the troika of nomadism, aversion to labor, and illiteracy. Such was the agenda of the All-Russian Gypsy Union, formed in 1925—to raise up their fellow Gypsies, the "ragged, dark, dirty" ones who "wander from place to place," as the organization's leaders proclaimed in a report to the Presidium of the Soviets' Central Executive Committee.[41]

Backwardness represented a ticket that select individuals from designated nationality groups could cash in to advance themselves and hopefully redeem their own people.[42] But the Roma sorely tried the limits of Soviet transformational optimism. Again and again—in 1926, 1928, 1932, and 1936—the All-Union Central Executive Committee and Council of People's Commissars would issue decrees encouraging them to make the transition to "a working, settled way of life" (to cite the title of the first decree). Each would proclaim the advantages of doing so and list various material incentives. The very repetition of the decrees, however, suggests that the gap between intentions and fulfillment remained yawning. Neither the Commissariat of Agriculture, nor the Kolkhoz Center, nor the Resettlement Administration, nor any other state bureaucratic agency seemed willing to tackle the issue with sufficient dedication and funding. Whether, as Brigid O'Keeffe suggests, this was because state officials "essentialized" the Roma "as peculiarly nomadic and inordinately backward and intractable," or because the Roma were too scattered and too few in number to bother about, remains unclear.[43] For their part, three prominent Romani scholars have asserted that "the very kolkhoz system contradicted Gypsy mentality . . . as soon as officials gave out loans, the 'collective farmers,' as a rule, disappeared." The few Romani kolkhozes that survived more than a few years required inventive, energetic, and even heroic efforts on the part of Romani activists who despaired at being able to replicate their experience.[44]

Because officials found it convenient to duck their own responsibility by casting the Roma as inveterate nomads and con artists, we should not take the opposite tack of romanticizing Romani resistance. Still, it is not hard to understand why, when faced with the grim prospect of life on some underfunded collective farm, many would choose to survive

41. O'Keeffe, "Backward Gypsies," 292.

42. As Yuri Slezkine argued in his justly famous article "The USSR as a Communal Apartment, or How a Socialist State Promoted Ethnic Particularism," *Slavic Review* 53, no. 2 (1994): 52–76.

43. Brigid O'Keeffe, "Becoming Gypsy, Sovietizing the Self, 1917–1939" (PhD diss., New York University, 2008), chap. 4. See also Brigid O'Keeffe, *New Soviet Gypsies: Nationality, Performance and Selfhood in the Early Soviet Union* (Toronto, 2013). For examples from 1936 of foot-dragging by the Resettlement Administration in confirming and funding the formation of "national gypsy kolkhozes" in Ukraine, see RGAE, f. 5675, op. 1, d. 158, ll. 9–99.

44. Nadezhda Demeter, Nikolai Bessonov, and Vladimir Kutenkov, *Istoriia Tsygan: Novyi vzgliad* (Voronezh, 2000), 203–4; O'Keeffe, "Becoming Gypsy," chap. 4.

otherwise by tried and true methods. The Romani group that, according to a Commissariat of Agriculture official, traveled from Moscow to Stalingrad, then to Groznyi, and finally to Baku, each time with free train tickets provided to potential settlers, was not unique, as we shall see.[45]

The Roma residing in and around Moscow and Leningrad proved less elusive—5,470 of them were among the "declassé elements" deported as labor settlers to Siberia in 1933.[46] Most, we learn from Vladimir Glodo, one of the survivors who was six years old at the time, had come to the capital from various parts of the country—"Kishinevites" from Nizhni-Novgorod, "Servitka Roma" from Ukraine, Vlachs from southern Russia and Crimeans from the eponymous peninsula—to escape the famine. Roused by the police from their tents one June morning near the Severianin Bridge, Glodo's Kishinevites were taken to a railroad station where, with other Roma, they were put in boxcars. After nearly three weeks, they arrived at the shore of the Chulym River in central Siberia. Another two weeks aboard a prison barge brought them to the site of a future lumber camp. But cutting timber was not in the future of Glodo's family. They escaped en masse and made their way back to central Russia, as the *chastushka* (ditty) Glodo cites had forecast:

I'm tired of us uprooting,	Надоела нам корчёвка,
Tired of being rooted out,	Надоело корчевать,
From Chikaiulskii settlement	С Чикаюлского посёлка
I wanted to run away.	Захотелось убежать.[47]

The historian V. N. Zemskov indicates that already by the fall of 1933 the entire contingent of Gypsy labor settlers had ceased to exist because almost all had escaped. He could find no record of any attempt to apprehend them.[48] Such was the advantage of itinerancy as a way of life that they easily blended in with other Roma.

The 1939 census counted 88,242 Soviet Gypsies, of whom nearly 70 percent resided in the RSFSR and 12 percent lived in Ukraine.[49] The Soviet annexations in 1939–40 of the Baltic states, eastern Poland, and especially the Romanian provinces of Bessarabia and Northern Bukovina surely swelled the Romani population to six figures. More arrived

---

45. O'Keeffe, "Becoming Gypsy," chap. 4, 15.

46. Ivnitskii, *Sud'ba raskulachennykh*, 48; Bessonov, "Tsygane," 816. See also chapter 7 of this volume.

47. Nikolai Bessonov, "Tsygane: Gody ssylok i pobegov," *30 Oktiabria* 6, no. 26 (2002): 10, http://gypsy-life.net/history08.htm (accessed June 3, 2013).

48. V. N. Zemskov, "'Kulatskaia ssylka' v 1930-e gody: Chislennost', rasselenie, sostav," in Zhiromskaia, *Naselenie Rossii*, 1: 308.

49. "Vsesoiuznaia perepis' naseleniia 1939 goda: Natsional'nyi sostav naseleniia po respublikam SSSR," *Demoskop Weekly*, http://demoscope.ru/weekly/ssp/sng_nac_39.php?reg=5 (accessed June 3, 2013).

during the Great Patriotic War, though not by choice. The Romanians under Ion Antonescu deported from Bucharest an estimated 25,000 Roma to Transnistria, their newly created province in southwestern Ukraine, and the Germans resettled several thousand from the Reich to ghettos in Lodz, Minsk, and Riga. As many as half sent to Transnistria died of typhus before liberation.[50] A reporter from *Izvestiia*, embedded with Soviet forces as they retook this territory in June 1944, described coming across "a strange procession" led by "men in tatters with holey hats, trailed by barefoot women with German camouflage gowns thrown over their shoulders, and semi-naked children bringing up the rear." These were Bessarabian Roma returning home.[51]

According to an order issued in December 1941 by the Reich Commissioner for the Baltic region and Belorussia, "the Gypsies wandering around the country" represented "a double danger." They "carry disease especially typhus," and they "are unreliable elements who cannot be put to useful work." They thus were to be treated "in the same way as Jews," though a later order from November 1943 spared sedentary Roma from this fate.[52] Estimates of the number of Soviet Roma who died at the hands of the Nazis and their collaborators are in the range of thirty thousand to thirty-five thousand.[53]

With the end of the war, survivors seemed intent on reviving itinerant traditions. Unimpeded by any revival of the party's earlier sedentarist campaigns, they appear to have succeeded. We thus return to Chernousov's letter of 1952. Much of it is devoted to describing the peregrinations of a group of 110 Roma. Although relatively insignificant in size, the group and its actions may have served as the ultimate provocation for this bureaucrat. The group, it seems, asked local authorities in the city of Kuibyshev to grant land in an industrial suburb where they could build homes for themselves. After being turned down, they traveled over 600 miles northwest to the city of Yaroslavl', where they again sought land. This time oblast' authorities stepped in and instructed district soviet officials in Danilov, a town some 40 miles to the north, to make land available and assist with materials, transport, and technical aid as well as jobs in local and cooperative industries. But the group did not "establish itself" in Danilov; instead, they left for Rybinsk, the second largest city in the oblast', and Arkhangel'sk far to the north, requesting . . . well, we know what they requested because they already had done so twice before. "Thus," Chernousov concluded, grossly generalizing from this one case,

---

50. Crowe, *A History of the Gypsies*, 133–34, 184.
51. *Izvestiia*, June 10, 1944, 3.
52. Heinrich Lohse, quoted in Crowe, *A History of the Gypsies*, 185–86.
53. The term *Porajmos* (also *Porrajmos*) has come into use in recent decades as the Romani equivalent of the Holocaust. For a forceful rejection of the term as "an unfortunate choice of words," see Tcherenkov and Laederich, *Roma*, 1: 184.

all attempts to employ Gypsies by ordinary means through local organs have failed. It is impossible under these circumstances to conduct political or mass cultural work with them. The majority of adults are illiterate, and the children of school age do not attend school. This creates a situation in which hostile elements can influence the Gypsies.[54]

Soviet authorities decided to crack down on these inveterate wanderers not in the years of Stalin's tyrannical regime but under Nikita Khrushchev, who actually was more of an interventionist in this respect.[55] In October 1956 the Presidium of the Supreme Soviet criminalized Romani nomadism as "vagrancy" (brodiazhnichestvo), and obliged each of the Union republics' Council of Ministers "to take measures to settle vagrant Gypsies in permanent places of habitation, and arrange employment and cultural and welfare services for them." Those who persisted in their vagabond ways would be subject to sentencing by a peoples' court of up to five years of corrective labor.[56]

But as an otherwise scurrilous article in Literaturnaia gazeta pointed out in 1957, "it is difficult to force Gypsies to settle by administrative measures alone." "Painstaking educational work by the progressive section of the Gypsy population" plus local soviets, educational institutions, and the Komsomol was needed to prevent the reappearance every spring and fall of Gypsy camps such as the one visited by the two reporters at Moscow's Yaroslavl' Station, which they described as "teeming with half-naked kids whose faces and little hands were covered with dirt, ulcers, and scabs, and who shouted, 'Uncle, give me a ruble,' while the older folks played cards, interrupting their game to ask, 'Do you have gold?' "[57] Scarcely three years after the law's passage, several institutions ranging from the trade union council to the Academy of Sciences's Institute of Justice advocated its rescinding. At about the same time a visiting English artist with Irish and Hungarian Roma roots could declare the compulsory settlement of Soviet Roma "an unworkable proposition," and describe in a much more positive light "Gypsies again travel[ing] the roads of the U.S.S.R.,

54. USHMM 22.027M, GARF, f. A-327, Reel 48, op. 1, d. 90, ll. 89–90. Rybinsk at the time was called Shcherbakov in honor of the Russian literary bureaucrat Aleksandr Sergeevich Shcherbakov (1901–45).

55. While party leader in Ukraine in the late 1940s, Khrushchev initiated a measure giving kolkhoz assemblies the right to exile "parasitical and criminal elements." See Sheila Fitzpatrick, "Social Parasites: How Tramps, Idle Youth, and Busy Entrepreneurs Impeded the Soviet March to Communism," Cahiers du monde russe 47, no. 1 (2006): 380. For other examples of his interventionism, see Oleg Kharkhordin, The Collective and the Individual in Russia: A Study of Practices (Berkeley, 1999).

56. Pobol' and Polian, Stalinskie deportatsii, 777–78; for the law "on bringing to labor gypsies occupied in vagrancy," see E. Iu. Zubkova and T. Iu. Zhukova, Na "kraiu" sovetskogo obshchestva; sotsial'nye marginaly kak ob'ekt gosudarstvennoi politiki, 1945-1960-e gg. (Moscow, 2010), 435.

57. Pavel Il'iashenko and Vladimir Strelkov, "Tsyganskii tabor," Literaturnaia gazeta, no. 15 (1957): 2.

plying their traditional crafts and trades . . . and playing their wild music in the towns and villages about Moscow and Minsk."[58]

Successive censuses recorded vigorous growth in the Romani population—more than doubling from 88,000 in 1939 to 209,000 in 1979.[59] Within the RSFSR, the southern territories of Rostov, Krasnodar, and Stavropol contained the largest contingents. Like the rest of the Soviet population, the Roma were becoming more urban: between 1959 and 1979 the proportion of urban-based Roma in the Russian republic more than doubled. They also became more Romani speaking.[60] This did not mean greater insularity, though, for the proportion claiming good knowledge of Russian as a second language also rose. Finally, it appears that the proliferation of cheaply produced manufactured goods and the reduced presence of horses in the countryside persuaded most Roma to abandon nomadism and its associated occupations. "There are no longer nomadic Gypsies," wrote a prominent Soviet ethnographer in the mid-1980s, meaning Roma not having a permanent place of residence. But, after noting that "this does not mean that customary trips around the country in summer have ceased," he added that Roma also change their permanent place of residence more often than anyone else.[61]

The upheavals that began with perestroika and intensified with the disintegration of the Soviet Union profoundly affected popular attitudes toward the Roma. Perceptions of Roma doing better via nefarious means while so many working-class Russians suffered led to pogroms against Romani settlements in the city of Yaroslavl' and in Sverdlovsk oblast' in 1990–91.[62] Taking advantage of its new freedom, the press printed lurid tales about Gypsies. Stories of Gypsy gangs robbing and killing isolated elderly people in the Smolensk countryside, of a Gypsy family in Azerbaijan kidnapping and enslaving a three-year-old girl, of desperate mothers in Cheliabinsk oblast' and Khabarovsk selling their children to Gypsies, and of Gypsies' relatively high birthrate exploited the public's already considerable

---

58. Zubkova and Zhukova, Na "kraiu" sovetkogo obshchestva," 451; Basil Ivan Raskoczi (1908–79), as quoted in Crowe, A History of Gypsies, 188.

59. Demoskop Weekly, http://demoscope.ru/weekly/ssp/sng_nac_39.php?reg=5; and http://demoscope.ru/weekly/ssp/sng_nac_79.php?reg=0. (accessed June 4, 2013).

60. M. B. Denisenko, "Osobennosti demograficheskogo razvitiia narodov Rossii v 1960–1970-e gg.," in Zhiromskaia and Isupov, Naselenie Rossii, 3: bk. 1, 92–93; Crowe, A History of Gypsies, 189–91. By 1979 just under three-quarters gave Romani as their native tongue.

61. L. N. Cherenkov, "Nekotorye problemy etnograficheskogo izucheniia tsygan SSSR," in Malye i dispersnye etnicheskie gruppy v evropeiskoi chasti SSSR (geografiia rasseleniia i kul'turnye traditsii), ed. I. I. Krupnik (Moscow, 1985), 13. See also Nikolai Bessonov, "Tsygane v Rossii: Prinuditel'noe osedanie," in Rossiia i ee regiony v XX veke: Territoriia—rasselenie—migratsii, ed. O. Gelzer and P. Polian (Moscow, 2005), 631–40. For a photographic collection of Gypsies from the Kazakh steppe and Odessa, ca. 1979–90, see Ljalja Kuznetsova, Shaking the Dust of Ages: Gypsies and Wanderers of the Central Asian Steppe (New York, 1998); for an online collection of photographs, see http://www.gypsy-life.net/foto-01.htm.

62. Izvestiia, December 19, 1990, 6; July 29, 1991, 8.

insecurities and anxieties about crime, the disintegration of the family, and ethnic Russian population decline. Even an article supposedly intended to enlighten readers about Gypsy customs began by noting the negative associations that "the majority of us" have about them, which was only natural given the "dirty, impudent beggars we see every day in the metro and on public transport." Little wonder that a survey of Ukrainians in 1997 found that nearly one in three opposed allowing Gypsies to enter the country—more than double the proportion for any other ethnic group.[63]

On the other hand, many Roma did benefit materially from their mobility, extensive family connections, and economic gumption. This was especially the case during 1989–94 when prohibitions against "speculation" from earlier in the Soviet era no longer existed but shortages of goods still prevailed. Twenty-seven-year-old Artur, who described himself as "head of a family business," was among them. He had a wife and four children living near Astrakhan, but had come to Moscow to sell cigarettes near the Riga metro station at twice the price he had paid for them.[64] Like others from elsewhere in the former Soviet Union and even Eastern Europe, he had gravitated to Moscow to escape desperate conditions. Liubertsy, the working-class suburb just outside Moscow's ring road, attracted more than its fair share; it included "representatives of nearly every subethnic group of Gypsies in Russia." By the end of the millennium improvised settlements in the Moscow region's forests reportedly housed Roma from as far away as Hungary and Moldava, and the Liuli from Central Asia. Obtaining money by begging in metro stations and at major intersections, they generally were shunned by Moscow's preexisting Romani population that in the meantime had come up in the world.[65]

Tramps

Aside from the Roma, Russian political space hosted other categories of people distinguished by their wandering. Their numbers waxed and waned over the century. In fact, such fluctuations are as good an index as any for registering the ravages visited on people close to the margin of survival. Most of the categories are imputed and some mutated over time. Overlapping in meaning, some are easier to translate than others. They include panhandlers

---

63. *Nezavisimaia gazeta*, January 30, 1998; *Kommersant*, March 25, 1998; *Segodnia*, February 21, 1996; *Pravda*, September 20, 1997; *Trud*, November 20, 1997; *Argumenty i Fakty*, no. 2 (1991): 4; *Nezavisimaia gazeta*, April 27, 1997 (emphasis ours); *Literaturnaia gazeta*, no. 35 (1997), all via East View Information Services Universal Databases. An earlier survey from Soviet Ukraine carried out in 1989 found attitudes toward Gypsies "predominantly unfavorable." See Valentin Sazhin, "Attitudes Towards Gypsies in Ukraine (1989)," *Nationalities Papers* 19, no. 3 (1991): 340.

64. Bessonov, "Tsygane," 824; *Argumenty i Fakty*, no. 2 (1991): 4.

65. Cherenkov, "Tsygane Moskvy i Podmoskov'ia," 9–10.

(poproshaiki), hobos (bosiaki), tramps (brodiagi), wanderers (stranniki/strannitsy), bums (bi-chi), and the homeless (bomzhi). Not all the people referred to by these categories had repertoires of migration. Most, however, tried to stay out of the way of the police, who tended to associate them with criminal activity.

Russians in earlier times had made other associations. In seeking the origins of the Russian "culture of giving," Adele Lindenmeyr notes that the theme of beggars as the incarnation of Christ recurred throughout eighteenth- and nineteenth-century Orthodox Christian sermons, quoting from the advice of one model sermon to "Remember, the Heavenly King—our Lord Christ Himself—visits us in the person of wanderers, the needy, beggars."[66] As the Slavicist Ewa M. Thompson pointed out, the strannik, the "one who wanders for God's or spirituality's sake" and whose "lack of worldly wisdom and . . . actions . . . seem motivated by . . . other worldly concerns," was "indistinguishable" from and the "moral cousin" of the iurodivyi—the Holy Fool. We meet his type throughout nineteenth-century literature: in Tolstoy, as Grisha in Childhood, who "went barefoot in both winter and summer while visiting monasteries"; as Platon Karataev in War and Peace; and as Dmitrii Nekhliudov in Resurrection. He appears as Nikolai Leskov's eponymous "Enchanted Wanderer," and as Prince Myshkin in Dostoevsky's The Idiot. He reappears in the twentieth century. Doctor Zhivago is a kind of strannik, leading, as Thompson notes, "an unsettled life."[67]

Actual wanderers populated the roads of the country—"countless singers, bandura players, witches, cripples, hobos, lyrists, religious mystics, old men, sorcerers, fortune-tellers, and vagrants"—returning hospitality and donations with songs, stories, and news. Thousands headed for Moscow and particularly its monasteries, churches, and cathedrals, where they could be sure of receiving alms, to the extent that those living near the Uspenskii Cathedral became known as Uspenskiis, while those settling near the Kremlin's Cathedral of the Archangel were called Archangelites.[68] "You shouldn't make fun of beggars, God help them," Maxim Gorky's pious grandmother once told him. "Christ was a beggar—and all the saints as well."[69] The journalist Vladimir Korolenko wrote in the last years of the nineteenth century, "Begging in Russia is an enormous

66. Adele Lindenmeyr, Poverty Is Not a Vice: Charity, Society, and the State in Imperial Russia (Princeton, 1996), 10.

67. Ewa M. Thompson, "The Archetype of the Fool in Russian Literature," Canadian Slavonic Papers 15, no. 3 (1973): 245–73. For a famous nonliterary reference, see Vasilii Surikov's gigantic historical canvas Boiarynia Morozova (1887), which includes in its lower right-hand corner a Holy Fool who is barefoot in the snow.

68. A. Iu. Gorcheva, Nishchestvo i blagotvoritel'nost' v Rossii: Rossiiskii zhurnal kak istochnik svedenii o sotsial'nykh prioritetakh obshchestva (Moscow, 1999), 16.

69. Maxim Gorky, My Childhood (Hardmondsworth, 1966), 161, quoted in Lindenmeyr, Poverty Is No Vice, 19.

popular force, volatile and resilient, absorbing a huge mass of people and then secreting them from its depths."[70]

Joseph Flynt, who made a specialty of studying up close those he labeled "voluntary beggars" or "professional tramps," lived "intimately with the vagabonds of England and the United States" during the 1890s, and then went to Europe where he tramped in both Germany and Russia. Flynt categorized Russian tramps as authorized and unauthorized, a distinction identical to the one the Resettlement Administration used and Soviet authorities would retain. Authorized tramps were religious beggars, "an inevitable church class . . . taken care of almost as conscientiously as the priests." They did not interest him. The unauthorized, known officially as brodiagi, called themselves victims of grief. They clearly fascinated Flynt by their internal organization or "clannishness," as he put it. "They are as organized as compactly as a trade-union," he wrote, with each group having its ataman, and "even in St. Petersburg, strict as the police are, they have their peculiar artel," each with its own lingo.[71]

Their itineraries varied. Some averaged 15 miles a day walking on the highway, but others covered scarcely more than 5, and one old man he met on the Kursk road between Tula and Orel in August 1897 limited himself to 2 miles, meaning that it would take him all autumn and into the winter to reach Odessa, his destination. Tramps in the countryside made their homes with peasants, sleeping in sheds and haystacks in the summer and in cabins during the winter. In the cities, they stayed in night shelters and lodging houses such as the Viazemskii House near the Haymarket (Sennaia) in Petersburg, where 35 kopeks would buy them a spot on a plank for a week. The distinction between rural- and urban-based tramps is misleading though, for Flynt describes a Moscow-based artel that twice a year hit the road for Tambov, Voronezh, and "so on down to the Don."

Flynt put the total number of tramps in European Russia at more than nine hundred thousand. They represented a greater proportion of the population in Siberia, although as we already have noted, this included fugitives as well as vagrants. "In no other country that I have visited," wrote Flynt, "are there so many women and families 'on tramp.'" Whether married or not, men and women cohabited in the lodging houses along with children. The children were valuable for begging purposes, and deformed and crippled children were the most valuable of all. In the case of one group of beggars known as the Reapers, the adults rented blind and deformed children from neighboring villages before departing on

---

70. Korolenko quoted in Lindenmeyr, Poverty Is No Vice, 17. For a discussion of worker-poets who in early twentieth-century Russia often engaged in wandering, see Mark Steinberg, " 'A Path of Thorns'—The Spiritual Wounds and Wandering of Worker-Poets," in Sacred Stories: Religion and Spirituality in Modern Russia, ed. Christine Worobec (Bloomington, 2007), 304–29.

71. Josiah Flynt, Tramping with Tramps: Studies and Sketches of Vagabond Life (New York, 1907), 3, 170, 205, 210–15.

begging expeditions.[72] By describing such practices, Flynt probably intended to shock his readers. Although rarely explicit about his own reactions, his skepticism about the genuineness of beggars' outward expressions of grief and his failure to interrogate the voluntary-involuntary distinction suggest that he shared the general attitude among educated Russians that unauthorized beggars were a scourge.

If Flynt approached his subjects as something of a participant-observer, then a volume published in 1929 took a more conventionally statistical social-scientific approach. Issued by the Moscow Office for the Study of the Criminal Personality and Crime, it focused on the capital's professional beggars and street children whose déclassé situation, in the editors' view, made them prone to a "semi-criminal way of life . . . often connected to the criminal world."[73] The contributors drew on data from the 1897 Empire-wide census, the 1923 census of Soviet cities, and the first all-Union census of 1926, but generally avoided making longitudinal comparisons. In view of the noncorrespondence of categories, this is understandable but it makes our lack of access to contemporary sources about begging during the years of war, revolution, and civil war all the more unfortunate. We assume that although mortality rates among "self-supporting beggars" rose, as they did for virtually everyone else, the breakdown of preexisting economic relations led to more people joining their ranks.

By the mid-1920s, the number of beggars, at least in Moscow, had stabilized.[74] Those practicing their profession did so at familiar places: in the streets, in churchyards and cemeteries, in apartment buildings, and in public institutions. War invalids and others with physical disabilities predominated among street beggars, although one also could encounter individuals who would implore passersby to "Help an old teacher," or "a former bookkeeper." The elderly, the lame, and the sightless frequented churchyards and cemeteries; former servants too old to continue their arduous tasks filled the courtyards of apartment buildings; and by contrast, children were most numerous at public facilities such as railroad stations and tram stops.

According to one contributor, peasants by social origin comprised over 60 percent of Moscow's beggars, far outnumbering workers at 22 percent. Most came from villages and provincial cities and over half began their "profession" as beggars only after arriving in Moscow. When asked what brought them to the city, a third answered, "to beg"; another third went to seek work; and the rest who responded sought a place in a nursing home or home for the disabled or went to visit relatives. Conforming to the gravitational model of

---

72. Ibid., 205, 209, 215–16.

73. E. K. Krasnushkin, G. M. Segal, and Ts. M. Feinberg, eds., *Nishchestvo i besprizornost'* (Moscow, 1929), 3. The Office also offered volumes on hooligans, murderers, and those who had committed sex crimes.

74. A contributing factor was the arrest in late 1925 of 1,744 "malicious poor" (*zlostnye nishchie*), many of them evidently disabled, and their expulsion from Moscow to the Solovki prison camp. See Baron and Gatrell, "Population Displacement," 94.

migration, Moscow pulled in people in roughly equal proportions from the central industrial provinces, other parts of the RSFSR, and the rest of the Soviet Union.[75] In short, just
as these people fell through the cracks of official accountability, so they fell through our
interpretive schema. Neither seasonal nor rural-to-urban migrants, "a large group of
peasants for whom begging was a kind of seasonal occupation" would arrive every year in
large cities, dressed in bast shoes and homespun coachmen's coats characteristic of
country folk.[76]

Let us look closer at some of those who wound up begging in Moscow. In their study of
"contemporary mendicancy" during the 1920s, Men'shagin and Edel'shtein cite twenty-
five "cases," of which twelve involved individuals who came from elsewhere. Several arrived in the city to find work but failed to do so. Abandoned by his wife and married son, a
fifty-six-year-old alcoholic peasant from Moscow province had been begging for six years
by the time the investigators interviewed him. A forty-six-year-old peasant woman from
Saratov province outdid him by two years. Widowed in 1919 and with five children all under
the age of ten, she placed three of them with relatives and brought the other two with her
to Moscow. Another woman bore a son out of wedlock and, determined to avoid shaming
by the village, brought him to Moscow with her.[77] None had family or community support
in the city.

In some ways the most interesting case was that of R., an eighty-five-year-old illiterate
woman who had spent thirty years living in Saratov with her husband but after his death
moved to Moscow. She traveled on foot to sacred sites throughout Russia such as the Solovki monastery (before its closure in 1920) and Kiev's Pechora monastery (ten times, the
last at the age of eighty-two!) and had even been to Jerusalem. A "genuine strannitsa," she
always wore black and was fed, as she said, "by what good people gave me." The investigators noted that she was unfamiliar with elementary facts about the country, and described
her as "old and weak in the head."[78]

Orphans

Another category of cases consisted of people at the other end of the age spectrum—
homeless children, called *besprizorniki*, who fended for themselves. Long before the

75. V. D. Men'shagin and A. O. Edel'shtein, "Sovremennoe nishchestvo," in Krasnushkin, Segal, and
Feinberg, *Nishchestvo i besprizornost'*, 72–84.

76. Ibid. 97.

77. Ibid., 93–96. For connections between pregnancy and cityward migration, see Rachel G. Fuchs and
Leslie Page Moch, "Pregnant, Single, and Far from Home: Migrant Women in Nineteenth-Century Paris,"
American Historical Review 95 (1990): 1007–31.

78. Men'shagin and Edel'shtein, "Sovremennoe nishchestvo," 101–2.

Bolsheviks came to power, parents were abandoning their children, but the children generally were illegitimate infants, too young to survive on their own.[79] The almost continuous warfare that occurred on Russian territory between 1914 and 1921 tore asunder millions of families. "Undoubtedly," we read in a source from 1925, "the present cultural squalor of the *besprizornyi* has its bitter roots in the massive waves of refugees" from both World War I and the Civil War.[80] Yet it was the famine of 1921–22 that produced more homeless children than either war—because it caused more parents to perish or give up on feeding their offspring. Children, orphaned or abandoned, either continued the itinerary they had been part of or initiated a new one. They were prominent among the famine victims who flocked to cities in large numbers beginning in the summer of 1921. Their numbers crested during the famine, when estimates range from 4 to 7.5 million abandoned and orphaned youths. In Ufa province their numbers nearly tripled from June to October; in the "Kyrgyz" republic they more than tripled to 408,000 in March 1922.[81]

These enormous numbers give an idea of the catastrophe, but they also disguise the fact that *besprizorniki* were created one by one, when the only surviving mother or father perished, when the child lost sight of a parent in a crowd, when life en famille became unbearable, or when a child was told to wait right here until mother returned—and the demoralized mother would never come back. "There were many like us," stated the boy from the city of Grodno whose family had fled for a village in Cheliabinsk province in the Urals during the war. His father had died in 1914, so the boy helped support his family by working for peasants rather than attending school. When the famine struck their village, the family—mother, two boys, and two girls—went to the city of Cheliabinsk for food. Housed in a typhus-ridden barracks, the boy lost his mother and a sister to the disease. Three days later, his other sister died, and when he was evacuated his remaining brother was not allowed to come along because he too had fallen ill.[82] Like all child refugees in time of famine, with or without siblings, he developed his own Plan B or got help from the state, if it was available—or developed a combination of the two.

Visitors to Russia, stationmasters, police, relief workers, and adult citizens remarked on the shocking groups of children on the loose—lice-ridden, filthy, hungry, dressed in rags and barely dressed at that. *Besprizorniki* were urban, for the most part, because cities

79. On the abandonment of children in tsarist Russia, see David L. Ransel, *Mothers of Misery: Child Abandonment in Russia* (Princeton, 1988). For orphaned and abandoned children elsewhere, see John Boswell, *The Kindness of Strangers: The Abandonment of Children in Western Europe from Late Antiquity to the Renaissance* (New York, 1988); Rachel G. Fuchs, *Abandoned Children: Foundlings and Child Welfare in Nineteenth-Century France* (Albany, 1984).

80. M. I. Levitina, *Besprizornye: Sotsiologiia, byt, praktika raboty* (Moscow, 1925), 107.

81. Alan Ball, *And Now My Soul Is Hardened: Abandoned Children in Soviet Russia, 1918–1930* (Berkeley, 1994), 1, 9–10, 16; V. Zenzinov, *Bezprizornye* (Paris, 1929), 76, 84.

82. Ball, *And Now My Soul Is Hardened*, 4; for the evacuation of children at this time, see page 100.

offered more possibilities with their markets, deserted buildings, and train stations. They gathered where travelers do, in junction facilities and stations because, for such young people, there was safety in numbers. They slept in tunnels under stations, sheltered niches of buildings, vats for heating asphalt, and more squalid places like garbage containers and disused lavatories. Many spent their days in the station, where there was heat, work to be had, and food to be gotten.[83]

The itineraries of orphans and abandoned children varied. While some traveled down the Volga to Samara or Saratov, others journeyed south to Odessa, Krasnodar, Rostov, or Crimea. Some wound up in the cities of central Russia such as Orel, Voronezh, and Nizhni-Novgorod, but others rode the rails as far as Siberia's Omsk and even Tashkent. According to a source from the mid-1920s cited by Alan Ball, about 10 percent of homeless children were constantly on the move.[84] Their hub, however, was Moscow, which the secret police chief Feliks Dzerzhinskii described as "the national refuge to which *besprizornye* stream from all ends of the country" and which the orphans and abandoned children regarded as the center of power with the greatest food possibilities.[85] Once, a member of the Central Executive Committee's commission to combat children's homelessness asked a crowd of children at the Riazan' railroad station where they were heading. "To Moscow," they replied. "What will you do in Moscow?" he asked. "We want to enroll in the *besprizornye*."[86] What many did was to gravitate to one of Moscow's rougher neighborhoods such as Mar'ina Roshcha or Cherkizovo, or find a place to sleep near one of the city's markets. They resorted to children's homes only during the coldest months, like Siberian escapees who returned to prison.

Two of the many who started out in Samara during the famine of 1921–22 later described their journeys to Moscow. Ivan Pomorin accompanied his mother and brother to Kiev; after they both died, he intended to travel to Tashkent, where his sister lived, but someone stole his money and papers and he wound up in Moscow instead. Leaving his parents in Samara, Grigorii Valentinov traveled with "several thousands" to Moscow, where he was taken to an orphanage and began his career in theft. After escaping from the orphanage, he "hung about the stations and the markets" and became a cocaine addict, stealing to feed his habit. When he told his story he had only just emerged from a clinic that he claimed had cured him.[87]

---

83. Witness testimonies abound in Ball, *And Now My Soul Is Hardened*. On sleeping places, see Zenzinov, *Bezprizornye*, 148, 153; A. A. Slavko, *Detskaia besprizornost' v Rossii v pervoe desiatiletie sovetskoi vlasti* (Moscow, 2005), 75.

84. Ball, *And Now My Soul Is Hardened*, 25.

85. Ibid., 22, and chap. 1, "Children of the Street," 21–43; see also 90–91 on Dzerzhinskii and children.

86. Zenzinov, *Bezprizornye*, 130, citing *Izvestiia*, May 15, 1927.

87. Zenzinov, *Bezprizornye*, 93–94. Readers of the English translation should be warned that "several thousands" is inexplicably rendered as "some millions." See Vladimir Zenzinov, *Deserted: The Story of the Children Abandoned in Soviet Russia*, trans. Agnes Platt (Westport, CT, 1975 [1931]), 75.

Those interviewed toward the end of the decade told of extensive travels that in each case ended in Moscow. They included a sixteen-year-old boy from Riazan' province whose father had died just before the war and whose mother passed away when he was ten. A year after he moved in with his grandfather, the latter also died. After traveling around the countryside for a couple of years, the boy came to Moscow in 1926 because he had heard one could survive there by begging. Another, a twenty-one-year-old former peasant, exhibited many of the repertoires already mentioned. After abandoning his family, he was placed in a children's home in Saratov but soon escaped. He tramped along the railroad through the North Caucasus to the Volga and back, traveling sometimes on goods trains and sometimes on foot. Considering himself to have a gift for poetry, he joined a circle of proletarian writers in the Caucasus. "Extremely affected (*maneren*) in speech and movements," he represented the secular equivalent to the strannitsa.[88] We note that both cases were boys. Evidently, two-thirds to three-fourths of all youths adrift were male, a gender imbalance that contemporary observers attributed to a combination of moral strictures among parents and youths' own inclinations. Among the various activities in which *besprizorniki* engaged, begging attracted most, but prostitution, petty trade, and stealing found practitioners too, though in what proportions of boys and girls we do not know.[89]

"Tragedy's offspring," in the words of Ball, the *besprizorniki* were pitied as long as they could be contained and taken care of. Peter Gatrell has observed that women refugees received the most aid when they were seen as "deserving supplicants or pitiful victims." So it was with children.[90] *Besprizorniki* who did not go into (or who escaped from) receiving stations or orphanages often traveled and worked in groups, displaying disrespectful and combative behavior that disgusted upright Soviet citizens and lent truth to an official's proclamation that "*besprizornye* are the breeding grounds of hooliganism."[91] By the mid-1920s, thanks to absorption by receivers, children's homes (*detskie doma*, shortened to *detdoma*), labor communes, and schools, their number was reduced to a few hundred thousand.[92] From there, the Soviet state made great efforts with inadequate resources to equip former *besprizorniki* for productive lives—like the young boy from Grodno mentioned above who was in school by the end of the famine, albeit the only survivor of a family of

88. Men'shagin and Edel'shtein, "Sovremennoe nishchestvo," 102–3, 110.
89. Ball, *And Now My Soul Is Hardened*, 60, 227–28.
90. Gatrell, *A Whole Empire Walking*, 127.
91. Ball, *And Now My Soul Is Hardened*, 73.
92. N. I. Ozeretskii, "Nishchestvo i besprizornost' nesovershenno-letnikh," in Krasnushkin, Segal, and Feinberg, *Nishchestvo i besprizornost'*, 141, cites a figure of 75,000 street children for the RSFSR in 1926.

six.[93] Those who stayed on the streets (or more accurately sheltered with others in obscure and in some cases well-hidden underground locations) to make a living by begging, pilfering, or prostitution would remain a thorn in the side of the state and society—the hooligans of their time.[94]

Beggars

We have more than once referred to collectivization as the cause of great displacement, and we must do so again. In addition to deportations of peasants identified as kulaks, rural-to-urban migration by those fleeing collective farms, and seasonal migration by those seeking a source of income to keep them and their families alive, we need to address the wandering of rural folk. "Wandering," it should be noted, is not necessarily an objective description, but rather what others who observed them assumed peasants, uprooted and desperate, were doing. Wandering and associated activity such as begging became ubiquitous during the famine years of 1932–33. Whole families, individual adults whose families had perished, and children all wandered. Sheila Fitzpatrick's indefatigable research has uncovered a "pathetic letter" that peasants, expelled from their collective farm in the Central Agricultural region, sent to President Kalinin in 1933. They described themselves as having "been turned into tramps, roaming the whole Soviet Union." They had been to the Northern Caucasus, Siberia, Central Asia, and even the Far East but, for inexplicable reasons, could not settle anywhere, and so returned to their home districts with "no strength and nothing to eat."[95] Something like fifty thousand homeless Kazakh children escaped the famine in their homeland in the latter half of 1933 by crossing the border into western Siberia. According to the head of that region's NKVD, Sergei Mironov, it also attracted large numbers of itinerants, Gypsies, beggars, criminals, and others on the loose and on the run.[96]

In Ukraine "masses of peasants" roamed the countryside in search of bread. Finding none, they crossed borders into the Central Black Soil region, traveled to the Volga, to Moscow oblast', the Western oblast', and Belorussia. On January 22, 1933, Stalin and Molotov issued instructions to regional authorities not to permit these movements, which they

---

93. Ball, *And Now My Soul Is Hardened*, 4, 87–175. Among the best known of children's homes were those Anton Makarenko established under the auspices of the NKVD. One of the homes, the Gor'kii colony in Poltava province, served as the basis for his fictionalized account *Pedagogicheskaia poema* (1934–37), translated as *Road to Life: An Epic of Education* (Moscow, 1955). *Road to Life* was the title of a popular film about the Gor'kii colony (1928), directed by Nikolai Ekk.

94. Ball, *And Now My Soul Is Hardened*, 12.

95. Fitzpatrick, *Stalin's Peasants*, 88.

96. Shearer, *Policing Stalin's Socialism*, 258.

attributed to enemy agents who had stirred up the peasants. Over the next six months, hundreds of thousands were arrested and either sent back home or prosecuted. Peasants also wandered into the cities of Ukraine. In early May, the Politburo of the Ukrainian party organization blasted local party and government organs for having allowed homeless children to leave villages for the cities and even in some cases encouraging them to go. According to G. I. Petrovskii, chairman of the Ukrainian SSR's Central Executive Committee, authorities were picking up 150 to 170 children from the streets of Khar'kov every day, 20,000 in Chernigov needed assistance, and the numbers were comparable in the mining towns of the Donbas. The Politburo identified adults who had made it to Khar'kov, Kiev, Odessa, and Dnepropetrovsk as "rogue elements" (brodiazhnicheskie elementy), a choice of words indicative of both a lack of compassion and a lack of understanding of what their agrarian policy had wrought.[97]

The policy the government pursued began with repatriations and ad hoc impressment into labor units for convict-like rock breaking and road building. It evolved into mass roundups, dispatch to NKVD labor colonies, and in the case of minors, return to their parents or relatives, confinement in children's homes, or prosecution. The more the security organs fretted about the security of the country's major cities and other strategically significant locations (border regions, ports, facilities of the armed forces), the more vulnerable the rural effluents and others subsumed under the category of "socially harmful element" became to these dragnets. The passport regime, introduced in several phases throughout the 1930s, served as the most effective—albeit blunt—technique for catching up with and expelling itinerants and other wanderers. From spring 1935 to fall 1937, nearly one hundred thousand homeless children were sent to institutions run by the Education and Health commissariats, and another forty thousand wound up in NKVD colonies or prison. These actions overlapped with the mass operations of 1937–38 that targeted for confinement in the Gulag or execution former kulaks still at large, passport violators, ex-convicts, the unemployed, and the homeless.[98]

People continued to beg, professionally and otherwise, during the war, and in what one historian describes as record numbers—two to three million—in the years immediately following. Begging by widows, the elderly, war invalids, and children became "commonplace," especially in the countryside. But many did not stay in the countryside; they headed

97. Danilov, Manning, and Viola, Tragediia sovetskoi derevni, 3: 670–71; Gorcheva, Nishchenstvo, 179; V. V. Kondrashin, Golod 1932–1933 godov: Tragediia rossiiskoi derevni (Moscow, 2008), 220–22; N. A. Ivnitskii, Golod 1932–1933 godov v SSSR: Ukraina, Kazakhstan, Severnyi Kavkaz, Povolzh'e, Tsentral'no-Chernozemnaia oblast', Zapadnaia Sibir', Ural (Moscow, 2009), 198–99.

98. Shearer, Policing Stalin's Socialism, 57–59, 231–32, 285–370. See also Hagenloh, "'Socially Harmful Elements,'" 286–308.

for large industrial centers. At the same time, hungry urban residents left the cities and gathered by the hundreds near starch factories hoping to obtain their edible pulp by begging. Lots of people—both adults and children—were apprehended and, in a reprise of the cycle from the early 1930s, either sent back home or, if repeat offenders, dispatched for short-term corrective labor. Laws passed in 1948 and 1951 against "parasitical and criminal elements" in rural and urban areas were aimed at beggars, vagrants, and tramps with "no definite occupation and place of residence."[99] In February 1954 the minister of internal affairs Sergei Kruglov reported that in the previous year the police had apprehended over 182,000 "antisocial, parasitical elements on city streets, and at railroad stations and river ports." Seven out of ten consisted of those incapacitated by war or labor, 20 percent were deemed temporarily indigent, and only 10 percent were professional beggars.[100] But how many were on the move, that is, migratory, is unclear, and probably was not known by Kruglov.

We do have some data for individual cities, though. According to Ministry of Social Services files, nearly three-quarters of those detained by the Moscow police for begging in June 1954 hailed from the nearby oblasts of Kaluga, Vladimir, Riazan', and Smolensk. In Leningrad, the police arrested 2,380 beggars on trams and trolleys, at the markets, and on the streets during the first nine months of 1954. Over 70 percent came from outside the city. The Ministry of State Control turned up evidence about the sending regions. For example, collective farmers in Kaluga oblast' "systematically traveled to supplement their income by panhandling in Moscow, Leningrad, and other populated points of the USSR." In Moscow alone between January and October 1954, the police picked up 313 people registered in Kaluga oblast', some of whom went on excursions of a week or two accompanied by children of preschool and school age. Also among the apprehended were family members of leading cadres from several collective farms.[101]

We have referred more than once to cemeteries, trains, train stations, abandoned buildings, and markets. These, as Juliane Fürst has observed, were liminal spaces where homeless children, beggars, tramps, and other "non-conformist outsiders, such as small-time

---

99. V. F. Zima, *Golod v SSSR 1946–1947 godov: Proiskhozhdenie i posledstviia* (Moscow, 1996), 217; Sheila Fitzpatrick, "Social Parasites: How Tramps, Idle Youth, and Busy Entrepreneurs Impeded the Soviet March to Communism," *Cahiers du monde russe* 47, nos. 1–2 (2006): 380–81. The number of homeless and vagrant children also reached "new heights" during the famine of 1946–47, according to Juliane Fürst, "Between Salvation and Liquidation: Homeless and Vagrant Children and the Reconstruction of Soviet Society, *The Slavonic and East European Review* 86, no. 2 (2008): 245.

100. "Doklad MVD SSSR v Prezidiume TsK KPSS o merakh po preduprezhdeniiu i likvidatsii nishchestva," RGANI, f. 5, op. 30, d. 78, ll. 41–46, available at Almanakh "Rossiia: XX vek," Arkhiv Aleksandra N. Iakovleva, http://www.alexanderyakovlev.org/almanah/inside/almanah-doc/1007415 (accessed June 10, 2013).

101. Zima, *Golod v SSSR*, 219–24, citing GARF, f. 8300, op. 1, d. 93.

criminals, drunkards and fugitives from Soviet law . . . developed a distinct and alternative culture of their own." Police might make forays into these territories to "flush out" their denizens, but because their very nature was to be in constant motion, new itinerants soon would arrive to take their places. Indeed, if not territorial war then musical chairs seems the appropriate characterization for this interaction. "At times," writes Fürst, "police themselves would shove [homeless children] onto a train to the next raion or oblast', where other local policemen had to tackle the problem."[102]

Over the next several decades as the general standard of living rose and Soviet state services improved, the problem abated but never disappeared. In the new Soviet town of Togliatti, the police detained 429 people during the first eight months of 1971 for vagrancy, panhandling, and failing to engage in socially useful work.[103] By this time, the subculture whose lineage could be traced back to the tsarist era received new infusions from Soviet hippies, draft evaders, and other dropouts. In 1980 as Moscow prepared to host the Olympics, police swept the city clean of homeless people, transporting them beyond the 100-kilometer zone that was off limits to convicted criminals. They soon returned. But Moscow was by no means alone in confronting this social scourge. Khabarovsk, a Far Eastern town whose population fluctuated more than most because of geographic, climatic, and occupational factors, was inundated with "bums" (bichi) "who lounge about the streets, railroad terminals and docks, near stores and in marketplaces," many of them recruited from elsewhere for particular jobs but "dismissed for negative reasons." This is another instance of our categories overlapping, for it turns out that the local demand for seasonal or temporary workers—to unload trucks outside stores, to bridge gaps at the vegetable depot, to haul bags of cement off railroad cars—kept them coming back for more.[104]

Soon, bichi had been joined by bomzhi, the acronym for "without definite place of residence" that police used in their reports and that caught on with journalists and the public. And so we meet Petr Gerasimovich Maslov. Our encounter takes place in November 1982 in an unnamed Uzbek village not far from Pskent, south of Tashkent. But it could have been earlier, in 1971 in Margelan, or 1977 in Tashkent, or six months after that at a remote railroad station southwest of the Uzbek capital. Those are the places, the police blotter tells us, where Petr Maslov was arrested for vagrancy. Except the last place. There, he was beaten unconscious by a bunch of kids and found by a local resident who gave him shelter. Maslov stayed not only overnight but for four years, until one September night he vanished without a trace.

---

102. Fürst, "Between Salvation and Liquidation," 248.

103. Upravlenie po delam arkhivov merii g. Tol'iatti (TGA Togliatti), f. R-94, d. 417, l. 122.

104. V. Razboinikov, "On Your Instructions: Season of Heavenly Apples," Sovetskaya Rossia, September 25, 1983, trans. in CDSP, November 9, 1983, 2–4. Bich also means "scourge." See also B. Reznik, "A Journalist Raises a Problem: For Whom Is This 'Scourge' a Scourge?" Izvestiia, February 4, 1985, trans. in CDSP, February 27, 1985, 9.

From his rescuer, we learn that Maslov was born in 1921—or so the tattoo on his right arm indicated, for he was paperless—and therefore had reached pension age but was without a pension. We also learn that he spent those four years from 1982 to 1986 earning his keep at his rescuer's house by doing odd jobs, fixing appliances, building a garage, and plastering walls. He was, as Albert Plutnik, the *Izvestiia* correspondent who tried to track him down, described him, "a strange and for our times unexpected phenomenon—a regular jack of all trades, part of the reserve army of labor . . . a latter-day nomad." Two years later, Maslov was found in a local hospital recuperating—perhaps vegetating is more accurate—after a stroke, no longer mobile, no longer a nomad. "What is to be done with these lost people?" Plutnik asks. "Who will register them? Who will provide accommodation?" And then, casting his view more broadly to include the changes swirling around what was still Soviet society, Plutnik notes:

> Suddenly it turns out that the society, always encouraging its prodigal children to return to a normal existence, is far from always facilitating this in reality. If previously such people voluntarily deprived themselves of many of their rights guaranteed to everyone in our society—to labor, housing, social security—then now, so to speak, just let them try to regain those lost safeguards. Will they succeed?[105]

The new freedom of economic enterprises to lay off workers or simply stop paying them, combined with the commodification of housing and the shredding of social services, produced a new cohort of vagrants in Russian cities during the 1990s. They included the homegrown variety but also, as before the October Revolution, in the hungry years of the 1930s, and again after the war, people from the countryside seeking but not finding work or just seeking food. Ex-convicts, ex-soldiers, and de-institutionalized alcoholics figured prominently. In addition, the collapse of the economy that had brought workers to far-flung places via the northern increment sent many fleeing back to the cities of the mainland, often in desperation and unable to find work.[106] Homeless children proliferated. By 1997, estimates of their numbers ranged from the Ministry of Internal Affairs' 587,000 to the Presidential Council's two million, a range that itself was disturbing. In Moscow, among *besprizorniki* brought by the police to the Center for Temporary Isolation of Juvenile Offenders, most were not local and almost half were from outside Russia. They included

105. Al'bert Plutnik, "Bomzh," *Izvestiia*, February 12, 1988, 3.

106. Irina Ovchinnikova, "Skol'ko v Rossii bomzhei?" *Izvestiia*, March 5, 1996; Mikhail Nikolaev, "Besprizornyi Sever," *Trud*, December 27, 1997, both via East View Information Services Universal Databases; Vladimir Shmyganovsky, "The North Has Conquered Russia," *Izvestiia*, January 12, 1999, 7, trans. in CDSP, February 3, 1999, 2–4.

Figure 8 The Luzhkovs as migrants, http://
agitka.net/oda4ibost1ncpic.html.

seven-year-old Oksana T. from Uzhgorod in Ukraine whose father was sent to prison and
whose mother remarried, selling her to Roma for five million hryvnia or rubles, she was not
sure which. Brought to Moscow and told to beg, she got lost in the metro and was taken in
by the police.[107]

Moscow as always served as a magnet, but Moscow under Mayor Iiuri Luzhkov was not
a very welcoming place, at least not for bomzhi. As the city prepared to celebrate its 850th
anniversary in September 1997, the police started escorting the vagrants to Yaroslavl', Tula,
Kaluga, and other towns. Nine months later, the prosecutor's office for the city's Smolensk
district brought suit against the director of the Kiev Railroad Station for permitting the station to become a haven for bomzhi. By the end of February 1998, the police were detaining
some sixty-eight people every day for living illegally in Moscow. Worse, bodies of individuals who had died of alcohol poisoning kept on turning up in and around the station. Later

---

107. Sergei Sergeev, "Besprisornymi det'mi zaimetsia," Trud, December 10, 1997; Ivan Sas, "Moskva be-
sprizornaia," Segodnia, December 6, 1997, both via East View Information Services Universal Databases. Most
besprizornye from Moscow were not taken to the Center but rather to orphanages and boarding houses.

that year, the World Youth Games occasioned a repetition of the 1980 Olympics purging of *bomzhi*, but as with the earlier event, they were expected to return at the games' conclusion.[108] Ironically, when in 2010 President Dmitri Medvedev booted Luzhkov out of office, he and his wife, billionaire Elena Baturina, were depicted as classic peasant migrants who will "somehow survive on $3 billion" (See figure 8).

Nomads

Toward the end of his first trans-Siberian journey in 2001, the American writer Ian Frazier decided to cross the Sikhote-Alin Mountains east of Khabarovsk. Just as he ascended the crest of the divide between the waters flowing west to the Ussuri and Amur rivers and east to the Pacific, he encountered an obelisk on which was inscribed (in Russian) "Crossed over this pass: M. I. Venyukov 1858; N. M. Pzhevalskii 1887; V. K. Arsenyev 1906." Frazier had to ask his Russian traveling companions about the first two pass-crossers, but he knew about Vladimir Arsen'ev both from Arsen'ev's "timeless wilderness adventure story" *Dersu Uzala* and Akira Kurosawa's film version from 1975.[109]

Dersu Uzala was a trapper who identified himself as a Gold, the tribe indigenous to the Maritime region. Arsen'ev encountered Dersu in 1902 during his first expedition to survey "Ussuria," a "steep, mountainous country . . . covered with dense virgin forest . . . in places almost impenetrable." Dersu reminded Arsen'ev of "the delight of my boyhood, Fenimore Cooper and Mayne Reid," that is, an authentic son of the forest—a noble savage—who "had spent his entire life in the *taiga* and was exempt from all the vices which our urban civilization brings in its train." "Here," Arsen'ev writes after observing that Dersu had left kindling and matches for anonymous hunters, "was this savage far more thoughtful for others than I." "Formerly," he adds, "I had thought that egoism was characteristic of savages, and feelings of charity, humanity, and love of one's neighbour were a speciality of Europeans and Christians. Was I not wrong?"[110]

For our purposes, Dersu's importance lies not so much in his nobility as in his itinerancy. Asked by one of the soldiers accompanying Arsen'ev where he lives, Dersu replies in stilted Russian (that in English translation sounds more like Tonto than

---

108. *Izvestiia*, July 16, 1997; Vitalii Romanov, "Za ozverevshikh brodiag otvetiat zheleznodorozhniki," *Segodnia*, March 5, 1998; and *Segodnia*, April 24, 1998, all via East View Information Services Universal Databases.

109. Ian Frazier, *Travels in Siberia* (New York, 2010), 320–21. An earlier Soviet film by the same title was made in 1961 (Agasi Babaian, dir.). For another recent invocation of Arsen'ev's classic, see John Vaillant, *The Tiger, a True Story of Vengeance and Survival* (New York, 2011), 28–31.

110. V. K. Arseniev, *Dersu the Trapper*, trans. Malcolm Burr (New York, 1941), 5, 9, 13–14, 28,

Chingachgook), "Me no got house, me all time live moving: light fire, make tent, sleep; all time go hunt, how have house?" The problem is that already by the time Asren'ev meets him, Dersu's way of life including his freedom to roam is being constrained by the increasing presence of Russian "urban civilization." Smallpox, the virus that accompanied Europeans to the New World, Africa, and Australia, had felled Dersu's wife and children some years before. When his eyesight starts to fail, Arsen'ev thinks he is doing his friend a favor by taking him to Khabarovsk after reassuring him, "You will always find a roof for your head where I am." But Dersu cannot adjust to town ways; he goes off on his own only to be murdered by robbers. Distraught, Arsen'ev arrives just in time to see him buried and marks the spot by two cedars whose boughs stretch over his resting place. But less than two years later, in 1910, when he goes to visit Derzu's grave, he can't find it: "Everything had changed. A whole township had sprung up round the station . . . they were felling the forest for sleepers. . . . My cedar landmarks had vanished. New roads had been made. There were quarry faces, dumps, embankments . . . all around bore the signs of another life."[111]

Arsen'ev structures his account around the primitiveness/civilization opposition, and, by reversing the vectors in favor of primitiveness, underscores the tragedy of Dersu's obliteration. Like many binaries, however, this one breaks down upon further inspection. A trapper whose survival depended on the meat of the animals he caught, Dersu developed an itinerary based on his acute ability to follow the tracks of his prey. He "was really astonishingly adapted to life in the taigá," Arsen'ev observes. But in fact, Dersu was enmeshed in a rather complex social network with multiple interdependencies. In the course of his travels through the taiga he met other itinerant hunters, as well as hermits, Chinese and Korean ginseng cultivators, Old Believer settlers, brigands, and the occasional Russian expeditionary team. Not unlike outside the region, some of the relationships among these people were mutually beneficial and others just exploitative. To enhance his survival in the taiga, Dersu availed himself of an old "berdianka" rifle, as well as a great many other manufactured goods: two old shirts, cartridge-cases, an old pickle jar, a little kettle, copper buttons, and assorted other odds and ends. Arsen'ev writes that he advised Dersu to throw away half of "his treasures," but that Dersu rejected the advice because "they would all come in useful some day."[112]

111. Ibid., 9, 303, 333–40.

112. Ibid., 114–16. The berdianka, actually, "berdanka," was derived from Hiram Berdan, an American military officer and engineer who developed it during the Civil War for use by sharpshooter regiments. See Mikhail Gruzdev, "Berdanka: Pochemu na Rusi ee nazyvali amerikanskoi, a v Amerike—russkoi vintovkoi?" at http://shkolazhizni.ru/archive/o/n-47407/ (accessed May 7, 2013).

In the Far North

Entire peoples lived far to the north of Dersu, from the Chukchi Peninsula in the East to the Yamal Peninsula at the mouth of the Ob River. They were inhabitants of the Siberian Arctic littoral north of the 60th parallel. Like Dersu, they had their own itineraries, but also like him, they experienced state intrusion of a kind. The Imperial government did not want to settle the Far North, but its hunter-gatherers had long attracted a tribute-hungry empire. Furs were the coin of this part of the realm, and their extraction supported the "fur empire" of the eighteenth and nineteenth centuries.[113] These were the Evenki and many of the other numerically "small peoples of the North" who populated—albeit sparsely—vast remote territories. We learn most about them from the ethnographers and cultural anthropologists who, since 1926, have lived and worked among them enough to appreciate the logics of their mobility.

At the beginning of the twentieth century, the northern natives paid in sable, fox, or squirrel skins, and traded with Old Settlers to acquire tea, flour, salt, liquor, and metal utensils. Russian officials, priests, and exiles made up the third group in the Far North. The native peoples were mobile. Life on the tundra and in the northern taiga demanded repertoires of mobility in harmony with the wildlife—the reindeer, fish, and game that appeared in an annual rhythm. Fundamentally, reindeer facilitated movement by pulling sleds and hauling fish and game, so the possession of reindeer enriched a household; moreover, reindeer were neither fed nor enclosed, but rather foraged on their own, so they not only facilitated but also required mobility. Movement complemented the minimalist built environment: portable conical tents for summer travel, covered underground huts, and a variety of unfinished timber cabins like the flat pyramid-shaped *balagan*.[114]

Evenki traveled along the lower Enisei river valley in northern Siberia and along the broad Khatanga Way into eastern Siberia. They moved not in large groups, but rather in households of five or six kin with small herds of about forty reindeer, using the reindeer for transportation. Evenki hunters took to the mountains, hunted migratory wild deer, and hauled smoked and salted fish twice a year to Russian trading posts to pay tribute and to purchase the goods they desired. They then would return to familiar valleys and mountain areas, where they met their own kin. These were not the wealthiest of the small peoples, so they paid taxes at the lowest rate: thirty squirrel skins, four ermines, or one arctic fox per

113. Hoerder, *Cultures in Contact*, 212–15; Yuri Slezkine, *Arctic Mirrors: Russia and the Small Peoples of the North* (Ithaca, 1994), 97. See also F. G. Safronov, *Russkie promysly i torgi na severo-vostoke Azii v XVII–seredine XIX v.* (Moscow, 1980).

114. David G. Anderson, *Identity and Ecology in Arctic Siberia: The Number One Reindeer Brigade* (Oxford, 2000), 54; John Ziker, "Subsistence and Residence in the Putoran Uplands and Taimyr Lowlands in 1926–27," in *The 1926/27 Soviet Polar Census Expeditions*, ed. David G. Anderson (New York, 2011), 250–51.

year.[115] Nonetheless, some did travel widely, using more than one language and covering great distances. When in the early 1990s the ethnographer David G. Anderson interviewed the oldest Evenk in the settlement, a woman who had been widowed in 1915, she spoke at length about caravans of her youth and named trading posts thousands of miles apart (specifically south to Tura, to Turukhansk, and Volochanka to the west). The translator (necessary because the interviewee Agrafena Khristoforovna Khutukagir intermixed two native languages and spoke no Russian) was embarrassed, thinking the old woman's senility caused her to describe travel over such fantastic distances. Anderson disagreed: "while it is true that commuting between these points would seem impossible to a villager dependent upon the monopolistic and inefficient schedules of the civil aviation authority, the old woman's stories do resonate both with the stories and practice of present-day *tundroviki* and the archival record."[116]

Indeed, *tundroviki* knew and understood the ostensibly hostile arctic territory as most Russians never could, and their peregrinations in search of and in response to those of reindeer, fish, and game long went uninterrupted. They were affected by outside events, however, because as ethnologists have discovered, hunter-gatherers like the indigenous northerners do "interact with states, agro-pastoralists, and traders" that impinge on their subsistence and social organization.[117] The Revolution and Civil War brought conflict to the Amur and Okhotsk coast, but the collapse of trade and consequent loss of such crucial goods as arms, ammunition, flour, salt, and strychnine to be used against predators affected people like the Enisei Evenki the most—some lost over 90 percent of their reindeer. The Saami to the west and Kamchatka Evenki to the east fared better, but nonetheless these years brought on starvation and a retreat farther into the tundra in many cases.[118]

The early Soviet years, by contrast, brought on study, observation, and documentation of the indigenous people more than the intervention, social engineering, and economic reorganization that would follow. Many of the interpreters and census takers who would come to the north in the 1920s were professional ethnographers. They worked on a heroic scale, especially those who traveled to take part in the 1926/1927 Soviet Polar Census Expeditions. One of them called the census a survey of places difficult to reach and also difficult to describe.[119] In an attempt to interview every household head, to note on a household card

115. Anderson, *Identity and Ecology in Arctic Siberia*, 44–45.

116. Ibid., 131.

117. Peter Jordan, "Seasonal Mobility and Sacred Landscape Geography among Northern Hunter-Gatherers," in Anderson, *1926/27 Soviet Polar Census*, 32.

118. Slezkine, *Arctic Mirrors*, 131–32.

119. David G. Anderson, "The Polar Census and the Architecture of Enumeration," in Anderson, *1926/27 Soviet Polar Census*, 7; Jordan, "Seasonal Mobility and Sacred Landscape Geography," 37; Slezkine, *Arctic Mirrors*, 167. The census is also analyzed for its key role in delineating the nationalities of Soviet peoples in Francine Hirsch, *Empire of Nations: Ethnographic Knowledge and the Making of the Soviet Union* (Ithaca, 2005), 101–44.

Figure 9   Reindeer herder family. Courtesy Krasnoiarsk Kraevoi Kraevedcheskii Muzei, from 1926 Polar Census.

kinship, demographics, subsistence, and migration itineraries, and to write a diary of each community, these ethnographers created an invaluable record of life in the north before full-tilt Soviet intrusion. They created not so much a surfeit of numbers as have other colonial enumerations, as a surfeit of questions: northern household structures did not correspond to European Russian expectations and for those who wished to attach each household to one primary location, the complex movements of the northern household were a nightmare. Moreover, northern peoples are not loquacious. Census interviews must have been equally puzzling for the indigenous people: the ethnographer David Anderson observes that the "notion that they planned their lives out in autonomously functioning units within a limited spatial and time horizon must have seemed a mystical idea."[120] After all, they moved in a land inhabited by spirits and by the gifts of wildlife.

The enumerators in the territory of the Middle Ob in western Siberia, inhabited by the Iugan Khants, found that these "people of the river" engaged in flexible and far-reaching itineraries. Some downriver communities were settled and even kept pasture animals, but

120. Anderson, "Polar Census," 17–18.

upriver communities traveled from 30 to 500 miles—downriver to summer fishing grounds, then in diverse directions to winter hunting areas. Fishing was a collective endeavor, but hunting was an individual activity, for which men would go on skis while women set up shelters, prepared wood for a fire, and processed the kills. Most communities gathered only from two to eight families and in some cases one household would travel while the other would stay in place for the winter or the summer. Not only did the Iugan Khants live in small communities, but also their itineraries reveal that many households were alone for long periods in remote forest tracts.[121]

When the Soviet ethnographer Boris Iosofich Dolgikh worked in the Kamen' region far to the northeast of the Iugan Khants, he conducted interviews for ten days in December 1926 and January 1927. Dolgikh spoke with households of hunters, fishers, and trappers engaged in long-distance travel for trade, seasonal movements for reindeer herding and hunting of migratory prey, plus local travel for hunting, fishing, trapping, herding, and fuel gathering. These trips took families and individuals across the Putoran highlands—the high, flat-topped mountains in central Siberia—and north into the Taimyr lowlands. These "people of the mountain" lived, worked, and moved together throughout the year.[122]

The settlement of Davyd Stepanovich Buatulu, an Essei Iakut, exemplifies the collective and peripatetic nature of mountain people's lives. He led a settlement of five households, all living in his balagan. This head was seventy, his wife thirty-five, and his five sons aged two to twenty-four (the eldest adopted). His household had 700 reindeer, some of which were used to supply sleighs to traders. The other four households consisted of a total of fifteen people who possessed another 150 reindeer and 160 deadfall traps intended for arctic fox and ermine. Davyd's household "was in charge of buying groceries" for this productive group that brought in nearly 4.5 tons of fish that was probably smoked or dried and consumed, and gifted or traded along with hundreds of pounds of wild reindeer meat and the harvest from its network of deadfall traps. The subsistence-based economy of these five households was substantial, then, and perhaps more members were supported, at least in the summer, for their herding assistance.[123]

The people of the mountain had a yearly round of travel in the 1920s that began with a trip to Lake Essei some 180 to 250 miles southeast for a meeting of kin. Beginning in January, this long journey and gathering would last into early March. Travel on snow was then still possible so that stopping to trade, to stock up and sell pelts, took place in the spring. The return to the rivers meant the beginning of a mobile fishing season in which women were active workers. With the ascent of the reindeer to the plateaus in the summer, an

121. Jordan, "Seasonal Mobility and Sacred Landscape Geography," 44–60.
122. Ziker, "Subsistence and Residence," 253.
123. Ibid.," 252–54.

arduous routine of nearly daily moves began, performed by young men. Over the year, women's primary job was to process the reindeer hides. Fall ushered in the primary hunting and trapping season. The hide-covered tents moved less often since hunting and deadfall traps were attached to specific locations. By late winter and the end of the hunting season it was time to trade again, along the Khatanga track, at Volochanka, or in Dudinka on the Enisei.[124]

Such a yearly round seemed grossly inefficient, unmodern, and uncivilized to Soviet officials, who looked to keep native peoples off their sleds and settled. As one remarked in 1929, " 'Correctly organized hunting requires the presence of the hunter in hunting areas only during specific seasons, so he does not need to wander all year long, dragging his wife, tent, and household possessions behind him.' "[125] In the early 1930s, rationalizing the nomads ostensibly was the reason for dekulakization and collectivization in the Far North. These were campaigns designed for grain-producing areas and especially ill suited to the life of circumpolar indigenous peoples. Natives of the Far North already lived collectively and shared resources, so assigning kulak status was especially problematic. The Enisei Evenki, described above, practiced posobka, taking in an unfortunate young relative to train, employ, and assign some reindeer, a practice that the First Territorial Officer saw as exploitation. Many people remember this practice fondly, however, and the head of the First Reindeer Brigade expressed gratitude years later for having been apprenticed with relatives after his parents died. The people of this region staged a rebellion at Volochanka that showed the failure of the policies and got the Russian head of the reindeer farm arrested. Interrogated in the investigation of the rebellion, the rebels were direct: " 'Why should we pay such high taxes and denounce our relatives. Who is a kulak anyway?' "[126]

The campaigns of the early thirties came to three results among the Enisei Evenki and many other indigenous peoples who lived from hunting, fishing, and reindeer herding. Many competent, experienced men were arrested and jailed, devastating some communities. Second, reindeer were expropriated from families with large herds, despite the fact that officials did not know how many reindeer a family needed to survive. Third, territorial officers organized native groups not into settled farms, but into associations. The Evenki who lived on the shores of Lake Khantaika (a location so obscure that they were missed completely by the 1926/1927 Polar Census) formed the "Red Trapper" association in 1931 with nineteen members. In 1939, upon receipt of a donation of 391 head of reindeer from a wealthy family, it was upgraded to the Red Trapper work unit (artel). And the innovation of

124. Ibid., 258–63.
125. B. E. Petri, "Karagasiia stroitsia," Okhotnik i rybak Sibiri 6 (1929): 9, cited in Slezkine, Arctic Mirrors, 205.
126. Anderson, Identity and Ecology in Arctic Siberia, 49–50, 137; quotation on 146.

the counting corral—to make it possible to enumerate the herd twice a year—spread to rationalize reindeer herding, or at least to render it legible.[127] In other words, nomadism as a way of life was to become nomadism as production.[128]

Nevertheless, while dekulakization and collectivization devastated much of the rest of the country, the people of the Far North remained relatively free in these years. The state enjoyed only limited success in its attempt to control the arctic littoral and collect hides, fish, and reindeer meat. Some seasonal fishing communities refused to comply because to do so meant starvation.[129] Pelts from trapped animals proved even more difficult to gather because hunters could always sell to a high bidder or take pelts home until a better price was offered. Hunting remained an individual activity, as one Evenk explained his attachment to his individual itinerary: " 'We don't hunt together, we hunt in different places. I know and like my place, and Pavel Mikhailovich knows his. I don't want some other kolkhoz member to check my traps.' "[130]

Like hunters, reindeer herders could offer mighty and effective resistance because they knew the tundra and taiga; moreover, the remote, relatively empty territory was hardly inviting or easy for Russians. As a consequence Evenki were able to frustrate plans like those of the territorial formation officers who mapped out "a single reindeer farm for a district the size of Great Britain" on the Khantaika River. They also demonstrated the unreality of the project to set up the farm as a model for socialist herding that would contain over 20,000 reindeer. These expropriations of reindeer provoked the effective rebellion in Volochanka in the spring of 1932.[131] If a state farm or work unit like the Red Trappers mentioned above were to receive some 300 reindeer from a wealthy family, as they did, it is likely that the family retained their own stock. Wealthy herders continued to travel widely and some herders changed their routes and moved to more remote areas to evade authorities. The people of the mountain included Taspai Buatulu, whose entire herd of 5,000 reindeer was confiscated in 1934. His brother Paibal, who seems to have had more reindeer, simply disappeared.[132] The 347,000 total reindeer that were taken into state farms died at a great rate (51 percent was the reported proportion dead), and others disappeared along with their herders.[133]

So on the one hand, the state acquired some reindeer herders who could both be successful in delivering quotas and maintain a schedule, while at the same time respecting the

127. Ibid., 49–51; Slezkine, *Arctic Mirrors*, 202–3.
128. Slezkine, *Arctic Mirrors*, 341.
129. Ibid., 210.
130. Cited by Slezkine, *Arctic Mirrors*, 206.
131. Anderson, *Identity and Ecology in Arctic Siberia*, 49.
132. Ziker, "Subsistence and Residence," 255.
133. Slezkine, *Arctic Mirrors*, 212.

"ethical imperatives which govern the relationship between people, animals, and tundra."[134] On the other hand, collectivization of the Far North failed, so that Evenki and other peoples continued to move with their reindeer, to fish and to trap. By 1939, the state could lay claim to only a quarter of the Khantaika Evenki's reindeer.[135]

Between 1937 and the 1960s, these people fed the state with furs, leased their reindeer for hauling, and provided wild deer venison and fish to workers. The Khantaika Evenki remember these years as a heyday because they traveled freely; women and elders fished on lakes and rivers in the summer while young men went with the reindeer to high pastures and in the winter checked their deadfall traps. Using sleds or saddled reindeer, communities traveled to visit kin within state farm territory and beyond. Their division of labor and seasonal routines maximized mobility over a large region while minimizing the ability of the state to control "the structure of the work-unit, the number of reindeer, and the uses to which they were put." Is it any wonder that the 1950s and 1960s are especially fondly remembered?[136]

This is not to imply that native peoples were alone in the Far North, for many of the people we introduced earlier—administrators, special settlers, and prisoners—came to northern Siberia as well. During the First Five-Year Plan alone, a state joint-stock company initiated mining for coal and graphite and brought in hard currency by selling lumber to Western Europe. Over three thousand families, plus as many seasonal workers, came to work in fishing in Kamchatka. About one million newcomers arrived in the north during 1926–32, most of whom were labor camp inmates. Those who fished in native fishing grounds or demanded transportation and cargo hauling impinged on native life the most. This age before the snowmobile and helicopter created considerable obligations to transport Russians and equipment on reindeer sleds—and in the case of the people who worked along the key Dudinka-Khatanga track, this imposition was considerable because it took a toll on winter hunting.[137] The people of the north had no interest in lumber or minerals extraction. On the contrary, the destruction of the land or the forest violated their relationship to their surroundings.

Eventually, the exploitation, rationalization, and industrialization of the north enforced changes in migration and work patterns that profoundly disrupted the lives of its nomads. Together, settlement policies and the industrialization of the Noril'sk region, for example, underlay dramatic changes that had some brutal consequences for Evenki of the lower

---

134. Anderson, *Identity and Ecology in Arctic Siberia*, 28.

135. Ibid., 50–51. Slezkine writes that only 10 percent of reindeer were owned by kolkhozes, 8.8 percent by sovkozes "all in all" (*Arctic Mirrors*, 210).

136. Anderson, *Identity and Ecology in Arctic Siberia*, 52–53.

137. This route was used by Dolgan, Nenets, Evenk, and Nganasan, and the proportion of men engaged in transportation increased from 41 to 70 percent, 1930–1932 (Slezkine, *Arctic Mirrors*, 266–67).

Enisei Valley and the mountain people. From 1936 to 1952, the Khantaika Nomadic Council consisted of two officers moving with the hunters, but in 1952 the council became a village council, and deportees (Volga Germans, Poles, and Balts) constructed a settlement. In the late 1960s, the pace of consolidation picked up, as twenty-five work units of the lower Enisei became six large state farms.[138]

Most dramatically, one day in 1969 a "'Russian with a loud voice' gave the Mountain People a single day to pack two bundles of possessions into awaiting military cargo planes."[139] They were to join the Khantaika Evenki in a lakeshore settlement that became increasingly crowded and unhealthy. Industry intruded on the settlement in the 1970s when the rising Lake Khantaika, transformed into a hydroelectric reservoir, became the third largest lake in Russia, flooding longstanding wild deer pastures in the process. Finally, the heavy metal and sulfur dioxide pollution from mining and metallurgical processing—especially the Nadezhda nickel smelter—poisoned the atmosphere so much that wild reindeer changed their migration routes, avoiding their former lichen pastures in the Enisei river valley, and thus put themselves out of the reach of the Mountain and Khantaika Evenki. A second reservoir and natural gas pipeline further impeded human and animal movement.[140]

These changes to settlement patterns and the landscape itself altered longstanding migration patterns. They forced specialization, restricting nomadism to herders alone, separating them from fishing groups that worked seasonally. Ironically, these changes compelled people to live close together in settlements and also to live apart. The resultant regime of "state nomadism" divided communities and separated male herders from most women for nine months of the year as they followed an arduous itinerary.[141] When there was snow, they lived in baloks, hand-made portable dwellings on sled runners pulled by reindeer and furnished with tin wood-burning stoves. Each day out with the reindeer began with a fire, tea, and a search for the deer (that could have found pasture at a distance of some 6 miles), herding them in, then relocating to a fresh pasture in the afternoon and gathering firewood and ice for water.

The Number One Reindeer Brigade of the Khantaika sovkhoz gives us an idea of itineraries for late Soviet herders. Brigadier Nikolai Savel'evich Utukogir, born in about 1943, led a brigade with nine full members including himself: five male herders, two female tent

138. Anderson, *Identity and Ecology in Arctic Siberia*, 54–55, 58, 61.

139. Ibid., 57.

140. Ibid., 57–58, 62–63, 139. On the Khantaika dam, see A. L'vov, "Proshchanie s Khantaikoi," in *Eniseiskii meridian* 3 (Krasnoiarsk, 1977), 334–37, http://library.kspu.ru/files/kzd2010/95.pdf‎ (accessed June 18, 2013).

141. Anderson effectively uses this term, and thanks Ian Whittaker of the Scott Polar Research Institute for suggesting it (*Identity and Ecology in Arctic Siberia*, 37).

workers, and a local apprentice. Other young apprentices came and went during the season. Anderson clarifies the role of the woman "tent worker," in this case the wife of brigadier Utukogir. She, Liubov' Fedorovna, not only cooked every meal but was also "a central figure, if not *the* central figure" of the brigade. "As the senior housekeeper and mother or aunt to many of the herdsmen, she directed the packing and unpacking of sleds, the management of skins for sewing, and often the distribution of meat between the *baloks*."[142]

This brigade began the yearly round of moving out onto the tundra in January or February, then corralling the deer in April for the semiannual count. It then split the herd, half going with the males, the others with the pregnant cows and their year-old calves, heading for summer pastures to the south. In late May or early June the brigade rejoined for the hectic season of calving and to enjoy the better weather and pasturage before the mosquito season. Then they would move to high plateaus for the summer, finding shelter in smoke-filled tents. Splitting again, the young men would go to the highest pastures, supplied with bread by the women who remained in the base camp. With September and the first snows, the return began, necessitating vigilance as herders kept their deer from going off with migrating wild herds. Arrived back at the settlement in November, herders built a counting corral and enumerated the herd to measure and validate their year's work. They then selected the deer for the slaughter that required about two days. Women bought supplies and men negotiated contracts for the coming year, procured licenses for trapping, acquired ammunition, "ideally" received their back pay, and moved into a long period of drinking, resting, repairing tools, and relaxing.

Brigadier Utukogir was about fifty when anthropologist David Anderson caught up with him in 1993. Anderson asked Utukogir why he had taken on this work, because he could have had an easier life by assuming the less arduous job of fishing or even by rising in the party, since he was one of the first Communists in the settlement. His reply came as a question: "Who would feed the village?"[143] Indeed, state nomadism did feed the settlement by bringing in food, pay, and reindeer hides to sell and sew for clothing.

Although kinship and participation in a *kollektiv* remained of primary importance, the implosion of the Soviet state found many Evenki resisting what was called reform. The goods for which they could trade became scarce and services diminished drastically. Moreover, the ways that state nomadism disconnected nomadic herders from the lifeways of an integrated hunting and fishing community rendered it an isolated and asocial way of life,

142. Anderson, *Identity and Ecology in Arctic Siberia*, 19–23, 37; quotations on 22–23. He specifies, "Like all senior women on the tundra she was a master seamstress and very knowledgeable about the nature of animals both alive and undressed." For an equally engaging portrait of a brigadier's wife, in this case of the 7th Brigade of Evenki north of Lake Baikal in the Sebyan, see descriptions of Granny, the matriarch described by Piers Vitebsky, *Reindeer People: Living with Animals and Sprits in Siberia* (New York, 2005), part 2, 63–148.

143. Anderson, *Identity and Ecology in Arctic Siberia*, 38–42; quote on 20.

attractive primarily to confirmed bachelors. Women found *tundroviki* less and less desirable. The community's children, sent to boarding school, had neither the training for nor interest in life on the tundra. More isolated communities, like those of Evenki in the region around Sebyan north of Lake Baikal, had great difficulty summoning or paying for transportation in this age of aviation.[144] The fortunes of the moose-hunting Yukaghirs of the far northeast who had been organized into kolkhozes and then sovkhozes in the postwar period diminished tragically when they came under the power of the state enterprise Sakhabult in 1992.[145] As the well-being of northern Siberia's industrial towns faded and its people suffered on the polluted landscapes, most children of herders and trappers turned to more settled livelihoods.

In Kazakhstan

Far to the south, a very different ecosystem sustained a migratory way of life quite unlike the hunting and gathering practiced by the native peoples of the north or by Dersu and his ilk. At least since the seventeenth century, Kazakhs of the Great, Middle, and Little federations or hordes pursued mobile (or to use an older term, nomadic) pastoralism. They drove herds of sheep, goats, camels, and horses from summer grazing grounds in mountainous terrain and northerly locations to winter pastures bordering on desert in an annual cycle intricately connected to social organization, religious observance, and gender roles.[146] The distance between summer and winter pasturage ranged from 125 to 625 miles depending on the density of herd populations, rival claims to land by other peoples, variations in topography, and annual rainfall.[147] Despite Russian conquest beginning in the eighteenth century and the intrusions of settlers and the market economy in the nineteenth, these migrations continued, although with considerable modifications discussed below.

As described in Mukhamet Shayakhmetov's account of his own childhood, they continued up through the 1920s. Born into a Middle Horde family in eastern Kazakhstan's Semipalatinsk province in 1922, Shayakhmetov recalls "following routes established by our forefathers. Each move was like a festival. . . . The caravan was headed by the most

---

144. See the vivid closing of Anderson, *Identity and Ecology in Arctic Siberia*, 216–18; and Vitebsky, *Reindeer People*, 251–365 ("How to summon a helicopter").

145. Rane Willerslev, *On the Run in Siberia* (Minneapolis, 2012), 41–44, 181–83.

146. Nurbulat Edigeevich Masanov, *Kochevaia tsivilizatsiia Kazakhov (osnovy zhiznedeiatel'nosti nomadnogo obshchestva)* (Almaty, 1995), 144–46. The term "nomad" came into ethnographic disrepute because of David Sneath and Caroline Humphrey, *The End of Nomadism? Society, State, and the Environment in Inner Asia* (Durham, 1999). As historians, we respect the longevity of its usage.

147. V. P. Kurylev, *Skot, zemlia, obshchina u kochevykh i polukochevykh kazakhov (vtoraia polovina XIX–nachalo XX veka)* (St. Petersburg, 1998), 79; Martha Brill Olcott, *The Kazakhs*, 2nd ed. (Stanford, 1995), 17.

respected woman of the aul, who rode on a horse, leading the camels which carried her family's possessions." First, in the early spring, the entire village moved from its winter camp, stopping long enough for lambing. As soon as the lambs were old enough to travel short distances, everyone would be on the move again finding new pastures. In June, the nomads headed up into the mountains or further north, reaching their final destination by July. By early September when the weather became cooler, the process reversed itself, and by the first snowfall, people moved into their winter dwellings where they would remain until the next nomadic cycle began. Shayakhmetov remarks that the moves "had been developed to a fine art." It took less than an hour and a half to dismantle the yurt, pack it and its contents, and load everything onto a camel.[148]

Not all Kazakhs practiced this seasonal movement between fixed winter and summer pastures and not all who did were Kazakhs. Our decision to track Kazakh (and to a lesser extent Kyrgyz) herdsmen and women rather than, say, Turkmen, Buriat, or Uzbek pastoralists was dictated by several factors: the extensive nature of their migratory repertoire and its symbiosis with grain cultivation, the abundance of primary sources and scholarship associated with it, and the occasional availability of Kazakh pastoralist voices.[149] We are particularly interested in the internal sociocultural norms of Kazakhs who practiced some form of nomadic pastoralism, their interaction with both state officials and settlers, and their adaptations—or the limits of their adaptability—over the long term. Our main argument is the same as for the indigenous peoples of the Far North: the weakening and progressive elimination of the nomadic repertoire occurred not because of its inherent inferiority to others, but as a consequence of others' ability to apply forcefully, if necessary, their own economic and ideological agendas.

Kazakh society consisted of clans, each of which claimed territorial rights based on patrimonial lineage. Although historically subordinated to a khan and other White Bone (aristocratic) descendants of Chingiz Khan, the clan leader, the bai (alt. biy), adjudicated disputes within the clan and negotiated with other clans on the basis of customary law. Clans in turn were subdivided into tent encampments or auls that ranged from two or three to a dozen or more families. As the Soviet anthropologist Anatolii Khazanov has noted, in the absence of clear ownership of the key resources of land and water, kinship ties served to knit together different auls into "a community of the second order. The members of the latter community use the same pastures and/or water-sources at specific times of year, join up for pastoral migrations, and are linked by various social, kin and other ties, sometimes

148. Mukhamet Shayakhmetov, *The Silent Steppe: The Memoir of a Kazakh Nomad under Stalin*, trans. Jan Butler (New York, 2007), 4–5.

149. On these other nomads, see Adrienne Edgar, "Everyday Life among the Turkmen Nomads," in *Everyday Life in Central Asia: Past and Present*, ed. Jeff Sahadeo and Russell Zanca (Bloomington, 2007), 37–44; S I Vainshtein, *Nomads of South Siberia: The Pastoral Economies of Tuva* (New York, 1980).

also by specific forms of mutual aid." For example, the clan leader's redistribution of animals enabled poorer auls to survive, a practice known as *saun*.[150]

Scholars have debated whether the changes experienced by Kazakh nomadic society under Russian imperial rule resulted from policies of the colonial administration or emerged from the interactions of Kazakhs with colonial authorities. If earlier accounts relied on the state's own records of the laws and order it imposed, more recent inquiries, reading against the grain of official documents, have stressed greater agency on the part of the colonized. Shifting the optic to the Kazakhs has demonstrated not only their role as co-creators of the world they inhabited but also that interactions with and challenges from predominantly sedentary societies long pre-dated Russian rule.[151]

Strongly influenced by postcolonial studies, recent historiography has gone further to disaggregate the stark categories of colonized and colonizers. Instead of the unitary state or "Russia," historians now refer to military officers and civilian bureaucrats who sometimes acted at cross purposes, Cossacks sent to the frontier to serve as buffers between nomadic and sedentary societies, and surveyors who fanned out across the steppe to chart parcels for settlement. Settlers, whom we encountered in an earlier chapter, were not state actors, although state officials had fond hopes that their sedentary way of life and civic-mindedness would set an example for the Kazakhs. They began arriving in the steppe in significant numbers in the 1880s and, encouraged by the extension of railroad service to Tashkent in 1906, continued to pour into the region right up to the outbreak of the First World War.[152]

These groups interacted with Kazakh nomadic society in complex ways. In Virginia Martin's interpretation, the Provisional Statute of 1868 created positions for Kazakhs to fill within the colonial administration that the Middle Horde Kazakhs she studied "learned to manipulate and reinvent . . . in order to suit their own legal and political needs."[153] But the notion that Kazakhs could entirely blunt Imperial designs to deprive them of much of their pasturage and convert them into grain cultivators and hired laborers clearly would be wrong. In the Steppe Statute of 1891, the government redefined Kazakhs' land as the "property of the state," a crucial step in giving resettlement authorities greater flexibility in the

---

150. A. M. Khazanov, *Nomads and the Outside World* (Cambridge, 1984), 130–35. Khazanov goes so far as to assert that "from the structural point of view communities are frequently based on ties of kinship and common descent" (135). Shayakhmetov claims women could serve as heads of families or even clans (8). On *saun*, see Didar Kaaymova, Zhanat Kundakbayeva, and Ustina Markus, *Historical Dictionary of Kazakhstan* (Lanham, 2012), 234.

151. Jeff Sahadeo, "Conquest, Colonialism, and Nomadism on the Eurasian Steppe," *Kritika: Explorations in Russian and Eurasian History* 4, no. 4 (2003): 953. The Khanate of Kokand was a case in point.

152. Virginia Martin, *Law and Custom in the Steppe: The Kazakhs of the Middle Horde and Russian Colonialism in the Nineteenth Century* (Richmond, UK, 2001), 42–43. The state had pursued this strategy in the Caucasus earlier in the nineteenth century by using religious sectarians. See Breyfogle, *Heretics and Colonizers*.

153. Martin, *Law and Custom in the Steppe*, 88.

conversion of pasture land to grain cultivation. One surveyor, after investigating land usage in the steppe oblasts of Akmolinsk and Semipalatinsk in the summer of 1899, did not mince words in his report to the Ministry of Agriculture and State Properties: "The primary aim of the investigation is nothing but the development of firm foundations for the subsequent conversion of the Kirgiz [Kazakh] land into resettlement plots."[154]

Accommodating Russian peasant settlers in the Kazakh steppe removed summer grazing grounds and compelled Kazakh herdsmen to rely on winter pasturage for more, or all, of the year. The greater water supply in the winter afforded production of fodder, which promoted a more sedentary existence. The more sedentary the Kazakhs became, the less pasture colonial authorities considered they needed, a conclusion that led to the opening up of additional lands for Slavic peasant settlement.[155] Kazakhs' progressive abandonment of long-range migration and summer pasturage also meant less reliance on kinship and other social ties, which undermined Kazakh solidarity and the effectiveness of resistance. Or as a Resettlement Administration study of Kazakhs in Akmolinsk oblast' put it in 1910: "there is considerable evidence of cultural progress in the free development of households and personality, the weakening of the nomadic cast of life, a decline in the number of large familial groups, and a decline in those groups of five or more auls descended from the same ancestor."[156]

The trajectories of the family of Mustafa Chokai, the future Turkestani nationalist, well illustrate the cultural progress resulting from the "weakening of the nomadic caste." The youngest of five children, Mustafa was born in 1890 in an aul located roughly halfway between Tashkent and the Aral Sea. Both his father and mother claimed descent from White Bone lineages, and his mother was literate in both Arabic and Persian. Although Mustafa's grandparents had pursued nomadic ways, his father practiced agriculture. Nevertheless, both his sisters married into nomadic families that, according to his widow, "were quite wealthy." Mustafa's aul, consisting of about thirty relatives, "was not considered wealthy" primarily because Kazakhs measured wealth in terms of head of cattle and, as agriculturalists, they had few.[157] Mustafa graduated in 1910 from the lycée in Tashkent, but the death of

154. Ministerstvo zemledeliia i gosudarstvennykh imushchestv, *Otchet revizora zemleustroistva Smirnova po komandirovke letom 1899 g. v akmolinskuiu i semipalatinskuiu oblasti* (St. Petersburg, 1899), 2. This investigation was part of the Shcherbina expedition of 1896–1903, a vast undertaking to determine the amount of land required for nomads' subsistence and the amount to be allotted for settlers. See Ian W. Campbel, "Settlement Promoted, Settlement Contested: The Shcherbina Expedition of 1896–1903," in *Movement, Power, and Place in Central Asia and Beyond*, ed. Madeleine Reeves (London, 2012), 65–78.

155. For a neat summary of these developments, see George Demko, *The Russian Colonization of Kazakhstan, 1896–1916* (Bloomington, 1969), 56–60, 158.

156. Pereselencheskoe upravlenie, *Kirgizskoe khoziaistvo v Akmolinskoi oblasti*, 5 vols. (St. Petersburg, 1909–10), 5: vii. The reference was specifically to Akmolinsk uezd, but the criteria were universal.

157. Mariia Chokai, *Ia pishu vam iz Nozhana . . . (vospominaniia, pis'ma, dokumenty)* (Almaty, 2001), 12–13.

his father two years later caused him to interrupt his legal studies and return to the aul to take up the hereditary responsibilities of bai. The majority of cases he handled concerned the denial by Russian settlers of winter pasture rights for nomadic families.[158]

There is evidence already in the 1880s of Kazakhs violently resisting encroachment on their lands by unauthorized settlers, but also recruiting them as tenants and working for them (as well as for Cossacks) as farmhands and animal herders. These disparate responses suggest the deep divisions that economic transformation was causing. Martha Brill Olcott cites estimates of 5 to 25 percent of the Kazakh population benefitting economically from settlers' demand for livestock and especially cattle, since demand drove up prices "spectacularly" in the early twentieth century. But that meant that the economic situation of most Kazakhs "was bad and growing worse."[159]

Kazakhs' differential responses to the increased presence of settlers are neatly mirrored in A. A. Kaufman's survey from the mid-1890s of settlers who rented land from Kazakhs in Turgai oblast'. Some had nothing but praise for their Kazakh "masters." Residents of the settlement of Aleksandrovskii described relations as "most friendly"; damage by migrating cattle did occur but "we settled [the issue] peaceably." Families were guests at one another's homes. Young Russians learned "Kirgiz" and the Kazakhs learned Russian. Peasants in the nearby community of Romanovskii, however, complained of a whole series of misunderstandings and "offenses," in Borisovsk of "permanent disputes with Kirgiz over advance payments," and in Vorovoi of Kazakhs' "hostility," the main manifestation of which was their theft of horses and bulls.[160]

Different conceptions of property and its use account for some of the disputes. The Vorovoi settlement, formed in 1881, remained unknown to authorities for six years until one Kazakh complained that the agreement the settlers had signed with a Kazakh from another aul deprived his animals of access to pastureland. Settlers elsewhere discovered to their dismay that an agreement with one aul did not prevent others from invading "their" land en route to summer or winter pasture.[161] Mustafa Chokai may have dealt with cases of this sort. As for animal theft, Virginia Martin notes when an issue had not been settled justly or at all, Kazakhs customarily resorted to barïmta, which she defines as "self-reprisal when other solutions were deemed untenable, with the ultimate aim of revenging insult and upholding personal and clan honor." Barïmta often took the form of seizure of

---

158. Ibid., 22–23. An enemy of the Bolsheviks, he emigrated to Paris and was arrested by the Nazis and brought to Berlin, where he collaborated with the Third Reich and died in 1941.

159. Olcott, *Kazakhs*, 96, 99.

160. A. A. Kaufman, *Pereselentsy-Arendatory turgaiskoi oblasti (2-ia chast' otcheta starshago proizvoditelia rabot Kaufmana po komandirovke v turgaiskuiu oblast')* (St. Petersburg, 1897), 7, 63–64, 163; supplement 7, 20, 25, 33.

161. Ibid., 27–30, supplement 33.

another's animal, "a powerful recourse in a culture where the well-being of one's herds . . . could determine the well-being of the entire community."[162]

Russian imperial law criminalized the practice, making it identical to theft. But according to Martin, who listened closely to "Kazakh voices audible within Russian texts," rather than curbing barïmta, criminalization transformed horse theft into a heroic act within the Kazakh community "because it symbolized resistance to the imperial legal order . . . [and] the presence of colonizers."[163] The ease with which the barantachi (performers of barïmta, but horse thieves to Russians) made off with their four-legged prizes and avoided punishment must partly explain its frequency. A survey of settlements in Tobol'sk province that we cited in chapter 1 described the theft of horses and cattle as a "serious obstacle to the development of the peasant economy," adding that in the case of one settlement typical of those arising on the steppe in the previous ten to fifteen years, "the Kirgiz [Kazakhs] can steal half the herd without the shepherd knowing it."[164] Kazakhs by no means were the only ones engaged in this highly remunerative practice: exiles, Old Settlers, Roma, and Cossacks also stole animals and sometimes served as fences for the Kazakhs. In some parts of the province, to the north of Kazakhstan's present boundaries, settlers actually paid the Kazakhs not to steal their horses. And in at least one settlement (Matasy, Teplodubrovok volost'), investigators were informed by settlers that they liked to employ Kazakhs as shepherds because their relatives were less likely to steal from them.[165]

While not gainsaying these accounts, we would be remiss if we did not note the absence of Kazakh voices. Thanks to his widow, we have Mustafa Chokai's testimony that twice his family had to vacate their home because settlers decided to use it for a school or to house school personnel. No less humiliating was the appropriation of their harvest by settlers and officials who divided it among themselves. And from poor Kazakhs, settlers allegedly "selected cattle and carried off sheep [and] cows." They took what they wanted not to symbolize resistance to the imperial legal order but because the Kazakhs, lacking Russian-language skills, were powerless to prevent them. This, at least, was how Mustafa explained his father's decision to send him to study law in Tashkent.[166]

For all their economic benefit and effectiveness as a symbolic reversal of power relationships, the Kazakhs' theft of animals and other illegal practices ultimately could not

162. Martin, *Law and Custom in the Steppe*, 141, 143. The redistributive dimension of the practice is emphasized by Khazanov, *Nomads and the Outside World*, 156.

163. Martin, *Law and Custom in the Steppe*, 148, 153.

164. Stankevich, *Materialy dlia izucheniia byta pereselentsev tobol'skoi gubernii*, 1: 152, 158. Peasants in another village are described as "deprived of the possibility to successfully struggle against it by themselves" because "the proximity of the Kirgiz steppe and sojourns of individual Kirgiz families among Old Settlers as shepherds, saddlers, and simple poor peasants . . . is sufficient to guarantee the success of the theft" (204).

165. Ibid., 233, 285.

166. Chokai, *Ia pishu vam*, 13–14.

compensate for the loss of land. The latter trend intensified during the last years of the old regime, as authorities removed restrictions on further peasant settlement of winter pasture lands, first in Semirech'e oblast' (1905) in today's southeastern Kazakhstan, and then in the Syr Daria oblast' (1911) in northern and central Kyrgyzstan.[167] Although leery of disrupting the modus vivendi they had established with the nomadic pastoralists, tsarist officials could not resist the temptation of permitting settlement in what the military governor of Semirech'e referred to in 1902 as "obviously empty territory with rich agricultural land."[168] Like European colonizers elsewhere in the world, their definition of emptiness seems to have hinged on a particular understanding of land use that excluded pastoralism. Thus, when in January 1906 official announcements began to appear in the press about "free state land completely appropriate for agriculture," a contemporary Russian critic noted that "freed land" would have been more appropriate to indicate that the state had removed "excess" land from Kyrgyz nomads according to surveyors' determinations.[169]

Just as Russians differed over whether to remove even more land from pastoralist use and if so how much, so Kazakhs and Kyrgyz were divided. Occasionally, clan elders organized or sanctioned raids against those who had abandoned nomadism in favor of settled agriculture. The few Duma deputies representing the indigenous population differed among themselves. Some advocated a total halt to new settlement; others, deemed "progressive" by Russian liberals, wanted land taken away from the state and converted to private property. The emergent Kazakh intelligentsia, divided between Islamic and secularist orientations, generally advocated at least partial settlement of nomads, arguing, for example along historicist lines, that "the present-day Russians and Tatars and other settled peoples first led nomadic lives [and] we are also able to live as they do."[170]

For a few years, Resettlement Administration officials were able to keep abreast of these divisions and even exploit them to their advantage.[171] But World War I reduced the state's maneuverability. Its requisitioning of Kazakh livestock, insistence that Kazakhs work on the homesteads of settlers recruited for military service, and finally conscription of males

167. N. E. Masanov et al., *Istoriia Kazakhstana: Narody i kul'tury* (Almaty, 2001), 247. This is an area of mixed Kazakh-Kyrgyz ethnicity. We will use both terms as appropriate.

168. RGIA, library, d. 86, ll. 148–49, cited in Daniel Brower, "Kyrgyz Nomads and Russian Pioneers: Colonization and Ethnic Conflict in the Turkestan Revolt of 1916," *Jahrbücher für Geschichte Osteuropas* 44, no. 1 (1996): 45.

169. O. R. Shkapskii, "Pereselentsy i agrarnyi vopros v semirechenskoi oblasti," *Voprosy kolonizatsii* 1 (1907): 29.

170. Olcott, *Kazakhs*, 101–9, quotation on 116.

171. A. L. Tregubov, "Pereselencheskoe delo v semipalatinskoi i semirechenskoi oblastiakh: Vpechatleniia i zametki chl. Gos. Dumy A. L. Tregubova po poezdke letom 1909 g.," *Voprosy kolonizatsii* 6 (1910): 104–72. Tregubov, a member of the center-right Octobrist faction, strongly advocated Slavic settlement in the region as a bulwark against the Chinese. See also *Voprosy kolonizatsii* 3 (1908): 315–21; and Olcott, *Kazakhs*, 99, 113.

into labor brigades to serve the army provoked rebellion. We have remarked in an earlier chapter on the rebellion's antisettler animus. Here, we note the correlation that Daniel Brower observed between its intensity and the recentness of settler intrusions. Brower contrasts Semirech'e's western region where the Kyrgyz had "moved into . . . the 'middle ground' between the new order of a conquering empire and the traditional native community" with the area around the Issyk-Kul basin where "the traditional clan order remained firmly established." He argues that the less the departure from nomadic ways, the more willing were the Kyrgyz to risk everything to return to a "nomadic golden age."[172]

The argument is intriguing, as is the analogy with the Sepoy mutiny, an earlier "desperate rebellion thrown up against the alien colonial intruders and . . . the decay of hallowed, native ways." But the argument runs the risk of presenting a false dichotomy between modernity as represented by colonial intruders and the retrospective utopia of nomadism. It also obscures the Kazakhs' adaptiveness, for by this time animal herding among most of the population coexisted with farming and other endeavors. Thus, in addition to the extreme categories of nomadism and sedentarism, contemporary observers (and subsequent scholars) refer to both semi-nomadism and semi-sedentarism. Indeed, although animal herding remained the dominant economic activity among Kazakhs, total reliance on nomadism had become rare: "On the one hand, many poor Kazak families worked in agriculture as an accessory activity to the animal herding of the richer members of the aul; on the other, economic exchange between the Kazak herdsmen and Russian peasants was widespread."[173]

Kazakhs' adaptiveness would be put to the test in the years following the rebellion. Thousands fled across the border to China to avoid punishment. Between 1916 and 1920—years of revolution, civil war, drought, and famine—Russian land seizures in the area most affected by the rebellion occurred on a scale described by Terry Martin as "massive." Then these processes were reversed. The pacification of the region by the Red Army between 1920 and 1922 brought with it the expulsion from Semirech'e of several thousand Russian peasants to which we already have referred. The total Russian population of Kazakhstan dropped by about 20 percent during these years, and the sown area of Russians' crops shrank by more than 50 percent.[174] The establishment of Soviet authority in the countryside

---

172. Brower, "Kyrgyz Nomads and Russian Pioneers," 51–52. The "middle ground" is the concept developed by Richard White in reference to the zone of interaction between indigenous North Americans and European intruders.

173. See Niccolò Pianciola, "Famine in the Steppe: The Collectivization of Agriculture and the Kazak Herdsmen 1928–1934," *Cahiers du monde russe* 45, nos. 1–2 (2004): 140–41 (quotation on 141). See also Isabelle Ohayon, *La sédentarisation des Kazakhs dans l'URSS de Staline: Collectivisation et changement social (1928–1945)* (Paris, 2006), 24–29.

174. Martin, *Affirmative Action Empire*, 60.

was also accompanied by a series of decolonizing or "affirmative action" measures—including a ban (albeit unenforceable) on Russian settlement—intended to favor Kazakhs in the distribution of uncultivated land. The general consensus, though, is that most Kazakhs lacked the means to take advantage of the state's largesse, which in any case was more limited in actuality than on paper.[175]

The "nativization" (korenizatsiia) of political administration had no more success, which meant "Kazaks remained essentially alienated from the state." At the local level, however, clan and subclan ties "now took on a new vitality," with the bai reasserting saun relations with poorer clan members. Ceding ownership of animals to the bai, the herdsmen continued to look after herds, retaining the right to consume or trade products obtained therefrom.[176] Thus, the "retraditionalization" of authority relations among the Kazakhs entailed the reinforcement of animal husbandry. According to the 1926 census, over 97 percent of Kazakhs lived in rural areas. Although less than 10 percent of Kazakh households migrated year-round, two-thirds were classified as semi-nomads because they moved with their herds to summer pastures in a classical pattern of transhumance. Most traveled short distances (less than 60 miles) to higher elevations with cooler temperatures and a relative abundance of water.[177] Judging by his childhood recollections, Mukhamet Shayakhmetov's family was typical in this respect.

All of this is crucial to understanding what happened when, in 1928, the Communist Party's Kazakh section decided to launch an offensive against the "feudal" power of the bai, followed in December 1929 by its resolution to "sedentarize" Kazakh nomads on collective farms. The equivalent of dekulakization in the rest of the RSFSR and among Russians within Kazakhstan, "debaiization" struck at the heart of kinship solidarities that governed Kazakh nomadic society.[178] As elsewhere, regional and local party cadres—particularly non-Kazakhs—often got carried away in subjecting Kazakhs to enormous tax burdens and requisitioning livestock, becoming, as Stalin would put it in March 1930, "dizzy with success." Those required to pay, like Mukhamet Shayakhmetov's uncle ("Toimbai-ata"), sought to exchange as many head of cattle or other livestock for grain, the designated medium for paying taxes. But "the large numbers of animals being brought to market caused prices to plummet." Toimbai-ata was among those arrested for nonpayment and exiled to

---

175. Olcott, Kazakhs, 161–64; Pianciola, "Famine in the Steppe," 145.

176. Olcott, Kazakhs, 162; Pianciola, "Famine in the Steppe," 140, 146. On korenizatsiia see Martin, Affirmative Action Empire, 133–34.

177. Ohayon, Sédentarisation des Kazakhs, 24, 371; G. F. Danshleiger, "Iz opyta istorii osedaniia kazakhskikh kochevykh i polukochevykh khoziaistv (do massovoi kollektivizatsii sel'skogo khoziaistva)," Sovetskaia etnografiia, no. 4 (1966), 12–13; Martha Brill Olcott, "The Collectivization Drive in Kazakhstan," The Russian Review 41, no. 2 (1981): 124. In Semipalatinsk province, a mere 2.5 percent of households moved more than 100 kilometers between winter and summer locations.

178. On the debaiization campaign, see Ohayon, Sédentarisation des Kazakhs, 35–69.

Ust-Kamenogorsk, 150 miles away in extreme eastern Kazakhstan. He managed without too much difficulty to escape on horseback and for a year stayed on the run, joining the class of people we discussed earlier in this chapter. However, "discouraged by his loss and convinced of the futility of life as a fugitive," he gave himself up to the authorities, who sent him to prison.[179]

In seeking to settle the Kazakh nomads, Soviet Communists pursued an objective common among states with substantial pastoralist populations. Saudi Arabia's policies toward the Bedouins, Tanzania's ujamaa village campaign of the 1970s, and Ethiopia's compulsory villagization during the mid-1980s reminds us that sedentarization required neither colonialism nor socialism. The privileging of grain cultivation over livestock breeding, faith in the applicability of scientific farming techniques, and, as James Scott has emphasized, a felt need for greater legibility of the population crop up as common features.[180] In the Soviet case, regional Communists considered sedentarization of the nomads "a prerequisite for the socialist reconstruction of the economy," meaning collectivization. Yet, according to Niccolò Pianciola, the process "remained a dead letter" in 1930 and as late as 1933 less than a third of the reported 230,000 nomad families actually had been settled. Why? Using Terry Martin's terminology, Pianciola argues that during the First Five-Year Plan (1928–32) sedentarization was a "soft-line" policy—a declared objective but one whose postponement to the indefinite future would not get the cadres in trouble. The application to nomads of livestock and even grain delivery quotas, which required them to sell their animals, was more urgent and thus a "hard-line" policy. As Pianciola writes, "forced grain requisitions . . . paradoxically hit hardest those who produced no grain—herdsmen—and set in motion a process that led to the near destruction of the region's livestock."[181]

Turning over livestock to the collective and state farms almost ensured their neglect through lack of fodder, shelter, organization, and in many cases, will. Gosplan's figures reflect the drastic loss of livestock for all of Kazakhstan between January 1929 and June 1933: horses declining from 4.1 million to just over 450,000, cattle from 7.2 million to 1.6 million, sheep and goats from 24.8 million to 2.7 million, and camels from one million to less than 89,000.[182] Mukhamet mentions a decision in his region to keep part of the confiscated livestock for breeding purposes, for which a sovkhoz, "grandly known as a 'model livestock farm,'" was organized. But the farm turned out to be too small to accommodate

---

179. Pianciola, "Famine in the Steppe," 150; Shayakhmetov, *Silent Steppe*, 17–18.

180. James C. Scott, *Seeing Like a State: How Certain Schemes to Improve the Human Condition Have Failed* (New Haven, 1998), 223–61.

181. Pianciola, "Famine in the Steppe," 156, 161–63, 179, 188; Terry Martin, "Interpreting the New Archival Signals: Nationalities Policy and the Nature of the Soviet Bureaucracy," *Cahiers du monde russe* 40, nos. 1–2 (1999), 117–18; see also see Ohayon, *Sédentarisation des Kazakhs*, 227–77.

182. Pianciola, "Famine in the Steppe," 166.

all the animals, so the nondairy stock was slaughtered. But the dairy livestock proved too weak and malnourished to make the journey, and thus they met the same fate. The plan was to let the carcasses freeze, stack them along the Irtysh River, and dispatch them downstream to riverside towns at the first thaw. But by the time the upper reaches of the river became navigable, "the stacks of meat were stinking to high heaven" and nearby residents had to move away.[183]

The herdsmen and women, deprived of their traditional livelihood, became refugees—*otkochevniki* in state parlance—"all thin, cold, rag-clad, hungry, and many begging for bread," in the words of a Canadian agronomist who encountered them along the Siberian-Kazakhstan border. True wanderers, they rustled cattle and otherwise preyed on the kolkhoz population; they gravitated toward the cities, the industrial sites, and construction projects; and they traveled by the hundreds of thousands north to Siberia and the Urals, south to Uzbekistan, and east to China.[184] We cannot be precise about how many died along the way or succumbed to starvation before they had a chance to depart, but according to the successive censuses of 1926 and 1937–39, the ethnic Kazakh population within Kazakhstan dropped from 3.7 million to 2.1 million.[185] Mukhamet, whose father was sentenced to two years in prison for failing to pay taxes and died in the winter of 1932 trying to escape, reckons that his clan lost forty-three of its sixty-nine members during the 1930s.[186]

Maltreated and homesick, the otkochevniki did come back, and in larger numbers than officials had expected. This was when the party got serious about sedentarization. It identified several thousand points for settling the former nomads, instructing local authorities to build housing and provide other services for them. But the operation lacked follow-through from state institutions, the locations for settlement made no sense, and the quality of the housing was poor. In this manner, Kazakhs who had once been nomads were encouraged to seek their livelihoods elsewhere—and many did in industry and transport, education, and the military.[187] To this story of devastation and adaptation we would only want to add that what scholarly accounts have failed to mention but what comes through loudly in Mukhamet's memoir is that denomadized Kazakhs relied heavily for shelter and sustenance on their relatives—both near and distant, related by blood and in-laws. But in the hungry winter of 1932–33, sometimes people "travelled great distances to find their

183. Shayakhmetov, Silent Steppe, 50–51.

184. On emigration to China and cattle rustling in western Siberia, see reports from the OGPU's political section from October 1931 and August 1932 in Danilov, Manning, and Viola, Tragediia sovetskoi derevni, 3: 209–13, 454–55. See also O. V. Zhandabekova, Pod grifom sekretnosti: Otkochevki kazakhov v Kitai v period kollektivizatsii. Reemigratsiia 1928–1957 gg. Sbornik dokumentov (Ust'-Kamenogorsk, 1998).

185. Olcott, Kazakhs, 184–85; N. Masanov, "Migratsionnye metamorfozy Kazakhstana," in Viatkin, Kosmarskaia, and Panarin, V dvizhenii dobrovol'nom i vynuzhdennom, 137.

186. Shayakhmetov, Silent Steppe, 70, 180.

187. Pianciola, "Famine in the Steppe," 175–84; Danilov, Manning, and Viola, Tragediia sovetskoi derevni, 3: 665.

relatives, only to learn when they arrived that their family had moved on." Too weak to return home, such people often died of hunger. And, as an elder tells him, "Some won't have anything to do with their relatives any more, you know." "Recalling all this now," Mukhamet writes in the twenty-first century, "horrifies me."[188]

Nomadic pastoralism disappeared as a way of life from the Kazakh steppe, but stock raising by transhumance continued. In subsequent decades, herdsmen brought animals to graze in summer pastures located in northern regions and higher elevations, lived in yurts or other makeshift dwellings, and in winter relied on stall-feeding much as they had before. The differences were several: the animals and the territory they traversed belonged to a sovkhoz or kolkhoz, herdsmen's families remained behind to engage in agriculture or care for milch animals and their offspring, and, as an International Labor Office (ILO) report from 1966 put it, "the seasonal movement of livestock to pasture land specifically assigned by the State to each *kolkhoze* [sic] and *sovkhoze* [sic] takes place at previously fixed times."[189] The participants from various North African and Middle Eastern countries who produced the report acknowledged—without necessarily agreeing with—the Soviet view that "the nomadic way of life is . . . an anachronism," and accepted that "neither nomadism nor semi-nomadism exists any longer in the two republics visited—Kazakhstan and Kirghizia."[190]

Nomads reappeared some three decades later, after the Soviet Union had ceased to exist and kolkhozes and sovkhozes, losing their lifeline to central institutions, had been disbanded. The predominant form of livestock and dairy production became the small household averaging 3.4 head of cattle each. The overwhelming majority of households in the country came to depend on communal grazing with rotational herding duties or a paid herder, and purchased feed and fodder for cattle in winter.[191] In some parts of arid central Kazakhstan, however, mobile pastoralism made a comeback with herdsmen tending to their flocks of sheep, erecting yurts, and gathering with their families in auls. The evocation of earlier times is a bit attenuated by the fact that they do not rely on horses or camels to move from one grazing ground to the next, but rather motor vehicles, and they are likely to communicate with each other by cell phone.[192]

Nomadism reemerged in another way in post-Soviet Kazakhstan—and elsewhere—with the release in 2005 of *Nomad: The Warrior*. Kazakhstan's official entry for Best Foreign Language Film in the 2007 Academy Awards, it tells the story of Ablai Khan, the

188. Shayakhmetov, *Silent Steppe*, 168.

189. International Labour Office, *Report on the Inter-regional Study Tour and Seminar on the Sedentarisation of Nomadic Populations in the Soviet Socialist Republics of Kazakhstan and Kirghizia (5 to 30 September 1966)* (Geneva, 1967), 61.

190. Ibid., 75.

191. Anton van Engelen, *Dairy Development in Kazakhstan* (Rome, 2011), 5.

192. Tom Stacey, "Introduction," to Shayakhmetov, *Silent Steppe*, xii. See also *The New York Times*, June 19, 2013, A8, which reports, "nomadic herders from the nearby steppe are moving into abandoned buildings in Baikonur, home of the Cosmodrome."

eighteenth-century leader of the Middle Horde who successfully defends his people from the Dzungars. The film attracted $40 million from the Kazakh government. It was, in effect, an investment in the creation of a mythological past, before Russian settlement, when Kazakhs roamed the steppe freely and fiercely as nomads.

Conclusion

The escapees, vagrants, Roma, wandering orphans, and beggars who lived in Imperial, Soviet, and post-Soviet Russia had much in common with their brothers and sisters elsewhere in the world. They too led lives of itinerancy in which they could not take for granted food and shelter even from one day to the next. They too did not so much engage in illegal practices as virtually inhabit social categories that were by definition illegal or at least extra-legal.[193] At the same time, conditions arose in twentieth-century Russia that made it impossible to meet the needs of the needy with long-standing practices such as peasant adoption of unfortunate children and the provisioning of holy beggars. After 1917 the state aspired to fill the void by settling, employing, institutionalizing, and otherwise looking after these marginals, albeit in a space so vast that many could fall between the cracks. The 1990s saw a return to an anterior reliance on charities and religious organizations, however inadequate their efforts to quell impoverishment and the collapse of Soviet-era social services. These years inspired the recently coined phenomenon of "migrantophobia," although the fear and suspicion of outsiders long pre-dates the disintegration of the Soviet Union.[194]

The native herding nomads of Kazakhstan and hunter-gatherers of the Far North had a much less acute dependence on others for food and shelter at the beginning of the twentieth century. Indeed they had few needs for manufactured goods and foodstuffs and in the north had an independent life despite the fact that they paid tribute to the state. Nonetheless, in its desire to rationalize indigenous food and game production, to make way for settlers (in the case of Kazakhstan), and for natural resource exploitation (in the case of the Far North), the territorial agents of the Soviet state effectively chipped away at both independence and mobility. With the end of the Soviet state in the 1990s, mobility became legally possible but difficult in actuality owing to overwhelming impoverishment and a seriously degraded natural environment.

---

193. See such classics as Gareth Stedman Jones, *Outcast London* (Oxford, 1971); Olwen Hufton, *The Poor of Eighteenth-Century France, 1750–1789* (Oxford, 1974); Catharina Lis and Hugo Soly, *Poverty and Capitalism in Pre-industrial Europe* (Sussex, 1979); Robert M. Schwartz, *Policing the Poor in Eighteenth-Century France* (Chapel Hill, 1988); and the more recent Anne Winter, *Gated Communities? Regulating Migration in Early Modern Cities* (Burlington, 2012).

194. Viktor Shnirel'man, "Migrantofobia i kul'turnyi rasizm," *Ab Imperio* 8, no. 2 (2008). For comparative assessments of state policies on homelessness, including Russia, see Carl O. Helvie and Wilfried Kunstmann, eds., *Homelessness in the United States, Europe, and Russia* (Westport, CT, 1999).

Conclusion

Amnesty International noted in its newsletter for June 2013 that "more than 42 million people worldwide have now been forcibly displaced by conflict and persecution." Of these, some 15 million are refugees who fled their country because of abuses or conflict, another 27 million consisted of "internally displaced people," forced from their homes by conflict within their home country but not crossing an international border.[1] Most of these people are from countries engulfed in civil war, subjected to occupation by a foreign power, or experiencing devastating famines or other untoward conditions misleadingly called "natural disasters."

We conceived of this book as being about migration within borders governed by Russian political authorities, but to a degree that both surprised and dismayed us, movement in Russia during the twentieth century presaged the current global situation addressed by Amnesty International. Millions found themselves forcibly displaced within their own country as a result of two world wars, a civil war, a war to detach peasants from lands they considered their own, and all manner of economic and technological disasters both associated with these wars and independent of them. Hundreds of thousands of deportees crossed what had been international borders before the USSR absorbed their countries. And after the breakup of the Soviet Union toward the end of the century, millions more crossed what had only just become international borders to reenter Russian political space. The most comprehensive effort to date to measure migration in Russia in comparison with

---

1. *AIUSA Group 81*, June 2013, 1, 4. See the United Nations' report on which AI based its own, "Refugees: Overview of Forced Displacement," www.un.org/en/globalissues/briefingpapers/refugees/overviewof forceddisplacement.html (accessed June 23, 2013).

migration elsewhere finds that Russia's rate significantly outpaced the rest of Europe, China, and Japan between 1915 and 2000.[2]

Throughout this study we have emphasized space and distance as conditioning the migratory regimes we discuss. The abundance of space enabled the state—both tsarist and Soviet—to send into internal exile criminals and other "undesirable" elements. At the same time, the noncorrespondence between demographic density and natural resource location virtually dictated a policy of resettlement, sometimes voluntary and sometimes anything but. If space and distance enabled the state to do certain things, they also disabled; the country's proverbial vastness worked against the state's ambitions—unusually sweeping in the Soviet case—to track and control the movement of its citizens. They also complicated migrants' designs. Traveling thousands of miles across thinly populated territory proved debilitating and even fatal for some, but rehabilitating for others. The chains in chain migration could be stretched very thin, but new careers and identities could be forged. Finally, crossing such immense spaces often resembled crossing international boundaries. Evacuees from the Soviet Union's western regions certainly felt themselves in an exotic land when arriving in Alma-Ata, Tashkent, or even Bashkiria. By the same token, Central Asians coming to Moscow to study or earn enough to remit back to their families experienced their new homes as foreigners, often unwelcome ones. This was the Soviet version of transnationalism—transnationalism in one country.

Another surprising dimension of movement in Russia during the twentieth century was, contrarily, how much of it occurred outside of state strictures and irrespective of policymakers' intentions. At the dawn of the century peasants from the Black Earth provinces of Russia and Ukraine took advantage of the newly built railroads to settle "irregularly" in Siberia and the Kazakh steppe, often in numbers that far exceeded those seeking permission. Simultaneously, peasants from farther to the north migrated in unprecedented numbers to Moscow, St. Petersburg, and other cities where they found work as factory workers and domestics, or to mines in the Donbas. These migratory booms are well known; less so were the growing presence of Chinese and Korean migrants in the Russian Far East, the migration of seasonal workers to and from the sugar beet and wheat fields of Ukraine, and, during World War I, the refugees who poured into the Russian interior from the western border regions under invasion.

Since Moshe Lewin coined the neologism of the "ruralization of the cities," many scholars of Soviet history have emphasized the significance of this massive migratory flow during collectivization.[3] But few have commented on the voluntary basis of rural resettlement

---

2. Jan Lucassen and Leo Lucassen, "Measuring and Quantifying Cross-Cultural Migrations: An Introduction," in *Globalising Migration History: The Eurasian Experience (16th-21st Centuries)*, ed. Jan Lucassen and Leo Lucassen (Leiden, 2014), 33. Cross-cultural migration is defined on 14–20.

3. Lewin, *Making of the Soviet System*, 218–21.

or the extent to which peasants scouted by themselves potential areas of settlement and otherwise informed one another through informal networks about living and working conditions. Likewise, postwar demobilization gave veterans a chance to try out different scenarios of habitation, and young people moved from villages deprived of amenities across the Russian heartland to cities for more education, occupational advancement, and the expansion of connubial possibilities. In the immediate post-Soviet period, the capacity of the state to control or even monitor migratory movements greatly diminished. Here, in fact, what surprises is not that people moved largely of their own accord, but that there were any limitations on their movements at all.

We do not wish to suggest, however, that migrant repertoires and state regimes were mutually exclusive. On the contrary, they often constituted each other. Peasants who resettled in the East thanks to land preparation and incentives provided by state authorities urged relatives, friends, and fellow villagers to join them, and many did. Seasonal laborers from collective farms contracted with state employers as groups at construction sites; their late Soviet equivalents did likewise, albeit traveling as self-organized work teams from elsewhere to collective and state farms to help build infrastructure. Most of the young men and women who voluntarily braved the isolation and intense cold of the Far North to take up jobs at mining and metallurgical enterprises probably would not have done so without the Soviet state's offer of high pay, the so-called northern increment. And many subjected to the system of job assignments upon graduation from higher educational institutions used connections, bribery, and subterfuges like fictitious marriage to steer the decision of where they would serve. In short, networks of contact and friendship meshed with institutional initiatives.

Still, if repertoires and regimes need to be understood as interactive, differences did exist in the nature of their interactivity. Sometimes they were complementary and mutually reinforcing, in other cases, more antagonistic and compensatory. The family emerges as a key site where this interplay happened. Both evacuees and state officials relied on it to determine to where and even whether people would be evacuated. More broadly, rights to depart from a village or kolkhoz, live in a "regime" city, or return to one after a prolonged absence depended on the presence and cooperation of family members. At the same time, mothers caring for young children and children caring for their elders subtracted from what the able-bodied could contribute to collective labor in special settlements and colonies. And family ties among Kazakh and Evenk herders got in the way of state agendas to de-nomadize or "more rationally" distribute the population.

Recognizing that all migration involves some degree of coercion, even if only the force of circumstances, we organized our study along a continuum from least to greatest external compulsion. Peasants and army veterans resettling with their families faced various constraints in terms of where they could settle and on what terms, but, as we argue, generally were seeking to reproduce a more economically secure version of their lives before depart-ing. Both tsarist and Soviet states facilitated resettlement partly to relieve population pres-sure and partly to promote colonization and economic development. But as with all types of migration, the relationship between institutional and familial agendas was messy. Com-plementarity and antagonism existed not as dichotomies but along a continuum.

Both seasonal and rural-to-urban labor migrants entered migratory streams largely be-cause of limited and often shrinking opportunities at home. This form of nongovernmen-tal coercion *to* migrate was counterbalanced by legal constraints *against* departures, registration requirements at point of arrival, and competition for jobs and housing. Mi-grants developed repertoires for navigating within this force field of regimes, most of which revolved around the utilization of familial and local ties.

With career and military migrations we reach the midpoint on the spectrum between voluntary and coerced movement. Some careers coincided more with personal dispositions than others. Aleksei Tatishchev, whose career we follow quite closely, seemed ideally suited for a resettlement administration official; the fit between young, urban-based proletarians recruited as Twenty-Five Thousanders and their assignment as collective farm chairmen often was not quite so perfect; and Petr Abovin-Egides, the "philosopher in the kolkhoz" during the late 1950s, seemed determined to get into strife and thereby have a relatively short career. Security personnel posted to and among the labor camps, contract workers traveling to remote locations at elevated pay, and graduates repaying the state for their higher educa-tion by serving wherever assigned all migrated under varying degrees of compulsion. De-spite early wartime enthusiasms, conscription followed by subjection to military discipline and socialization turned soldiers into the most violent migrants of all. Compensatory reper-toires included (on a continuum of personal risk) pulling strings, deceit, and desertion.

Refugees and evacuees had even less room to maneuver. Writing to authorities, they employed strategies emphasizing neediness and worthiness, and ranged from what Golfo Alexopoulos has called "victim talk" to ringing assertions of the Soviet self.[4] The general aim was to be rescued—from the danger of falling under occupation in both world wars, from starvation during civil war and famine, from discrimination due to "ethnocratic" re-gimes, and from the effects of disasters unfathomable before the nuclear age. We learn of the inventive ways people in need of rescue pushed back against bureaucratic ineptitude, heartlessness, and lack of resources.

Deportees had the least opportunity to improve their situation. Deportation entailed using the remoteness of destinations from home (or, for that matter, anywhere else) to punish. Imperial Russian authorities applied it to both individuals who had committed

---

4. Golfo Alexopoulos, "Victim Talk: Defense Testimony and Denunciation under Stalin," *Law and Social Inquiry* 24 (1999): 501–18.

crimes and, during the First World War, collectively to ethnic Germans and Jews. Under Stalin, entire social categories such as kulaks and "déclassé elements" and about a dozen national groups received this treatment. Some former deportees report that state authorities deceived them into believing their compulsory dislocation was for their own benefit, to protect them from a foreign foe, for example. Whatever the pretext, once in exile, deportees combatted disorientation and despair in a variety of ways but none so definitively as flight.

The arc we trace of increasingly coercive migration regimes and corresponding repertoires stops at this point. Our excursion among migrants ends with those who fit neither into Imperial nor Soviet modernizing schema and who continued to occupy precarious ground in post-Soviet Russia—fugitives, Roma, beggars, homeless children, and nomads. What united these otherwise disparate groups and distinguished them from others we treat was their itinerant lifeways and subjection to regimes—of capture and incarceration, sedentarization and collectivization—that were essentially antimigratory. Ironically, itinerancy often was itself the result of state policies, or in the case of the upsurge of beggars and homeless children toward the end of the century, of the collapse of state institutions and practices compounded by the marketization of the economy.

Although moving in Russia was constant, its amplitude rose and fell throughout the century. Less and more coercive forms of migration occurred simultaneously, sometimes provoking or reinforcing each other and at other times having little if any connection. The first quarter of the century saw millions of peasants resettling and moving to cities, soldiers on the march, and urban and rural folk fleeing from war, epidemics, and starvation. After a brief hiatus, the period of the First Five-Year Plan saw the highest rate of urbanization in recorded history, anywhere. During the Great Patriotic War, several kinds of movement reached their peak: military migrations, evacuations, factory relocations, and deportations pushed the rates of migration to the high that characterized Europe during and just after World War II.[5] Until the 1990s, the preponderance of migrants went from rural areas and small towns in Russia to cities throughout the Soviet Union, generally moving from west to east. If that process began to reverse itself already before the Soviet Union disintegrated, then the out-migration of ethnic Russians from the "near abroad" comprised the most significant population shift of the first post-Soviet decade, followed in short order by labor migrants from the Caucasus and Central Asia in numbers nobody quite knows.[6]

What do we think we have added to the perspectives of historians of Russia in the twentieth century and to historians of migration? For Russianists, we have tried to elucidate the many ways that mobility was part and parcel of normal life in the twentieth century as well

5. Lucassen and Lucassen, "Measuring and Quantifying Cross-Cultural Migrations," 21–23.
6. For one of many attempts at quantification, see Rybakovskii, *Transformatsiia migratsionnykh protsessov*, parts 3–4.

as a key component of the century's spectacularly transformational events. Different cultures of mobility marked annual and life cycles across the "broad land." Not only did the subjects of the Empire and citizens of the USSR and the Russian Federation themselves move by the season or for education and work to cities and villages, or move by coercion, but they also lived among newcomers. There was plenty of mixing.

Russianists long have stressed the outsized role of state initiative and power never more so than during the Stalin era. What we demonstrate is that the major undertakings of those decades—collectivization, industrialization, mass terror, repulsion of invasion, and territorial expansion—depended for their success on people moving or being moved. Additionally, the extraction of natural resources on a grand scale, which continued well beyond the Stalin era, involved populating outlying regions in the Far North and eastern Siberia. We repeatedly were struck, however, by the state's inability to fulfill its promises to deliver necessary resources to those people it had moved or encouraged to move.

Yet people were not putty in the hands of the state. While not denying the forcefulness of state coercion in the name of security and expanded production, we found ample evidence of people's resourcefulness in disembarking at the "wrong" station, casting themselves in the most deserving light, bonding with distant kin, evading surveillance, adjusting to new environments, and otherwise taking advantage of opportunities presented by crises. Nearly forty years ago, Charles Tilly wrote rather grandly that "the history of European migration is the history of European social life."[7] Analogously, we have found that the perspective of mobility yields fundamental insights into Russia's history of the twentieth century. For example, along with using available means of transportation to "flit" from one worksite to another, laboring people engaged in self-organization and contract negotiations to a surprising degree. Temporary workers were considered by the state to be "irregular" or "wild" because they disrupted planned labor deployment. In carving out their own itineraries, though, they demonstrated not only neediness but also the flexibility and creativity exhibited by their antecedents of the late Imperial and early Soviet periods and post-Soviet equivalents. Temporary labor is only one of the practices under discussion here that provides another angle on the study of labor, so neglected in the past few decades. More generally, we offer to those most interested in Russia this observation: the regimes of migration and the repertoires of migrants have helped to shape the country's history at the level of family, community, region, and state.

For students of migration, we have sought to present the repertoires of people in Russian political space in a recognizable form. This has been the logic behind the organization of this study by kind of migrant. If Russia has been the Siberia of migration studies—distant and foreboding—we have endeavored to bring it into the conversation by going

---

7. Tilly, "Migration in Modern European History," 68.

beyond its reputation for coercion, as well deserved as it is, to present the full range of migratory mobility in the twentieth century.[8] This has involved extending our optic beyond European Russia to take in Siberia, the Russian Far East, the Far North, and Central Asia in order to move these areas into the view of a broader readership. In the process, we have tried to embellish the understanding of what an ambitious state can and cannot achieve in the control of its own people's movement and distribution over its territory. Those migration scholars who came to this study looking for fresh or improved data will have been disappointed, but that was not our goal. We have been more willing to spend our energies on the process of migrations, and have left finding and cleaning data to those better equipped to do so.

As we indicate in chapter 3, the city has been the winner of the twentieth century; a paltry 10 percent of subjects in Russia lived in urban areas in 1897; by the beginning of the twenty-first century, the proportion was at 73 percent. Moreover, Moscow continues to grow, having outpaced St. Petersburg early in the twentieth century to contain a larger proportion of people in Russia than ever before.[9] In sum, a century of population movement has been kind to the city, but has fallen far short of the erstwhile Soviet dream of a more even distribution of benefits among cities' residents. Our goal, however, has not been to trace population concentration or urbanization, but rather to give a more comprehensive and varied portrait of human movement. We think of urbanization as one net effect of a great many migrations.

Russia's twentieth century had the Great Patriotic War as its centerpiece, with the movement of soldiers, the evacuation of civilians, refugees, and deportees, all of whom numbered in the millions. Yet throughout the century, the temporary workers who harvested crops and built cities and infrastructures, the wanderers, the settlers to the East all teach us that internal migration, especially in a space as broad as Russia, is no small matter. And indeed, that is our point. As international migrations receive the lion's share of attention in this globalizing age, the internal migrations that are part of every country are equally as important in shaping its society and marking its people. In Russia (Imperial, Soviet, and

---

8. Russia is usually ignored in collections of global migrations such as Donna Gabaccia and Dirk Hoerder, *Connecting Seas and Connected Ocean Rims: Indian, Atlantic, and Pacific Oceans and China Seas Migrations from the 1830s to the 1930s* (Leiden, 2011). But Gijs Kessler's work "Migration and Family Systems" is included in Hoerder and Kaur, *Proletarian and Gendered Mass Migrations*, 133–50. Lucassen and Lucassen, "Mobility Transition Revisited," 347–77, include European Russia in their creation of migration datasets, and the whole of Russia in *Globalising Migration History*, which also contains Gijs Kessler, "Measuring Migration in Russia: A Perspective of Empire, 1500–1900," 71–88.

9. The urban figures are not for the same geographical areas; the 1897 figure is only for the territory encompassed by the USSR, and the 2002 figures for the Russian Federation alone. Timothy Heleniak, "The 2002 Census in Russia: Preliminary Results," *Eurasian Geography and Economics* 44, no. 6 (2003): 430–421; Lewis and Rowland, *Population Redistribution in the USSR*, 199–242.

post-Soviet), with its multiple cultural and linguistic boundaries, transnational migrations were masked within one political space.

Though comprehensive, this study is far from complete. Where to go from here? While we frequently have mentioned particular nodal points of the migration experience—most notably the railroad station throughout the century—we have not given due consideration to these kinds of places (e.g., markets, construction sites, bivouac points, way stations) within Russia's spatial vastness. Our study eschewed an overarching temporal approach in favor of one structured according to type of migrant experience. We did this so as to interrogate the differences among political regimes, but one of the potential advantages of a temporally based narrative structure would be enhanced insight into the simultaneity and interactiveness among different migrant experiences. A systems approach, emphasizing connections between origins and receiving areas, likely would better illuminate the operations of chain migration. And, of course, no approach can match the insights into everyday life gained from longitudinally based local studies.

Because internal and international migrations operate in tandem, it would be worthwhile to connect the migrations that have been our concern here to two other phenomena. The first would constitute the connections of Russia to the great currents of international migrations in the Pacific, the Baltic, the Black Sea, and the Caspian Sea, across the borders with Central Asia, and with the vast nation that is China as well as with Eastern Europe.[10] The second would be the history of the borderlands—that is, regions such as the Far East, the southwest, and the northwest; southern Tajikistan and western Kazakhstan; Armenia and Azerbaijan—where the exchange of peoples had an irregular and discontinuous history over the twentieth century and where cross-border activity has entailed so much more than emigration and immigration.[11] Because we have found the concepts of repertoires and regimes enormously helpful in framing our study, we encourage scholars to test their utility in examining other spaces and places.

---

10. For example, see Chia Yin Hsu, "Frontier Urban and Imperial Dreams: The Chinese Eastern Railroad and the Creation of a Russia Global City, 1890–1917," in Randolph and Avrutin, *Russia in Motion*, 43–62; Yuki Umeno, "Han Chinese Immigrants in Manchuria (1850–1931)," in Lucassen and Lucassen, *Globalising Migration History*, 307–34.

11. Much of this work is beginning, with, for example, Jaeeun Kim, "Colonial Migration and Transborder Membership Politics in Twentieth-Century Korea" (PhD diss., University of California, Los Angeles, 2011); Kitty Lam, "Shared Space, Varied Lives: Finnish-Russian Interactions in Dacha Country, 1880s–1920s" (PhD diss., Michigan State University, 2013); Alyssa Park, "Borderland and Beyond: Korean Migrants and the Creation of a Modern Boundary between Korea and Russia, 1860–1937" (PhD diss., Columbia University, 2009).

Selected Bibliography

ARCHIVES

Rossiiskii Gosudarstvennyi Arkhiv Ekonomiki (RGAE)
    F. 478 RSFSR People's Commissariat of Agriculture [op. 6, op. 7]
    F. 5675 USSR Ministry of Agriculture
        op. 1 Main Resettlement Administration (1925–1949)
        op. 7 Management of Organizational and Collective Farm Affairs (1939–1959)
Rossiiskii Gosudarstvennyi Arkhiv Sotsial'no-Politicheskoi Istorii (RGASPI)
    F. 591 Editorial office of *Sel'skaia zhizn'* [Rural Life] [op. 1]
Rossiiskii Gosudarstvennyi Istoricheskii Arkhiv (RGIA)
    F. 391 [Imperial Russian] Resettlement Administration [op. 1, op. 2].
United States Holocaust Memorial Museum (USHMM)
    RG-22.018M Gosudarstvennyi Arkhiv Rossiiskoi Federatsii (GARF)
        F. 9458, Personal Archives of Meer [Khaimovich] Bomash, member of State Duma, 1908–1917
    RG-22.020 Gosudarstvennyi Istoricheskii Arkhiv Chuvashskoi Respubliki (GIAChR)
        F. 827 Complaints of evacuees and families of Red Army soldiers on collective farms in 1943
        F. 835 Shemurshinskii district executive committee general office [op. 1]
        F. 1041 Presidium of Supreme Soviet of the Chuvash Republic [op. 1]
        F. 1263 Office of Evacuation of Chuvash Republic Council of People's Commissars [op. 1]
    RG-22.027M Gosudarstvennyi Arkhiv Rossiiskoi Federatsii (GARF)
        F. A-327 Main Resettlement Administration under the RSFSR Council of People's Commissars [op. 1, op. 2]
    RG-22.030 Tsentral'nyi Gosudarstvennyi Arkhiv Sankt-Peterburga (TsGA SPb)
        F. 7179 Executive Committee of Leningrad Oblast Soviet [op. 11]
    RG-22.033 Tsentral'nyi Gosudarstvennyi Arkhiv Sankt-Peterburga (TsGA SPb),
        F. 330 City Evacuation Commission of Leningrad City Soviet [op. 1, op. 2]
    RG-31.053 Memoirs of Abram Tseitlin
    RG-31-089 Sigal Family Papers, 1920–1947
    RG-31.113 Diary of Anna Dashevskaia
    RG-50.226.0008 Oral History Interview with Genya Batasheva (April 1992)
    RG-50.226.0024 Oral History Interview with Dimitri Vasilievich Mironyenko (August 1994).

RG-74.002 Tsentral'nyi Gosudarstvennyi Arkhiv g. Almaty (TsGA Almaty)
  F. 1137 Council of People's Commissars of Kazakh SSR Administration [op. 6, op. 9]

DISSERTATIONS

Dale, Robert. "Re-Adjusting to Life after War: The Demobilization of Red Army Veterans in Leningrad and the Leningrad Region, 1944–1950." PhD diss., University of London, 2010.
Edwards, Kristen. "Fleeing to Siberia: The Wartime Relocation of Evacuees to Novosibirsk, 1941–1943." PhD diss., Stanford University, 1996.
Kessler, Gijs. "The Peasant and the Town: Rural-Urban Migration in the Soviet Union, 1929–40." 2 vols. PhD diss., European University Institute, 2001.
Kim, Inna Penkhvaevena. "Razvitie territorii, prisoedinennykh k SSSR posle vtoroi mirovoi voiny (Vostochnaia Prussiia, Yuzhnyi Sakhalin, Kuril'skie ostrova), 1945–pervaia polovina 1949 gg." Avtoreferat, Yuzhno-Sakhalinsk, 2010.
O'Keeffe, Brigid. "Nomads into Farmers: Romani Activism and State Passivity on Gypsy Kolkhozes." PhD diss., New York University, 2008.

NEWSPAPERS AND PERIODICALS

Current Digest of the Soviet Press
Izvestiia
Komsomol'skaia Pravda (1966–1981)
Literaturnaia gazeta
The Moscow Times
Nezavisimaia gazeta
Pravda
Rossiiskaia gazeta
Sel'skaia molodezh (1970–1974)
Vestnik Evropy (1876–1910)
Vestnik statistiki (1984–1992)
Voprosy kolonizatsii (1907–1917)

PUBLISHED SOURCES

Abovin-Egides, Petr. "Filosof v kolkhze (Fragmenty iz knigi)." Kontinent 42 (1984): 200–239.
Adams, Bruce F. The Politics of Punishment: Prison Reform in Russia, 1863–1917. DeKalb: Northern Illinois University Press, 1996.
Afontsev, Sergey et al. "The Urban Household in Russia and the Soviet Union, 1900–2000: Patterns of Family Formation in a Turbulent Century." The History of the Family 13 (2008): 178–94.
Alexievich, Svetlana. Voices from Chernobyl. Normal, IL: Dalkey Archive Press, 2005.
Amanzholova, Dina A. "Iz istorii zemle ustroistva Evreev v SSSR: Neskol'ko obshchikh zamechanii." Cahiers du monde russe 45 (2004): 209–40.
Anderson, David G. Identity and Ecology in Arctic Siberia: The Number One Reindeer Brigade. Oxford: Oxford University Press, 2000.
——, ed. The 1926/27 Soviet Polar Census Expeditions. New York: Berghahn, 2011.
Applebaum, Anne. GULAG, A History. New York: Random House, 2003.

Arseniev, V. K. *Dersu the Trapper*. Translated by Malcolm Burr. New York: E. P. Dutton, 1941.

Aziatskaia Rossiia. 3 vols. Edited by G. V. Glinka and Pereselencheskoe Upravlenie. St. Petersburg: A. F. Marks, 1914.

Babchenko, Arkady. *One Soldier's War*. Translated by Nick Allen. New York: Grove Press, 2006.

Babel, Isaac. *1920 Diary*. Edited by Carol J. Avins. Translated by H. T. Willetts. New Haven: Yale University Press, 1995.

Bachmann, Berta. *Memories of Kazakhstan: A Report on the Life Experiences of a German Woman in Russia*. Lincoln, NE: American Historical Society of Germans from Russia, 1983.

Bade, Klaus. *Migration in European History*. Cambridge: Blackwell, 2003.

Bade, Klaus et al. *The Encyclopedia of Migration and Minorities in Europe*. Cambridge: Cambridge University Press, 2011.

Ball, Alan. *And Now My Soul Is Hardened: Abandoned Children in Soviet Russia, 1918–1930*. Berkeley: University of California Press, 1994.

Barnes, Steven. *Death and Redemption: The Gulag and the Shaping of Soviet Society*. Princeton: Princeton University Press, 2011.

Baron, Nick. "Remaking Soviet Society: The Filtration of Returnees from Nazi Germany, 1944–49." In *Warlands: Population Resettlement and State Reconstruction in the Soviet East European Borderlands, 1945–50*, edited by Peter Gatrell and Nick Baron, 89–116. Houndmills, UK: Palgrave Macmillan, 2009.

———. *Soviet Karelia: Politics, Planning, and Terror in Stalin's Russia, 1920–1939*. London: Routledge, 2007.

Baron, Nick, and Peter Gatrell. "Population Displacement, State-Building, and Social Identity in the Lands of the Former Russian Empire, 1917–23." *Kritika* 4 (2003): 51–100.

———, eds. *Homelands: War, Population, and Statehood in Eastern Europe and Russia, 1918–1924*. London: Anthem Press, 2004.

Bek, Anna. *The Life of a Russian Woman Doctor: A Siberian Memoir, 1869–1954*. Translated and edited by Anne D. Rassweiler. Bloomington: Indiana University Press, 2004.

Berdinskikh, V. A. *Spetsposelentsy: Politicheskaia ssylka narodov Sovetskoi Rossii*. Moscow: Novoe literaturnoe obozrenie, 2005.

Bessonov, N. V. "Tsygane." In *Mnogonatsional'nyi Peterburg: Istoriia, religii, narody*, edited by I. I. Shangina, 810–15. St. Petersburg: Iskusstvo, 2002.

———. "Tsygane v Rossii: Prinuditel'noe osedanie." In *Rossiia i ee regiony v XX veke: territoriia—rasselenie—migratsii*, edited by O. Gelzer and P. Polian, 631–40. Moscow: OGI, 2005.

———. *Tsyganskaia tragediia, 1941–1945: Fakty, dokumenty, vospominaniia*. vol. 2. St. Petersburg: Shatra, 2010.

Beznin, M. A., T. M. Dimoni, and L. V. Iziumova. *Povinnosti rossiiskogo krest'ianstva v 1930–1960-kh godakh*. Vologda: Volgodskii NKTS TSEMI RAN, 2001.

Borodkin, L. I., and S. V. Maksimov. "Krest'ianskie migratsii v Rossii/SSSR v pervoi chetverti XX veka (makroanaliz struktury migratsionnykh potokov)." *Otechestvennaia istoriia* 5 (1993): 124–43.

Bradley, Joseph. *Muzhik and Muscovite: Urbanization in Late Imperial Russia*. Berkeley: University of California Press, 1985.

Breyfogle, Nicholas B. *Heretics and Colonizers: Forging Russia's Empire in the South Caucasus*. Ithaca: Cornell University Press, 2005.

Breyfogle, Nicholas B., Abby Schrader, and Willard Sunderland, eds. *Peopling the Russian Periphery: Borderland Colonization in Eurasian History*. London: Routledge, 2007.

Brower, Daniel R. " 'The City in Danger': The Civil War and the Russian Urban Population." In *Party, State, and Society in the Russian Civil War*, edited by Diane P. Koenker, William G. Rosenberg, and Ronald Grigor Suny, 58–80. Bloomington: Indiana University Press, 1989.

———. "Kyrgyz Nomads and Russian Pioneers: Colonization and Ethnic Conflict in the Turkestan Revolt of 1916." *Jahrbücher für Geschichte Osteuropas* 44 (1996): 41–53.

———. *The Russian City between Tradition and Modernity*. Berkeley: University of California Press, 1990.

Brown, Kate. *A Biography of No Place: From Ethnic Borderland to Soviet Heartland.* Cambridge: Harvard University Press, 2003.

Brubaker, Rogers. *Ethnicity without Groups.* Cambridge: Harvard University Press, 2004.

Buck, Pearl. *Talk about Russia with Masha Scott.* New York: John Day, 1945.

Buckley, Cynthia. "The Myth of Managed Migration: Migration Control and Market in the Soviet Period." *Slavic Review* 54 (1995): 896–916.

Buckley, Cynthia, and Blair Ruble, eds. *Migration, Homeland, and Belonging in Eurasia.* Baltimore: Johns Hopkins University Press, 2008.

Bugai, N. F. *L. Beriia–I. Stalinu: "Soglasno Vashemu ukazaniiu . . ."* Moscow: AIRO-XX, 1995.

——, ed. *Iosif Stalin–Lavrentiiu Berii: "Ikh nado deportirovat": Dokumenty, fakty, kommentarii.* Moscow: Druzhba narodov, 1992.

Bugai, N. F., and A. M. Gonov. *Kavkaz: Narody v eshelonakh (20–60-e gody).* Moscow: INSAN, 1998.

Bugai, N. F., and M. I. Mamaev. *Turki-Meskhetintsy: Gruziia, Uzbekistan, Rossiia, SShA.* Moscow: Grifi K, 2009.

Burds, Jeffrey. *Peasant Dreams and Market Politics: Labor Migration and the Russian Village, 1861–1905.* Pittsburgh: University of Pittsburgh Press, 1998.

——. "The Social Control of Peasant Labor in Russia: The Response of Village Communities to Labor Migration in the Central Industrial Region, 1861–1905." In *Peasant Economy, Culture, and Politics,* edited by Kingston-Mann and Mixter, 52–100.

Bushnell, John. "Peasants in Uniform: The Tsarist Army as a Peasant Society." *Journal of Social History* 13 (1980): 565–76.

Carr, E. H. *Socialism in One Country, 1924–1926.* 2 vols. Harmondsworth: Macmillan, 1958.

Castles, Stephen, and Mark Miller. *The Age of Migration: International Population Movements in the Modern World.* 4th ed. New York: Guilford, 2009.

Chang, Felix B., and Sunnie T. Rucker-Chang, eds. *Chinese Migrants in Russia, Central Asia, and Eastern Europe.* London: Routledge, 2012.

Cheney, Glenn Alan. *Chernobyl: The Ongoing Story of the World's Deadliest Nuclear Disaster.* New York: Discovery, 1993.

Chokai, Mariia. *Ia pishu vam iz Nozhana . . . (vospominaniia, pis'ma, dokumenty).* Almaty: Kainar, 2001.

Coquin, Francois-Xavier. *La Siberie: Peuplement et immigration paysanne au XIXe siècle.* Paris: Institute d'études Slaves, 1969.

Crowe, David M. *A History of the Gypsies of Eastern Europe and Russia.* New York: St. Martin's Press, 1994.

Danilov, V. P. "Krest'ianskii otkhod na promysly v 1920-kh godakh." *Istoricheskie zapiski* 94 (1974): 55–122.

Danilov, V. P., and S. A. Krasilnikov, eds. *Spetspereselentsy v zapadnoi Sibiri.* 4 vols. Novosibirsk: EKOR, 1992–1996.

Danilov, V., R. Manning, and L. Viola, eds. *Tragediia sovetskoi derevni: Kollektivizatsiia i raskulachivanie: Dokumenty i materialy v 5 tomakh, 1927–1939.* 5 vols. Moscow: ROSSPEN, 1999–2006.

Dedlov, V. L. *Pereselentsy i novyia mesta.* St. Petersburg: M. M. Lederle, 1894.

Dekel-Chen, Jonathan L. *Farming the Red Land: Jewish Agricultural Colonization and Local Soviet Power, 1924–1941.* New Haven: Yale University Press, 2005.

Denisova, L. N. *Ischezaiushchaia derevnia Rossii: Nechernozem'e v 1960–1980-e gody.* Moscow: Institut Rossiiskoi istorii RAN, 1996.

——. *Zhenshchiny russkikh selenii: Trudovye budni.* Moscow: Mir istorii, 2003.

de Windt, Harry. *The New Siberia: Being an Account of a Visit to the Penal Island of Sakhalin, and Political Prison and Mines of the Trans-Baikal District, Eastern Siberia.* London: Chapman and Hall, 1896.

De Witt, Nicholas. *Education and Professional Employment in the U.S.S.R.* Washington, DC: U.S. Government Printing Office, 1961.

Diatlov, V. I., ed. *Migratsii i diaspory v sotsiokul'turnom, politicheskom i ekonomicheskom prostranstve Sibiri rubezhi XIX–XX i XX–XXI vekov.* Irkutsk: Ottisk, 2010.

Dune, Eduard M. *Notes of a Red Guard.* Urbana: University of Illinois Press, 1993.

Economakis, Evel G. *From Peasant to Petersburger.* Houndsmills, UK: Macmillan, 1998.

——. "Patterns of Migration and Settlement in Prerevolutionary St. Petersburg: Peasants from Iaroslavl' and Tver Provinces." *The Russian Review* 56 (1997): 8–24.

Edele, Mark. *Stalinist Society, 1928–1953.* Oxford: Oxford University Press, 2011.

——. "Veterans and the Village: The Impact of Red Army Demobilization on Soviet Urbanization, 1945–1955." *Russian History* 36 (2009): 159–82.

Edgerton, William, ed. *Memoirs of Peasant Tolstoyans in Soviet Russia.* Bloomington: Indiana, 1993.

Eichler, Maya. *Militarizing Men: Gender, Conscription, and War in Post-Soviet Russia.* Stanford: Stanford University Press, 2012.

Engel, Barbara. *Between the Fields and the City: Women, Work, and the Family in Russia, 1861–1914.* Cambridge: Cambridge University Press, 1994.

——. "Freedom and Its Limitations: A Peasant Wife Seeks to Escape Her Abusive Husband." In *The Human Tradition in Imperial Russia,* edited by Christine Worobec, 115–27. Lanham, MD: Rowman & Littlefield, 2009.

——. "St. Petersburg Prostitutes in the Late Nineteenth Century: A Personal and Social Profile." *The Russian Review* 48 (1989): 21–44.

——. "The Woman's Side: Male Out-Migration and the Family Economy in Kostroma Province." *Slavic Review* 45 (1986): 257–71.

Engel, Barbara, and Anastasia Posadskaya-Vanderbeck, eds. *A Revolution of Their Own: Voices of Women in Soviet History.* Boulder, CO: Westview Press, 1998.

Feferman, Kiril. "A Soviet Humanitarian Action? Centre, Periphery, and the Evacuation of Refugees to the North Caucasus, 1941–1942." *Europe-Asia Studies* 61 (2009): 813–31.

Ferrando, Olivier. "Soviet Population Transfers and Interethnic Relations in Tajikistan: Assessing the Concept of Ethnicity." *Central Asian Survey* 30 (2011): 39–52.

Fierman, William. "Central Asian Youth and Migration." In *Soviet Central Asia: The Failed Transformation,* edited by William Fierman, 255–82. Boulder, CO: Westview Press, 1991.

Filippova, E. I. "Rol' kul'turnykh razlichii v protsesse adaptatsii russkikh pereselentsev." In *Identichnost' i konflikt v postsovetskikh gosudarstvakh: Sbornik statei,* edited by Marta Brill Olkott, Valerii Tishkov, and Aleksei Malashenko, 134–50. Moscow: Moskovskii Tsentr Karnegi, 1997.

Filtzer, Donald. *Soviet Workers and Late Stalinism: Labour and Restoration of the Stalinist System after World War II.* Cambridge: Cambridge University Press, 2002.

——. *Soviet Workers and Stalinist Industrialization: The Formation of Modern Soviet Production Relations, 1928–1941.* Armonk: M. E. Sharpe, 1986.

Fisher, Harold H. *The Famine in Soviet Russia, 1919–1923.* New York: Macmillan, 1927.

Fitzpatrick, Sheila. *Education and Social Mobility in the Soviet Union, 1921–1934.* Cambridge: Cambridge University Press, 1979.

——. "The Great Departure: Rural-Urban Migration in the Soviet Union." In Rosenberg and Siegelbaum, *Social Dimensions of Soviet Industrialization,* 15–40.

——. *Stalin's Peasants: Resistance and Survival in the Russian Village after Collectivization.* New York: Oxford University Press, 1994.

Flynn, Moya. *Migrant Resettlement in the Russian Federation: Reconstituting "Homes" and "Homelands."* London: Anthem, 2004.

Flynt, Josiah. *Tramping with Tramps: Studies and Sketches of Vagabond Life.* New York: The Century, 1907.

Frank, Stephen P. *Crime, Cultural Conflict, and Justice in Rural Russia, 1856–1914.* Berkeley: University of California Press, 1999.

Frazier, Ian. *Travels in Siberia.* New York: Farrar, Straus & Giroux, 2010.

Fuchs, Rachel G., and Leslie Page Moch. "Pregnant, Single, and Far from Home: Migrant Women in Nineteenth-Century Paris." *American Historical Review* 95 (1990): 1007–31.

Fürst, Juliane. "Between Salvation and Liquidation: Homeless and Vagrant Children and the Reconstruction of Soviet Society." *Slavonic and East European Review* 86 (2008): 232–58.

Gal'chenko, V., with Nina Maksimova. "Zhitie odnogo shabashnika." *EKO* 3 (1987): 101–36.

Galuzo, P. G. *Turkestan-Koloniia (Ocherk istorii Turkestana ot zavoevaniia russkimi do revoliutsii 1917 goda)* Oxford: Society for Central Asian Studies, 1986 [1929].

Gatrell, Peter. *The Making of the Modern Refugee.* Oxford: Oxford University Press, 2013.

———. *Russia's First World War: A Social and Economic History.* London: Longman, 2005.

———. *A Whole Empire Walking: Refugees in Russia during World War I.* Bloomington: Indiana University Press, 1999.

Gelb, Michael. "An Early Soviet Ethnic Deportation: The Far-Eastern Koreans." *The Russian Review* 54 (1995): 389–412.

Gentes, Andrew. " 'Beat the Devil!': Prison Society and Anarchy in Tsarist Siberia." *Ab Imperio* 2 (2009): 201–23.

———. *Exile to Siberia, 1590–1822.* Basingstoke, UK: Palgrave Macmillan, 2008.

———. "Vagabondage and Siberia: Disciplinary Modernism in Tsarist Russia." In *Cast Out: Vagrancy and Homelessness in Global and Historical Perspective,* edited by A. L. Beier and Paul Ocobock, 184–208. Athens: Ohio University Press, 2008.

Glickman, Rose. *Russian Factory Women: Workplace and Society, 1880–1914.* Berkeley: University of California Press, 1984.

Gorbachev, O. V. *Na puti k gorodu: Sel'skaia migratsiia v tsentral'noi Rossii (1946–1985 gg.) i sovetskaia model' urbanizatsii.* Moscow: MPGU, 2002.

Goskomstat Rossii. *Chislennost' i migratsiia naseleniia Rossiiskoi Federatsii v 2002 godu (Statisticheskii biulleten').* Moscow: Goskomstat, 2003.

Greene, Robert H. "Bodies in Motion: Steam-Powered Pilgrimages in Late Imperial Russia." *Russian History* 39 (2012): 247–68.

Grinberg, I., G. Karataev, N. Kropivnitskii, eds. *Evakuatsiia v Kazakhstan: Iz istorii evakuatsii naseleniia zapadnykh raionov SSSR v Kazakhstan, 1941–1942.* Almaty: Fortress, 2008.

Gritsenko, V. V. *Russkie sredi russkikh: Problemy adaptatsii vynuzhdennykh migrantov i bezhentsev iz stran blizhnevo zarubezh'ia v Rossii.* Moscow: Insitut etnologii i antropologii RAN, 1999.

Gur'ianov, A. E., ed. *Repressii protiv poliakov i pol'skikh grazhdan.* Moscow: Zven'ia, 1997.

Hagenloh, Paul M. *Stalin's Police: Public Order and Mass Repression in the USSR, 1926–1941.* Washington, DC: Woodrow Wilson Press, 2009.

Hamm, Michael, ed. *The City in Late Imperial Russia.* Bloomington: Indiana University Press, 1986.

Heinzen, James. *Inventing a Soviet Countryside: State Power and the Transformation of Rural Russia, 1917–1929.* Pittsburgh: University of Pittsburgh Press, 2004.

Heleniak, Timothy. "An Overview of Migration in the Post-Soviet Space." In Buckley and Ruble, *Migration, Homeland, and Belonging in Eurasia,* 29–68.

———. "Growth Poles and Ghost Towns in the Russian Far North." In *Russia and the North,* edited by Elana Wilson Rowe, 129–86. Ottawa: University of Ottawa Press, 2009.

Henze, Charlotte E. *Disease, Health Care, and Government in Late Imperial Russia: Life and Death on the Volga, 1823–1914.* London: Routledge, 2011.

Herlihy, Patricia. *Odessa: A History, 1794–1914.* Cambridge: Harvard Ukrainian Research Institute, 1986.

Hirsch, Francine. *Empire of Nations: Ethnographic Knowledge and the Making of the Soviet Union.* Ithaca: Cornell University Press, 2005.

Hochstadt, Steve. *Mobility and Modernity: Migration in Germany, 1820–1989.* Ann Arbor: University of Michigan Press, 1999.

Hoerder, Dirk. *Cultures in Contact: World Migrations in the Second Millennium.* Durham: Duke University Press, 2002.

Hoffmann, David. *Peasant Metropolis: Social Identities in Moscow, 1929–1941.* Ithaca: Cornell University Press, 1994.

Holmes, Larry E. *War, Evacuation, and the Exercise of Power: The Center, Periphery, and Kirov's Pedagogical Institute, 1941–1952.* Lanham, MD: Lexington Books, 2012.

Holquist, Peter. " 'In Accord with State Interests and the People's Wishes': The Technocratic Ideology of Imperial Russia's Resettlement Administration." *Slavic Review* 69 (2010): 151–80.

——. "To Count, to Extract, and to Exterminate: Population Statistics and Population Politics in Late Imperial and Soviet Russia." In *A State of Nations: Empire and Nation-Making in the Age of Lenin and Stalin,* edited by Ronald Grigor Suny and Terry Martin, 111–44. Oxford: Oxford University Press, 2001.

Hough, Jerry F. "The Changing Nature of the Kolkhoz Chairman." In Millar, *Soviet Rural Community,* 103–20.

International Labour Office. *Report on the Inter-regional Study Tour and Seminar on the Sedentarisation of Nomadic Populations in the Soviet Socialist Republics of Kazakhstan and Kirghizia (5 to 30 September 1966).* Geneva: I.L.O., 1967.

Isupov, V. A. "Demograficheskie protsessy v tylovykh raionakh Rossii." In Zhiromskaia, *Naselenie Rossii v XX veke,* 2: 82–105.

Ivakhnyuk, Irina. *The Russian Migration Policy and Its Impact on Human Development: The Historical Perspective.* U.N. Human Development Reports, Research Paper 14. New York: United Nations, 2009.

Ivanova, Galina Mikhailovna. 2000. *Labor Camp Socialism: The Gulag in the Soviet Totalitarian System.* Translated by Carol Flath. Edited by Donald Raleigh. Armonk, NY: M. E. Sharpe, 2000.

Ivnitskii, N. A. *Sud'ba raskulachennykh v SSSR.* Moscow: Sobranie, 2004.

Johnson, Robert E. *Peasant and Proletarian: The Working Class of Moscow in the Late Nineteenth Century.* New Brunswick: Rutgers University Press, 1979.

Jolluck, Katherine R. *Exile and Identity: Polish Women in the Soviet Union during World War II.* Pittsburgh: University of Pittsburgh Press, 2002.

Kanatchikov, Semën. *A Radical Worker in Tsarist Russia: The Autobiography of Semën Ivanovich Kanatchikov.* Translated and edited by Reginald E. Zelnik. Stanford: Stanford University Press, 1986.

Kassymbekova, Botakoz. "Humans as Territory: Forced Resettlement and the Making of Soviet Tajikistan, 1920–38." *Central Asian Survey* 30 (2011): 349–70.

Kaufman, A. A. *Khoziaistvennoe polozhenie pereselentsev vodvorennykh na kazennykh zemliakh tomskoi gubernii: Po dannym proizvedennago v 1894 g., po porucheniiu g. tomskago gubernatora, podvornago izslenovaniia.* 2 vols. St. Petersburg: Bezobrazov, 1895–96.

——. *Pereselentsy-Arendatory turgaiskoi oblasti (2-ia chast' otcheta starshago proizvoditelia rabot Kaufmana po komandirovke v turgaiskuiu oblast').* St. Petersburg: Bezobrazov, 1897.

——. "Pereseleniia i pereselencheskii vopros v Rossii: Pereselencheskaia statistika." *Entsiklopedicheskii slovar'* 31 (1914): 506–48.

——. *Sibirskoe pereselenie na iskhode XIX veka, istoriko-statisticheskii ocherk.* St. Petersburg: Kirshbaum, 1901.

Kennan, George. *Siberia and the Exile System.* 2 vols. London: J. R. Osgood, McIlvaine, 1891.

Kessler, Gijs. "Migration and Family Systems in Russia and the Soviet Union, Nineteenth to Twentieth Centuries." In *Proletarian and Gendered Mass Migrations: A Global Perspective on Continuities and Discontinuities from the 19th to the 21st Centuries,* edited by Dirk Hoerder and Amarjit Kaur, 133–50. Leiden: Brill, 2013.

——. "The Origins of Soviet Internal-Migration Policy: Industrialization and the 1930s Rural Exodus." In Randolph and Avrutin, *Russia in Motion,* 63–79.

——. "Russian and Ukrainian Seasonal Laborers in the Grain Belt of New Russia and the North Caucasus in the Late 19th and Early 20th Centuries." In Bade et al., *Encyclopedia of Migration and Minorities in Europe,* 658.

Kessler, Khais [Gijs]. "Krest'ianskaia migratsiia v Rossiiskoi Imperii i Sovetskom Soiuze: Otkhodnichestvo i vykhod iz sela." In *Sotsial'naia istoriia: Ezhegodnik 1998/99,* 309–36. Moscow: ROSSPEN, 1999.

Khazanov, A. M. *Nomads and the Outside World.* Cambridge: Cambridge University Press, 1984.

Kheifets, L. *Pereseliates' k nam na Sakhalin.* Iuzhno-Sakhlainsk: Pereselencheskii otdel pri sakhalinskom obliapolkome, 1954.

Khlevniuk, Oleg V. *The History of the Gulag: From Collectivization to the Great Terror*. Translated by Vadim A. Staklo. New Haven: Yale University Press, 2004.

Khokhlov, G. T. "Puteshestvie ural'skikh Kazakov v 'belovodskoe tsarstvo.' " *Zapiski imperatorskogo russkogo geograficheskogo obshchestva po otdeleniiu etnografii* 28, no. 1 (1903): 3–101.

Khorev, B. S., and V. N. Likhded. *Zhitel' sela—Rabotnik goroda*. Moscow: Finansy i statistika, 1982.

Kingston-Mann, Esther, and Timothy Mixter, eds. *Peasant Economy, Culture, and Politics of European Russia, 1800–1921*. Princeton: Princeton University Press, 1991.

Kir'iakov, V. V. *Ocherki po istorii pereselencheskago dvizheniia v Sibir' (V sviazi s istoriei zaseleniia Sibiri)*. Moscow: I. N. Kushner, 1902.

Kirss, Tiina, and Rutt Hinrikus, eds. *Estonian Life Stories*. Budapest: Central European University Press, 2009.

Klimin, I. I. *Rossiiskoe krest'ianstvo v zavershaiushchii period sploshnoi kollektivizatsii sel'skogo khoziaistva (1933–1937 gg.)*. St. Petersburg: VVM, 2012.

Koenker, Diane. "Urbanization and Deurbanization in the Russian Revolution and Civil War." *Journal of Modern History* 57 (1985): 424–50.

Kolonizatsiia Sibiri v sviazi s obshchim pereselencheskim voprosom. Edited by Komitet Sibirskoi Zheleznoi Dorogi. St. Petersburg: Gosudarstvennaia tipografiia, 1900.

Kommunisticheskaia partiia sovetskogo soiuza v rezoliutsiiakh i resheniiakh s"ezdov, konferentsii i plenumov TsK (1898–1988), 9th ed. Moscow: Izd-vo polit. Litry, 1983–90.

Kornilov, Gennadii. "Refugees in the Urals Region, 1917–25." In Baron and Gatrell, *Homelands*, 156–78.

Korobkov, Andrei V. "Post-Soviet Migration: New Trends at the Beginning of the Twenty-First Century." In Buckley and Ruble, *Migration, Homeland, and Belonging in Eurasia*, 69–98.

Kotkin, Stephen. *Magnetic Mountain: Stalinism as a Civilization*. Berkeley: University of California Press, 1995.

——. "Peopling Magnitostroi: The Politics of Demography." In Rosenberg and Siegelbaum, *Social Dimensions of Soviet Industrialization*, 63–104.

Krasnushkin, E. K., G. M. Segal, and Ts. M. Feinberg, eds. *Nishchestvo i besprizornost'*. Moscow: Moszdravotdel, 1929.

Kulischer, Eugene. *Europe on the Move: War and Population Changes, 1917–47*. New York: Columbia University Press, 1948.

Kumanev, G. A. "Evakuatsiia naseleniia iz ugrozhaemykh raionov SSSR v 1941–1942 gg." In Zhiromskaia, *Naselenie Rossii v XX veke*, 2: 60–81.

Kurtsev, A. N. "Bezhentsy pervoi mirovoi voiny v Rossii (1914–17)." *Voprosy istorii* (1999): 104–13.

Lahusen, Thomas. *How Life Writes the Book: Real Socialism and Socialist Realism in Stalin's Russia*. Ithaca: Cornell University Press, 1997.

Larin, A. G. *Kitaiskie migranty v Rossii: Istoriia i sovremennost'*. Moscow: Vostochnaia kniga, 2009.

Lewin, Moshe. *The Making of the Soviet System: Essays in the Social History of Interwar Russia*. New York: The New Press, 1994.

Lewis, Robert A., and Richard H. Rowland. *Population Redistribution in the USSR: Its Impact on Society, 1897–1977*. New York: Praeger, 1979.

——. "Urbanization in Russia and the USSR, 1897–1970." In *The City in Russian History*, edited by Michael Hamm, 205–21. Lexington: University Press of Kentucky, 1976.

Lohr, Eric. *Nationalizing the Russian Empire: The Campaign against Enemy Aliens during World War I*. Cambridge: Harvard University Press, 2003.

——. *Russian Citizenship: From Empire to Soviet Union*. Cambridge: Harvard University Press, 2012.

Lucassen, Jan, and Leo Lucassen. *Globalising Migration History: The Eurasian Experience (16th–21st Centuries)*. Leiden: Brill, 2014.

——. 2011. "From Mobility Transition to Comparative Global Migration History." *Journal of Global History* 6 (2011): 299–307.

——. "The Mobility Transition Revisited, 1500–1900: What the Case of Europe Can Offer to Global History." *Journal of Global History* 4 (2009): 347–77.

Manley, Rebecca. *To the Tashkent Station: Evacuation and Survival in the Soviet Union at War.* Ithaca: Cornell University Press, 2009.

Markwick, Roger, and Euridice Charon Cardona. *Soviet Women on the Frontline in the Second World War.* Houndmills, UK: Palgrave Macmillan, 2012.

Marples, David. *Social Impact of the Chernobyl Disaster.* New York: St. Martin's Press, 1988.

Martin, Terry. *Affirmative Action Empire: Nations and Nationalism in the Soviet Union, 1923–1939.* Ithaca: Cornell University Press, 2001.

——. "The Origins of Soviet Ethnic Cleansing." *Journal of Modern History* 70 (1998): 813–61.

Martin, Virginia. *Law and Custom in the Steppe: The Kazakhs of the Middle Horde and Russian Colonialism in the Nineteenth Century.* Richmond, UK: Curzon, 2001.

Matthews, Mervyn. *The Passport Society: Controlling Movement in Russia and the USSR.* Boulder, CO: Westview Press, 1993.

Mazurin, Boris. "The Life and Labor Commune: A History and Some Reflections." In *Memoirs of Peasants Tolstoyans in Soviet Russia*, edited by William Edgerton, 27–108. Bloomington: Indiana University Press, 1993.

McKeown, Adam. "Global Migration, 1846–1940." *Journal of World History* 15 (2004): 155–89.

——. *Melancholy Order: Asian Migration and the Globalization of Borders.* New York: Columbia University Press, 2008.

McNeal, Robert. *Tsar and Cossack, 1855–1914.* New York: St. Martin's Press, 1987.

Meier, Andrew. *Black Earth: A Journey through Russia after the Fall.* New York: Norton, 2003.

Merridale, Catherine. *Ivan's War: Life and Death in the Red Army, 1939–1945.* New York: Metropolitan Books, 2006.

Millar, James R., ed. *The Soviet Rural Community: A Symposium.* Urbana: University of Illinois Press, 1971.

Mixter, Timothy. "The Hiring Market as Workers' Turf: Migrant Agricultural Laborers and the Mobilization of Collective Action in the Steppe Grainbelt of European Russia, 1853–1913." In Kingston-Mann and Mixter, *Peasant Economy, Culture, and Politics*, 294–340.

Moch, Leslie Page. "Connecting Migration and World History, 1840–1940: Demographic Patterns, Family Systems, and Gender." *International Review of Social History* 52 (2007): 97–104.

——. *Moving Europeans: Migration in Western Europe since 1650.* Bloomington: Indiana University Press, 2003.

Mochulsky, Fedor Vasilevich. *Gulag Boss: A Soviet Memoir.* Translated and edited by Deborah Kaple. Oxford: Oxford University Press, 2011.

Moine, Natalie. "Passportisation, statistique des migrations et contrôle de l'identité sociale." *Cahiers du monde russe* 38 (1997): 587–600.

Moiseenko, V. M. "Migratsiia i emigratsiia v Rossii v 1960–1970-e gg." In Zhiromskaia and Isupov, *Naselenie Rossii v XX veke*, 3: bk. 1, 107–18.

Molodikova, Irina, and Alla Makhrova. "Urbanization Patterns in Russia in the Post-Soviet Era." In *The Post-Soviet City: Urban Form and Space Transformations in Central and Eastern Europe after Socialism*, edited by K. Stanilov, 53–70. Dordrecht: Springer, 2007.

Moon, David. "Peasant Migration and the Settlement of Russia's Frontiers, 1550–1897." *Historical Journal* 4 (1997): 859–93.

Motrich, E. L., and S. A. Kravchuk. "Gosudarstvennaia politika khoziaistvennogo osvoeniia i zaseleniia Dal'nego Vostoka s kontsa XIX v. do serediny 1980-kh godov." *Vestnik SVO RAN* 6 (2006): 121–28.

Mukomel', Vladimir. *Migratsionnaia politika Rossii: Postsovetskie konteksty.* Moscow: Institut sotsiologii RAN, 2005.

Murphy, Patrick. "Soviet Shabashniki: Material Incentives at Work." *Problems of Communism* 34 (1984): 48–57.

Nekrich, Aleksandr M. *The Punished Peoples: The Deportation and Fate of Soviet Minorities at the End of the Second World War*. Translated by George Saunders. New York: W. W. Norton, 1978.

O'Keeffe, Brigid. " 'Backward Gypsies,' Soviet Citizens: The All-Russian Gypsy Union, 1925–28." *Kritika* 11 (2010): 283–312.

Ohayon, Isabelle. *La sédentarisation des Kazakhs dans l'URSS de Staline: Collectivisation et changement social* (1928–1945). Paris: Maisonneuve et Larose Institut français d'études sur l'Asie Centrale, 2006.

Olcott, Martha Brill. *The Kazakhs*. Stanford: Stanford University Press, 1987.

Ostapenko, I. P. "Izmenenie demograficheskogo sotava gorodskogo naseleniia RSFSR v 1939–1959 gg." In Zhiromskaia, *Naselenie Rossii v XX veke*, 2: 206–17.

Oversloot, Hans. "Soviet Migrant Construction Workers (Shabashniki)." In Bade et al., *Encyclopedia of Migration and Minorities in Europe*, 687.

Pallot, Judith, and Laura Piacentini. *Gender, Geography, and Punishment: The Experience of Women in Carceral Russia*. Oxford: Oxford University Press, 2012.

Panfilova, A. M. *Formirovanie rabochego klassa SSSR v gody pervoi piatiletki*. Moscow: MGU, 1964.

Patenaude, Bertrand. *The Big Show in Bololand: The American Relief Expedition to Soviet Russia in the Famine of 1921*. Stanford: Stanford University Press, 2002.

Perevedentsev, V. I. *Molodezh' i sotsial'no-demograficheskie problemy SSSR*. Moscow: Nauka, 1990.

Pervaia vseobshchaia perepis' naseleniia rossiiskoi imperii, 1897 g. Edited by N. A. Troinitskii. 89 vols. St. Petersburg: TsSK MVD, 1899–1904.

Pianciola, Niccolò. "Famine in the Steppe: The Collectivization of Agriculture and the Kazakh Herdsmen, 1928–1934." *Cahiers du monde russe* 45 (2004): 137–92.

Pikalov, Iu. V. *Pereselencheskaia politika i izmenenie sotsial'no-klassovogo sostava naseleniia Dal'nogo Vostoka RSFSR (noiabr' 1922–iiun' 1941 gg.)*. Khabarovsk: Chastnaia kollektsiia, 2003.

Pilkington, Hilary. " 'For the Sake of the Children': Gender and Migration in the Former Soviet Union." In *Post-Soviet Women from the Baltic to Central Asia*, edited by Mary Buckley, 119–40. Cambridge: Cambridge University Press, 1997.

———. *Migration, Displacement, and Identity in Post-Soviet Russia*. London: Routledge, 1998.

Pintner, Walter McKenzie, and Don Karl Rowney, eds. *Russian Officialdom: The Bureaucratization of Russian Society from the Seventeenth to the Twentieth Century*. Chapel Hill: University of North Carolina Press, 1980.

Piore, Michael J. *Birds of Passage: Migrant Labor and Industrial Societies*. Cambridge: Cambridge University Press, 1979.

Platunov, Nikolai Ivanovich. *Pereselencheskaia politika sovetskogo gosudarstva i ee osushestvlenie v SSSR, 1917–iiun' 1941 gg*. Tomsk: Tomskii gosudarstvennyi universitet, 1976.

Pobol' N. L., and P. M. Polian, eds. *Stalinskie deportatsii, 1928–1953 gg*. Moscow: Materik, 2005.

Pohl, Michaela. "The 'Planet of One Hundred Languages': Ethnic Relations and Soviet Identity in the Virgin Lands." In Breyfogle, Schraeder, and Sunderland, *Peopling the Russian Periphery*, 238–61.

Pokrovskii, N. N., ed. *Politbiuro i krest'ianstvo: Vysylka, spetsposelenie 1930–1940*. 2 vols. Moscow: ROSSPEN, 2006.

Polian, Pavel. *Against Their Will: The History and Geography of Forced Migrations in the USSR*. Budapest: Central European University Press, 2004.

———. *Ne po svoei vole: Istoriia i geografiia prinuditel'nykh migratsii v SSSR*. Moscow: OGI-Memorial, 2001.

Priimak, G. A. *Tsifrovoi material dlia pereseleniia v Sibir', sobrannyi putem registratsii pereselentsev, prokhodivshikh v Sibir' i vozvrashchavshchikhsia iz Sibiri cherez Cheliabinsk v 1898 godu/ pod rukovodstvom G. A. Priimaka*. Moscow: n.p., 1904.

Prociuk, S. G. 1967. "The Manpower Problem in Siberia." *Soviet Studies* 19 (1967): 190–210.

Randolph, John, and Eugene M. Avrutin, eds. *Russia in Motion: Essays on the Politics, Society, and Culture of Human Mobility since 1850*. Urbana: University of Illinois Press, 2012.

Ransel, David. *Mothers of Misery: Child Abandonment in Russia*. Princeton: Princeton University Press, 1988.

Rashin, A. G. *Formirovanie rabochego klassa Rossii, istoriko-ekonomicheskie ocherki*. Moscow: Sotsekgiz, 1958.

Rawicz, Slavomir. *The Long Walk*. New York: Harper, 1956.

Reeves, Madeleine, ed. *Movement, Power, and Place in Central Asia and Beyond*. London: Routledge, 2006.

———. "Black Work, Green Money: Remittances, Ritual, and Domestic Economies in Southern Kyrgyzstan." *Slavic Review* 71 (2012): 108–34.

Retish, Aaron. *Russian Peasants in Revolution and Civil War: Citizenship, Identity, and the Creation of the Soviet State, 1914–1922*. Cambridge, Cambridge University Press, 2008.

Roman, Meredith. "Making Caucasians Black: Moscow since the Fall of Communism and the Racialization of Non-Russians." *Journal of Communist Studies and Transition Politics* 18 (2002): 1–27.

Rosenberg, William, and Lewis H. Siegelbaum, eds. *Social Dimensions of Soviet Industrialization*. Bloomington: Indiana University Press, 1993.

Roshchin, Iu. V. *Migratsiia naseleniia v sud'be Rossii*. Moscow: Avangard, 2008.

Rozenberg, Lena Jedwab. *The Girl with Two Landscapes: The Wartime Diary of Lena Jedwab, 1941–1945*. New York: Holmes and Meier, 2002.

Rybakovskii, L. L. *Transformatsiia migratsionnykh protsessov na postsovetskom prostransteve*. Moscow: Academia, 2009.

Ryndziunskii, P. G. *Krest'iane i gorod v kapitalisticheskoi Rossii vtoroi poloviny XIX veka*. Moscow: Nauka, 1983.

Sahadeo, Jeff. "The Accidental Traders: Marginalization and Opportunity from the Southern Republics to Late Soviet Moscow." *Central Asian Survey* 30 (2011): 521–40.

———. *Russian Colonial Society in Tashkent, 1865–1923*. Bloomington: Indiana University Press, 2007.

Samoilov, F. N. *Vospominaniia ob Ivanovo-Voznesenskom rabochem dvizhenii*, vol. 1, 1903–1905 gg. Moscow: Gosizd-vo, 1924.

Sanborn, Joshua A. *Drafting the Russian Nation: Military Conscription, Total War, and Mass Politics, 1905–1925*. DeKalb: Northern Illinois University Press, 2003.

———. "Unsettling the Empire: Violent Migrations and Social Disaster in Russia during World War I." *Journal of Modern History* 77 (2005): 290–324.

Schmidt, Matthias, and Lira Sagynbekova. "Migration Past and Present: Changing Patterns in Kyrgyzstan." *Central Asian Survey* 27 (2008): 111–27.

Shayakhmetov, Mukhamet. *The Silent Steppe: The Memoir of a Kazakh Nomad under Stalin*. Translated by Jan Butler. New York: Overlook/Rookery, 2007.

Shcherbakova, Irina, ed. *Puti sledovaniia: Rossiiskie shkol'niki o migratsiiakh, evakuatsiiakh i deportatsiiakh XX veka*. Moscow: Memorial, 2011.

Shearer, David R. *Policing Stalin's Socialism: Repression and Social Order in the Soviet Union, 1924–1953*. New Haven: Yale University Press, 2009.

Shilovskii, M. V. *Sibirskie pereseleniia: Dokumenty i materialy*. 2 vols. Novosibirsk: Nov. Gos. Universitet, 2003–2006.

Shiokawa, Nobuaki. "The Collectivization of Agriculture and Otkhodnichestvo in the USSR, 1930." *Annals of the Institute of Social Science* 24 (1982): 129–58.

Shishkin, V. I., ed. *Sibirskaia vandeia*. 2 vols. Moscow: Demkratiia, 2000.

Shulman, Elena. *Stalinism on the Frontier of Empire: Women and State Formation in the Soviet Far East*. Cambridge: Cambridge University Press, 2008.

Siegelbaum, Lewis H. "Another 'Yellow Peril': Chinese Migrants in the Russian Far East and the Russian Reaction before 1917." *Modern Asian Studies* 12 (1978): 307–30.

———. *Cars for Comrades: The Life of the Soviet Automobile*. Ithaca: Cornell University Press, 2008.

———. "Those Elusive Scouts: Pioneering Peasants and the Russian State, 1870s–1953." *Kritika* 14 (2013): 31–60.

Siegelbaum, Lewis H., and Andrei Sokolov, eds. *Stalinism as a Way of Life: A Narrative in Documents*. New Haven: Yale University Press, 2000.

Simpson, James Young. *Side-Lights on Siberia: Some Account of the Great Siberian Railroad, the Prisons and Exile System*. Edinburgh: Blackwood, 1898.

Slavko, T. I. *Kulatskaia ssylka na Urale, 1930–1936*. Moscow: Mosgorarkhiv, 1995.

Slezkine, Yuri. *Arctic Mirrors: Russia and the Small Peoples of the North*. Ithaca: Cornell University Press, 1994.

——. *The Jewish Century*. Princeton: Princeton University Press, 2004.

Solov'ev, F. *Kitaiskoe otkhodnichestvo na Dal'nom Vostoke Rossii v epokhu kapitalizma (1861–1917)*. Moscow: Nauka, 1989.

Solzhenitsyn, Aleksandr. *The Gulag Archipelago, 1918–1956: An Experiment in Literary Investigation, V–VII*. Translated by Harry Willetts. New York: Harper & Row, 1978.

——, ed. *Voices from the Gulag*. Translated by K. A. Lantz. Evanston: Northwestern University Press, 2010.

Stankevich, Andrei. *Materialy dlia izucheniia byta pereselentsev tobol'skoi gubernii za 15 let, s kontsa 70-kh godov po 1893 g.* 2 vols. Moscow: Tipografiia Obshchestva rasprostraneniia poleznykh knig, 1895.

Steinwedel, Charles. "Resettling People, Unsettling the Empire: Migration and the Challenge of Governance, 1861–1917." In Breyfogle, Schraeder, and Sunderland, *Peopling the Russian Periphery*, 128–47.

Stepakov, V. N., and E. A. Balashov. *V "novykh raionakh:" Iz istorii osvoeniia karel'skogo pereseika, 1940–1941, 1944–1950 gg.* St. Petersburg: Nordmedizdat, 2001.

Stronski, Paul. *Tashkent: Forging a Soviet City, 1930–1966*. Pittsburgh: University of Pittsburgh Press, 2010.

Sumkin, M. V. *Sibir' za zemlei (iz kaluzhskoi gubernii v semipalatinskuiu oblast'), zapiski khodoka*, Moscow: Zemliak, 1908.

Sunderland, Willard. "The 'Colonization Question': Visions of Colonization in Late Imperial Russia." *Jahrbücher für Geschichte Osteuropas* 48 (2000): 210–32.

——. "Peasant Pioneering: Russian Settlers Describe Colonization and the Eastern Frontier, 1880s-1910." *Journal of Social History* 34 (2001): 895–922.

——. *Taming the Wild Field: Colonization and Empire on the Russian Steppe*. Ithaca: Cornell University Press, 2004.

Tatishchev, A. A. *Zemli i liudi: V gushche pereselencheskogo dvizheniia, 1906–1921* Moscow: Russkii put', 2001.

Teptsov, N. V. "Ssyl'nye muzhiki: Pravda o spetsposelkakh." In *Neizvestnaia Rossiia, XX vek*, vol. 1, edited by V. A. Kozlov, 184–268. Moscow: Istoricheskoe nasledie, 1992.

Thurstan, Violetta. *People Who Run: Being the Tragedy of the Refugees in Russia*. London: Putnam's Sons, 1916.

Tilly, Charles. "Migration in Modern European History." In *Human Migration: Patterns and Policies*, edited by William McNeill and Ruth S. Adams, 48–72. Bloomington: Indiana University Press, 1978.

——. "Transplanted Networks." In *Immigration Reconsidered*, edited by V. Yans-McLaughlin, 79–95. New York: Oxford University Press, 1990.

Treadgold, Donald. *The Great Siberian Migration: Government and Peasant in Resettlement from Emancipation to the First World War*. Princeton: Princeton University Press, 1957.

Tsentral'noe statisticheskoe upravlenie pri Sovete Ministrov RSFSR. *Chislennost' i sostav naseleniia SSSR, po dannym Vsesoiuznoi perepisi naseleniia 1979 goda*. Moscow: Finansy i statistika, 1984.

——. *Itogi Vsesoiuznoi perepisi naseleniia 1959 goda RSFSR*. Moscow: Gosstatizdat, 1963.

——. *Itogi Vsesoiuznoi perepisi naseleniia 1970 goda, vol. 7, Migratsiia naseleniia, chislo i sostav semei v SSSR, soiuznykh i avtonomnykh respublikakh, kraiakh i oblastiakh*. Moscow: Statistika, 1970.

——. *Narodnoe khoziaistvo RSFSR v 1985 g.* Moscow: Gosstatizdat, 1986.

——. *Narodnoe khoziaistvo RSFSR v 1989 g. Statisticheskii ezhegodnik*. Moscow: Gosstatizdat, 1990.

Tuan, Yi-fu. *Topophilia: A Study of Environmental Perception, Attitudes, and Values*. Englewood Cliffs, NJ: Prentice-Hall, 1974.

Turchaninov, N. *Itogi pereselencheskago dvizheniia za vremia s 1896 po 1909 gg. (vkliuchitel'no)* St. Petersburg: Pereselenchekoe Upravlenie, 1910.

Tyuryukanova, Elena. *Forced Labour in the Russian Federation Today: Irregular Migration and Trafficking in Human Beings*. Geneva: International Labour Organization, 2005.

Valetov, Timur Ia. "Mekhanizmy samoorganitsii sezonnykh trudovykh migrantov v SSSR i na postsovetskom prostranstve." In *"Sovetskoe nasledstvo": Otrazhenie proshlogo v sotsial'nykh i ekonomicheskikh praktikakh sovremennoi Rossii*, edited by L. Borodkin, Kh. Kessler, and A. K. Sokolov, 253–78. Moscow: ROSSPEN, 2010.

——. "Migration and the Household: Urban Living Arrangements in the Late Nineteenth- to Early Twentieth-Century Russia." *History of the Family* 13 (2008): 163–77.

Verbitskaia, O. M. "Demograficheskaia kharakteristika sel'skogo naseleniia v 1960–1979 gg." In Zhiromskaia and Isupov, *Naselenie Rossii v XX veke*, 3: bk. 1, 41–74.

——. "Krest'ianskaia sem'ia v 1920–1930-e gody." In Zhiromskaia, *Naselenie Rossii v XX veke*, 1: 191–218.

——. "Migratsiia sel'skogo naseleniia." In Zhiromskaia, *Naselenie Rossii v XX veke*, 2: 275–90.

——. *Naselenie Rossiiskoi derevni v 1939–1959 gg., problemy demograficheskogo razvitiia*. Moscow: RAN, 2002.

——. "Planovoe sel'skokhoziaistvennoe pereselenie v RSFSR v 1946–1958 godakh." *Voprosy istorii* 12 (1986): 13–26.

Viatkin, V., N. P. Kosmarskaia, and S. A. Panarin, eds. *V dvizhenii dobrovol'nom i vynuzhdennom: Postsovetskie migratsii v Evrazii*. Moscow: Natakis, 1999.

Viola, Lynne. *The Best Sons of the Fatherland: Workers in the Vanguard of Soviet Collectivization*. New York: Oxford University Press, 1987.

——. *The Unknown Gulag: The Lost World of Stalin's Special Settlements*. Oxford: Oxford University Press, 2007.

Vitebsky, Piers. *Reindeer People: Living with Animals and Sprits in Siberia*. New York: Harper Collins, 2005.

von Hagen, Mark. *Soldiers in the Proletarian Dictatorship: The Red Army and the Soviet Socialist State, 1917–1930*. Ithaca: Cornell University Press, 1990.

Vorderer, Susan M. *Migration Patterns, Occupational Strategies, and Work Experiences in a Large Textile Town: The Case of Ivanovo-Voznesensk*. Carl Beck Papers 1403. Pittsburgh: University of Pittsburgh Press, 1999.

Werth, Nicholas. *Cannibal Island: Death in a Siberian Gulag*. Translated by Steven Rendell. Princeton: Princeton University Press, 2007.

——. "Les déserteurs en Russie: Violence de guerre, violence révolutionnaire et violence paysanne—1916–1921." In *La violence de guerre, 1914–1945: Approches comparées des deux conflits mondiaux*, edited by Stéphane Audoin-Rouzeau et al., 99–116. Brussels: Éditions complexe, 2002.

Wildman, Allan. *The End of the Russian Imperial Army: The Old Army and the Soldiers' Revolt (March–April 1917)*. Princeton: Princeton University Press, 1980.

Wimbush, S. Enders, and Alex Alexiev. *The Ethnic Factor in the Soviet Armed Forces*. Santa Monica: Rand, 1982.

Wimbush, S. Enders, and Dmitry Ponomareff. *Alternatives for Mobilizing Soviet Central Asian Labor: Outmigration and Regional Development*. Santa Monica: Rand, 1979.

Yaney, George L. "Agricultural Administration in Russia from the Stolypin Land Reform to Forced Collectivization: An Interpretive Study." In Millar, *Soviet Rural Community*, 63–35.

Zaionchkovskaia, Zh. A. *Novosely v gorodakh (metody izucheniia prizhivaemosti)*. Moscow: Statistika, 1972.

Zaslavskaia, T., ed. *Migratsiia sel'skogo naseleniia*. Moscow: Mysl', 1970.

Zemskov, V. N. " 'Kulatskaia ssylka' v 1930-e gody: Chislennost', rasselenie, sostav." In Zhiromskaia, *Naselenie Rossii v XX veke*, 1: 277–310.

——. *Spetsposelentsy v SSSR, 1930–1960*. Moscow: Nauka, 2003.

Zenzinov, V. *Bezprizornye*. Paris: Sovremennyia zapiski, 1929.

Zhiromskaia, V. B. *Demograficheskaia istoriia Rossii v 1930-e gody, vzgliad v neizvestnoe*. Moscow: ROSSPEN, 2001.

——. "Liudskie poteri v gody velikoi otechestvennoi voiny: Territoriia i naselenie posle voiny." In Zhiromskaia, *Naselenie Rossii v XX veke*, 2: 128–65.

——. "Naselenie Rossii v 1970-e gg.: Chislennost', razmeshchenie, demograficheskie protsessy." In Zhiromskaia and Isupov, *Naselenie Rossii v XX veke*, 3: bk. 1, 244–68.

——, ed. *Naselenie Rossii v XX veke: Istoricheskie ocherki v 3-kh t.*, vol. 1, 1900–1939. Moscow: ROSSPEN, 2000.

——, ed. *Naselenie Rossii v XX veke: Istoricheskie ocherki v 3-kh t.*, vol. 2, 1940–1959. Moscow: ROSSPEN, 2001.

Zhiromskaia, V. B., and V. A. Isupov, eds. *Naselenie Rossii v XX veke: Istoricheskie ocherki v 3-kh t.*, vol. 3, 1960–1979. Moscow: ROSSPEN, 2005.

Zielinski, Konrad. "Population Displacement and Citizenship in Poland, 1918–24." In Baron and Gatrell, *Homelands*, 98–118.

Zima, V. F. *Golod v SSSR 1946–1947 godov: Proiskhozhdenie i posledstviia*. Moscow: Institut Rossiiskoi istorii RAN, 1996.

Zubkova, E. Iu., and T. Iu. Zhukova. *Na "kraiu" sovetskogo obshchestva sotsial'nye marginaly kak ob'ekt gosudarstvennoi politiki, 1945-1960-e gg*. Moscow: ROSSPEN, 2010.

On-line Sources

Asadov, Sabir. "Deportatsiia azerbaidzhanstev iz armianskoi SSR (1948–1953 gody)." http://azerbaycanli.org/ru/page136.html.

Cherenkov, Lev Nikolaevich. "Tsygane Moskvy i Podmoskov'ia." http://gypsy-life.net/history26htm.

"Ia Pomniu/I Remember: Vospominaniia veteranov VOV." www.iremember.ru.

Khaniutin, Aleksei, dir. *Piatachok*. 1987. http://films.academic.ru/film.nsf/9498/Пятачок.

Kovriga O. "Kak my shabashili." http://pro-shabashku.narod.ru/Part2_1.html.

"O pereselenii azerbaidzhantsev." http://www.hrono.info/dokum/194_dok?1948031azer.html.

"O raspredelenii vypusknikov i o posylkakh." http://sovietdetstvo.livejournal.com/259782.html.

Oxford Russian Life History Archive. www.ehrc.ox.ac.uk/html/ehrc/lifehistory/archive.htm.

Perevedentsev, Viktor. "Migratsiia kak sud'ba." *Otechestvennye zapiski*, no. 4 (18) (2004). http://www.stran-oz.ru/2004/4/migraciya-kak-sudba.

"Polozhenie o raspredelenii vypusknikov uchrezhdenii obrazovaniia, poluchivshikh professional'no-tekhnicheskoe, srednee spetsial'noe ili vysshee obrazovanie." December 10, 2007. http://job.bseu.by/help/assignment.htm.

"Postanovlenie ot 29 maia 1948 g. N 1840 ob uporiadochenii raspredeleniia i ispol'zovaniia molodykh spetsialistov, okanchivaiushchikh vysshie i srednie spetsial'nye uchebnye zavedeniia." http://bestpravo.ru/sssr/gn-gosudarstvo/jor.htm.

"Postanovlenie Sovmina SSSR ot 28.11.1951 N 4881 ob uporiadochenii provedeniia organizovannogo nabora rabochikh." http://pravo.levonevsky.org/baza/soviet/sssr6272.htm.

"Postanovlenie Sovmina SSSR ot 21.12.1951 N5263 o l'gotakh po pereseleniiu na 1952 god." http://www.lawrussia.ru/texts/legal_586/doc586a391x339.htm.

"Postanovlenie Sovmina SSSR ot 31.05.1973 N364 o l'gotakh po pereseleniiu." http://bestpravo.ru/sssr/gn-normy/c6n.htm.

"Postanovlenie Sovmina SSSR ot 19.06.1973 N 421 ob uporiadochenii otkhodnichestva kolkhoznikov na sezonnye raboty." http://pravo.levonevsky.org/baza/soviet/sssr4652.htm.

"Postanovlenie TsK KPSS, Sovmina SSSR ot 21.54.1964 N 499 o srokakh podgotovki i uluchshenii ispol'zovaniia spetsialistov s vysshim i srednim spetsial'nym obrazovaniem." http://www.libussr.ru/doc_ussr/usr_6082.htm.

Sandul, Irina. "Time Runs Out for Russia's Foreign Workers." *The Russia Journal*, 13 May 2002. http://russiajournal.com/node/6205.

"Sheftel', Il'ia Bentsianovich (1920–1976)." http://www.famhist.ru/famhist/sheftel/0002c21f.htm#0002f09.htm.

Tiuriukanova, Elena. "Trudovaia migratsiia v Rossii." *Otechestvennye zapiski*, no. 4 (18) (2004). http://www.strana-oz.ru/2004/4/zapadnyy-dreyf-vnutrirossiyskoy-migracii#t1.

"Tsoi K. A. Chukotskie meridiany." http://pro-shabashku.narod.ru/Content.htm.

"Vsesoiuznaia perepis' naseleniia 1989 g.: Chislennost' gorodskogo naseleniia RSFSR, ee territorial'nykh edinits, gorodskikh poselenii i gorodskikh raionov po polu." Demoskop. http://demoscope.ru/weekly/ssp/rus89_reg2.php.

"Vsesoiuznaia perepis' naseleniia 1939 goda: Natsional'nyi sostav naseleniia po respublikam SSSR." Demoskop Weekly. http://demoscope.ru/weekly/ssp/sng_nac_39.php?reg=5.

Index

CPSIA information can be obtained
at www.ICGtesting.com
Printed in the USA
LVHW101946130619
621017LV00016B/54/P